INVISIBLE POWER

Sherrill MacLaren

INVISIBLE POWER

A Seal Book / November 1991

For information address: Seal Books.

ISBN 0-7704-2341-8

Canadian Cataloguing in Publication Data

MacLaren, Sherrill Maxwell
Invisible power : behind the scenes with Canadian women of influence

Includes index.
ISBN 0-7704-2341-8

1. Women in public life - Canada. 2. Power (Social sciences). I. Title.

HQ1236.5.C2M33 1991 305.43'32'0971 C91-094893-3

PRINTED IN U.S.A.

(Printer's ID) 0 9 8 7 6 5 4 3 2 1

INVISIBLE POWER

THE WOMEN WHO RUN CANADA

Sherrill MacLaren

DEDICATION

In memory of Anna French

CONTENTS

INVISIBLE POWER

Women need to stop being afraid of power.
They need to take it and use it.

Jeanne Sauvé

ACKNOWLEDGEMENTS

Researching a book throughout the vastness of Canada is so costly that without sponsorships it would be impossible. I am grateful to Canadian Airlines International, Zenith Data Systems, and Loomis Courier Service in Vancouver, all of whose generosity made it possible for me to meet with several hundred women from coast to coast and into the North.

The four years of work on *Invisible Power* were a constant reminder that creating non-fiction can be achieved only through collaboration. The vision of E.B. White holding a single piece of blank parchment in a bare room is a fantasy to be emulated only by novelists, poets, and dreamers. Countless times when I was tempted to napalm my Vancouver office cluttered with newspaper articles, texts, memos, faxes, and illimitable telephone messages, Michelle Barker, my assistant and researcher, encouraged me to continue. I would never have completed this book without her support. While I was meeting with interesting women and men across Canada, Michelle became a one-person industry—transcribing interviews, scouting newspapers and magazines from across the country, building and cross-referencing a superlative filing system—until one day she escaped to sail the Pacific. Five months later she returned to subject this manuscript to fact-checking scrutiny, making hundreds of telephone calls to verify facts and chronology, and to update the ever-changing climate of socio-economic conditions.

Our work was aided by a number of librarians and researchers nationwide who in their own time provided valuable assistance. Most notable were Denise Turnbull of Alcan, Julie Kirsch of the Toronto *Sun*, Lorraine Harvey (assistant to Martha Blackburn) of the *London Free Press*, Vivienne Moody of CBC, and the supersleuths in all departments of the Vancouver Public Library.

Despite a previous commitment to a major work, Janet Craig, editor nonpareil, assumed the task of editing *Invisible Power* and juggling the demands of two frantic authors. She not only brought her gifted eye to weeding out my tangled literary garden but lent me her Victoria home in which to work. Then, at the eleventh hour and much still to be done, editor Kay Lusty McConnell dropped everything to assist Janet. Combined with the computer skills of my son Douglas MacLaren, editor Felicity Stone and eighteen-hour days, the editors met the publisher's deadline. Bravissimo.

Leaving Anna Porter, Canada's most successful publisher/businesswoman, out of a book that includes entrepreneurial power risks invalidating the work. At the last minute I removed the story of women publishers due to her immovable determination to elude even a hint of conflict of interest. In assiduously avoiding the creative process of this book, Porter became for me a mysterious black hole in the publishing galaxy. Her absence — and thus that of other women publishers and agents — arguably has rendered her a greater power.

Several stories in *Invisible Power* are so complex that, although I spoke with the principals in them, I relied upon the expertise of authors who had already recorded the dramas in order to follow up the intricacies of each. And to keep the work contemporary required the aid of newspaper, magazine, and television journalists too numerous to mention. Over the four years, every single one of them returned any calls made by myself or Michelle Barker, and I am indebted to them all. Particularly helpful were columnists Michael Valpy, Linda McQuaig, Harvey Enchin, Charlotte Gray, Peter Newman, Stevie Cameron, Hana Gartner, Rosemary Sexton, Rod McQueen, and, for good humour as well as pithy points, Allan Fotheringham. Ian Brown, author of *Freewheeling*, brought sense to the labyrinth of the Billes Canadian Tire story; and for the lobby assembled to enshrine women's rights in the Constitution, I found Penney Kome's books, *Women of Influence* and *The Taking of Twenty-Eight*, essential texts.

Most of all, I am grateful to the hundreds of contributors, many of whose names do not appear in these pages, who made *Invisible Power* possible. They were the experts, and the innumerable statements and quotes that appear unattributed throughout the book come from my taped interviews with them. Although I had expected resistance to researching *Invisible Power*, instead, in response to over three hundred requests for interviews, only four women refused outright and three did not reply. One said yes twice, then each time suffered a headache and cancelled; her power was societal, while the others, as corporate vice-presidents, were driven underground through apprehension rather than any sense of superiority. An overwhelming majority of women wanted to share their lives as they related to power. And in the spring of 1991 when Michelle Barker telephoned almost every one of them to update their stories, she was received with enthusiasm, courtesy, and only occasional alarm.

The only qualifications I brought to the research were curiosity and ignorance. As a child during the Second World War, a nurse, a homemaker, and the full-time mother of four children, my background is that of the care-giving traditionalist bound by the restrictions of a Victorian society. The concept of women and power was at first so inconceivable to me that the project I chose to tackle was as intimidating as it was intriguing. My ignorance of feminist history made me representative of the suspicious traditionalists countrywide. My naive questions brought initial looks of shock to the faces of former university president Margaret Fulton, constitutional expert Mary Eberts, economic sociologist Senator Lorna Marsden, and former MLA Rosemary Brown—each of whom has spent her adult life fighting for equitable conditions for women and minorities—looks invariably replaced by an earnest and courteous effort to inform. The speech of Rosalie Abella, chair of the Ontario Law Reform Commission, to the Canadian Clubs of Vancouver in February 1988 became the historical thread connecting my search for power from "The Grassroots Movement" through "The Age of Meritocracy." For all of this cheerfully proffered help and superlative expertise, my gratitude is unending. Any flaws or excesses remain mine alone.

During the past four years, the impact of a hectic schedule and a hazardous subject was softened and enriched by the enthusiasm each woman had for her particular interest, and by the exceptional kindness shown by strangers in every region of Canada. In a country so fragmented by its geography and cultural singularities, this became the unifying gesture of a national family. Everyone, from native trappers to Establishment billionaires, welcomed me with curiosity and courtesy before handing me on to their own friends. From Upper Battery Road in St. John's to a sky blue house in Inuvik, they served me exotic meals, shared secret hideaways on magnificent lakes, sheltered me in historical homes and included me in their social events. When I was stranded on the Beaufort Sea, the pilot of a charter plane carrying dynamite flew me out. One midnight my mariner host and hostess, clad in black tie and ball gown, ferried me by open launch across a stormy Lake of the Woods. Following a cross-country ski trek on L'Île d'Orléans, and while a snowstorm raged, I slept peacefully beneath the eaves of a two-hundred-year-old stone farmhouse. A Justice of the Supreme Court of Canada invited me to lunch with her illustrious colleagues. The studio visit with a Newfoundland artist epitomized the serene power of our Canadian landscape. Over coffee in Rideau Hall, Her Excellency Governor General Jeanne Sauvé smiled, "I have sought power since I was fifteen years old." Then she produced a recorder and taped her interviewer. These extraordinary experiences compelled me occasionally to include the reader in the journey of "the traveller."

Although I have identified some women as "wife of" to establish for the reader the core of their clout, as more women assume executive roles in the decision-making processes, it is my hope that meritocracy will render such titles obsolete and end the need for books that separate the genders.

SM Spring 1991

INTRODUCTION

The Illusion of Power

If you like power, you never have enough of it.

LISE WATIER[1a]

I am a power junkie. I like to feel that in the the air.

ANNA MURDOCH[2]

Publisher/provocateur Jack McClelland introduced me to the potential for a book on Women in Power in 1986 when he ventured the notion that it is really women who run Canada. A wicked curiosity impelled me to seek reactions to this declaration. These ranged from hostility to hilarity and roused hot debate. Some men insisted that women and power were contradictory terms and predicted a book would be a slim volume. Author/activist Doris Anderson scoffed at McClelland's claim, "That's bull. Women don't have any power." Joan Fraser, editorial page editor of the Montreal *Gazette*, nearly buried the idea when she exploded, "What a sexist remark!" Then journalist Joan Sutton Straus and interior designer Susan Curry,[3] Insiders married to Establishment wealth, disinterred it by declaring, "What took Jack so long to figure that out?" Heated discussions over just what power is and whether or not women had any, enlivened dinner tables from coast to coast.

The controversy was expected. For millennia, a patriarchal culture defined women by the terms "mistress" and "motherhood." In the words of B.K. Sandwell, editor of *Saturday Night* in 1938, "The business of women is to keep house and to keep quiet." Despite the fact that women won the right to vote and the right to be recognized as Persons, attitudes toward their function remained static. Then in three decades, 1960 through 1991, women at the grassroots level struggled through legal inferiority and public ridicule to achieve a voice that was heard. Through a professionalism manifested in the House of Commons, the Supreme Court of Canada, corporate structures, the clergy, and a social elite raising huge funds for charity, women's influence shifted to the inner sanctums of power. Six months of questioning why they wanted power, how they got it, and what they do with it, finally compelled me to write the book.

Relating women to power invariably became entangled with a perception of feminism, the most divisive word to trouble four years of research. Many still see "feminist" as the counterpart to "male chauvinist," and one prominent businesswoman worried that "talking with too many bra-burners might turn you into a butch." Her concern illustrates society's tendency to equate "power" with "coercion", and "feminism" with "masculinity." The notion of women competing for power continues to be so hazardous that even in the more open society of the 1990s, successful women tend to cling to the polite façades imputed to them through the centuries. In general, women tend to deny their power. Men compete. Women pursue excellence. When skater Elizabeth Manley won her silver medal at the 1988 Calgary Olympics, she talked about "doing her best." When skater Kurt Browning won the world championships in 1989, he shot his fist into the air and laughed exuberantly, "We kicked butt!"

My softening of the title from the original *Women in Power* to *Women and Power* did little to appease the critics. The juxtaposition of the nouns buried the nuance. The irony was that although women denied it, plenty of them had power and used it. My wish to acknowledge both this irony and the secrecy with which power is secured, led to the title *Invisible Power*.

In the late 1980s, there were two metaphors for visible power, "Brascan" and "Trevor Eyton."[4] Time and again men and women would express a gut feeling when they argued, "There are no female Trevor Eytons running Brascans, so there can't be a book on women and power." That response revealed an attitude that has been entrenched in society's collective consciousness for generations. Power is money. Existing in the upper echelons of the corporate elite means having the clout to get things done in almost any other field. I expanded "Brascan" to include the institutions of government and the professions. Except for the judiciary, few women were visible in the power elite.

Researching *Invisible Power* became a quest to understand the relationship between women and power within the contexts of history, institutions, and perception. Categorizing is perilous, but it became clear through hundreds of interviews that within the ramifications of power there were Insiders—represented in the Establishment and the executive of Institutions—and Outsiders, reflected through the Activists and Individuals. The Futurists operate in either sphere. These young women, whose mothers were defined by what they could not be, define themselves and operate in a world that now accepts freedom of choice. None of these divisions is mutually exclusive and Inspirational Power is common to them all.

The only constant I found in power is that it is ephemeral and as the Wizard of Oz knew all too well, public perception can play a larger role than reality. Jane Pepino, for example, previously acknowledged by *Toronto Life* as a powerhouse lawyer/activist/member of boards and commissions for three levels of government, was placed in its 1990 "Dropouts" list just because she did not seek the leadership of the Ontario PCs. Another "dropout" was none other than Edward Bronfman because he was "bowing out of high finance to work in the volunteer sector."[b] Scoring in the power game means enjoying massive corporate clout or personal financial resources, winning legislative change or, in the charity stakes of social competition, raising at least $150,000 in an evening.

One of the most compelling reasons for examining the nature of women and power was to learn how the various groups of women dealt with their power and how they viewed each other. The activists who seek equality and social justice are known to criticize supporters of the status quo, particularly those of Establishment wealth who throw gala fund raisers for "respectable" charities rather than marching for social change. Many imply that if you are not a feminist, you are anti-woman. In turn, the Establishment scorns the activists for their strident style. Diametrically opposed special-interest groups—the feminists' National Action Committee and the fundamentalists' REAL Women—have exacerbated the divisions.

My original curiosity led to the hope that a book including the whole spectrum of women and power might foster a mutual appreciation if not a synthesis of ideas. After all, it was the grassroots movement that was so vital to ensuring the freedoms that women enjoy today, and it is Establishment wealth that has the power to support the activists. The goals that inspire a pursuit of power may differ with each individual, but everyone seeking it is motivated by a desire not only to participate in the game but also to create the rules by which it is played. Bringing them together could realize a power of unimaginable dimensions.

How to choose the women to include in *Invisible Power* from among the hundreds interviewed remains a matter of debate. With the largest population and head offices of most major businesses located in Ontario, more women of power reside in central Canada than anywhere else. But women who may enjoy star profiles in Toronto—or, for that matter, in Vancouver or Winnipeg—remain unknown beyond Mississauga, Mission, or Portage La Prairie. It was after travelling for some months that I referred to "Toronto and the extremities of Canada," understanding just how much this is a nation of communities defined by geography and regionally inspired parochialism. The power of most women and the style they bring to its expression are shaped by individual communities. Therein lay a problem.

With each visit I made, men and women presented to me dozens more names of women whose influence was making a difference in their communities. If I had given equal weight to each region the work would have become unwieldly. This made it essential to deal with issues, and therefore the stories are symbolic rather than comprehensive. Excluded is the powerful but silent support system through which women raise new generations and perpetuate the quality of their communities. Perhaps someday the care-givers and the educators will be recognized for their collective and unfathomable power, but worthiness was not a criterion for *Invisible Power*. The YWCA Women of Distinction Awards annually name hundreds of women across the country who are both helping to develop and inspire their communities. Many of these nominees, however, sustain the harsh thesis that women are care-givers who follow, not power-brokers who lead. My task was to seek out the latter. There was nothing fair or scientific about this selection, but neither of these elements is instrinsic to the whim of power. This is a book about women who, through heritage, prestige, achievement, wealth, moxie, or sheer perseverance, are becoming indispensable to the institutions and organizations that run this country. Increasingly these women are demonstrating that despite historical restrictions they are astonishingly resourceful in accessing power. It also became clear that power won through inspiration, skill, or excellence was not the exclusive domain of women any more than that grasped through manipulation, coercion, or dominance was the sole territory of men.

Invisible Power personalizes women's individual and collective routes to power. If the decision to include one woman but not another appears singular, it at least validates the claim that power—however briefly held—may be neither fair nor impersonal.

SM SPRING 1991

INTRODUCTION NOTES

1. Watier's private Montreal-based company Groupe Watier includes a beauty spa in Outremont and Lise Watier Cosmetics, with 1988 sales estimated at $15 million.
2. Author/socialite Anna Murdoch is the wife of Rupert Murdoch, the Australian-born publishing magnate.
3. Straus is a former columnist and current force in the fund-raising world of New York where she lives with her husband, Arnold Straus, a Guggenheim. Curry is the wife of Peter Curry, former deputy chair of Power Corporation, herself a former co-chair of the Montreal Musée des Beaux Arts Ball, one of the premiere charity events of the season.
4. The crown jewel of the Edper Bronfman empire, Brascan controls some of the largest Canadian companies in natural resources, financial services, and consumer products. *The Globe and Mail Report on Business Magazine* in December 1988 described president and CEO Trevor Eyton as ''the chief hired gun'' for the Edper group of companies, which controls in excess of $100 billion worth of North American assets. In 1990 Brascan's gross revenues exceeded $6.8 billion, with a net income of $281 million. In 1989 Eyton, COO Jack Cockwell, and other colleagues in Brascan's Hees International became ownership partners with Peter and Edward Bronfman. In May 1991, Senator Eyton was named chair and Cockwell became the president and CEO.

PART I

SOCIAL POWER

Positioning. That's the game of life if you want to be in it.
Corporate society today is nothing but a paid deal six nights a week.

SUZANNE BANFIELD LOUNT

C H A P T E R   O N E

The CEOs of Social Power

It's very important never to tell the truth.
It is important to talk in code.
BRENDA KINSELLA

No one minds giving away money if they are having fun doing it.
JEAN SOUTHAM

Ask two hundred Establishment women to define power in relation to themselves and you get three hundred intensely personal interpretations, all of which relate to someone else. *Opéras bouffes* abound as traditionalists clasp their hands, recoil at the inference, and trill, ''I am Charlie's wife . . . I have no power.'' Ask Establishment women what they do for the community and they will tell you. Ask with whom they do it, and even if it is done publicly with a thousand people in attendance, their eyes fog over at the impropriety. They clam up as if asked to reveal the code number of the family vault, banishing the interviewer with the chill of terminal frostbite. Social power is the impenetrable mantle of a secret society, its members denying they are seduced by it while pursuing it with the stealth of cat burglars.

Women socialized in the pre-1960 era of Calvinist taboos and patriarchal control continue to deny power while executing it in the restaurants and theatres of the nation with haute couture fashion and extravagant staging that would have enthralled Shakespeare. They became experts at the game in a childhood restricted by a plethora of conventions. As young women they were discouraged from professional disciplines in favour of motherhood. Snaring a mate became the prescribed raison d'être, and they grew up affecting the composure of saints while exercising power in their limited sphere through the art of exclusion, or cutting their rivals out. Humans are herd animals who cannot bear to be ostracized. Rejection is one of the worst forms of punishment, or the most effective forms of power, depending upon where you are standing. Women also know that sharing information dilutes the power source, or as Margaret Atwood put it, "Knowledge is power only as long as you keep your mouth shut."[a]

All through lunch at the Rideau Club in Ottawa, Susan Peterson, then Privy Council staff member and one of the Prime Minister's personal friends,[1] greeted a flock of mandarins and MPs who paused to share a friendly word. Yet she insisted she had no power. Access is power. Diana Kirkwood brilliantly played the role of chatelaine in Paris, Athens, and Bonn for her ambassador husband and, say observers of the social milieu, she has replaced pre-eminent economist Sylvia Ostry as the supreme hostess of Ottawa. Kirkwood's apartment is decorated with the elegant chic of one who operates at the centre of the social cosmos, yet she shrinks from the notion of power, wishing to be recognized only as a successful real estate agent in Rockcliffe, which she is. Kirkwood's and Peterson's denials reveal a delusion about power—it is something you might actually have but can rarely use. After all, should either woman suddenly leap at Brian Mulroney during a state dinner to demand that he increase tax deductions for charitable donations, she might find herself finishing dessert on the river bank below the Rideau sewage station. And Pat Buckley, who rules New York society and fashion trends with the tilt of her Vancouver upper-class chin, continues to impute her power to her famous husband, William. In the Wolfian vernacular, however, it is she who is master of the social universe.[2]

Fair or not, since time immemorial, social power has held a peculiar pre-eminence that transcends all other rules of civilized society. Rulers came only from the most notable families and, without Establishment status, ability alone rarely got you to the top. In this contemporary age of meritocracy, that image is fading, but for centuries social power, institutionalized through marriage, was women's only access to that enclave of name and wealth. For some, social power in Canada circa 1991, is manifested in Toronto's Hilary and Galen Weston[3] who summer at Fort Belvedere on the grounds of Windsor Castle and polo or picnic with Prince Charles and Diana, Princess of Wales. Others would prefer to trek with Montrealer Sandra Kolber and Vancouverite Natalie Veiner Freeman, their senator husbands, and former prime minister Pierre Trudeau, along Marco Polo's trade routes through China, before having audiences with Deng Xiaoping and billionaire financier Li Ka-shing.

Each of the women known for her social power pursues a serious career or significant volunteer work about which she would prefer to talk, yet she cannot escape the public perception of herself as the female avatar of social access, the power that opens — or closes — almost any global door. "Wife of" or "daughter of" is a woman's most direct and traditional route to power, and those who travel it successfully do so with skill, subtlety, and, considering their fund-raising panache, extraordinary consequence. Women who can raise $2 million in a single night, as did the committee for the Toronto Symphony Orchestra in 1987, personify social power. In fact, the Charity Gala has become the barometric measure of society, the social equalizer of the twentieth century and an axis of the power game. Of the four billion charity dollars raised annually in Canada, only about 15 percent is funded by corporations and foundations. Tens of millions are enticed out of donors' pockets by a legion of imaginative women who combine executive skills with social power in all its ramifications, most often through the gala, a monster of their own creation.

Anatomy of a Fund Raiser

At the British Columbia Club during Expo 86, a small private luncheon was held for Jack McClelland, who was promoting the fledgling Writers' Development Trust. Also present was the lovable if irascible Jack Webster, whose own annual dinner has raised thousands of dollars for promising B.C. journalists. Pia Southam, former television anchor/actress and co-founder with her late husband, Harvey, of *Equity* magazine, arrived with an unexpected Montreal guest, her jet-setting sister-in-law Nancy Southam.

The wine flowed with the conversation until, just into the entrée, McClelland began his pitch for throwing the Great Literary Dinner Party to support the Writers' Development Trust. His idea was to hold soirées in cities across Canada, for one glorious evening a year, uniting authors and readers into a great literary family. To illustrate the cause, McClelland launched into a saga about novelist Marian Engel, whose struggles to complete her final manuscript when terminally ill had been compounded by encroaching poverty. Fifteen minutes later McClelland was still warming up. Webster began pushing his salmon furiously around his plate and mumbling, his voice a soft but ominous drum roll to McClelland's patter.

When McClelland reasoned that because the Great Literary Dinner Party at $200 a head was already a roaring success in Toronto, Vancouver should join the trend—anything that "goes" in Toronto is considered a national trend—Webster suspected a Toronto plot. He exploded that the idea was "too highbrow . . . too intellectual and not my cup o'tea." Then he stomped out of the room leaving behind an awkward silence and a luncheon that wilted before dessert. The fiasco was an omen for serendipitous events at future Great Literary Dinner Parties.

McClelland's vision of a cross-country fund raiser might have faded away had ink not run in the veins of the publishing Southams. The story of Engel had touched Nancy, the ebullient youngest daughter of Gordon and Jean Southam and a friend of the Who's Who wherever.[4] She believed in the cause and recognized a wickedly delicious potential for mixing mischievous writers with the conventional powerhouses of society, business, and politics. McClelland and Southam had never met, but they spotted in each other kindred spirits of incendiary proportions. A genius at collecting talent to effect his extravagant ideas, McClelland invited Southam to stay on for a brandy. Three hours and several snifters later, Southam agreed not only to host a Great Literary Dinner Party in Montreal but also to expand the existing Toronto and Ottawa dinners into a national event. Unite two forces like Southam and McClelland in a cause and the result is a tornado that sweeps up even the suspicious or the resistant. Wired to power more intricately than Bell Telephone, Southam sat down and dialed the country.

Montreal and Toronto responded immediately. Both have politicians and celebrities to burn, as well as the only donors who would pay $400 a couple for anything other than airplane tickets. Or so everyone thought. Ottawa was known only for its thirty-dollar luncheons until about the same time, when the queen power-broker of the nation entered the volunteer sector. One evening over dinner at Sussex Drive, Mila Mulroney mentioned to Edmonton Oilers owner Peter Pocklington that she was looking for a cause. Pocklington remembered a poignant story he had seen on TV about a child with cystic fibrosis. A few months later, Mila and Peter threw a sellout $5,000-a-plate cystic fibrosis bash complete with movie stars and hockey teams, proving that Ottawa, along with the rest of the country, could be lured into anteing up the cash. The successful formula had been less the cause than the celebrities.

Armed with this information, Nancy Southam and Great Literary Dinner Party supporter Edith Cody-Rice struck a committee of women central to Ottawa's fund-raising dynamics. It featured Diana Kirkwood and communications expert Starr Solomon. They contrived a list of writers and political celebrities and sold out the $200-a-plate author roast. Platoons of government luminaries came to see their *bêtes noires* on the firing line. Outsiders who sought access to cabinet ministers snapped up the remaining tickets. During the entertainment, politicians gleefully watched the authors hammer each other unmercifully—until the writers turned on the politicians. With the expression of a beleaguered bloodhound, Marjorie Nichols, parliamentary columnist with the Ottawa *Citizen*, brought down the house with line after bawdy line about free trade and the tangled love lives of the squirming politicians. The evening was off the record but the word spread; as calamity draws crowds, tickets for the following year sold faster than those for the Indy 500.

When resistance to $200 tickets continued in Vancouver and Calgary, Southam called upon two forces of nature — her own mother, philanthropist Jean Southam, who gives so much money to charitable causes every year that no one can refuse her, and Margaret Atwood, a founder of the Writers' Development Trust. That summer, Atwood slipped into Calgary to take tea with philanthropist Arthur Child, promising to be his guest of honour if Child would host an October dinner. He would and she did, welcoming Calgary into the fold. In Vancouver, Jean Southam decreed that eighty friends pay and show up at Cynthia Woodward's[5] submarinal soirée among the fish tanks at the Vancouver Aquarium. The nervous Woodward introduced newly paroled author Stephen Reid[6] with a spellbinding account of the bank robberies performed, not by his characters, but by the author himself.

That same week at the Montreal Great Literary Dinner Party, Southam herself gathered a potpourri of old and illustrious political rivals,[7] and such media celebrities as Leonard Cohen and Adrienne Clarkson. A cluster of Greek shipping magnates added the international flavour so much the cachet of Montreal. Somewhere between the soup and the entrée, the usually bilingual Southam struggled through the pain of a toothache and the din to request that the authors "move à la droit à l'autre table—ah, change places—s'il vous plaît." It was the only French that had been spoken by the executive all evening. A furious Alice Parizeau harassed her tablemate Gérard Pelletier, former federal cabinet minister and Canadian ambassador to the United Nations, until he strode to the microphone and demanded silence. Before a hushed crowd, he noted that Southam had failed to welcome the Quebec authors in French, scolding, "Do not call this a Canadian Great Literary Dinner Party. It is an *English* Great Literary Dinner Party!"

Pelletier's reprimand had the effect of an electrical failure in the Ritz Bar, uniting everyone in a common disaster and ensuring the unqualified success of the evening. Months later when friends asked McClelland why he hadn't bailed out the mortified Southam, he asked in amazement, "Was I there?"

Even René Lévesque played a posthumous role in bringing national exposure to Southam's party. While participating in the GLDP predinner press conference he had felt ill and left. He died later that evening. The media flooded Southam's after-party at her fabulous, renovated Cedar Avenue fire station with calls and the next morning the nation learned not only about Lévesque's death but also about a gala known as the Great Literary Dinner Party. National curiosity was piqued. By the fall of 1988, Southam-engineered dinners were proliferating. In Montreal, the Conservatives threw a Canadian National Railways dinner for forty in the company's corporate dining room. Following a superlative meal, each of the four guest authors was asked to say a few words, it was hoped, in appreciation of the dinner. Quebec novelist Hélène Holden[8] stood up and exclaimed, "Thank you for this elegant dinner.

Take an author to bed tonight!'' and sat down. Diane Francis acquitted herself with equal eloquence.

Then Tom Naylor of McGill University rose to joke, ''I'm curious. There is a preponderance of investigative business writers here—Diane Francis wrote *Controlling Interest* and *Contrapreneurs*—I wrote *Hot Money and the Politics of Debt* and I'm now working on a book on laundering money. Just what is CN up to, anyway?'' He grinned, waiting for the laugh.

Instead, he got CN chair Brian Gallery who leapt to his feet with the roar of an outraged father defending his daughter's honour. Naylor stuttered apologies while then Montreal *Gazette* publisher, Clark Davey, commanded in Churchillian tones, ''Never apologize! Never apologize!'' Mesmerized guests wondered who would be first out the eighteenth-story window. When Gallery paused for breath, Phil Johnston, former vice-chair of the Royal Trust, told a joke about a bull called Pompadour. Guests broke into near hysterical laughter. Strangers became newest best friends. Gallery apologized, uncorked more wine, and news of another delicious disaster spread across the country.

The oversold Ottawa GLDP in 1989 comprised an elite of 250 politicians, senators, the Speaker of the House, authors who flew in from everywhere, and a liberal representation of Fine Old Ottawa Families. The only couple in town left at home were the Mulroneys, uninvited because the committee did not want to stifle the fun with protocol—said to be taken seriously by Mila. In a much publicized gaffe, broadcaster Larry Zolf delivered his funny seven-minute speech, which had been approved the previous day by Cody-Rice. Then, pulling up a chair, he began reading twenty-five pages of his own intense prose. Guests quaffing champagne but thirsting for blood waited for the punch line that never came. Shouted pleas to stop were met with Zolfian bellows of ''Fuck thee!'' Cody-Rice had no wind-down signs, and Nancy Southam was strolling the beaches in Lamu. A sea of waving handkerchiefs finally drove a humiliated Zolf from the podium.

By the politicians' measure, Zolf had set himself up, perpetuating the GLDP tradition of calamity. By the fall of 1989 the Great Literary Dinner Party had become the social event of the nation. Nancy Southam's own itineraries and telephone bills resembled those of a federal political campaign, but in her second year of chairing and attending almost every dinner—not quite all on the same night—her hostesses, committees, the cast of writers, and about one thousand guests raised hundreds of thousands of dollars for the Writers' Development Trust. By 1990 the event had become an institution. In Toronto, where there are more celebrities in the audience than there are authors, seventy-two GLDPs were held, with a cross-country total of one hundred. The money will be held in trust by Wood Gundy until an endowment of $2 million has been reached.[9]

The GLDPs confirm the sine qua non of successful fund raising that the event, including the audience, must be at least as attractive as the cause. Unlike the heart and cancer fund raisers, the Writers' Development Trust in its early days was cheerfully nebulous about its intention. For the first two years as it grew in popularity, authors would openly puzzle over why they were there, while guests would examine the likes of Atwood, Fotheringham, or Musgrave and blurt out, ''You don't look like indigent writers.'' Eventually, it didn't matter. Surprise engendered intrigue until the event became the cause, and everyone had to be there. Broker Gordon Gekko said it in the movie *Wall Street* when he viewed an artistic atrocity that had appreciated in value from $200,000 to $2 million: ''Nurture the illusion until it becomes reality, and when it does . . . everyone has to own it.'' In other words, everyone has to be there—even at $200 a plate, and even if you are Jack Webster and had stormed out of the GLDP founding luncheon.

In October 1989, the great Webster himself bought his own ticket to escort Nancy Southam to Pia and Harvey Southam's GLDP for authors Margaret Atwood, Diane Francis, and William Deverell. Pia had sold out her guest list of eighteen in as many minutes. The only no-show was investment dealer Peter Brown, who refused to dine with Francis, a Vancouver Stock Exchange basher. The evening became so boisterous that Atwood scrapped her reading, and in the pre-dawn hours Webster joined Francis and a handful of other highbrow intellectuals who were not his cup o' tea in tiptoeing through the hedge into the Shaughnessy garden of Jean Southam, shedding his black-tie ensemble and jumping skinny into the swimming pool.

****

Why do these women, who ''have everything,'' do it? The simplest answer is that they care about the Cause and only the cruellest cynic would dismiss this gut rationale. Prominent women have long given their names and administrative expertise to major campaigns. Millie Lande, a Bronfman through the Rasminskys who was president of the 1987 multi-million-dollar Montreal Jewish Community Foundation Drive, is happiest wearing a lab coat and working in the volunteer sector on the hospital ward. Tannis and George Richardson[10] of Winnipeg lost a daughter to diabetes; Tannis became a leading force for the Juvenile Diabetes Foundation. In Montreal, Sheila Kussner, who survived cancer herself, founded Hope and Cope, a support group for patients and their families. The Belzberg's Bel-Fran Foundation is a major force behind the Simon Wiesenthal Center in Los Angeles and a flagship for research into dystonia, a muscle disorder suffered by the daughter of Sam and Fran Belzberg.

But caring about a cause is a one-dimensional answer that fails to define the motivation behind the thousands of hours donated by virtually hundreds of volunteers for each major event. Commitments to creating galas have implications far beyond the cause. The need for creative validation seems to be inherent in humankind, and is inextricably connected to the conviction that one person can make a difference. The power volunteers are driven by those needs expanded. The first is to be visible as an individual entity, not merely as Mrs. Wife Of, but to seek community at a level that gives control. Margo Bindhardt, former president of both the Canadian Opera Company and the Art Gallery of Ontario, noted, ''The fun is working with a team of people and seeing your ideas taking shape.'' The second is to make a political statement by upholding one's democratic right to choose where one's charity dollar goes. A third need is to expand one's potential from house-to-house canvassing to negotiating in the boardroom, where participation in the creative building process transcends the event. The fourth, and most signficant, is to meet with and learn from the male volunteers who are powerful executives from the corporate, financial, political, and professional institutions.

With talk of the recession, galas are switching from balls to barbecues, but money still needs to be raised, and the Charity Gala remains a phenomenon of excess in which the Establishment seeks power and personal identity while reaffirming its traditional status. It is also a game that the masses want to play or no one would go to the party. Anyone who dismisses as insignificant or frivolous the social implications of fund-raising luncheons, dinners, and balls, might consider the argument of Allan Gotlieb,[11] former Canadian ambassador to Washington: the cocktail soirée, the black-tie dinner, is *the* avenue to access, information, and power. In describing power Washington-style, Allan Gotlieb inadvertently elevated the role of society hostess to that of ambassadress-cum-pre-eminent power-broker, validating a woman's historical seat of influence. Author Sandra Gwyn, underscoring the importance of social access, has described the newspaper columns featuring the gala not as gossip but as sociological commentaries on the fabric of power.[12]

Men use the gala pipeline too. At the 1989 Great Literary Dinner Party in Ottawa, a lobbyist for Rogers Cable joggled the elbow of a cabinet minister, introduced himself, and arranged to meet with him that week. It beat fighting his way through four secretaries and a deputy. The political overtones cloaked in the niceties of social functions are stupendous. Lucy Johnson, daughter of former United States president Lyndon Johnson, observed from her Toronto home, ''The greatest thing I ever learned from my father was how to work a room.'' Anyone watching Mila Mulroney press the flesh at a banquet for 1,200 knows why this skill is revered. Former Ontario premier Bill Davis said publicly to the Prime Minister during the 1984 election campaign, ''I want you to understand, Brian, that if you win, Mila will have won at least half of your votes for you.'' He was not joking.

Does everyone really care about the Cause? Montreal social and political denizen Brenda Turner Norris,[13] who delivers sage zingers with such humorous agility that fans believe she might have been better suited—or at least more fun—than her brother John to run the country, replied, "Of course not." Others agreed. Norris further broadened the definitions of the Gala Game when she revealed that it is the wife who most often organizes the social events, decides which of the avalanche of invitations she and her husband will accept, and who will sit at their table. Men who make business contacts at parties are apparently blissfully unaware that their *eminences grises* have manoeuvred them like pawns on a chess board.

Social power is a façade for leverage in action. Anyone who purchases tickets to a thousand-dollar-a-plate fund raiser may well give initial thought to the cause, but the purchase can have as much, or more, to do with the patron list, peer pressure known as "business development," celebrity guests, and the gala committee itself. A galling reality is that powerful husbands can be reached through current wives (which in the institution of the Establishment makes the position vital and new wives so immediately acceptable). This was never even whispered about among the Old Guard, where the service of fund raising was synonymous with modesty and anonymity.

Passion for a cause is often superseded by that unmistakable breeze fluttering through the mists of altruism: "What's in it for me?" Pursuing social power must take a place beside the gift concept as a force behind volunteerism. In *The Fashion Conspiracy* Nicholas Coleridge noted, "Charity . . . provides both a purpose and a justification for buying couture dresses."[b] Blending social games with causes reflects one of the intriguing dualities of the human race. Few philanthropists sit at home and write large charity cheques, but they do attend galas that amuse them out of their money or bring them into contact with power. Winnipeg business and society power Suzanne Banfield Lount observed, "Home entertaining has been replaced by the Charity Gala as the only social event of the city." Shrewd chairs recognize these churning needs for inclusion and harness that energy into quality work for their cause. "Greed, guilt and fear," said Bluma Appel with a searingly candid eye to the game, "that's how you sell everything. There are so many people who get something out of it, whatever it is you want to sell—pollution, perfume, or philanthropy—it's still those three motivating things. It's what makes the world go around, and I love it." In the growing 1990s auction rage, many guests are simply seeking a good deal, and regardless of motivation, the collective pursuit of gala goers and their money produces a kinetic energy that circulates down — or up — through the system to play a major role in running this country.

Canadians do not admit to the desire for inclusion, but the more confident Americans rejoice in the notion. *Fortune* magazine journalist Julie Connelly observed of the New Money financier Saul Steinberg that his wife Gayfryd (the daughter of a clerk in the British Columbia telephone company) has connected him through respectable charities to members of the Old Guard. Canadian Posy Chisholm, writer/entrepreneur/adventurer/ international jetsetter who loves to blend the Establishment, the nouveau riche, and the ethnically diverse, said, "There's a whole group of Outsiders who are struggling to be at the top of the social ladder. They do these marvelous jobs, but they are not necessarily going to be invited to go duck shooting in the family marsh. . . . They're all going to get the Order of Canada, which they deserve, but the sad thing is, they struggle for power, and they're never going to make it where they want to be."

Each morning, social architects from coast to coast leap from their beds to design strategies for wooing the charity dollar for their hospital, university, or ballet, while social aspirants rush to join their committees, the post-graduate sororities of the city. To lure guests to the gate, Brenda Norris said, takes a combination of politics and quality entertainment. Montreal gala organizer Sandra Kolber agreed, explaining, "I am not just promoting a cause, I'm selling entertainment." Money pours into the coffers of non-profit organizations as creative thinkers have expanded the gala concept to include dinners, celebrity tennis matches, a Wrecker's Ball for Juvenile Diabetes, Susan Bassett's Worst Oil Painting in the World auction for the Canadian Paraplegic Association, the Vancouver Symphony on top of Blackcomb Mountain, Multiple Sclerosis Society's Auction-a-Bachelor Night and Mary Connacher's ZooDo, in 1991 called the "Hogtown Hoedown . . . All the beautiful people will be here—and a couple of incredible boars."[14] North American fund-raising antics have skyrocketed from the $200 church bazaar to the $2,000,000 Cecil B. de Mille spectacular thrown for the Toronto Symphony Orchestra's farewell to Walter Homburger.

****

How do they do it? Gala organizers know that the real art in fund raising is to render the element of coercion as subtle and appealing as a *Traviata* aria. The skill can be seen best by browsing through any performing arts program in the country and turning to the donor lists. Few, if any, givers still disguise themselves with the time-honoured title of "Anonymous." As the Canadian Establishment and monied elite in each community know each other, non-contributors are conspicuous by their absence. Donors who see their neighbours in a higher category are encouraged to increase their gift from benefactor to patron before the next program is published.

Smart organizers understand that positioning guests has everything to do with the politics of inclusion. As everyone has paid more or less the same amount of money, just who gets to sit by fashion guru Oscar de la Renta at the Genesis dinner or opposite Pavarotti at the gigantic Montreal Symphony Orchestra ball, and who languishes in obscurity two hundred yards away between a waiter's station and the kitchen?

Committees devise pecking orders to lessen the odds, selling corporate tables at $10,000 and single seats at $1,000, $500 and $300. Still, seating arrangements can lead to committee clashes and temper tantrums by disgruntled guests that make the Stanley Cup finals look like a stroll down Harmony Lane.

Committees have softened the pain of presumed rejection with a pre-dinner cocktail hour in which guests can check out the hundreds of thousands of dollars of fashion competition for the fifth time that week, mingle undeterred by social and ethnic barriers, pigeonhole business prospects, and chat with the Rosedale, Westmount, or Shaughnessy set who might otherwise pass them by on the street. Like Cinderella in her magic moment, under the guise of supporting the Cystic Fibrosis Foundation, the Vancouver Museum, the Royal Winnipeg Ballet, or the Montreal Symphony, the satellites can share fois gras with the magnates of business, politics, and society, flirting with the notion that they are all flying together in the stratosphere.

Power swirls around galas with more pirouettes accelerando than a Bolshoi ballet, and demonstrates the primary difference between events that raise $20,000 and those that bring in $350,000 or more. Galas realize mega success when the cause takes second billing to the guests, allowing the celebrities, politicians, and socialites of the audience to become their own enamorata. At a Toronto ''Auction-a-Bachelor Night'' the in-gossip had it that a mother lost her head in the frenzy, and spent $10,000 winning a date for her daughters with a Canadian rowing crew, after which they all took off to Club Med for the weekend. Raconteurs could not remember the name of the charity, which raised over $250,000 in one evening, but they couldn't wait for the event next year.[14c]

Nowhere in the land is the Gala Game played with more awesome success than in Toronto, the head office of Canada, which houses the CEOs of national and international institutions. To a financier, the intersection of Bay and King may look like a cluster of vertical boardrooms, but to an impassioned fund raiser of the National Ballet company, the soaring glass and concrete towers resemble a flock of dancers reaching toward the sun. Toronto is the mecca of charitable pursuits into which Canada's most prominent wives channel pipelines from their husbands' corporate donations to their specific cause, and they compete for those funds with elegantly concealed ferocity. Women do not have to be the source of wealth—just connected to working capital. Wives of prominent CEOs are fiercely wooed as chairs, not only for their personal skills but to access their husband's corporate generosity. Then they help each other out: you donate to my Toronto Symphony gala and we'll donate to your Irish Relief Fund. It's all part of the unspoken game. Each table bought with corporate funds can bring in $10,000. Combine this with individual ticket sales of $250, and any gala can realize over $200,000 in a one-night stand.

In the frenzied competition for donations, billions may be raised, but the amount is grossly insufficient to meet the needs of 60,000 Canadian charities. Keeping one's cause afloat depends upon superlative volunteer skills equal to the professional expertise of fund-raising companies, which can cost 50 to 80 percent of the take. Well-meaning amateurs have been known to make "huge" profits that may cover the expenses, or even cause the charities to lose small fortunes.[15] It takes a special kind of courage combined with executive skill to raise money. What sounds like fun and frivolity is work that would exhaust a financial analyst in a corporate takeover.

Margaret Atwood had founded the Writers' Development Trust in 1976 with a series of dinner parties in her own home before she, Graeme Gibson, Pierre Berton, Margaret Laurence, and significant others got a tax number and in 1982 held a fund raiser called the Night of One Hundred Authors. Although their enthusiasm was boundless and the evening was a smashing success, it left them $60,000 in the hole.[16] Hard at work on a novel at the time, Atwood offered to write *The Great Literary Cookbook* to help pay off the debt. Everyone thought it was a terrific idea. "So," groaned Atwood, "I had to write the damn thing."

Former Ottawa resident Belle Shenkman is the grande dame of corporate galas. Her penchant for theatre is reflected in her tony London flat, where entering her opaque-viridian kitchen is equivalent to swimming in a Perrier bottle. Royalty frequently attends her spectacular events for visiting Canadian companies or when she brings the Royal Ballet to Canada. Due to the brilliant pioneering promotions of women like Shenkman, major corporations are shifting their charity money into the advertising budget, acknowledging up front the marketing value of the charity/business combination.

Toronto's counterpart to Shenkman is Margo Bindhardt who initiated the idea of winning corporate sponsorships and springboarding fund raising into the world of big business. She was involved with the Canadian Opera Company when it was housed in a run-down factory reeking of maraschino cherries, and was raising about $25,000 annually. For two years Bindhardt nagged her board friends to help her set up a business sponsorship as her mother (Mrs. Gilbert W. Humphrey) had done so successfully in New York. But Bindhardt needed more power to win over the CEOs. She recalled, "They all thought I was nuts." Then Monty Larkin became president and in 1973 told Bindhardt to go ahead. Backed by Eph Diamond of Cadillac Fairview, whose wife, Shirley, was on the women's committee, and Lorenz Blaser, a senior officer of Gulf Oil, Bindhardt grabbed a cheap recording of a medley of operas that needed sponsors and breezed into the offices of CEOs with "Have I got a deal for you!" Later she recalled with embarrassment, "Oh, I could just die!" About the same time she lost her nerve, the idea took off, launching Business and the Arts as an industry. By 1989, the corporate sector was sponsoring the Canadian Opera Company to an annual aria of $840,000.

That corporate structure has helped to create a massive infrastructure to support galas, one that is making some fashion designers, florists, caterers, and event planners very rich. They will tell you they do it for cost, but if this were true, they would all go out of business because they are doing it every night of the week.

Chasing the charity dollar provides unlimited opportunity for deadly competition even within a single charity. In 1987, Anne E.P. Armstrong[17] chaired the first fund raiser for the Genesis Research Foundation,[18] providing the ambience of Green Meadows, the famous thoroughbred horse farm of her late uncle, Argus mogul John Angus ''Bud'' McDougald. Friend Sherrill ''Sherry'' Eaton[19] helped co-ordinate the Racing Gala, her pal Mila Mulroney came as guest of honour, and political star Barbara McDougall satisfied the requirement for political celebrities. Four hundred guests paid $300 each to view the antique auto collection of motorcyclist and former Olympic skating champion Maude ''Jimmy'' McDougald, to dine and dance in a giant marquee decorated in the family's blue and pink racing colours, and to race broomstick hobbyhorses across a lucite floor laid over the swimming pool. Armstrong's gala raised $100,000 and entered the short list of Toronto's In fund raisers.

Then, just four months after the McDougald spectacular, Armstrong's committee was astounded to learn that Nancy Raeburn Paul[20] and boutique owner Sharon Batten were holding their own Genesis gala at the Four Seasons Hotel, featuring the great Oscar de la Renta himself. Red-and-black art deco invitations the size of placemats were showered upon Toronto, advising the guests to come ''Black tie and Beautiful.'' More than a charity fund raiser was at stake: Sharon Batten owned a Hazelton Lanes boutique that sold gowns by Oscar de la Renta.[21] Fearing that Genesis would suffer from overkill, women sprang to their telephones with cries of ''Don't go!'' and ''Listen to your conscience!'' Still, the gorgeous Oscar was coming with his sensational show of spring and summer gowns.[22] Conscience lost. The Event had superseded the Cause, and it sold out at $400 a plate. Unparalleled in opulence, the evening featured black-and-white satin bows on every chair, ice sculptures on every table, door prizes (including a de la Renta gown), a magnificent menu, and the promised fashion show. To their embarrassment, some committee members were ordered to advertise the exclusive gowns by wearing them throughout the evening. Nevertheless, Genesis and the ecstatic medical research team realized another $100,000 and broad community support.

Even though Batten had personally paid $4,000 for the invitations — in the fashion business, four grand would pay for little more than the décolletage of one de la Renta gown. The event was a brilliant marketing coup worth a fortune in free advertising for Batten. One of her salespeople admitted that for days after the event business in her Toronto boutique had soared. So what? Everyone won. An entrepreneur scored on a cause, the charity benefitted from the entrepreneur, and the guests enjoyed a splashy affair where they were wowed by Oscar. Who's to moralize?

Raeburn Paul had devised a formula based on acquisitive desires and social needs. Shortly after the de la Renta marvel she did it again, drawing 1,200 guests to a luncheon fashion show for cancer that featured the popular New York designers Carolyne Roehm and Arnold Scaasi, both of whom also sold through Batten's Yorkville shop. Philanthropist Bluma Appel observed of this luncheon, "A group of women took it over and made it into the social event of the season. What it was for was of no consequence. If it had been for kittens with two ears in the wrong place they still would have sold out."

It is this kind of Malcolm Forbes revelry that drives Calvinist Canada wild with rage and sets columnists sharpening their pencils to skewer the extravagant and champion the dispossessed. It seems bad enough that the rich should be privileged, but must they have fun too? Journalists are known to rail against women who lavish more on their gowns and decorations than they do on charities.[d] Detractors forget, however, that these women's annual family taxes are already immense, only 44 percent of each dollar donated is deductible, and their husbands' corporations have probably sponsored the events. The harsh reality is that women are merely acting as the facilitators in a game that society chooses to play. Many supporters are there waving the flag and being good sports, but the charity gala works because it is a marriage of convenience between two pursuits: money and social power.

****

The logistics in organizing a ball for one thousand guests in a setting such as the Montreal Musée des Beaux Arts are worthy of their own legend. Money is committed months in advance; orchestras and halls are rented; liquor, flowers, menus, table decorations, and entertainment are procured. Women who have direct access to the CEOs' offices realize more on the bottom line. The 1988 Montreal Musée des Beaux Arts Ball committee had despaired after three failed attempts to get the liquor donated, but co-chair Andrée Beaulieu called pal Charles Bronfman[23] and within moments Seagrams agreed to supply the booze for the bash.

In the days and hours before, women juggle schedules, menus, transportation, and the onerous task of seating guests along with their personal commitments to family and home. Nothing can be set up until the art gallery closes on the eve of the event. Then, after tables, decorations, place settings, dance floor, orchestra space, and ambient lighting are in place, a catering staff with makeshift kitchens swoops in like a set change at La Scala. At the stroke of midnight the frenzy is repeated in reverse, in order to return the setting to a gallery before morning. Faced with a similar challenge, Cinderella's fairy godmother would have tossed up her wand and quit. Sandra Kolber[24] opened the books on the 1986 Montreal Symphony extravaganza starring Rudolph Nureyev, which included a mind-boggling shift of 1,100 guests from the Place des Arts theatre to the Queen Elizabeth Hotel for a midnight supper that featured gold-flecked consommé. The elaborate staging was typical of Kolber, an author and filmmaker.

The gala underscored a truism that to make money you have to spend it. Guests at the black-tie event bought tickets for $250 or $500; sales brought in $380,000. Nureyev alone cost $50,000. After artists, accompaniment, stagehands, busses, and a stunning dinner were paid for, costs had swelled to $160,000. In the end, the profit to the symphony was $220,000 or, in fund-raising terms, a commendable 43 cents on the dollar. The numbers rarely match, but Kolber noted that "comparisons are invidious." In 1984, she had raised $300,000 with Danny Kaye because he came for free, but she laments that there are no Danny Kayes left. In 1989 she had to pay so much to get Pavarotti to sing at the symphony that, despite luring 2,000 donors and netting $750,000 for the orchestra, she could not bear to reveal his fee. Kolber deals in big numbers and horrible risks: Pavarotti is notorious for last-minute cancellations, but she would have pulled it off even if she had had to warble in his place.

Veterans of galas like Kolber and Eve MacDougall[25] are so swamped with requests to chair or to attend functions that the problem for them is not how to get in but how to get out, how to say no. MacDougall estimated that Establishment Torontonians can easily donate, annually, $35,000 of their personal funds. The demand is out of hand, which is a better reason than hard times for any reduction in giving, and unless a witty note from a prominent patron friend is scribbled on the invitation, chances are it will land in the G file. This is conferred power personified.

****

Numerous women like Margo Bindhardt shrink from running balls and will chair fund-raising campaigns only if there is direct contact to government or the CEOs. Philanthropist/activist Bluma Appel, chair of the Canadian Foundation for AIDS Research (CanFar), reflected on the tough new approach: "The only way you can get money from the government is to prove that it costs less to give [it] now than to pay later. It has nothing to do with ideals, it has nothing to do with humanitarianism. [Just] show them how much it's going to cost to treat . . . all these AIDS patients and it will blow their minds." Approaching corporate CEOs is a process that tests the highest power of access: rejections can be tough but wins can be big. Publisher Avie Bennett queried the value of charity balls when he said, "Ten guys can get together over lunch and raise a million dollars."[26] Elizabeth Tory agreed with Bennett; the social and business dynamo wife of John[27] sat on the board for financing the building of Roy Thomson Hall in the late 1970s. The $20 million raised, including $4.5 million from Kenneth Thomson, was the largest fund-raising sum ever achieved in the private sector.[28] In Montreal, Sheila Kussner of Hope and Cope is one woman who single-handedly raised a million dollars over a private luncheon.

As board members of Toronto's Wellesley Hospital, Vice-chair Kelly Meighen[29] and Joanna Black,[30] put a new slant on direct contact when they agreed to help the gynaecology department raise $135,000. Instead of seeking out the CEOs, they approached the Wellesley doctors who in turn involved their women patients. Within two months they had exceeded their goal, raising $210,000 in a fifth of the time needed to prepare a ball, and 100 percent of the money went to the cause. In Vancouver, Barbara Brink devised the most respected fund raiser for the Junior League and Science World by combining the social nuances of the gala with internationally renowned speakers such as Henry Kissinger, Lee Iacocca, and Benazir Bhutto. Sellout crowds welcome the variation from the gala format of designer gowns and expensive decorations.

Martha Cohen and Vera Swanson[31] unabashedly acknowledged the power of their husbands' positions when they sought $15 million to build the Calgary Centre for Performing Arts. They headed for the corporate head offices in Toronto, where no one refused to see the wife of either Harry Cohen of Sony or of a Southam publisher. Furthermore, Cohen's well-publicized birthday present, from an adoring Harry, was a million dollars to build the Martha Cohen Theatre in the CCPA complex, and the power to donate money always establishes the peer pressure to get it. CEOs ready to sign cheques for $2,000 to $10,000 were startled by these two dynamos requesting $100,000. They rarely got less than $25,000. The $15 million raised through the leadership of Cohen, Swanson, and Calgary volunteer extraordinaire Sandra LeBlanc,[32] combined with government funds, produced a three-theatre acoustical marvel. Vera Swanson became the first person ever to get a million-dollar donation from Calgary's Mannix construction family. It was used to buy a famous Casavant organ built in St. Hyacinthe, Quebec.

When the power of the cause merges with the competitive drive of the human species, the results can be astounding. The British Columbia Children's Hospital fund raisers used to be earnest but mediocre affairs until Isabel Diamond was appointed to the board. In 1987 Diamond created and co-chaired with Fran Belzberg[33] the Children's Hospital Crystal Ball. They included in the dinner menu a Wish List of twenty specialized pieces of medical equipment costing as much as $100,000 each. Initially she and Belzberg had hoped that the 250 guests would take the Wish List home, think it over, and mail in a donation. On the evening of the ball, however, somewhere between the smoked veal and the pomme torte, Rosalie Segal[34] bought a $4,800 transport monitor for infants. The news galvanized the party. Segal's act of generosity inspired that competitive mania that lurks near the surface of the human psyche. In an hour-long purchasing frenzy, guests bought every item on the Wish

List and the hospital was $500,000 richer. Within twenty-four hours every hospital in the country knew about it.

The myth that guests attend fund raisers solely to support the charity dwindles with each gala and was never more evident than on the eve of October 23, 1986, when the Famous People Players (FPP), the fabulous black-light troupe of mentally disabled artists, opened on Broadway. This event enjoyed more clout at the chair level than any other in memory. Mila Mulroney served as honorary Canadian chair while co-chair Hilary Weston organized a planeload of 160 friends to fly down for the event, valued from $300 to $1,000 a seat. The New York chairs, Joan Sutton Straus, Kenneth Taylor, and Eunice Shriver, sister to Jack, Bobby, and Ted Kennedy, had spent ten gruelling months first ensuring the essential collection of illustrious patrons and volunteers, then juggling the committees[35] of two countries to produce a guest list that would have impressed the Queen. Canadian and American acceptances poured in from the wealthy, the famous, the ambassadorial, the aristocratic, and the merely powerful.

In her autobiography *Dare to Dream*, FPP founder Diane Dupuy described what was to have been the greatest night of her troupe's collective life—a successful Broadway debut.[101] At the final curtain call, however, the performers, who had struggled from the obscurity of a church basement to stardom, stood in the wings entirely forgotten as Prime Minister Brian Mulroney swept to the stage to give his regards to Broadway. For the organizers who accompanied him, it was a well-deserved moment. It had been the first hazardous chairing of a New York mega gala by Mrs. Oscar Straus III, as Joan Sutton is known in New York[36]—and her committee had pulled it all off by attracting a celebrity audience and raising a substantial sum of money. Who would have shrunk from the chance to hold a microphone on a Broadway stage? Not the Canadians. Brian spoke. Mila spoke. Joan spoke. The thirsty audience of celebrities clapped appreciatively, wondered who was sitting four rows away and dreamed of the next attraction, the Lincoln Center and a gala dinner dance.

According to Dupuy's memoirs, it was Ken Taylor who suddenly ran back on stage, and blurted, "Oh, we forgot the next best thing to the Mets score—Diane Dupuy!" Maureen McTeer and Catherine McKinnon cheered the forlorn Players onto the stage to thunderous applause. It should have been Dupuy's finest hour but she committed a fatal gala gaffe. She used the platform to promote her cause. After thanking everyone for coming she challenged, "And now you . . . the leaders of this country . . . are in a position . . . to open up your companies and employ handicapped people!" The silence was deathly, underscoring Bluma Appel's sage observation that moral wrangling and audience commitment are not part of fund raisers. Donation yes, commitment no. Two lone reporters leaped to their feet and began clapping. The audience recovered in a buzz of conversation, and, Dupuy wrote, "left so fast that you might have thought the theatre was on fire."[f]

Looking back, Dupuy spluttered that "the audience were the idiots," and she may have a point. But her primary objective, raising funds for an FPP theatre, had been eclipsed by the very human desire for recognition. Beyond the cause, the illustrious guests had their own agenda. The Prime Minister also understood what his audience wanted. New York loved Mulroney; later at the dinner dance when a woman offered $25,000 more for FPP if the PM would sing, he responded by crooning "Paper Doll." Money is so easy when the game is played right. Celebrities who are willing to shed a little dignity can attract an audience who will pay to be surprised. FPP was merely the backdrop for the primary entertainment of the evening.

When the Stratford Festival's *Stratford Express* pulls out of Toronto's Union Station for opening night, the organizers understand that Shakespeare is not to be taken seriously. The brilliant idea of VIA -Railing guests from Toronto to the stage some two hours away was chaired in its inaugural year by Joanna Black, followed by Eve MacDougall, who doubled the numbers to 750 and who missed her calling as a stand-up comic or a set designer for the Canadian Opera Company. Months later that same year, hundreds more guests scrambled for $200-a-seat tickets to see Don Harron's post-modern Shakespeare, *Much Ado About Something*, performed at the Inn on the Park by the Toronto social and business elite. Plucked from their regular role as audience, the Gilt-Edged Players included heavy hitters Hal Jackman, Marlene Del Zotto, Conrad and Joanna Black, Trevor Eyton, John Craig Eaton, Sherry Eaton, and Julian Porter. Had Stratford performed a classic *Macbeth*, the reaction might have been ho hum. Instead, the audience got a huge laugh at Canadian celebrities playing the gentle fool, Stratford got $112,000 dollars more, ample publicity, and Shakespeare was possibly also amused.[37]

Arguably the most successful events occur when clever chairs reach beyond the regular donor pool to enkindle a response from the general public. In this case the power is generated by an inspired media that appeals to a collective community heart. In Vancouver during the summer of 1985, "Take the Art Gallery to Court" fund raisers Margaret Pitts and Joan Keevil created Pyramid Parties. A volunteer would host a luncheon at which every guest gave only three dollars to the art gallery. Then each of those guests became a hostess at another luncheon whose guests would pay three dollars and in turn become hostesses. The game caught the imagination of British Columbians. Thousands held picnics on boats, beaches, and mountaintops from English Bay and Vancouver's East End to Alta Lake and Whistler, from Saltspring Island to Prince George. The parties raised $22,000, but better still, new members and donors jammed gallery telephone lines to become involved in the bigger campaign, which went over the top. On another occasion, Margaret Pitts and Fran Belzberg overlaid a $75,000 Rauschenberg painting with a graph, which they then sold off by the square inch. A delighted public oversubscribed.

At the once flagging Metropolitan Toronto Zoo, rejuvenated by former chair Mary Connacher, and at the Vancouver Aquarium, chaired by Jane van Roggen,[38] wild animals and alligators can be bought or adopted by the public. At the zoo, a corporation bought a rhino and a Grade 6 class parented a nest of baby snakes. At the aquarium, a Grade 3 class bought a school of fish, and for Nancy's birthday Jean Southam bought Bianca the killer whale.

****

In Vancouver, the Countess Aline Dobrzensky, the Irish-born daughter of Sir John and Lady Galvin, has become the pivotal member of the country's "royal set" and a premier force in the Vancouver charitable community.[39] The countess achieves a subtle balance between an Irish lass's gentle demeanour and a business executive's intellect, which she daily employs to scan a dozen financial newspapers, oversee the running of numerous office buildings around Vancouver's Hastings Street, a shopping centre, and ranches in B.C. and California. Besides caring for her young children, she also volunteers in an East End soup kitchen, ran the family compound at Cap Ferrat until it was sold in 1991, recuperates with Mick Jagger and Joan Carlisle Irving[40] on Mustique, and attracts international nobility to help sponsor such fund-raising events as Panache, an exhibit of women's fashions dating over the past 200 years. The difference between Countess Dobrzensky and other women of social power in Canada is that she not only has the title and the fortune, but she runs the business. What she lacks is that image of institutional clout that propels the fund-raising efforts of a Hilary Weston into the stratosphere.

****

Mila Mulroney may achieve a gross of $2.4 million for cystic fibrosis in a single night, but as the nature of her power is political, her days are numbered. It is Hilary and Galen Weston who qualify as Canada's royalty by dint of popular acclaim and through power that endures because it is social, historical, and institutional. The Westons are also one of a mere handful of couples who hold the key to the inner sanctum of British royalty and may be the only couple on the continent with the panache combined with (his) blood lines, the wealth, the corporate resources, and royal friendships,[41] to conceive and execute the impossible charity weekend: a $3-million fund raiser for their favourite cause, the United World Colleges.[42] When the access is disguised through support for one's favourite charity, the proposition becomes irresistible to those who enjoy the game. The Westons flew two hundred Canadians and Americans on two chartered Concordes from Toronto and New York to London. Then, in the concentrated space of three days, they bussed them all over southern England to castles, manor houses, and gourmet meals, with less time to visit the loo than to change from spectator silks for polo into gowns for a ball at Blenheim Palace, and on the fourth morning sent the most cynical home raving that they had had such a great time they forgot to suffer jet lag.

Hilary Weston is neither a calculating business executive nor a chilly socialite; her personality fluctuates from savvy buyer/marketer for Holt Renfrew to hilarious flake. Friends and staff find her human traits endearing as do her innumerable house guests of international stature. When the Westons took up racing, a friend reportedly asked Hilary, ''What are your colours?''

Hilary queried, ''What are colours?''

When she and Nicole Eaton were preparing their garden book,[43] they clambered over Winnipeg fences in early May, searching the still frozen ground for exquisite landscapes. Now the vice-chair of Holt Renfrew, Weston was once a model and buyer for the Weston family's Brown Thomas Department Stores in Ireland where she had first met Galen. Later she modelled in Edmonton, where she had gone to further her career and to decide whether or not to marry the greatest catch since caviar.[44] Hilary Weston balances upon that delicate line between Establishment woman and community player, a chameleon who pursues her own career without endangering her marriage or her privileged position.

****

Toronto fund-raising luminary Posy Chisholm,[45] globe-trotting journalist, pal of English Lords, Malcolm Forbes, Italian counts, Indian raj, and anyone who amuses—titled or merely outrageous—has the body of a match stick and the energy of a 747. In India a few years ago at the invitation of her friends, then prime minister Rajiv Gandhi and his Italian wife (with whom Chisholm had worked in Rome as foreign correspondent for the *Telegram*), Chisholm became the only pilot in history to balloon over the Taj Mahal, and praying thousands, with the airsick minister of tourism hanging over the side. The event was a metaphor for social power. But Chisholm is most loved by the children and staff of orphanages in India and Sicily and the women of a dozen villages around Cuernavaca, Mexico. She not only enjoys life's whimsies but has also shared her wealth and, most significantly, the process of how to effect change. Canadians who shovel snow through the bleakness of northern Februaries while those dreadful rich are supposedly languishing on the white sands of some tropical idyll can take heart that, more often than they slather on the suntan oil or quaff mimosas under the palm trees, these tycoons of social power could be building orphanages, expanding hospitals, or empowering the homemakers of indigent villages.

CHAPTER 1 NOTES

1. Peterson's husband, Thomas d'Aquino, is the president and CEO of the Business Council on National Issues, was a special assistant to Prime Minister Pierre Trudeau (1969-1972), and is linked through endless boards, professorships, and councils to government and business in Canada, the United States, and Europe. Peterson moved to the finance department where she holds the illustrious title of director general of Federal-Provincial Relations Division and Social Policy Branch, and she is the assistant to Russell Robinson, Assistant Deputy Minister of Finance.
2. Pat Buckley is the wife of William, the archetypal voice of conservatism in America. In *The Fashion Conspiracy*, p. 67, Nicholas Coleridge refers to Pat as "one of the three power charity queens of Manhattan." *Chatelaine*, in April 1988, described her as the epitome of Tom Wolfe's "social X-ray"—"a woman starved to near perfection" in a Bill Blass gown—adding, "No Manhattan party quite makes the A-list if she's not there."
3. Both in their forties, the Westons are among Canada's most glamorous and popular Establishment couples. Hilary is vice-chair of the family fashion company, Holt Renfrew (bought, some say, for her by Galen for $43 million). Galen's $3.5-billion food empire on two continents listed its 1988 North American revenues at $11 billion. Family holdings in Great Britain and Ireland are extensive.
4. Southam's maternal grandfather was the legendary H.R. MacMillan who came west as a young man dying of tuberculosis, founded the MacMillan Lumber Company that became the giant integrated forest conglomerate MacMillan Bloedel, and lived into his nineties.
5. Woodward was Cynthia Shaw, daughter of Neil Shaw, chair of Tate & Lyle, the largest sugar company in the world. She is the wife of Christopher "Kip" Woodward, a son of the late department store owner C.N. "Chunky" Woodward and Rosemary "Posie" Devlin.
6. Author of *Jackrabbit Parole*, Reid is married to author/poet Susan Musgrave.
7. Present were former Quebec premier René Lévesque, former prime minister Pierre Trudeau, current Parti

Québécois chief Jacques Parizeau and his wife, the author Alice, Michael Pitfield, former Clerk of the Privy Council, aspiring Liberal leader Paul Martin, Jr., and socialite-backroom-politico Brenda Norris.

8. Sister of Niky Papachristidis of the Greek shipping line, Papachristidis Canada Ltd.
9. GLDP funds are directed toward memorial lectures, awards, Writers in Electronic Residence, which links students to Canadian writers by computer, and support of established but impoverished writers.
10. George is the fourth generation of the Manitoba grain and financial management family. James Richardson and Sons Limited was originally established in 1912 and is the parent company Richardson Greenshields of Canada.
11. Allan is the Husband Of Sondra, who is the author of several books including *Wife Of . . . An Irreverent Account of Life in Washington,* as well as of the famous Secretarial Slap. Allan Gotlieb is currently delivering his message to aspiring diplomats from his chair at Harvard University, while Sondra embodies media power: on June 14, 1991 she devoted her *Financial Post* column to defending Allan's innocence in expediting the immigration papers of former Iraqi defense minister Mohammad Mashat.
12. The most notable columns are those of Rosemary Sexton, a lawyer turned social commentator who replaced Zena Cherry in the *Globe and Mail,* Thomas Schnurmacher in the Montreal *Gazette,* and jet-setting bonne vivante Valerie Gibson, whose internationally flavoured and amusingly bitchy "Top Dollar" appears in *Vancouver* magazine.
13. The daughter of Phyllis Turner Ross and sister of former prime minister John Turner, Norris has her own real estate company. She is a backroom Liberal worker and a director of Roosevelt Campobello International Park Commission, once an exclusive seigniory and now the site of a prestigious Canadian-American think tank.
14. That was the Bachelor Classic held for the Multiple Sclerosis Society of Canada, which in 1990 sold out at 1,100 tickets. Actually, it was not a rowing crew, but a bachelor trio up for auction and yes, they did go to Club Med with the woman's daughters.
15. In 1990, two Vancouver neighbourhood societies joined forces, held a lottery, and lost a reported $426,000.

16. Clarkson Gordon now provides fiscal guidance to the GLDP.
17. A law partner in estate planning at Toronto's McMillan Binch, the super-achieving Armstrong has written textbooks, is a mother, teacher, wife of lawyer Doug Gibson, and an impassioned advocate of the credo that resting on one's name and wealth is déclassé.
18. Genesis was established to research women's health issues, particularly in the field of reproduction.
19. Sherrill Eaton is the former wife of department store chair John Craig. As a member of the Montreal Webster family, she belongs to old Establishment wealth in her own right.
20. Nancy Raeburn Paul is in real estate; her husband is in business.
21. By 1990, Batten had become director of the designer boutiques at Holt Renfrew.
22. The event with Oscar had actually been sewn up by his friend, fashion writer and future vice-president of Oscar de la Renta's company, Princess Marina Sturdza, whose mother is the sparkling Ioana Soutzo Malone, the Romanian princess who survived as a refugee by running a pig farm in Saskatchewan.
23. The Musée des Beaux Arts Ball is co-chaired by French and English women. Among the chairs have been Penelope Price and Denyse Bazin, Susan Curry and Andrée Lessard, Pattie Cleghorn and Andrée Beaulieu.
24. Wife of Senator Leo Kolber and prominent through her own expertise, Sandra operates from the apex of social and business power. When representing Claridge Incorporated, the Samuel Bronfman family's interests, on the board of Cineplex Odeon, Kolber headed the search committee for a buyer for Cineplex. In 1990 she retired from the board of Cineplex to accept an order-in-council directorship with the CBC, which apparently made her the only non-Conservative member of a board charged with guiding the CBC through a period of massive budget cuts ($180 million) and a pending Broadcast Act.
25. Eve Gordon MacDougall, a former Montrealer, is the wife of Hartland MacDougall, chair of Royal Trustco. She is famous for the casually elegant style in which she launches events.
26. To launch the Toronto Sky Dome fund drive, Trevor Eyton called up twenty-eight friends to raise $5 million

from each for a total of $140 million. The Sky Dome is known as ''The house that Trevor built.''

27. Elizabeth ''Liz'' Tory has not only run her own successful travel agency, which she subsequently sold to American Express, but has her securities certificate and enjoys business connections to Senator Trevor Eyton, a childhood buddy, and Imperial Oil head Arden Haynes. She is known as a board member who delivers and when a major roast was held for Eyton, Tory was the only woman asked to speak. In an evening of illustrious speakers, her delivery was brilliant.
28. Liz Tory's husband, John, is righthand man to press and retail magnate Kenneth Thomson but she insisted that John bends no arms for her. Nevertheless, the Thomson family is widely known as a difficult philanthropic sell, and public perception puts Liz Tory at the heart of the $4.5 million coup.
29. Kelly, the wife of Senator Michael Meighen, is a Toronto organizer par excellence, had her own career with General Foods, is a volunteer in the campaigns of Barbara McDougall, and is a board member of the Meighen family foundation, Themadel.
30. Joanna, formerly Shirley Black, is the wife of business executive/publishing magnate Conrad. When she changed her name in 1991, a bemused press speculated that it was to hasten Conrad's predicted peerage. But friends insist that Joanna has always despised the name ''Shirley'' and they admire her gutsiness in ignoring the inevitable ridicule from the press.
31. Vera Swanson is the wife of Frank, former Southam publisher. She began polishing her fund-raising skills years ago in Ottawa with the grand Pooh Bah of fund raising, Belle Shenkman.
32. LeBlanc, a former member of the Canada Council, headed the volunteer organization of 15,000 for the 1988 Calgary Olympics.
33. Isabel is the wife of business executive Charles Diamond. Fran is the wife of Sam Belzberg of First City Financial Corp. Ltd., and the namesake of Bel-Fran Investments, the company's philanthropic arm, which in 1989 donated a million dollars to the library of the Simon Fraser University downtown campus.
34. Rosalie has raised over $81,000 for charity by making her own fashion hair bows at home, absorbing 100 percent of the costs, and selling them throughout the

Vancouver retail trade. She is the wife of Joe Segal, who built and later sold the retail empire that included Fields, Marshall Wells, and Zellers Department Stores. At one time he was the largest shareholder of the Hudson's Bay. His Kingswood Capital Corporation includes real estate holdings and retail stores.

35. The patron list included the Prime Minister and Mila; David Peterson, then premier of Ontario, and his wife, Shelley; Bob Johnston, then consul-general of Canada, and wife, Popsie; Joe Clark, then minister of external affairs. A committee member in New York was Canadian lawyer Marilou McPhedran.
36. Sutton Straus's husband, Oscar, told the *Globe and Mail*'s Zena Cherry that his personal contribution was "one or two tables . . . plus the use of his house, office and wife for one year."
37. Don Harron did it again in 1990 with "The Shaming of the True," a parody played by business and political luminaries Hal Jackman, David Crombie, Bob and Arlene Rae, Senator Michael Kirby, and Gerry Caplan.
38. The wife of Jimmy Connacher of Bay Street giant Gordon Capital, Mary Connacher created "The ZooDo," a fund-raising safari night complete with elephant and camel rides when guests tire of dancing. Jane, the wife of Liberal Senator George van Roggen, is also president of the B.C. Cancer Agency.
39. Countess Dobrzensky launched her volunteer career as a young woman in Rome through the Knights of Malta, which is where she met Count Enrico during a dinner party given by a Russian prince. Her current focus is on the Vancouver Museum for which she has increased annual donations over a hundredfold. With her own connections plus those through her sister, Princess Patricia de La Tour d'Auvergne, and her brother Sean (whose sister-in-law is best friends with Fergie and therefore linked to British royalty), as well as through her own husband, who is cousin to Prince Hans-Adam II, head of state in the monarchy of Liechtenstein, and to Princess Caroline of Monaco, Countess Dobrzensky's board shines with the aristocracy of business and blue blood including Countess Pilar Crespi of New York, Hilary Weston of Holt Renfrew, and Sonja Bata of Bata Shoes.
40. Vancouverite Carlyle Irving was once married to Arthur Irving of the New Brunswick Irvings.

41. The Westons were invited to purchase Belvedere Palace, formerly the Windsor home of the Prince of Wales. They attend church on Sundays with the Royal Family; in Toronto, the Queen Mother stays at the Westons'; and on the first night of their Royal Weekend, at a Savoy Hotel dinner, Hilary and Galen were summoned upstairs to visit with the Queen Mother, who was celebrating her eighty-ninth birthday.
42. First chaired by Lord Louis Mountbatten, the United World Colleges promote peace through international understanding pursued through colleges that accept teenagers from countries around the world in Grades 12 and 13, in an international baccalaureate system. Galen Weston is the chair of the Lester Pearson College of the Pacific on Vancouver Island.
43. *In a Canadian Garden* shot onto the best-seller list. It is a combination of superb photography and commentaries by the rich and famous, inviting the public to peer into their private worlds with a measure of propriety.
44. The Westons' wedding took place in England. Guests arrived in costume à la Edmonton's Klondike Days. The festivities included punting the turn-of-the-century entourage down the Thames.
45. The widow of Robert Chisholm, a former president of Dominion Stores, Posy Chisholm married New Yorker William Feick Jr. in 1989 but continues to keep bases in London, Rome, and Toronto.

CHAPTER TWO

The New Establishment

Where are the Idle Rich?

Give it, get it, or get off the board.

At a Vancouver event sponsored by Texaco, western power player Jane Heffelfinger saw women whipping business cards out of their décolletages the way their grandmothers withdrew lace hankies and overheard one husband say to another, "Have you noticed that the women are all talking business while the men are standing around looking decorative?"

****

In 1987, when a talented and well-known Establishment woman was welcomed to the predominantly male board of a Toronto hospital, she was handed a name tag that read "Mrs. John Smith." To her own amazement, she returned it, explaining, "My name is Jane Smith." In the awkward silence that followed, she realized that it was not her expertise they had sought but her husband's name for their letterhead. Deference had been innate to this woman's identity, but she suddenly turned to leave and heard herself saying with the intransigence of a full-fledged feminist, "I will return when you make me a new name tag." For weeks the board attempted to shame her into changing her mind, but she stood firm. In the end the chair gave her a name tag reading "Mrs. Jane Smith," the antiquated title of a divorcée. Her stance had been less a power play than a simple wish to be invisible no longer.

****

The members of the New Establishment move in the fast lane of the community highway. In their vernacular, you are either a Player or a Sweeper—the latter describing their own friends who dare to give their names but not their time, or who do not aspire to board memberships. Peer pressure to participate at the executive volunteer level is far heavier than feminist criticism of women who stayed at home ever was. Volunteerism in the 1980s defined a New Establishment based on meritocracy. Its women are identified by pace and profile. Recognition has replaced anonymity and they expect to be taken seriously. "Just as long as you are having fun, dear," is a 1970s epithet few husbands would dare think, let alone utter. Establishment women seeking directorships covet the boards of banks and corporations, but failing those, they look to prominent community institutions such as hospitals and universities or other advanced educational institutions.

Nonetheless, a harsh reality of appointments to charitable boards and non-profit institutions is that they have less to do with specialized expertise than with the ability to raise money. In the scramble for the charity dollar, board members such as Elizabeth Tory or Countess Dobrzensky can mean the difference between taking in $25,000 or raising $1,000,000. Joan Randall, the able former chair of the Governing Council of the University of Toronto, said, "It took me quite a long time to realize that talent aside, volunteer boards really only ask you if you are in a [financial] position to support their causes." Randall accepted her challenging position, but noted with a sly smile, "Some of my long-term interests are going to be best served only when I die."

Although board appointments are rarely token placements any more, a few still come through the old boys' network and the power of social access. In 1988 the CEO of a major oil company remarked to the wife of a friend as they were riding up a chairlift in Banff that he needed a woman on his board. Rather than seek out expertise among women oil executives, economists, or financial experts in the industry, he appointed his friend's wife before the downhill run. "I know nothing about oil companies," she laughed to a friend. However with the rising liability factor, directorships are not for the faint of heart, and there is a growing trend for incumbent directors to approach head-hunting consultants to find women with specific qualifications.

****

Scrambling for health-care dollars from hospital boards in today's climate of shrinking funds, for example, is the equivalent at the community level of running a high-risk business. The repercussions of hospital staffing problems and soaring costs first hit the media in 1987 when several Toronto hospitals sought a collective $100 million in private-sector donations. The competitive nature of the New Establishment was embodied in the Meighen family when Kelly served as vice-chair of the Wellesley Hospital while her husband, Michael, sat on the Princess Margaret Hospital board. Both hospitals were vying for $138 million from the provincial government. There could be only one winner, and it was eventually the Princess Margaret.

The funding of health-care facilities is becoming so critical that women serving on hospital boards with $100-million annual budgets are frequently competing against their friends on rival boards not only for the donated dollar but for government funds as well. They also wrestle continually with provincial policy concerning the future and identity of hospitals, and survival by amalgamation is a major issue. The most corrosive battle between Establishment friends began in 1989 when the board of the Women's College Hospital approved a government proposal to merge with the Toronto General. Some directors were for it; others believed the quality of such specialized care as the neo-natal clinic would suffer, and voted against it.

The board split, with the incumbent chair, Ruth Grant,[1] and the hospital president and CEO, Elaine Smith, supporting the merger, while Gail Regan[2] and her team sought continued autonomy. While Grant worked in the privacy of the boardroom with her equally illustrious directors to promote the merger, Regan recruited a group that she named "Friends of the WCH," implying that Grant's group was the enemy. Battle veterans Doris Anderson, impresario Tina VanderHeyden (producer of *The Phantom of the Opera,* who had garnered $209,000 for the hospital through a gala night with the play) lawyer Laura Legge, former lieutenant-governor of Ontario Pauline McGibbon, and Helen Phelan, (Regan's own mother and longtime supporter of WCH), operated from the outside like corporate raiders.

Procuring a list of WCH doctors, volunteers, and donors, Friends won a majority over to their side and signed up enough new WCH members to meet constitutional requirements for voting out the incumbent board. Grant, accused Friends of "turning the hospital into a war zone"[a] and took her case to the Supreme Court of Ontario. To fight the merger, Helen Phelan collected around $80,000, which came in from anonymous Friends who could not stomach the impropriety of a public fight. When the Supreme Court ruled that Regan's organization was within its constitutional rights, Grant, Elaine Smith, several doctors, and eighteen other directors resigned. The board is now controlled by Friends with Regan in the chair. The victory raises questions about the future of WCH, but, for now, Regan holds the power. Smith called the battle "the most distressing, the most personally devastating experience of my life."[b] She cited Regan's use of "outside lobbyists . . . litigation, and . . . community activism as if [the hospital issue] were voter registration.'' Exactly. In women's groups or women's deals, the competitive edge has invaded the once courteous domain of voluntary service. While Grant harbours no bitterness of this new age *coup d'état*, she observed that the event must cause men and women to reassess the nature of volunteer service at the board level, circa 1990.

****

Still, they serve. Jean Forest, successful business executive, educator, and human rights activist who became chancellor of the University of Alberta and chair of St. Stephen's Theological College, was pivotal to a 1984 committee that submitted a report to the Canadian (Roman Catholic) bishops with recommendations that women play a wider and more responsible role in the church. The bishops turned it down but later were forced to reconsider. Also in Alberta, Jennifer ''Jenny'' Belzberg chairs The Banff Centre, a complex tri-disciplinary institution combining performing arts master classes with business and a conference centre. Women have served as chancellors of a number of Canadian universities, although with few exceptions that position has remained purely honorary.[3] A number of women prefer executive positions to chancellorships because they provide a greater opportunity to affect policy. But the great attraction is that all board positions, whether paid or voluntary, connect women to the male professionals and financiers who form the axis of corporate and academic power in this country. The result is not only an outstanding learning experience, but the hands-on feeling of participating in a process of significance to Canada.

Margo Bindhardt takes her executive volunteer positions at least as seriously as any paid employment.[4] ''I worry just as much as if I were selling shares. You have to get the product out there, to get people to buy into your dream or your institution, or whatever. You've got to assemble a good team that can help you. You can't do it all yourself. You've got to deal with the staff. If it's a well-run institution, it runs like a corporation with a good CEO, a strong board, a good administration that is fiscally responsible. We are playing the corporate game without the financial recognition.''

****

In three generations society has swung from the rigid restrictions on grandmothers to the free-wheeling lifestyles of their granddaughters and the world of DINKS and POSSLQs.[5] It is the middle generation that represents this cultural antipode, women rooted in the patriarchal era functioning in the uncharted future. How well these women remember mothers and grandmothers of towering intimidation who had operated independently when husbands were away at one or both world wars.

The Canadian Establishment had always been a rock-solid institution composed of old, distinguished British and European families, preferably monied and frequently integrated through marriage. Women defined themselves through the family unit, class, and community service, often governing their households, children, servants, and guests with the imperious calm of divine right. Long before governments had a role in social and cultural programs, these women had perceived the quality of their communities as an extension of their families. Men were an intrinsic part of this concept, but as they were tending their cattle, drilling for oil, and running the country, they let their wives shape the community.

Working within the narrow framework of their position and exercising their administrative skills, women established schools, libraries, hospitals, symphonies, operas, and ballets.[6] When government grants began to supplement gifts from the private sector, their creations often achieved size and quality and are now memorials to the timelessness of their contributions. There was only one flaw: women founded organizations or institutions, but men ran them. From the earliest time, the churches and the cultural mores of the ruling class continued to regiment and restrict Establishment women.

Few enjoyed freedom in the flamboyant style of American-born Nova Scotian Dorothy Ruth Killam, who swept through life like Halley's Comet. She once tried to buy the Brooklyn Dodgers and she helped to form the New York Mets. It was her own legacy that her husband used to build the family fortune, and when he died, the government used the 50 percent tax on his estate to found the Canada Council. Dorothy Killam then built her remaining estate from $40 million to $100 million and gave most of it away to universities and hospitals.[7]

Other women of privileged birth put aside distinctions of class, religion, and culture to work for change at a time when "women" and "power" really was a contradiction in terms. Their goal was not power as an end in itself, but as a route to effecting desperately needed reforms, particularly in family and property law. An early example was Lady Ishbel, Marchioness of Aberdeen and Temair, wife of Canada's seventh governor-general,[99] an upper crust imperialist with a futuristic style. Empowered from childhood by wealth, name, and a political conscience, Lady Aberdeen, as she was called, became particularly adept at political games. Like a turn-of-the-century Madame de Pompadour, she connived with her husband to promote Sir Wilfrid Laurier as the candidate for prime minister, battled with Ottawa's Roman Catholic archbishop over opening an uncensored public library, supported suffrage for women, and founded activist women's groups both nationally and internationally. In a similar vein was Evelyn Farris, the New Brunswick-born wife of future Senator John de Beque Farris, who stated that educated women had "a public duty as well as a private one" and in 1907 founded the equality-seeking Vancouver University Women's Club. Nonagenarian Senator Muriel Fergusson, who became a lawyer in the 1920s and was the first woman Speaker of the Senate, has been a lifelong champion of women's rights.

With the departure of their men for Europe in the advent of World War II, women found the doors unexpectedly opened to management roles. The organization of the Junior League became the correct club for the Protestant Establishment volunteer. Admission to its ranks was tribal, depending upon who your mother was and/or whom you had married. Regardless of its exclusivist principles, the League, like the National Council of Jewish Women, functioned on the leading edge of social change. It not only founded community institutions such as the first shelters for battered women, but also recognized the importance of leadership training through volunteerism. Paragons of Winnipeg's social register established the Volunteer Bureau, which became a prototype for similar services throughout the country. During the wartime years, women enjoyed such extraordinary freedom in community participation that many felt pivotal to the administrative process of the country.

In 1941, when the government responded to women's request for war service by establishing the Canadian Women's Army Corps, the Royal Canadian Air Force, and the Women's Royal Canadian Service, more than 45,000 women volunteered. Some defied their husbands, who feared their wives would be considered "loose women." It was the male chiefs of staff who chose young, well-educated members of the Establishment to head the women's forces. Their leadership qualities were bolstered by aristocratic style, that slightly intimidating demeanour characteristic of those who know they belong. Colonel Margaret Eaton,[8] Wing Officer Willa Walker,[9] Captain (N) Adelaide Sinclair, and Colonel Mary Dover[10] became famous for their ability to boost troop morale and convey an inimitable sense of purpose.

During that era two superwomen emerged. When the prominent Winnipeg grain baron and broker James Richardson died in 1939, his wife and closest confidante, Muriel Sprague Richardson, stepped into the chair and expanded James Richardson and Sons like a modern-day acquisitor. During the 1941 blockade of Great Britain, Phyllis Turner, a young widowed economist, was appointed to the Wartime Prices and Trade Board to negotiate with merchants and government officials in Ottawa, New York, and Washington. Both were raised in an atmosphere that made their accomplishments even more extraordinary and their subsequent denials expected. When the war ended in 1945, Phyllis Turner married industrialist Frank Ross, moved to Vancouver, and listed her occupation as "housewife." And although Muriel Richardson ran James Richardson and Sons until the 1960s, when historian Donald Creighton finished the first draft of the family history, she would not allow it to be developed. Her daughter, Agnes Benidickson, said of her mother's decree, "She felt it made the women look too strong."

In the delicate task of reuniting families after the war, women did relinquish their fledgling powers, returned to the home front, bore babies, shouldered monumental volunteer projects, and reinstated their husbands as society's sole decision makers. The Establishment retrenched itself in the status quo, resisting or ignoring post-war conditions that saw increasing numbers of women joining the work force out of economic necessity. Establishment daughters were still trained for motherhood under the old rules that made growing up a hazardous experience. In subtle ways they were taught that marriage and motherhood was their duty, and that to snare a mate, passive comeliness remained as essential as chastity. Boys never made passes at girls who wore glasses, and the goods had to be pure. The degradation of a debutante who had lost her virginity could be as monumental as the pride shown by a father when a son had lost his. Girls were consumed by the demands of steering a cautious course through a moral and social minefield, one in which any stray step could result in being ostracized by their family, church, and peers.

Time and again women from that era come up with no other explanation of their lifetime role than, "I did what I did because . . . it was expected of me." Their childhood inculcation focussed on their limitations rather than their potential. Following the ceremony of holy matrimony in which the young bride was handed from her father, whom she had always obeyed, to the groom, whom she then promised to honour and obey, she relinquished to her husband her name and frequently her dowry. It was not unusual for a husband to purchase a home with his wife's money but register it in his own name. Wife Of was a woman's identity and children grown to adulthood as God-fearing citizens her chief reward. Even though the world order as the Establishment had known it was crumbling by the early sixties, husbands and wives clung to that battered status quo like anchors grasping at sandy ocean floors in the turbulent riptides of history.

Two post-war revolutionary factors, television and the Pill, heralded greater freedom for women, but debutantes continued to watch brothers being groomed for power while they were trained for care-giving professions with abominable pay structures. Nurses, home economists, and teachers continued to be regarded as sweepers rather than players, and upon marriage they relinquished their jobs and concentrated on the home. At a Toronto cocktail party in the 1980s, Establishment-activist Nancy Jackman remarked to a grandmotherly socialite how much her generation owed theirs for the volunteer work they had done and the organizations they had founded. The woman seized Jackman's elbow in a frightening grip and demanded, "Don't you see that it was the only way out of the house?"

Most women, Establishment or not, had a tough time breaking free of the stereotype. In the 1940s, Toronto philanthropist Helen Phelan was prevented by her father from taking a master's degree because marriage and motherhood were to be her career. In 1987, she gripped her Louis Quatorze fork and rap-rapped its handle on her polished mahogany dining-room table, announcing with a steely softness, "It's time this story was told." Most women, Establishment or not, had a tough time breaking free of the stereotype. In Quebec, when Deputy Premier and Minister of Energy Lise Bacon, the brightest member of her family, had wanted to attend university in the fifties, her father directed her to work as a secretary to put her brother through instead. During that same era in Montreal, Cornelia Vaughan graduated in commerce and expressed a wish to continue with an MBA. Her father replied, "Your brother gets the MBA. You get your wedding." Then the Catholic Cornelia married Protestant Stephen Molson of the brewing family at a time when mixed marriages were unacceptable. Their wedding was private, and after marriage ended in divorce without the presumed generous financial settlement, Molson worked her own way to an MBA at l'Université de Montréal. She is now president of Covan Corporate Capital.

Some mothers who gave their time exclusively to caring for their families later faced painful disdain from their own children who believed their mothers should have done more. As a teenager, future senator Thérèse Casgrain had idolized her father, Rodolphe Forget, a banker and Conservative MP. He *did* things, like founding schools for underprivileged children, while her mother, Casgrain wrote almost scornfully in her memoirs, "and her ladies bountiful . . . took baskets of food to the poor but never questioned the causes of poverty." Casgrain seemed to consider her mother's lifestyle to be irrelevent. Yet, circumscribed as they were by cultural taboos, the Mamans Forgets did their best. As they could not insult their husbands by becoming activists for social justice or working for a salary, they could not earn funds to finance more enduring gifts such as special schools.

Economic independence makes a significant difference. Penney Kome wrote in her book *Women of Influence*, "Experience shows that only women who have property of their own, be it political, intellectual or financial, can expect men to treat them as equals and on their own terms."[d] Jean Southam, a woman of good humour, wealth, and empowerment, agreed, reasoning that she has always held a strong position in her long and successful marriage to a member of a prominent family because she controls her own legacy. She also acknowledges the benefit of a famous father who instilled in her the belief that she was the equal of any of the loggers or executives who worked for his forestry empire. The ebullient matriarch has passed on that same sense of strength to her five daughters, who are intimidated by no one—except occasionally by Mrs. Gordon T. Southam herself.

It was in the rebellious sixties that the Establishment was finally convinced that the old rules didn't seem to count any more. Emboldened by the feminists, traditionalists ventured out to work in flower shops,[11] real estate offices, and art galleries. Alarmed husbands devised diminishing repartees to underscore that these roles outside the home were inconsequential. They probably were, in the larger scene, but jobs were connecting women in deadly earnest to the survival of self-esteem, won through society's measuring stick of a salary. No matter how infinitesimal it was, that income to spend as she chose was the reward that changed everything.

Today, New Establishment women are choosing the volunteer executive directorships with the satisfaction once reserved for salaried positions. What has changed? *Society's perceptions*. It both respects the voluntary service and its accompanying power. Being a player means that besides being CEO, one must be seen to be involved in the community in high-ranking volunteer positions. That was why Brascan's Senator Trevor Eyton, frequently named the most powerful CEO in the country, had a higher public image than the company's financial genius, Jack Cockwell.

****

Two of the most successful women pioneers who blazed this modern-day executive trail are Mary Alice Burton Stuart and Joan Walwynn Randall. In historic continuity, these two evolved from young homemakers seeking extended educations to executives without salaries.

In 1988, Mary Alice Burton Stuart was called upon by university chancellor John Black Aird to co-chair with him the $100-million University of Toronto Breakthrough Campaign. Aird chose her not because she was rolling in disposable cash, which the distaff side seldom is, but, he said "because she's the best." She had the voice, the clout, and the organizational skills. With a merchant's eye to the bottom line, Stuart created a mobile office by wrangling from Ford Motors and Cantel the use of a Lincoln and a cellular phone. By the time the university kicked off the public drive in March 1989, the high-powered team already had guarantees of $50 million. Stuart's marketing talent, inherited from her grandfather C. L. Burton, founder of Simpson's department store, combined with her innate leadership skills, and a natural affinity for contract law, are the tools she uses to sell educational futures through the CJRT open learning radio station and the university campaign.

Stuart is Establishment by birth, entrepreneurial in discipline, and impresario in style. Working out of her cubicle on Victoria Street, also known as the Ryerson radio station, she greets visitors with the contralto voice of an orator and the energy of a producer about to present Andrew Lloyd Weber's latest blockbuster. Stuart swept an arm towards the progress charts of her radio station, and the cluttered office disappeared as the curtain rose on the star performer and she began to speak. The broad smile never faded as she brought alive flow charts, spread sheets, comparative sub totals, bottom lines, and successful infiltration of the commercial market by CJRT. Her spellbinding delivery, at once kinetic and casual, evoked images of a dynamic CEO convincing his directors of a profitable takeover, or of a rainmaker drawing in the curious townfolk to see her elixirs, en route to explaining yet another concept, winning yet another convert. The rain falls, the elixirs rejuvenate, and the directors donate a million dollars for the university campaign. Cynics are either bewitched by Stuart or simply succumb to her positive pressure. There is no middle ground. Failure does not exist in her lexicon. If this fund-raising tycoon fears her visitors missed her point, she has been known to make inspired telephone calls at midnight. The recipient nods sleepily, convinced that someday Stuart's CJRT will be a national institution, and that the university will not only make its $100 million but that it will go over the top.[12]

One of Stuart's great strengths in this campaign was having her old friend, Joan Randall, presiding in the chair of the University of Toronto Governing Council, from where she made all facilities of the institution available for Stuart's inspired drive. These two were always brilliant strategists at hacking through the cultural jungles of yesteryear. In 1949, Mary Alice Burton, gold medalist in English Language and Literature at the University of Toronto, married Sandy Stuart, then consulted her former professors about the three courses she needed to get her masters. The men who had so respected her scholarship chorused, "You're a married woman! You couldn't possibly do it." With Sandy working long hours building a chemical engineering company, Stuart stared at the walls of her apartment and felt useless. Then she convinced the Toronto *Telegram* to hire her as a free-lance book reviewer. Payment was her byline and the book.

Prevented from pursuing advanced educations, and in the tradition of their resourceful mothers and grandmothers who had done the same, Stuart, Randall, and seven others formed what was essentially an underground university, benignly called a "reading club." At a time when the Junior League membership was WASP by invitation, Randall's and Stuart's club was secular and their assignments sufficiently ambitious to reflect the professionalism of research papers. By 1955 the club began seeking challenges for their administrative skills. Half of them, including Stuart, volunteered at the Art Gallery of Ontario, while the others, with Randall, formed the first women's committee at the Royal Ontario Museum.

While Randall was nurturing the ROM, Stuart was eyeing the restoration of the Grange, one of Toronto's oldest homes, and part of the AGO. The challenge was ideal for a woman whose talent lay in creating the structure, solving the problems, and then turning it over to a new team and moving on.[13] In this instance, Stuart convinced a sceptical women's committee, which until then was pleased to be raising $10,000 annually, that it could raise the $100,000 restoration cost in a year. It was an unheard of sum, but another member responded to Stuart's enthusiasm and devised the idea of playing an Art Game in the press. It amused the entire city, and the gallery raised the unprecedented $100,000. When the revised cost for restoration of the Grange came in at $700,000, Stuart concluded that the money raised by special events—auctions, balls, Art Games — was token. "It's P.R. from my point of view. It's not fund raising." Not wanting to involve the exhausted women's committee further, she raised the other $600,000 herself. Once you have your first 25 percent, she explained, it's easy.

But Stuart also had the eye for choosing talent, and she had social access to information at the top corporate levels. When the Ontario government asked Stuart to take on the flagging CJRT educational radio station, her first choice as a fellow board member was the youthful Dick Thompson, destined to become CEO of the Toronto-Dominion Bank.

Then in her gleeful description, she "got rid of the dead weight—fourteen board members—who were government patronage appointees and didn't want to attend board meetings, let alone work." CJRT became the reading club phoenix, an open college reaching out to those who either must, or prefer to, remain at home. Offering university credit courses by radio, audio cassette, and correspondence,[14] it has become a thriving community-supported station.

When Joan Randall approached the ROM , museum administrators saw no need for "society ladies," but Randall emphasized that they would do translations and other work for free. She and her committee also started the ROM on the road from community obscurity to such popularity that today almost every Toronto Player who isn't on the boards of the Art Gallery, Ballet, or Symphony wants to be involved with the museum. Randall's volunteers also raised capital to found the reproduction shop, which quickly repaid all initial expenses and earns a profit.

In her mid-forties, Joan Randall lost first her father, then her mother, and then her husband. Faced with a flood of financial management challenges of three estates, she took a securities course and subsequently served on the financial committees of the ROM. She also sat on the politically thorny board of the National Museums of Canada, a two-year term to oversee devolution of museum boards from central government control. By 1989 she was chairing the university's Governing Council, participating in policy development, and collaborating with Stuart.

Randall suspects that this management phase of her life might not have happened had her husband lived. In the most positive context, she feels that being on her own has enabled her to move beyond cultural restrictions to seek change, pursue excellence at an administrative level, and best of all, to be welcomed by the exhilarating academic community. At the close of her tenure in 1990, she chaired the search committee for the new president of the university. Armed with the power to realize the noblest visions of a beneficent society and to hone executive skills, Randall laughed at the memory of her former lifestyle. Then, in fear of being considered elitist, she added hastily, "Some of my best friends are Establishment!"

****

Rather than unique, the accomplishments of Joan Randall and Mary Alice Stuart reflect those of women in every region and community of this country. Margaret Norrie McCain, whose mother was Senator Norrie and whose husband is Wallace McCain of the multinational frozen food company, lives in the family's Florenceville, N.B. compound and flies to appointments in one of two jets from the runway outside her home. But most often McCain is seen driving to Mount Allison, Canada's second-smallest university with the highest number of Rhodes scholars per capita, where she presides as chancellor. In Saskatchewan, Peggy McKercher, whose regal stature caused people to mistake her for the governor-general when the Right Honourable Jeanne Sauvé was in office, took on the communities, the government, and her own friends to win for Saskatoon virtually miles of land for parks with paths for bicycling and cross-country skiing.

Through personable warmth, and attention to finances and detail, Calgarian Margaret Southern[15] has turned her family's Spruce Meadows equestrian centre into one of the world's finest, drawing world class competitors from Germany, Japan, France, Ireland, Mexico, and the United States, with international sports coverage. The riders themselves consider it to be one of the most popular equestrian events anywhere in the world.

The ubiquitous Vancouverite Natalie Veiner Freeman is a subtle power who can neither be labelled nor slotted. Eloquent and insightful, Veiner Freeman is a master at defining concepts, policy, and the nature of power. Sociologist, backroom politician at the local level, former policy co-ordinator at the Asia Pacific Foundation, writer, Inheritor, Veiner Freeman is the Gail Sheehy of Canada, jetting around the world and chronicling the lives of philosophers, economists, artists, and the powerful.[16]

****

Reva Gerstein, a PhD psychologist, built her reputation through order-in-council research projects on public policy and post-secondary education, and task forces on the economy. Although she divorced from Bertrand Gerstein of People's Credit Jewellers and eventually remarried, Reva strategically kept the high-profile name recognized by the community. After raising $50 million for Sick Children's Hospital, she joined Stuart in the University of Toronto Breakthrough Campaign. Gerstein's current community presence has little to do with her new married persona and everything to do with her redoubtable skills. Besides her brilliant fund-raising capabilities, she was appointed in 1991 to the internationally respected board of The Canadian Institute for Advanced Research.

Many corporate women and executive volunteers who will not volunteer at the "elementary" door-to-door canvassing level, anymore with causes to sell or skills to share are recognizing that the consequence of secrecy is a continued anonymity that no longer works. Prominence is acceptable if it sells their cause, and those who are pursuing professional careers want to be respected. Lisa Balfour-Bowen, a member of the Southam family and one who is said to throw the most intellectually stimulating soirées in Toronto, shrinks from the moniker "socialite," insisting, "It's *Walter* who gives those parties." Balfour-Bowen wants to be known only for the credible journalist and art critic that she is.

Elizabeth Nichol,[17] who founded the internationally respected Equinox Gallery in Vancouver, remarked that Maryon Pearson's snappy line of the 1970s, "Behind every successful man is a surprised woman," has become "Behind every successful woman is a surprised woman." Many traditionalists are astounded not only by their own success in the business or administrative arenas but by their discovery that it is exhilarating and fun.

Winnipegger Suzanne Banfield Lount, a glamorous member of the Establishment, "married well" in 1961, and anticipated a life of privilege. The Junior League, winter trips to Aspen or Europe, and summers at Lake of the Woods were *de rigueur* for her social set. One day while she was a young mother of four small children, her architect/oil investor husband arrived home and announced, "I've got thirty-eight dollars in the bank." It was the early 1970s, and he had lost not only his economic footing but also his competitive spirit.

Lount promptly removed her apron, passed the exams for a real estate licence and soon cornered the elite market of her own turf, the tony Tuxedo Park and the stately Wellington Crescent, one of the most beautiful residential streets in Canada. Establishing her own company with two women partners, Ellie MacFarlane and Lilian Jean Evans, she discovered that she loved business and took her boutique company to annual revenues of $20 million and a generous six-figure income for herself. In a city where spurts of economic growth are rare, her revenue represented a generous portion of the residential market. Instead of paying nannies, Lount hired her children to help do the housework, gardening, and grocery shopping. She put them through private school, and with the funds that they earned from summer jobs at Lake of the Woods, all have graduated with university degrees. Friends called her the Real Estate Queen of Manitoba. When jealous competitors called her the Barracuda, the effervescent Lount ignored them as whiners.

With the look of a *Vogue* cover model and the moxie for cutting hard deals, Lount was the first woman to sell a million-dollar Winnipeg home, the first woman member of the Associates of the Faculty of Administrative Studies at the University of Manitoba, and, contrary to all her proper upbringing, the first to sue a lieutenant-governor, her friend John McKeag—for reneging on a real estate deal. No one pushed around the Barracuda, and after Lount won the case the two remained friends. Lount is said to "think like a man," which simply means she can separate business from personal issues, an essential precursor to success and one of the toughest lessons for women to learn.[18] Twice engineering financial bail outs of her former husband's business ventures, Lount beamed, ''Women don't know what they are capable of until survival becomes their responsibility.''[19]

****

New Establishment women are showing extraordinary resourcefulness in joining the game. Less than a decade ago when society was easing into a more liberal mode, and spousal expectations in the home were less rigid, appointments of women to the boards of banks, insurance companies, and non-profit organizations were still rare and went almost invariably to Wives Of who could be trusted to behave appropriately. Husbands were asked for permission before wives were invited to join, and the guys had a standing joke about the women carrying ''bullshit briefcases.'' Many of these ''safe'' pioneers were as capable as they were intelligent,[20] having won valuable experience in the volunteer sector. Louise Vaillancourt of Montreal, one of the best-connected women in Canada, was first invited to join the Hôpital Marie-Enfant board, where she worked with the future chair of Bell Canada Enterprises, Jean de Grandpré. Subsequently, Vaillancourt was appointed to de Grandpré's BCE, and a flood of invitations followed,[21] including governor of l'Université du Québec, the body that determines the policy and financing for a network of Quebec universities and institutions, such as the bio-medical Institut Armand Frappier where she is president of Fondation Armand Frappier. Vaillencourt remarked unapologetically of tokenism, ''Women my age have a duty to open doors while boards are under pressure to appoint women, and to prove we can be competent without being . . . aggressive.'' Women are, however, learning to tread the fine line between aggression and assertion. One is suicidal, the other essential.

By the mid-1980s husbands were encouraging their wives' exodus to the office. Their jobs came less from dormant university degrees in arts, teaching, or home economics than from experience gained during a quarter-century spent on running a home, working through the volunteer hierarchy, juggling priorities, and adapting to everyone else's shifting needs. Homemakers have accumulated organizational and administrative skills that are of corporate value. Male chairs and CEOs who once prided themselves as the public representative of the family are providing offices for their wives just down the hall from their own, as well as secretarial services and the use of the company Cadillac.[22] This is not patronage to wife or neighbourhood. It is a recognition of the growing profile of their wives and an appreciation of the cross-pollinating power in the mainstream of their community. In turn, many women are attributing their stellar successes not just to their own determination and navigational skills, but to husbands and male mentors who showed the way, opened the doors, and encouraged them to pursue their potential.

As for housework, no one seems to have time for it any more. A young Toronto entrepreneur started a business called "Rent a Wife," which takes on every challenge usually covered by homemakers, and grossed a small fortune in its first year of operation. Home cooking? This is the age of decorator kitchens and delectable catering.

For years some women have exercised a subtle, significant power through foundation directorships. Two billion dollars in annual interest accrued by Canadian foundations is directed, often by women, to provide funding for myriad causes. The top fifty range from the $7-million Kathleen Richardson Foundation in Winnipeg, to the largest at over $318 million in the J.W. McConnell Foundation, run by Derek Price but whose wife Jill McConnell Price is an active director. Another, the $56-million Macdonald Stewart Foundation, is run by Liliane (Mrs. David) Stewart. Her sister-in-law, Bea Molson of the brewery Molsons, also sits on the board, which dispenses nearly $5 million annually. In Toronto, Themadel, the Meighen family foundation, has on its board Kelly, wife of Senator Michael Meighen, and his mother, Margaret (Peggy) Meighen Molson, who in 1990 married Senator Hartland de Montarville Molson. The interrelations of Montrealers in particular, where most of the great Canadian fortunes were founded, create a powerful network of women and foundation assets.

****

The Aspirants are a special breed pursuing power. They are the fascinating and colourful hopefuls of the New Establishment, illuminated by New Money, sexual politics, haute couture style, and a lust for competition. The 1980s marked a new age of unprecedented wealth, freedom of expression, and a measure of success rooted in the exhilaration of winning. The aspirants are judged by how much each can raise, how much leverage one has in extracting corporate donations for the ROM the hospital, the ballet, how many women she can get to a fashion show for cancer research, how many $1,000 seats she can sell for the Great Gathering. It was the Great Game of the 1980s and, in his book *Old Money*, author Nelson W. Aldrich Jr. observed that Old Money is identified by status and property, whereas New Money is realized through talent and exhibited with toys.[101] He might have added that worthiness is often judged by the style in which the game is played: who throws the best party, who wears the latest fashion, who hobnobs at the latest In restaurant, who makes the biggest charity donation, who sports the new young wife—or which young woman snares the most powerful CEO. In the institution of marriage, power goes with the position and sexual power still reigns supreme.

Some husbands who felt threatened in the 1960s if their wives worked, were by the 1980s trading in their paragons of domesticity to marry what *Fortune Magazine* christened "Trophy Wives." *Fortune*'s list of executives and CEOs who married a second time indicates that over 50 percent marry women twenty to thirty years younger who come armed not only with gorgeous bodies and a self-image distinctly expressed in their sense of fashion, but with MBAs. The first wife adhered to family budgets, drove the kids to soccer games, music lessons, and the doctor, in between cooking to entertain her husband's boss; the trophy wife has neither aspirations to domesticity nor hang-ups about spending her husband's money.

The trophy syndrome works both ways. American Bonnie Swearingen, who married the former chair of Standard Oil, told *Fortune*, ''I didn't just marry a CEO. I married one of the world's outstanding business leaders.'' Another woman boasted that she is the only woman in America to have been married to two CEOs of *Fortune* 500 companies.[102] Canadians raised in the ethic of propriety demurred from making such claims. Some young wives did confide that when their husbands retire from their CEO positions and all their directorships, thus disqualifying them from using the company jet and limo service, *their* trophy loses its lustre. Where's the fun and glamour in travelling by taxi or standing in the economy line at airports?

It's all about belonging, about being inside. ''Positioning,'' repeated Suzanne Banfield Lount, ''*is* the Game.'' And when the game escalates to power, the players require physical proof of status. Acquisition, whether of a painting or a spouse, became the 1980s metaphor for positioning. As Sotheby's head, the Earl of Westmorland, told Peter Newman in *Maclean's*, ''People are acquisitive. They love owning something . . . that will impress those who [view] their canvasses.''[8] He was speaking of New Money. Old Money drives tired cars and sits on worn upholstery. Liliane Stewart, sits on fabulous antique chairs with stuffing pushing through fraying silk, and Mary Alice Stuart's CJRT offices look like a welfare hangout on the Yonge Street Strip. Nobility in Canada is manifested in that innate courtesy, dignity of carriage, and the inculcation of noblesse oblige so discreet, yet so instantly recognizable in the historically privileged. The quiet scions such as Pam Holt Dunn of Montreal, daughter of the famous Sir Herbert Holt,[23] personify third-generation Establishment wealth bound by discretion. By comparison, and in joyous celebration of their second-generation wealth, Canadian Tire heir Fred Billes, and his new wife Barbara, built a 30,000-square-foot home and spray-enamelled tires, brake discs, and tail pipes a brilliant white, to hang as mobiles above their indoor swimming pool. A comparable Establishment stunt would be for Signy Eaton to suspend diamond patterned socks, boxer shorts, and tea pots from her patio. In fact, Mrs. Eaton's home is aged like fine wine, flavoured with a gentility so imperceptibly gracious that outsiders who visit might despair of ever belonging.

Patience. It just takes patience; about three generations of it. Then the Establishment will forget where you and your money came from, and will swing open its doors and welcome your grandchildren with their

Old Money. In the meantime, the recession and the Gulf War in the spring of 1991 rendered talk of aspiration unseemly, but the game goes on, and if positioning means accessing the inner circles of power, money still opens the doors. In the movie *Wall Street*, Gordon Gekko said it all when he announced his appointment to the board of the New York Zoo: ''Cost me a million.'' Contribute a bundle to the opera, the ballet, or the charity of your choice, get invited to sit on the board, and in you go. New Money has so much of it that Old Money, with its air of gentility, breeding, and a million or two, cannot afford to ignore the generosity of the *arrivistes*. Vancouver investment dealer Peter Brown, chair and CEO of L.O.M. Western Securities, commented to Peter Newman in 1980 that with one-hundred-million-dollar deals going down, you can't even begin to play any more until you have at least $15 million.[h] Women are often front and centre to this game.

For example, Old Money sends invitations to former British Columbian Gayfryd Steinberg, of Manhattan's aspiring New Establishment. Recruited to PEN by celebrity author Norman Mailer, Gayfryd Steinberg threw a cocktail party for the cause in her thirty-four-room apartment, and in twenty minutes her wealthy husband, Saul, raised $200,000 for her pet, PEN, merely by cruising among the guests.[24] This hustle may gall the old guard but, perform and you're in, to a degree. Fail and you're yesterday's news. When outsider Robert Campeau bought the Federated Department Stores chain, including Bloomingdale's in New York, he was received by Establishment attitudes ranging from rejection, to overwhelming curiosity, to cautious inclusion. When the women's committee of the National Ballet organized a $1,000-a-plate black-tie dinner at the Campeau home in 1987, tickets sold out within hours. Organizers lamented that they could have charged $2,000 or printed twice as many tickets because so many people wanted to see how the Campeaus lived. By the spring of 1990, having filed for protection under Chapter 11, Campeau had faded from the invitation lists.

Diehard Establishment elitists south of the border, who are masters in the art of exclusion, chill to the annual migration of Canadians to Florida. A few winters ago, one of the most powerful New Money Canadians, Montrealer Paul Desmarais, and his effervescent wife, Jacquie, entertained a heady selection of prime ministers, media stars, and financial power brokers at their new $10-million hideaway in Palm Beach. Old New York Money wintering close by, sat up and snapped, ''Desmarais? I wouldn't know a Desmarais if I fell over one.'' The American doyenne's own lineage includes a robber-baron grandfather but as that was two generations ago, she had long since entered the inner sanctum of the Establishment to be revered as a national philanthropist. Leaning conspiratorily forward, she confided of both the Steinbergs and the Demarais with an upper-class Vassar inflection, ''They are NOCD. Not our class, dear.''

In this age of meritocracy, Frosty Intimidation — that self-perceived supremacy, that contemptuous attitude towards a lower class—remains the hallmark of a dwindling sector of the Old Establishment and their progeny who have no identity beyond name and wealth. The imperiousness of that ''Do you know who I am,'' glare can halt an interloper at fifty feet. If forced into closer proximity, the use of the limp-wristed, glaze-eyed, ''How do you do drop dead'' handshake dispels any doubt in the mind of outsiders that whatever their community contributions, they are of no social consequence. Gayfryd Steinberg observed with cynical amusement to *Vanity Fair's* Tina Brown, ''One of the most unattractive things about the wealthy is that they think they deserve to be.''[i] Old Money is renowned for its belief in divine right, and its power can be defanged only when it anoints the newcomers with the honour of an invitation and they do not bother to show.

****

Regardless of individual successes, the lifetime priority of the New Establishment woman remains with her husband and family. Few build major enterprises, enter politics, or campaign for equality. For that matter, movements such as affirmative action probably do not fall within her political philosophy. For the most part, the community involvements of the privileged set have been confined to the respectable endeavours of surrounding hospitals, art galleries, educational institutions, museums, and the performing arts. Issues such as day-care centres, maternity leave, and the millions of dollars needed to meet the pay equity requirements, continue to challenge the propriety and bottom-line headaches of her husband's corporation, and therefore are rarely addressed.

Lawyer and activist Marilou McPhedran described Establishment women as walking a very fine line. They live with high-powered men who operate in a pressure cooker environment, and while they may enjoy a world of material privilege, demonstrations for social justice may be hazardous to their health. Whatever their community commitments, New Establishment women try to plan for a flexibility that allows them to fly on a moment's notice to London, Frankfurt, or Jakarta. It was political and charitable gala organizer Marlene DelZotto who most honestly expressed the gut motivation of New Establishment volunteers when she said, ''I never had an identification. Zena Cherry always listed me along with ''the spouses'': '''Mr. Conrad Black, [Senator] Trevor Eyton, [Senator] Michael Meighen, Mr. Elvio DelZotto, *and spouses*.' Now I finally have a name.''

In Toronto one winter evening, at a cocktail party featuring Old Establishment wealth, a prominent dowager was considering the New Establishment, its choices, and society's increasing acknowledgement of women for their participation in the game of power. When asked what she would do if she could do it all over again with today's freedoms, the woman fell into a reflective silence before revealing the homemaker's duality: ''Well . . . I would like to have been someone.''

> Are you talking about fund-raising dinners? Is that what you call running the country? The social women don't have any power at all outside of their little group. You have to go to those women who can change the course of this country.
>
> BLUMA APPEL

CHAPTER 2 NOTES

1. An experienced volunteer at the executive level, Ruth Grant was also special assistant to former secretary of state David Crombie, chaired the campaign for all eighteen ridings in Metro Toronto in 1984, played a major role in the campaign of Barbara McDougall, was the first woman on the board of TVOntario, and rose to the position of vice-chair.
2. Regan is president of Cara Holdings, the billion-dollar (system-wide sales) food-services corporation, and the controlling shareholder in Cara Operations, whose 1989 net earnings were $30 million plus on revenues of $308 million. It was Regan's mother, Helen Gardiner, who brought the mammoth Scott Hospitality line to her marriage with Paul Phelan, founder of Cara Holdings.
3. Women chancellors of Canadian universities include Phyllis Ross, British Columbia; Pauline Vanier, Ottawa; Pauline McGibbon, Toronto; Raynell Andreychuk, Regina, (where she had a hands-on participation in policy development); Barbara Rae, Simon Fraser; Agnes Benidickson, Queen's; Ruth Goldbloom, Mount Saint Vincent; Sylvia Fedoruk, Saskatchewan; Margaret McCain, Mount Allison; and Rose Wolfe, Toronto.
4. The employees at the Canadian Opera Company number upwards of a thousand in various disciplines, and as president of the AGO, Bindhardt was responsible for an operating budget of $10 million.
5. Translated, Double Income No Kids, and Persons of Opposite Sex Sharing Living Quarters.
6. The list of prominent women who founded symphonies, Red Cross chapters, hospital volunteer services, and such mammoth fund raisers as Vancouver's Endeavour, an annual auction that raises over $700,000 in one evening for charity, includes Mary Early, Pauline McGibbon, Julia Ruby, and Jean Tory in Toronto; Muriel Sprague Richardson, Peggy Sellers, and Dime Riley in Winnipeg; Hazel Harrington and Barb Whitley in Montreal; Mary Dover in Calgary; Eleanor Malkin, Evelyn Lett, and the musical Europeans Elsje de Ridder and Thea and Iby Koerner of Vancouver.
7. Killam donated funds to Dalhousie, the Universities of British Columbia and Alberta, the Montreal Neurological Institute, and the Canada Council. She established

the Isaac Walton Killam Hospital for Children in Halifax.

8. When Colonel Eaton, the daughter of Sir John and Lady Eaton, was asked to head the CWACs, she refused at first, citing her sole qualifications as ''knowing the best night clubs in London and hunting with the best packs'' as in horse and hound. To the chief of staff, that, of course, was what made her so eminently eligible.
9. As wing officer of the 17,000-woman air force training camp at Rockcliffe near Ottawa, Willa Walker finally tired of having men and women sneaking in and out of the camps and ordered the removal of the barbed wire perimeter. From St. Andrews, New Brunswick, Walker is a first cousin to Margaret (Peggy) Meighen Molson and, as a friend of Phyllis Turner Ross who summered at St. Andrews, was a frequent guest of Prime Minister Mackenzie King. Despite turning out a weekly 500 airwomen trained as drivers and technical operators, Walker was forbidden by her CO to enter the officers' mess. Even in –10 degree weather, she was left to eat lunch in her car.
10. Colonel Dover, daughter of the Alberta industrialist and rancher A.E. Cross, was appointed commanding officer of the huge women's army training camp near Kitchener, Ontario. On trips to England during the war, Colonel Dover met with her counterpart, Mary Churchill, daughter of Winston, and stayed with family friend and former prime minister, Viscount R.B. Bennett.
11. In British Columbia, homemaker Grace McCarthy started up a flower shop, ran for provincial office, and for over two decades was one of the most powerful, influential politicians in Canadian history. In 1991, she joined the Social Credit leadership race and placed a close second to incumbent Premier Rita Johnston.
12. On November 22, 1990, Mary Alice Stuart, who had not been allowed to pursue her masters degree at the University of Toronto in the 1940s, was awarded an LLD from that university. The Breakthrough Campaign had raised $125 million.
13. In those days Stuart was not above galas. Making $4,000 on a costume ball, she and her committee used it to purchase a Henry Moore bronze named The Seated Warrior for the gallery. Today it is arguably worth close to $1,000,000.

14. The Ontario government provides a little more than half of CJRT-FM's annual operating revenue. The balance is donated by the business community and CJRT listeners. Its Open College department provides university courses accredited by York University, and its signal reaches throughout Ontario from Kenora to Cornwall.
15. Margaret's husband, Ron Southern, turned ATCO, his fledgling trailer company, into an international giant. He has always credited "Marg" with being a full partner in his endeavours, particularly in the development of Spruce Meadows.
16. Among those whom Veiner Freeman has met with and written articles on are: economist/environmentalist Lady Barbara Ward Jackson; scientist/actress Jean Houston; artist Judy Chicago, internationally renowned for her work *The Dinner Party*; and Hong Kong financier Li Ka-shing.
17. Elizabeth Nichol is the wife of former senator John Nichol (former bag man for the Mike Pearson administration, and the inspirational force behind the founding of the Lester B. Pearson College of the Pacific).
18. McKeag's wife Dawn, herself a player as president of Walford Investments, and director on such major boards as The Hudson's Bay, Royal Bank of Canada, Goodyear Canada, has yet to reconcile the friendship. This is fairly typical of women who attack each other rather than the issue. A major board battle in Canada caused one woman on a rival board to describe another as wearing "dumb hats and tea rose perfume that is so overpowering that other directors want to throw open the windows in the middle of winter." Men do it differently. When Jimmy Connacher (Gordon Securities) squared off against Jimmy Pitblado (CEO Dominion Securities), Pitblado sent Connacher a dead fish; Connacher sent him a live turkey. Then they continued doing business together.
19. Banfield divorced in 1984. She married Graham Lount, founder of Shelter Corporation, in 1987, sold her company, and now hones her handicap at her husband's championship golf course near his hotel in Naples, Florida. Lount served on the board of Lester B. Pearson College of the Pacific and sits on the University of Manitoba Advisory Council for the School of Business.
20. Six of the most competent, most sought after early women directors were, and are: Inheritor Mona Camp-

bell of Dover Industries, a director of Toronto Dominion Bank, Rothman's Pall Mall Canada; Sonja Bata of Bata Shoes, a director of Canadian Commercial Corporation, Alcan Aluminum; Mary Alice Stuart, a director of Bank of Montreal, Johnson & Son; Agnes Benidickson, a director of James Richardson and Sons, Chancellor of Queen's University, Mutual Life, National Trust; her sister, Kathleen Richardson, a director of Gulf Oil, Barclays Bank of Canada, Sun Life Assurance; Dawn McKeag, a director of Walford Investments, The Hudson's Bay, Royal Bank of Canada, Goodyear Canada.

21. Vaillancourt was appointed a director of the National Bank of Canada, Carling O'Keefe, F.W. Woolworth, United Provinces Insurance, Institute for Research on Public Policy, Niagara Institute, Montreal Stock Exchange, Conference Board of Canada, Royal Canadian Geographical Society, Vanier Institute of the Family, Air Canada, and IRCM (Clinical Research Institute of Montreal).
22. Montreal's Sandra Kolber and Susan Curry, Toronto's Heather Reisman, wife of Liberal powerhouse Gerry Schwartz and president of her own company Paradigm Consulting, and Betsy Taylor, wife of Austin, CEO of ScotiaMcLeod, also have at their disposal limousines with chauffeurs whose executive dress barely disguises their dual role of bodyguard.
23. An engineer who guided the building of CPR through the Rocky Mountains, Sir Herbert was head of the Royal Bank and controlled some $3-billion of assets in hundreds of companies by the 1920s.
24. A world association of poets, playwrights, essayists, editors, and novelists, PEN has been instrumental in championing the cause for dissidents imprisoned or endangered within their own countries. Prominent Canadian members include Margaret Atwood and Adrienne Clarkson.

PART II

ACTIVIST POWER

Power does things, influence changes things.

PETER NEWMAN[a]

Establishment women just get mad. Activists change the laws.

NANCY JACKMAN

CHAPTER THREE

The Grassroots Movement

Wives, submit yourselves unto your own husbands, as unto the Lord. For the husband is the head of the wife, even as Christ is the head of the church . . . as the church is subject unto Christ, so let the wives be to their own husbands in everything.

EPISTLE OF PAUL THE APOSTLE TO THE EPHESIANS, CHAPTER 5: 22-24

On February 5, 1988, in the Four Seasons Hotel, forty-two-year-old former judge Rosalie Silberman Abella, chair of the Ontario Labour Relations Board, player/catalyst/futurist, rose to address a room packed with members of the collective Canadian Clubs of Vancouver. Many guests were either Establishment women who would not walk across the street to listen to a feminist, or CEOs of corporations under the populist gun of implementing employment equity as recommended by the Abella Commission.[1] They came to hear Abella the judge. Stereotypes intruded: she looked too feminine and was too humorous to be a feminist; she was too youthful to have been a judge. Appointed to the bench at the age of twenty-nine while seven months pregnant with her second child,[2] Abella has degrees and honorary doctorates that guarantee her success is grounded in scholarship, and her accomplishments can be measured by the month rather than the decade.[3]

Gathering a team of tireless experts, she collects and collates information and then, faster than most could read a judgement, publishes a definitive report identifying the problems and recommending solutions. By her early thirties she had entered the ponderous institution of the law, risen to the top, and become indispensable to the legal machinery that influences policy and, ultimately, attitudes.[4] *Toronto Life* publisher Peter Herrndorf has said that Abella intersects every level of the community, that she is a "powerhouse in six different fields: law, women's issues, the Jewish community, public policy, arts and journalism, and the academic community, [with] a kind of influence in all those fields that is almost unparalleled."[a]

The question hovered over the Canadian Club luncheon: what drives her? After cracking a joke, the petite Abella peered over the lecturn and commanded, "Let me explain myself." The story that followed was a manifesto of power inspired by historical tragedy. Before the Second World War, Abella's mother, Fanny Krongold Silberman, participated in running her family's manufacturing business in Poland. Abella's father, Jacob Silberman, was a practising lawyer. They were youthful parents and popular members of the Polish Jewish Establishment. Then Hitler invaded. Under Nazi rule Jacob could not practise law and the Krongold factories were nationalized. The couple was split up in separate concentration camps and their two-year-old son was killed. Each survived the Holocaust and, in the aftermath of the war, the redoubtable Fanny[5] tracked down Jacob, by then a leader of the revived Jewish community in Stuttgart. In 1946 they had Rosalie, and four years later, as refugees, the Silbermans arrived in Canada.

Abella is consumed by this history of a torn and tortured family, by the outrage that those she loves could have had their lives "ripped up . . . when everything was so great. Who would have expected it?" Beneath her veneer of humour is a drive bordering on compulsion, fuelled by her conviction that freedom could suddenly be snatched away and the horror could recur, even in Canada. Signs were once hammered up on Ontario beaches that read "No Jews, Dogs or Blacks," and in 1990 Nazi swastikas were painted on headstones of Jewish graves in an Ottawa cemetery. Such incidents make her words of 1988, "I have a sense of the limits of time," eerily prophetic. Rather than surrender to paranoia or a siege mentality, however, Abella views her world with optimism, evoking a pragmatic tone of objectivity while sharing her experience.

Choosing law as a discipline was as simple a decision for Abella as her commitment to equality and community is indelible. As her father could not practise law without a Canadian degree, she would do it. Jacob and Fanny Silberman had instilled in Abella and her sister "an intractable faith in the art of the possible, an unshakable sense that nothing and no one is to be taken for granted, and a ferocious commitment to justice." By joining an institution of power and earning an executive position, she fights inequality by influencing legislation that will prevent any group or culture from ever again being subjugated. She is particularly concerned with alleviating pain for women, who, have for centuries been treated legally as a minority, although they are 51 percent of the population.

Abella's life embodies that devotion through stewardship to the democratic process, a responsibility embraced most passionately by new Canadians or the progeny of families that have experienced oppression. They recoil from the complacency fostered by generations of entitlement in Establishment Canada. To Abella, maintaining human rights depends upon eternal vigilance. Two months before she graduated from law school in 1970, Jacob Silberman died, and she became, for her family, the personal guardian of this trust.

Having authenticated her position, Abella proceeded to take the Canadian Club audience on a historical journey to explain where her generation of activism was coming from and what is at stake today for women.

****

Most activists up until the 1980s were outsiders, those who had not made it inside the power system. To Toronto lawyer Jane Pepino and Rosalie Abella, policy makers who have made it, power means creating new and equitable legislation for women in the fields of family and labour law. They are the professional activists who, along with legions of homemakers (such as Berenice Sisler of Winnipeg) who became experts in their fields, make up the army that knows how to infiltrate the legal, political, and media strongholds, to amend laws, and to raise social consciousness—to fight for a world that is fair.

In the twentieth century, four significant events brought Canadian women from legislated subordination to constitutional self-determination, and closer to a mandate of equality. The first was achieving the vote in 1918. The second occurred in 1929 when the Privy Council in England, overturning a decision of Canada's Supreme Court, decreed that Canadian women were "persons" having all the rights and privileges thereof. The third did not happen until thirty-eight years later, following the 1960s climate of social anarchy, and innovations in media technology that would enable well-educated women to begin achieving the changes they so assiduously sought. It was the federal government's Royal Commission on the Status of Women, and it led to a heightened consciousness of women's issues and a gradual shift in public attitude, if not legislation. As a result, activists and a growing number of women lawyers mobilized themselves in 1981 to win the fourth and most significant victory of the century in 1982—the enshrining of women's rights in the Constitution.

At the turn of the century the primary injustices to women fell under the category of family and property law. Single women had many of the same rights as men, but once married, women became the legal property of their husbands, who had the right to decide on surgery for child or wife, to administer community holdings unilaterally, and to spend their wives' savings.[6] Fathers could, and did, marry their daughters off as early as age twelve. For a divorcée, the courts awarded financial support only if the wife's behaviour had been impeccable, a judgement based presumably on the testimony of the husband. Since many provinces did not allow women to sit on juries,[7] all verdicts were made by men. In 1989, ninety-year-old former lawyer and senator Muriel Fergusson remembered wryly of that era, "There weren't many rape convictions."

Determined to protect the moral quality of their homes and communities, women banded together through the church and volunteer sectors to call for control of alcohol and prostitution, and a higher age of consent to protect their daughters. As the turn-of-the-century expectation by men of "loving persuasion" from women had not improved laws, women sought voting power through legislated suffrage.[8] Gradually they earned their way into the institutions that controlled their welfare, but it was a long and tedious struggle. Emily Howard Stowe had studied medicine in the United States, and in 1867 when she returned to practise in Canada, she defied the law that prevented women from practising. As for the legal profession, the Law Society of Upper Canada changed its rule in 1897 and admitted Clara Brett Martin, but twenty years later the Quebec Bar remained closed to McGill graduate Annie Langstaff. Mr. Justice Saint-Pierre decreed that admitting her "would be nothing short of a direct infringement upon public order and a manifest violation of the law of good morals and public decency."[b]

By 1917, there were women "judges" in two provinces, magistrates Emily Murphy and Alice Jamieson in Alberta, and juvenile court judge Helen Gregory MacGill in British Columbia. Their appointments were not in accordance with written law, but all three played prominent roles in improving conditions for women. The day Emily Murphy moved to the bench, a lawyer correctly argued that, as she was not legally a person, she had no right to deliver judgements. A brilliant organizer who recognized the strength of group lobbying Judge Murphy refused to resign and led the "social feminists" to spearhead the drive for reform of family law and to win the Persons Case in 1929. Heralding the modern-day Judge Abella, she also fought for the rights of immigrants and minorities, and wrote *The Black Candle*, a trailblazing book on drug abuse used by the League of Nations Narcotics Division as a textbook.

When Agnes Macphail became the first non-person elected to Parliament in 1921, the press called her a "freak." Careful to play by the unspoken rules of the existing hierarchy, she worked for social reform in general rather than specifically for women, and stayed in the House for nineteen years. But Macphail was no pushover. When an opposition member leaped to his feet and roared, "I bet you wish you were born a man!" Macphail responded with Churchillian aplomb, "I bet you wish you were too!"

It was also in 1921 that Nellie McClung, homemaker and mother of five children, was elected to the Alberta legislature. Despite her speeches in favour of female representation in all divisions of government, three successive prime ministers — Borden, Meighen, and King — refused to appoint any women to the Senate. Women, they continued to argue, were not persons. With the resolution of the Persons Case in 1929,[9] women qualified for any discipline, but no one said men had to accept them as players in the game.[10] In fact, feminist causes dwindled with the suffragist and Persons Case victories. Young women were more interested in university degrees than equality demonstrations. The one exception was in Quebec.

****

Forty-seven-year-old litigator Lorraine Duguay can freeze a client with her hooded glare that persuades witnesses to tell the truth, and she speaks with contralto tones that convince juries of her veracity. Like so many other Quebec women whose ancestors were restricted by the dual vise of church and state, she absorbed her fierce sense of liberation as a child at her grandmother's knees. Once the most oppressive province for women, Quebec became within a decade the most liberated. And this backroom federal-Conservative powerhouse, broadcaster, business executive and activist is typical of the extraordinary number of Quebec women who have access to a network of male and female colleagues that crosses every discipline and all persuasions. Said Duguay of her vast contacts, ''We all know each other. We meet at the same meetings, attend the same conferences or receptions. When I phone someone — [Supreme Court Justice] Claire Dubé or Brian Mulroney — they answer.''[11] From 1989 to 1991 Duguay has served as a member of the Immigration and Refugee Board, an administrative tribunal that judges refugee cases.

In the early 1900s, Lorraine Duguay's upper-middle-class family had challenged church dogma and for its unpardonable sin was excommunicated. Rather than creep out of town in disgrace, they welcomed their freedom. One daughter, Anne Garneau, Duguay's grandmother, married at the age of seventeen, moved to Massachusetts, had three children (one of whom was Duguay's mother), divorced, and returned to Quebec. Garneau married twice more — to prominent Protestants. ''She was fantastic,'' reflected Duguay on the manner in which her grandmother charted her way through life. Duguay's mother also grew up a rebel by Roman Catholic standards and was criticized by her peers for bearing only three children instead of the customary ten. Lorraine Duguay was encouraged in the forties and fifties by her nurse mother and doctor father to seek a profession, to become ''autonomous.''

Duguay became entangled in the political world as a small child living on the fashionable Côtes des Neiges. Premier Maurice Duplessis was a frequent visitor to her home, and when her father became a deputy minister, he used to carry her into the legislature to hear his speeches. When Duguay's father died at forty-five and her mother had to return to nursing, the autocratic Duplessis assumed the role of family guardian.

The premier considered the children far too strong willed, particularly when Duguay's brother began to write for *Le Devoir,* exposing the powerful Duplessis to the discomfiting challenge of a new and defiant generation. Duplessis once exclaimed to Duguay's mother that she had never taught her children to respect authority and admonished her, "You should take care of [them]!" as if raising a child to be an independent thinker was equivalent to abandonment. Duguay's mother cheerfully advised her children to follow their instincts, live with their consciences, and, if necessary, pay the consequences of their actions. The only order she ever gave to Duguay was to spend one Saturday a month caring for the children of a poor family so that their mother could get out of the house.

Another frequent visitor to the Duguay home was Thérèse Casgrain, Quebec's most famous daughter and Duplessis's most ardent opponent. During the twenties and thirties, Casgrain presented innumerable briefs to the provincial government demanding the right to vote, recommending changes to the civil code, and requesting the admission of women to the Quebec Bar and the Society of Chartered Accountants, both of which were open only to men.[12] She was publicly ridiculed and on one occasion politician Dr. Ernest Poulin announced that "female suffrage is contrary to the spirit of the Catholic Church and [will] accomplish no useful purpose."[99]

Casgrain enjoyed an upper-class childhood among the elite of French and English Canada including judges, titled Englishmen, and prime ministers. It would have been a carefree life but for the all-pervasive politics to which Quebec children were exposed. Married in 1916 to Pierre Casgrain, a Montreal lawyer who would become prominent in business and a Liberal politician, Casgrain dined with the glitterati and intelligentsia by night, while by day fighting to change the fossilized attitudes of church and state. The organizations she helped create became essential components of the crucible from which would emerge the Quiet Revolution. In her memoirs she describes what must have been her greatest triumph over Duplessis: in 1945 when Family Allowances[d] were introduced, she learned that the Premier had instructed the federal government to issue the cheques to fathers, instead of to mothers as elsewhere in Canada. Believing that most women handled the family budget and that giving the money to the fathers would, she wrote, "demean the mothers of Quebec in the eyes of all Canada by letting it be seen that they were legally incapable," Casgrain called right through to her friend Louis St. Laurent, federal Minister of Justice and future prime minister. Then she quickly organized a massive Montreal publicity campaign to get mothers to flood the Minister of Health and Welfare with letters and telegrams of protest. She succeeded, causing Prime Minister Mackenzie King to telephone his friend Thérèse Casgrain to agree to the change.

In 1946, when the provincial Liberals prevented her from campaigning for a seat in a sure riding, a discouraged Casgrain left the party to join the Co-operative Commonwealth Federation and led its Quebec wing from 1951 to 1957, known as Le parti social démocratique du Québec.[13e] In an era that intensified a political consciousness among men and women as in no other province of Canada, her sympathizers included Pierre Trudeau, Gérard Pelletier, Jean Marchand, and Jeanne Sauvé, future power-brokers of Canada. A young Lorraine Duguay campaigned in Outremont with Casgrain and recalled that the great woman never won a seat. As a purist, she would never deliberately seek real power. When Pierre Trudeau joined the Liberals to promote federalism, Casgrain never considered going with him; instead, she felt betrayed. Even if she saw that he made the move to gain the necessary leverage to effect reform, she clung without compromise to the NDP . Her power lay in setting the stage for reform by founding grassroots groups that would win respect in the 1970s and 1980s following the confluence of societal forces. Despite her international renown as a humanist[14] and her access to influential circles through her Establishment roots, she operated perpetually outside the political executive that counted. It would be her younger protégés, Jeanne Sauvé, Monique Bégin, Lucie Pépin, Lorraine Duguay, who would get inside by joining the Liberals or the Conservatives, the traditional the ruling institutions of the country.

****

In her sweep through history, Rosalie Abella employed an Atwoodian style to seduce then shock her Canadian Club audience. "The forties was a time," she said, "when the public danced, swooned, and fantasized to Benny Goodman, Irving Berlin, Vera Lynn . . . consumed by a cataclysmic war, a nuclear bomb, a holocaust, a time in Canada when Japanese Canadians were disenfranchised and dislodged." Economist Phyllis Turner Ross became a senior government negotiator at the international level. Muriel Sprague Richardson took over the helm of James Richardson and Sons and became the most successful woman CEO so far in this century. The redoubtable Charlotte Whitton was on her way to a career as the mayor of Ottawa. Elsie MacGill, the daughter of Judge Helen Gregory MacGill, was the first woman to graduate in electrical engineering from the University of Toronto and, in 1929, the first to take a master's degree in aeronautics at the University of Michigan. In 1938 she was elected the first woman member of the Engineering Institute of Canada. During the war she was appointed head of all engineering work in the Canadian production of the Hawker Hurricane fighters used in the Battle of Britain, and later of Curtis-Wright Helldivers for the U.S. Navy.

During the flat, grey decade following the war, a lone woman's voice was heard in federal politics from Ellen Fairclough, a Hamilton chartered accountant. Parents continued to encourage their daughters to become nurses, teachers, and home economists rather than explore the worlds of corporate or professional power. Only a handful thundered ahead: lawyer Margaret Hyndman,[15] the first woman in Canada appointed to the board of a trust company, Anne Dubin and Laura Legge, who formed law partnerships with their husbands, and lawyer Marjorie Bowker, who was appointed to the bench in the 1960s. In fact, change in the 1960s would come only from those women who had no fear of being expelled from the tribal elite.

CHAPTER 3 NOTES

1. Appointed in 1983 to conduct a Royal Commission on Equality in Employment in eleven Crown corporations, Abella prepared a report that was used in developing the federal Employment Equity Act. It required Crown corporations to implement employment equality programs immediately, and federally regulated employers with one hundred or more employees to establish targets and timetables for hiring and promoting women and minorities.
2. Rosalie Abella is married to Irving Abella, historian and co-author of *None Is Too Many*, a study of Canadian anti-Jewish immigration policy in the face of the impending Holocaust.
3. In 1982, Roy McMurtry, then attorney general of Ontario, commissioned Abella to examine the rights of the disabled. The result, "Access to Legal Services by the Disabled," was vintage Abella—both a critique and a road map. Many of the one hundred recommendations have since been implemented by the Law Society of Ontario. For her commission on employment equity, she invited briefs from all over the country, held hearings in seventeen cities in six weeks, met with over a thousand individuals, and fourteen months later submitted the results, complete with recommendations.
4. In 1984, with an eye to evolving social conditions and the legal upheaval following the patriation of the constitution in 1982, Judge Abella and Quebec Court of Appeal Justice Melvin L. Rothman conceived and ran a conference for judges entitled "Law and Justice Beyond 1984." Lay speakers such as Margaret Atwood were invited to the oversold conference, and the resultant speeches and papers were published under the futuristic title *Justice Beyond Orwell*.
5. Fanny Silberman, who became a Toronto real estate agent with Royal LePage, helped develop trendy Queen Street with artist Charles Pachter. The septuagenarian, who is said to equal Rosalie in energy, acted as agent for the deceased Marian Engel and has bought and sold property for many prominent writers and artists such as Margaret Atwood and Michael Snow.
6. Many husbands were deeply insulted if their wives worked. Author Isabel Bassett wrote in *The Parlour Rebellion* about Peggy Shand, a woman who worked appalling hours during the Klondike Gold Rush. Even-

tually when she was offered an impressive $15 a day to bake in a hotel, her husband refused, explaining, "I will not allow my wife to [earn money] as long as I am able to care for her." Yet he allowed her to continue working long, hard days for the rest of her life, keeping her husband's pride intact.

7. Former Vancouver judge Nancy Morrison recalled that although women have been allowed to be jurors since the 1950s, it was common to choose jurors from the lists of property owners, and as hardly any women owned property, women jurors did not begin to appear until the early 1970s.
8. The federal vote, won in 1918, did little for Quebec women whose concerns for social and educational change were provincial matters based on the civil code from Napoleonic law. It was not until 1939 that the Liberal minority recognized the potential of what would be identified in the 1980s as "gender politics" by inviting forty women delegates to its convention. When Premier Maurice Duplessis of the Union Nationale called an election, La Ligue des droits de la femme and L'Alliance pour le vôte des femmes du Québec, both founded by Thérèse Casgrain, publicly backed the Liberals, who won. On April 25, 1940, Quebec's new government passed the women's suffrage bill.
9. When the Persons Case went to the Supreme Court of Canada, the chief justice argued that "it would be dangerous to assume that by the use of the ambiguous word persons, the Imperial Parliament meant in 1867 to bring about so vast a change affecting Canadian women as would be involved in making them eligible [to join the male worlds of politics, business, and the professions]." Judge Murphy, MLA McClung, Louise McKinney, Irene Parlby, and Henrietta Muir Edwards then took the case to the Judicial Committee of the Privy Council in England where, in 1929, it rapped the knuckles of the fusty colonial justices and overturned the ruling.
10. The first woman senator was Liberal Cairine Wilson, appointed February 20, 1930. In 1949 she also became Canada's first woman delegate to the United Nations.
11. In the 1984 federal campaign, Duguay was a prominent if unsuccessful candidate. Doors in Ottawa remained open, however, and Prime Minister Brian Mulroney attended her huge fund raiser for Accès 51 (a registry of female talent for business and the professions).

Board memberships have at various times connected Duguay to the social powers at the Montreal Symphony, the Musée des Beaux Arts, and Thêatre du Nouveau Monde. Her directorships include Radio-Canada, and her membership in the Canadian Bar gives her links from coast to coast. Her 1988 vice-presidency of the Montreal Chamber of Commerce linked her with Manon Vennat, president, then chair, of the Montreal Board of Trade, and with the thriving milieu of the Montreal business community where the acquisitory styles of women have placed them in the national ranks of corporate players. Quebec journalists know Duguay through her years of broadcasting and her position as press attaché for seventeen theme pavilions at Expo 67. Her former sister-in-law, the defiant Dr. Lise Fortier, founded the first birth-control clinics in Quebec.

12. In 1930, the Society of Chartered Accountants allowed women in anyway.
13. In 1961, the CCF was renamed the NDP.
14. Casgrain achieved international renown through the peace movement Voice of Women. She represented Canada at world seminars, conventions, and congresses. Her friends and acquaintances included Prime Minister Golda Meir and King George VI. Prime Minister Pierre Trudeau appointed her a senator in 1970.
15. Hyndman, who died in 1991 at the age of eighty-nine, was also the second woman in the British Empire to be made a King's Counsel. She was appointed to the board of Canada Trustco Mortgage in the forties. She held the presidency of the Canadian and International Federation of Business and Professional Women's Clubs, and during the Second World War she helped persuade the Canadian Bar Association to provide free legal services to military personnel and their spouses, an agreement that marked the advent of legal aid in Canada.

CHAPTER FOUR

The Turbulent Decades

The Sixties

> We awoke from the somnolence with a trajectory of energy. We blushed with Gerda Munsinger, watched . . . McLuhan's Global Village invade our living rooms . . . listened and gyrated to the Beatles. It was our most turbulent decade. . . . We were existential, Jungian, Freudian, nihilist.
>
> ROSALIE ABELLA[a]

Author Christina McCall once said, "Scratch any woman deeply enough and you find a feminist." But few would admit to it. The F-word drove even sympathizers underground; other women rejected it on principle as passionately as many embraced it, and the word became synonymous with "man-hater," polarizing the sexes and violating the sensibilities of middle-class America. Men's worst nightmare had come true. Tennyson had predicted it long ago in his 1874 poem *The Princess*: "Man to command, and woman to obey: All else confusion." The feminists' demonstrations bombarded television with a ferocity that spilled into the living rooms of an appalled North America. "Women's Libbers" tore off their bras (which, contrary to folklore, they never burned), donned overalls, and demanded the right to compete with men. This time reformists had banded together for good. Although their protests were not a renunciation of womanhood but a denunciation of cruel convention, they antagonized, offended, and even frightened politicians and the business world who were suddenly expected to welcome these Gorgons into their caucuses, offices, and boardrooms. No one was exempt from their wrath as minority groups seized upon the phenomenon of media technology to share their message with the world, to emerge from centuries of invisibility, and become lobbying forces of international prominence.

The ever adaptable Thérèse Casgrain envisioned the ''*global village*'' before Marshall McLuhan coined the term and quickly learned the art of attracting international attention for her causes. In 1962, as Soviet ships steamed to Cuba with their missiles, Casgrain, representing the Voice of Women peace movement, prepared to accompany Mrs. Cyrus Eaton of American Women Strike For Peace on her private plane to meet with Fidel Castro. They were about to take off when the dictator backed down and the ships turned back. In 1963, Casgrain took a Japanese girl burned by the Hiroshima bomb to visit the Pope. But her finest hour was in Paris, en route home from a meeting with Israeli Prime Minister Golda Meir, when she and Voice of Women co-founder Kay Macpherson[1] were jailed for inciting a demonstration. Twenty-five years later, in a radio interview with Peter Gzowski, Macpherson recalled the ''look of ecstasy on Casgrain's face'' as the police ushered them into the paddy-wagon, successfully turning the incident into an international media event.

It was the Pill that released women from the greatest threat of all: the terror of illegitimate pregnancy and the choice of public shame or back-alley abortion. Virginity or abstinence were no longer the only forms of birth control; the church had lost its moral imperatives of fear and condemnation. The new freedoms expanded from sexual to educational and societal. Homemakers who were untrained for anything but motherhood began to experience divorce, desertion, and poverty on the one hand, but unparalleled opportunity to join the workforce on the other.

One such homemaker was Lucie Pépin, the elegant, Establishment-born Quebecker who had been educated at private schools and, in a reverse pattern, was steered by her father towards medicine. Instead she became a nurse and homemaker before the unthinkable happened. Pépin found herself a divorcée with two daughters to raise and no money. She collaborated with Dr. Lise Fortier to found Quebec's first family planning and vasectomy clinic, simultaneously lobbying for an end to the ban on dissemination of birth control information. Pépin had become an activist. She recalled the time she addressed an audience of nuns, describing to them the anguish she had felt in her youth when at church she had watched husbands approaching the altar to take communion while their humiliated wives had to remain in the pews. Exhausted mothers of ten to twelve children, they had practised rhythm birth control, which was acceptable to the church but condemned by their culture, which demanded acquiesence to their husbands. The sacrament was no longer about sanctity but obedience. The sisters gave her a standing ovation.

When Betty Friedan's book *The Feminine Mystique* was published in 1963, "it hit," recalled Doris Anderson, "like a bomb." The quiet rumblings of the 1950s burst into revolution. The question "Why?" and its attendant thirst to know became the fulcrum of the decade. The visionary Anderson, editor of *Chatelaine*, had seen it all coming and had hired journalists Michele Landsberg and Barbara Frum, who, along with associate editor Christina McCall, had already begun shifting *Chatelaine*'s focus from the joys of domesticity to the feminist polemic. Anderson recalled, "We were ahead on articles on abortion, divorce laws, child abuse, poverty of women, working women." She does not recall that Frum, McCall, or any of her writers were card-carrying feminists, but as equality was a hot issue it was assigned to the staff writers, who became catalysts to change.[2]

Still the traditionalists clung to the status quo, and the laws of divorce and family property remained unchanged. Husbands were still entitled to give or to take away. It was only the feminists who had no fear of being ejected from the Establishment because for the most part they had never belonged. They had the freedom to work and gain some economic independence.[3] Many, such as seventy-year-old Laura Sabia, founder of the National Action Committee, or forty-five-year-old Chaviva Hosek, former Ontario MLA and former NAC president and now director of the Liberal Caucus Research Bureau, were second-generation Canadians whose immigrant parents had been barred from the Establishment despite prodigious achievements. Hosek suffered a further obstacle in Montreal when she was shunned by her wealthy Jewish classmates because her family was poor. Whether or not ostracism has more to do with economics than culture, the thrust for power is overwhelmingly driven by the emotional engine of exclusion.

Growing numbers of women began moving into the institutions of law, finance, politics, education,[4] and the church,[5] but throughout the educational system children rebelled at every time-honoured custom. Parents or university administrators who were raised within the strictures of duty, and had survived a depression and possibly two world wars, were dismayed by spoiled kids who were obsessed with "finding themselves," choosing their own curricula, and rejecting traditional deportment out of hand. In one enraged outburst, students trashed the computer centre at Sir George Williams University in Montreal. Puzzled university deans shuddered as their powerful chairs teetered on the edge of chaos. Students were directing their rebellion against the rigidity of an arcane system, against a generation that was clinging to the past rather than grappling with the future. No one was protected. Private families of rock-solid foundations were being torn asunder by offspring questioning truths no one had ever dared address. Instead of studying law or business, they talked about marching for peace and saving the environment. Ellen Fairclough became the first woman cabinet minister, Judy LaMarsh the second.[6] LaMarsh challenged women's groups by calling them the engine that keeps Canadian political parties functioning—the machinery rather than the engineers.

****

Laura Sabia was ahead of her time. It was 1974 in Montreal, at the annual meeting of the Royal Bank of Canada, one of the most venerable, impenetrable institutions in the country, its board an old-boys' club boasting the cream of the Canadian business community. The ritual event was open to shareholders—predominantly male, pin-striped executives—and journalists who sat quietly at the back of the room waiting to record yet another boring annual report. On the stage, banker Earle McLaughlin prepared to deliver his address. He smiled at his directors, his shareholders, and the press. It was a moment of profundity, reflecting everything power has to offer the Chairman of the Board. Suddenly a lone woman emerged from the audience, stepped up to the microphone, and demanded, "Take Idiot Mary off the air!" The startled McLaughlin peered down expecting to see a one-share dissenter, one of those nuts who were beginning to disrupt the meticulous choreography of annual meetings. What he saw was his old adversary, homemaker-broadcaster Laura Sabia, also chair of the Ontario Advisory Council on the Status of Women. They had tangled before over a promotional booklet called "Let's Pretend We Work in a Bank," which Sabia had argued stereotyped men's roles as managerial and women's as secretarial. Now Sabia was using this very public and dignified vehicle, the annual meeting, to demand that the bank cancel its advertisement depicting a mother saving funds to send her little boy to medical school. Stereotyping was a hazard of the times. What was wrong with sending your son to medical school?

Familiar with Sabia's media skills, McLaughlin agreed to meet with her the following day. Journalists scribbled happily, correctly visualizing front-page headlines. Sabia knew that two essential elements would give women power in the institutions: organized support, in this case the threat of gender power, combined with media exposure. No one was more aware than McLaughlin that, collectively, the "Marys" controlled a large part of Canada's wealth. What if they pulled their accounts? He took Idiot Mary off the air.

In 1976, when a beleaguered McLaughlin invited Sabia into his office to ask, "What do women want?" she took along reporters and challenged the chair to appoint a woman to the Royal Bank board. McLaughlin scoffed that there were no women qualified to sit on it. The media ecstatically created another national row. Sabia was prepared. She presented to McLaughlin, and the media, the name of Montrealer Mitzi Steinberg Dobrin, business executive/lawyer/supermarket heiress who lived in the Royal Bank's own backyard. Duly appointed, Dobrin became the second woman to crack a bank board.[7] Sabia recalled that when Bill McLaughlin, the son of the Royal Bank chair, met her years later, he told her that from the stories his father had told in the 1960s, he had imagined her to be a werewolf.

Laura Louise Villella Sabia, a second-generation Canadian-Italian with roots in Montreal, had no fear of being expelled from the Establishment because she neither belonged nor aspired to it. But her father had. Like Helen Roman-Barber's mining czar father, Stephen, Sabia's father had arrived in Canada in his teens and built up his own construction company. Both men enjoyed the perks of financial success, but neither their great wealth nor their community contributions was sufficient to make a place for them at the Establishment dinner table. While Roman-Barber insisted that her father had no wish to belong, Sabia admitted that the rebuff had broken her father's heart. Both women became super-achievers, consciously or unconsciously reacting to the rejection by the Montreal and Toronto elite.

"Money makes the difference. I had money," said Sabia of her marriage. Dr. Michael Sabia, the traditionalist for whom she left law school, could control his wife only by extracting a promise that she would not demean him by earning a salary. Family wealth provided her with a sense of freedom and empowerment unknown to the financially dependent who, she said, are afraid of everything — of being criticized, of being considered too aggressive, of being cast aside. On one occasion after Sabia had spoken with the Hamilton *Spectator* in 1967 about "women's biological beat of bed, board and babies," she recalls that the Etobicoke *Press* shot back: "Women don't want to be equal . . . their place . . . is to complement [their husbands]."

The Sabias lived in St. Catharines, where Victorian traditions were as revered as was Doctor Sabia of the St. Catharines General Hospital. It was also the place where Laura Sabia had her children, Maureen[8] and John, kept hired help, and grew bored. Unable or unwilling to join the doyennes of the St. Catharines volunteer circuit, Sabia amused herself by tackling the venerated institutions of religion, education, and politics.

In 1955, she noticed that the Roman Catholic Separate School Board was a quasi old-boys' club that hadn't had elections for seventeen years. Membership was by tacit agreement. In her view, board and church needed shaking up, and she summoned the press to announce that she was running, not just for a board seat but against the Monsignor. She achieved so much publicity that another trustee stepped aside to let her in. Sabia proceeded to shake up the moribund system and, before long, to win a seat on city council. That wasn't enough and the brilliantly organized superwoman soon cast around for more to do. In 1964, when she was invited to host a radio talk-show, her alarmed husband suggested she take a trip to Europe. "Why work?" he puzzled. That was all the challenge Sabia needed. She took the job but donated her thousand-dollar-a-month salary to the founding of a women's centre. Then, to her husband's horror and the dark fascination of the community, Sabia proceeded to tackle the taboo subjects of incest, homosexuality, prostitution, abortion, and the arcane structure of the Roman Catholic church. The reaction of St. Catharines housewives amused her: "It blew their lid off. Every woman in the city could have killed me." Even though a woman's place was still in the home, Sabia continued blithely smashing down the walls of colonial silence. Today, friends laugh at "the awful things she used to say." There was hardly a radio in the city that wasn't tuned in every morning.

Whenever the mortified Dr. Sabia entered a nursing station at his hospital, the staff would lunge for the volume control on smuggled radios. His wife reflected, "Michael thought he was marrying a traditional housewife, and suddenly he's got a viper in his bosom." Dr. Sabia once rushed home because everyone at the hospital was discussing her morning program on incest. "My God!" he exclaimed, "Next thing you know they'll be saying that *I'm* doing something." His comment illuminates the greatest societal control — fear of ridicule and rejection through being identified with a taboo merely by proximity. Public discussion of AIDS and homosexuality is finally helping Canadian society to get over that awful suspicion that anyone who discusses aberrant behaviour without condemning it might be condoning it or even participating in it.

One day Sabia learned that the famous Dutch prostitute, Xaviera Hollander, author of *The Happy Hooker*, was in Toronto. Sabia phoned and invited Hollander to join her on the talk show.[9] Noted for the exuberance with which she regarded her profession, Hollander was delighted to share her message, so Sabia picked her up and brought her home for the night. Dr. Sabia was appalled. Jesus Christ might have given Mary Magdalene metaphorical shelter, but He didn't have a son attending Ridley College. "What will the neighbours think?" took on a whole new meaning.

Hollander's upcoming show received top billing and a local bookstore owner who had stocked five hundred copies of *The Happy Hooker* later said he could have sold two thousand—mostly to the housewives of St. Catharines. Once Dr. Sabia got over the shock of having a prostitute in his home, he found Hollander a bright conversationalist, but he nearly suffered cardiac arrest when she told him the best prostitutes in her New York salon were housewives. It was their way of earning some secret spending money while maintaining a public image of propriety as non-working wives.

At the appointed hour, a hoard of extra radios brought into the hospital by staff and patients' relatives began broadcasting in quadraphonic clamour down the hallways, about the wards and even through the ever-so-hushed operating rooms. Dr. Sabia's hospital had become a scene from "M*A*S*H*" with Hot Lips Hoolihan rebounding off the walls. At every patient's bedside, Michael Sabia cringed at the voices of his wife, Hollander, and St. Catharines phone-in afficionados — all muffled and disguised — grappling with sexual dysfunctions and laughing with Hollander.

In 1965, Sabia chaired a coalition of thirty-five women's groups calling for what would become the third landmark in the history of the women's movement to study Canadian women. The late Margaret Hyndman, who had been expressing concern about women in economic straits who were being ignored, encouraged Sabia to organize the national policy meeting, which included Quebec contingents headed by Thérèse Casgrain and Réjane Colas. Naming themselves the Committee for the Equality of Women,[10] they debated the issues, reached a consensus, and then approached the federal cabinet as a united front. Sabia, who had tired of women fighting against each other in public, laughed, "The politicians were amazed that the two cultures got along so well."

Chatelaine ran a questionnaire on the pros and cons for the proposed royal commission and acted as an open forum for the country. Charlotte Whitton, by then an Ottawa alderman, backed the status quo, arguing that the doors were already open and women didn't need that kind of support. Her do-it-yourself attitude reflected that of more recent players who have "made it" and wonder why other women cannot. Prime Minister Pearson must have agreed with Whitton, for he turned the proposal down. MP Judy LaMarsh called Sabia with the news just before a *Globe and Mail* reporter called to probe, "What are you going to do now?"

"There's a million things you could do," said Sabia boldly.

"Name one," pushed the reporter.

Sabia bluffed, "I'll march two million women to Ottawa and we'll see what Mr. Pearson has to say."

"Thanks," said the reporter and hung up. The following morning, the *Globe and Mail*[b] screamed, "Two million Canadian women may . . . march on Ottawa if the . . . government fails to announce . . . a Royal Commission. . . . Mrs. Michael Sabia of St. Catharines claims her organization representing two million women . . . has given an ultimatum. . . . "[11] Sabia was petrified. The woman who would successfully corner 100,000 Bell Canada[12] proxies in a lobbying coup knew she could not possibly deliver, physically, one million women, let alone two million. Many of the supporting organizations' members were ladies of the Junior League and other traditionalists who might send money but would never join a public march. But even Sabia had underestimated the power of the press. Minutes after the *Globe and Mail* hit the street, Judy LaMarsh telephoned Sabia to relate a conversation she had just had with the Prime Minister. "Who the hell," he had asked, "is this Laura Sabia?" LaMarsh had warned that she was a St. Catharines housewife with a talent for mobilizing large numbers of women. According to Sabia, Pearson promptly announced the Royal Commission on the Status of Women. Shaking her head some twenty years later, she marvelled at media power, "We would never have had [it] but for that headline."

Sabia's greatest strength as a feminist was that she amused while getting her message across. Her power through the media was as good as, if not better than, that of a bank chair. Free agent, fearless, fun, she was impossible to control or to ignore. She still is. More recently a columnist for the Toronto *Sun*, she had become a model for outsiders seeking access to institutional power. Asked why she spent so many years battling the odds to build a national army of women to assault the institutions, why the radio talk show, the politics, the school board, the St. Catharines city council, Laura Sabia replied, "It's being in the public eye." Fighting anonymity. Playing the game. Shaking up the system that had not accepted her immigrant father in spite of his New World success. She would be neither overlooked nor forgotten. In excluding Laura Sabia's father, the Canadian Establishment became an unwitting catalyst in the emancipation of women.

By 1968, a new act had broadened the grounds for divorce but made no changes to family law. Yet out of the turbulent, confusing 1960s would emerge first the Royal Commission on the Status of Women, then commissions on human rights, a civil rights act, and talk of affirmative action. Rosalie Abella said of that era, with finality, "We were never the same again."

The Seventies

> [The decade] started . . . with a Royal Commission on the Status of Women and Watergate. We learned . . . that democracy was an unquenchable public thirst. . . . It was a time of hopeful dialogue and, in retrospect, a time of innocent vitality.
>
> ROSALIE ABELLA

Now in her eighties, former senator Florence Bird still has her expansive smile and her snow-white hair still coiffed in an unruly chignon, epitomizes the way she races through life. It was this prominent, American-born journalist-broadcaster whom Lester Pearson called upon to chair the Royal Commission. She had been trying for weeks to get an interview with Pearson for an article on Commonwealth relations, and when she heard his unmistakable lisp on the telephone, she assumed the call was about that interview. She never got it. Pearson was calling about the RCSW, and after her initial reluctance, she agreed to replace her broadcasting job and home life with three years of extensive travel on its behalf.

Pearson's choice of Bird angered the feminists, who viewed her as a Liberal partisan of Establishment origins.[13] Sabia believed the real reason for Bird's hesitation had been a fear of being tainted with feminism, which, at that time, "was a dirty word. The Liberals wanted a token person and came up with Bird." It was Sabia who engineered the appointment to the commission of two experienced feminists, sociologist Monique Bégin[14] and electrical engineer Elsie Gregory MacGill.

In fact, as a practical bridge between the factions, Florence Bird was the perfect choice. Her Establishment roots allowed her to operate in the inner circles of institutional power and win the trust of those dedicated to the status quo, while her American forthrightness combined with her own work ethic enabled her to deal with the public in a way that was assertive but unabrasive. Bird had travelled the country during the Depression with her journalist husband John and had observed reactions ranging from apathy to antagonism from colonial-minded anglo-Canadians towards Quebec. She had written about the need for a new constitution to give Quebec a better deal, and in Winnipeg during the war she had broadcast a radio program for youth and challenged married women to get out into the workforce, to "take on the discipline and the toughness of a professional job."[c] But even she succumbed to the proscription of embarrassing one's husband with a higher profile, a salary, or progressive opinions: Bird wrote under the pseudonym of Anne Francis.

In 1968, the commission spent nine weeks touring seventeen major cities, listening to repeated accounts by women—many of them widows or single mothers—of family breakups, default on child support, inequitable salaries, discrimination in the marketplace, the unattainable wish to develop latent talents after the children left home and the desire to become more productive in society. In so many voices and in so many places, they expressed a sense of invisibility and uselessness. It was the first time anyone had listened officially, and the commission heightened the country's awareness of such great activists as Mary Two-Axe Earley, who fought for years to win for native women the right to keep their status upon marriage to non-natives. In her memoirs, Bird described a meeting with a northerner in Yellowknife in a "cold, bare room, empty except for a chair and a single-burner electric stove on the floor."[d] Offering her chair to Bird, the woman sat on the floor and told a story of childbearing in dirt-floor shacks without heat or running water, and of her feeling of hopelessness. Bird persuaded her to appear at the hearings the next day. It took extraordinary courage, but native women unaccustomed to television cameras, bright lights, and microphones did come before the commissioners to tell their heart-rending stories with quiet dignity.

Royal commissions are famous for being shelved. Even Prince Philip had asked Bird during a Government House reception if she didn't think hers would be pigeonholed and forgotten. Bird shot back an emphatic no, knowing that the groundswell of activism and professionalism would never let their advantage slip away. The emerging power came from the remarkable number of women graduating from the university faculties of medicine, business, and law.[15e] Doris Anderson put journalist Barbara Frum on the telephone lines in 1971 to encourage women across the country to run for public office. Women still staffed party constituency offices for men, rarely fielding or supporting one of their own. In a subsequent *Chatelaine* article, Frum listed 105 possible candidates, and over the next ten years, women mayors and provincial politicians said it was Frum who inspired them to run. The night before his surprise wedding to Margaret Sinclair, Prime Minister Pierre Trudeau made a speech encouraging women to run for Parliament and said if he were re-elected, he would appoint women to government boards and committees. The subsequent 1972 election marked the first time that the Liberals welcomed women into safe ridings. Monique Bégin and Jeanne Sauvé won and entered the upper echelons of Canadian political power.[16]

The toughest job ahead would be implementing the recommendations made in the Royal Commission's report. Seeking to preserve the power of the national women's organizations that had lobbied for it, Laura Sabia became chair of the newly named National Action Committee for the Status of Women, which over the next fifteen years came to represent some five hundred organizations and approximately four million women.[17] The grassroots activists became further legitimized through government structures — the ministry for the status of women and the Canadian Advisory Council on the Status of Women. As the federally funded Advisory Council enjoys an autonomous mandate, in essence the government is monitoring itself. Should inequities arise, the CACSW night-riders could charge the Hill with vigilante force.

The rising profile of women mushroomed through the work of the RCSW. Lorna Marsden won the vice-presidency of the National Liberal Party in 1975, followed by Iona Campagnolo, who later became its first elected woman president. In 1976, Flora MacDonald won the position of national secretary of the PC Association of Canada. The NDP Participation of Women committee (POW) began to take part officially in the creation of party policy. But the polarization between the activists and the traditionalists remained extreme. Rather than give feminists credit for their own growing freedom, Establishment women never really wondered why they could now take jobs without condemnation.

Despite the progress of the late 1960s and early 1970s, Penney Kome wrote in *Women of Influence* that little had changed.[f] The RCSW had recommended equal pay in the federal public service, the largest employer of women in the country, and hoped that provincial and municipal governments and even the private sector would follow suit. "Example rather than legislation" was the key, but to paraphrase Abella, it takes the passage of laws to provoke attitudinal change. Another fifteen years would pass before that happened. The nine women members of Parliament elected in 1974 would not become ministers of major cabinet portfolios, and the one major facelift they achieved in the House was changing the sign on the restroom door from Parliamentary Wives' Lounge to Parliamentary Women's Lounge. Even incremental steps were significant.

The Eighties

> Talking about Canadian women in power is kind of phoney. Women don't have any power.
>
> DORIS ANDERSON, TORONTO, 1988

> Doris Anderson . . . was . . . the most powerful woman in the country. She [had] built a constituency at all levels of society—the public service, the politicians, the women's movement, the activists. . . . She gave away that power. Just gave it all away.
>
> SENATOR LORNA MARSDEN, TORONTO 1988

Speaking about Section 15 of the Canadian Charter of Rights and Freedoms, Christie Jefferson, the executive director of the Legal Education and Action Fund, LEAF, said, "The definition we have of equality, particularly the section that says equal protection and benefit under the law, is revolutionary around the world." Yet, like the proposed Equal Rights Amendment in the United States,[18] it might never have happened. Section 15 and Section 28 were conceived and born of an acerbic battle in 1981 between Doris Anderson, president of the CACSW, and Lloyd Axworthy, Minister Responsible for the Status of Women.[19] This Anderson-Axworthy debacle stemmed from a cancelled meeting, with the Advisory Council caught in the middle, and the subsequent, year-long lobby by women to enshrine their rights in the constitution, epitomized the thrill of winning, the tragedy of losing, and the ephemeral nature of power. No one could have predicted the explosion of events that would build the national conference, planned for February, 1981, into an historical political event. The hour-by-hour, day-by-day evolution of Section 28 of the charter, including the work of the players who made it happen, has been meticulously documented by Penney Kome in her book, *The Taking of Twenty-Eight*.[g]

In January 1981, prior to a major CACSW conference on the constitution, Anderson claimed that Axworthy had "leaned on the executive to cancel its conference—the government was debating the issue in the House [and he saw the meeting as a potential embarrassment]." Interference by government in the CACSW contravened its mandate, but when Anderson approached her own executive—which included Berenice Sisler, an old pal of Axworthy—for support, it voted to comply with the government's request. Anderson's furious resignation, with the charge of government interference, was like plunging off the Queen Mary, and demonstrates a sine qua non of power: to keep it, you have to stay in the game. She was left treading water while CACSW executive member Lucie Pépin assumed command of the bridge. In the House, Conservative and NDP MPs unsuccessfully demanded Axworthy's resignation.[20]

Not only did Anderson lose her power but it would be two years before she would be offered a job by anyone. Although she lost that battle, it is generally acknowledged by everyone, except the embarrassed Liberals, that she was the catalyst that won the war. Her resignation inspired a core group of talented women to mastermind a year-long lobby that would result in women's rights being entrenched in the constitution. Flora MacDonald reflected in 1989 of Anderson's resignation, "I doubt we would have got the legislation otherwise."

In the fall of 1987, Senator Lorna Marsden, former sociology professor with expertise in work/labour markets, gazed out of her office window onto the rain-soaked grass of Massey College's common and, in tones ringing with friendly authority, reflected on those bizarre events of 1981. Never before had women been so politicized, so constant, in conducting a sustained lobby to achieve what has so far proven impossible in the United States.

The Canadian women's movement had its martyr. In the Senator's view, Anderson had symbolized leadership. Her ability, vision, and activism had been expressed not only through *Chatelaine* magazine, but also through her "magnificent job of stumping the country and rousing women to consciousness about the . . . Constitution." While helping Anderson campaign in a 1978 federal by-election, however, Marsden had observed that Anderson "lacked an understanding of politics on the ground," or the concept of the team before the individual. "Journalism," noted the Senator, "[makes you] a bit of a maverick. It doesn't put you into that organizational world—and Doris suffered from that." Berenice Sisler also described Anderson as a woman used to being at the top of the heap, to giving orders. On a previous occasion, she also broke a hierarchical taboo by appealing directly to the Prime Minister. That further damaged her position and suggested that Anderson did not understand the principles of institutional power, the survival tactics employed in staying in the game.

Anderson's power as president of the CACSW was arguably greater than that of senior politicians, unparallelled, Marsden said, by that of any other woman—including cabinet ministers who receive their positions from the Prime Minister and have to live with whatever he decrees. In resigning, Anderson relinquished her access to high places in government, to the elite in business and, said the Senator, "to all those other constituencies that are so important to get anything changed in this country. . . . She overreacted. Just blew up and quit."

In her partisan observations, Senator Marsden nevertheless underscored the reality that institutional power belongs to the position—not to the individual. Or does it? What happened next indicated that it can also belong to the group, in this case, to the quasi-institution of gender power. Almost immediately after the resignation, Anderson supporters regrouped to organize an unofficial conference on the constitution to be held in Ottawa just three weeks later.[21] The "faceless bureaucrats," the secretaries, two-thirds of whom are women, made it possible. Government telephones suddenly became conduits to women's organizations across the country. Regular business slowed as secretaries in the Langevin Block and on Parliament Hill surreptitiously prepared, then photocopied and distributed, information papers.

Flora MacDonald remembered that "the constitutional battle was the most significant event of the century. My office was in the West Block, so we made it the working headquarters for people to use. My secretary co-ordinated most of it."[22] MP Margaret Mitchell of the NDP vacated her office to provide space for the organizers. Various ministries arranged consultations with boards and commissions to coincide with the proposed conference so that women could be flown in from remote areas of Canada courtesy of the government. Billeting, day care, and meals were organized for the three hundred women expected to arrive for the unofficial conference. No one had fully anticipated the national furore that would be raised over Anderson's resignation. When the event began on February 14, 1981, over 1,300 women registered. MP Marion Dewar rushed out and rented a larger hall. Many who could not attend sent donations. Maureen McTeer and Joe Clark had offered to have a Stornoway reception for those originally expected but instead they threw one for the two hundred and fifty women who had come from farthest away.

This time it was the Liberals who were left out in the cold. The Anderson-Axworthy battle had eliminated ideological differences as traditionalists joined with feminists, Francophones with Anglophones, Conservatives with New Democrats to devise recommendations for constitutional change. Illustrating the principle of collectivity: that while one woman might not have power, together women made up a huge lobbying force that was impossible to ignore. For ten months the core group persistently lobbied the MPs, some of whom wondered aloud just what it was women wanted. In particular, they wanted the correct wording in the constitution, having rejected Sections 15 and 28 as framed by the experts in the office of the minister of justice, Jean Chrétien. Although columnist Geoffrey Stevens wrote that the words were already carved in stone, the National Association of Women and the Law[23] revised the wording twice and the lobbyists then moved to have the final draft inserted in the new charter. But when the premiers known as the "gang of eight" hustled in Section 33,[24] giving them the power to override constitutional provisions, both Section 15 and Section 28[25] were defanged. The exhausted women lobbyists set aside their home lives and businesses once again to regroup and to get those two sections exempted from the override clause.

Judy Erola,[26] who had replaced Axworthy as minister responsible for the status of women and became the lone Liberal to assist the lobby, recalled Trudeau's warning to her that agreement of all the premiers was now obligatory to change anything in the wording of the constitution. A committee of six,[27h] with the support of Erola, spent hours telephoning women's groups across the country, as well as each premier, securing their approval to exempt Section 28. On November 24, 1981, then justice minister Chrétien complied with the change. The struggle originally begun by the suffragists, continued by Emily Murphy in the Persons Case, bolstered by the Royal Commission on the Status of Women and culminated on April 17, 1982, in a single constitutional decree: Notwithstanding anything in this Charter, all the rights and freedoms in it are guaranteed equally to male and female persons.

Erola served champagne in her office and Penney Kome wrote: "Only later was it apparent how much political respect we had won and how much public sympathy had been aroused by the fight."[i] Jean Chrétien publicly applauded the lobbyists for their excellent work, and journalists Allan Fotheringham and Richard Gwyn commented that it was the most skillful lobbying they had ever seen on the Hill.[j] Senator Marsden saw it differently, citing the division between Liberal women and the lobbyist force. At one time united across lines of party, religion, culture, class, and region through issues of social justice such as family law, the women's movement had begun to be divided by politics. Nevertheless, the victory marked the end of a decade that had seen an unparallelled assault by grassroots associations on institutions, the evolution of social activism, and the emergence of a new professionalism. Organizations such as the National Association of Women and the Law had functioned effectively under the eye of experts and would continue to press for implementation of the RCSW report and to contest the abuse of constitutional rights through the courts. Using the Royal Commission's work as a comprehensive road map and the constitution as their legitimate vehicle, women finally had the tools and the credibility to pursue equality.

Male politicians accepted the fact that women were a force to recognize, to court, and to incorporate into the political structures of the country. The term "gender politics" and its potential power was bandied about the Hill, and parties promoted women as never before. Sociologist Lynn McDonald, past president of NAC, took the nomination from popular NDP stalwart Gerry Caplan in a 1982 Broadview-Greenwood federal by-election and then defeated Peter Worthington, a prominent Torontonian and former Toronto *Sun* editor who ran as an Independent. When she ran again in 1984, McDonald won by 3,000 votes and was one of twenty-seven women elected to the federal parliament.

Eight years after the Anderson-Axworthy quarrel, in 1989, the wounds had still not healed. Pépin denied that she had been a Liberal partisan in 1981 when she replaced Anderson as the CACSW head, but Anderson claimed that all the participants who voted to cancel the famous conference were rewarded: "Lorna Marsden was appointed a senator by Trudeau in 1984, in 1986 Berenice Sisler won the Persons award [commemorating the 1929 landmark]. Lucie Pépin replaced me as president of the Advisory Council, and in the 1984 federal election her nomination for Outremont was endorsed at the highest level. And she served in the federal shadow cabinet. If the Liberals had won, she would have been given a cabinet position." On February 15, 1991, Peter Gzowski looked back on Doris Anderson's resignation and its inadvertant sparking of the drive for constitutional reform, and asked her if she ever wondered whether or not she had done the right thing. Anderson, who has written a lightly disguised novel on the period, *Affairs of State*, replied in that deep, assured voice, "No. Not once."

As for Doris Anderson's dictum that women do not have power, Marilou McPhedran, who was awarded an Order of Canada for her contribution to the constitutional lobby and is a student of the nature of power, considered the nature of institutions and their intrinsic rigidity. She told Penney Kome, "To make any lasting change you have to participate in the workings of the institution. . . . We [the constitutional lobbyists] assaulted the institution and forced it to respond."[k]

The Great Debate—Resolved: Affirmative Action Is Reverse Discrimination

> When they have to resort to a euphemism for a euphemism, as using the term "employment equity" for affirmative action in the hideous Abella Report, they are not only uncomfortable with the truth, they are dishing up abominable lies.
>
> BARBARA AMIEL

> I want to say how relieved I am to find that Barbara Amiel is as poisonous in person as she is in print.
>
> ROSEMARY BROWN

> Let's arm the women. I would rather be the one at the front with the M16 than the one left at home in the barn defending the homestead with a pitchfork.
>
> NANCY MORRISON

> Nancy . . . you have one of the best pitchforks I've ever seen, and what you dished out certainly came from the barnyard.
>
> MORRIS SCHUMIATCHER

The Canadian Bar Association debate on August 26, 1987, was brilliant, corrosive, funny, and provided the kind of thought-provoking challenge that makes bar meetings the envy of all professional associations. Few of the approximately one thousand members who attended will ever forget it. Barbara Amiel and lawyer Morris Schumiatcher argued for the affirmative while former judge Nancy Morrison and former NDP politician Rosemary Brown defended what has become, as Judge Abella predicted, one of the most hotly disputed issues of contemporary society. The arguments of Amiel and Brown still evoke the fascination reserved for some cataclysmic occurrence in nature: violently executed and awesome to behold. The debate was inspired by noteworthy events of 1983-84.

One of the most smoothly expedited commissions of inquiry ever undertaken began in 1983 when Lloyd Axworthy, then Liberal minister for employment and immigration, appointed Judge Rosalie Abella to conduct the Royal Commission on Equality in Employment regarding women, minorities, the disabled, and native people and studying eleven Crown corporations. The judge promptly expanded the mandate to include government and the private sector in Canada. She completed the task in 1984 just after the Conservatives had won the federal election.

Instead of shelving the report, Flora MacDonald, the new Minister of Employment and Immigration, used it to frame Bill C-62. Supported by Brian Mulroney, she ushered it quickly through cabinet without a detailed analysis and then accomplished the impossible by introducing it into House debate within six months of its initial drafting. It passed, went to the Senate, and became the Employment Equity Act on June 27, 1986.[28] To Abella's surprise, the press all but ignored Bill C-62 and the resultant Act. Calling it "one of the most significant pieces of social legislation to come out in a decade, " Abella marvelled, "The impact could be monumental and the media overlooked it."[29] That is, almost all media persons did, but not Barbara Amiel, celebrity journalist, TV hostess, author, provocateur.

Schumiatcher and Morrison had delivered low-key speeches for the affirmative and negative respectively, the former preferring excellence and ability to quotas, and the latter lauding employment equity as a progressive remedy. Morrison cited the voluntary affirmative action taken by women following the Second World War when they had relinquished their jobs and higher education to make way for the veterans. Taking a good-natured swipe at the CBA's all-male executive, she called for widespread advertising of jobs, instead of canvassing the old-boys' network, and fair recruitment practices. "Discrimination is an illness . . . affirmative action is an imperfect solution." Then came Morrison's parting shot: "Discrimination does not affect the very beautiful, as Rosemary can tell you; it does not affect the very smart, as Barbara can tell you; it doesn't affect those who have both beauty and brains, as Morris Schumiatcher can tell you." She put the audience in a jovial mood.

The moderator, Gordon Fairweather,[30] never saw Barbara Amiel coming. Known to mesmerize entire audiences as effectively as she does individual men, Amiel incapacitated him so completely in her opening statement that he lost control and never regained it. She simply recalled her televised interview with Fairweather a decade earlier when she had asked him, as the new Human Rights Commissioner, "Might not affirmative action programs that give preference to women be a violation of the great liberal idea of equality?"

Fairweather had unabashedly replied, "Reverse discrimination, you mean, Barbara—I'm not afraid to use the phrase. Sure I favour it, and it's going to be around for awhile . . . until the year 2000.'' With a few deft quotations, Amiel had transformed Fairweather from the disinterested moderator into a participating opponent, an ethical faux pas on the part of the CBA. Amiel, who never just nicks her victims, deepened the wound with, ''I find it intriguing that the CBA would have as a moderator over affirmative action, the man charged with implementing it. . . . I would not try a case in court under those circumstances, and I doubt if any one of you here would either.'' Embarrassed laughter rippled through the hall. Most debaters might have moved on, but not Amiel. Her perfect British accent lent authority to her scalpel as she carved each accusation. She referred to an article her then husband, George Jonas, had written in the *Canadian Lawyer* describing Fairweather's affirmative action policies as reverse discrimination. Fairweather had protested in a letter to the editor that he had never used the phrase. Now, a decade later, Amiel was exposing his ''inconsistency'' before 1,200 of Fairweather's professional colleagues. Then, having rendered the moderator irrelevant, she turned on Rosemary Brown. Four years later, male lawyers and judges still remark that they would never have gone at each other the way these women did.

Repeatedly employing the personal approach rather than referring to ''my honourable colleague,'' Amiel disposed of ''Nancy's'' lightweight argument describing discrimination as a bad habit that could be broken — with all the benign encouragement of an evangelist murmuring that you too, can give up smoking. Then she focused on ''the hideous Abella report.'' Tossing out the constitution, the human rights acts, and court precedent as irrelevant to the resolution, Amiel likened pay equity to ''all the paraphernalia of a coercive society.'' Then she dismantled the term ''discrimination'' like a particle physicist examining the elemental components of Napalm.

Amiel's power lies in articulating what the public might think but hasn't the nerve to say. In the starkly analytical style of a trial lawyer, she built her argument: that since discrimination exists in almost any kind of selection, it follows that as ''in the past we favoured white, able-bodied males, today we [are] favouring black, handicapped women,'' that those who implement the law ''simply want to create a situation in which . . . candidates being equal in ability, a woman or a homosexual will be given the first crack at a job. . . . '' The audience punctuated her speech with bursts of nervous laughter and clapping. Expanding on her premise, she argued, '' . . . [it] becomes excruciatingly clear if you use the same grammatical construction and say in a very reasonable tone, 'All things being equal I prefer a white male for the job,' that is discriminatory and only a fool and a thoroughly intellectually dishonest person would say otherwise.'' Having delivered that zinger, Amiel personalized the argument by listing the moral and intellectual deficiencies of those who disagreed.

The very existence of affirmative action, in Amiel's view, "requires that we offend our most basic idea of equality and fairness . . . and posit the idea that something so bad is happening in Canada that our great tradition of liberal tolerance and equality must be put aside." In a soft but adamant tone emphasized by clipped consonants, Amiel pounded home her conclusion that the principle was "contemptible . . . mindless nonsense. . . . I find it ludicrous to suggest that the Canada that we live in today is systemically sick and prejudiced against groups." Someone who had been refused a job could rationalize the rejection by blaming culture or gender discrimination rather than recognizing that he or she happened to be a jerk.

"Would a society that is racist and sexist pay for the extraordinary bureaucracies and studies that give a living to Mr. Fairweather?" Amiel asked. "Would they provide jobs for Ms. Brown as a Status of Women committee member? What government could afford to spend millions on such things as the Abella Report and all the enforcement that goes along with it if this society were basically sexist or racist?" Her tones of derision were as unmistakable as her language was eloquent, and she expelled the words "Abella Report" as if ejecting lemon seeds from behind her teeth.

Amiel is a survivor, solely responsible for all that she has accomplished, and she would have it no other way. Schumiatcher himself had inadvertently sketched a picture of her when he said that affirmative action "does a disservice to those minority groups who wish to be the masters of their own fate and destiny, who resent the interference of government for good or for ill." She is Jewish, a member of a minority, and she struggled out of a painful childhood of parental and experiential heartbreaks. Leaving home at fourteen, she put herself through school by working in a peach-canning factory where her hands and arms were torn by the jagged edges of tin. Amiel made it by applying her incisive, analytical mind and, at times, unapologetically, her extraordinary beauty. None of her accomplishments, which include being editor of the Toronto *Sun*, an author, and a top print/TV journalist/columnist in England and Canada, were assisted by affirmative action programs. She enjoyed an occasional seat at the dinner table of then British prime minister Margaret Thatcher and still savours the camaraderie of intellectuals to be found in the British parliament. Her male companions, say friends, "ooze power." Barbara Amiel is one of the most discussed journalists on two continents. That she enrages is part of her success.

"What Rosemary and Nancy and Gordon stand for," Amiel warned, "is *parity* . . . a statistical concept [or the implementation of percentages] . . . introduced immediately as part of a coercive social engineering." As ours has been a patriarchal society for two thousand years, she noted sardonically, we could hardly assume that removing barriers would mean that 50 percent of the female work force would immediately become presidents of chartered banks. It was the kind of comment for which she is famous and that often brings business executives cheering to their feet. Reintroducing the concept of moral propriety, she mused, "Some of us at least have the decency to be ashamed of this." She then suggested that those who think Canada is sick should "try and implement the Abella Report in South Africa or . . . pay equity in sexist Iran." Stripping her arguments to the bare bones of logic and definition, Amiel appealed to her audience's intellectual discipline honed through jurisprudence. Then she moved in for the kill, merging the scenario of affirmative action in Canada into a deadly analogy with the horrors of Nazi Germany, a result of liberalism denied.

A thunderous ovation was showered upon Amiel as Rosemary Brown set aside her prepared speech, tapped her microphone, then announced, "I want to do a voice check because I want to be absolutely sure that you hear every word I am about to say." The hall fell silent as Brown apologized to Fairweather for "Barbara's cheap shot." Shivers of anticipation rippled through the crowd as Brown anointed Amiel with the sobriquet of "poisonous." Morrison recalled, "It was like Wimbledon. Heads were swiveling back and forth each time the ball sizzled into the enemy court." They had gone too far. Atwood's ever-lurking Cordelia was inspiring the women to fling insults directly at each other, transgressing the formalities of debate. Too often women with a mission expect loyalty and appreciation from all women, and when someone expresses an opinion incompatible with their ideology, the response may take an irrational turn into a personal attack on the arrogance of her wrong-minded thinking.

Brown had fallen into the trap with, "When we talk about seeing the world through the eyes of our experience we also—those of us who are *normal* human beings—try to see the world through *other* people's experiences too. I was hoping that, somehow, Barbara and Morris had an ability to experience the world even superficially through our . . . experiences." Brown then put Amiel's speech down as "nonsense. Her thinking is confused, her arguments convoluted, her information false. . . . We have been subjected to the most incredible case of ethnocentrism that I have ever experienced."

Without referring to a single note, Brown held the eyes of each of the thousand or more CBA members while delivering an oration in which every word sprang from a history of discrimination and the positive power of affirmative action. Brown spoke with the articulate, modulated tones of authority that had taken her to the third ballot against Ed Broadbent at the 1975 NDP national leadership convention. Rather than dissect definitions or acknowledge Amiel's logic, she focussed on the positive, intangible forces of self-esteem and dignity. The distinguished-looking black woman, whose face is framed by a shock of tightly curled white hair, was speaking from a childhood background in upper-middle-class Jamaica in a family of self-reliant women, followed by her years at McGill University during which she could find no woman who would room with her. Brown's speech was spare, her demeanour at times indignant, her impact stunning. Statistics, she argued, have little to do with affirmative action, which ameliorates individual disparities. As it was, the government itself that had set up many of the discriminatory barriers—such as that it would not employ married women.[31] How could redressing that wrong be beyond its power? The oversight, she allowed, occurred "not because men are evil, bad or malicious—but because they are not women, black, disabled, Francophone, or native."

"Affirmative action is not discrimination . . . [it] is not designing narrow eligibility rules and regulations that say you cannot enter here unless . . . you have these qualifications or those qualifications." Her own law career had stumbled, she confessed, because of atrocious LSAT scores. UBC had said, "'We don't care if you are black and female, we're not letting you in here.' So I went into politics instead." The laughter from the audience was warm and appreciative, and respectful. She continued, "Affirmative action is . . . the most positive, non-discriminatory kind of vehicle that can help us to work towards true equality. Now Barbara said, in her infinite wisdom, and this is an incredible talent which she has for mind reading, that what Nancy and I were speaking about was parity and not affirmative action. Well, she has as much talent for mind reading as she had for fairness. She was wrong. I did not use [that word]. I speak English 'good.' When I say parity I mean parity, and when I say equality I mean equality."

Expressing pride in her gender and race, which give her enriching assets, Brown commanded with all the authority of her roots and life experience: *"I want you to respect them.* If there is one country in this world that can have a concept as powerful . . . as affirmative action, it's going to have to be us." Brown closed with the determination of a settler's wife defending her family with a single bullet in her gun: "I am not going to let go until we do."

Ultimately, the debate had not only underscored Rosalie Abella's power and what she had wrought through due process of law, but also forecast the future effect of the Pay Equity Act on society as a whole. It validated a century of progress beginning with women winning the vote and culminating in entrenching their rights in law. It also clearly established just who has the power. Barbara Amiel and Rosemary Brown can challenge and inform, but they cannot legislate. Abella had engaged that higher process when heading the royal commission on pay equity in 1982, and Flora MacDonald had completed it by using her political position to manoeuvre Abella's report first into Bill C-62 and then into law. The distinctive difference between Amiel's and Brown's influence and MacDonald's legislation lies in winning institutional power.

CHAPTER 4 NOTES

1. Toronto journalist Lotta Dempsey, Kay Macpherson, and Maritimer Muriel Duckworth founded the anti-nuclear movement Voice of Women. In Quebec, Thérèse Casgrain and Senator Marianna Jodoin organized a VOW chapter in 1961 and Casgrain was elected president. Although the Quebec women of the church movement Action catholique canadienne described VOW as falsely humanitarian and misguided in its political aims, by 1962 the VOW national membership stood at 10,000.
2. While married to Peter C. Newman, Christina McCall worked with him on the initial phases of some of his books. In 1982 she wrote *Grits*, the definitive work on the Liberal party of Canada, and in 1990 she co-authored, with her husband, Stephen Clarkson, the award-winning analysis of Trudeau's years in power: *Trudeau and Our Times*, Volume I. Michele Landsberg became a columnist for the *Globe and Mail*, best known for her gutsy articles on New York, written while she was there with her UN Ambassador husband, Stephen Lewis, and for her book *This is New York, Honey*. She now writes for the Toronto *Star*. *Journal* host Barbara Frum first gained international accolades as host of the CBC radio talk show "As It Happens" and wrote a book, *As It Happened*.
3. Activists come from everywhere but the Establishment with the exceptions of the late Senator Casgrain, current Nova Scotia NDP leader and MLA Alexa McDonough, former NDP MP Lynn McDonald, and Toronto Conservative Nancy Jackman.
4. As recently as 1963, when future university president Margaret Fulton, then in her forties, requested that A.S. Woodhouse, dean of graduate studies at the University of Toronto, let her write a doctoral dissertation on the writer/wife of Thomas Carlyle, Woodhouse replied that if she did, she could forget about her degree. Fulton understood the nature of power. Limiting her defiance to picketing with a handful of other women to win the right to dine with the male graduate students, she wrote her thesis on Thomas Carlyle and got her doctorate. Her acquiesence marked one of the rare times in her illustrious career that she complied meekly with the system. Woodhouse announced of the women at one meeting, "Well, gentlemen, we are

scraping the bottom of the barrel. We are going to have to make some of the women teaching fellows." Author Susan Crean defied her dean when he decreed that no woman could write on "Strategy and Tactics of the Peloponnesian Wars," and, thanks to family experts in the field, did just that. Her professor castigated Crean and lowered her mark for being disobedient.

5. In 1964, UBC Anglican Theological College student Elspeth Alley was forbidden to eat in the dining room or study in the library of the college. In 1972, amidst threats on her life, she was the first woman deacon to be ordained in the West. At the time there were only five other women ministers in Canada. She became the rector of Holy Trinity Church in Vancouver. In 1980 and 1986 respectively, the Very Rev. Lois Wilson and Anne Squire were appointed moderators of the United Church. Wilson became the first woman president of the World Council of Churches. Sister Mary Jo Leddy of Toronto, a prolific writer in Church publications, advocated a more liberal approach to including women in the executive of the Church.
6. In 1963 LaMarsh was appointed minister of health and welfare. She spent much of the following two years bringing in the Canada Pension Plan. Her next portfolio was secretary of state at a time when that ministry had approximately fourteen different departments under it.
7. Madame Pauline Vanier, wife of Georges, the governor-general of Canada, had been appointed to the Bank of Montreal board in 1967.
8. Maureen Sabia, a childhood friend of Barbara Amiel, became a Toronto lawyer, a proponent of right wing politics, and a member of prominent boards.
9. Judy LaMarsh was another issue-oriented broadcaster who featured Hollander on her radio show.
10. In 1966, Sabia was also president of the Canadian Federation of University Women. The Committee For the Equality of Women included, among other organizations, the Business and Professional Women's Clubs and the University Women's Clubs.
11. Two million denoted the number of members in the organizations covered by the Committee for the Equality of Women.
12. At the 1969 annual meeting, Sabia threatened a major proxy fight if Bell did not begin to hire more women. She threatened to depute someone in every city to col-

lect women's proxies. The burgeoning meeting went on for an extra hour and a half and turned into an uproar over the hiring issue. The following year she showed up with 100,000 proxies to make her point and stated that the appointment of Helen Hogg, a McGill professor, and Pauline Vanier to the Bell Canada board was tokenism. She expected the company to hire up to 25 percent women within ten years. In 1991, out of seventeen directors, three were women: Guylaine Saucier, Jean Casselman Wadds, former High Commissioner to London, and Claire Paradis Bertrand.

13. Florence Bayard Rhein was born into Philadelphia society, the daughter of a neuro-psychologist father and a writer mother whose ancestry included a long line of senators. While Bird credits both parents with instilling in her a sense of self-worth and capability, she acknowledges her father as the one who patiently guided her explosive temper into a process of reason.
14. Bégin, a political protégée of Thérèse Casgrain and vice-president of the newly formed Fédération des femmes du Québec, was appointed executive secretary-general of the commission.
15. In 1920 Canada had 26 women lawyers; in 1950 there were 113. Then in the decade from 1971 to 1981 there was a 563-percent increase in the number of women lawyers from 780 to 5,177.
16. Trudeau appointed Senator Muriel Ferguson Speaker of the Senate and named five women judges, a deputy minister (Sylvia Ostry became head of Statistics Canada), and Pauline McGibbon as lieutenant-governor of Ontario, minister of health and welfare from 1977 to 1979 and from 1980 to 1984, Monique Bégin strengthened the health insurance system by amending the health law in 1984. Jeanne Sauvé presided as minister of state for science and technology in 1972, minister of the environment in 1974-75, during which time she brought in the first legislation for environmental control minister of communications, in 1975-79, Speaker of the House, in 1980-83, governor-general, in 1984-90, and honorary chair of the Jeanne Sauvé Youth Foundation, in 1990.
17. Two of the NAC's most prominent leaders were future senator Lorna Marsden and future MLA Chaviva Hosek. Hosek led the successful 1984 challenge to the three federal leaders to include women's issues their famous, and for John Turner, fateful, television debate.

NAC's aim was to attack the inequities publicized by the RCSW and to provide a forum where special interest groups could present their briefs to the government.

18. Although some states do have their own equal rights amendments, the amendment to the federal constitution that would have affected all women and minorities, though passed by Congress in 1972, has yet to be ratified by a sufficient number of states to become law.
19. Section 15 deals with equality: "Every individual is equal before and under the law. . . . " Section 28 deals with equality of the sexes: "Notwithstanding anything in this Charter, the rights and freedoms referred to in it are guaranteed equally to male and female persons."
20. Particularly vocal were Flora MacDonald, Pauline Jewett, Margaret Mitchell, and Ed Broadbent.
21. Those who helped to organize the unofficial conference included Voice of Women co-founder, Kay Macpherson, Laura Sabia, lawyer Marilou McPhedran, Linda Ryan-Nye and Nancy Jackman. One prominent speaker was Jill Vickers, professor of political science at Carleton University.
22. Beth Atcheson and Beth Symes, former law students of constitutional expert Mary Eberts, along with Marilou McPhedran, and Ryan-Nye, would become the power behind the constitutional battle.
23. NAWL was helped by NAC and the CACSW.
24. Section 33 became famous when Premier Robert Bourassa cited it to override the Supreme Court of Canada decision on language and implement French-only signs in Quebec. It can render Section 15 useless, and for this reason many women fought against the 1990 Meech Lake Accord, which would have given the provinces greater autonomy in government.
25. Section 15 didn't come into force for another three years (April 17, 1985) to give legislatures the opportunity to remove legislation from the books which was sex discriminatory. Section 15 is still subject to the override clause.
26. The fifty-seven-year-old businesswoman and politician was elected in 1980, enabling her to become a champion for women during the constitutuional events. Erola was also minister of state for mines, and minister of consumer and corporate affairs. She was minister responsible for the status of women from 1981 to 1984. After being defeated in 1984, she was immediately

appointed president of the Pharmaceutical Manufacturing Association of Canada.

27. They were Linda Ryan-Nye, Pat Hacker, Rosemary Billings, Vaughan Jeliffe, Marilou McPhedran, and Tamra Thomson.
28. Employment equity is tougher and more comprehensive than affirmative action legislation, and while it differs from equal pay legislation, it includes it as a critical component.
29. Critics say the law will cost millions and in 1991 the Ontario government reported that it would cost $50 million in hospital salaries, but Abella countered that ultimately it will save billions in human resources.
30. Fairweather was appointed head of the Immigration and Refugee board in 1987.
31. At the end of the First World War, women were strongly encouraged to leave the workforce and the government passed legislation to keep married women off its payroll.

PART III

INSTITUTIONAL POWER

Individualities may form communities, but it is institutions alone that can create a nation.

BENJAMIN DISRAELI

Everybody, including the Pope, is replaceable.

JUDI KORBIN

CHAPTER FIVE

Winners in the Power Game

I cannot, when I have a job before me, render a bad decision in order to be nice to an institution.

JUDGE ANDRÉE RUFFO

What makes women winners or losers? Is it era or aura? Specific experience or performance on the bench, in the House, on the hustings, or at the bottom line? In politics, why was cabinet minister Judy LaMarsh so pummelled and ridiculed when half a decade earlier colleagues had listened to Ellen Fairclough when she harangued the caucus? Why did Sheila Copps have problems making her points, while Jeanne Sauvé had a ready audience? Why did Flora MacDonald never quite achieve the clout of Pat Carney or Barbara McDougall? Considering women's historical disadvantages, how has anyone at all made it to the top? For a gender identified for centuries by such terms as "mistress," "maiden," and "mother," why do women even want institutional power?

Benjamin Disraeli supplied an answer to the last question in an 1866 speech at Manchester. For all the frustrations they impose, the waiting to climb one more rung on the ladder that often ends in mid-air, institutions alone can make a nation.[1] And it was Lenin who wrote, "Political institutions are a superstructure resting on an economic foundation."[a] In 1988 at an Ottawa conference on women and power, Professor Jill Vickers warned that if women want to challenge the shape and logic of power, they must learn how to enter the institutions and work from within, or create their own.[b]

Bluntly, women have not been there. The vast majority of women in senior management or vice-presidencies have presided over human resources or legal services. That is changing, but as Judi Romanchuk, Calgary vice-president and director of the Dean Witter Reynolds (Canada) brokerage house, candidly observed, "Power in our industry is money, and if you run a big organization that wields a lot of money, you've got power. [Except in rare cases] women in this country who have headed major corporations are inheritors, not women who have come up through the ranks, and they are not women who've bought it through an LBO."[2]

Until the 1980s, only a handful of women got inside. The shrines of power—the government, the professions and their omnipotent associations, the corporate sector with its multinationals, banks, trust companies, insurance, and brokerage houses—functioned in hierarchical systems rooted in tribal law. Talent continually clashed with gender. Few women became judges and politicians, and in the world of finance, no women could be found among the corporate executive. Winning a platform was next to impossible for women whose male bosses were socialized in an earlier age when Marilyn Monroe steam and Doris Day domesticity were still the reigning stereotypes. As recently as 1985, CFTO documentary producer Isabel Bassett wrote *The Bassett Report*, illuminating the difficulties still faced by women who intended to advance into the executive sphere and expected to be regarded as colleagues by their counterparts.

One pioneer was Ellen Fairclough, who had earned a CA in the 1940s and successfully integrated into a business world still foreign to women. She had also served as a city councillor and deputy mayor but when she entered politics, it was probably inevitable that she would be characterized as "female" before "CA." In 1957 when elected prime minister, John Diefenbaker was forming his cabinet but kept ignoring the increasing pressure to appoint a woman. He ran out of excuses when Bill Blair, a trusted team player, died, but continued to delay announcing his cabinet for days after the funeral, perhaps hoping Fairclough would vanish into the mist. Finally he summoned her one evening after everyone had left, kept her waiting in the hall for half an hour, then grumbled, "It looks as though I'll have to form my cabinet from amongst my enemies, (Fairclough being one of those for voting against him at the leadership convention). You can be Secretary of State."

Instead of swooning as Diefenbaker had expected, Fairclough was ticked off. As Labour critic, she had hoped for that at least. Snapping, "I'll let you know," she walked out. It was George Drew, former Ontario premier and high commissioner to London who convinced her to accept the token post. Marjorie LeBreton, deputy chief to staff of Prime Minister Brian Mulroney, said in 1989 that when Fairclough entered cabinet as secretary of state, later becoming minister of citizenship and immigration and then postmaster general, she was respected as a businessperson when she challenged the caucus. In 1965, however, when then Liberal MP and economist Pauline Jewett informed Prime Minister Pearson that she had spent two years learning the ropes and would be interested in a cabinet position, Pearson, who already loathed having Judy LaMarsh in cabinet, regarded Jewett with genuine amazement and exclaimed, "But we already have a woman minister."[3]

Not even skill as a criminal lawyer was sufficient for Judy LaMarsh to command respect in the House. Her former law partner, Nancy Morrison, remembered that while other cabinet ministers could telephone directly to the Prime Minister, Pearson screened calls from LaMarsh to an appointment secretary. "Pearson treated Judy like shit," remembered Morrison. "She used to come back in tears after speaking with him." Yet her contribution to Canadian politics was valuable. In her first portfolio as minister of national health and welfare from 1953 to 1965, LaMarsh brought in the Canada Pension Plan and set up the medicare system. Then as secretary of state in charge of some fourteen departments, she exhausted her own funds crisscrossing the country to promote Canada's Centennial Year celebrations, establish the Royal Commission on the Status of Women, and encourage women to get involved in politics. While her mission aided the Liberal cause, gaining public recognition was also her way of reinforcing her territorial imperative. Pearson was saddled with LaMarsh, unable to dismiss the woman who, Morrison acknowledged, "was big and tough and strong and swore too much." Though adept with actuarial tables and accountancy, LaMarsh lacked business experience. Worse, she lacked feminine chic, and her parliamentary colleagues never forgave her for that. When asked about the way LaMarsh was treated, one of her former colleagues exclaimed, "Well, can you imagine going to bed with that?!" For women, politics was guerrilla warfare.

In the early seventies, when CTV and CBC financial analyst Dian Cohen, was first invited to speak on business panels at conferences, it was less because she was a superlative communicator than because she was young and attractive. "You'll brighten the panel up," her colleagues would say. Cohen remembered that for a long time her role was to wear a red dress and keep her voice soft. She played the game and was eventually recognized for her financial and communications savvy. Bruna Giacomazzi, a Vancouver-based vice-president of personal (retail) banking at the Hongkong Bank of Canada, recalled of those years, "I had to fight gracefully for every job." Invisibility went with the role. In 1972, while a manager at the Mercantile Bank, she accepted an invitation to accompany senior vice-president Duncan Campbell to a Vancouver Club reception for the bank's new president. She was the boss of some of the men who would be present and was respected as a competent player. But instead of entering honourably, she found that women were not allowed into that male enclave at that hour, and Campbell sneaked her in via the fire escape and the freight elevator, as if he were smuggling a stripper into a stag party. When the pair finally entered the private dining room, the party of men fell silent with embarrassment. Quelling the awful feeling that she had no right to be there, Giacomazzi smiled with as much dignity as she could muster. Women who faint, cry, or shriek are stricken from the team. Suddenly, as if cued by a choral director and by way of an indirect apology, the men began stammering about the shameful discrimination against Indians and Jews.

In 1984, when Pat Carney was in Calgary as the federal minister of energy, mines and resources dismantling the National Energy Program with oil magnates from Canada and the United States, she could not attend the breakfast meetings, where everyone did their deals, because they were held at the men-only Calgary Petroleum Club. It had never occurred to the multinational executives to hold them anywhere else. Despite being voted "oilman of the year," Carney was on the outside. The problem was not the women but the era. One could give the men the benefit of the doubt—reasoning that they made the meal reservations absentmindedly, viewing these women as colleagues. After all Mercantile did it again just a few months later.

Former labour negotiator Judi Korbin, now a vice-president of Canadian Airlines International, recalled that when she held her first meeting with the pilots' union, the forty men present were so disgruntled over having a woman in charge that they would not allow her into the room. She won them over by joking, "Listen, guys, just pretend I'm a gender mistake."

In 1982, Donna Bridgeman, formerly in management with the international chemical company Monsanto, requested an alternative date for her CA tax exam as her baby was due on that date. After consulting the Chartered Accountants of British Columbia, the teacher replied, "Sorry, the association does not allow changes for trivial reasons." Bridgeman studied in hospital before having her baby, then showed up five days later carrying the trivia to write the exam on the set date. She received the second highest mark in the province.

When business strategist Lynne Hall, noted for her financial skills honed over the years with AT&T, General Electric, and Shell Oil, was appointed to the board of Canadian Tire in the early 1980s, she expected to contribute to the board in a capacity commensurate with her corporate experience. But she recalled that at her first meeting, the acting chair saw only a woman and declared, "You look like a socially responsible person so we'll make you chairman of the social responsibility committee." Tire was unusual in having four women directors on its board, and they proceeded to shake up its culture and wrench it into the twenty-first century.[4]

Why did women keep struggling to get inside and climb the institutional ladder? Because institutions run the country and being a player in their ranks means winning the right to exercise unparallelled economic, political, or judicial power. Professional institutions form the backbone of civilization, and at the brain stem is the law, its members an erudite elite whose moral integrity is expected to be sacrosanct by definition. Any unprofessional conduct is disciplined internally, rendering members accountable to no one but themselves. That alone is a privilege enhancing the mystique and prestige of professional power. Women who broke through the glass ceiling of the judiciary during the 1980s were the Justices of the Supreme Court of Canada Bertha Wilson, Claire L'Heureux-Dubé, and Beverley McLachlin, previously Chief Justice of the Supreme Court of British Columbia. Mary Batten, a former Chief Justice of the Court of Queen's Bench in Saskatchewan, was the first woman to achieve that post. Chief Justice Constance Glube currently presides over the trial division of the Nova Scotia Supreme Court. Lynn Verge served as minister of justice and attorney general of Newfoundland.[5]

In the economic game of leveraged buyouts and corporate takeovers in the 1980s, banks were central to the action. Giacomazzi of the Hongkong Bank, this country's largest foreign bank, whose parent corporation has world-wide net assets of approximately $150 billion,[6c] expressed the sentiments of virtually every on-line vice-president in corporate institutions when she reasoned, "Where else could I manage $3.5 billion in assets, learn about so many different facets of one discipline, be connected to a global network, and have such an opportunity for advancement?" The most prominent woman in Canadian banking during a time of monumental change for that monolithic institution is forty-year-old Helen Sinclair, formerly vice-president of the Bank of Nova Scotia, and currently president of the Canadian Bankers' Association.

****

By the late eighties management was dropping its adversarial stance and humanizing its corporate structures. Women were being headhunted for expertise peculiar to the boards rather than for their social background or how they looked. The handful of trailblazers who had entered the upper echelons of institutional power had managed to sidestep or conquer the historical impedimenta and downright hazards littering the path to acceptance. Not the least of these, after centuries of conditioning, was a lack of belief in themselves. Women who succeeded in management in the fifties, sixties, and seventies became adept at harnessing skills honed, not only on the job but through homemaking, volunteering, and the delicate world of gender diplomacy.

There are four specific characteristics by means of which women have succeeded or failed, and will continue to win promotions or sabotage themselves in the 1990s: business experience, secret agendas, deportment, and tone of voice.

First, business experience reigns supreme among the accepted routes to power. Flora MacDonald came to Ottawa as a secretary and the memory lingered. It was from the position of chief of Tory headquarters that she built a national network, ran regional campaigns, and became better known than any other Conservative except the prime minister. She skilfully adapted her bookkeeping experiences and her penchant for world travel to enter politics and rise to cabinet minister in the posts of External Affairs and Communications, but perception counts, and she continued be regarded as a secretary, a helper who conveyed a sense of earnestness rather than that sustained image of authority so essential to leadership. Old images are hard to shake.

Business experience makes the difference. The women most respected in cabinet are those who have proven track records on the Bay Streets of Canada. MPs Judy Erola, Pat Carney, Mary Collins, and Barbara McDougall all operated in the world of commerce before entering politics. Erola had already run her own successful company[7] before dealing in the early 1980s with the rough diamonds of the mining world as the first woman junior minister in Energy, Mines, and Resources. Then, as minister of consumer and corporate affairs, she was the first woman member of the Priorities and Planning Committee, and as minister responsible for the status of women, Erola played a key role in the lobby to enshrine women's rights in the constitution. In life after politics, she was hired as president of the Pharmaceutical Manufacturers Association of Canada and appointed to the board of Inco. Like Jeanne Sauvé, Erola had broadcasting experience and possessed a commanding voice that was heard, but most significant, she had been welcomed into politics as a businessperson.[8]

Women with the clout of a business degree and experience in the contentious world of finance may or may not be better debaters, but they are recognized as coming to the political table with a tacit acceptance of the game. Male politicians are confident that women from Bay Street can take part in acrimonious debate with smiles and otherwise inscrutable expressions. The burden of gender fades in the face of skill. No one cared whether or not Carney had feminine chic. They just cared that she could deal. When Simon Reisman or Adam Zimmerman haggled with Carney over free trade or stumpage rates, neither man feared a quivering chin, and the Reichmanns knew that her tears would never spill into Gulf Canada's oil. Carney was no sissy. She set aides' knees shaking and won the upper hand in deal-making by exuding a kind of implacable authority conveyed through an abstruse frown.

Women without business experience but with a sophisticated sense of how to play the game had been welcomed into the old boys' network at an earlier stage. Conservative backroom player Manon Vennat of Montreal was a buddy at university of Michael Meighen, archetypal Conservative and close friend of Brian Mulroney. During the 1940's Jeanne Sauvé first developed contacts through the Jeunesse étudiante catholique and firmly rooted her friendships with Gérard Pelletier and Pierre Trudeau. She later parlayed her own considerable skills to join them in running the country.

A law degree did not help Maureen McTeer who, in the 1970s, followed the traditional woman's role by sacrificing her final year of law school to help her husband, Joe Clark, campaign his way to prime minister. But she scandalized the country by keeping her maiden name. Today the issue of a woman's surname is passé and in Quebec women retain their maiden names by law, but McTeer never shook her image as a ball buster. Although she later finished her degree, McTeer is perceived to be a journalist and feminist rather than a member of the legal profession. Even in the supposedly enlightened era of 1988, when McTeer ran for a federal seat at the same time as her husband, shockwaves reverberated across the land. What if she won and Joe did not? Regardless of Clark's obvious pride in campaigning for his wife and the fact that they were seeking seats for the same party but in different ridings, in the marvellous convolutions of human logic one prominent businessman choked, "This time she's gone too far. Wives shouldn't compete against their husbands."

The second requirement, adhering to secret agendas, means that women must learn to play the game in the corridors of institutional power. In a paradox for a gender known for its secrecy, women are still learning this. Ten years ago, finding a woman director in business, government, or education was as rare as sighting a Siberian tigress in Fred Eaton's Forest Hill garden. For those few pioneers, functioning in that milieu of the old boys' club was like orienteering without a compass. A strange game was afoot, one of subtle competition between administrators and directors, with an etiquette of procedure and a language of negotiation. As directors are ultimately accountable to an institution but must not interfere in its operations, the hockey puck in this game was the secret agenda couched in the cautious exchange of information. Scoring goals meant retaining the balance of power.

In a practice that even pre-dates the Roman Empire, men know that issues are passed at board meetings but debated beforehand. Women are more accustomed to dealing with issues up front, charging into domestic frays, organizing volunteer events or solving small business emergencies with an entrepreneurial exuberance. When elected to boards, they were amazed to find themselves lacking a voice at the table. Institutions shoot messengers and newcomers to boards learned the hard way that voicing criticisms or asking provocative questions in the boardroom is akin to tearing off a goalie's face mask. And a decade ago some women directors typified the cliché. They could not read a balance sheet, and they kept raising issues outside the safe boundaries of finance, and inside the realm of those terrifying "soft" concerns in management territory—staff well-being and equality of positions. When one such woman asked her first blunt question, she was met with chilling silence. Later, another board member — a male business executive — drew her aside to explain that subjects like that were never raised nor debated during formal meetings. "You deal with those ahead of time in the pub over a beer." As she had not been invited to the pub, she had not been privy to the game plan.

In the mid 1980s, Jalynn Bennett, then a vice-president of ManuLife and seasoned board member at the corporate, political, and policy, making levels, told journalist Anne Collins,[d] "For awhile I couldn't understand why I would propose something . . . and there'd be absolutely no reaction . . . until the same idea would come out of somebody else's mouth, and the group would consider it." At first Bennett reasoned that no one had heard her. Then she suspected that it might be some kind of male plot, that women were seen but not heard. She finally deduced that the concept at play was one of team participation. Once a woman is accepted by her board, and recognized as someone of substance, it becomes OK to listen and respond. There is no hurrying the tribal dance. It must be observed, even if a woman's continued silence implies a tacit acceptance of all that she may detest.

To initiate change, women must first be secure at the top, and getting there means mastering the art of obfuscation — or keeping their agenda secret. Activists call this selling out to the system and they are probably right, but that is why they are still on the outside. As Marjorie LeBreton, has said, you can't use power if you don't have it in the first place. Barbara Rae, president of Office Assistance and chancellor of Simon Fraser University, added,[9] "Most male executives know how to cover their ass. Those of us who come by a less traditional route never even think of it." Rosalie Abella put her message across to an Establishment audience in her 1988 speech because her reputation as a judge provided her with the institutional credibility that Abella, the feminist, could not command. Had she presented herself as the latter, the Vancouver Canadian Clubs might never have invited her to speak in the first place, or she would have spoken only to the converted. As a former judge, Abella was able to convey her feminist message to the traditionalists with the eloquence of an Alice Munro and the punch of a Sugar Ray Leonard.

Secrecy and denials of power are less a façade of propriety than a mode of institutional self-defence. The gloves are off but the fists must remain invisible. Longtime Alberta cabinet minister Elaine McCoy,[10] whose mentor was Premier Peter Lougheed, insisted, "We are not in power. We are in government." Petro-Canada's Stella Thompson is a death-defying skier and corporate risk taker who thrives on the vastness of a conglomerate with assets of over $7 billion and on the team-oriented dynamics of problem solving and futures strategizing. But ask her for an interview and she chokes as if drowning in a barrel of crude. Ask the same question of Louise Cannon, vice-president of the Bank of Nova Scotia, and her voice constricts over the telephone as if she has just been demoted to teller. Even Tory cabinet minister Barbara McDougall shied away from a lengthy interview and refused to acknowledge any particular clout in the political hierarchy, laughing like a society doyenne over the notion that she has power in an institution that enjoys an unparallelled concentration of it. To McDougall, power means calling uncontested shots and she insisted, "There is still only one person who has the final say—the Prime Minister."

At the best of times, entrenched power invites neither introspection nor the will to change, and women who speak out too frankly, too quickly, learn that appointment does not translate into approbation. Preserving power is the first line of defense in a good corporate offense. Change terrifies institutions. Just mention the word "restructuring" and watch faces pale. In the corporate vernacular that means lethal shifts in power and often reversals of fortunes. When Martha Blackburn "restructured" the Blackburn Group, it meant early retirement, demotions, and some employees even being required to reapply for their own jobs. Institutional power emanates from the position, not the individual, and denizens of power who have been removed from their lofty levels, know that the company jet, car, driver, condo in the Bahamas, and even the power "friends" can vanish as fast as a twenty-eight dollar barrel of oil.

Loyalty to the team is an essential component of secret agendas that is connected to fear of excommunication. Only blatant incompetence is a stronger cause for dismissal than saying the wrong thing. And unless you stand on the top rung of the ladder, institutional success demands an appearance of humility, and power must be perceived to belong to a team. Breaking that code transforms winners into losers. During the eleven months that Suzanne Blais-Grenier, Tory MP for Rosemont, was federal environment minister, she bought into the delusion of power by running up what the press called her $64,000 overseas junkets[e] said by government insiders to involve more pleasure than business. From her lofty perch the minister had fogotten that real power belongs to the mahout sitting between the elephant's ears. Defy the conventions and the great beast who controls your destiny can trumpet your death knell or drive you to the lower end of the jungle. Mulroney demoted Blais-Grenier to the position of secretary of state for transport. She left the cabinet and retreated to the backbench. Had she taken her punishment silently, she might have worked her way back into favour. Instead, she charged her own government, via *La Presse*, with receiving kickbacks for awarding federal contracts, and alleged that a secret patronage network existed. She may have been right, but by all counts she had failed the accountability requirements, and the code of silence/loyalty intrinsic to the team. She was suspended from the Quebec caucus, was perceived by the public as a loser, and lost her seat in the 1988 election.

One who survived the wild crap shoot of British Columbia politics was Bill Vander Zalm loyalist Rita Johnston. Her name was inextricably linked with that of the Premier right from volunteer days in the Socred backrooms. Whenever he made another explosive statement, such as refusing to fund abortions even in cases of assault including incest, or advising single mothers whose welfare cheques had been reduced to ''pray to Jesus,'' Johnston steered a ''no comment'' course in silent support of her boss. She received portfolio after important portfolio, and when he was banished in shame from the top job in 1991, without distancing herself from him, she won his vote, which helped her win the caucus's approval as the first woman premier of a Canadian province. Immediately, Johnston changed horses to address social issues that Vander Zalm had rejected. She looked at providing hot meals in schools, and focussed on women and children by expanding the cabinet portfolio headed by Carol Gran to include minister of women's programs, government services, and responsible for families. Then she blasted the judgement of Supreme Court Justice Sherman Hood as ''terribly inappropriate'' and ''unacceptable'' when he acquitted a man of sexual assault on the grounds that ''no may mean maybe.'' The legislative power is never supposed to interfere with the judicial power, but she did it anyway. Her process of reaching the top had required combining loyalty to a difficult leader with the kind of delicate balance essential not only to surviving, but to winning power. At the July 1991 leadership convention, Grace McCarthy, longtime aspirant to the premier's chair and the real power in the Socred party, lost to Rita Johnson who had never in her wildest fantasies entertained the notion of becoming premier.

One woman who did not keep her agenda secret was Maureen McTeer. During her 1988 campaign for the federal seat of Carleton-Gloucester, she polarized her riding by emphasizing her feminist views, such as championing the pro-choice abortion cause, even though she is a Roman Catholic. Not only did she upset many of her constituents, but Gilles Belisle, the auxiliary Bishop of Ottawa, publicly condemned her pro-choice stand. Abandoning her fractious platform to jump on her party's free trade bandwagon might have been the politically astute move, but she remained honest and open to a fault and for that, she was beaten at the polls.

In the 1988 federal campaign, loyalty proved to be suicidal for MP Lucie Pépin. As Liberal child-care critic, she had devised, in consultation with several experts, a financially sound day-care plan on which she was prepared to campaign. Marc Lalonde recalled that Pépin's complete policy had been presented to and endorsed by caucus. Yet the night before she was to hold her press conference, a new sheet of figures that conflicted with those in her plan was sent to her with orders from Peter Connolly, then Liberal chief of staff, to present them to the nation. Pépin did not believe the figures came from Liberal leader John Turner, but Lalonde recalled, ''Those involved had not participated in the preparation of [Pépin's] policy yet they had changed it and modified it without informing Lucie.'' Pépin knew the bottom line was incorrect and said so privately. As a loyal party member, however, she presented the faulty figures to the nation and was blown out of the water. Effecting damage control on national TV is shatteringly difficult. Lalonde insisted, ''Lucie [hadn't made] any mistake. That was not her policy.'' But she protected her leader and took the fall for it.

During the 1990 evolution of the bill to return abortion to the Criminal Code, Justice Minister Kim Campbell swallowed her pro-choice principles in order to sell her government's unpopular compromise. She may have been privately relieved when it failed to pass, but politically it was a black mark against her. She has similarly supported a gun control bill that is reputed to be a watered-down version of what activists are seeking. Many view these stands as inconsistent with Cambell's activist background and she faces the charge of being the puppet of a greater power. But in politics, winning and making your team look good, even at your own expense, means everything.[11]

The biggest joke circulating in political circles the day following the January 31, 1991, Senate vote that killed the abortion bill, was that a savvy veteran like Senator Carney had actually believed the government's pronouncement that senators could vote with their conscience. What the crafty senator actually did was inform the party whip that she would not be present for the vote. As she had missed a number of sittings, he believed her, tallied up his ''yes'' votes and knew he would win by one. Then, just before the historic event took place, Senator Carney slipped into the upper chamber and cast her ''no'' vote which created the 43-43 tie and killed the bill. Other Conservative senators who had voted No had been accounted for. Carney had set her team up with unforgivable conceit, if not deceit, and internal justice was swift. The following morning Senator Lowell Murray removed her from the Senate House of Commons joint (amendment) committee on the Constitution, the plum appointment that had lured her to accept the senate position and all that cross-country travel in the first place. An enraged Senator Carney accused that chamber of sober second thought of being ''the last pigpen of chauvinism left in the western hemisphere,'' and swept into the next sitting, said a CTV reporter, ''like a pirate ship in full sail.''

With her vote and her reckless public salvos, Senator Carney had assaulted the tribal code and made her institution lose face. She has to be finished with the inner sanctum of the PMO even though she cannot be fired. And adhering to party line can mean mere embarrassment,[12f] survival, promotion, or even patronage. For those who wish to remain politicians, there is a price—the ultimate test of political power is at the polls.

A growing number of women who reached safe plateaus in institutional power are now sharing their real agendas, jolting the system with seismic force and, in the view of those who have long benefitted from the perquisites of the old ways, with distressing repercussions. Within the hallowed judiciary, public statements from the bench have been considered inappropriate if not unethical. But the beauty of judges' power is that they cannot be voted out, and only in the rarest cases can they be removed. Judge Andrée Ruffo sued her own chief judge because he ordered her to stop criticizing the Youth Protection Branch of the Quebec provincial government. The case was dismissed, which in essence allowed her to continue speaking out. Chief Judge Albert Gobeil then launched a countersuit against her—and asked her to step down during the hearing, which she did. But he could not fire her and the recalcitrant Ruffo is now back on the bench.

Madame Justice Bertha Wilson of the Supreme Court of Canada astounded the legal profession in a February, 1990, speech[g] at Osgoode Hall Law School by calling for the formation of judicial task forces across the country to find ways to neutralize male bias and humanize the law. The unspoken corollary was that conduct in the courts was sexist and the law was not humane. Whether or not one agrees with what they did, Ruffo and Wilson waited until they had reached positions of inviolable power before going public. Ruffo can have no aspiration to higher benches. She almost surely relinquished promotion in pursuit of a different—a public—power.

The third characteristic essential to winning is deportment, the ability to handle power itself if, in fact, women really want it. The dearth of women at the executive level is not the sole fault of the old boys' network. Women seeking a balanced identity are victims of their own mixed messages. Some seek power, get it, and then circle it with wariness and mistrust, as if it were a time bomb. Vancouver business psychologist Lynda Bentall, whose expertise is crisis intervention in the corporate milieu, has observed that some female executives who were socialized in an era of passivity remain fundamentally conditioned to want protection. Quebec lumberwoman Guylaine Saucier agreed. When she was CEO of her own company, she became exasperated trying to hire and promote women into management because they preferred to seek secure work with the government. Marjorie LeBreton, chief of federal government appointments, has tried repeatedly to appoint qualified women to ambassadorial positions abroad, or within the country to executive posts which require moves, but the candidates were not willing to uproot families and leave town. Centuries of conditioning still cause women to identify with service on the home front, and women are still seeking that hazardous balance between a quality lifestyle and corporate productivity.[13] Others, learning to confront confusion and fear of power, still want approval so badly that they deny their titles. B.C. MLA Carol Gran, Minister Responsible for Women's Programs, pleaded in a 1990 speech to commemorate the twentieth anniversary of the Royal Commission on the Status of Women, "I'm not one of the guys. I'm not a politician."[h] In rejecting the institutional power that she had earned, Gran destroyed her own credibility and substantiated the suspicion that she was merely an extension of former premier Vander Zalm.

On the other hand, rather than deny it, some women seize it like Boadicea charging into battle against the Roman legions.[14] Lynda Bentall has observed that the pleasant temperament of some women who win power begins fluctuating between chippy school-girl behaviour and parental bossiness. Rather than project the positive and trust their team, they seize their territory, and hoard power to the point where they antagonize their staff, shoot themselves in the foot, and will never make it to the top. Everyone has jokes about avoiding women police, customs, or immigration officers. The suspicion that they will be overbearing is not entirely mythical. Even other women avoid them in the cities or at the border crossings of the world. Belligerent male executives are legendary, but the culture has accepted them. One of the hazards of being a woman, is that aggressive female behaviour is resented.

Until women emerge with a deportment nurtured through empowerment, the attempt to bring more women into executive positions will expose one of the follies of affirmative action. Gillian Steward, former managing editor of the Calgary *Herald*, observed that the little girl syndrome just won't disappear, and she found few women willing to assume the responsibility of leadership. In newsroom promotions, she found that women tended to wait for someone to anoint them, to make them powerful instead of assuming the power that went with their title and getting on with the job. With an exuberant fearlessness she stated in 1988, "Management should push as hard as it can [without worrying about approval]. I'm paid to take calculated risks, and if I overstep the line it's my publisher's job to tell me. It's not my job to hold myself back." Deanna Rosenswig, senior vice-president of corporate electronic banking services at the Bank of Montreal, agreed. She described her years in commercial banking as "a gutsy, meaty job, not for the faint-hearted." As women who have found the essential balance, Steward's and Rosenswig's successful behaviour is not masculine as some would charge, but it is adult and it is professional.

Deportment in the most confident of women is demonstrated by the comfort with which they own their power, their skill, and their appearance. In other words, they are comfortable with an integrated self. Liberal backroom powerhouse and corporate lawyer Kathryn Robinson is typical of such women leaders. She has painted her Toronto offices dusty pink, tossed out the power shoulder pads in favour of a softer look, and couldn't care less if a business reporter adds a vignette about the pattern on her blouse or the colour of her office. She is busy getting on with being a professional. Putting appearance off limits keeps the whole person from being seen and sustains that anonymity from which they are trying to escape. As Maureen Forrester said, " . . . part of the secret [of professionalism] is knowing how to put yourself on display."[i]

In the delicate balancing act between decree and inspiration, the best of male leaders have had more time—centuries of it—to practise power as an art form. Their identity emanates more from accomplishment than from external perception, and power is part of the package. They are more familiar with the concept of team games; going out and bashing a ball around and then sharing a draught. This translates into the business world as hotly debating ideas and then having lunch. Many women have yet to learn that an attack on a concept or an ideology is not an attack on the self. Men have proved capable of making an absolute botch up of power. But the very best CEOs handle it with courtesy and consideration. Almost all of the successful female vice-presidents who have waded through this hazardous minefield have named a male mentor or mentors — from supportive fathers to executives who have encouraged and guided them through to the top.

In the 1960s and 1970s, when women were emerging from the passive stereotype, Bruna Giacomazzi developed a business style that enabled her to deal with men without being considered either a wimp or a shrew. ''Speak [men's] language, emulate them, and I don't mean [assume] a masculine perspective. Dress femininely, talk the way they do only don't swear—ignore it when they do. Smile when they head off to the pub for a beer or to the locker room. Keep your self-respect when they make a decision during a break in the john in the middle of a strategy meeting. It was probably tribal and unintentional, but frustrating to you because now you have to catch up, and if you disagree, you are climbing Mount Everest. Develop a presence without getting a chip on your shoulder. It is a fine line to walk. Over and over you have to convince them that you can do the job.''

Futurist Susan Eng, a lawyer, noted about bureaucracy in particular, ''Getting something done from the inside is like throwing yourself at elephants — sometimes something lands in an ear and something happens. The key is not to keep riding the elephant.'' On a more positive note in the shifting attitudes of 1991, Anne Fawcett, managing partner at Caldwell Partners International, said that the most competent women are not those who were trained within the traditional corporate hierarchies, but rather those who juggle ''home, family, corporate and social lives . . . [it] makes women executives more comfortable with ambiguity in a fast-paced business climate.''[j] As a result, they are bringing to the executive suite a more entrepreneurial, flexible, style that is beginning to have a noticeable impact on institutions.

The fourth overwhelmingly important characteristic of a winner is voice. Barbara McDougall's low pitch is an essential element for women seeking institutional credibility. Better yet, her speech is leisurely paced with reason and humour rather than punctuated by high-pitched indignation. Associate Minister of Defence Mary Collins can talk faster than a speeding CF-18, rebutting from a mental encyclopaedia of stats in sonorous tones that she could bottle and sell to Sheila Copps. Then there was the case of Ann Medina, veteran broadcaster of various wars, who was bumped as the host of Saturday Report on CBC-TV in the mid-1980s because her voice was considered too low. Sometimes you just can't win, but women whose voices rise with virago shrillness in concert with the passion of their arguments send audiences scrambling for the exits.

More than one staunch Liberal has refused to attend a speech by the competent MP Sheila Copps because, they say, cringing, "Who wants to be screeched at?" Writing about House debates, *Saturday Night's* Robert Mason Lee noted that Copps's greatest impact may lie less in what she says than in how others react to her voice. In her wilder Rat Pack days, she used it to send the cleverest debators into a frothing rage. Lose your temper and you have lost the game. In her own memoirs, *Nobody's Baby*, Copps recalled that her first question concerning women to Prime Minister Mulroney left him so stunned that he diverted it by delivering a critique on her voice. A Toronto *Star* list of in-House attacks on Copps's voice and scrappy demeanour included MP Jack Shields's non sequitur, "Can you imagine being married to that?"[k]

Copps is more warmly received in 1991, and reaction to her famous voice has turned from irritation to amusement. On March 9, 1991, on CBC, the Royal Canadian Air Farce sketched a scene of her as Deputy Leader of the Official Opposition, visiting Jean Chrétien in the hospital. As Sheila chattered away in rising decibels, Chrétien pleaded, "Quieter, Sheila, please whisper," to which Copps replied, "I AM WHISPERING, JEAN, I AM WHISPERING!"

The voice of former Alberta judge Marjorie Montgomery Bowker rings with the resonance of God speaking and for decades her tones of conviction have underscored her credibility. During the 1988 federal campaign, she wrote a book exposing the weaknesses of the free trade deal and became the catalyst for escalating ordinary debate into one of the most deafening political roars of the century. In rebuttal, John Crosbie dismissed her as an elderly citizen, before trotting out ninety-year-old former Supreme Court justice Emmett Hall to rebut her. Bowker then appeared on national TV and with her sonorous voice won the full attention of Canadians and lent veracity to her scholarship.[15]

Women who have won respect in the House, on the campaign circuit, and on the bench know that the trick is to vocalize in the masculine tenor while clinging to the feminine mystique. For some, the effective delivery comes naturally. Others take voice lessons. Manitoba Liberal Leader Sharon Carstairs speaks as if she has just swallowed helium but has successfully marketed her voice as an endearing idiosyncrasy. Aiming for the top has meant balancing on the androgynous high wire or, as author Hugo Young said of Margaret Thatcher who has perfected the technique, "Without discarding womanhood, she has transcended it."[l]

Who ever said power was fair?

****

As the 1990s loomed, society was on a roll, and the phenomenon of change had infiltrated the corporations. Taboos were falling away as strategists realized that more open discussion did not destroy, and decision by team consensus was an effective if not inspiring kind of power built on trust. Rigid attitudes towards women were softening. This was seen most dramatically in the career of Kim Campbell, who, while breaking the rules that used to be political liabilities, shot up from law student in British Columbia in 1980 to justice minister and attorney general of Canada in 1990.[16] Campbell practised law only briefly, has never been in business, nor has she ever had a secret agenda. NDP MLA Gary Lauk defeated her in a 1983 provincial election and noted that she was brilliant but not smart enough to play dumb. At the time he was right. During the 1986 leadership convention in which she ran as a candidate against Vander Zalm, she said of the future premier with extraordinary prescience, ''Charisma without substance is a dangerous thing.'' Her frankness cost her. She became an MLA under Vander Zalm, who kept her on the backbench. Two years later, after Campbell won the Vancouver Centre riding in the federal campaign by 279 votes and moved into the House of Commons, Prime Minister Mulroney acknowledged her multilingual scholarship and scrappy, articulate forthrightness by appointing her, in February 1990, justice minister and attorney general of Canada. At a youthful forty-four, and as a member of the coveted Priorities and Planning Committee, Campbell had reached the top just when the streams of social and legislative change had merged. To paraphrase Jocelyne Pelchat, former publisher of Montreal's *Le Journal,* the importance of one's gender decreases as personal power increases.[m]

There is one last characteristic of women in institutional power. Former cabinet ministers Sauvé, Carney, and MacDonald, and current ministers Collins, Campbell, and McDougall charted their way into power specifically by *not* becoming champions of minority or special interest groups. This angers activists who believe that women should get into politics primarily to improve conditions for women, children, and minorities. In power parlance, this is naive. Some women want to be involved with budget matters rather than human rights, and purposely dissociate themselves from what are known as the ''soft issues.'' Others want to be alone at the summit and proffer a silent warning to those who expect to be given a hand up the ladder: some senior executives are quite capable of sawing through the rungs beneath them.[17] Margaret Thatcher is the world's most awesome example of a woman who neither reached the pinnacle nor remained there by promoting her female colleagues. In Sherry Atkinson Cooper's[18] opinion, as expressed to Anne Collins in *Canadian Business,*[n] there is a considerable advantage in being the only woman at the top because when you speak, people listen. The corollary, of course, is the consequence of stumbling. Atkinson Cooper warned that mistakes are more visible when you are up there all alone. One slip and the reaction is, ''Women don't know how to do the job.''

Several successful women insisted that the fastest way to improve the lot of all women is to improve their own and just demonstrate the process, but Nova Scotia Chief Justice Constance Glube suggested that women stop competing and start relying upon each other the way men do. Bruna

Giacomazzi helps women who were previously passed over for promotion if she is certain that they really want to make it in senior management. She warns, "Too many potential executives have a distorted view of the sacrifices essential to making it at the top. Men have always accepted that senior executives have to put in long days, evenings, and weekend work." Some industrial psychologists believe that women just can't have it all, that corporate commitment is the child. Giacomazzi grills women aspirants concerning their goals and willingness to give extra time to the corporation. If convinced, she will lobby to promote them into middle management with doors open for advancement.

Some women reject any kind of traditional power, and call for a change in the infrastructure. Linda Crompton, a vice-president of the Vancouver City Savings Credit Union wrote to *Report On Business* magazine,° "Many female executives . . . openly reject the legitimizing [by the old-boys' club] of workaholic, aggressive, competitive values in favor of co-operative, ethical and, most importantly, human ones." Considering that our capitalist society is based on competition, that could take time. Institutions are built on procedures based on ritual designed to protect individual pockets of power. Levels of hierarchy must be recognized, and if everyone approached his/her particular task with entrepreneurial alacrity, fear of chaos or even anarchy would rumble in the bowels of the beast. An innovative idea can be trampled under committee meetings, centralization, decentralization, paper work, computer printouts, consultant thinktanks, delegation, hidden hierarchies, peripheral committee meetings, and luncheons. The implementation of that idea means more delegations, legal consultations, committee meetings, dinners, delays from statutory holidays, summer breaks, lawyers, executive decisions, receptions, more luncheons, and expense accounts that outclass the incomes of the upper middle class—and the elephant wiggles an ear or perhaps takes two steps. Not always forward.

By the time the elephant moves, the original concept has been diffused into innumerable variables, its creator sidelined, possibly forgotten and powerless. The result may be half the original idea, no visible change, or—and this is the monumental strength of institutions, if someone in power has listened and approved—a result exponentially greater than originally anticipated. And that is what makes it all worthwhile. Complaints about the beast may be rampant, particularly because most women are on the outside looking in, but within institutions themselves one finds the care and nurturing of a traditional family and the cooperative spirit of a team. Institutions may be complex, but Lynda Bentall argues that corporate structures, at least, are not inherently hostile, that they only appear that way to women who enter them with the attitude of a victim.

Whatever the difficulties, there are women who say it is worth their while to get to the top in corporations because multinationals have the resources to cross boundaries, link nations and cultures, and alter public opinion.[19] Ultimately, institutions have more potential to impact positively on their respective environments than they have to destroy them. Women are positioning themselves to play a part in shaping that future. Stella Thompson, whose titles shift upward monthly at Petro-Canada, argued that enlightened leaders are counterbalancing the negative effect of an *Exxon Valdez* (read Petro-Canada). It is the internal culture of an organization, the power of which is centralized in the CEO, that guides a portion of its huge financial resources into community activities. Corporate giants like Alcan and Northern Telecom have become major supporters in the philanthropic sector, demonstrating that they have the power to set a tone of responsibility for our future society.

For other women, the costs of advancement are too high and increasing numbers of senior executives in the business world are leaving. Statistically, women are still shouldering the bulk of domestic and child-care duties as well as their executive commitments and, for Elizabeth Parr-Johnston, a Shell Canada economist, the price was too high. Realizing that, after ten years, she was not going to move up any further, she accepted the position offered in 1991 of president at Mount Saint Vincent University. And like Dianne Hall of Nova, and so many before and after her, Jalynn Bennett traded her ManuLife position for what many consider the greatest power of all—entrepreneurial freedom.[20]

The Elephant and the Gnats

For a decade before being called to the bench, Quebec Judge Andrée Ruffo had practised as a children's advocate, struggling to deal with the Youth Protection Branch of a social services ministry that had backlogged some three thousand cases of abused children. Although the delay was annoying she was particularly disturbed to see government social workers privately advising judges based on criteria other than need. That the advice was reflected in the judgements was clear evidence to Ruffo that the provincial government had hijacked the court. Saying nothing until she was appointed to the inviolable position of judge in 1986, Judge Ruffo then proceeded to turn the institutions of law and government upside down with her public criticism, ordering homeless adolescents to be delivered to the office of then minister of health and social services Thérèse Lavoie-Roux, in an attempt to force her to provide safe homes for the children.[21]

In June 1988, a director of the social services centre in the Laurentian region north of Montreal laid fifty-eight complaints against Judge Ruffo before the disciplinary board of the Magistrate's Council for destabilizing the system. This merely provided the judge with a vehicle to expose the ministry's weaknesses. In response, Judge Albert Gobeil, the Chief Judge of the Provincial Court, wrote Judge Ruffo a letter in which he called her a "critic of the state," and a "public figure," and forbade her to speak or write further on the subject. Her public attack on the government was unacceptable to a man on whom a sense of professional propriety had been imprinted in an age of reticence. Former Supreme Court Justice Willard "Bud" Estey agreed with him: "If you are on the bench, you keep quiet."

Judge Ruffo disagreed. Voluntarily taking a leave of absence from the bench, she sued Judge Gobeil in the Quebec Superior Court, arguing that judicial power must not be subject to legislative or executive rule. Interference in judgements were antithetical to the fundamental philosophy of a democratic society. The Superior Court dismissed the suit, with the decision that while the Chief Judge had the authority to issue the directive, it was not legally binding on judges. Judge Ruffo was free to continue speaking out and she stated defiantly, "Now no chief judge [of Quebec] can tell a judge to keep quiet."

Of the fifty-eight complaints laid by the social services ministry, four remained and a reprimand was ordered against Judge Ruffo by the Magistrate's Council. Judge Ruffo has retaliated by appealing the reprimands. Alain Blaise, director of a youth reception centre, testified in February, 1990, that if he were asked to stay with the old system, he would hire lawyers to fight for the changes demanded by Judge Ruffo. In November 1990, Chief Judge Gobeil laid new complaints against Judge Ruffo before the Magistrate's Council, of which *he* is the Chair. The case went to the Superior Court in March 1991 and whatever the results, the repercussions of Judge Ruffo's very public stand against certain aspects of the judiciary and the government have extended beyond Canadian provinces to governments in France, Belgium, and Switzerland. Having encountered similar problems, they have requested her book on the inadequate system of care for abused children, entitled *Parce que je crois aux enfants*.

Judge Ruffo had kept her agenda secret until she was, more or less, safely on the bench. Only then was she able to confront what she believed were faulty processes in two of society's most powerful institutions. She was brave, and she was also lucky. Few women find themselves so protected when they challenge the inflexible beast. She returned to the bench in the winter of 1991, and of the continuing law suits, she told a Canadian Press reporter in Montreal, "I became a judge to help these children, and I'd be shirking my legal and moral responsibility if I didn't."[p] Her ultimate power may lie not in the bench but in the supportive opinions of the public and even of some judges.

Micheline Beauchemin

Renowned Quebec artist Micheline Beauchemin, whose 30-by-15-metre National Arts Centre screen took two years to create and whose colossal woven sculptures hang in museums and corporations throughout the world,[22] lives in the once pristine village of Les Grondines on the banks of the St. Lawrence River. Beauchemin had traded the exciting environs of Montreal for her three-hundred-and-ten-year-old farm, a hundred kilometres west of Quebec City, in order to devote more disciplined time to her work. For inspiration she drew upon the pastoral setting and the regenerating forces of the river.

Beauchemin's heritage home and lands were an artist's haven complete with steaming scones baked in the wood stove, jam made from the farm's own wild strawberries, and omelettes from the eggs of her chickens. Beyond her windows and the snow piled fence-high, grazing lands stretched northward to the woods. Above her living room, winter light beamed into a skylighted loft to radiate off a forest of copper wiring, twisted and woven into delicate folds and spiralling into a multidimensional cornucopia. It was a piece commissioned for the new building of the giant engineering firm Lavalin International. Maquettes of other sculptures revealed the same muscular creativity, the steel-spined character of its gentle creator.

Upon completion of a work, Beauchemin would use as many as twelve snowmobiles to haul it out onto the river, then photograph it looming above, yet blending with, the shards of ice, their interior light gleaming with the same intensity as her steel and silk creations. Filaments of natural and ever shifting light would rebound off metal, ice, and opalescent moire threads to create a vast, surrealistic landscape undefiled by buildings, cables, or bridges.

Suddenly, in October 1985, an event occurred that shattered the artist's tranquility and impelled her to challenge the second largest corporation in Canada. Beauchemin was in Montreal when one of her international students phoned her from Les Grondines to say that unidentified men had arrived by helicopter, landed in her pregnant mare's paddock, and were testing the soil. The mare soon aborted her foal and died of shock. Beauchemin rushed home to find workers clearing her land for the towering steel pylons of the James Bay-New England States $1.72-billion Hydro-Québec project. Lofting the heavy wires over the St. Lawrence River would mean first separating her pasture and students' quarters from her house before desecrating the river itself. Pressed to complete the job by the 1990 deadline, Hydro-Québec was bashing the power line through before the sleepy villages of Les Grondines on the north shore of the river and Lotbinière on the south realized what was happening.

Until that moment, Beauchemin had never had a political bone in her body but she felt violated. For some inexplicable reason, the route was taking a lengthy dog-leg jog around the industrial and agricultural villages of Becancour and St. Prosper to come through her land at an estimated cost overrun of millions. Ordering the men to stop, she rushed back to Montreal and confronted Hydro president Guy Coulombe, whose planning staff had already made the detour under pressure from a vociferous and successful lobby by the Union des producteurs agricoles, headed by Paul Couture, future mayor of St. Prosper. Coulombe's reaction was, it's tough, but billions of dollars were at stake and the line had to go somewhere.

But Delphis Duhamel, who lived near Lotbinière, challenged that logic ''We wonder why Hydro dropped its original plan to cross the river in Becancour to come to our places instead.''[q] Why lay waste to the agricultural and tourist region of Les Grondines so far to the west? Hydro spokesman Jean-Guy Ouimet denied that the utility had ever changed its mind about the power line's route. Beauchemin drew up a petition, signed by 557 of the 560 villagers who grouped together under the name *Contestension,* and presented it personally to Premier Bourassa and to Guy Coulombe. The press joined in, and its articles alerted the environmentalists. She met with Bourassa, Coulombe, and John Ciaccia, the Minister of Energy. According to Beauchemin Ciaccia said it was crazy to put the line through a tourist area when there was an industrial area that could be used, and Bourassa ordered Hydro to return to its drawing board.

A relieved Beauchemin returned home only to find the institutional Hydro elephant lumbering on, placing survey markers across her land, and the farms in Lotbinière on the south shore. There, shocked farmers drove their tractors into the Hydro trucks and pushed them onto the main highway. The police arrived, handcuffed the farmers, and laid criminal charges against them for attacking the Hydro workers—who had trespassed in the first place.[23] It was like a re-enactment of the Red River Settlement in 1869, when Sir John A. Macdonald had sent his surveyors onto Métis land with no warning. Beauchemin had no institutional structure to assist her and her life became a costly nightmare of organizing petitions, writing letters, research, and making endless trips from Les Grondines to Montreal and Quebec City. Consumed by her quest, she drew repeatedly on her own funds first to bail out the farmers and then to hire lawyer Guy Bertrand to fight for *Contestension* against Hydro-Québec.

Why it had happened at all is conjecture, but St. Prosper citizen Paul Couture had vociferously opposed the proposed route through his village. A prominent landowner with friends in high places, Couture had been president of the farmers' union, a member of the Régie des marchés agricoles, and he had sat on an administrative tribunal for agricultural markets. In the second half of 1983, he was appointed to the Hydro board of directors. Environmentalists claim that during this time, the dog-leg route was created. The surveyors arrived on Beauchemin's land in October 1985. In January 1986, Couture retired from the board of Hydro-Québec and attended to his new duties as mayor of St. Prosper.

Beauchemin's cluster of copper, silk, and wool spiraling through the loft would hang untouched until she resolved her nightmare with Hydro. She marshalled a committee that included Jean de Grandpré, then chair of BCE, artist Jean-Paul Riopelle, and friend Pierre Trudeau — who believed the issue could be fought on the constitutional argument that expropriation of land for a product meant solely for export was a federal, not a provincial, matter. Hydro had denied the existence of feasibility studies for submerging the line because it was quicker and cheaper to go over the river. When the research was discovered early in the fall of 1987, the company was accused of concealing information and became mired in delays caused by environmental hearings, which included *Contestension*, and government demands for extended studies. Still the beast lurched forward to meet its 1990 deadline and Beauchemin's illustrious committee faded away. In the environmental hearings, Hydro explained that they could not comply with the government's order because they were running out of time.

In 1987, the Quebec cabinet decreed that Hydro-Québec would have to cross the St. Lawrence underground. By 1990, the tunnel was built but huge pylons still loomed over Beauchemin's farm, the home she had built for her students, and the river. A 122-by-244-metre building to house the cable machinery was placed underground, but another structure was scheduled to be built in the spring of 1991. Forty acres of her land have been consumed to accommodate the pylons, three of which are built on a jetty that juts out half way across the St. Lawrence River. Beauchemin was still in court in August of 1990 and predicted that she would be in debt for the rest of her life. Hydro announced to the press that it had paid her one million dollars for the expropriated land. In fact, it paid $250,000, every cent of which went into legal fees.

Beauchemin's personal battle may have already been lost in 1983 with the appointment to the board of an astute man who had the power of access, institutional support, and who knew how to play the game. Her victory lay in politicizing two farming villages and creating a *cause célèbre* that resulted in the decree that Hydro reroute the James Bay cable partly under the St. Lawrence River.

In the winter of 1990, Beauchemin held a show in the Place des Arts de Montréal "in homage," she said, "to the St. Lawrence River." Her completed copper sculpture was already hanging in the new Cambridge Center building in Boston, but her other magnificent hangings created a fabulous show. On the cover of the program is her "Les Ailes nordiques couleur du temps 1981," Nordic Wings, a work of glistening aluminum, threads of gossamer silk, and hues of the Northern Lights, all reminiscent of the pristine mid-winter river and pastoral Les Grondines in the era before Hydro. The completion was a personal triumph for the artist but the cost was prohibitive. Financially and emotionally drained, Micheline Beauchemin has learned first hand about institutional power.

Yvonne Lavallee

In 1977 Yvonne Lavallee, a young native mother, could see from her kitchen window in the Algonquin Park, Sabine Township, the massive Ontario Hydro towers supporting transmission lines to Toronto, two hundred miles south. Each one took up an acre of Lavallee's own land, yet like hundreds of other homeowners in rural communities, she had no electricity, no plumbing, no water. Besides substandard housing, her village had no insulation, no fire protection, and no telephones. Twenty years earlier Ontario Hydro had convinced the natives, many of them illiterate, to sign contracts that allowed Hydro to build power lines on the land. Many had understood that they would benefit, but Lavallee's father-in-law, a respected elder and adviser, had been requesting electricity for two decades in vain. Lavallee said that her people had been used "to pump power to the big corporations." As taxpayers who had never gone on welfare, the Lavallees believed they had citizens' rights and Yvonne decided to attempt the impossible — challenge Ontario Hydro. But Sabine Township had no political structure and Lavallee had no idea how to begin. Worse, instead of joining her after she began her fight, her own MLA expressed disapproval of her temerity in the Ottawa *Citizen*.

Lavallee got together a town meeting, incorporated her group, then began writing letters by lantern-light after putting the children to bed. For years she pursued a lonely quest, writing to Ontario Hydro, two levels of government, the Ontario Human Rights Commission, and native organizations. The giant corporation stuck to its argument that because Sabine Township did not fall within company guidelines, the town did not qualify for electricity. Lavallee doggedly expanded her campaign to include the federal government and three Ontario ombudsmen. Her boxes of accumulated documentation hold letters of regret from a prime minister, a secretary of state, two different ministers of energy, and ministers of Indian affairs. "I went through three Hydro chairmen," she recalled: "Hugh Macaulay, Milan Nastich, and Tom Campbell. I went through premiers Bill Davis and Frank Miller. They all gave the same answers for years. I even wrote to Frank Miller's wife." Ironically, Tom Campbell's wife, Mary Mogford, was Deputy Minister of Natural Resources but Lavallee did not find out who she was until years later. One of Hydro's stipulations was that they could not bring in electricity unless the houses were fixed up, so Lavallee went to the federal government to win funding to improve the homes in Sabine.

In the 1980s world of material luxury, Lavallee's four children studied by kerosene light, collected their water from an outdoor pump, and used an outdoor privy. "We were absolutely broke," Lavallee recalled, but her family encouraged her not to quit. Learning when Hydro workshops and seminars were being held throughout Ontario, Lavallee would get on a bus and travel to attend them, including those for professional engineers. At first she was treated like an industrial spy, but gradually she was regarded as a non-threatening, if not respected, presence, and officials began to inform her of meetings. She became as knowledgeable about the operations of Hydro as the employees.

Seven years later Sabine Township fortunes turned when Lavallee and the media discovered each other. Photographing her children in front of a huge power station with a picture of her father-in-law in full regalia and the caption, ''Grandfather's dream is our dream. Help light up our lives,'' she sent to the Ontario media, to Hydro, and to governments across Canada. As press support and public interest grew across the country, the case became a symbol of hope for similar rural communities. Ombudsman Dan Hill reopened the case. The native woman from Sabine had learned how to play the game.

It took eight years but Lavallee won electrical power—not only for her town, but for rural Ontario. Campbell expressed admiration for her because the grassroots politician had accomplished her goal without militancy or slander. On the day that Sabine Township lit up, Rabbi Gunther Plaut, a director of the Ontario Human Rights commission, called Lavallee to rejoice that it had happened during Hanukkah, the Jewish Holiday of Lights.

In 1987 Lavallee slammed into another institution. When she applied to the Canadian Political Science Association Internship Program operated in conjunction with the Ontario Legislature, she was told she did not qualify. The association was looking for bright young university graduates with degrees in political science. Lavallee argued that she had a lifetime of practical degrees but the institution was required to adhere to guidelines. It was the Toronto *Star's* Ottawa Bureau Chief Rosemary Speirs,[24] a member of the Committee for '94, who reached out to Lavallee. The committee, whose goal is to see women make up fifty percent of government representatives, by 1994, was looking for women with experience and a knowledge of government. The Sabine Township homemaker concluded, ''You are talking about me.'' In Toronto she met with Speirs, and with Liberal backroom players Maria Minna and Wanda O'Hagan, who named her their special intern. Lavallee recalled that the Canadian Political Science Association Internship program condescended with, ''We'll let her tag along.'' She cared not what they thought, but only that she had won admission.

Assisted by a small stipend from the association and another from the Ontario government, Lavallee used her own money to move to Toronto and participate in the program. When she could, she bussed home to Sabine Township. She worked in a Conservative constituency at the provincial level and with a parliamentary assistant to help shape a private member's bill for Liberal MP Sheila Copps at the federal level. When she completed the course, Lavallee was hired by the Ontario Ministry of Natural Resources to develop a prototypical program designed to foster northern initiatives amongst the isolated citizens of remote North American communities.[25] After all those years, she is now in a position to create positive change. In March, 1989, in Ottawa, Lavallee was named Woman of the Year.

Five months after the lights went on in Sabine Township, Lavallee's mother suddenly died, having waited, Lavallee believed, for the electricity, the fulfilment of her father-in-law's visions, and the validation of the family's quest. Of her successful challenge to the rigidity of institutions she said, "It was no longer for survival. It was symbolic."

CHAPTER 5 NOTES

1. For the purposes of *Invisible Power*, the term ''institution'' includes any major corporate, governmental, or professional body that is hierarchical in structure, as opposed to those that are individual and/or entrepreneurial.
2. LBO: leveraged buyout. Women, many with MBAs, are appearing at the top in middle-sized companies. Sheelagh Whittaker, president and CEO of Cancom (Canadian Satellite Communications Inc.), which is controlled by Western International Communications, was the first of a diminutive number of presidents and CEOs of publicly traded companies who did not inherit the position. Cancom is a service company with revenues of $60 million. She was formerly a partner in the Canada Consulting Group. Patty Stonesifer, general manager of Microsoft Canada, and Sue Miller, president of the $300-million Merisel Canada, both have strategic positions in companies whose annual revenues exceed $30 million.
3. In 1972, Jewett quit the Liberal party and ran successfully for the NDP in 1979.
4. The four were Jean Pigott, Martha Billes, Maureen Sabia, and Lynne Hall.
5. In 1991, Verge serves as Opposition Critic for the Status of Women, Justice, the Constitution, and Culture.
6. In 1990, the Hongkong Bank of Canada purchased the $190-million Lloyd's Bank Canada, giving the Hongkong Bank of Canada a total asset base of $10.5 billion. On December 19, 1990, the bank reported an income jump of 40 percent over 1989.
7. Erola was co-owner and operator of a marina and tourist-
outfitting business. In 1990 she was appointed with John Tory (junior) to co-chair the $5-million LEAF campaign.
8. When former businessperson and MP Pat Carney retired from the House of Commons, she was appointed director of B.C. Sugar, Pacific Press, and Rogers Communications. She was also made executive-in-residence at the commerce faculty, UBC. On the other hand, Liberal MP and sociologist Monique Bégin, who broadened the mandate of health care through the Canada Health Act, did not run in 1984 and, viewed as

an academic rather than a business executive, she could not find a job in Canada. After teaching in the United States at Notre Dame University, she moved to the joint chair in Women's Studies at Carleton University and the University of Ottawa.

9. In her position of chancellor, Rae works with such business luminaries as Sam Belzberg and Joe Segal. She is a director of B.C. Telephone, MPR Tel. Tech., Microtel, Seaboard Life Insurance, and *Imagine* (National Advisory Council). She has also chaired the United Way and served with Junior Achievement.
10. Since 1989, McCoy has served as minister of labour with responsibility for women's issues, the human rights commission and personnel administration. The Advisory Council on Women's Issues also falls under her ministry.
11. On April 21, 1991, in an act of strong support, the Prime Minister initiated a major cabinet shuffle, at Kim Campbell's request, left her in as justice minister and attorney general of Canada.
12. In July of 1987, as minister of state for privatization, Barbara McDougall flew into Edmonton for an inner cabinet meeting at which it was to be announced that Air Canada was on the block for private buyers. Just as she landed and headed for the waiting press, she learned that Mulroney and senior ministers had cancelled the plan without telling her. Political columnist Carol Goar wrote that "McDougall was left sitting in an ante-chamber outside the cabinet room trying to explain why she had flown 2,000 miles for no apparent reason."
13. Failed domestic relationships remain alarmingly high among executive women. A *Globe and Mail ROB Report on Business* article in October, 1990, listed statistics showing that 52 percent of executive women had never been married, were divorced, or widowed, and 61 percent had no children. A similar study of male executives in 1979 found that only 5 percent of the men had never married or were divorced and only 3 percent had no children. The comparison is flawed, but reports point overwhelmingly to the continuing reality that women bear the responsibility for home and family.
14. Boadicea (also spelt Boudicca), a Celtic chief in the first century A.D., had good cause. The Romans had dragged her daughters into the town square and publicly raped them to humiliate her. She responded by

being one of the few commanders in recorded history to destroy two Roman legions.

15. Bowker did it again over the Meech Lake debate. She wrote a best selling dissertation on the topic, and in a Toronto *Star* interview with George Oake, December 26, 1990, dismissed a Triple-E Senate as "another Commons clone."
16. Campbell is the first female minister of justice of Canada and one of the first in the world. Another, thirty-two-year-old Monica de Greiff of Colombia, was appointed in July 1989, but received so many death threats from drug lords that she resigned that September.
17. In a letter to the editor in *Report on Business Magazine,* December 1990, Wayne Ralph wrote that he had once worked in a company where a young woman was promoted to a technical position, and the female director of personnel vetoed her substantial pay increase which made the woman's salary higher than her own. Senior male managers had to intercede before the young woman received the correct salary.
18. Cooper is chief economist and director of bond and money market sales, at Burns Fry, in Toronto. Every year since 1985, she has been ranked the number one economist in Canada in GNP and interest rate forecasting by an independent U.S. surveyor of Canadian institutional accounts.
19. H.J. Heinz Star-Kist Seafood, the world's largest tuna canner, announced in 1990 that it would no longer buy tuna trapped by nets that kill dolphins. Their stand was followed by other companies that produce nearly three-quarters of the canned tuna sold in the United States.
20. The well-connected Bennett is president and CEO of her own Toronto consulting firm: Jalynn H. Bennett and Associates.
21. Lavoie-Roux retired as minister in 1989 and was appointed to the Senate in the 1990 addition of eight Conservatives to the upper house.
22. Inspired by her mother, who sewed brilliantly, and her civil engineer father, Beauchemin's work reflects her combined disciplines of fine arts and marine architecture. Her first creations were exhibited and sold at the 1958 Brussels World Fair and one still hangs in the London City Hall.

23. Albertan farmer Connie Osterman ran successfully as an MLA and became a cabinet minister, all because she had looked out her kitchen window one day to see Calgary Power invading her land as egregiously as Hydro Quebec had invaded Beauchemin's.
24. Speirs is the author of *Out of the Blue,* a study of the Ontario Conservative government.
25. Lavallee has worked as an employment equity officer, Northern native coordinator, and is now manager of education, training, and employment for the Ontario Ministry of Natural Resources. In education, one of the programs involves distance learning to bring schools to native communities rather than uprooting native children to study in a foreign environment. Another involves cross-cultural training to foster greater understanding of native and white cultures and to put an end to stereotyping.

ECONOMIC POWER

CHAPTER SIX

The Senior Executives

St. Peter told three executives that they had to pass a little test to get into heaven.

''Spell God,'' St. Peter told the first. The man did and was admitted to heaven. The second
man got the same word and was also admitted.

The third, a woman, [said]: ''In life I had to work twice as hard for half pay, and now I'm
being tested again. O.K., what is it?''

Said St. Peter, ''Spell Czechoslovakia.''[a]

The entire group of on-line, senior women vice-presidents in corporate Canada is so small that it really could dance on the head of a pin. Outside Toronto, few know each other, and as they are not part of the old boys' network, many of them feel isolated. In the oil patch, the men all meet at the Calgary Petroleum Club,[1] but Petro-Canada's Stella Thompson has never met former Shell vice-president Lynne Hall or Shell's former senior manager Elizabeth Parr-Johnston. In 1989 the Hongkong Bank's Bruna Giacomazzi[2] of Vancouver had never met the female vice-presidents of the six major banks in central Canada. When Vancouver-based Judi Korbin was vice-president and chief labour negotiator of Canadian Airlines International, she had no female counterpart. Giacomazzi once mused of women vice-presidents, ''I almost met one,'' as if sighting a trumpeter swan while out birding on Howe Street.

In Toronto, investment counsellor Mary Susanne Lamont continues the luncheons originally begun at the Albany Club by Barbara McDougall and Jalynn Bennett that bring together up to forty of the most powerful women in Canada. Corporate sponsors cover the actual costs and the thirty dollars charged is donated to a charity. The donation is minor; the players are major.[3] Holiday or fashion chatter is usually abandoned in favour of discussions about acquisitions, management restructuring, bottom lines, liabilities, mergers, and the effect of the GST on charitable donations. Business cards float about like snowflakes, although most of these guests know each other. Plenty of Establishment stars attend, but the only real criterion is accomplishment. Lamont includes newcomers, such as successful entrepreneur, Futurist, and west coast native indian Kaaydah Schatten. These powerbrokers see each other often in Toronto where the corporate action is. Such power luncheons do not occur in the extremities of Canada.

Wherever they are in the country, women vice-presidents are generally unwilling to endanger their hard won positions by giving expansive interviews or revealing their innermost ambitions. It has been tough sledding, and many who have adapted to the institutional restrictions inherent in corporate culture have done so with the visions of entrepreneurs. Pioneer women bankers, like vice-presidents Giacomazzi and Gwyn Gill of the Royal Bank, learned that arriving meant combining Zen philosophy with the patience of Mother Teresa, while exercising the agility of a gazelle.

While it is difficult to imagine any male vice-president not hungering for that ultimate title of CEO, some women believe that public perceptions of titles can be fallacious. Jalynn Bennett, former VP of the $25-billion ManuLife, argued that the senior VPs were already operating at the top. This consummate communicator said, ''I care [more] about what I'm doing . . . than what I'm called. The question of 'up' doesn't seem to be particularly relevant — we are working with the CEO. There isn't any up place to go to.''

At one time, frustrated by her sluggish progress relative to her personal ambition, Bennett began to chair major community organizations as much for the executive challenges as for the causes. In a symbiosis, as her community profile increased with volunteer successes, so did her institutional promotions, and for this financial expert and backroom Conservative, order-in-council appointments began to roll in. Executive headhunter Douglas Caldwell, chair of Caldwell Partners International told *Maclean's*[b] in 1990, ''Part of getting to the top is being perceived as being out in the world. The [complaint] we often hear is, 'I don't see him around much.'''

Bruna Giacomazzi

The experiences of Bruna Giacomazzi reflect the mythology of institutions. One of the first women to tackle these male bastions, she took an advanced secretarial course instead of going to university because she noticed that women commerce graduates were being hired as typists. Joining Household Finance in 1965, she secured the job of training supervisor at the age of twenty-one. Then she aimed for branch manager, the position for which she was already training men, and substituting for them when they were absent. When she applied for management, she was told women were not promoted beyond her present job.

In the United States around the same era, Household Finance lost millions of dollars in a class action suit launched by a group of women blocked from promotion. The fallout blew north. In 1971, Giacomazzi was offered the promotion to branch manager if she would first take her own training course given by the staff she had trained. She responded by quitting to join the Mercantile Bank, a subsidiary of the aggressive Citibank, where she convinced vice-president Brian Romer to let her set up the department for residential mortgages. She recalled of her boss, ''He not only took a chance on me but became my mentor.'' A year later Romer invited her to join the corporate lending team as the first woman senior account manager. Giacomazzi was free to hustle for business. She remembered, ''We did a lot of deals.''

In the mid-1970s, when she accidentally saw a male colleague's pay slip that revealed an annual salary of $10,000 higher than hers, Giacomazzi confronted her boss. It was a risky decade in which to complain: CTV had fired Joan Donaldson for requesting equal pay. But Giacomazzi's boss responded positively. It took two years of raises to catch up but she had made her point; however, she had also compromised. The name of the game was survival and continual, if incremental, progress. By 1985 as a vice-president for Western Canada, Giacomazzi had begun to believe her own myth — that business executives were more concerned with management and bottom line efficiency than with sex, colour, or religion. She had been through all levels of the corporate structure, thus acquiring the practical degree equal to the one she had always coveted from a university. She had even given seminars to the senior MBA bankers. Then in 1986 the Banque Nationale took over the Mercantile and she found herself junior to a man with less experience.

When word spread that she was job hunting, Giacomazzi discovered that she had a network of support among her male colleagues. Gary Poroznick, a managing partner of Coopers and Lybrand, recommended her to Jim Cleave, president of the Hongkong Bank that had just targeted the Bank of British Columbia for takeover. Cleave hired Giacomazzi without a vice-president's title to manage the $600 million in problem loans inherited from the Bank of B.C. She accepted, once again prepared to prove that management skills and the bottom line would speak for themselves. They did. She received credit for being a skilled negotiator and problem solver, and within months was appointed the vice-president of personal banking (retail, in other banks). Within two years she had reduced the problem loans to $100 million.

When Cleave introduced Giacomazzi to the branch staffs not only as the new VP of personal banking[4] for all of Canada but also the only woman VP in Western Canada, women employees at the White Rock branch cheered, clapped, and stomped their feet in a spontaneous outburst of delight at having won gender representation in the upper echelons of banking. By 1989, the forty-four-year-old Giacomazzi was one of the top executives in the $150-billion Hongkong Bank of Canada. She and Anne Lippert, vice-president of retail banking, at the Royal Bank, are of that rare breed seldom seen—women senior corporate executives of prominent financial institutions.

Anyone in the banking world who thought that women could not organize, finance, or negotiate a deal obviously did not have the same experience Giacomazzi had as a child watching her mother participate in business decisions and manage the proud men in her Italian family with the skill of a CEO. Along with her brother and sister, Giacomazzi had participated at all levels in the running of her family's large Aldergrove dairy farm east of Vancouver. Gender had never been an issue. She learned the delicate art of negotiation, a skill that few university courses can teach.

Helen Sinclair

There are currently 60 women in a total of 1,019 vice-presidents and senior vice-presidents sprinkled about the top banks in Canada, and one former VP, Helen Sinclair, is the president of the Canadian Bankers' Association. The banks' top lobby with government and the public, the CBA represents areas of common interest to sixty-six chartered banks with assets of $461 billion. Sinclair is charged with the sensitive task of restructuring an industry reluctant to have new competitors in its territory, but resigned to the reality that to compete, they must provide broader services. Sinclair must reconcile the traditional philosophy of the institutions with a Bank Act facing revision and new legislation. The only bankers more powerful than Sinclair are the CEOs, and her salary allegedly makes her one of the best-paid female executives in Canada. Sinclair has served on a task force on retail banking, represented the banks in free trade and GATT discussions, and she has dealt with such divisive issues as allowing Amex to enter the Canadian market, while waiting for Ottawa to introduce financial services reform to make banks and financial institutions competitive as international conglomerates. She is also faced with improving the banks' community image, which was tarnished by high service charges and huge loan losses, accusations of offering women less than fair employment and management opportunities, and discriminating against women seeking business loans.[5]

Sinclair is a prime example of the winner who has the ability to balance her own agenda with the patience essential to advance to a position of sufficient power to enforce it. First hired at the CBA at the age of twenty-nine in 1980 by then president, the combative Robert MacIntosh, she actually resigned in 1985 from the position of director of public affairs to wait for a more agreeable climate. (Translation: the CBA was a fractious place in which to work.) In 1989 MP Donald Blenkarn, chair of the House of Commons Finance Committee, told journalist Jonathan Ferguson that MacIntosh "was a goddamn disaster for the industry."[c] With her positive negotiating skills, even old style bankers are optimistic that the advent of Sinclair in this age of deregulation means more effective leadership.

Behind the extraordinary accomplishments of Sinclair lies yet another achiever who, like Marjory LeBreton, Nancy Jackman, and Martha Billes, competed as a child against older brothers, and, like Rosalie Abella and Chaviva Hosek, has a family history of resistance to oppression. Her grandmother, ninety-year-old Frida Morawetz, escaped from Czechoslovakia in 1939, and in 1974 when Mikhail Baryshnikov defected, Sinclair's mother, author and businesswoman Sonja Sinclair, hid the dancer at their home for a weekend. Sinclair also embraces life with a clarity known mostly to men and women whose ill-health has tested the outer limits of mortality. At twenty-four, about to embark on a promising career, she was halted by a brain tumour. The risks of surgery included death or permanent disability, but she survived and returned to the world with renewed energy and a pace that would exhaust Olympic sprinter Florence Griffith-Joyner.

Sinclair's CBA presidency is both fortunate and challenging. The movement of women into upper-level bank management is gathering momentum, and the banks claim they are in the vanguard of companies promoting women into jobs for which they were not considered suitable as recently as ten years ago. There is another factor. With the changing marketplace and the multiplicity of financial institutions to choose from, banks must alter their attitudes towards women whose financial needs differ completely from those of the homemaker thirty years ago. Financial services, in general, have moved too slowly in addressing the fact that the majority of businesses today are being started by women. This trend for women to take hands-on control of their business affairs is affecting trust companies whose management histories contain horror stories of 4 percent returns on estate investments during the 1970s and 1980s booms. Widows who once entrusted their stocks to the care of these companies now have daughters or granddaughters with MBAs, law degrees, stock broker licences who are competent money managers. Financial institutions that meet new needs with innovative responses will be on the leading edge of change in a dinosaur industry.

The 1990s could see the advent in Canada of Women's World Banking, and should see the big banks relaxing their stance toward women seeking loans. The record of women in small business has become too impressive to ignore. In the past, most women who went to lending institutions needed men as guarantors. In the case of Kaaydah Schatten, only after her business was worth a solid $20 million, thanks to the help of offshore banks, did Canadian banks begin dealing with her. Today's schools of business administration respect the qualities of entrepreneurship and communication, skills that enable institutions to survive in a global market. Corporations with management trained in this more flexible style of conducting business are creating the kind of energy-filled atmosphere of which Judi Korbin spoke: "Candour and openness are the way of the future. Show the guys a different way of looking at things and they may not always accept your conclusion, but they sure want to open up the dialogue."

Judi Korbin

One day when a television news reporter pushed a microphone and camera at Judi Korbin, then labour negotiator for Canadian Airlines International and demanded, "How much money do you make?" the vice-president cracked, "Lots!" and walked on. A student of the Henry Ford school of confidence — "never complain and never explain" — Korbin believes that women apologize too much. Korbin's style demonstrates the ebullience of an enterpreneur convincing you that anything is possible. A staunch team player, she sees herself as a catalyst with the team that negotiated and reduced, in a hectic fifteen months, thirty-two separate labour agreements among twenty-two bargaining units in the acquisition by Pacific Western Airlines of Canadian Pacific (which had purchased Nordair and Eastern Provincial), into seven contracts and five bargaining units. In one case, eleven different contracts had to be reduced to two, for 6,000 of the total number of 17,000 employees. Multitalented teams worked in other spheres of the contracts, but by interacting directly with senior management, Korbin's crew had the overall scope and power to maintain a balance, so that the clerical employees' contract would link with the pilots', which would mesh with the flight attendants', all of which would consider distinctive regional differences. Recollecting all the pressure, travel, hotel rooms, and long nights of negotiations, Korbin grinned, "All of a sudden this mess comes together into a structure with a signature at the bottom. There it is. They've got conditions of pay and job security that satisfy them, and a deal that not only won't bankrupt the company but keeps it competitive. It's creative. It's an art form. It's the same kind of high."

Korbin credits her background of teaching teenagers for learning the negotiating skills of composure and effective communication under pressure, and developing an ability to anticipate unpredictable responses with good humour. When she was young, her father Harold Freeman, a committed Zionist turned his home into a recruiting centre for Canadians fighting for Israel. He was one of three Canadians invited to participate in piecing together Israel's constitution. Ironing out the right of a people to exist as a nation under law in an area as politically complicated as the Middle East made a huge impression on the future negotiator. Years later, when Korbin's parents were drifting toward separation, the teenager would listen to them talk and note inwardly their areas of common ground rather than their differences. Problem solving through quality communication, so often lost in the emotions of dispute, became an intrinsic process for her. B.C. union mediator Vince Ready has said that Korbin's great ability is to slice through to the heart of a problem.[d] An aura of *joie de vivre* and empowerment about her conveys the convincing impression that everything is possible, and she has almost proven that. No sooner had she and her team successfully completed the seven contracts than a rapacious little PWA swallowed Wardair, sending Korbin and her team on the road again.[6]

Louise Roy

In 1985, this youthful and compelling communicator accepted the presidency of the Montreal Urban Community Transit Corporation: 1,800 buses, 659 subway trains, 8,000 employees, over 1.2 million daily passengers, and the crises and crimes endemic to the tangle of municipalities in Canada's most volatile urban territory. Roy deals directly with what journalist Peter Black described in 1986 as ''the city's most obstreperous union'';[e] twenty strikes occurred in the thirteen years before her ascendency. Since then only one bus driver strike in 1989 has brought the city to a near halt. Roy maintained essential services, restructured management, and in 1990, without major turmoil, signed three-year contracts with all five unions. Her concern for the internal dynamics of human resources has fostered greater self-esteem and a reduction in absenteeism among staff in the sprawling city department. Concerned with physical spaces, density, and how they relate to the well being of citizens, Roy successfully argued that humanizing the institution is both valuable and cheaper in the long run.

The Wonder Woman of Métro has created a more congenial city in which to travel by winning funds to give underground stations spectacular face lifts, including fabulous murals and bicycle racks, improving access for the disabled, reducing crime, and responding quickly to complaints both internally and from the general public who love her. Known to ride the systems where she has become a celebrity, Roy has also cheerfully scolded the bus drivers for jumping off in the middle of their runs for unscheduled coffee breaks. Only in Montreal.

Despite a formal education encouraged by her father that included a masters in sociology from l'Université de Montréal, and a PhD in urban studies at the University of Wisconsin,[7] Roy believes that skills from her life experience are even more significant to her job. She recalled that her mother and her aunts, when teenagers, had to work to finance the studies of their brothers. During the war, her mother was promoted from bank teller to senior accountant and then in 1946 demoted back to teller. In a volatile family setting, her mother was the peacemaker, the one who coped. During the 1960s and the Quiet Revolution, the lives of Quebec women were still controlled by the male-dominated church and state, yet Roy and other women in their mid-forties describe the influence at home as matriarchal. Unable to taste freedom themselves, the mothers and grandmothers of earlier decades impressed upon their daughters the importance of individual achievement and the protection of their rights.

Roy was a student in the late 1960s when the Montreal universities were caught up in human rights movements. Students attended classes by day and participated in demonstrations by night. Roy also joined a citizens' activist group. She saw students developed into intelligent, committed adults accustomed to functioning in an atmosphere of dissension. "I am part of a generation mobilized by collective ideologies. Ideas . . . make me run in life. This is the difference between my mother's generation and mine." Attractive as well as personable and competent, she has more than once been encouraged to quit the Métro job and run for mayor. Roy is keeping her options open.

Annette Verschuren

A Futurist through and through, Annette Verschuren, vice-president of the giant Imasco,[8] plays a game that is neither male nor female. It is the Verschuren game. The daughter of a Dutch immigrant father, she grew up on a Cape Breton farm and now cultivates an individual style to survive and thrive in the corporate world. Coming from the far east coast of the country is what actually gave her the leverage that ultimately vaulted her into the upper echelons of the corporate sphere. With a bachelor's degree in business administration, she became chief planner of a coal mining company before being hired by the Cape Breton Economic Development Corporation and the CDIC, the privatization arm of the federal government then under Barbara McDougall. Verschuren credits childhood setbacks for her swift success and positive attitude. At age eleven, when her father had a heart attack, she and her twelve-year-old brother ran the farm. At age sixteen, she contracted a kidney disease and, after four operations, she focused "not on my liabilities, but my opportunities, and the recognition that I had no boundaries."

In 1985, Verschuren met Imasco chair Purdy Crawford when presenting strategic options open to the Cape Breton Development Corporation. Although the Nova Scotian government did not respond to her report, Crawford was impressed with a plan she presented to make the coal companies profitable. A couple of years later when Crawford ran into Verschuren in Toronto, he convinced her to come to Imasco as vice-president of corporate development. It was an attractive offer in a company that is comprised of only sixty people and whose flattened hierarchy actively involves its executive in decision making. Verschuren handles strategic planning, mergers, acquisitions and divestitures. She has developed a style that is open, frank, and friendly, and she anticipates that the increasing numbers of women coming into the business world will mean the end of secrecy, and promote the co-operative spirit that is beginning to permeate the marketplace. Her connections to federal and provincial governments, to the corporate sector, and to the Establishment through boards are growing.[9] Thirty-four years old and irrepressibly optimistic, Verschuren intends to hone management skills in working towards the CEO position of, if not Imasco, then another large business enterprise.

Diane Schwartz

"I'm the only person in the world who prays for rising interest rates and a weak Canadian dollar, because it's good for my business." The speaker was Diane Schwartz, senior VP and general manager of ManuLife's United States and Caribbean operations. On-line management has been the route to the top for Schwartz, and also for Zané Stait-Gardner, senior vice-president and general manager of ManuLife's re-insurance operations. No other women in North America run insurance departments this large. Stait-Gardner's department has no issuable figures, but Schwartz's departments runs around $2 billion, with two thousand employees. Schwartz observed with satisfaction that ManuLife has never treated her as a woman, but as a general manager, or vice-president, or whatever her position was at the time.

In a new-age departure from tired corporate customs, the forty-four-year-old Schwartz successfully lobbied for her on-line track from a staff position, an unlikely scenario in the executive structure of a bank. Educated in business and finance, and inspired by a grandmother who was a gold medalist at McGill, she wanted the action, responsibility, and accountability of running a business. She is known for her decisiveness in downsizing, restructuring, or changing the game plan when necessary and said, "It's a constant challenge. You just can't stay still. You lose sleep, but you feel like you own it."

Describing ManuLife as a great place for anybody with initiative and ambition who's prepared to take charge and take risks, Schwartz noted that the insurance company is hardly a sleepy investor wallowing in blue-chip stocks, but an aggressive trader in the marketplace. While she stresses the value of on-line experience, Schwartz credited ManuLife's former CEO Sydney Jackson, a father of three daughters, as having run a dynamic institution that involves women at the executive level and adapts rapidly to changing market conditions. He was also the one who opened the doors enabling managers to take different routes to the top.

Of Schwartz's style, an office worker observed, "Diane is a very tough boss and she's got a very high profile around the building." Schwartz concedes that she is not known as a guardian angel, nor should a woman be expected to be one. "I am a good marketer," she explained with the candour more often expected of her American colleagues. Unlike her former colleague, Tory Jalynn Bennett, Schwartz claims not to be politically oriented and says headhunting was the reason for her order-in-council appointment to the council of regents for the Community Colleges of Ontario. Like other senior vice-presidents her age, she is in high demand for the ABCs[10] of the community.

Would she ever leave the institutional structure as did Jalynn Bennett? Only for a piece of the action. The opportunity to build owner equity, something that management cannot do in a mutual life company, could lure her away from her current challenges and an excellent salary. For some executives, like Dianne Hall and Jalynn Bennett who did choose a more entrepreneurial world in which to spend their future, the wish to build equity together with freedom and control, was the critical factor.

Judi Romanchuk

A vice-president and director of the brokerage firm Dean Witter Reynolds (Canada) in Calgary, forty-five-year-old Judi Romanchuk runs in the fastest lane of all these driven vice-presidents, weaving her international connections into a linkage more complex than a fishing net and speaking the Acronym patois of federal finance more fluently than anyone else in the West. She serves on the board and the audit committee of EDC,[11] and the financial sector of SAGIT[12], which, she explains breezily, is a sub-advisory group of ITAC.[13] Romanchuk sits on the board of the University of Calgary business school, and was appointed to the board of the new Belzberg-Vencap venture Alberta Television Network.

Although frequently on the move to Ottawa and Europe, Romanchuk is determined to live in Calgary, a city that up until the late 1980s revolved around the price of oil. Smiles or frowns on 6th Avenue became a civic symptom in the rise or fall of the dollar value of a barrel of oil. "It's a one-horse town," explained Romanchuk, who diversified early and extended her business operations overseas. By 1990, numerous unemployed Calgary oil executives had diversified into different businesses and Romanchuk is focussing on attracting value-added industries to the area. Still, oil reigns supreme.

Romanchuk epitomizes the businessperson with an entrepreneurial temperament who manages to exist within the framework of a large corporation, albeit one that is more loosely structured than a corporate body such as Petro-Canada or Shell Oil. Dean Witter is so concentrated in Ontario and has so many vice-presidents and partners that Romanchuk places no great significance on the title. It helps in Europe but not in Canada. Building her portfolio around investment counselling that takes her beyond the confines of regionalism and Calgary oil, Romanchuk considers business to be her first love, but has expanded her volunteer capacity from her own community to federal and international financial, political, and ambassadorial participation. It extends into federal and provincial Tory fund raising, and into Toronto through the board of the National Ballet. She hosts fascinating business/ambassadorial/political soirées in this country and Europe. Her friends would kill for her bizarre adventures, but it is clearly her ability to blend spontaneity with design that brings success. How Romanchuk became honorary consul for Finland is typical of the way in which those "adventures" occur.

In 1979, following several weeks in Europe explaining the National Energy Program to the West Germans, Romanchuk returned to New York on the Concorde. Thanks to an all-night surprise thirty-third birthday party thrown for her by one hundred of her nearest and dearest friends and business colleagues in a hunting lodge outside of Munich, Romanchuk barely made her London connection. Upon arrival at Kennedy Airport, she exhaustedly collected her luggage and absent-mindedly threw it into the open trunk of a giant blue limousine that had just backed up in front of her. She opened the door to find someone already in the car. It was the vice-chair of Neste Oy, Finland State Oil Company.

Two weeks of warbling statistics on the National Energy Program had made Romanchuk a mine of information, and she spent the limo ride into New York answering the gentleman's queries on import and export prices and the impact of the NEP on the Canadian oil industry. They lunched the next day, and weeks later when the chair had occasion to visit central Canada, they spoke again. By coincidence the Finnish government was seeking an honorary consul for Calgary, and a representative asked if Romanchuk would let her name stand with six others being considered. She agreed, then rushed to the library to read every book on Finland she could find. On a subsequent trip to Ottawa for a Tory convention, Romanchuk lunched with the Finnish ambassador to Canada and his wife. "Tell me something more, Mr. Ambassador," beamed Romanchuk, "about your peat bogs in Finland as an alternative source of energy. . . ."

"You know about our peat bogs?" exclaimed the ambassador, and launched into a detailed discussion of marketing the fuel. At the end of the luncheon he said, "You know more about Finland than most Finns."

A few months later he called to inform Romanchuk she had been chosen — the youngest person and the first woman ever to be appointed to a Finnish consular post. In the decade since, Romanchuk has returned the honour tenfold as a superlative trade intermediary between Canada and Finland. In 1985, while at a dinner meeting in Finland, she spoke with the chair of a petrochemical company that was considering manufacturing MTBE[14] in Quebec but whose negotiations were faltering. It was a $280 million project, and Romanchuk suggested that he consider Alberta as an investment alternative. The chair expressed interest. Romanchuk returned to Canada and called her EDC board members as well as the Alberta Minister of International Trade to learn more about the chemical.

"I decided it was the perfect venture, not only for Alberta, but to convince the Europeans that the National Energy Program was gone, that we were open for business again," she commented. "Oil prices were still on the skids and it was an excellent time to bring a triple-A corporation from northern Europe into our province." When Petro-Canada executives expressed doubts, Romanchuk courted other partners; then, eventually, Petro-Canada did join with Neste Oy as a 50-percent partner. February 1990 saw the MTBE project, grown to $350 million, become a reality. It would never have happened without Romanchuk. In 1988, during a formal dinner at the Winter Olympics in Calgary, the Prime Minister of Finland presented to Romanchuk his country's highest award for her contributions: the Knight's Cross, First Class, Order of the White Rose of Finland.

Romanchuk's lifestyle demonstrates once again that the power of social access — dinners, volunteer boards or galas, consular titles, and political hobnobbing — provides the conduit for the refinement of crude contacts into the high-grade oil of deal making. She frequently holds forums and dinners in Calgary for business and corporate leaders such as John Crow of the Bank of Canada, Fred Gorbet, Deputy Minister of Finance, and the CEOs of such corporate giants as TransCanada PipeLines, PWA, NOVA, and Canadian Forest Products.

The vice-presidents of banks and oil companies enjoy generous company expense accounts and high community recognition, but in a brokerage company like Dean Witter, the more individual focus allows Romanchuk the freedom to develop European contacts while remaining discouragingly anonymous at the head office in Toronto. "My head is so sore from knocking against the glass ceiling," she mused. The obvious place for her to live would be Toronto, but Canadians embrace their regions as they might ducal seats in England and whatever the cost, are determined to thrive in the financial hinterlands. In fact, Romanchuk burns over the parochial mentality that grips Toronto as fervently as it does Vancouver. She once took a Dean Witter colleague from Toronto to a possible underwriting, and during the discussions he suddenly interjected to the potential client, "Well, if you moved to Toronto we could do it, but who the hell is going to invest in an Alberta-based company?"

Romanchuk has chosen to maintain a base where she finds the outdoor lifestyle as appealing as the friendly Calgarians, and where the central core of the city has so many glass buildings that at sunrise it is a radiant city of mirrors. A strategic presence in Alberta, with extraordinary European contacts, she is well positioned in the game. Her happy rationale or the international trade and investment opportunities is, "Once you get into Zurich, London, or Frankfurt, Toronto seems like pretty small fish."

Diane Hall

The Alberta oil companies and resource and pipeline businesses are still traditionally and overwhelmingly male or, as NOVA's Robert Blair described them, "male biased," with most women employees functioning at the middle management level. Dianne Hall was the first woman on-line senior vice-president of Alberta's petrochemical and natural gas transmission giant, NOVA, and was arguably the most prominent female executive in the country. She was with the company as it rode the extraordinary equity growth curve from assets of $500 million to $6 billion, and she participated in many of its acquisitions. In her executive capacity she supervised the marketing plans of subsidiaries in the United States and Italy, bought and sold properties — one of which was the property on which their own building stood. The sale price of $175 million was a complex transaction that netted NOVA one of its highest capital gains ever.[15]

The job brought to Hall what every man or woman seeks in climbing to the stratosphere of a major corporation, beyond love for the job itself, money, or power—an earned prestige. She was known and accepted by the Canadian business community, and she sat on boards at the corporate and government levels.[16] All were huge steps for the eldest child in a family of seven children whose parents could not afford to educate them beyond Grade 11. Like Bruna Giacomazzi, and against all odds, Hall had made it. Suddenly, in 1987, Hall resigned, claiming that she needed more control over her time. She headed first for Queen's University, where she lectured on the advantages and disadvantages of women in corporate power; then she moved to Vancouver and into the entrepreneurial world with her own business. Did Hall duck out when the heat was on and NOVA CEO Blair was under heavy criticism from shareholders? In the fluctuating 1980s, she oversaw the painful "restructuring" moves that sliced over 2,800 employees out of 10,000 from the payroll. She admitted that laying off so many talented and hard-working employees had become intolerable for her and had crystallized a desire for a different quality of life.[17]

Blair described Hall's effort in the strenuous decade of the 1980s as "tremendous," adding, "I've never thought she left because the going got tough. She did a lot of things against the odds. Of all the top people that have been with us, I would think of her as the least susceptible to feeling the pressure of work, demands, and the tough times.'' Blair has always based promotion on ability but, to date, no other women have risen as high at NOVA. He said that Husky Oil is the only company under the NOVA net that has encouraged female financial officers. In fact, it has the largest concentration of women at the vice-presidential or senior management level in the oil industry. Dianne Hall has been the only woman ever to serve on the NOVA board, and Blair believes that her participation may have effected this change.

Hall's departure illustrates a growing trend among women in their mid-forties who had blazed the trail into senior positions to abandon the corporate world and hard won vice-presidencies in order to expand their lifestyle to include what they perceive to be those of greater quality. Until 1990, Hall's own company, Sea Island Group, included among its assets a 33,526-square-metre hanger at Vancouver International Airport to accommodate 737s, DC8s, 727s, or any number of private jets, and single-engine and float planes. Hall will not discuss balance sheets, but she does savour achieving her chief priority, which is being able to inject a greater ''human element'' into her business than she could in the multinational world. In the fall of 1990, she chose to sell the hangar in favour of operating an air charter company for couriers. Entrepreneurship brings flexibility and freedom.

Stella Thompson

Canada's most senior woman in the oil industry[18] gives only cautious interviews typical of women near the top. A vice-president of Petro-Canada, Stella Thompson's knowledge of the business began when she was a child at her father's side. Charles Lee was a prominent geologist and one of the first independent oil executives in Calgary. Lee taught Thompson to fish, ski, and do carpentry, and by some osmotic process his technical knowledge filtered into her veins during their meanderings through the world of exploration, strikes, and crude oil. Thompson never had to study about oil or multinationals. She became it.

Following a master's degree in economics from the University of Alberta, Thompson launched a career that in the last twenty years has spanned work as an economist linking Alberta with the federal government, responsibility for purchasing and delivering up to $1 billion dollars in crude, regulatory affairs, forecasting prices of natural gas and crude oil, strategizing investment opportunities in petrochemicals involving major projects around the world, and energy futures trading. She had worked with PanCanadian Petroleum, and Pacific Petroleums, before moving to Petro-Canada just as the NEP and FIRA were established. She weathered the dreadful consequences of those two programs, as well as optimizing production schedules at six refineries across Canada. In 1985 when the new federal government swung from NEP to deregulation, her responsibilities expanded to preparing Petro-Canada for the change.

Through a plethora of multidisciplined duties relevant to the huge oil industry, Thompson comes into daily contact with other senior executives of Petro-Canada. After being appointed vice-president of business strategy in January of 1990, in the hierarchical complexity of institutions, Thompson's level of vice-president was elevated, again, to a position just below that of senior vice-president. Being a member of the management committee gives her executive responsibilities in running Petro-Canada's refining and marketing company.

****

In April, 1989, *Fortune* magazine ran a cover story entitled ''The Workaholic Generation,'' detailing the enthusiasm of the baby boomers for the eighty-hour work week. Considered obsessive by some, the corporate executives who are featured talk about the creative high they get from their work along with the augmented sense of self-esteem. All vice-presidents say extensive overtime hours are essential in reaching the top. Male executives are prepared to give them, and women who are not should get out. The gruelling reality about women executives is that many still feel they are carrying the full domestic burden.

Giacomazzi remained single until 1991. Judi Romanchuk has never married. Hall's first marriage was a casualty of her NOVA success. Three years into her entrepreneurial life, she remarried. Those who manage to do it all show a remarkable stability thanks to highly supportive husbands, indispensable nannies, and a network of homemakers who throw out a safety net. Judi Korbin has thrived in her executive career thanks to a CA husband and two adult children who regard corporate demands on their mother's time with bemusement. ''Groceries!'' Korbin once exclaimed when asked how she coped. ''What are groceries? We turned our kitchen into a flower pot.'' Friends of senior law partner Mary Eberts say that her toddler learned to speak with the cockney accent of his English nanny. Diane Schwartz of ManuLife has two live-in housekeepers and recaptures the sense of family bliss by escaping to the Schwartz's century-old farmhouse on Friday afternoons with her two small children and tax-lawyer husband. Stella Thompson, her husband Dr. Derrick Thompson, and their teen-aged son retreat to the mountains to replenish their dynamic lifestyles. Helen Sinclair married James Coatsworth, a partner at Coopers and Lybrand, in her late twenties when her career was already launched. She credits her husband with the enthusiastic parenting that makes her staggering schedule possible. She took one month off to have her first baby and three weeks for her second, but kept her briefcase with her while in hospital. She rises at 5:30 a.m., works out for an hour, breakfasts with the family, then often remains at the office until 8 p.m.

****

The challenge for women seeking power in industry, according to the activists, is to become a force for change without feeling they have to buy into the system. But many who have made it, and the young comers who are single, like the system the way it is. Why should they resist it, or change it? Many see that as a worse stereotyping of women than the old restrictions of the 1950s. Almost without exception, the women who have made it to the top possess an overwhelmingly positive attitude, a sense of humour that blends well into the male culture, an easy, cooperative manner in handling and sharing power, and a stylish self-esteem that helped put Stella Thompson onto the cover of the *Globe and Mail's Report on Business Magazine*.[f]

Judi Romanchuk provides the last word on women, corporate institutions and power in a capitalist culture in which positions of directors and administrators have been staunchly in the male domain. "Frankly," said Romanchuk of women at the top, "how many women are chairmen of the board or CEOs of major corporations? They aren't there. So you can't expect them to catapult into the hallowed halls of secrecy and male dominance because they happen to be female. They have to earn their way. And they are, slowly but surely. But they're [still] not as visible; they're just simply not there." In 1991, 60 percent of companies still have no women on their boards; those that do, often have only one token woman. In Alberta, for example, major corporations such as NOVA, Alberta Energy, and Vencap Equities had no women on their boards as of the spring of 1991. TransAlta Utilities had, as of 1989, just one—Diane S. Kaufman, a partner in the law firm of Stikeman Elliot, and a member of an Old Montreal family.[19]

Money gets you into the game and Romanchuk describes the essential scenario: "If Jane Smith started up an oil company and sold it to Petro-Canada for $300 million, which she then banked with one of the Big Six banks, she might be invited onto the bank's board. Then, if she donated to the coffers of the ruling federal party she might find herself on a Crown Corporation board. A donation of a million dollars to a university would make her a patron and put her into the running for chancellor, although large university gifts in the 1990s are common. All of a sudden, she'll find herself being courted as a player. Connections are great, but money is power." Romanchuk's observation emphasizes that the women who control the real source of economic power are the Inheritors who have moved to implement their own visions through executive positions in their own corporations.

CHAPTER 6 NOTES

1. Women were first admitted as members to the Calgary Petroleum Club in 1989.
2. Bruna Giacomazzi is a vice-president and one of the top executives in the Hongkong Bank of Canada.
3. The events intermittently include Diane Schwartz, vice-president of ManuLife; lawyer and Ontario Liberal president Kathryn Robinson; Julia Ruby Foster, campaign manager for Barbara McDougall in 1988; Gail Regan, president of Cara and Chair of the Women's College Hospital; Toronto Hospital board member and former chair of the Toronto Metro Zoo Society, Mary Connacher; psychologist and mega fund raiser Reva Gerstein; publishers Anna Porter and Martha Blackburn; lawyer/activist Marilou McPhedran, chair of the College of Physicians and Surgeons of Ontario's Task Force on Sexual Abuse of Patients; former chair of the University of Toronto Governing Council Joan Randall; and Laura Legge, former treasurer of the Law Society of Upper Canada.
4. Giacomazzi's job description includes personal loans, residential mortgages, RRSPs, term deposits, and Mastercard. All branches report to her and/or to the VP of commercial banking.
5. Marni Kinsley, the newly appointed vice-president of the Bank of Montreal, has been charged with leading an internal task force on the advancement of women in the Bank of Montreal.
6. The Vancouver-based Korbin dealt with the ministry of labour in Ottawa, with the senior officers in labour relations and human resources in other airlines, Bell Canada, the banks, and the Conference Board of Canada. In August 1990, Korbin's vice-presidential duties shifted, requiring her to spend two days a week in the Canadian Airlines International head office in Calgary. In 1991 she was appointed to the Economic Council of Canada.
7. Roy's thesis dealt with the crisis of developing suburbs and the related social and transportation equipment in cities. Before joining Métro, she taught urban studies at l'Université de Montréal and worked on transportation issues, policy making, planning and development for the Montreal area.
8. Imasco, a company that has in its stable Imperial Tobacco, Canada Trust, Shopper's Drug Mart, and

Hardee's Food Systems, had 1990 revenues of $5 billion and profits of $295 million.

9. While working with the CDIC and its privatizations, Verschuren sat on five or six boards at a time. She sits on the boards of Skydome, the CBDC, and the Sunnybrook (Hospital) Foundation, which brings her into proximity with fellow directors Maureen Sabia, Martha Billes, and formerly, Elizabeth Tory.
10. The ABC's are the thousands of agencies, boards and commissions in all three levels of government throughout Canada, most of which are staffed through the volunteer/patronage system.
11. Export Development Corporation.
12. The Sectoral Advisory Group for International Trade.
13. The International Trade Advisory Committee to the minister of international trade. Initially struck to advise the government during the talks on free trade (FTA), ITAC became a sub-group to advise the ministry on the Uruguay round of GATT negotiations in Geneva. Chair of the financial sector of SAGIT is Jalynn Bennett, who also sits on ITAC.
14. Methyl Tributyl Ethylene.
15. In 1972, NOVA had assets of $500 million, earnings of $11 million, and a staff of four hundred. It peaked in the early 1980s with assets of $6.5 billion, earnings of $180 million, and a staff of ten thousand worldwide.
16. Hall has been a member of the Advisory Committee to the National Economic Conference, the Task Force on Telecommunications, and the boards of the Federal Export Trade Development Board, the Conference Board of Canada, the US Conference Board's International Council, the Advisory Council of the C.D. Howe Institute, NOVACOR Chemicals, and T.C.C. Beverages.
17. One year later, following a $2-billion takeover of Polysar Energy and Chemical Corporation, and an infusion of Hong Kong cash by financier Li Ka-shing into Husky Oil, NOVA was written up as a healthy, $8-billion company. Blair was once again a hero, but Hall was gone. Then on December 31, 1989, reports showed NOVA profits had plunged to $186 million from $396 million a year earlier.
18. Also strategic players within their companies are Gwyn Morgan, senior vice-president of Alberta Energy Company and president of the AEC oil and gas division;

and Sue Evans, vice-president of law and corporate secretary of ENCOR, a $1-billion public oil and gas company spawned a decade ago when Dome Petroleum divested itself of excess foreign investors to qualify for the Canadian PIP grants.

19. A good choice, the competent Kaufman family has its own foundation, and Kaufman sits on the CRB Foundation of Charles R. Bronfman.

CHAPTER SEVEN

The Inheritors

A poor relation—is the most irrelevant thing in nature.

CHARLES LAMB[a]

In the spring of 1989, seven members of CAFE, the Canadian Association of Family Enterprises, met at a private luncheon in an exclusive club in a major Canadian city. The six women there represented hundreds of millions of dollars worth of family holdings. The mood was friendly but a sense of purpose hovered over the intimate proceedings of a nearly secret society. Their chief purpose, like that of the hundreds of other members across Canada representing untold billions, is to protect the continuity of family fortunes, to avoid painful and embarrassing court cases over deep pools of money through in-fighting among proliferating progeny, often passive recipients if effective stewards.[1]

Those present at this particular luncheon represented the founding generation. Except for one, the women were unadorned by Guccis and Giorgios, choosing to shade their wealth in a purdah of stylish anonymity. One after another related with the passion of motherhood how she had nourished a fledgling business from conception through bookkeeping to staff relations. Later, when human children came, and the businesses grew into corporations and then into giant entities, these women remained connected as confidantes and advisers to their husbands. Explaining the children's point of view, Maureen Prendiville, president of Prendiville Lumber, noted how her father had founded the firm and groomed his two sons to inherit it: ''His children were . . . important to him, but — I'm sure a lot of children would say this — I always felt his business was his first child.''

The guests at the CAFE luncheon, who care more about the health of the company and staff than they do about the fortune, expressed concern about the second- and third-generation offspring, who have experienced the trappings of success more than the sacrifices of building. Some of the second generation do remember the tougher years and function with visions compatible with those of their parents, but by the third generation, too many offspring threaten to confuse corporate operations. Many identify with a territorial imperative but lack that gut feeling for the business, while in a cruel joke, tax shelters have made some children rich beyond their wildest dreams, while their parents or even grandparent founders remain locked into relatively modest incomes and lifestyles.[2]

Some children in these ensuing generations enter the business because they are expected to, others resemble the original founder with a genuine passion for the business, but most want in because the company is not only their destiny but their identity. The more generations that pass, the greater is both the distance from the trunk of the family tree and that proof of their identity. Even if they have inherited the business rather than created it, or even if they have been shuffled aside and denied a piece of the action because there can be only one or two leaders, there exists that immutable sense of belonging, that desire to be connected. The gnawing whisper that they are poor cousins or that they haven't earned the wealth and position impels them to cling to their birthright even if doing so overrides good business sense and portends the death knell of their progenitor's creation. Inheritors may also go for control as revenge or vindication for ancestral wrongs — father pushed aside by a more powerful brother, or a Mother or even a grandfather diminished by the anonymity and decreased earning power so common to the distaff side.

No matter what impels the ones who become CEOs, no matter how fine a steward or even an acquisitor may emerge in an ensuing generation, there remains that spectre of the founder and the nagging query of whether they could have made it on their own. This albatross binds them to a destiny that can be as oppressive as it can be ultimately self-defeating.

Over dessert, the women at the CAFE luncheon discussed who if any of their children, including daughters, should step into the position of CEO. What if no one were interested? What if one aspired but was incompetent? Should the company be sold? How can parents improve communication between siblings, cousins, and the generations to avoid fractured families and messy court battles? How do the women gain a voice and participate? The format and subjects for a major symposium to address the role of women in the Inheritor family were discussed, following which the members dispersed onto the street, mingling with a lunch hour throng that was unaware that women with collective assets of well over a billion dollars had just entered its midst.

In 1986, *Financial Post* columnist Diane Francis wrote a book called *Controlling Interest*, an account of the thirty-two families who control a disproportionate chunk of corporate Canadian wealth, and enlivened the notion of family omnipotence, of manorial lords overseeing their national or international fiefdoms. The public continues to measure power by the Bronfman score card (or by that of the Reichmanns, Westons, or Desmarais), shrug their shoulders, and conclude that there are no women in the country worth counting. Judging by bottom lines, they are correct. Publisher Martha Blackburn, and Cara president Gail Regan, who is hovering in the wings of the CEO office, oversee businesses with assets ranging from $200 million to over a billion, less than one-sixth the size of a Brascan, or one-fortieth the assets of a National Trust. Blackburn poses little threat to the publishing empires of Ken Thomson or Conrad Black, and the Steinberg sisters have fractured the vision of a female clan to rival the Eatons. Women are still struggling to play on the first string and, rather than pursuing power with the rapacious appetite of a Robert Campeau, they are cleaning house and tending their businesses with courage tempered by caution. They are validating both their potential for growth and the hypothesis that competition and nurturing are characteristics not of gender but of human nature.

Muriel Sprague Richardson

> If you don't like the way we do business, there's the door!
>
> MURIEL RICHARDSON

Mrs. James, as she was called, is a sovereign member in the rarified ranks of corporate dealers. She is a secretary who married her boss and then became a grain broker without ever appearing to overstep the social boundaries of the rigid Winnipeg Establishment. In 1939, just prior to the Second World War, when the prominent Winnipeg grain baron James Richardson died, leaving a young family, Muriel Sprague Richardson, his wife and his closest confidante, promptly moved into his chair. Peter D. Curry, former deputy chair of Power Corporation, remembered that Richardson's talented staff at first looked askance at a woman running a company. "It was a gutsy thing to do," recalled Curry. Many things were at stake, not the least of which was the future of the four Richardson children for whom Mrs. James intended to preserve the family estate.

Not only did she run the company for twenty-seven years, but Mrs. James guided it into growth with exponential swiftness. Focusing on grain, she made line elevators and terminals a leading factor within the private trade, then turned to expanding the stock and bond business through branch offices across the country. In 1944, she initiated pension plans, and Richardson's Pioneer Grain expanded its investment into twenty-six cities, more than doubling its capacity to handle grain. In 1950 she established group life insurance and other benefits for her employees. In the next decade she launched into real estate and pipelines. Today, Richardson Greenshields of Canada, an offspring of the original company, is the largest privately owned national integrated investment dealer in Canada.

In the spring of 1989, Bob Richards, a partner in the 1940s, did not remember the deals they made but he recalled of Mrs. James, "She was tough. We loved her." For decades Muriel Richardson was the only woman listed in the Canadian Business Hall of Fame, but her legacy may be less that of corporate power than of having instilled in her children a sense of noblesse oblige. Today's Richardsons of Winnipeg are western Canada's royalty. The four children of the third-generation grain and securities family are as firmly woven into the philanthropic history of their community as they are into the financial fabric of the country.

The most visible family members are George T. Richardson, chair of Richardson Greenshields and former governor of the Hudson's Bay Company, and his wife, Tannis a regal descendant of the Icelanders of Gimli. Like so many western Establishment families, the Richardsons reflect a humility fostered by the land. As concerned with the cattle on their farm as they are with their billion-dollar business or philanthropies, the family keeps its anchor in life's fundamentals—ploughing fields, feeding horses, and building flood gates. George has been known to attend an evening at the Royal Winnipeg Ballet with the whiff of manure on his shoes, and he defies snowstorms by flying his own Bell Jet Ranger helicopter between the farm, their home at Lake of the Woods, and the heli pad on the roof of Richardson's in downtown Winnipeg. Tannis and her Jewish friend Irene Walsh employed an entrepreneurial, SWAT team approach to raise money for the Winnipeg Symphony Orchestra. The two "cross pollinated" their ethnic and cultural contacts to complete the job in record time.

George's sister Kathleen Richardson, a woman of towering height and Eartha Kitt humour, is the den mother of the Royal Winnipeg Ballet. It is with the protection of her financial safety net and spirited encouragement that the ballet corps has achieved international status. Best known for her renditions of the Queen and for pitching in during ballet practices to shift a grand piano or a prop, she must realize a vicarious, exhilarating freedom in the airy gifts of principal ballerina Evelyn Hart. Kathleen's sister Agnes Richardson Benidickson has lived an illustrious life as the wife of former MP and senator, the late William Benidickson, and as a major force in the Ottawa philanthropic and volunteer communities. Like her siblings, Benidickson influences the worlds of finance, education, and health through her directorships.[3]

Family holdings are vast and the Richardsons' community involvement is comprehensive. Typical of Canada's Establishment royalty, the clan is not involved in changing systems. The focus could shift, however, with the advent of the fourth-generation Futurists who have been charged both with serving on the board of the family foundation, and with identifying its philosophy and future direction.

With the notable exceptions of Muriel Sprague Richardson and Dorothy Ruth Killam, most Canadian women have had their legacies cared for by trust companies and/or solicitous husbands, brothers, uncles, and cousins, some of whom were known to have dipped into the assets for not-so-successful investment. By the late 1980s some women were rejecting the passive receipt of dividends to assume their own fiscal responsibility. They want in, not only to the boardroom, but to the action.

Although Helen Gardiner Phelan[4] stayed home to raise her family, in 1983 her daughter, Gail Regan, was appointed over her brothers' heads as president of Cara Holdings, the $1.6-billion family company that presides over Cara Operations. In January 1990, the *Financial Post* noted that with little debt and a ''war chest'' of $30 million, Cara was looking for an acquisition in the range of $100 million.[5b] Armed with an MBA and a PhD, Regan as president is nevertheless a woman in waiting, both at her Cara office — an exquisite renovated home off Bloor Street — and at the Women's College Hospital where she is presiding as chair. Although she is the most ardent suitor of the CEO post, her personality is viewed as more academic than charismatic and she may not be the primary choice to front the family business.

****

The women who are becoming the most prominent and successful CEOs of their companies are those whose fathers not only encouraged them to enter the business but groomed them for it. Montrealer Niky Papachristidis and her brother, Basil, are the second generation in Papachristidis Maritime, their Greek father's shipping line, founded in 1946. Phrixos Papachristidis always took Niky, his youngest daughter, as seriously as he did Basil, while training them both to co-run the company. Upon his death she became president and CEO of the renamed Papachristidis (Canada), with assets estimated at $43.1 million. Basil formed a new company in England, Papachristidis (U.K.) Agencies.

In Newfoundland, Janet Dawe Gardiner runs the Chester Dawe Construction companies (using the title treasurer) with her sister, Sonia Dawe-Ryan (secretary of the company). In an amicable arrangement, their founder father retired and handed over control to his daughters. Janet Gardiner is the power, and connects to corporate Canada through corporate directorships.[6]

In Alberta, Cathy Roozen, the daughter of surgeon and business magnate Dr. Charles Allard, is, along with her brothers, active in her father's companies with assets estimated at $160 million.[7] She is the most elusive and unapproachable of the new generation known as the Futurists.

Accompanying the huge influx of Asian capital to Canada—up to $200 million every month in the late 1980s—are multigenerational families. In 1987, Canadian Business published an article on the Hong Kong immigrants and noted that the ties of kinship are inseparable from the imperatives of profit. Hong Kong women are considered to be highly capable business operators. The indomitable Sally Au Sian controls 60 percent of the Sing Tao Group, a $150-million publishing, property (apartments, office complexes and shopping plazas), and pharmaceuticals company that puts out two of Hong Kong's dailies and Chinese-language newspapers in Canada.[c]

****

Not only are women Inheritors joining the game, but they are breaking the age-old rule of taking their husbands' names. Money is power and it allows Helen Roman-Barber or Martha Billes, whose former husband legally changed his name to Daniel Gardiner Billes, to bring historical asymmetry into balance. If "corporation" is a synonym for economic power, then the women who have not only inherited companies but who are actively running them are positioning themselves or their children to play in the major league. Wives and daughters with commerce degrees, MBAs, and brokerage licences are foregoing holidays, hideaways, and weekends to shake up their companies and forge growth and change. Blake Bromley, Vancouver lawyer and family foundation expert, predicts that the next generation could bring a distinctive shift in which women take a hands-on role in managing their money and their companies, if not moving directly into CEO positions.

Those Deadly Trusts

It happened to Nancy Jackman, Martha Billes, Mitzi, Evelyn, and Marilyn Steinberg, Rachelle Campeau, Mary Elizabeth Ballard, to say nothing of brothers, and cousins, spouses, and children. Only 1 percent of family companies survive to the third generation, and the horrendous fallout from trust management could have a lot to do with it. Many have gone awry because fathers settled upon their young children deep pools of wealth in the form of company shares—as much from the goodness of their hearts as because of the tax benefits to their empires. Each child is supposedly treated equally, and the event is usually celebrated by naming those trusts with a folksy acronym incorporating the names of the beneficiaries. Suddenly, and often before the father even retires, huge companies are put at risk because of internecine squabbles among once friendly sisters, brothers, and parents that have less to do with running the business than with the power plays and jealousies of childhood. Put adult brothers and sisters together to deal with business or inheritance issues and long-suppressed resentments erupt like chicken pox. Rather than discuss projected sales or diversification plans calmly, siblings and, worse, their spouses, attack each other with the viciousness of pit bulls. In the end, the only winners are the lawyers.

The most famous cases of 1989 were those of the children of Robert Campeau and Harold Ballard Sr., but it was the actions of the fathers themselves that started it all. In 1987, Robert Campeau sued his children, Rachelle and Jacques, over the voting rights to a block of shares in Campeau Corp. that he had placed in trust for them. They were supposed to get their shares when they turned thirty-five, but Campeau claimed they should not get the attendant voting rights. The children, who were more farsighted than Campeau's board or the investing Reichmanns, became alarmed over their father's reckless extension of his empire, pleaded loss of confidence, and fought for voting control over their frozen shares. Campeau was purchasing Federated Department Stores for $8.2 billion and would subsequently file for protection under Chapter Eleven of the United States Bankruptcy Code. The children lost their case and Jacques went to court a second time to get his nearly two million shares released, but it was too late. The shares plummeted in less than one week from $22.25 to $13.50, a paper loss of $17 million. By January 1990, they had fallen to $2.70, and on April 19, 1990, they closed at ninety-nine cents.[d]

In hopes of regaining control of his company, the irascible Harold Ballard Sr. bought the shares of his children Mary Elizabeth and Harold Ballard Jr. in HEBL (Harold E. Ballard Limited), the holding company that owns the Maple Leaf Gardens, for $15.5 million and $21 million respectively. Along came son William, who went to court to win control of the Gardens. Despite the fact that Harold Sr. had bestowed the shares upon his children in the first place, William believed that he had the right of first refusal on his brother's shares. While Harold Sr. was trying to regain control of his company, the children wrestled not only with their father, but with the staff at the Gardens and Harold's live-in, Yolanda Ballard, while the board of directors suffered a collective migraine.[8e]

****

One family that intends to survive is that of Philippe and Nan-b de Gaspé Beaubien, who founded their Télémédia conglomerate on a potato chip distributorship that Philippe ran first in Montreal and then in Toronto, where they were physically threatened by rival distributors. The couple are first-generation empire builders nurturing the second generation with long-range family visions. They are the founders of Télémédia, broadcasting and publishing company, which in 1991 owns twenty-seven radio stations, twenty-five community newspapers, and eighteen consumer magazines. Out of concern for so many family businesses ending in disaster, in 1991 the de Gaspé Beaubiens established, through their family's charitable foundation, the International Centre for

Family Enterprise. They intend to put on videocassette Harvard Business School case studies on topics combining family and business issues to provide a forum for exchanging views, and formal educational materials for guidance. Their three children, two sons and a daughter, all have their MBAs from Harvard. They are a family united. Meanwhile, battles rage on.

The Steinberg Sisters

Mitzi Steinberg Dobrin, as fiercely competitive as she is petite, is the daughter who most closely resembled her driven father, Sam, the son who turned his mother's grocery store into a $1.5-billion business (with annual sales of $4.5 billion). Returning to university after raising a family, Dobrin earned a law degree and then, at the age of forty-two, became general manager of the family's troubled Miracle Mart food division. Shortly afterward she joined her husband Melvyn, who was already on the executive committee of the board. One of Mitzi's younger sisters, Marilyn Steinberg Dobrin, spent the seventies running Hermms Investments, the acronym holding company that Sam had devised and divided equally among his grateful daughters. By the time he died in 1978, Hermms had assets of over $150 million.[9] Eased out of the daily running of Steinberg in 1985 by its chief Irving Ludmer, who threatened to quit unless she stopped undercutting his authority, Mitzi Dobrin took arbitrary steps to help Marilyn run Hermms Investments. Marilyn resented the intrusion. Enter the Older-Better-Educated-Sibling Syndrome, a condition which reopens the wounds of childhood and transmogrifies mature adults into quibbling eight-year-olds.

In 1987, Mitzi was keen to accept an offer on the family's 380 stores, all in need of a cash transfusion and general restructuring, but her sisters, Evelyn Steinberg Alexander and Marilyn, wanted to keep the company and refused an informal offer of over $1 billion. As her sisters had bought voting shares worth $3 million in the first half of 1987, Mitzi suspected they were aiming for control. Marilyn had already asked Irving Ludmer to force the Dobrins off the board and to replace them with Evelyn and herself. Ludmer refused. In September 1987, the daughters and their mother, Helen, battled over redeeming preferred shares of a holding company, and at one meeting, Marilyn ousted her eighty-year-old mother. By early 1988, suit and countersuit had been filed. How Helen must have wished Sam were still alive.

In January 1988, Steinberg was formally put up for sale. Three years later Dobrin divested herself of all her directorships except the Royal Bank, Mont Saint-Sauveur International, and DBRN Holdings. Hermms was being closed down, and the once inseparable family seemed irretrievably divided. As Alan Gray put it in the *Financial Times of Canada*, "Marilyn has stopped talking to her sister Mitzi. Mitzi says Marilyn lacks education. Evelyn and Marilyn aren't even letting Mitzi use her own office. And lately, the brothers-in-law haven't played much golf together.''[f]

By 1989, Steinberg was in desperate need of cash and the sisters had reunited as a block, scrambling to sell or dismantle some three hundred Steinberg stores. The buyers were a partnership between the Caisse de dépôt et placement du Québec (the $37-billion public pension fund) and Socanav, and the Toronto-based consortium named Oxdon Investments, which included Galen Weston's Loblaws, in an agreement with the unions for Loblaws to buy and operate some of the supermarkets. The latter was a better deal. Oxdon was union supported, offered more per share, and had agreed to parent Steinberg through its flagging sales crisis. On the other hand, Socanav had expressed its intention to restructure some stores and sell off others, which meant lost jobs. Oxdon charged that the marrying of Socanav and the Caisse violated the Quebec Securities Act. Whatever the dénouement, the sisters, mother, and grandchildren stood to make, at $75 per voting share, about $260 million.

Enter the power of politics. As an Ontario company hungering after one of Quebec's natural resources, Oxdon was an undesirable alien. Premier Robert Bourassa publicly blessed the Socanav offer to keep ownership of Steinberg in Quebec despite the cost to employees, and privately called to chat with Mitzi Dobrin. Despite the soundness of economic power and good business judgement, political clout prevailed and the sisters sold to the Caisse/Socanav.

Martha and other Billeses

Jarislowsky calls me the poison pill.[10]

MARTHA BILLES
CALGARY, 1988

I was [seen as] a usurper in the boardroom.

MARTHA BILLES[g]

As if a passing eighteen-wheeler had blown its tires at high speed, the freeway of Canadian Tire and its extended family is littered with the shredded rubber of fractious power plays, each providing a window onto the murky, turgid waters of inherited wealth, sibling rivalry, multiplying progeny, and a female[q] inheritor trying to claim her right. In just one lifetime Alfred Jackson ''A.J.'' Billes, the father of Martha, Fred and David, and his older brother John Williams, ''J.W.,'' the father of Dick, turned a Toronto garage worth $1,800 into a $3-billion quasi-department store, and tore a family asunder. The seventy-year, convoluted saga of Canadian Tire is a theme for a Shakespearean tragedy—or the Geraldo Rivera Show.

In Calgary, just days before the 1988 Winter Olympics, Martha Billes, one of the three controlling shareholders of Canadian Tire, arrived for lunch at the Skyline Restaurant. Tall, thin, fortysomething, she was swathed in varying shades of autumn hues, from her tumbling copper hair and owlish glasses to her red-brown paisley dress. The only outward sign of wealth was her fur coat, which had slipped from her shoulders in the style of a soignée librarian. Martha's gentility was a disguise. She could, and did, halt the Canadian Tire juggernaut.

Announcing with her mystical smile that she was returning to Toronto to convince the Class A shareholders to "get rid of my brothers," she described her part in the saga. In October 1986, Fred and David announced that they intended to sell Canadian Tire to the dealers, deeply hurting their father, who had given away his 49-percent shares to his three children and could do nothing but watch the ghastly scenario unfold. But Martha's one-third shares were essential for the deal to go through.

That was her power. Martha's brothers needed her shares. She had no intention of selling them, but without saying so she began fishing for their value before determining whether she could afford to buy out her brothers and run Tire herself. There was more. In *Freewheeling*,[11] the story of the Billeses, author Ian Brown wrote that A.J. knew that Fred was not presidential material, yet the father gave the son the flagship Canadian Tire store in Toronto—presumably to cultivate an image commensurate with his position of primogeniture. Martha understood business and had always wanted to be in the game but A.J. and the boys had kept her out. Now everything counted on her. Finally, it was the divine rapture of controlling an older brother who had always had the upper hand. When Fred offered to sell Tire to Martha at the inflated price of $140 million, she hesitated, saying neither "no" nor "yes." Crafty Martha in turn tempted then rejected Fred with the cryptic phrases by which she likes to communicate. Fred wanted information, Martha wasn't giving it, and her air of sang-froid exasperated him. As she explained in Calgary over lunch, "I am able to compartmentalize." Translation: "I can play their game." That strategic calm is a skill of self-defense learned by many little girls mounting counterattacks against older brothers.

Ian Brown wrote that the family might have avoided the public spectacle of a court battle had their meeting to discuss it all proceeded with civility. But Fred was so frustrated by his sister's fence-sitting that he began flinging disparaging epithets at Martha, who merely ignored the non sequiturs in favour of getting on with the business. It was Martha's husband who was stung by Fred's cracks; Dennis Gardiner Billes demanded apologies be extended to Martha. Fred refused. Rather than discuss the company's future, they broke up the meeting, wrote Brown, just six minutes later, and from there it was all downhill to court.[h]

In 1983, Fred, David, and Martha had collaborated in winning control of Tire by buying out Uncle J.W.'s estate shares, originally willed to charity but freed for auction by the Ontario Supreme Court. Together, the three had set aside differences in order to outbid J.W.'s own son, cousin Dick. As her brothers had purchased more shares beforehand, Martha said it had cost her an extra $15 million just to reach a percentage equal to theirs, and their collective purchase had cost them a premium $76.7 million. Then Fred and David offered to sell their shares to the dealers from the four-hundred-odd Canadian Tire stores. To be successful they needed Martha, who continued her evasive tactics.

When the Dealers offered an irresistible $7.5-million non-refundable bonus to each brother, Martha still remained silent. No one knew where she stood, until the Dealers offered her, to her brothers' amazement, a *fifteen-million-dollar* bonus to sell her shares to them. Finally Martha moved. As the brothers were going to sell anyway, she could not win control of Tire so she went for the deal—at least she said she would. The trio stood to make $290 million in a transaction that excluded the non-voting shareholders. This ploy was not legal and Martha knew it. In planning for a future sale beyond his lifetime, A.J. had signed an agreement called the Aldamar that decreed each child have the right of first refusal, and Dean Muncaster, then CEO of Canadian Tire, had convinced A.J. to add a coat-tail provision requiring non-voting shareholders to be included in any takeover bid. It was a clever caveat that would haunt the Billes children, who viewed the company as their birthright.

Envy born in primogeniture is what had really spawned the mess. In 1922, A.J. had put up the larger portion of the $1,800 to buy the garage, but his elder brother, J.W., took the controlling percentage. Martha, Fred, and David spent their lives watching their frustrated father try to gain control. Legitimizing is vital to Inheritors, particularly those who feel they have been disenfranchised. J.W.'s death in 1956 caused an exacerbation of pain on all fronts. He left his large block of shares to charity instead of to his co-founding brother, or even to his own son, Dick. Dick had expected to run the store, but was soon kicked out by A.J., even though the senior founder had no legitimate control because his shares belonged to his children.

It is fathers with economic power whom offspring most desire to please, and who unintentionally foster lifelong sibling rivalries. A.J. Billes thought he had treated his children equally in the share split, but he was a turn-of-the-century man who believed fulfilment for his sons would be business, and for his daughter, motherhood. In A.J.'s world, sons could win their father's approval and a store simply by being male, but even though Martha turned out to be the brightest, she was forbidden to play the game.[12] When she had wanted to study civil engineering, A.J. had refused her as firmly as he did her repeated requests to join the Tire board. She pleased him by graduating in Home Economics.

Martha was inside with her equal number of shares yet outside the action. Only three board seats were allotted to the A.J. Billes family and neither brother would step down. The directors thought her request was ridiculous, anyway. Of their chuckling rejection Martha recalled, ''They seemed to think that I should run the cafeteria or [at best] become an expert on the new Kevlor radials.'' Corporately speaking, Martha was invisible. Fred grew up believing *he* was the heir apparent; Martha became the frustrated aspirant. She seemed to be the child who really cared about the quality of the business, and her illimitable drive both for ownership and recognition by her father would become manifest in a competitive nature equal to that of any male who had ever stalked a controlling share. Canadian Tire was her father's first child and it was Martha's identity denied.

Fed up with the home corral in Toronto, Martha rode west to Calgary in 1978, sold some Class A Tire shares to raise capital, incorporated a company named Marlore Enterprises, invested in oil-producing properties, and made strikes! Martha became the business success.[13] Not only was it fun, but she said that her holdings outside Tire came to form a considerable balance of her total worth. Then, with an intuition that must have made her father proud, Martha turned most of her assets into cash just before the 1981 oil crash. She said that the $15 million she used to bolster her percentage of Tire in 1983 came from Marlore Enterprises. While she had luck and acknowledged wise advisers, Martha had clearly exercised good judgement. Having demonstrated that her business acumen was as sound as her timing, she renewed her efforts to join the Tire board. When Fred and David refused to relinquish either board seat, A.J. himself stepped down for Martha. One woman board member, Jean Pigott, was already there, but Martha insisted upon, and got, two more women: lawyer Maureen Sabia and Lynne Hall, a former senior executive with AT&T and Shell Oil.

Directors of corporate or non-profit boards have been paradigms of club psychology, particularly in the days before directors could be sued and began asking more about operations. Management may still regard directors as little short of private investigators and in the early 1980s, Martha as a director was a star performer. On her own volition, she set out to determine what was happening with Tire's American retail chain, called White Stores, purchased with board approval but on the professional advice of Tire CEO Dean Muncaster. By 1983, White's was losing a million dollars a week and, with the enthusiasm of corporate Amazons, Martha and Jean Pigott swooped down to check out the American management scene before returning via the Canadian West to examine Tire stores there. In British Columbia, their spot checks and criticisms created high-volume angst amongst the Dealers, many of whom had become millionaires and were more interested in their ocean toys than selling radials. Muncaster was caught in a Catch-22 and in polite boardroom vernacular was said to be alarmed by Martha's zealous participation in operations. But White's losses were Martha's losses, and she held Muncaster responsible.[14] With brutal directness, the board fired a shocked Muncaster in a public announcement just minutes before the 1985 annual meeting. It was, said Martha, a consensus decision, but there is no doubt in most minds whose opinion had prevailed.

In 1987, the Ontario Securities Commission squelched the Billes children's sale to the Dealers, as Martha had known it would all along. Fred and David left town, Martha walked away with $15 million *and* launched a suit against her brothers for breaching the Aldamar Agreement. They countersued for a stake in the extra $7.5 million she had received from the Dealers. By 1989, each side agreed to drop all suits provided Martha pay up $2.5 million to each of the brothers. She did, and the saga ended—until the children of the next generation, now in their twenties, decide they want to become the president or sit on the board. Martha and Fred are still directors, only the Dealers lost and Tire is enjoying an extraordinary period of success when other retail stores are suffering.[15] One might have a better understanding of what Mona Lisa had really been up to by studying the mysterious Martha Billes. It seems that Dean Muncaster and everyone else had underestimated her power.

Nancy Rowell Jackman

> Philanthropy . . . is a way to launder money.
>
> NANCY JACKMAN[i]

> My hunch is it's terrifying for [the Establishment] to deal seriously with feminism. A radical feminist is someone like Mary Eberts, who is a partner at Tory Tory . . . not someone who wears a jean jacket and is part of the lesbian caucus of the National Action Committee annual convention.
>
> NANCY JACKMAN

Nancy Rowell Jackman—pagliaccia, United Church theologian, wanderer, holder of a master's degree in applied behavioural sciences, candidate for the federal Conservative nomination in Rosedale,[16] activist, catalyst, philanthropist, champion of the dispossessed—is a woman born in Establishment wealth and raised into inextinguishable anger. Her personality fluctuates from a caring comedienne to a feminist raging over what she views as a manipulated legacy and the repression of women and minority groups. Her pain emanates from an immutable link to the walking wounded. Wealth and Rosedale may shield her from hunger and exposure to the elements but they serve as scant protection from the ridicule and control she experienced as a child. Like numerous middle-aged women, Jackman cites privileged brothers as one of the major sources of her supersonic drive.[17]

Incapable of guile or finesse, Jackman strode through her house expressing herself with an eloquence bolstered by her master's degree and the gestures of a professional clown. Her emotions ranged from the warm winds of a chinook to a Force 10 hurricane. She was wild, black, funny, rude, compassionate, and shared her truths in scene after spellbinding scene. Some of Jackman's more awesome performances have mesmerized entire tables of strangers. In one Vancouver restaurant, guests stared as she warmed to her dinner in concert with her attacks on pro-lifers, child batterers, and sexual assaulters. Building to a crescendo, she suddenly set aside utensils and dove into her coq au vin, causing the sauce to fly in all directions, dismembering legs and wings with the raging gusto of a black-belt karate expert demolishing a would-be mugger.

Beware of Jackman, for she walks with mirrors, reflecting Establishment protocols while revealing their layers of deceit. An Inheritor who enjoys the financial security inherent in wealth, she refuses to succumb to its conventions. Changing systems is what Jackman is about rather than providing the Band-Aid therapy for which the Establishment is renowned.[18] ''Wealthy women and their galas — are they working for charity or justice? It's Justice. Charity for Just Us! They function for the preservation of a male society!'' Charity involving galas, balls, and entertainment is distinctively different, she noted, from philanthropy. Jackman embraces the indigent, the oppressed, the abused, carrying their pain on her own broad shoulders with an aggressive bluster, frightening away both demons and, sometimes, those who would try to understand and help her cause.

Jackman's father, Henry, was larger than life as head of his huge empire, and with his wife, Mary,[19] instilled in the children the philosophy of noblesse oblige. Jackman came from a family of super achievers. Her mother and grandmother received university degrees and two of her cousins were lawyers, but her home remained rooted in an atmosphere of dictatorial patriarchy. In the late 1970s, after taking the securities course, Jackman asked to join one of the family companies but her father refused to let her in. A disenfranchised daughter went to work for a management consulting firm.

Jackman's sprawling brick home, situated on a Rosedale ravine, has a sign on the door announcing ''Nuclear-free zone.'' It provides the perfect setting for her dichotomous life. She is the compleat *Tamara*, a movable play in every room, beneath every archway. At the start of the interview in the den, her tone of compassion for immigrant women and single mothers on welfare merely hinted at the mistral wind that suddenly sent her roaring toward the kitchen, the decibels an escape hatch for her mounting pain. The traveller followed, both apprehensive about and intrigued by her first encounter with a woman described by her brother Hal as a ''militant feminist.''

Stirring a pot of homemade soup, Jackman suddenly whirled, raised her wooden spoon, half-baton, half-weapon, to roar, ''Do you know why I went into the Church? It was for power! That's where the power was!'' God did not seem to have a lot to do with Jackman's ecumenical experience. She had earned her theology diploma but so unnerved the United

Church, whose authorities could not begin to guess what colourful language she would use in the pulpit, that she was not given a congregation. Furthermore, the church required her to petition the Toronto Conference for acceptance annually. When it rejected her the second year, she sued it, and won the appeal.[20] The first time Jackman met Mary Eberts, she had asked the lawyer how much it would cost to sue the Pope for refusing to ordain women. In her fury, Jackman became a catalyst for promoting gender awareness in the Protestant Church, including the change of language used in United Church literature. To this day, she speaks of the church as an institution based on the power of repression rather than on love.

Jackman then directed her outrage toward the $30-million Jackman Foundation and, with crescendos and whole bar rests of pain, she described how the individual foundations were set up to provide the boys' inheritance with liquidity, and the women with shares in Hal's companies. "My brother Hal is the power in the family, there isn't any doubt about that, anywhere," Jackman judged correctly. Nancy and her mother each had about $5 million, which they wanted to extricate from the family foundation so that they could make independent choices about the recipients.[21] Mrs. Jackman gave her $5 million in shares to universities and hospitals, amongst others. LEAF received a million-dollar combined gift from the two women which, of course, was in shares. Jackman said, "Then we had to go and negotiate with Hal as to price and so did every other charity that got those shares, while Eric [who had not left his father's foundation] gets away scot fucking free because he still has liquid assets!" It was years before they would sit down to a prickly family dinner again.

Jackman paused in her expansive front hall to interject, "I was going to sell this house once, put it on the market, and guess who arrived at the door to view it? Barbara Amiel!" Peals of laughter reverberated through her home. But despite their antithetical ideologies, Amiel and Jackman share a similarity — they are the only two women who wear their honesty on their sleeves, saying openly what many people feel but dare not articulate even to their friends. This earns them a grudging respect from some of their detractors. Jackman swept on, through her upstairs office, which looks like the nerve centre of the women's movement. She had first become involved with it when she gave $5,000 from her foundation to the National Action Committee, and more recently she sponsored the flagging Ad Hoc Committee of Canadian Women on the Constitution. She has been present at major events of the women's movement: the constitutional battle (her maternal grandfather, Newton Rowell, was the lawyer in the 1929 Persons Case), and the founding of LEAF. She has opened her home to almost every feminist cause imaginable, and she became a major financial supporter when LEAF took its 1989 Roadshow across the country.

Returning downstairs, Jackman plunged into a chesterfield in the sunken living room overlooking the ravine filled with trees. It is a lovely home, surrounding its owner with a serenity that could not begin to assuage the turmoil in her soul. Suddenly she was up, swinging her arms like a tormented Lady Macbeth, swooping toward the den while analyzing power in families, governments, religious systems, and other institutions. Her knowledge is vast and sophisticated, particularly on how to infiltrate bureaucracies. Long ago Jackman disdained Establishment titles and was subjected to the ridicule reserved for eccentrics, but in 1988 at a LEAF fund raising dinner in her honour organized by Establishment powerhouse Susan McCutcheon, the hall was filled with corporate tables, including one for National Trust bought by her brother Hal. For all her ferocity, Toronto has embraced this champion of social justice as a singular institution.

Phyllis Lambert

> Scholarship without public involvement is arcane; public involvement without scholarship leads nowhere.
>
> PHYLLIS LAMBERT[j]

Phyllis Lambert has no Deadly Trusts because the family wisely dissolved Cemp (a holding company for Sam's children) at the first hint of family dissention. She does not hail from a Troubled Feifdom, scorns gala fund raisers although she is the matriarch of all philanthropy, and she will not be slotted, categorized, labelled, or even tracked down for an interview. The elusive Lambert is, simply, an Inheritor extraordinaire. On a spring day in 1989, Phyllis Bronfman Lambert with her family, Prime Minister Mulroney, Premier Robert Bourassa, and Deputy Premier Lise Bacon gathered to open the world-renowned Canadian Centre for Architecture.[22] Built in the rescued 1874 Montreal mansion known as Shaughnessy House, it is an edifice unparallelled almost anywhere in the world both for its acquired treasures and for the magnitude of Lambert's personal gift. Architect and former Museum of Modern Art curator Philip Johnson wrote that Lambert's acquisitions are of such high quality that they have "made even MoMA look foolish,"[k] and Paul Goldberger of the *New York Times* observed that the building's "quiet dignity and great strength . . . weaves together several generations of architecture with considerable grace."[l]

In combining financial generosity with her multidisciplined expertise as an architectural restorationist, Lambert has earned what she has sought for herself—her own place as a citizen of the world. Hers is the eternal paradox of some of the wealthiest Inheritors who seek to distance themselves from their social positions and names while enjoying the luxuries that continue to render them illimitably famous. Lambert's Shaughnessy House is a monument to the children born into wealth and privilege who, through some unfathomable depth of inner vision, regard their world differently from their happy playmates or parents. Being Someone is the antithesis of what they want. Nelson Aldrich Jr., author of *Old Money,* touched on their dilemma when he wrote, "A child of riches is not at the beginning of anything. He, or she, is all outcome, ending, goal. . . . An inheritor is a mere *effect*"[m] — rendered irrelevant simply by being born into a lavishly wealthy family.

Like Nancy Jackman, Lambert marches to her own drummer, driven by a father who became a legend in his own time, and who conducted his life in a way his daughter would not have chosen. Lambert's life should have been glorious under the care of her wonderful philanthropist mother, ninety-five-year-old Saidye Bronfman, who lives on in a magnificent Westmount mansion filled with sunlight, roses, and Renoirs. But the home became a crucible of acute discomfort for the young Phyllis. A shy, brooding child who began sculpting at the age of nine and exhibited in the Royal Canadian Academy by age fourteen, Lambert escaped from a family ambience with which she could not come to terms to attend Vassar College, where she studied modern history. At twenty-two, she married French banker Jean Lambert, ostensibly to free herself from the too-famous Bronfman name; a luxury that neither Charles nor any other "son of" has ever managed. With over $50 million worth of assets in her own foundation, Lambert can hardly expect to escape the shadow of her family tree. A more candid route to the freedom she sought might have been to give it all away and, indeed, with the Canadian Centre for Architecture, she almost did.

Lambert's fortune has given her the freedom and manoeuvrability to move in the stratosphere of her chosen profession. In 1954, while she was in Paris studying painting and sculpting, she became intrigued by architecture and wrote a sixteen-page critique of the proposed New York building for the Bronfman's Seagram. The critique so impressed her father that he invited her to supervise the job. She chose Ludwig Mies van der Rohe to design what became the award-winning $41-million bronze Seagram Building. Van der Rohe was a man whom she admired for his modernist philosophy, and she subsequently received a master's degree under his tutelage at the Illinois Institute of Technology.

Dividing much of her time between Los Angeles and Chicago, Lambert also designed the Saidye Bronfman Centre in Montreal and gained respect as a restoration architect through her own company, Ridgway. One of her award-winning creations was the restoration of the Los Angeles Biltmore Hotel. In the 1970s, during a trip back to Montreal, her current neighbour, music critic Eric McLean, took her to the Sherbrooke Street block where historic buildings were being demolished. Her modernist bent was transformed overnight. With a core group,[23] Lambert and McLean formed the Heritage Montreal Foundation and, creating a lofted home in what was once a nut and dried-fruit factory in the area, Lambert became a leading force in the restoration of Old Montreal. Her work in the old city and her determination to build a great architectural museum have earned her the appreciative sobriquet ''Joan of Architecture.''

Single-minded dedication to the huge CCA project sent Lambert through dozens of young architects and draftspeople. Three months of sixteen-hour days was the predicted burn-out time as she drove her charges relentlessly in pursuit of her goal. The joke around the curatorial circuit of central Canada was, ''You mean you haven't worked for Phyllis yet?'' One former, and still exhausted, senior aide remarked, ''Phyllis has had unlimited wealth for her entire life and it's cut her off completely from any understanding of how other people actually live. She thinks of every one of us as being her chauffeur.''[25] But she demands nothing she doesn't also give. She just has no time for frivolity.

Frowning as she does on society galas and even philanthropy, Lambert fails to distinguish between them. Her critiques land on the well-intentioned efforts of those Inheritors who accept the task of philanthropic disbursements with a pride in family and community activism.[24n] But Lambert cares little what others think, and the loner has been known to sit glumly silent through entire dinner parties. In her most creative stages she is a professional who dresses in baggy overalls, wore round scholar glasses long before they became the rage, and styles her hair for androgynous anonymity. A brilliant writer, and a lecturer, photographer, and political activist in her city, Lambert presents herself less as a human being than as an instrument of design. It is her own creation, the Saidye Bronfman Centre, that most succinctly reflects the paradox of an inscrutable, and often unapproachable, woman who protects herself behind layers of public relations people.[25] Her mother's building is designed in the openness of modernism, a glass structure allowing passing pedestrians an unimpeded view of its inner core.

The Troubled Feifdoms and their Inheritors

By the mid-to-late 1980s an increasing number of women were inheriting their family chairs. Cynics who claim that they were bequeathed the positions and therefore do not count, might consider that, for centuries, men have inherited chairs without sacrificing respect. Utilizing high-priced expertise to supplement their own talents, several families have launched their third to sixth generations of inherited wealth: the Bronfmans, the Eatons, the Molsons, and the Birks. When women began moving into the chairs, however, the concept was so novel that street and media speculation focused on how women inheritors might botch the job. Tough decisions by CEOs perceiving the need for change have never before been seen as indications of malice or whimsy but the media was galvanized into an *analyse nouvelle* over the ascendency of the two women most strategically placed in the country to access economic power. When Martha Blackburn of the Blackburn Group and Helen Roman-Barber of Roman Corporation dismissed their top executives and cleaned their respective houses, it was new sport for cute headlines. Martha Blackburn has endured "She's the Boss"; "A Union at the Free Press? Her father must be turning in his grave . . . the daughter is stumbling in his shoes"; and "Buy, Buy Blackburn"—a critical commentary on her move to diversify.[o] Roman-Barber's press clippings were more serious, but she had to expect an article entitled, "The Roman Empress."[26p] By 1991, with the devastating plunge taken by Roman Corporation, the press was addressing the companies and general management abilities rather than the gender of those in control.

Differentiation of Inheritors skills based on gender is a senseless exercise when that view belongs to imaginative boys or girls raised by the founders. Inherited companies do not always come in top-flight condition. Denison Mines was already precariously positioned and debt heavy in 1988 when Helen Roman-Barber assumed the position of CEO upon her father's death. The Blackburn Group's *London Free Press* readership and profitability had plummeted to half the industry's average. Canadian Tire was losing a million a week on the American venture when Martha Billes collaborated in firing CEO Dean Muncaster. Winnipegger Maureen Prendiville took control of what she described as a "haemorrhaging company." Jean Pigott rescued the family bakery when sales were as flat as unleavened bread. A widowed Wendy McDonald took over a family company with $250,000 in sales and multiple problems.

These companies were at least one, and as many as four, generations old. They reflected some or all of the symptoms of malaise—corporate veins blocked with the cholesterol of high living, operating lungs labouring under the pollution of economic change and social conditions, budgetary muscles gone flabby from carelessness, and managerial strength bloated by complacency or weakened by rampant expansionism. Medical assessment decreed quadruple bypass surgery, a focus on behavioural change, and the installation of positive health programs. In several cases, it was by dint of primogeniture that some women have engineered the restoration to health. Ultimately, whether or not Blackburn, Roman-Barber, Billes, Prendiville, Pigott, or a handful of other strategically placed women succeeded or failed, they possessed that infallible conviction of power implicit in anointment by inheritance.

Martha Blackburn

> [Martha] had inherited her father's lust for power. . . . And she knew she had everything at her fingertips to make or break things.
>
> PETER WHITE[q]

It was the end of a marriage for Peter White, president and CEO of the estimated $200-million Blackburn Group. On September 3, 1986, it was also the end of his job. His estranged wife and the Group's sole shareholder, Martha Blackburn, fortyish, great-granddaughter of the 1853 company founder Josiah Blackburn, fired him and assumed the chair of Blackburn Group. Then she initiated major changes throughout the company, particularly in the *London Free Press*.[27] By 1991 she was overseeing a company that controls communications systems in London, Ontario (extending also into Buffalo and Cleveland), as well as expanding into a consortium of publishing, broadcasting, distribution, and market analysis companies with offices across Canada. There are approximately 2,300 employees with $125 million in annual revenues. For a woman whose abilities were regarded with scepticism, Blackburn is relishing the job and its expansionist philosophy.

The youngest child of Walter and Marjorie,[r] Blackburn had become a director in 1975. In 1976 her husband became president of the *London Free Press*, and in 1983 president of the family holding company, now the Blackburn Group. But blood runs thicker. Despite his faith in Peter White's ability, Walter was dying of cancer and his only son had died. Believing Martha to be the Blackburn capable of running the business, Walter instructed her to buy out her sister's shares.[28] The most competitive Blackburn in two generations was the natural choice to take control at a time when a hint of ruthlessness was essential to survival. Martha had always spent much time with her father and, like so many other women, had learned the business by osmosis. She was with him when he died, and the following month, with Peter White as the CEO, she assumed the positions of publisher and chair of five companies.

By fall 1986, their marriage was disintegrating. White and Blackburn were still operating out of adjacent offices, and White was living with another woman. Blackburn was trying to do what was best for the company, and one day, faced with the immediacy of a deal maturing, and unable to track White down, she secured the board's support in removing White. It was a shock to his employees. White was popular and his dismissal could have hurt company morale, but before leaving, he gathered his staff, discussed his future plans without critique of Martha, thanked each of them personally, and walked out. There was hardly a dry eye in the room. Immediately after his departure, Martha Blackburn entered to face a silent staff. If she felt bitter — or even avenged — she didn't show it. Instead of slamming White, she looked around the room and said, "If I had been here, I would have applauded him too." It was a class act. Bob Elsden, president of Blackburn's CFPL Broadcasting and a forty-year employee, said that management agreed they could never have been that gracious. It is that extraordinary dignity founded in internal toughness and a sense of heritage that has made Blackburn a recognized player in the corporate sector.

Until 1984, Blackburn's life had been focussed more on family and community interests,[29] but making deals is such a part of her nature that relatives and friends from university days recall incidents hinting that she might revel in running the family business. Appointing Jim Armatage as CEO, and giving him the mandate to force financial fitness on the four-generation-old company, Martha oversaw a drastic change in staff management. In the amiable Walter's day, the Blackburn Group had been known, as journalist Rod McQueen wrote, as "the velvet coffin (comfortable and forever)."[30s] Peter White had already begun modernizing the paper, but Blackburn set to sculpting the company with a sharper knife and swifter strokes. Reorganizing the umbrella administration into decentralized units, Blackburn got the various companies running autonomously and competing with one another. The *London Free Press* shifted from being publisher-driven to becoming market-driven with community input, a new format, and increased advertising. Concomitant with that were staff shakeups, firings, and the requirement that some employees reapply for their own jobs. Blackburn retired some older stalwarts and ruffled the feathers of others, which drew unfavourable publicity right in her own newspaper. In 1990, the editorial employees formed a union and went on strike. She hadn't just shifted the comfortable pew, she had upended it. Yet a year and a half after she had started it all, Elsden noted that the changes were remarkably for the better: "If Walter [were] alive today he couldn't have managed [the company] the way it was thirty years ago. You have to change."[31]

In August 1989, Blackburn established Blackburn Marketing Services, a subsidiary of the Blackburn Group, to start or buy businesses in non-traditional media areas such as marketing, communications, and media research. In other words, it will stay out of the publishing and broadcasting fields of BGI. Blackburn has survived her first four years as CEO with style, but a strike, decreasing circulation, the refusal of the CRTC to sanction the Blackburn Group proposal to merge its television stations with Maclean Hunter's CHCH station in Hamilton, and the reality that the *London Free Press* is one of the last remaining independent dailies, portends a tough decade. Harmonious staff relations are important to Martha Blackburn and the strike rankled. Nevertheless, Canada's counterpart to Katharine Graham of the Washington *Post*[32] will not be bullied. As for the hovering question "will she succeed?" Blackburn critics speculate she is controlled by consultants and professional managers,[t] rather than being in control. It appears, however, that, like any astute CEO, she makes good use of the talent around her and delegates authority with discretion. In the world of power, access is crucial, and few Canadian women combine business and social power with the style of a Martha Blackburn.

Confidence oozes like sap from Blackburn's Establishment veins and enables her to damn the consequences of talking freely with the press. Moving in the stately, easy style of the thoroughbreds she trains in dressage,[33] her blue eyes confront one with unswerving forthrightness and her voice sounds as if she were trained in choral speaking classes—modulated, cultured, and slightly theatrical. She thinks quickly, states opinions without apology, and is not afraid to make a mistake. With an eye to nurturing business connections and an alertness that embodies a sense of fun, Blackburn connects to the world with that irrefutable confidence of one who belongs—particularly to the Ontario and New York Establishment circles of society, business, politics, charitable organizations, and the performing arts. That kind of community presence was cited by *Canadian Business* as being an essential component of power. When Conrad Black sends out his most coveted invitations to the annual Hollinger Dinner at the Toronto Club, featuring speakers such as Margaret Thatcher (1988) and Ronald Reagan (1989), Martha Blackburn is one of the handful of women who have been invited into that enclave of old-boys' pre-eminence.[34] Few spouses attend because Black bases his invitations strictly on meritocracy. Guests agree that the invitation epitomizes "making it," however one chooses to keep score.

Helen Roman-Barber

In March 1988, Helen Roman-Barber moved into the CEO chair of the $1.4-billion Denison Mines and Roman Corporation. She was also chair of the Lawson Mardon (packaging) Group, a director of both the Standard Trustco and the Stephen B. Roman Foundation. The family owns 61 percent of Roman Corp. stock, and family members own 41 percent of Denison. The family worth of Mrs. Roman and the seven children was estimated at $200 million. Helen was dedicated to her father's visions but she had inherited companies in desperate need of overhaul.

In 1985 Stephen Roman was forced to write off the soured B.C. Quintette project, costing Denison Mines $240.7 million. Exploration errors had failed to determine the percentage of gravel mixed in with the coal so the coal was selling for less than production costs. Fluctuations in the commodities market worsened Quintette's position and that of their potash mines, and by 1988 when Helen took over, there was a glut of uranium on the world market. (In 1954 at Elliot Lake, Stephen Roman had built the world's largest uranium mine.) The highly leveraged company was caught at the end of a boom with no cash. Losses at Roman Corp. were $97.3 million for the first nine months of 1990.

Saving the company meant divesting fast, and at her first annual meeting she had announced, "If the Denison of tomorrow differs in any significant way from the Denison of today, it will be because I have implemented, not departed from, the long-term strategy and plans of my father." The claim allowed for drastic changes that might slice away the losers gathered under the corporate umbrella by her father, while crediting him for their divestiture. Roman-Barber had intended to get

Denison out of the oil and gas business, concentrate on its uranium operations, and raise $217 million in loans and equity. But uranium was not in demand, and the company's largest mine, Koongarra, in Australia's Kakadu National Park, was locked in the ground by government policy. Potash values were low, and real estate prices plummeted.

Unstable markets and world conditions have played a major role in Roman Corp's condition, but Roman-Barber's personality was also a factor. When Martha Blackburn, fourth generation WASP had taken over her father's offices, she contemporized and feminized them into dusty pink. A year after Roman-Barber had assumed the Denison chair, however, her father's Royal Bank Plaza office still reflected the omnipresent aura of the founder. His elaborately carved desk was the size of a Douglas fir and with the petite Roman-Barber sitting behind it, evoked images of Brobdingnagia and the impression that Stephen Roman's spirit was still hovering over the new CEO. Roman-Barber's thinking seemed to reflect, rather than succumb to, the spectre of Stephen Roman. Her reticence enshrouded a core which seemed determined, shrewd and astute.

She was also wary, her mistrust of the media ingrained in her by Stephen Roman and by the fact that she still felt like an outsider. As a second generation Roman Catholic Slovakian immigrant, she regarded the Toronto social jungle with suspicion. Heading down a mine shaft with Quintette Coal dust wafting through the air would have been preferable to an old boys' dinner with Conrad Black. Roman-Barber had a strong sense of who she was, but not where she stood in the community. Her worlds were mining and international law and if the CEO was going to hang out with anyone, it was her family, a couple of old school friends, or the straight shooters of the mining world — in whom any trace of pretension was as rare as trace gold in uranium. In 1989, however, when Conrad Black invited her to dine with Reagan, Roman-Barber's acceptance marked a tentative step towards the Establishment net.

A degree in international law, a business background, and fifteen years at her father's right hand may be insufficient for Roman-Barber to save the unwieldy corporation. In December 1990, she hired Bill James, the John Wayne of the mining industry, to take over the reins and salvage what he could, but he presided more over a fire sale of individual companies. Roman-Barber then appointed financial and management consultant Juri Koor as CEO of Standard Trustco, but that, too, was too late. By April 25, 1991, Standard had declared bankruptcy and Roman-Barber was being criticized for not riding herd on Standard management, who had done much of their lending in an inflated real estate market. And on April 30, 1991, Denison's Elliot Lake mining operations shut down, putting a thousand people out of work. Hiring outside help sooner might have been the most astute move of an Inheritor in control. Roman-Barber is experiencing the disheartening reality of watching the whole house of cards come tumbling down. As Carlyle Dunbar, editor of the *Investor's Digest*, understated, "Mining is a risky business."

The Industrialists
Maureen Prendiville

Lumber companies evoke visions of cleat-booted, towering lumberjacks, IWA heavies, machinery the size of 747s and bank accounts in the billions.[35] It is the last place one would expect to find a woman and, despite the fact that Jean Southam could have harvested and sold board feet faster than her father H.R. MacMillan, the idea of a woman running a forestry company a generation ago would have been preposterous. In 1973, however, Winnipegger Maureen Prendiville was a twenty-one-year-old college graduate whose experience with her father's companies consisted of travelling with him as a child was about to do just that. The only fights she had ever had were with her nineteen-year-old twin brothers over their cars in the driveway. Her father, a rough-talking, hard-drinking Irishman who had founded Prendiville Industries in Flin Flon, wanted Maureen to go into the antique business. He was training his two sons to take over the lumber company. She recalled of her father, "He was the original entrepreneur . . . his left hand didn't know what his right hand was doing." He was also an alcoholic and, following her father's sudden stroke and two years of management indecision, Maureen returned from a trip in Europe to find Prendiville Industries sliding towards bankruptcy.

When Prendiville moved into head office with the title of family representative, she found a $500,000 discrepancy between audited statements and their own year end accounts. Her young brothers were locked in a management struggle with the comptroller, who was more concerned with power than with straightening out the books. Management was a nightmare. For five years, her father had been hiring his drinking buddies out of bars. Employees with expense accounts and company cars were arriving at 10:00 a.m. and leaving at 2:00 p.m. Someone had purchased a computer system that would have serviced IBM itself. Her father had expanded into an insurance company about which he knew nothing, and he had purchased businesses in B.C. that had neither timber rights nor licences. Sales were excellent but as Prendiville said in logging vernacular, "We were peeing the profits out the window."

Firing the comptroller in 1975, Prendiville spent eleven months learning from the general manager before firing him too. When the Royal Bank threatened to pull out, she shut down the Winnipeg distribution business and fired most of the management. The bank still held much of Prendiville's assets as collateral, and when she watched the staff walk out the door, past their company cars and into taxis, it struck her that she was all that stood between Prendiville Lumber and bankruptcy. To complicate matters, her father had regained sufficient use of his limbs to walk, but only partial speech, and had returned to try and run the office. In fits of frustration, he fired staff indiscriminately until Prendiville took control and told him to deal only with her. By 1982, Prendiville was losing

$2,000 on every truckload of milled lumber that left the yard. She closed down and sold the mills rather than take another nosedive. Rival tradespeople said she was crazy, but Prendiville survived while her detractors ran themselves into the ground. "It was a matter of trying to stop the bleeding," recalled Prendiville, who quickly perfected a juggling act in negotiating peace between the warring factions while realizing her business objectives. Eventually she sold all of her timber rates in an excellent deal to Manitoba Forest Products, a Crown corporation in the NDP government and, when the economy improved, she was perfectly positioned for a profit-making opportunity.

During this crisis time, Prendiville discovered that not only was she financially oriented and sensitive to personnel but she loved the job, discovering, as Inheritors often do, that she already knew much of the business by osmosis. She still negotiates her own employee contracts. Prendiville is an expansionist who is adept at second-guessing a fluctuating economy. In 1978, she modified their mill and enlarged operations in Neepawa, and like Martha Blackburn, she runs each of the companies independently in an interrelated system. She and her brothers, who run marketing and sales, are amicable, equal partners, and they continue to do business with the Royal Bank. From 1982 to 1987 their sales doubled, and Prendiville's prediction of a 10-percent increase annually over the next five years is proving to be correct.

Married to lawyer Paul Jensen, and mother of two young children, Prendiville has nation-wide connections through her directorships.[36] Crediting Manitoba MP Dorothy Dobbie with breaking ground for her, Prendiville was the first and only woman member of the coveted YPO (Young Presidents Organization) Canada.[37] Ultimately, Prendiville's ability to nurture peaceful resolutions to her father's personality problems, once combative brothers, and union negotiations, combined with her business acumen, have meant the survival and continuing success of Prendiville Lumber.

Guylaine Saucier

> Strikes? We haven't had any. Oh, but those 1,200 [employees] are fantastic.
>
> GUYLAINE SAUCIER, 1988

Second-generation lumber inheritor and former president and CEO of the forestry company Le Groupe Gérard Saucier, the petite, blonde, Guylaine Saucier[38] was born in Noranda and raised in Val d'Or, Quebec. She is proof that the business acumen of the French-Canadian women is as dynamic and impressive as their politicians are adroit. Her office is decorated with photographs of huge lumber trucks and massive machinery engaged in the deployment of logs, part of her operation that, by

1988, Saucier had taken from $17 million to $90 million in annual sales, $50 million in assets (350 million board feet of lumber), and sold to Donohue, the integrated forest products company. In the spring of 1990 she was waiting for better market conditions and the right manufacturing company to buy back into the game.

In 1985 at the age of thirty-nine, Saucier was the first woman elected president of the Quebec Lumberman's Association and in 1987 was voted president of the Quebec Chamber of Commerce, the umbrella federation for the Montreal Board of Trade, chaired by prominent businessperson Manon Vennat. The Lumberman's Association was a distinctive vote of respect for Saucier as both a businessperson and negotiator who, despite a relatively small company, sat on SAGIT[39] during the free trade negotiations and represented all Canadian forest companies. Besides conducting negotiations on stumpage and countervailing duties, Saucier was an intermediary between the industry and the Quebec government, which was renegotiating its agreements with each forest industry company. Under her leadership the companies won increases in ten-year contracts to twenty-five-year government land leases, and new forest management plans. Recalled Saucier, "It was not only a big job, but a big fight."

Saucier is a seventeen-year veteran of the family business, begun in 1966. The oldest of six children, she got her chartered accountant's degree and was considering a career in corporate law, when her father offered her a job as chief comptroller in his company, Produits Forestiers Saucier. Annual sales were $10 million. She accepted, with the intention of returning to law school in five years. Four years later, after her father and his partner died, the twenty-nine-year-old Saucier committed herself not only to running the business, which had grown to $17 million in sales, but to expanding it. The company was several millions in debt to the bank, and colleagues warned her that as a woman she would have problems getting capital. She promptly met with National Bank of Canada president Germain Perreault, declaring, "My father died. I'm the new president. I'm only twenty-nine but I have a CA, I know the books, and this is what I would like to do. Will you help me do it?" And he did. She ran Saucier International without a comptroller and brought it into a successful growth pattern. She kept the books, formed a profit-sharing system for employees, and often donned a hard hat to join the crews.

Saucier brims with the positive energy of the successful merchant. During the 1988 free trade uproar, she noted that she already conducted 60 percent of her business with the United States. Once deeply concerned and vocal about Quebec and its cultural future, Saucier looked startled when asked about Bill 101, as if jolted into another world. "What is important [to Quebec]," she said, "is to have a sound economy." Then, like so many successful Quebec women for whom the fun of business has superseded politics, Saucier said, "[As] French-speaking people, and as women, we are more confident, more secure in business. . . . [Quebeckers] don't need to be that much protected."

No joiner of women's groups, which she believes encourage an unreal world, her association is with business people, period. "Just doing it [business]," she said, serves as a better role model for other women than seeking legislation to equalize job opportunities.

Saucier's view is supported by Vancouver-born, Canadian Forest Products (Canfor) lumber executive and Inheritor Barbara Bentley Hislop. Hislop is the thirty-five-year-old granddaughter of Canadian Forest Products co-founder Poldi Bentley, and the daughter of crack golfer Sheila and urbane European aristocrat Peter Bentley. Vice-president of corporate sectors and a director of the company, Hislop has worked her way through marketing, accounting, finance, and other aspects of the multilayered divisions of the $1.2-billion company. Juggling a family of four children with business presents no problems to Hislop, who shares the parenting with her equally capable husband John. She said in a voice of equanimity, "I don't see what the big deal is in today's environment. We love our four children and our work." Hislop's goal includes participating at the top. In lumbering, banking, and other corporate fields in which women talk about isolation, it is interesting that Prendiville, Saucier, and Hislop have never met.

Wendy McDonald

> Wendy McDonald? Never heard of her.
> She must be a hamburger.
>
> TORONTONIAN

Her employees call her "Mrs. Mac," and if Wendy McDonald lived in Toronto she would be one of Canada's most celebrated businesspeople, the toast of "Morningside," an authority on "The Journal," a director of multinationals and perhaps even a guest at Conrad Black's dinner table. Instead, she is known only in the Far West, where she is one of British Columbia's natural resources. A young mother widowed as the result of an accident in 1950, McDonald knew something of the esoteric world of ball bearings from running the company while her husband was overseas in the Second World War. Hiring nannies, she headed for the Vancouver office of B.C. Bearing Engineers founded by her husband. It had annual sales of $250,000, a half-built machine shop with no architect, and union problems. McDonald completed the buildings, negotiated her own union contracts, and opened the new works by Christmas. Then the city built the Granville Street Bridge and, breaking its promise, expropriated her building as a site to construct a pillar.

When her second husband was killed in an accident, McDonald continued juggling more children, nannies, and the expanding business, eventually marrying a third time to become the mother of a total of ten children. Selling to industries such as aircraft (Boeing), shipyards, and pulp mills, McDonald moved three times into progressively larger quarters and branched out into the United States, Mexico and Singapore, with agencies in Taipei, Bangkok, and Istanbul. Then McDonald's third husband died.

Keeping her sanity, McDonald raised all the children while developing B.C. Bearing into a solid international company with annual sales estimated at $60 million. Although some of her children came into the business, McDonald, who looks fifteen years younger than she is, continues to run the company, serves on a flock of industrial boards, and loves to deal in the male world as much as it enjoys and respects her. In 1990, she became the first female chair in the 104-year history of the Vancouver Board of Trade. Chairing the Asia Pacific Initiative's export services committee connected her to the players in the Pacific Rim countries. When Veuve Cliquot named McDonald Canadian Businesswoman of the Year in 1982, the champagne company honoured her with a vine in its French vineyards, *Wendy McDonald*. Stomping one's own grapes and quaffing the vintage represents about as delicious an accolade of power as some ever dream. A few years ago, on her sixtieth birthday, her namesake fastfood chains provided her children with flags to fly in her front garden: *Wendy's* and *McDonald's*. Some hamburger.

Jeannine Guillevin-Wood

Man of the Month[40]

> We always look at acquisition because it goes faster. We believe in the company that it's better to make an acquisition in a new territory than [to start] from zero.
>
> JEANNINE GUILLEVIN-WOOD

When fiftysomething Jeannine Guillevin-Wood was led to her table by the maître d' of The Beaver Club in the Queen Elizabeth Hotel, male business executives deep in conversation paused to greet her with appreciative nods acknowledging that the former homemaker-turned-CEO is one of them.[41] Widowed twenty-five years earlier, with a teenaged daughter, she had inherited F.X. Guillevin & Fils — a thirty-five employee, $1.5-million household appliance company. Instead of selling out, Guillevin-Wood stepped into her husband's position with the aplomb of one who had always been there. The banks responded with full support when she asked to increase the operating loan of the cash-thirsty Guillevin, and then continued to back her when she expanded into the international sphere. Her longtime employees taught her the business in order to survive and the year after she took over, the Canadian

Electrical Distributors Association invited her to join. At her first conventions there were 200 men, fifty wives, and Jeannine Guillevin-Wood, but she was both warmly received and eventually elected president. Nervous about making acquisitions at first, Guillevin-Wood sought help from her young comptroller rather than outside consultants. Their first purchase was a small company in Trois-Rivières and from the start it was a success.

Guillevin-Wood then launched the company on an acquisitory bent that frustrated male competitors. Renaming her company Guillevin International, she went public with a company that now has 1,470 employees and 82,000 products, operates over 118 distribution centres around the world, and deals with five hundred international suppliers.[42] In the period 1985-90, Guillevin International has increased its sales nearly fourfold from $109 million to $428 million, a net earnings per share increase of 250 percent. She now believes that anyone with motivation and willingness to work and learn, can do anything.

****

> I've met more women who fail because of self-pity . . . and worrying about their pride. My definition of courage is that you hang on five minutes longer than the other guy. Don't blink.
>
> JEAN PIGOTT

"I'm sixty-three, chum!" It is less her round face and slightly protruding upper teeth that give former Conservative MP Jean Pigott a hint of beaverlike caricature, than her perpetual motion. Her halo of white hair is neat, yet brushed with the absent-mindedness of someone on a higher mission, and her face is luminous with the enthusiasm and energy of an entrepreneur closing her first deal. As far as family corporations go, Morrison Lamothe Bakery and its $19 million in annual sales and other income is like a blip in a column of figures to a Canadian Tire, a Blackburn Group, or a Roman Corporation. But Jean Pigott and her sister Grete Hale personify the strength of inheritor families. They credit their father, who armed them with homilies that they used to save their heritage, run the company, and see its peaceful passage to a third generation.

The head of this family is not a son, uncle, or male cousin who claimed control like J.W. Billes, but a woman who subscribes to the Scottish convention of female primogeniture. As the eldest child, Jean Pigott assumed the role of matriarch with all the traditional gusto associated with patriarchy. Pigott stated, "The difference between Grete and myself is very simple. I was born first."

In 1967, when her seventy-four-year-old father relinquished the company and its problems to his daughters, the bank summoned her to say she had three months in which to restructure or they were calling in their loan. A furious Pigott hired a management consultant with the proviso that she be made CEO, and immediately sold four of the family companies to raise cash, reducing a work force of 1,000 to 350. Laying off staff loyal to Morrison Lamothe for decades was a terrible experience for Pigott, but it was the only way to save the company. All the while, she put on a confident front and wielded her power with the poise of an Amazon. Two years later, when Morrison Lamothe was stabilized, the head of the bank's credit committee admitted, "You know Jean, if your name had been John, we would have given you twice the working capital and twice the line of credit."

Pigott reminds everyone of their favourite sister, pal, cousin, or aunt. A direct descendent of working families who came to the Gatineau Valley in 1800, she said proudly, "We're not Establishment. We're strong," as if refinement might be synonymous with weakness. Her style is folksy, her welcome a hearty "Howrya doing!" as she throws open the doors of her 1828 home to fledgling MPs. (It helps if you are a Tory, like Pat Carney and Barbara McDougall, both of whom enjoyed Pigott's hospitality when they were newcomers to Ottawa.) Her home echoes with the charitable and political activities of more than 160 years. Pigott's zest for life stems from a childhood spent in bed with rheumatic fever, arthritis, and pneumonia. Doctors predicted that she would either be dead by eighteen or spend her life in a wheelchair, harsh news for a family that had already lost a daughter to meningitis. But Pigott read voraciously and discussed politics, business, and leadership strategies with her father. She most valued his observations on the nature of people. Cured by surgery at the age of fourteen, Pigott joined the world with a fierce defiance of adversity and an insatiable thirst for life. She participated in everything from theatre to sports to running the school. To this day she exudes bumptious energy both in the style of her language and her expansive gestures.

It was the old story in 1945—the universities filled with veterans and Pigott could not attend. But rather than advise her to marry and settle down, her father suggested she learn about the working world beyond Morrison Lamothe and seek leadership experience. Advising her to learn to make decisions, to pay the consequences for bad ones, and to build teams, Pigott's father would say, "When you learn to harness the energy of the bullies . . . when you can get the people who are scared stiff . . . to make a contribution, I can use you." His most valuable maxim by which she was expected to live was, "your word is your bond." Pigott still lists his maxims off with the zeal of an evangelist: self-awareness, building a powerful team, decisiveness, strategic focus, tenacity, personal integrity, accountability, responsibility, and timing. Of the latter Pigott said, "Everything in my life has come at the wrong time. Each time doors open, you just have to recognize it and walk through that door. The priorities sort themselves out, people grow around you. It's got nothing to do with rational thought.'' Pigott sniffed the air of opportunity as if savouring the scent of freshly baked bread.

In true Scottish style, and as the eldest member of her generation, Pigott has maintained control of the estate. Trust and a sense of family and community are her only checks and balances. The CEO post of Morrison Lamothe has moved on from Grete Hale to Pigott's thirty-three-year-old son John, an understudy of his aunt who was but an able caretaker in the hierarchy. One wonders how accepting of primogeniture Pigott might have been had she had an older brother.

Only once has Pigott experienced the invisibility felt by so many lone women directors on all-male boards. In the early seventies, while serving on the Bakery Council of Canada, she attended a long, drawn-out meeting in Ottawa where everyone was fighting. Suddenly Pigott had an inspiration, suggested a solution, and within ten minutes crisis and meeting were over. ''Thanks, Pigott,'' the others said good-naturedly, and as they spilled onto Richmond Street one of the men exclaimed, ''Let's go to the bar and we'll have a drink on this. Goodbye, Jean.'' Pigott was left standing speechless on the street. At the next meeting, which proved just as divisive, she remained silent until the chair said, ''Jean, you helped us the last time. What's your answer?'' She replied, ''I think this is what you should do. . . . '' Everyone heaved a sigh of relief and said, ''God! Thanks, Pigott.'' Then to their amazement she resigned, revealing the deep insult she had felt at not being included for a drink as a member of the team. It had never dawned on them to invite her. Pigott's role, as so many other women working alone, was that of trailblazer. It would be Grete Hale who joined the board. In 1974 Hale was elected the first female president of the Bakery Council of Canada.

The great matriarch has designed her own epitaph. Pigott's tombstone will be divided into four sections for her equally valued four careers some of which happened at the same time — motherhood, politics, business, and Chief of the National Capital Commission. Pigott wants everyone to know that all her married life she has paid for teeth, tutors, ski holidays, bicycles and cars. To prove that Morrison Lamothe was not controlled by the banks, she will include a graph showing the increase in its working capital. And because she wants the world to know that she loved revelling in controversy,[43] Pigott will add the words,

Chairman of the NCC.
Closing the gates of Government House.
Signing the American Embassy.

''What a conversation in the graveyard! A hundred years from now can't you just hear people say, 'What a broad!' ''

CHAPTER 7 NOTES

1. CAFE members such as Martha Blackburn and Gail Regan oversee holdings of up to, or over, a billion dollars, and a flock of new fortunes, including those of Ron and Marg Southern of Calgary and Philippe and Nan-b de Gaspe Beaubien of Montreal and Toronto, whose Futurist children are now involved, belong to CAFE, but no Eatons or Molsons acknowledge being among its ranks.
2. An irony of the tax laws is that the children can become immediate beneficiaries of family success but the wife cannot. The long years she may have devoted to helping her husband establish his business can never be recognized in a retroactive salary or gift. Wives must remain dependants.
3. Agnes Benidickson serves as chancellor of Queen's University and has sat on the boards of Mutual Life, National Trust, National Trustco, James Richardson & Sons, and the National Gallery Association. Kathleen Richardson sits on the boards of Sun Life Assurance, Barclays Bank of Canada, and James Richardson & Sons.
4. In March of 1989, the family sold off her father's Holiday Inn chain for $285 million.
5. Since 1988, Cara Operations has acquired the master franchise for Days Inn, bought Grand & Toy Ltd. for $105 million, and agreed to buy Arvak Ltd. for $34 million; Cara's 1990 figures show a slight slowdown in profits since its acquisition of Grand & Toy. Still, in a recession year it was an impressive performance with revenue for the third quarter up 31 per cent to $661.4 million and net income down two percent to $25.3 million from $25.7 million in 1989.
6. Gardiner was a director of Mutual Life and currently sits on the boards of Canada Bay Lumber, Fishery Products International, Labrador Hydro-Electric, and Better Homes, a division of Chester Dawe.
7. Most prominent of Allard's companies are Canadian Satellite Communications and Allarcom Pay T.V.
8. Columnist Diane Francis explained the tangled intrigue in the *Financial Post*, 31 Jan 1991. William waged a lawsuit against Harold Ballard Jr., who gave William and partners an option to buy his third of Harold E. Ballard Ltd., then changed his mind and sold it to his father instead, giving the old man control just before he died.

If William wins, he and his partner will control the Gardens. Rachelle's role is rarely recorded.

9. The Steinbergs had a 52 percent block of voting shares through the holding company Rockview Investments, whose parent is Hermms, and through Sam's estate, which went to Helen Steinberg, Sam's widow. Another 36 percent of voting stock was held by other branches of the Steinberg family, so 88 percent of voting stock was in family hands.
10. Stephen Jarislowsky, a Montreal investment manager, formed the Shareholders' Action Committee to defend the rights of shareholders.
11. The Tire story is vividly documented in Ian Brown's 1989 biography, *Freewheeling*, a book written in a tone of bemused incredulity that, combined with the Ontario Securities Commission hearings, has made public a once intensely private family.
12. In Canada's greater or lesser family retailing dynasties —Eaton's, Simpson's, Woodward's, Canadian Tire, Sobey's, Finning Tractor, Weston's—daughters were encouraged as children to visit the store and to attend company picnics, but as adults they were forbidden to sell bananas or gas, let alone become management or directors. If they married, like Martha Blackburn, Mary Margaret Finning Young, Mary Twigg Woodward White or Mitzi Steinberg Dobrin, their husbands were the ones invited in to run the companies and/or sit on the boards.
13. Martha diversified into real estate—her holdings are in Ontario and British Columbia—and into leasing equipment during the building of the B.C. Railway. She rolled her oil and gas properties into a drilling company called Newmat Drilling (Western), of which she is chair, major shareholder, and executive vice president of oil and gas operations.
14. Tire took a $141-million writedown on White's Stores.
15. Canadian Tire enjoyed 1989 revenues up 12 percent to $3 billion from $2.6 billion, and a net income of $149.6 million, up 20 percent from $124.9 million.
16. In 1988, Jackman ran against Douglas McCutcheon, prominent Establishment Torontonian, and David MacDonald, who was brought in from Ethiopia where he served as ambassador. A former cabinet minister, MacDonald was supported by Barbara McDougall and most of the party establishment. He won. Jackman's conso-

lation prize was an appointment to the ECC. The council quivers.

17. Nancy Jackman is the daughter of former Rosedale MP Henry Rutherford Jackman, who amassed the National Trust financial empire. The National Trust, founded in 1843, is a holding company with subsidiaries including National Trust Company, Victoria & Grey Mortgage Company and the Premier Trust. It includes banks, insurance companies, and trust companies. Her father's equal share split of $30 million to her and three older brothers—Hal, who chairs National Trustco, Eric, a psychologist and business executive, and Edward, a Dominican priest—was complicated because Nancy and her mother were given non-negotiable stock while her brothers received liquid assets. It was her brother Hal who went solo in building National Trust into a company with total assets estimated at $45 billion.
18. Jackman has an honorary degree from Mount St. Vincent University and sits on its board, as well as those of Casey House Hospice, Womanly Way Productions, International Institute for Concern for Public Health, and the Canadian Women's Foundation, which she founded. She is a cornerstone of LEAF, and is involved in the Association for Creative Change and Feminist Spirituality.
19. Mary Rowell Jackman started the first day-care centre in Toronto in the 1930s, a time when many Establishment women were unaware that some mothers had to work.
20. A few years later Jackman was appointed interim associate minister at the Metropolitan United Church in downtown Toronto.
21. Nancy Jackman's foundation is named NaRuth.
22. Founded in 1979 by Lambert, the CCA started as a place to house her three-decade collection of photos, drawings, books, and models, and to foster an appreciation of the history of architecture. The CCA houses approximately 20,000 drawings and prints, 55,000 photos, and 130,000 books (the library ranks in stature with the Royal Institute of British Architects) worth over $50 million, $30 million of which was given by Lambert. It opened with one hundred employees, twenty of them librarians.
23. Included was Blanche van Ginkel, who received her degree in architecture from McGill in 1945 and was the

real pioneer in the efforts to save Old Montreal from demolition.

24. The traveller learned firsthand of Lambert's separation of herself from the realities of other people's expenses. After being granted an appointment, the traveller flew across Canada, arrived at Lambert's St. Catherine's Street office and was directed to her public relations office. It in turn required her first to visit Lambert's public relations guru on Mountain Street, Mr. Richard Gervais. There, a crisis was unfolding. Gervais's gold-plated Victorian telephones were ringing off their hooks on his antique gilded desk as he tried to round up three barrels of bluepoint oysters for a fund-raising gala that evening. The originals had gone astray in a Maritime snowstorm and were rotting in places unknown. Between calls he swept about his office naming the glitterati in the hundreds of photographs decorating his dusty pink walls; Gervais was shaking hands with every prime minister, potentate, governor-general and movie star, with his wife, Marie Chevrier, close at hand, his performance was a cross between a kinetic Robin Williams and a debonair Richard Chamberlain, coiffed with a hair advertisement for *Gentlemen's Quarterly*.

    Time was running out. Reminded that the traveller had arrived for an interview with Phyllis Lambert, Gervais alighted momentarily to check his appointment book, a magnificent work of art worthy of a pen-and-ink Salvador Dali. Yes, Lambert was in town, he concluded as he waved his arms north, south, east and west, but she was so busy coming and going, "Zaire, Brazil, Yugoslavia . . . " he ran out of breath. Then he exclaimed, "Well, the person you should really interview is my wife!" Enter the Game. The traveller made a shameful trade-off and headed for Mt. Pleasant Avenue for an hour's visit in the eclectic home of the charming Marie Chevrier Gervais, lawyer, a daughter of Lionel Chevrier, (famous Quebec politician) and an organizer of the Canada Day celebrations. The traveller returned to Vancouver without the interview with Phyllis Lambert.

25. Lambert is active in the Montreal Citizens Movement, and she spearheaded the move to save an entire Montreal neighbourhood slated for destruction and redevelopment. With a group of concerned citizens and the help of government, she established the largest

co-operative non-profit project for urban home renewal in Canada. In her address to the Bélanger-Campeau Commission on the political and constitutional future of Quebec, she favoured Quebec sovereignty when she said, ''I think Quebec should go for it.''

26. Intrigue over the Roman-Barber and Blackburn ascendancies can be better understood when considering that, just months beforehand, the three Steinberg sisters and Martha Billes had also headed into court.
27. Blackburn is the controlling shareholder, president, and chairman of The Blackburn Group and its subsidiary companies: London Free Press Printing Company Limited, CFPL Broadcasting Limited, CKNX Broadcasting Limited, Blackburn Marketing Services, Compusearch Market and Social Research, Netmar, and, on the personal front, Kilbyrne Investments.
28. Women are not the only ones who had stereotypical roles imposed upon them. Walter Blackburn junior anguished over his presumed role of heir apparent to the family business. While still a young man, he committed suicide. His shares were split between the two sisters. Susan, the eldest, spends much of each year in Florence, Italy.
29. Blackburn's directorships include Blackburn Holdings and the Walter J. Blackburn Foundation. Community boards are: Junior Achievement and The World Wildlife Fund, and the board of the Elgin and Winter Gardens with Elizabeth Tory and Hilary Weston; the *Imagine* board with prominent national representation, and at the University of Western Ontario, the advisory committee for the Women in Management Research Project, which also includes Maureen Sabia, CAFE, and the board of administration and finance committee of the Anglican Diocese of Huron.
30. *London Free Press* circulation was down to 60 percent, or 128,000, from a high of 90 percent. A survey showed that readers thought it was dull. Michael Nolan, author of A Man For All Media, suggests that Walter Blackburn's vision had been circumscribed by the perimeter of London.
31. Diversification included Compusearch Market and Social Research, Pennysaver Publications, and Netmar (a weekly advertisement distribution system reaching two million homes across Canada), which was sold in 1991 to Southam. The company also purchased the

London edition of *Ontario Living* magazine from Comac Communications of Toronto, and attempted unsuccessfully to acquire CHCH-TV from Maclean Hunter.

32. Graham is chair and CEO of the Washington *Post* Company, a $1.4-billion media empire, one of twenty of the most profitable companies in the United States. *Working Woman* magazine calls her the most powerful woman in America. (November 1989, Mary Rowland.)
33. Blackburne's farm, Kilbyrne, is becoming a prominent centre for advanced dressage.
34. Besides Blackburn, other women invited to the 1990 Hollinger dinner were: Barbara Frum of "The Journal"; economist Dr. Sylvia Ostry; Rosalie Abella, chair of the Ontario Law Reform Commission; economist Marie-Josée Drouin who sits on the Hollinger board of UniMedia in Quebec; Anna Porter, publisher of Key Porter, and Seal-Bantam; Heather M. Reisman, president of Paradigm Consulting; Helen Roman-Barber, then CEO of Roman Corp. and Denison Mines; and from the United States, A. Devon Gaffney, director of Research Smith-Richardson, New York; and Katharine Graham.
35. Calling herself a small business, Prendiville cites $20 million in annual sales compared to $3.3 billion for MacMillan Bloedel.
36. Prendiville has served on the boards of the Central Forest Products Association, and the Winnipeg contingent of former trade minister Pat Carney's ITAC (International Trade Advisory Committee), which included George Richardson and clothing magnate Peter Nygard as well as Lise Watier, cosmetic queen of Montreal. She is a member of the Manitoba Round Table on Environment and the Economy. She is also a member of CAFE.
37. Requirements for membership in YPO are $4 million in annual sales, at least fifty employees, and the title of president before the age of forty. Prendiville's company has approximately $20 million in sales and two hundred employees.
38. Saucier, who sold her company in 1988 and is seeking another, is connected as a board member to some of the major corporations of the country: Metro Gas until 1988, when she stepped up the hierarchy to join Noverco, Metro's parent Dale-Parizeau, Bank of Canada, Bell Canada, Laurentian General Insurance,

Sodarcan, Hawker Siddeley Canada, and Roy Fund Equity.

39. A multidisciplinary body, the Sectoral Advisory Group on International Trade was struck to deal with free trade, and now deals with GATT. Saucier still sits on the committee dealing with forest products.
40. Guillevin-Wood was twice anointed with this title by the Montreal business Establishment.
41. In March 1989, Guillevin-Wood was awarded the Mercure Award, presented to the Business of the Year by the Quebec Chamber of Commerce. It is one of the most prestigious business awards in Quebec. Her directorships include Chair and CEO of Guillevin International, BCE, CDME (France), Hydro-Québec, Laurentian Bank of Canada, Provigo, Royal Insurance of Canada, Sun Life Assurance of Canada, Business Council on National Issues, Fondation de L'Hôpital du Sacré-Coeur, and the Musée des beaux arts. Her presidencies include Les Placements Guillevin and Guillevin Holdings.
42. In 1990 Guillevin International posted net earnings of $5.9 million on sales of $428 million, with total assets of $153 million. From 1988 to 1990 Guillevin-Wood invested over $4 million in modernizing her equipment and extending operational capacities. Acquisitions since May 1989 include GIR DEL Hydraulic Services, 70 percent of Rocmer, and National Cable Specialists and its subsidiaries.
43. The NCC chief did give up her plan to turn parkland bordering the classy residential village of Rockcliffe into an embassy row, starting with the American Embassy, when citizens caused an uproar.

POLITICAL POWER

CHAPTER EIGHT

The Political Pyramid

[Getting into] politics is very, very hard . . . and it's partly women's fault. We looked at ourselves as being support . . . content with the backroom, with the teacakes, licking the stamps. I blame the women.

JEAN PIGOTT

If you can balance a household budget on today's wages, [direct staff, or put on a dinner party for fifty people], you can bloody well do anything. Home is one of the better training areas for involvement in the community, the province, territory or the country because it's a mindset no different than business, or politics. Just alter the mindset and change the venue.

PAT McMAHON
MAYOR OF YELLOWKNIFE

The Volunteers

It was never really the railway that connected this country but the machinery of federal politics. Its volunteers are the energy and the glue that bind Northerners to Torontonians, Calgarians to Montrealers, Charlottetowners to British Columbians, and everyone to Ottawans. The political pyramid is the foundation of a free society that connects cabinet ministers with backroom strategists, envelope stuffers with senators, professional lobbyists with mandarins. It is through volunteer efforts that NDP Leader Audrey McLaughlin, Liberal leadership hopeful Sheila Copps, External Affairs Minister Barbara McDougall, and Justice Minister Kim Campbell find themselves, like legions of men and a few women before them, at the pinnacle in the House of Commons.

The 1989 NDP leadership victory of Yukon MP Audrey McLaughlin showed that it doesn't matter from what corner of Canada you come, you can play in the Ottawa game. In the 1988 federal election Ethel Blondin, a Liberal and a Déné, became the first NWT woman to win a federal seat, but her campaign manager, Lynda Sorensen of Yellowknife,[1] former president of the National Liberal Women's Commission, had been linked with Ottawa since the Trudeau days. After twenty years of dealing with Ottawa ministers, Nellie Cournoyea, NWT MLA and minister of four portfolios,[2] knows more about all parties and the Ottawa bureacracy than the federal government itself.

Volunteers in the federal Liberal and Conservative parties have enjoyed, historically, the greatest connections to power. Those from Whitehorse, St. John's, or Regina who play major roles in supporting political winners have been appointed into the ABCs — the 260 federal government agencies, boards, and commissions. Add to those the powerful tribunals, and the judgeships of the Citizenship and Immigration courts and you have electrifying connections into which thousands of ''ordinary'' Canadians can be directly plugged into the central station of power. One volunteer and former MP who reached the puissant post in the 1970s was Jean Casselman Wadds when she became high commissioner to Great Britain. Another party stalwart, Bettie Hewes, currently an Alberta Liberal MLA, topped a career beginning with occupational therapy, ranging through leadership positions in numerous community boards, through a decade as an Edmonton councillor, with an appointment by the federal Liberals to the plush chair of the Canadian National Railway. In 1988, CN president Ron Lawless remembered Hewes as running the best meetings of any chair under which he has served.

With the Conservatives in power for nearly eight years, the ABC seats are filled by party faithful who have paid their dues. Winnipegger Diane McDonald is a citizenship court judge and Helen Arpin serves on the Immigration Appeal Board (tribunal). Vancouver Conservative Sally Warren sits on the board of the mighty CRTC, and Calgary investment dealer Judi Romanchuk, with Toronto lawyer Maureen Sabia, heads off for meetings of the $7.5-billion Export Development Corporation (EDC) to ponder financial and insurance credit proposals for such projects as Lavelin's multi-billion-dollar contract to build the subway system in Bangkok. In the spring of 1991, Prime Minister Mulroney appointed Sabia chair of the EDC.[3] Former York mayor Gayle Christie became a director of Air Canada. The lieutenant-governor positions connect those who hold the honour to every national or international figure who visits their province including, of course, the Royalty that they represent.[4]

To be flown to Ottawa from the far reaches of Canada courtesy of the government can be heady stuff, and appointees take the responsibility seriously. Should their reward be a position on a board like the Canada Council, they will spend many hundreds of hours working on behalf of artists across the country. Diva Maureen Forrester figured that she has lost about $500,000 in concert fees by chairing the Canada Council, travelling the country, holding hearings, and evaluating requests for grants on its behalf. Accepting a parole board position, as Vancouverite Liberal backroom force Sarah McAlpine did, means that long hours, angst, and even public outrage can accompany the perks.

If the demands are so heavy, why do so many volunteer?

First because they believe in the democratic system in which one person can make a difference. But beyond political ideology, an appointment to the federal ABCs connects the individual to a dynamic and specific community. Often it marks the first time a woman has been recognized beyond her regional sphere of volunteerism, and is her first opportunity to test her voice at the policy-making level. Skilled volunteers, backroom strategists, or political aspirants like Liberals Lorna Marsden, Joyce Fairbairn, Anne Cools, Muriel Fergusson, and Conservative Mira Spivak of Winnipeg, longtime toilers in the trenches, were rewarded with senatorships that, whether they are abused or not, come with a "global budget" requiring no accountability.

Senators have the greatest freedom/power on the Hill. Whether or not they avail themselves of all the privileges, they can hire relatives, give away their over one hundred airline passes on to family or friends, and they can use their free travel on their frequent flyer program. Janis Johnson of Winnipeg (former wife and speech writer of former Newfoundland premier Frank Moores), mastermind of Brian Mulroney's political campaigns, was appointed to the board of the Canadian National Railway and then was appointed a senator in 1990. Rumour has it that she found CN more fun.[5]

Rather than view the exalted seat as a sinecure that will get them the best restaurant or theatre reservations in town, most drive themselves relentlessly trying to make a difference. When she was seventy-four, Thérèse Casgrain was appointed a senator and shamed her colleagues with the number of committees on which she served, reports she wrote, and speeches she made in her continuing quest for reform. Of equal energy is Senator Mira Spivak who, in her "spare time," when she was not in committee or commuting from Winnipeg, founded "Winning Women," conferences on how to enter politics that have become sellouts across the country.

The senators are heartened by having the final say. Although accused for years of being irrelevant, in 1988 the Liberal Senate majority guided by Opposition Leader John Turner, forced the Conservatives into an election that year without a vote on the child-care or broadcast bills. In the spring of 1991, the child-care bill was still in limbo and the broadcast bill had yet to go through. In 1990, the display of Liberal bell-ringing and the slinging of vitriolic abuse among senators fighting over the proposed Goods and Services Tax transformed this "chamber of sober-second-thought" from the ultimate haven of power into the land's most infamous kindergarten. Still, it had the power.

To the partisan volunteer, loyalty to one party is as immutable as religious convictions, and those on the outside have faith that their time will come. Look what has happened in Ontario. The New Democrats have come in from the cold and all those ABCs will start filling up with the party faithful. Patronage is as inevitable in the democratic system as is its occupational hazard, obsolescence. In 1984, the departing Pierre Trudeau dumped approximately two hundred appointments on incoming Prime Minister John Turner, which meant turfing out many of the incumbents. *Globe and Mail* reporter Stevie Cameron broke the story and Opposition Leader Brian Mulroney used it to help win the election. Once ensconced in the PMO, Mulroney then played the same game. Sheila Copps reported that after serving ten years as judge of the citizenship court, her mother's appointment was not renewed. When Geraldine Copps asked why, the reply from Deputy Prime Minister Erik Nielsen and Walter McLean, then minister of state for immigration, was, "[Your daughter] has been vocal in her opposition to the government." The sin of the daughter was visited upon the mother. Then sixty, Geraldine ran for a seat on Hamilton city council and won.

The Conservative government, through the PMO and its deputy chief of staff, Marjory LeBreton, has actually increased women's appointments enormously. Critics will argue that many appointees in the consular or agent general field are simply loyalists who can throw great parties, an opinion that recalls the thesis that information, the greatest source of power, is frequently gleaned from the cocktail circuit. In 1984, longtime Mulroney pals and faithful backroom supporters Pierrette Lucas and Joan Price Winser of Montreal were appointed consuls general to Boston and to Los Angeles respectively. Both won rave reviews from Americans for their facilitating styles. Following her successful Massachusetts posting, Lucas was promoted in 1989 to chief of protocol for the PM, a job that connects her to every state, world, or god-like figure who confers with the Prime Minister or with the Minister for External Affairs. A mine of knowledge on who's who in anywhere from Malta, to Capetown, to Odessa, Lucas has that essential ability to remain amusing, aware, and articulate after five rugged hours on the banquet circuit.

To suggest that Conservative patronage appointments relegate the best Liberal talents beyond the Canadian Shield until the Opposition regains power, or that NDP talent is never used, is to argue that expertise lies only in the opposition parties. In 1985 when Janis Johnson was appointed to the board of CN, CJOB talk show host Peter Warren scoffed over the airwaves, "She doesn't know the difference between a caboose and a cowbell." Johnson parried, "You can't tell me that all the men appointed [to boards] for the last hundred years have been intellectual giants." Then she proceeded to digest, and become conversant on, every piece of information available on the company.

The most valuable volunteers are the backroom strategists who mastermind the whole election process starting with the tough nominations, and they come from every background. The profession of nursing has produced a number of crisis managers. Vancouverite Virginia Richards figures that nursing prepared her perfectly for politics. Both require the organizational skills of a juggler, the patience of a saint, the stamina of an oilrigger, and an adaptability for trench warfare. As Richards put it, "My bent is getting people elected. I like the chase, the adrenalin, the crisis management, and a finite end. It's like being in the operating room."[6]

Brenda Kinsella, a political veteran raised in the United States, first tasted politics when she worked on John Lindsay's 1968 mayoralty campaign, and marched to 52nd and 5th with Betty Friedan and Gloria Steinem. Kinsella moved to B.C. when her husband, Patrick, was hired as principal secretary to Bill Bennett. "The first thing you have to do [for a campaign] is raise money," said Kinsella, pointing to women's eternal and monumental problem in entering politics.[7] With a pragmatism notably American, she said, "I have no doubt why people answer my phone calls — it's because of Patrick." Close association with a major government player around helps when fund raising for women politicians, but Brenda's name is mentioned about town as much as Patrick's, both being central to the federal systems as well as the wacky world of B.C. politics.

The Vancouver backroomers connected with their central Canadian counterparts when Richards and Kinsella co-founded, with Sally Warren and Lisa Woodward, the group called Tories for Choice, then promoted it across the country. It dealt with the abortion question, and while the group received no publicity in Vancouver, it was amazed at the media response in Toronto. Thanks to prominent Conservatives Lynn Golding, Susan Fish, and Jan Diamond, the organization became a cause célèbre on the Toronto talk show circuit. The network works.

****

In Toronto, Jalynn Bennett, then a vice-president with ManuLife, was a member of Barbara McDougall's original nominating campaign. In 1986, she was appointed chair of the financial sector of SAGIT, a private sector thinktank reporting to the federal government on the pros and cons of international trade for financial services. Inherent in the pyramidal system is knowing when not to use the power of access. "We had a tacit agreement," recalled Bennett, "never to discuss the business of finance when Barbara was minister of state for finance." She believed her name had been proposed for the SAGIT position by the Investment Dealers Association, but the open line from private sector to the heart of government was unmistakable.

****

Jane Pepino, Toronto lawyer and shaper of policy change at three levels of government, puts hundreds of hours into her boards, committees, and commissions, "because of all those women out there . . . who've been slugging their guts out for years, picketing, letter writing, pushing. Pushing." A 1970 gold-key graduate of Osgoode Hall Law School, Pepino at first sought to article with a Toronto law firm. It accepted her but warned there would be no litigation for her: it did not want a woman taking the firm's name into court. Pepino in turn demanded that the dean's office bar the firm from interviewing graduating students at Osgoode but the dean saw nothing wrong with the firm's decree.

A senior partner with Aird and Berlis, Pepino practises municipal and land development law, with the DelZottos of Tridel high on her client list. Always on the run, she has combined her profession with marriage, three children, volunteer work for METRAC (president), the United Church, and a dozen other community commitments including pulling strings in the campaigns of Roy McMurtry, David Crombie, and Barbara McDougall. It is her clout at three levels of government that inspires the public perception of Pepino as one of the most powerful women in the country.[8] In 1989 when she was being pressured to run for the Ontario Tory leadership, Pepino faced the dilemma of being against Meech Lake when the PMO was trying to sell it. She remained publicly silent, loyal to the party, while delivering to the official committee her well-informed argument against the Accord. She finally exploded when Senator Lowell Murray said in a special hearing, "OK, we've heard from the women, now let's hear from the experts."

****

Politics is as rough in the backrooms as in the front, and no one knows better than Torontonian Sarah Band,[9] a woman of great administrative abilities and wide community recognition. She met her Waterloo in 1983, the year of the Conservative leadership convention in Winnipeg when Joe Clark and Brian Mulroney were battling it out for the top job. Band ran for national president of the party and blames her loss on Mulroney for "scuttling me out of winning." According to Band, Mulroney had privately assured her backers that she had his team's support, but his team's most ardent goal was less one of electing Band than beating Joe Clark, and that meant winning support in the West.

Once in Winnipeg, Band was surprised to see one of her opponents, Edmontonian Peter Elzinga, wining and dining the crowd and enjoying splashy campaign headquarters. Band knew he had no money and believed that Mulroney's team was funding Elzinga so that he could win the West. Elzinga was also chair of the leadership convention and with the doubly high profile, won the presidency. Mulroney won the leadership and took off for a holiday to Palm Beach. Exhausted and disappointed, Band also headed for the Florida hideaway with Monty, and Conrad and Joanna Black. One day, when she collided with the Mulroneys at a luncheon party, Brian made stumbling apologies to Band, blaming complex backroom strategies for her loss. Band had plenty to say to Mulroney about lying and backstabbing, and she pulled away from the double dealing to end her political career. In 1991, following eight years of silence, she wrote a strong letter to the Prime Minister outlining the steps he should take to win back national confidence. These ranged from economic recovery and national unity, to government expenditures and political image. Mulroney responded by welcoming her back and appointing her to a top backroom job.

****

Ask almost anyone in the know whom they consider to be the most powerful woman in the Conservative Party and just as often as they say, ''Barbara McDougall,'' they will opt for ''Marj LeBreton.'' Aged fifty-one, the tall, dark-haired dynamo epitomizes the heights to which a volunteer can ultimately reach. LeBreton was a Tory even before she was old enough to join the Young Progressive Conservatives. She would become secretary and confidante to three prime ministers and one leader of the Opposition. Now, as deputy chief of staff and special assistant, appointments, she has a direct hand in filling the 2,746 order-in-council positions in the ferris wheel of federal agencies, boards, commissions, and tribunals that help to make this country work. From 1986–1988, she claims to have single-handedly increased women's appointments by just over 31 percent.[10] Her sister, the highly qualified Kay Stanley, was co-ordinator of the status of women in Canada, then became Deputy head, reporting directly to the minister responsible for the status of women.

LeBreton talks candidly, unhampered by the slick rhetoric typical of appointment secretaries and chiefs of staff. Screwing up her face, her eyes as bright as a mad scientist's hot on the trail of a new discovery, she claimed that she has Canada's best job. Her rise from volunteer to one of the most powerful managerial positions in the country began with the 1950s privileged-older-brother syndrome, the crucible for so many women of achievement.

Marj and Kay were daughters of C.W. Mulvagh, a dairy farmer whose Conservative politics were as vital to him as his thriving Carleton County operation southwest of Ottawa. Like so many other girls of that era, the sisters were expected to become nurses, teachers, secretaries, or, recalled

LeBreton, ''stay-at-homes.'' The idea of university education was as distant as farm labour was omnipresent. From childhood, both girls drove tractors and trucks, loaded hay, and twice a day helped to milk seventy-five cows. Afterwards they assisted their mother with the dishes and beds and every Saturday cleaned and baked, jobs their older brother never had to do.

One day Marjory's father brought home a big shiny green Ford cattle truck with *C.W. Mulvagh and Son, Registered Jerseys* painted on the side. Decades later, her eyes flashed with the anger she had felt that day. ''If he wouldn't put our names on that truck, [we] weren't doing the work.'' Flinging ultimatums in the face of parental decrees during the 1950s was hazardous stuff, but LeBreton convinced Stanley to go on strike with her. They infuriated their father; cows, hours late for milking, bellowed their way through two days of chaos. They do not recall their mother saying anything but feel that in a subliminal way, she may have planted the idea in their heads. Mrs. Mulvagh had worked in her own family's lumber company, which was handed down through the male line, and although she might have liked to continue working after marriage, she never had the choice. Mr. Mulvagh refused to change the sign on his truck and so to ease the cows' suffering, the girls returned to the barn. That incident was a turning point in Marjory's life. It moulded her sense of initiative and self-reliance, and she gained wisdom about patience and strategy. Never did she or Kay consider themselves victims.

LeBreton's future hinged on a few fateful events. After attending business school she worked as a secretary, and as a Young Progressive Conservative, she volunteered for the 1957 election. When she heard through a friend about a secretarial opening at Conservative headquarters, she dashed over in a wild March storm and was interviewed by Flora MacDonald, executive secretary of the party and one of the great backroom strategists of all time. MacDonald was building her own grassroots support and would become a minister in senior portfolios. Twenty years later LeBreton said of her future career, ''Flora was the key.''

When LeBreton heard of an opening in the PMO, she applied for, and got, the job. It was in a rather perverse way that Diefenbaker persuaded LeBreton to promote women into the broad spectrum of government. The wild-eyed, buck-toothed, wavy-haired Dief was a frustrated combination of Harold Pinter and Laurence Olivier. He manipulated his female staff members by summoning them all into his office as though he were gathering an audience for opening night. Then he would call LeBreton his Irish girl, or say that she reminded him of a Gibson Girl. Once, before all of them, he gave LeBreton one of the few remaining original copies of the Bill of Rights. The others burned with envy and made LeBreton's life hell. This pitting of women against each other as a ploy in sexual politics continued to be prevalent into the 1980s. The jobs of women secretaries in particular depended upon the men who hired them, and they had neither a human rights code for protection nor an individual sense of empowerment to stop such gambits. Diefenbaker's behaviour made an indelible impression on LeBreton, who vowed to do whatever she could for the women coming after her. Her appointments to the ABCs, and her advocacy of a co-operative, government and private-sector funded child-care program lend testimony to her will.[11]

But there were perks for women staff on the Hill. For women relegated almost exclusively to secretarial work, it provided a rare opportunity to participate in the excitement of running the country. Federal political power is omnipresent and seductive, and offices throughout the West and East Blocks of Parliament and the Langevin Building across the street are littered with photographs of female—and male—staff associated with the power that runs Canada. Some fawn over the paunchy bodies of MPs and prime ministers, their eyes burning with an adulation usually reserved for Mel Gibson or Sean Connery. Others just want to be where the action is and Liz Coburn, executive secretary to John Turner when he was Leader of the Official Opposition, recalled ruefully of her appointment in 1988, "I thought I had arrived." Short months later, with word of massive Liberal debt leaking out to the press, Turner's staff vacated the office like sailors leaping from a sinking ship.

While working with Robert Stanfield during the imposition of the War Measures Act in 1970, LeBreton broke out of the secretarial mould and entered executive roles. In 1976 she became party organizer and registrar for the convention at which Joe Clark was elected leader. In 1983 she acted as a convention co-ordinator, having already computerized the PC party in a move that left the Liberals out in the cold. In 1984 she supervised Mulroney's election campaign tour, and in 1988, as Mulroney's deputy chief of staff, she was appointed executive director of the Tory campaign. The atmosphere in the PMO differs vastly from the Diefenbaker days, and LeBreton finds Mulroney willing to listen to her views on any issue. It is possible that she comes as close to influencing the core of power as the most powerful cabinet ministers. Like an executive assistant to corporate CEOs, LeBreton has the access and the trust, and she is heard.

Entrusted with speech making all over the country, LeBreton functions as much as a political power as she does an office facilitator. She believes she has influenced policy through open discussions and debates in the weekly senior staff meetings with such heavies as Derek Burney, former chief of staff to Mulroney and currently ambassador to the United States. She has repeatedly voiced her opinions on both abortion and child care, explaining, "I owe it to myself and to the [grassroots] party not to be restricted." When Mr. Mulvagh refused to let his daughters' names be painted on his truck, he had no idea that his restrictions would foster the discipline, determination, and defiance that developed LeBreton into the power-broker she is today.

The Bureaucrats

> There are three official languages in Canada: French, English, and Acronym. In Ottawa, if you speak Acronym, it is not necessary to speak either of the other official languages. Bureaucrats speak Acronym when travelling on government business because they know that no one outside the capital and the NWT understands it. Acronym is the language of an elite society.
>
> THE TRAVELLER

Boston, 1987. Pierrette Lucas, then Canadian CG to Boston, hosted a luncheon attended by Margaret Catley-Carlson, then DM of CIDA, Stan Carlson—husband to C.C., and SS to the PC—and S.S. and B.P., gallery owners in Boston who knew all about "Explorations" at the CC. Save for the traveller, everyone there had their Master's in Acronym. While sipping Camparis the bureaucrats discussed CIDA's concern with SIDA, and described CIDA's multitentacled global connections through the NGOs, the IC, the BCB, and the BBC. They reminisced about days in Tanzania and Uganda, and sang the praises of the IBRD and the IMF in Acronym quintet, a lilting cadence reminiscent of the Russian Army Chorus. Over pasta it was the WERDP, the KTTC, the EEC, ECC, CUSO, and UNICEF. Figuring that she had cracked the code, the traveller joined in with commentaries on the IRC, the IDC, the IUD, and the IODE, later departing to Ottawa with the confidence to meet the mandarins, the real aristocracy in a city that remains, to most Canadians, an incomprehensible, faceless, inexorable force.

The public might think that cabinet ministers control their departments but they come and go according to the vagaries of the electorate and the PM, while the omniscient bureaucrats stay on to grow more knowledgeable, more irreplaceable, and more powerful. Senior mandarins are veterans in the arts of diplomacy and survival. They have experienced at least one change in government and several ministers, and they not only know each other, but like former CIDA chief Catley-Carlson, Deputy Minister of National Defense Bob Fowler, CSIS head Reid Morden, and John Weekes, ambassador to the GATT hearings, many have trained together as bureaucrats and enjoy the lifelong camaraderie of a private club. Catley-Carlson's original 1966 external affairs class once struggled to learn about this vast country. Now they are running it.[12]

Margaret Catley-Carlson

> Examiner: Who is the premier of Ontario?
>
> Catley-Carlson: I don't know, sir. I don't know the Ontario politicians, but I can tell you the names of the president of France, the

undersecretary of state in Washington, or the president of the Ivory Coast.

Examiner: Well, who is Leonard Cohen?

Catley-Carlson: I said, sir, that I don't know any Ontario politicians.

UBC, 1965

In her 1988 position of deputy minister of the Canadian Industrial Development Association (CIDA) with a budget of $2.6 billion, Catley-Carlson used the title of president and oversaw Canada's global responsibilities in the style of a corporate CEO.[13] Her computerized mind deftly links trillions of intricate governmental and private-sector systems. If knowledge is power, Catley-Carlson is indispensable to any ruling government, in particular to any new cabinet minister floundering through what Auditor General Kenneth Dye called the most complex department in Ottawa. During her presidency, Catley-Carlson executed CIDA's work through some 300 NGOs (non-governmental organizations), 80 degree-granting institutions, 1,500 exporters, 3,000 consultants, and endless Canadian producers and transporters in fisheries, forestry, and shipping. It was the task of the humorous, cool-thinking bureaucrat to keep CIDA stable, enabling it to operate over planning periods of up to seven years, through changes in government and policy. In 1989 she moved on to become deputy minister of health and welfare, responsible for 33 percent of Canada's total spending.

''Bureaucrat'' and Catley-Carlson seemed a contradiction in terms. Although she was locked in the proverbial tangle of red tape and multi-departmental systems of that sprawling institution, her view of developing countries was boldly entrepreneurial. Her sense of pragmatism and initiative emanated from twenty-five years of operating through External and living in the countries with which she dealt. Over the past two decades Catley-Carlson has not only watched the Third World evolve from helplessness into development, but she has guided government policy from nurturing do-goodism to fostering self-help. A philosophy manifested in the Business Co-operation Branch (BCB), restructured and streamlined by her in 1985 into a partnership between the private sector and CIDA. Aiming to help Canada's private sector play a full role in ripening world markets, BCB works with some 700 private companies to transfer Canadian technology to developing countries, and to build dams, roads, and hydro power systems, in addition to creating employment. To Catley-Carlson, the ''scariest'' statistic on Canada's future is our woeful position in the world game. We do only 8 percent of our business with 80 percent of the developing world's population, and she urged, ''We must form more sophisticated technological, institutional, and trade linkages with a Third World which is rapidly moving into a status of high consumerism.''

When with CIDA, Catley-Carlson trained her staff to help Third World women establish cottage industries. "Preaching human rights or doling out food will not stop the dreadful exploitation of women in Third World countries," she noted. "My image of a Third World woman is of a very tough lady. We just need to teach her process."[14] Her comments could be a manifesto for the welfare system in Canada. Her promotion from the international sphere into Canada's Health and Welfare Ministry initially seemed a waste of her world view and credo of individual initiative. In fact, Health and Welfare is the Canadian system most susceptible to the stagnation typical of Third World countries. The Deputy Minister's visions encompass the principles of entrepreneurship with programs to teach individuals how to grab hold and pull themselves out of financial slumps, how to shed the smothering blanket of dependency in favour of initiative, process, and empowerment.

In 1988, while still chief of CIDA, Catley-Carlson invited the traveller to her Gatineau Hills hideaway for cross-country skiing with old bureaucrat friends. Her home is a maze of wood and glass, and a gallery of treasures garnered during her years with External that trace the political and cultural history of Africa and its prime ministers. Acronym skill does not necessarily translate into skiing expertise, and the traveller raced smugly ahead of the pack while senior mandarins, including secret service chief Reid Morden, fell into drifts along the Gatineau trails. But the bureaucrats had the final word. That evening, with wind and snow gusting against the walls of glass, and in the candlelit intimacy of friends, these powerful mandarins huddled together and shared their state secrets—in Acronym. The traveller drank a lot of wine and understood why the bureaucrats run the country.

Jean Pigott

> Don't be bamboozled by the cookie jar. . . . She's Margaret Thatcher . . . hard-nosed, knows how to establish a power base and how to get money on the table.
>
> ANONYMOUS DEPUTY MINISTER[a]

The "political godmother nonpareil to women of all political stripes,"[b] Jean Pigott rose to speak at a 1989 fund-raising roast of Pat Carney, in Vancouver, on the occasion of her retirement from politics. On the subject of female invisibility, the white-haired Pigott told of the time she was standing at the Chateau Laurier intersection in Ottawa when an elderly gentleman turned to her and said, "Good morning, Madame Sauvé."

Pigott replied cheerfully, "Sorry, I'm not Madame Sauvé."

The light changed and they stepped from the curb. In mid-street the gentleman stopped and said, "A-ha! Good morning, Honourable Pat Carney!"

Pigott smiled again and replied, "I'm not Pat Carney."

At the other side the man said crossly, "Well, who in hell are you?"

She said, "My name is Jean Pigott, and once upon a time I was an *MP*."

The gentleman groused, "Ah, you old grey-haired broads all look alike."

After four careers, which she identified with equal pride as motherhood, volunteerism, business, and politics, Jean Pigott was given the ultimate patronage payoff—she chairs of the National Capital Commission, with $350 million in real estate, and power over the mansions of famous tenants.[15] "I've got the best job in Canada . . . guarding the soul of the country," she chuckled to writer Charlotte Gray.[c] Some would demur at Pigott's claiming Ottawa as the national soul, but in the hierarchy of chatelaines, she certainly has the power. Former governor-general Jeanne Sauvé, Cate Fraser, wife of the Speaker of the House, Mila Mulroney on Sussex Drive, and even the indomitable Geills Turner while at Stornoway, all had to take orders from Jean Pigott. The public attacked Sauvé for allegedly shutting them out of the Rideau Hall gardens with a $650,000 fence and then spending over $700,000 to give the kitchen a face lift. Quick to take the blame, Pigott said, "Sauvé got unfair press over that." The NCC chief wanted it understood that it was she, and not the GG (or the SH or the PM or the OLO), who ruled their official residences.

Furious at Pigott over closing the Rideau Hall grounds, Ottawans called her dictatorial, arrogant, and power hungry. She was delighted to report that, "The amount of steam and heat was incredible." She did it again by announcing that Ottawans would be charged parking fees in Gatineau Park and skating fees on the Rideau Canal. "Unfair!" howled the citizenry, and labelled the NCC "non-accountable." Pigott was described as "an iron-fisted decision-maker who cannot satisfy a thirst for power."[d] The NCC chief reacted like a bemused parent, retorting that Ottawa is not a playground merely for the residents, although they get to use it the most. Then she relented on the canal charge and hit them with just the parking fees, which was probably what she had intended to do all along. Pigott has also been described over the decades as funny, optimistic, folksy, "one who looks out for the little guy."[e] She is all of these things, but *matriarchal* may suit her best. As the eldest of two siblings, she has subscribed to the concept of primogeniture and has always ruled her family with the divine, if compassionate, right of a feifdom chief. She believes that she knows best on almost any subject, and, for all she has experienced, she probably does.

Pigott will tell you that she orchestrated her way into the male-dominated world of politics by making herself noticed and heard, but she also had a proven track record in business. While serving as an MP, Pigott, Flora MacDonald, and Grace McInnis of the NDP were the only women in the opposition. Since then, Pigott has cajoled and inspired women to get into politics and donated her unprecedented *surplus* campaign funds from 1980 to establish a Women's Bureau in the PC party as well as caucuses across the country. The advent of so many younger women in the Conservative Party is largely the result of Pigott's initiative, and many new MPs stay at her home until they get their bearings.

Following the short-lived Clark government, Pigott ran and lost in 1980, the last Trudeau triumph. She loved the battle and was annoyed at being pushed out of the fun. She worked for John Crosbie's 1983 leadership campaign, which dismayed Joe Clark but delighted Brian Mulroney. Impressed by her prodigious organizational skills, Mulroney appointed Pigott to his transition team when he won the party's leadership.

Give Pigott a tough project and she plunges in with the gusto of a Stormin' Norman. With the sixteen-person NCC uninhibited by elected members, her power over Ottawa is far greater than that of the mayor. A master planner who plots her course with graphs by the week and up to ten years in advance, Pigott organized a long-term plan to restore city parks and boulevards, and the official residences, which had fallen into scandalous disrepair. When Geills Turner moved into Stornoway after the Clarks, she found a two-by-four propping up the ceiling in the middle of the den.

Although some checks and balances were eventually introduced into the NCC management structure, Pigott reigned. The Prime Minister got a "bum rap," she said of all the accusations about redecorating the NCC houses, but the scandals inspired changes. If the Speaker wanted a waterbed in place of a four-poster in his bedroom, she would take him to the government warehouse to rummage around for one. "But," grinned the former baker with a smack of her hands as if whomping the dough into shape, "we ain't agonna buy you one. And those are the new rules."

Pigott's unprecedented, three-term tenure will end in December 1991, but her NCC legacy is the awesome fifty-year, multi-billion-dollar facelift for Ottawa and its "shrines — like the White House." Her ardour is understood in the city more prone to navel-gazing than any other in Canada. Entering Ottawa for the first time is like crashing a giant family business with a sophisticated, interrelated hierarchy in which everyone has the same employer, knows everything about the others, and speaks an incomprehensible language. Pigott's greatest bequest, however, is her enthusiasm in showing other women how to get involved in the political process.

Barbara Joan Reed

Chair of the Competition Tribunal and judge in the trial division of the Federal Court of Canada, Reed's powers are sweeping. Her mandate is to determine that corporate mergers and acquisitions are in accord with Canada's competition law. She had the power to put a temporary halt to the $5-billion takeover of Texaco Canada by Imperial Oil. Writer/lawyer Harvey Enchin described Reed as bright, fearless, bad-tempered, opinionated, and humorous. He added, "Her opinions helped shape the Canadian constitution. Her rulings as a Federal Court judge led to the world's first trial decision giving copyright protection to computer software. And her judgements may provide the impetus for a national policy on telecommunications."[f]

The Economists

In 1988 when Bernard Ostry, head of TVOntario, accepted an invitation to speak at the Vancouver Canadian Club, club members all received the usual brochure with a bio on the distinguished visitor. At the luncheon itself, the hapless individual assigned to introduce the guest speaker rose and read from the brochure of Ostry's distinguished career. Western guests were suitably impressed to hear that he was ambassador for multilateral trade negotiations and personal representative of the prime minister for the 1988 economic summit. Then Bernard approached the microphone, thanked the speaker for his flattering introduction, and wondered who they thought was coming to address the club. "The person who is described in your brochure," he explained, "is not I. You have just read a biography of my wife, Sylvia."

Economists are advisers, social scientists who seek an understanding of how society works, specifically in the areas of production and consumption. In any set of objectives that requires a country to make trade-offs in the percentage mix of market forces, social services, and welfare, decisions must be made about balanced growth, high employment, low inflation, and other vital aspects of a healthy capitalist economy. The economists' power lies not only in giving advice, but also in having it followed. It imbues them with a certain elitism, and a certain internal rivalry: with the exception of Judith Maxwell and Sylvia Ostry, other women economists receive mixed reviews from their colleagues. One will applaud a particular economist as having street sense, while another will complain that she is incomprehensible.

Because the system is in operation, there is no way to discern what the government would have done in the absence of the research, opinion, and general input provided by the economists. It is almost impossible to pin down individual power among them. In the broadest terms, they all have some impact as they submit different views that will provide a healthy range of policy objectives from which to choose a direction. By way of example, Jalynn Bennett described a publication of the ECC on restructuring the taxation of capital gains and income that inspired five published dissents from individual council members. "Hopefully," said Bennett, "reports are written in such a way that most people can follow what the issues are, and you can see very clearly what the pressure points are on government when they have to come and make a choice." In structuring the policy, of course, the final decision rests with the government.[16]

The economists seem to be pivotal to public policy, but determining what, exactly, they do is difficult. They dash with the speed of "hot money" between the corporate sector and the inner sanctums of the ministry of finance, the Business Council on National Issues, the Economic Council of Canada, and the institutes—C.D. Howe, Hudson, and Fraser. Elizabeth Parr Johnston,[17] Judith Maxwell, and Wendy Dobson come and go between the private and public sectors. When C.D. Howe head Judith Maxwell left to become chair of the ECC and became, in the opinion of board member Dian Cohen, the first chair in over a decade to make that board relevant, she met incoming C.D. Howe president Wendy Dobson, a former nurse who has her PhD in finance, had served with CUSO in India, and who would subsequently move into the department of finance as Michael Wilson's deputy and aide for the Group of Seven club of nations.

Dobson intends to remain in the field of international economics and trade but has accepted a nomination of visiting fellow at the Institute for International Economics in Washington, D.C.[18] Both Sylvia Ostry and Dobson are fellows at the University of Toronto, Ostry as the chair of the Centre for International Studies, and Dobson in the Faculty of Management. The economist with the highest public profile is Dian Cohen who, in her morning report on "Canada AM," informs and influences an audience far wider than she could reach through her own consulting firm, Dian Cohen Productions, or her positions on numerous corporate boards.[19] In general, the economists belong in the sophisticated networks that link the corporate, bureaucratic, and academic worlds.

Marie-Josée Drouin of Montreal combines business acumen with lofty connections in international society fostered partly through her own expertise and partly through her husband, the wildly popular Charles Dutoît, conductor of the Montreal Symphony. Montreal is more of a pied-à-terre, their real home is a Swiss hideaway in a mountain village. Executive director of the Hudson Institute and reporter on the economy for the *Financial Post*, Drouin was described by former Power Corp. vice-chair Peter Curry as an economist with street sense. On the other hand, a professor of economics will not even accord Drouin the title of economist. Her long list of directorships includes the boards of Canadian Imperial Bank of Commerce, Seagram, and Standard Life.

Although the ECC acts collectively, Maxwell plays a pivotal role in the chair. "She is highly respected," said UBC economist John Helliwell: "She had enormous integrity as a journalist because she gave balanced treatment." Maxwell is known to influence colleagues with persuasive but nonabrasive arguments. She has also built a team with a significant number of women, not there by coincidence, said Helliwell, but thoughtfully chosen. Under her the organization runs effectively and she achieves results.

The most memorable female players in the government economist game are Phyllis Turner Ross and Sylvia Ostry. Phyllis Ross, née Gregory received degrees in economics[20] in the 1920s, was widowed, and in 1934 became chief economist with the Dominion Tariff and Industry Commission, often writing reports for the Minister of Finance. A strikingly handsome woman, she soon became an international negotiator, and a tour de force of the capital's professional and social milieu. In 1941 she was appointed to the Wartime Prices & Trade Board, making her the most senior woman in the public service. Her son, John Turner, remembers her days as sixteen-hour marathons of meetings, speeches, negotiations, and homemaking. The Montreal *Standard* once raved of her, "She can preside at a meeting of the biggest manufacturers of . . . competitive industries, secure the co-operation of all, [and] resolve their conflicting interests."[g] Later, as the chatelaine of British Columbia's Government House, she delivered such polished speeches that many saw her second husband, Frank Ross, who had the lieutenant-governor's title (and the money), as consort to his wife.[21] In 1967 the National Council of Jewish Woman presented Phyllis Ross and Thérèse Casgrain with Woman of the Century awards for their commitment to the Canadian public. In a tragic twist, Ross became a victim of Alzheimer's Disease, and when wheeled before a television to watch John Turner become prime minister, Ross did not recognize the son whom she had ostensibly groomed for the job.

Despite Ross's academic papers on fair pay and working conditions for women in the late 1920s, the Ottawa politicians and bureaucrats were not threatened by hints of feminism. Men listened to her professional advice, and she operated with the confidence of an education in economics and an understanding of how to play the game on the Hill. Whatever she may have thought, Ross the professional economist portrayed the image of the steel-spined woman of propriety, highlighted by the Establishment precepts of feminine deportment and inscrutability, all survival tactics that she employed with the subtlety of an undercover agent.

Sylvia Ostry played a similar game but in the 1960s was far more outspoken in her field of expertise. Before going to Ottawa, she was already known as a specialist in labour economics. In 1991 Donald Munton, president of the Canadian Institute for International Affairs, described Ostry at a Vancouver Board of Trade luncheon as an economist who delivered "incisive, unvarnished, hard hitting briefings." During the Trudeau era, the diminutive woman with the authoritative voice, dry wit, and a shoot-from-the-hip style kept the capital hopping, first with hard facts as chief statistician, then later with fiscal forecasts and, on the side, with the most interesting parties in town. Social power. Everyone wanted to go to Ostry's soirées. That's where the fun was, and the information. She was a senior mandarin who fostered harmony among the politicians, bureaucrats, the Establishment, academics, and ambassadors, and she did it with style. Power for Ostry the bureaucrat was achieved by sidestepping party politics to move about Ottawa as a free agent. Many Ottawans mourn the fading of the capital's dynamism after the noble priestess of the social and intellectual communities departed. Helliwell admires Ostry not only for her intelligence, but also for her skill for developing ideas and then, with "extraordinary toughness, pushing through inside and outside negotiations to get results." Ostry is not just a theorist; she is a deal maker, known to be a telephone junkie adept at networking with men and women. She knows who the international operators are, or, as Helliwell put it, "Sylvia knows who to talk to. She operates in a male way in a male world."

Until 1989, Ostry was ambassador for multilateral trade negotiations and personal representative of the prime minister for the economic summit. Of her standing, Carleton University economics professor Christopher Maule observed that she was one of the few mandarins who could write and deliver her own speeches on the international stage without first being required to pass them through the PMO—but that is also what got her into trouble on the last day of the 1988 economic summit in Toronto. Following a gruelling night of drafting the final summit communiqué on free trade with representatives from the European nations, Ostry handed it in for a press release due the next afternoon, delivered a copy to Derek Burney, the Prime Minister's chief of staff, then at 5 a.m., headed for her hotel and the bathtub.

According to *Toronto Star* national affairs columnist Carol Goar, everything was fine until about 7 a.m. when Burney got to the first sentence of paragraph 15. It said, "We welcome the free trade agreement between Canada and the United States." In diplomatic language, that was a watered-down version of what the PMO wanted. Burney hit the roof, summoned Ostry out of her bath and raged at her in front of some twenty senior officials. The communiqué had already been leaked to the European press and was picked up by Canadian reporters, but the Prime Minister pooh-poohed it as just pieces of paper floating around. By 3:45 p.m., the word "strongly"—"We strongly welcome the free trade agreement. . . . "—had been accepted and officially released. Goar wrote that Mulroney aides whispered about Ostry's arrogant temperament, and officials from the finance and external affairs department countered that those aides were running damage control for the PM who is known to hate bad press.[h]

A few months later, Ostry accepted the prestigious five-year post at the University of Toronto, financed by a $2.9-million grant from the Ontario government for strategic research on international economic issues. The mandate provides for the inclusion of multinational corporations and even foreign governments in the analysis of global economic issues.[22] As CTV's Pamela Wallin put it, "She was in a bit of trouble but that's not going to stop Sylvia. She [is still] a very, very powerful person."

In 1989, international respect for Ostry's expertise was emphasized when she was invited to be the western co-chair of the Hungarian-International Blue Ribbon Commission, designed to advise Hungary's return to a market economy. She remains co-chair as the commission heads into Phase Two.

In January of 1989, Pamela Wallin attended a private dinner at Rideau Hall given by the Right Honourable Jeanne Sauvé for her old friend Sylvia Ostry. Guests included the American and Japanese ambassadors, Barbara and Murray Frum, Max Yalden, Stanley Hartt,[23] Michael Wilson — mostly former colleagues of Ostry. Wallin said, "If I've ever stood in awe [it was there], because it is women like that who had this town by the balls."

CHAPTER 8 NOTES

1. Lynda Sorensen is a key player in training northern women in the bureaucratic process, in policy implementation, and in political campaigning. She was the power behind the federal campaign of Ethel Blondin.
2. Cournoyea played a crucial part in winning the Inuvialuit land claim in the Western Arctic, worth $240 million to her people. By getting lands classified as 7A included, those with the highest oil and gas potential in the North, Cournoyea ensured that the land claim could realize billions in the event of a pipeline. At a time when the NWT government is taking control of its own portfolios from the federal government, Cournoyea is an MLA and, as of March 1991, was minister of health, minister of energy, mines and petroleum resources, minister of public works, and the minister responsible for NWT power corporation.
3. Maureen Sabia has served as general counsel to Redpath Industries, solicitor to Canadian Pacific, assistant counsel to the Ontario Law Reform Commission, and solicitor to the Ontario Securities Commission. She sits on the boards of Canadian Tire, Laurentian General Insurance, and the University of Guelph, as well as chairing the Women in Management Research Project at the University of Western Ontario's School of Business Administration.
4. Women lieutenant-governors have included Sylvia Fedoruk in Saskatchewan; Pearl McGonigal in Manitoba; Marion Reid in Prince Edward Island; Pauline McGibbon in Ontario; Helen Hunley in Alberta.
5. Johnson was reportedly heading for the Senate four years ago, but her father was made lieutenant-governor of Manitoba and one reward per family was deemed enough. Janis would have to wait. In 1990, when eight emergency appointments to the Senate were sanctioned by the Queen to even the odds in a House dominated by Liberals, Janis became Senator Johnson.
6. Richards has organized campaigns for Senator Pat Carney and Justice Minister Kim Campbell. She was also on Vancouver Mayor Gordon Campbell's election team.
7. Following her 1990 bid for the Liberal party leadership, Sheila Copps was over $40,000 in debt.

8. Pepino was the first woman police commissioner on the Metro Toronto Police Commission, and sat on the Ontario Human Rights Commission in 1980-82, where she insisted that protection from sexual harassment be included in the provincial code. At the federal level she was special adviser to Brian Mulroney on women's issues, and has been an executive member since 1986 of the Advisory Council on the Status of Women. Many issues such as pornography, immigration, and child-care policies overlap in these agencies.
9. Inspired by Jean Casselman Wadds, former Canadian high commissioner to Great Britain, Band entered politics in the early 1970s, then set up the ultra-right-wing National Citizens' Coalition office in Toronto. Following a job as special assistant to the tough MP Margaret Scrivener, Band headed the 1979 and 1980 federal Conservative campaigns for the twenty-three ridings in Metro Toronto. One of the best connected women in Canada and England, Band's "Sarahband" is one of the best known gift shops in Toronto's upscale Yorkville.
10. In 1984 there were 307 women serving on federal ABCs. That number has increased to over 880 and includes women on the bench, in the foreign service, and women who head such government institutions as the Economic Council of Canada, the Science Council of Canada, and the National Gallery of Canada.
11. It was not until Jeanne Sauvé as Speaker of the House established a centre on the Hill that civil servants had day care. LeBreton recalled her distress at leaving her children in the care of women hired, sometimes hastily, from newspaper advertisements.
12. All the other women in Catley-Carlson's class have quit the government.
13. CIDA uses corporate terms to spare the ministers and heads of government of small countries from, as Catley-Carlson put it, "conversing with the incomprehensible titles in Ottawa," such as associate undersecretary.
14. In Africa where 80 percent of the manual labour on farms is done by the women (who could never get bank loans even to buy fertilizer for their farms), millions of aid dollars were poured into training the men. Then in March 1988, the Minister for External Relations Monique Landry announced a $3-million credit for African women.

15. Pigott's budget of $82 million (1989-90), includes the running of 48,000 hectares of green space (spring landscaping includes over 450,000 tulips), all of the federal government buildings, parks, residences, trails, the Rideau canal, and overseeing 1,000 employees.
16. In 1991 women serving on the ECC are Judith Maxwell, Caroline Pestieau (deputy chair and director), Judi Korbin, Nancy Jackman, Mary Mogford of Mogford Campbell Associates, and Dian Cohen of Dian Cohen Productions.
17. Formerly an economist who taught at UBC, and then in Ottawa who worked with Judith Maxwell and Wendy Dobson, Elizabeth Parr-Johnston joined the private sector with Shell Canada first as a vice-president in strategic planning and information systems, then in the marketing of oil products. In 1991 she left to become the president of Mount Saint Vincent University.
18. Dobson has also been appointed to the boards of DuPont Canada, IBM, and the Toronto-Dominion Bank.
19. Cohen lists ten boards on which she sits, plus her own company, and she is a governor of the Canadian Institute of Chartered Accountants.
20. Phyllis Gregory Turner Ross became a fellow in the department of economics at Bryn Mawr, then won two more fellowships, and attended the London School of Economics.
21. In a 1957 midnight fire, the original sprawling mansion on Rockland Avenue in Victoria burned to the ground, leaving the Rosses and the staff standing in their nightgowns on the driveway. They lost virtually everything, including personal papers. John Turner remembered that Premier "Wacky Bennett was so impressed with my mother . . . he came over and just said, 'Mrs. Ross, here's $2 million, fix it up.'"
22. Ostry was also appointed chair of the Council of Canadian Institute of International Affairs. She is also a visiting fellow at the Council on Foreign Relations in New York, and, along with Allan Gotlieb, she has been appointed to the International Advisory Council of the Bank of Montreal.
23. At that time, Max Yalden, former External Affairs senior mandarin, was chief commissioner of the Canadian Human Rights Commission; Stanley Hartt was Mulroney's principal secretary.

CHAPTER NINE

The Mayors

Interviewer: Why did you run?

Cynthia Hill: They shot my dog.

Inuvik, NWT

Elsie Wayne: The council was corrupt. I got flooded out from lousy town planning.

Saint John, New Brunswick

Pat McMahon: Council wanted to build an apartment building on our ball field.

Yellowknife, NWT

Marion Dewar: In public health nursing in the schools I saw the kids experimenting with drugs, sex, the adults blocking it out—'none of that exists.'

Ottawa, Ontario

May Cutler: My building was zoned for seventeen 'professions' from engineers to chiropractors, but no book publishers were allowed. I couldn't move in.

Westmount, Quebec

All mayors will tell you *they* have the best job in Canada, although few grew up yearning for it the way one aspires to becoming a doctor, a teacher, or a lawyer. Something negative usually happened to fire them into action. Independent thinkers known to speak up in outrageous ways, mayors have little fear of antagonizing their respective parties or being banished to the back bench. They are prime ministers of their mini-dominions, hands-on politicians who can make appreciable differences in the immediacy of what counts most—our families and communities. The mayors are an essential force in making this country work. St. John's Mayor Shannie Duff, a successful entrepreneur with an up-market furniture store, does not lead a life defined by jet lag and the PM's decree: she gets to go home every night — late — but home. The changes she initiates are directly visible to her constituents. Rather than operate in the loneliness of the House of Commons, Duff enjoys the proximity of friends and supporters, even if the corollary is immediate contact with her detractors.

Mayors are vivid raconteurs, specializing in their respective cities with the thoroughness of a historian describing life in a seventeenth-century village. Ask them about comparative mill rates over the last century, the weather during civic festivities on July 1, 1953, the percentage of seven-year-olds in the inner city, and they spew out the information like a computer running amok. Ask the same questions about their neighbouring jurisdictions, and they are struck dumb by the non sequitur. Mayors from Whitehorse to Charlottetown want you to understand that theirs is the only terrific city in Canada, and they have the statistics to prove it.

Hundreds of other women who serve across the country as councillors, formerly known as aldermen, are able to politic by day and return home at night. Former Vancouver councillor Carole Taylor was a national CTV host of "Canada AM" and "W5" for years, best known for her on-the-spot coverage of the Yom Kippur War and Allende's Chilean revolution. Married to former Vancouver mayor Art Phillips, and the mother of two children, she served two terms, having first lost her party nomination, then topping the polls as an Independent.[1]

May Cutler

> The city had treated its citizens like high strung neurotics too long. Westmount needed shaking up.
>
> MAY CUTLER[a]

"You live in a community. You make it work," explained the mayor of the tiny, perfect city that perches above Montreal. May Cutler is the feisty chief executive of Westmount, one of Canada's wealthiest, most educated, most sophisticated, enclaves with two-thirds of its 20,000 citizens representing the country's oldest and tightest clique of WASP society. Originally from the French-speaking east end of Montreal, Cutler shocked most residents when she ran against Westmount Mayor Brian Gallery, Mulroney pal and former chair of CN. It was not only that Cutler was a woman; it was that she was *not one of them*. Historically, the Westmount Municipal Association operated the city as a private club and elected its mayors from within its own ranks by acclamation. No outsiders had ever challenged them, but Cutler believed Westmount was going downhill, and a new species of Westmounter agreed with her. They were the francophones, allophones, and the anglophone academics from McGill University who moved in when a real estate recession followed the FLQ crisis in the early 1970s.

Cutler is the owner of Tundra Books, a successful international publishing house that produces elaborately illustrated, bilingual stories for children. She does not even know the old guard, is said to have received huge support from women voters, and is somewhat contemptuous of the "self-congratulatory closed-shop gentlemen's club" of the Westmount Municipal Association.[b] Egged on by friends to give it to the old boys, Cutler adopted the slogan "May for September" and swept the polls. A senior herself, she said the former civic government treated its magnificent mini-city as an old person might a home in which he/she had lived for eons without noticing the worn furniture, torn wallpaper, or peeling paint. "When you say no [to new ideas]," she bristled, "you don't have to do anything."[c] Cutler briskly began shaking up council whose meetings, she claimed, used to take five minutes. She sparkled with the pyrotechnical brilliance of a high-voltage wire coming down on Dorchester Boulevard. In fact, when Montreal proposed renaming Dorchester "Boulevard René Lévesque," Cutler was incensed along with Anglophone Westmount, and won the fight to keep the road's historic name where it crosses into Westmount. A voluble opponent of nationalism, she is infuriated by its excessess: "I despise nationalism!" she snapped. "Quebec nationalism. Canadian nationalism. Toronto nationalism. It's all the same. Jingoism. Ugly."

Mayor Cutler is one who never felt circumscribed by neighbourhood, parental expectations, or career limitations. As the daughter of an Irish policeman in the 1920s, she saw enough ghettoizing to last her a lifetime, and she deplores the fact that she could continue her education while French kids had to leave school after Grade 9 unless they were from rich families or were going into the church. It annoyed her that francophone children were also not allowed to speak English, so that the breadth of their universe shrank even further. Following graduation from McGill in the early 1940s, Cutler headed for the Columbia University School of Journalism, each step a defiance of her strict traditional upbringing. She studied by day and worked by night, then returned from the United States after marrying a Montrealer. What she retained was that sense of self-determination and entrepreneurship so prevalent in the American character.

Cutler's first manuscript from Anne Blades was refused a Canada Council grant so she raised the money herself to launch Blades on what became an illustrious international career. It had never occurred to Cutler to depend upon local markets. It is her world view that separates her from the Westmount old guard and makes her so refreshing for that city.[2] Referring to the free trade issue in 1988, Cutler told Matthew Fraser of the *Globe*,[d] ''Canadians should grow up. No one is going to take away *my* cultural identity. This country is full of cowards and sycophants. . . . Americans are horse-traders and we've got to be horse-traders too.''

Elsie Wayne

I believe in honest government. I took council to court.

ELSIE WAYNE, ST. JOHN

Fearless Elsie has also taken the powerful Irving family to court to expropriate land to build flood gates. The city needed it: the Irvings wouldn't sell. The lives of New Brunswickers living at the confluence of the St. John River and the Bay of Fundy are ruled by monster thirty-foot tides. The phenomenon of the flood tide racing toward the downflowing river creates a reverse waterfall drawing tourists from afar. In times of extreme tides and strong winds, it also caused extensive flooding to nearby residences, including Wayne's. In the absence of town planners or building controls, development had gone unchecked, and homes were built and sold on flood plains. Council, charged Wayne, ''was being run as a little clique,'' and she was one of the victims. She organized the Greater Glenn Falls Flood Committee and for three years used her own money to travel between Fredericton and Ottawa, negotiating with environment ministers Jeanne Sauvé and Romeo LeBlanc and winning $2.2 million for a flood reduction program. The Irving land battle marks the only battle from which she eventually backed down and found other solutions, one of which was to get involved in municipal government.

Possibly the best known woman mayor in Canada, Elsie Wayne is the consummate promoter who can talk non-stop without breathing. Print and television media love her, and her white hair, gap-toothed smile, and saucer-sized glasses make her a cartoonist's dream. Wayne is so approachable. Walk down the street with her and people holler ''Hey Els!'' Yet the mayor assumes the stance of an athlete on guard, of a girl who had to establish space among five brothers. Elsie Wayne is fun to be with, but she will not be pushed around.

When first elected to council, Wayne was shocked by what she called ''terrible corruption.'' She said that for fifty years, St. John City Hall, like Westmount, had been run as a private club. The aldermen were so resentful of having a woman on council that they required Wayne to support all her positions with written documentation even though they themselves made unsupported oral presentations and then voted upon them. Worse, Wayne quickly realized that their decisions were often made before the vote.

As mayor, she hired professional talent from across the country to help balance the city's books, then embarked on a civic promotion with the enthusiasm of Klondike Kate. She founded Sur Mer, a festival by the sea, and insists it brings in the largest bus tours in Canada. Like so many other successful women, Wayne has no time for women's movements. "Just get out and do the job. Prove yourself and men will accept you." When reporters need information, they call Wayne. She always makes them laugh, gets herself lots of press, and usually makes her point. She is Peter Gzowski's Maritime link on "Morningside"; when Brian Mulroney gave Dalton Camp a job in the PMO and the next day gave Nova Scotia $250 million for oil exploration, Wayne quipped to the press, "Well, how do you think I feel? Nova Scotia gets $250 million and we get one job for Dalton Camp."[3]

Pat McMahon

> In the 1960s I remember a number of women who moved up here from Ottawa who left in straight jackets. They couldn't hack 'the isolation.' Isolation is something you do to yourself.
>
> Women have effected the greatest changes in the North. Mind you, I'm not a feminist.
>
> PAT McMAHON

"To put it bluntly, he was a real jerk," recalled Pat McMahon of her second boss in Toronto. Royal Trust consultant Llewyle Staples had run through approximately seventeen secretaries and executive assistants in less than three years. As an accountant in another department, McMahon had spent eight hours tracking down a mistake made by Staples. Finding and correcting it, she then stormed past his secretary into his office and demanded of the nonplussed consultant that he check his work before he took up eight more hours of her time. Then she turned around and marched back to her office. He ran after her and hired her. They fought constantly and she stayed for two years.

"If somebody gets in your way," McMahon's mother used to say, "try going around them, and if you can't go around them, go through them." Born in northern Ontario, McMahon grew up speaking Inuktitut and Cree as well as English, and her mother always told her that with hard work she could do anything she wanted. In her first real job at the age of eighteen, McMahon was trained by her boss to take over when he left. The day he did leave, she requested his post but was told, "Women can't go into management in this company." She quit, but on her way out she stopped at the coffee rooms on every floor and, like

Norma Rae galvanizing the factory workers, told the secretaries what had happened and challenged them: "Get your act together or you'll be stuck as typists for the rest of your lives. *Do* something." Shortly afterward, they went on a one-day strike, and the company changed its policy.

Within two years, McMahon had married an aircraft engineer and returned to Yellowknife where they built a house and had children. Four years later, she was doing volunteer work with the Daughters of the Midnight Sun and was president of the Yellowknife Rate Payers Association. She ran for city council and lost twice. On the third try she won and served on almost every committee. In 1984 she ran for a seat in the territorial government and lost. In 1988 she made it to mayor. Her message is: don't quit. In fact, her greatest thrills are teaching women how to participate in government, and watching change in northern attitudes. In 1983 McMahon organized the Northern Women's Coalition Conference with the future MLA Eliza Lawrence, and Cece McCauley, a Métis chief of the Inuvik Dene Band, journalist, and entrepreneur. With help from the Secretary of State and the territorial government, they brought together native and white women from numerous towns and hamlets scattered about the North to discuss ways and means of organizing and empowering communities. The women were accustomed to isolation and found being together for the first time electrifying. McMahon continually drew a parallel between "domestic engineering" — running a home — and running the government. She admits she nags women to get into politics with the argument, "You are so disenfranchised now, you have nothing to lose." Then she teaches them how.

McMahon's vision for the North includes using party affiliations to increase accountability and abolish the current division by territory. She would eventually like to see provincial status for the NWT, but believes Northerners must first learn to manage an expanse of land equal to one-third of Canada with a thinly scattered population of 79,000.

Paradoxically, the children of families like the McMahon's are among the best connected in Canada. All winter long they hold bottle drives and bake sales to finance trips to Ottawa and points east and west. She figures that such trips, combined with her international contacts made with people who come north, make her kids about as knowledgeable as any in the South. "We're a close-knit community that literally has global ties." That's as good a reason as any for seeking power in the mayor's chair.

CHAPTER 9 NOTES

1. In 1991 Taylor resigned from City Council and became a columnist for the Vancouver-*Sun*.
2. Culter's books, *New Ideas,* are based on her own philosophy, and she intends to write *Rising Senior Power,* a manifesto for octogenarian activism.
3. In November 1990, Wayne was appointed to the Spicer Commission on National Unity.

CHAPTER TEN

The Parties

THE LIBERALS

In August 1989, Their Highnesses the Prince and Princess of Wales were hosts to a luncheon at Highgrove, their Georgian summer residence, for two hundred North American social cyclones and business tycoons who had anted up a total of $3 million to spend a weekend with Their Royal Highnesses in aid of the United World Colleges. Twenty impeccably laid tables were sprinkled about a striped marquee in the royal gardens. Sometime after the hors d'oeuvres an American business potentate turned to regard the stately looking woman with the halo of white hair sitting beside him, nudged her, and asked, "So, honey, what's your name?"

"Sauvé. Jeanne Sauvé," came the reply, richly accented with the French nuance.

"*Jan*. What kind of a name is that? Spell it." She complied.

"That's *Jeen-ee!*" he boomed triumphantly. "So—what do you do?"

A Toronto guest leaned over to whisper, "Her Excellency, Madame Sauvé, is our governor-general—the Queen's representative in Canada."

"The Queen's rep?" The American raised an eyebrow and said, "Your husband must be an important guy. What does he do to get you this job?" Maurice Sauvé grinned delightedly from the far end of the table.

Her Excellency's eyes smouldered. Forgetting she sat in the presence of royalty, the carpenter's daughter pounded on the table with each word, enunciating with all the resonance of a former broadcaster and the authority of a former cabinet minister and Speaker of the House of Commons: "I. GOT. THIS. JOB. MY. SELF!!"

" OK-OK, honey," the American soothed. "Don't get yourself all riled up!"

Get the job she did. It is one of the hazards of history that Sauvé will be best remembered for what happened most recently — closing the grounds of Rideau Hall to the public, which Jean Pigott did. In fact, Sauvé had wanted to move into the little house on the property and use Rideau Hall only for official purposes but Pigott said no. But Sauvé's history long antedates her time in Rideau Hall and these teapot tempests. Jeanne Sauvé has done it all: minister of three portfolios, Speaker of the House of Commons, a university degree earned later than most women of that era, opting out at the age of thirty-seven to stay home for a few years to care for her child, and even playing her part in the Quiet Revolution—first as a youth speaker and later as a broadcaster. In her own estimation, she belonged in Rideau Hall, claiming her power like a well-earned prize. The confidence, conviction, and dignity with which she welcomes power reflects a century of Francophone women in Quebec who conceived a vision of freedom and went for it.

Born in 1922 in Prud'homme, Saskatchewan, and raised in Ottawa, Sauvé sought a platform in Montreal in the 1940's shortly after Quebec women had won the right to vote. Her father, Charles Benoit, may have been the source of her phenomenal drive. At first he encouraged his daughter's intellectual curiosity as well as her performing skills, but when Sauvé won a university scholarship, he not only forbade her to accept it, but he would not allow her to earn the entrance fees. When she was first offered a job in Washington with the Canadian Information Office, Benoit forbade her to go. He was unwittingly preparing Sauvé for a public life, while expecting her to take her place in the home.

Sauvé continued to push and finally, when she was twenty, her father permitted her to accept the job of "propagandiste" offered by the Montreal chapter of the Jeunesse étudiant catholique, the popular Roman Catholic youth group associated with Action catholique canadienne, which was bent on spiritual revival and social change. Within a year of joining the centrale, Sauvé's ability to inspire others had made her a principal recruiting speaker. Her original motivation in joining may have been religious, but travelling caused her to shift her political thinking from nationalism to federalism and the JEC gave her a platform from which to promote this philosophy. Somehow in the repressive atmosphere of Quebec, the bright young minds of the JEC managed to include the dogma of the parent church while preaching "Look, Judge, Act," helping to politicize a generation glimpsing wider horizons. Political affiliations were proliferating in Quebec and the cross pollination brought Sauvé into proximity with such friends and future colleagues as Jean Marchand, Maurice Sauvé, Alexandrine Leduc who would marry another member, Gérard Pelletier, a friend and colleague of Pierre Trudeau, who co-founded the periodical *Cité libre*. As the friendships and careers of the men crystallized into political power, Sauvé as a broadcaster parlayed her considerable skills and rising profile to accompany them.[1]

In 1952, Sauvé began broadcasting on CBC radio on "Opinions," a program directed toward youth in the decade leading into the Quiet Revolution. Dorothy Zolf, then a young Edmonton homemaker caring for small children, recalled of Sauvé's broadcasts that were so filled with good humour, "she understood." In two words, Zolf, who years later earned her PhD in communications, encompassed the power of Sauvé — her ability to empathize equally with the frustrations and dreams of women who either chose to stay home or who sought to build careers.

Back in the 1930s, Thérèse Casgrain had broadcasted on "Femina" trying to inspire change, but the time wasn't right, and she never accessed the power of Sauvé. Older by a generation, Casgrain became the leader of the Quebec CCF/NDP party, founded the Quebec branch of the Voice of Women for peace and disarmament, and called for women's equality. A trailblazer who had set the stage for Sauvé's career, she had faced crushing adversaries in Premiers Taschereau and Duplessis, as well as in the church, a traditional society, and a Liberal party reluctant to support women politicians. Casgrain had created a voice for women but, like a Jiminy Cricket struggling to influence a national conscience, she could be heard and then ignored. It would be Jeanne Sauvé and her friends, the "three wise men," Pierre Trudeau, Jean Marchand, and Gérard Pelletier, who had left-wing sympathies with Thérèse Casgrain, but who would take the decisive step of joining the federal Liberals to access a traditional route to power. Political savvy and personal skills aside, Sauvé happened to be in the right place, at the right time, with the right people and she offered a more attractive message, emphasizing positive change rather than calling for women's rights.

When Trudeau became leader and prime minister to an adoring country, the golden age of the Liberal Party dawned anew. Sauvé was at home raising a son, but by 1972 she was ready to enter the political fray. Maurice Sauvé had lost his seat in 1968, fallen out of favour with the Liberal machine, and gone into business; he supported Jeanne Sauvé's nomination for a federal seat, which she won. Trudeau immediately appointed her to cabinet where she proved to be remarkably adept at assimilating complex issues. Astute and confident, what Sauvé didn't know, she made up as she went along or learned on the job.

Sauvé's personality is reminiscent of another winner and friend, Margaret Thatcher. Sauvé's power may be rooted in her skills but that sense of empowerment is ultimately conveyed through deportment. She has packaged her political aspirations, her tough-minded intentions, and her activist views in an acceptable, attractive style. In the early 1950s she was inspiring Quebeckers to form unions and she understood how to deal in the rough and tumble of politics, yet she was never called feminist or accused of stridency. In a 1983 speech to graduating students of Mount Saint Vincent University, she charged that feminists were polarizing and alienating the sexes, something that she never did despite some very tough operations. Calling upon women to "rectify the irregularities of the system through the appropriate legal and political avenues" she demonstrated that if you want to play the game, you have to have the power, and to have the power, you have to get inside the system. She did it, maintained it, and effected change by focussing on the positive and conveying her image as a political leader rather than a feminist.

When Maurice became a cabinet minister, Sauvé was pressured out of her broadcasting job with the CBC. Instead of creating an uproar, she joined the Liberal party. As minister of science and technology she was also responsible for the environment, and her steps to clean up the St. Lawrence River, warn of PCB dangers, and pass the Environmental Contaminants Act in 1975 were visionary. In Communications, she tackled the complexities of a national broadcasting policy and the concept of pay TV.

Sauvé has also taken what might be termed very feminist actions such as fighting the males-only rule of the Rideau Club by simply refusing to attend functions until women were accepted. As her power increased, so did the club's embarrassment. As Speaker she cited the government discrimination policy and stopped government patronage of the club. When the sexist barrier crumbled under such pressure, it gave Sauvé satisfaction to see Conservative colleague Jean Pigott admitted as the first woman member. The club burned down shortly after — some say from shock. Jean Pigott quipped, "When you deal with 'hot broads,' things start to sizzle."[97] Speaker Sauvé was also instrumental in opening a daycare centre on the hill and effecting a budgetary crackdown on parliamentary expense accounts. One of her most famous demands for attitudinal change toward women happened during Question Period. Tory MP Mike Forrestall was recognized and talked for so long that Sauvé demanded, "Does the honourable member have a question?"

Forrestall replied, "I certainly do, my dear."

Sauvé leaped up and snapped, "Don't call me 'my dear.' Call me Madame Speaker."

"Tokenism," say the feminists, dismissing Sauvé's accomplishments. Nancy Jackman charged that any woman who gets inside the system has a duty to champion women's causes and the feminists have never credited Sauvé with that. Sauvé's critics were never far away. Some believed that as gg^2 she had entertained on too grand a level and had not made the ordinary Canadian feel welcome; others complained that she did not address the grimmer side of life such as AIDS, drug abuse, and poverty. She had reigned in a transitional era between the opulence of the mid-1980s when pomp and circumstance was still expected of the Queen's representative, and the end of the decade, when the common touch was coming back. Sauvé has been judged as a power seeker who sold out to the system. Even her lifelong devotion to the development of youth is seen only as an abstract value. However, her supporters see the Jeanne

Sauvé Youth Foundation to be a challenge of lasting international value, and future conferences that attract the youth of the world will carry on a tradition of Look, Judge, Act.

The real secret of holding the reins of power for so many decades lies in believing that you belong. Sauvé grasps the word *power* as if seizing a halogen flashlight and beaming a brilliant path through the political jungle. Even her departure from the governor-general's post was controversial when she delivered her New Year's message to the country. Meech Lake was on everyone's lips but it should not have been on those of the governor-general, who is supposed to remain impartial. Not Sauvé. She created a storm by unapologetically urging the Mulroney government or "the parties involved" to "ratify their pact and . . . not let Canada drift into an unforseeable future."[b]

An Ottawa friend once said that Jeanne Sauvé had come from the wrong side of the Saskatchewan tracks. But when asked if, as a child, Her Excellency had considered herself a member of the Establishment, she arched a little higher from the downy cushions of the Rideau Hall chesterfield, thought for a nanosecond, then squashed the notion that wealth or name are prerequisites for membership in that enclave. "Of course!" she exclaimed. "As teenagers, we were the intelligentsia. We *were* the Establishment!"

****

In the summer of 1987, Sharon Carstairs was operating out of a cubbyhole in the NDP-controlled Manitoba legislative building. With papers piled high on the desk and surrounding table tops, the room barely had room for Manitoba's sole Liberal MLA. Serving coffee in paper cups, the cheerful Carstairs made it clear that she was merely passing through this cluttered closet en route to the premier's spacious office.

The Conservatives formed the official Opposition at the time, and have long been the government, so why be a Liberal in Manitoba? Carstairs, her eyes gleaming behind glasses the size of dinner plates, explained with enthusiasm that the Liberals were on their way into power. By the summer of 1987, in less than two years, this articulate, squeaky-voiced educator had made a nearly extinct party with no stated policy into a provincial power. She had won the leadership in 1986 by chalking up 200,000 kilometres driving to meet with the grassroots, uniting the rural-urban divisions, and producing a slate of fifty-seven candidates, then running the election in the black. When the 1988 provincial election approached, pollster Angus Reid said of Carstairs, "She has these apparent political disabilities in terms of voice—and she's short and she's fat, and like, who'd ever want to vote for her?"[c] Lots of people, as it turned out. Four days after Angus Reid's query the Liberals won twenty seats, pushed to twenty-one by a Conservative defection, and the country met Sharon Carstairs.

A maverick in the disguise of a Wellington Crescent matron with the resolute debating skills of her father, Senator Harold Connolly of Nova Scotia, Carstairs is actually a clever behind-the-scenes dealer. She frequently, and privately, debated issues and sought consensus with NDP Premier Howard Pawley, thus influencing his decisions in the Legislature without his losing face. It was her survival ploy against the particularly disputatious Manitoba Conservatives.

Meech Lake bashing brought Carstairs favourable press coverage until Conservative Premier Gary Filmon suddenly decided that he didn't like the deal either. The press suggested he somersaulted to seduce popular opinion away from Carstairs and neutralize her, but in the spring of 1990 when the decision came down to Mulroney's ''crap shoot'' at the eleventh hour, Carstairs and NDP leader Gary Doer travelled to Ottawa to deal alongside Premier Filmon, who was presiding over a minority government. It was unfair, but Sharon Carstairs was suddenly being dubbed the ''mother of deconfederation,'' and her star began fading in popularity. During a fall 1990 election campaign she said she needed tranquilizers to sleep and complained that her opponents were belittling her debate of serious issues, implying that she couldn't take the pressure because she was a woman.[d] Her position was out of character for a political veteran, and if there is anything the public has come to dislike, it is women who appear to be weak or are hiding behind their own skirts. The election resulted in a minority win for the Conservatives, a big rise in NDP seats, and a drop from twenty-one seats to seven for the Liberals. It was a blow, but in the vicissitudes of politics she is simply in a state of eclipse.

Sheila Copps

On March 24, 1987, during Question Period, a very pregnant Sheila Copps was yelling and haranguing the Conservative government, a verbal pugilist interjecting ''Ha!'' and worse into her opponents' speeches with the dissonance of some rasping musical instrument. Most women find it tiring to stand in the final hours before childbirth, let alone fight, but not Copps. Her barbs were grating on everyone's nerves, the air was heavy, and a battle royal threatened the proceedings. Then Speaker John Fraser intoned mournfully, ''And soon there'll be two.''

A few days later, there were. Copps had remained in the House until she felt the pangs of labour: a woman driven by some internal mission that will not allow her to rest. Within two weeks she was back on the job —harping, harassing—just as when she had leaped over chairs to chase Sinclair Stevens out of a meeting and into a conflict of interest inquiry. Her Rat Pack days were passing but the moniker, given by Toronto *Star* writer Bob Hepburn to a group of six Liberal MPs who had united after the 1984 Conservative sweep, stuck. They were like modern-day Robin

Hoods, making sudden hits behind the enemy line to champion the needs of the underdog.

When John Turner decided to retire in 1989, Copps tested the waters for a try at the federal Liberal leadership. She carefully presented to the public a mellowed image of a politician who would still go to the wall for her principles. At a Liberal breakfast meeting held in Vancouver, Copps was to be the guest speaker. Just before she arrived, a campaign manager growled, ''I don't know what I'm doing here, subjecting myself to a half hour of being screeched at.'' There was a sympathetic echo from men and women around the table and not one prominent Liberal could be seen in the room. Even in that partisan gathering, Copps had not shaken the baggage of yesteryear.

As the guests sipped their coffee, some of them recalled that Copps may sear nerves, but she also provided some of the more hilarious comic relief of the decade. After all, she coined the word *Bulroney*! And in her joyful leaping to her feet (on 236 issues in her first two years in office)[e] to say anything but say *something*, Copps has been known to tie the House up in metaphoric knots with such malapropisms as, ''I have seen [Erik Nielsen's] Velcro lips sink into the political sand for the last time!'' When Copps and Co. accused John Crosbie of dispensing patronage in Newfoundland, Crosbie became so apoplectic in defending his integrity that Copps shot up, shouting, ''Is there a doctor in the House?''

Likening the Rat Pack to loud-mouth punks and poltroons, Crosbie roared at Copps, ''Just quieten down, baby . . . ''

Copps retorted, ''I'm thirty-two years old, I'm an elected member of Parliament from Hamilton East, and I'm nobody's baby!'' She then sat down and penned an autobiography with that title in the hope of inspiring more women to enter politics. Her political career is filled with extraordinary milestones. She worked on federal campaigns for Hamilton MP John Munro, and municipally for her father, Vic Copps. At the age of twenty-four she ran for a provincial Liberal seat and lost by a mere fourteen votes. Four years later, in 1981, she won that seat to become the only woman in the Ontario Liberal caucus and one of only six women in the entire legislature. At the age of twenty-nine when Copps made a bid for the provincial leadership, she was ridiculed by the Liberal caucus, and the press foresaw a replay of the Flora Syndrome. It was predicted that Copps would receive verbal support beforehand only to face betrayal on the first ballot. Instead, she placed a strong second to future premier David Peterson, noting the anxiety of the power establishment that had written her off as a token woman. Encouraged in 1984 to run for the Hamilton East seat by federal heavies Marc Lalonde and Keith Davey, Copps found herself in a strategic quagmire. She left the Ontario government just as it was entering power and won a federal seat just as the Liberals were losing it.

Sheila Copps is a driven politician. A second-generation political animal who speaks three languages fluently, her leftist platform and lack of business experience make the corporate world nervous. But Copps is bringing a revolutionary style into politicking of the 1990s. In Vancouver, with her toddler in tow, she directed part of her message to women saying, "the single biggest factor holding women back is the fear of failure," especially the fear of holding power in what is considered a "man's world." Yet no fractious statements alienated men. No high-pitched shrieks shattered nervous ear drums. Copps communicated in articulate tones and with a speed that kept everyone's attention. The consummate politician, she sounded genuine, and answered questions forthrightly. When challenging the leadership, she did a cross-country marathon of thirteen appearances over twelve hours, flinging barbs at candidate Paul Martin Jr., who represented big institutions but said he was unable to find qualified women to serve on their boards.

Copps still gets excited and falls off the dignity wagon. When Audrey McLaughlin won the leadership of the NDP, Copps was approached for a comment. She might have welcomed her opponent into the House in the smooth manner adopted by the Prime Minister and John Turner, particularly as McLaughlin was pioneering the way for women as national leaders. Instead, Copps told the press that the 1989 NDP leadership convention was "Mickey Mouse" and that McLaughlin was "fluff . . . a has-been . . . "[f] Perhaps she realized her gaffe later that day as Susan Delacourt wrote that Copps was applauding the New Democrats who had "blazed a trail for her by choosing a woman to lead their party."[g]

While Copps spoke at the breakfast meeting her daughter played at the foot of the podium, occasionally reaching up toward her mother, who hugged her without missing a beat. Toward the end of the question period the two-year-old child, who as an infant had napped through evening committee meetings on the Hill, began tugging gently at her mother's skirts, a little hour-glass signalling time was up. Travelling with babe in arms was at first judged a catchy ploy, but this new age politician, a Futurist juggling the dual responsibilities of motherhood and federal politics with a determination to be pre-eminent in both, was sincere. In January 1991, Jean Chrétien, the new Leader of the Opposition, appointed Copps as deputy Liberal leader before entering hospital for surgery. In his absence, Copps won national respect for her skills in raising and debating relevant issues.

Ethel Blondin

In the North, Liberal MP Ethel Blondin is the woman with the power potential. She is the first woman from the NWT ever to sit in the House of Commons. Appalled that the North was not mentioned even out of courtesy in the Meech Lake Accord, the thirty-eight-year-old Blondin decided to run for parliament in the November 1988 elections. Her campaign manager, Lynda Sorensen, had originally found Blondin in the Department of Information in Yellowknife and hired her to translate a video into Slavey. Sorensen carefully structured the campaign to win the nomination away from two male candidates on the first ballot. Blondin succeeded in a landslide victory. In the opinion of northerners, she has no enemies, quite an accomplishment in tundra politics.

From the start, Blondin's credibility quickly solidified during the emergency debate on the Exxon Valdez oil spill. She so impressed even the opposition with her knowledge and expertise on that disaster that Pierre Cadieux, the Minister of Northern Affairs (formerly of labour), requested a meeting and went to Blondin's office. She is not a frightened, inexperienced northerner as some veteran politicians had suspected, but a phoenix rising from her people's harsh history to fly towards a clearly defined goal. Speaking requests have flooded in from across the country as cross-party support from such veterans as Barbara McDougall have helped ease Blondin into the fabric of Ottawa.

A graduate from the teacher education program in Fort Smith, Blondin earned a Bachelor's of Education from the University of Alberta. She worked for twelve years in the Public Service Commission in Ottawa as national manager for a program in northern careers and native development, and knows her way through the bureaucratic system. Blondin's visions for the North are crystallized through creative survival and she intends to entrench the identity and roots of her people deeply into the soil of Canada's constitution. In 1990 during the Meech Lake debates, Blondin said, "You should be able to look into the Constitution and see yourself in it."

THE NEW DEMOCRATS

> Vicky Gabereau: I don't think there will ever be an NDP federal government in my lifetime.
>
> ROSEMARY BROWN: IT WILL HAPPEN[3h]

On September 7, 1990, the morning after Premier David Peterson and his Establishment Liberals went down to defeat, TV cameras zoomed in on the NDP woman who had won his London Centre riding. Soon-to-be-cabinet-minister Marion Boyd was slouched on a sofa wearing a tattered T-shirt and blue jeans, looking like a couch potato about to take charge of her remote control. But Boyd's laid-back demeanour was a disguise. Formerly the executive director of a battered women's advocacy clinic in London, the blue-jeaned Boyd heralded the arrival of the common folk. She is a no-nonsense loyalist who intended to whip her Ministry of Education into a model for the twenty-first century.

Except in Saskatchewan, Manitoba, British Columbia, and the Yukon, members of the NDP have been scorned or considered irrelevant to the ruling landscape of Canada. Members such as Stanley Knowles, Pauline Jewett, and Stephen Lewis may be esteemed, but they have never had legislative power to implement change. In the national forum, the federal NDP has enjoyed the power to criticize without having to define economic policy, balance a budget, or implement a comprehensive economic platform. As a consciousness-raising catalyst for social justice, however, the NDP has used media power to push for legislative changes finally made by the Liberals and Conservatives. Ultimately, that may be its greatest power.

The New Democrats' win in Canada's wealthiest province under the leadership of Bob Rae has changed all that. The country is paying close attention to his NDP policies and his management. Suddenly it doesn't matter much whether Audrey McLaughlin's television performance is lacklustre or schoolmarmish. Her message takes on a whole new significance. She really could become the prime minister. In Ontario when Premier Rae appointed eleven women[4] to his new cabinet and decreed that he intended to appoint women to at least one-half of twenty-seven new provincial judgeships, and four new appointments to the Judicial Advisory Appointments Committee, he ushered in a Golden Era for women in political and judicial power.

The Ontario NDP astonished even itself by winning a majority government and boosting its ratings across the nation. British Columbia and Saskatchewan are shifting back to the left, and the Manitoba party increased its seats in 1990.[5] And the personable Alexa Shaw McDonough, who presides over the Nova Scotia NDP, may find her fortunes rising as annoyed citizens react to the RCMP investigation of former premier, now senator, John Buchanan, for allegedly accepting kickbacks. Retaining her seat in the 1988 provincial election by less than thirty votes reflected not upon McDonough but upon the polarization of voters by the free trade issue, McDonough remains popular. Sharon Carstairs, a former Nova Scotian and friend of McDonough, still sees the NDP leader's policies as pro-Liberal in philosophy.

As a member of a wealthy Establishment family, McDonough is an illuminating case of competence sidelined by conscience. A Liberal in the 1970s, she was so frustrated with then premier Gerald Regan's intransigence on what she deemed poor social policy that she rejected the notion of survival politics, joined the NDP, and diluted her power potential. Save for McDonough and Elizabeth Weir, the outspoken leader of the NDP in New Brunswick, all NDP members, like all opposition members, are outsiders. Espousing the ideology of a shared power, of consensus government, they are masters of patience, willing to wait and maintaining the image of a national conscience.

Shirley Carr

> Social taboos are still the strongest isolator and the strongest motivator of all.
>
> SHIRLEY CARR

In Niagara-on-the-Lake in the 1940s, there was no social elite contributing to the war effort through the Junior League and officers' corps in the part of town where the Boutilier family lived. Mary Geraldine Boutilier, a Nova Scotian who was chiselled from the same Cape Breton rock as her father, watched four of her seven sons and her husband leave for the war in France. Then, despite the aftereffects of a stroke, she worked for six years in a chemical factory to supplement the men's minimal pay. One of her two daughters remaining at home was eleven-year-old Shirley, seventh child of nine, who helped supplement the family income by cleaning floors after school. Each day in class, Shirley suffered the searing lesson that wealth and position, rather than ability and service, were what invited you in or shut you out. Ridiculed by her peers because she wore slippers to school, she was never invited into any of the clubs, lost an election to the student council, and remained an outsider until two of her brothers were killed in the war. Then her classmates made overtures to her, but Shirley knew pity when she saw it and declined. Within the crucible of her childhood germinated the embryo of an equality-seeking feminist.

After the war when the men returned home to find only periodic work, the family moved further out to a farmhouse, with Mary Boutilier—who had two more strokes—supplementing their welfare cheques by working in a paper-box factory. The education in criminal law that the sixteen-year-old Shirley wanted was out of the question. She took a fifty-five cents-an-hour job at Brewers Retail. When she learned that the truck drivers were earning more than the women who worked equally long hours inside, she became a vocal activist. At the age of nineteen she married Bruce Carr, joined CUPE, the Canadian Union of Public Employees, and a decade later became shop steward. Then she joined the NDP, ran and lost provincially in 1971, continued championing the rights of workers and in 1974 she was elected executive vice-president of the Canadian Labour Congress.

Shirley Carr's name became a household word in Canada as she tangled with management on her way to becoming the first woman president of the CLC, and presided over the total membership of 2.2 million in 78 affiliated unions comprising 59 percent of all unionized employees in Canada[6]. She won international recognition negotiating with politicians both nationally and through the International Labour Organization. Once, during a lengthy IWA strike in British Columbia, she came to the rescue of IWA boss Jack Munro by using the CLC Ottawa building as collateral for a million-dollar loan.[i]

Although in the more conciliatory tone of the 1990s Carr's profile is less visible, in May 1988 she came to verbal blows with Prime Minister Brian Mulroney in Vancouver. The feud was really rooted in 1986 and her ascendency to the CLC presidency when Mulroney had kept her waiting for six months for an audience. No city was big enough to hold the two of them and Carr was particularly angry that the Prime Minister had the effrontery to storm Vancouver when she had booked first. On that weekend, the Hotel Vancouver, was her turf. Just down the street in the Hyatt Regency Hotel, the Prime Minister raged to the press that Mila had been elbowed in the stomach during an angry demonstration by an anti-privatization crowd in Moncton. They had been incited to riot, he insisted, by the NDP and by CLC president Shirley Carr who had used "the language of war," as if warmongering terms had never been used in Conservative circles.

While the more than 2,800 delegate Canadian Labour Congress continued its annual meeting in the Vancouver Convention Centre below the Pan Pacific Hotel, its president was actually ensconced far from the madding crowd on the gold-key floor of the Hotel Vancouver. The dark-haired, fifty-nine-year-old Shirley Boutilier Carr, the outcast child of the forties, looked every inch a member of the Establishment. Walking tall in stylish heels, a taupe suede skirt, and a grey silk shirt draped by a strand of pearls the size of acorns, the closet capitalist who earns $97,000 annually explained unapologetically, "I have never been against success." With her was Mary Boutilier, her mother, who accompanies Carr on travels that have included trips to Ottawa to be invested with the Order of Canada, and to four Canadian universities for honorary doctorate degrees.

Less a union scrapper than a matriarch caring for her union family, Carr reminisced about the International Labour Organization[7] in Geneva through which she has befriended or conferred with the likes of Ronald Reagan, Mikhail Gorbachev, and in particular, Lech Walesa of Poland. From the corporate world, both Bob Blair of NOVA and Thomas d'Aquino, president and CEO of the Business Council on National Issues on which Carr serves, have expressed respect for her open-minded approach to business if not to the federal politicians.[j]

Shirley Carr is a woman who encompasses the graciousness of propriety and success, the negotiating skills of a corporate CEO, and the fighting instincts of a mother grizzly. Ask if her union members have ever been violent and she snorts, "Never." She reasoned that slashed tires and baseball-dented trucks during the construction battle of Expo '86 union members vs. non-union labour, or postal strikes when scabs were attacked for trying to drive across picket lines and "steal union jobs," are acts not of aggression, but of self-defence. In the CLC vernacular, her boys were simply protecting their livelihood. Carr uttered the word "scabs" with the palpable disgust reserved for a festering, gangrenous wound. Through the 1970s and into the 1980s, colleagues were never quite sure which Carr they were going to get. Surprise is part of her power: it is how she survived during those years of street language and threats then common to the union world.

Today, unions are characterized by ivy league negotiators, and Carr has cooled her rhetoric. By 1991, she had survived several palace revolts at a time when union membership is shrinking away from socialist control towards the philosophical centre. She has walked the high wire, ruling in the days of the abrasive, cigar-chewing Dennis McDermott, and hanging in with the waning membership, and she continues to chart her own course. At the 1989 NDP leadership convention, Carr ignored the tacit pressure on women to support one of their own and publicly backed Dave Barrett over Audrey McLaughlin. It became a tactical error when McLaughlin won, but the leader was interested only in mending fences and in 1990 was invited to address a cheering throng of 600 from the CLC's Biennial National Women's Conference. Carr still rules. Despite calls from within the unions by members who wish to disassociate themselves from the NDP in order to better negotiate with the two major parties of the country, she continues to support the NDP through mandatory union dues.

Pauline Jewett

Another veteran of the political wars of the 1960s, Pauline Jewett came highly qualified into the House. As a Liberal MP she was rejected by Mike Pearson as cabinet material because he already had Judy LaMarsh, and one woman was plenty. Jewett remained on the Liberal backbenches until her defeat in 1965, then served as the vice-president of the national Liberal party until 1970, when she was not re-elected. In 1972 when Trudeau invoked the War Measures Act, she had had enough, crossed the floor, and joined the NDP who respected Jewett's individual accomplishments such as degrees from Queen's, the London School of Economics, and a PhD in political science from Harvard. In 1974 Jewett became the first female president of a major university when she accepted the hazardous position at the politically volatile Simon Fraser University. In 1979 she ran as a New Democrat, won, and sat in the House until 1988 when she retired. She became involved in the 1981 constitutional lobby by supporting the unofficial conference and made the opening comments with Flora MacDonald. She was also the founding president of the Canadian Research Institute for the Advancement of Women.[k]

Audrey McLaughlin

> One day you can be a hero and the next day you can walk down the street and see the story of your life half price in a bookstore.[1]
>
> AUDREY McLAUGHLIN

Born in Dutton, Ontario, and married at eighteen, Audrey McLaughlin has raised two children, managed a mink ranch, and earned a master's degree in social work. A fearless adventurer, she spent time teaching in Ghana, and once paddled down the Amazon River catching and eating piranhas with a man who spoke no English. Divorced by 1979 and seeking a change, she bought a truck, piled in her belongings and drove to Whitehorse, where she set up her own business as a social policy consultant working with women's and native groups. Like Lynda Sorensen in the NWT, and Raynell Andreychuk in Regina, McLaughlin became a pre-eminent force by getting away from the accepted centre of power then creating her own. Competing against the men at the 1989 leadership convention was probably her least frightening challenge; McLaughlin told *Maclean's* magazine that the only advantage a male politician has over a female politician is comfortable shoes.[m]

McLaughlin is a twenty-year veteran of the NDP who has sat on the federal executive, organized election campaigns such as that of Yukon's Justice Minister Margaret Joe, and attended to the 1975 leadership convention, where she backed Rosemary Brown. In 1987, when Conservative Erik Nielsen retired, McLaughlin became the first NDP member for Yukon in the by-election. She was re-elected in 1988, became chair of the national caucus, and hasn't looked back.

Continually under attack, McLaughlin was described by some old pros at the 1989 leadership convention as lacking experience, being geographically remote, giving a dull performance on the stage, having an ill-defined policy platform, and speaking mediocre French. Gender might get her elected, leadership contender Dave Barrett's corner argued, but it would be insufficient to sustain her through the poison darts of Question Period. In a Vancouver *Sun* article, Charles Lynch, former chief of Southam News, was even harsher. He predicted of McLaughlin, "She will get clobbered."[n] Her election as leader, he argued, would be a gift for the other parties. Lynch warned that she would fall victim to what is known as the Flora Syndrome, "and Flora," he declared, " . . . was light years ahead of Audrey McLaughlin in political smarts." Lynch seemed to forget that in 1984 Brian Mulroney was inexperienced, and Ed Broadbent's French was unintelligible. Time could bring to McLaughlin not only sounder platforms, but the sparkle, confidence, and performing skills so essential in today's election-by-media.

The NDP entered a different era of national prominence during the 1989 leadership campaign and the introduction of scandal. CBC wired candidates and became privy to secrets behind closed doors. Proud of its consensus leadership and equitable policy, the NDP was stunned to hear Dave Barrett offering candidate Simon de Jong a deal for his support. But it was all for naught, because while Barrett was creating his mini scandal in the back room, Audrey McLaughlin was out mixing with the masses, flanked by Nova Scotia NDP chief Alexa McDonough and Canadian Auto Workers union president Robert White. On the fourth ballot,

Simon de Jong crossed the floor to support not the deal-making Barrett, but the first woman to lead a major national political party in North America.

In the spring of 1991, following a year of unparallelled squabbling among Canadians over Meech Lake and Oka, McLaughlin had yet to discover her full voice. Not as coolly magnetic as Barbara McDougall nor as brash as Sheila Copps, she struggled to break from the unwitting image of a lacklustre pedagogue. Supporters say that public perception differs from the more private reality where she shines as a backroom administrator and conciliator. In the meantime the NDP's popularity continued to rise through the spring of 1991, to 32 percent of popular vote. Critics call her style the "social worker approach . . . heavy on consensus-seeking and light on decision-making,"[o] but if she warms up her media persona and develops a viable economic policy, McLaughlin could well be the first woman to lead a country disenchanted with its traditional power parties.[8] It is also possible, however, that the electorate will be so disgruntled over Ontario Premier Bob Rae's 1991 deficit budget that the national fortunes of McLaughlin as well as those of the NDP will plummet. In that case, McLaughlin's political fortunes could be seriously affected.

THE CONSERVATIVES

Pat Carney

> The public Pat Carney is a large lady who smokes while others are eating, who is hard-nosed and determined, tough, smart, impatient, sarcastic, someone who would never do a thing to ingratiate herself with anybody.
>
> JULIET O'NEILP

April 14, 1989: the Vancouver Pat Carney Farewell Roast. The apex of the Conservative pyramid was present in person or on video — federal and provincial politicos, the Prime Minister, the Speaker of the House, former prime minister Joe Clark. Scattered throughout the hotel ballroom among the tables of oil executives, were the western backroom players who made it all happen — co-chairs Diana Lam and Jack Webster, and Virginia Greene and Virginia Richards, Brenda Kinsella, Sally Warren, Lisa Woodward, who represented their counterparts in every riding in Canada. Then there were the managers, the personal aides Donna Mackie and Pierre Alvarez, aide to Northern MLA Nellie Cournoyea, who was also present.

John Crosbie paid his respects by video, as did then B.C. Minister of economic development, Grace McCarthy, who never missed an opportunity to wave the flag. One of the most articulate champions of the westernmost province and a woman who understood the nature of power so well she survived over two decades of political life in the inner sanctum of decision making, McCarthy praised Carney by talking about their collaboration on the B.C. Trade and Convention Centre, the Asia Pacific Initiative, and lauding Carney's work on the free trade agreement.

MP Mary Collins appeared on the Carney Roast stage to lead the Tory Caucus Chorus in a hammed-up adieu. Collins's star should be rising, but in the 1989 cabinet shuffle, it was Kim Campbell, the most junior member, who won the most senior position of justice minister, while Collins was appointed deputy minister of defense just three months before her budget was slashed by $8 billion and the proposed nuclear subs cancelled. By then she had also received the additional burden of minister responsible for the status of women, in which over $1 million was cut at about the same time that she toasted John Crosbie as a national treasure after he had crooned "Pass the Tequila Sheila . . . lie down and love me again." Every which way Collins turned seemed fraught with landmines and her 1990 message of "negotiate" rather than "demonstrate" angered the women's movement. Despite a consulting background and a mettle compatible with corporate dealing, in the spring of 1991, Collins had not received a major portfolio.

At the Carney roast podium Barbara McDougall rose to take credit for Carney's career[9] (as would Joe Clark and Allan Fotheringham), describing the time in 1979 when she and David Crombie had met with Carney in the Hotel Vancouver lounge and persuaded her to run for office. Later, Carney expanded on the story: As a successful business consultant and a former journalist, Carney wasn't at all sure she wanted to relinquish her freedom to enter politics and asked Crombie and McDougall what a candidate was supposed to do. McDougall replied, "Well, you have to go and stand in front of liquor stores and hand out pamphlets . . . shake the hands of perfect strangers."

Carney was aghast. "I couldn't do that. That's impossible. Nobody does that. I don't want to go up to strangers and say, 'Hi, I'm your Conservative candidate.' Well, they took me outside and I stood at the bus stop . . . and I accosted people . . . and said, 'Hi, I'm Pat Carney, your Conservative candidate,' and people smiled and shook my hand and I thought, well this isn't so bad.

"So I went to a little old lady who was crossing the street and I said, 'Hi I'm Pat Carney, I'm your Conservative candidate,' and I held out my hand and she said, 'My hand will shrivel and drop off before I ever shake hands with a Conservative.'"

Once settled into politics, Carney executed a series of fiscal deals that will continue to impact on the economic structure of Canada and its citizens. In 1983 as opposition energy critic, she was already developing policies such as the Atlantic and Western Accords,[10] which were signed in principle with opposition leader Brian Mulroney. When the Conservatives won in 1984, Carney was ready to move swiftly. Within her first six months in office as minister for energy, mines, and resources, she had signed the Accords, dismantled the National Energy Program, cutting some $4 billion from energy expenditures, and kept up the gruelling pace while deregulating the price of natural gas. Driven by mid-year tax deadlines, she jumped into the field of haggling with the gusto and skill of a Jack Munro, garnering both criticism for an abrasive personality and praise for deadpan humour.

Known for a tough negotiating style, Carney is most pleased at ''winning over [Cabinet's] dead bodies'' the right for Petro-Canada to buy the downstream assets of Gulf, and enabling Paul Reichmann to purchase the upstream assets of Gulf (which made the huge Amauligak oil reservoir Canadian owned). The first move, which would create the cash flow essential to finance their 50 percent share of Hibernia, actually contradicted government privatization policy. Instead of downsizing Petro-Canada, it made it the second-largest oil company in Canada.

Had Carney not put the Petro-Canada/Gulf package together, the two largest oil reservoirs in Canada—Amauligak and Hibernia—would still be American owned. She said with satisfaction, ''We are talking billions and billions and billions.'' To accomplish the deal, Carney negotiated with Mobil Oil U.S. — through Investment Canada — to complete the Hibernia purchase. Running an American company with a Canadian subsidiary was a major headache for the Mobil chair. As Carney put it, ''You really had them by the balls because you could demand of them fairly outrageous things in order to approve this acquisition. . . . They came to me—oil men will fly anywhere. They were fun.'' And they were rebellious, at first, over the premise that Canada had the right to interfere in the purchase of one American company by another American company, both just happening to have Canadian subsidiaries.

One aspect of Carney's power was having the authority to close a deal without consulting cabinet. She recalled that, ''all I had to do was phone the PM and say I've closed.'' Carney would have already worked out the boundaries with Mulroney, who trusted her to get the job done. How she did it was her choice. ''You couldn't do that now,'' she said. ''A lot of ministers don't have the chance to say 'we're going to deregulate oil, deregulate gas, increase Canadian ownership; we're going to bring on Hibernia.'''

Carney's operational freedom stemmed directly from her business skills. In 1970, when she was a thirty-four-year-old single mother, working as a business columnist at the *The Province*, a paper that said it would never put her in management, she found herself on strike. She had to find alternate means to support her son, a nanny, and a mortgage, and she believed, as she often said to Allan Fotheringham, ''men will only take you seriously when you've made some money.'' She knew the North and loved it, having covered an oil story that broke in 1968. Carney guessed that this sleeping giant was about to awaken and with the courage that puts entrepreneurs on the leading edge, she moved with her son J.P. to Yellowknife. There she freelanced for TV, the Toronto *Star* and

Maclean's, and when Alberta Gas Trunk Line (now NOVA) asked her to be its northern consultant, she founded Gemini North, the first economic consulting company in the western Arctic. Carney recalled, "We had no competition in Yellowknife."[11] Gemini's baseline studies, often effected with native expertise, are still used in the North. As minister for international trade responsible for negotiating the 1988 free trade deal, Carney enshrined the Atlantic and Western accords into the agreement.

Back at the Roast, B.C.'s beloved tough guy and IWA labour leader Jack Munro approached the podium and gushed admiration for his old friend's ability to carry out the tougher assignments "like explaining the oil agreement to Don Getty."[12q] Once described by *Report on Business Magazine* as one of Canada's ten toughest bosses, Carney also earned Munro's undying respect over the 15 percent countervailing duty levied by the U.S. on exported softwood lumber. When the consequent softwood agreement was heavily criticized by the lumber industry, Munro growled, "[Pat] was the only federal minister who had the guts to tell Adam Zimmerman publicly to go get goddamned stuffed."

Carney later justified the toughness Munro described. "When I went to Ottawa I spoke very quietly and I shut the doors gently, but nobody listened. I found . . . it takes some determination and some yelling . . . to get the attention."

Munro said that his favourite Carney quote was when she called chief trade negotiator Simon Reisman "'a little pipsqueak' when he was trying to screw things up, and the Prime Minister was trying to make him the hero of Canada." Later in her townhouse, Carney agreed that "Simon was outrageous," adding quickly, "I'm fond of Simon" (as in some of my best friends are named Simon). The difficulty, she explained of Reisman's ego, was his contempt for operating within the mandate. As Carney's job was to uphold the cabinet process, the two were destined to clash.

When he reflected upon that time, Reisman responded to the question of just who had the power during the free trade negotiations by explaining that the Prime Minister had backed his pre-eminence in the House. Reisman added with a jocular sweetness, "Pat and I got along just fine once she accepted who was boss."

Carney retorted, "Simon failed to get an agreement. He needed the ministers." She negotiated tariffs and the Minister of Finance approved them. On the final weekend before the free trade agreement was signed, and facing a Saturday midnight deadline, Finance Minister Michael Wilson, Pat Carney, and Derek Burney representing the Prime Minister, holed up in James Baker's office in the Treasury Building in Washington and thrashed out the final wording. It had been ten days of frenzy and, Carney recalled, "Mike Wilson did all of the work on the financial institutions, I did the trade elements, and Derek Burney did the dispute settlement. [We] did the key issues." In the final hours the drafts were rushed back and forth, debated, and finally completed. Derek Burney called Mulroney an hour before the deadline to say they had a deal.

CTV host Pamela Wallin added a postscript to who accomplished what: "In this town when you're expressing an opinion, it depends on whether you're agreeing with the guys. If you're with them then you're one of them. If you happen to be against them—well, Pat had a horrible reputation in this town as being impossible. But she didn't get where she got by being Cinderella. . . . The revisionism about who really did the hard, slogging work on free trade is interesting. To hear the story told now, Derek Burney and Michael Wilson wrote the free trade deal and negotiated every square inch and somehow Pat was this loony broad running around firing her staff because it was that time of the month."

With the denouement of free trade, Mulroney appointed Carney president of the Treasury Board, a sort of on-side auditor general who examines and approves government spending. Some considered it to be the plum job in cabinet while others saw it as a vote of non-confidence from Mulroney over the trade ministry issues of stumpage and free trade. Carney saw it differently: "The secretary presents the case and the Treasury Board says yes or no. In terms of actual power, Treasury Board had the most power of any of my ministries." Through it, Carney took the opportunity to establish a major task force on the barriers to the advancement of women in the public service. Called *Beneath the Veneer,* it was researched by Jean Edmonds, Edna MacKenzie, and the ubiquitous backroom Tory, Jocelyne Côté-O'Hara.[13]

It was not one person or spectral ogre who brought Carney's political career to a close, but ill health—an occupational hazard worsened by the brutal travel demands on western politicians. Carney is not an easy person to know; pain was making it harder. Her dry humour and warmth, which draw support, can just as quickly be replaced by a wall of apparent hostility. Yet insiders believed that her famous outbursts and rebukes to her staff emanated more from arthritic pain than from any personal displeasure with her department.[14] In August, 1988, two months before the election writ was issued, Carney was approaching the steps of an airplane when she was so overwhelmed by pain that, she remembered, "I couldn't climb into it." Even so, she considered running in the fall elections. In the end it was her doctor who told her that she could not get through a campaign and she retired.

Kim Campbell

Following the 1988 elections, Carney and Barbara McDougall headed for Hawaii—McDougall for the tennis courts and her weary, joint-stiff friend for the beach. But, well, there was this hot real estate situation in the Pacific and Carney couldn't pass up a deal. She sold her Hawaii condo and got into development, the maverick patient in every physician's nightmare, the businessperson who can't stop dealing. At first Carney hadn't wanted to enter politics, but once given the power to effect policy change pivotal to the country, she was wired. As Donald Trump would say, deals were her art form. As Carney dreamed of being left in peace, she kept setting herself up to be connected. Liked and respected by the corporate business world, she received a flurry of invitations to join major boards,[15] and she has a listed telephone number, just in case anyone needs her.

In the summer of 1990 the Prime Minister appointed Pat Carney to the Senate. Through the media, the annoyed Premier Vander Zalm called upon Carney to play fair, step down, and run for a seat in the Senate. It was one of Carney's finest moments, when power and victory were absolute. Facing the television cameras, Senator Carney smiled and replied to Vander Zalm in her droll but definitive tones, "Thanks I think I'll pass."

Carney's cousin through marriage, then British Columbia MLA Kim Campbell, was openly frustrated by her boss, Premier Bill Vander Zalm, who had kept her on the backbench. To resign and run federally in a volatile riding was a big risk, but Carney knew that Campbell had become a seasoned politician while chair of the Vancouver School Board and she was a professional campaigner. So Carney called Campbell and urged her to run in Vancouver Centre, where the NDP's popular national president, Johanna den Hertog, had already declared. Campbell was hesitant, but Carney's polls had indicated strong support (newspapers speculated otherwise). The lure was a streamlined campaign team and a ready-made war chest. Campbell resigned her Socred seat and accepted the nomination.

After a ferocious fight, Campbell won by 279 votes in a province that voted largely NDP. She was appointed minister of state for indian and northern affairs, a junior position that enabled her to connect with Cabinet while learning Acronym. An unknown force in central Canada, Campbell then astonished the Prime Minister with her bilingual ability and gutsy debating, and in an unprecedented move in February 1990, he appointed her minister of justice and attorney general of Canada.

Flora MacDonald

> Flora was well liked. She was a drinking buddy, but [in 1972] she was, well, a secretary. We didn't think of her as a politician.
>
> GOWAN GUEST

On February 22, 1976, at the Conservative leadership convention, minutes before the first ballot count was announced, anticipation in Flora MacDonald's corner was high. Everyone at the convention knew her, and IOUs from coast to coast abounded. In earlier days when there was no staff, politicians everywhere had called upon MacDonald as the national executive secretary to help run their campaigns. She always responded, and her combined constituency of members and aspirants ranged from janitors to CTV's John Bassett, from lumberjacks in B.C. for whom she once worked, to the late New Brunswick premier Richard Hatfield.

Raising money has always been one of the toughest challenges for women in politics, and it was Toronto lawyer Eddie Goodman, MacDonald's chief fund raiser, who sent out a plea to the country.[16] She was known everywhere as an indefatiguable campaigner, one of the first to introduce door-to-door canvassing, and she always responded personally to telephone calls and letters. Of the $140,000 raised, $40,000 came in on one and two-dollar donations from strangers, testimony to her grassroots support. Others were uncertain about the chances of any woman winning. Conservative heavies such as Ontario Premier Bill Davis claimed they were behind her all the way, but she would understand that they just couldn't back her publicly. Author Heather Robertson[r] explained that while MacDonald was popular with the media, she came across as a Red Tory rather than one marked with the elitist character of the Conservative party. Certain factions never did want to see her become leader.

MacDonald was a risk taker. In 1966, Dalton Camp and Finlay MacDonald called for a leadership review of John Diefenbaker, then chickened out over going on with the executive meeting. Flora stepped in to organize the meeting, but was fired by Prime Minister Diefenbaker. Out of all those who had participated in the palace revolt, and despite the fact that others had started it and then faded to let her front it, she was the only one fired. When she went to Queen's University to teach and ran up a telephone bill of $600 organizing the subsequent Conservative executive meeting, she was investigated by the RCMP, who suspected she was running a call business. What else would a woman be doing phoning all those men in the 1960s? The meeting was held, the leadership convention scheduled, and Flora ran Robert Stanfield's campaign. He won and the membership-at-large reclaimed Flora MacDonald by electing her national secretary of the party.

MacDonald's political aspirations in 1956 were some twenty years ahead of the general movement of women into the work force and politics.[17] The 1970s was still a rough decade for women to be in politics, and the early 1980s were only incrementally better as their numbers slowly increased. When MacDonald had first won a seat in 1972 there were only five women MPs and her 1976 quest for leadership found insignificant support from women because so few could identify with being a politician, let alone the leader of a federal party or prime minister.

In 1976 the large roster of leadership candidates — eleven of them, including lawyers Joe Clark and Brian Mulroney — would make the results unpredictable, but MacDonald expected to be a strong second on the first ballot. She has an effective speaking voice and any plainness in style faded before her enthusiasm, and her large, friendly smile that beamed across the nation. When the announcement of the first ballot results was about to be made the convention hall fell silent, television cameras searched the faces of the candidates like predators—Oscar Night in the PC party. The news broke. From more than 2,000 delegates, MacDonald had won a paltry 214 votes. Cameras zoomed in, microphones shot forward to record the shock registering on her face. It was immediately followed by a dry-eyed steely resolve, an honest expression of disappointment conquered by upbeat hope, marks of courage that would be a hallmark of MacDonald over the coming decade. Politics is no place for wimps.

Following the second ballot MacDonald, her support decimated, moved over to Joe Clark, sealing her fate. Clark won, evoking an almost palpable bitterness on the face of young Brian Mulroney. Subsequently, Clark's prime ministerial career bombed, Mulroney assumed the leadership of the party, and although Flora MacDonald went on to serve in major portfolios and to sit on the prime minister's planning and priorities committee, insiders say that Mulroney never forgot her 1976 allegiance to Clark.

Gender would continue to plague MacDonald as she struggled to excel and be identified with the job. Later in 1979, MacDonald as secretary of state for external affairs first coordinated on a living room floor the famous escape of six Americans to the Canadian Embassy in Tehran. Three months later, Ambassador Ken Taylor executed the plan and MacDonald held a press conference. Amazed that the whole episode had occurred without a leak, a male interviewer asked MacDonald, "Tell me, Madame Minister, how was it that a woman was able to keep a secret like that for three months?"

On another occasion, MacDonald accompanied Prime Minister Clark and Maureen McTeer to Africa to the Commonwealth Conference. At the time, MacDonald was the only female foreign minister in the world. En route, the Canadian team stopped to pay its respects to the prime minister of the Republic of Cameroon in West Africa and to enable MacDonald to meet with the foreign minister as a prelude to their formal talks. When the plane landed, Clark and McTeer disembarked with MacDonald directly behind them, followed by their entourage. There were two rooms in the airport. In one were the Prime Minister and the Foreign Minister of Cameroon. In the other, to which McTeer was ushered, the spouses gathered to await the social hour. As Clark went in to greet the West Africans, the Canadian ambassador turned to MacDonald and said, "Would you mind waiting in the other room with the women?"

MacDonald froze. The ambassador had made the fatal mistake of regarding his boss as a woman rather than as the minister. A moment later she commanded, "That plane turns around and goes back to Canada. And you're on it.'' Then, smiling brilliantly, MacDonald accompanied Clark to meet the ministers of Cameroon.

In her decade of assorted ministries, MacDonald's goals and promises, which ran the gamut of disciplines and issues, were continually impeded by fiscal cutbacks and such hazards as free trade. Life in caucus is a constant scrapping over the dollar, and MacDonald's perceived accomplishments or frustrations of the 1980s had little to do with being a woman and much to do with the formidable reality of playing hardball as a cabinet minister. Possibly her toughest assignment was snaring an elusive broadcast act.

In 1986, following Employment and Immigration, the woman from Cape Breton whose childhood entertainment had consisted of family singsongs to a piano and a fiddle, became the minister of communications, a $2.2-billion imbroglio of broadcasting, cultural spheres, and telecommunications, all of them interconnected and each with its own internal problems yet having to be guided in the context of cultural sovereignty. Her primary challenge was to create the long-awaited broadcast act. Previous ministers including Jeanne Sauvé had been stymied by the job since 1968 when the old act bound the various facets through technology which kept changing. Cable TV, for example, had rendered the act obsolete.

MacDonald did produce a broadcast bill that extended beyond future technology and it included every corner of the country. To her dismay, late in 1987, when the CRTC gave the CBC permission to form an all-news channel, the government placed guidelines on the CBC and put the broadcast act on hold. It all suggested that MacDonald was losing control, as columnist Hugh Winsor wrote: ''MacDonald is a weak minister with few allies in cabinet and she has not as yet been able to articulate any clear vision about the future of Canadian television.''[s] Eventually critics in the House supported her bill (with the exception of the film distribution section) to get it passed quickly and it cleared on September 29, 1988.

Then the Liberal senators stopped it along with the child-care and trade bills, part of a larger plot to force the Conservatives into a pre-Christmas election, which in turn buffeted the bill in the rough waters of free trade.[18] Cultural sovereignty pitted MacDonald against trade minister Pat Carney and her negotiating team. At the time MacDonald was struggling to keep the culture Canadian, while the artistic community, led by Adrienne Clarkson and Margaret Atwood, worried volubly that Simon Reisman was giving it away. With the loss of her seat in 1988, MacDonald was out of the game, but she claims authorship of Bill C-40, the revised draft of which by March 1991 has been approved in the Senate.[19] If politicians ever tried to measure their success or their power by the legislation they've put through the House, they would go mad. Flora MacDonald reflects not with bitterness, but with the fire of competition in her eyes and that upbeat enthusiasm as she said, ''The communications portfolio was a really tough, hot deal—the most exciting, interesting time I've ever spent."

Early in 1989, the former MP sat in her Ottawa apartment surrounded by political memorabilia and a silent telephone. Months passed and tributes rather than job offers poured in. Rumour had it that no distinguished appointments would come Flora's way from the PMO. A retiring Erik Nielsen got the chairship of the National Transportation Agency and an annual salary of somewhere between $120,000-$140,000. Once safely ensconced, he wrote a book, *This House Is Not a Home,* which included critical pieces about the Conservative party. Retiring NDP leader Ed Broadbent was named head of the newly created International Centre for Human Rights and Democratic Development. MacDonald received no major payoff. She had left External eminently qualified with a vast global knowlege of the intricate systems of business and government. Rumours rumbled about decades-old wounds, the institutional beast, its driver, and her banishment to the lower end of the jungle.[20] There was a poignancy surrounding this politician who considered her constituency her family and politics her life, and who still had much to give.

In fact, the Prime Minister did offer MacDonald high commissioner to India, but she turned down that illustrious job in the hope of winning the position of United Nations high commissioner for Refugees, for which her talent in coordinating global resources would have made her an ideal choice. She was nominated by Canada for the job, but the United Nations chose Japan. By 1991, MacDonald was fiercely claiming independence from any kind of government patronage. She is a free spirit who prefers to get her own jobs, and in 1991 serves as special adviser to the Commonwealth of Learning, which involves distance education to the forty-nine countries in the Commonwealth.

Ask Flora MacDonald and Rosemary Brown about their biggest disappointment in political life and they will mention their failed leadership bids.[21] The hype of conventions is fuelled by public energy and adulation, rocketing the candidates into stratospheric dreams of achieving the impossible. Becoming leader and perhaps prime minister confers greater power than being CEO of a multinational. It is the power to change legislation, to influence the course of a country according to one's visions, and it can all begin at the leadership convention. Adulation suspends disbelief and fuels the exhilaration of anticipated victory. Losing must be devastating, but in 1987 publisher Mel Hurtig had told the *Globe and Mail* that MacDonald adored the process of politics.[t] She would have to. Defeat, false promises, and grudges are all a part of that process, and she has seen it all. MacDonald took up hang-gliding in 1990, a pastime arguably less risky than the hazards of a political career.

MacDonald's greatest power may still be invisible. Not only does she receive letters from younger women whom she has inspired to accept extraordinary challenges, but she has also collaborated with Marjory LeBreton in engineering significant appointments of women to the policy-making levels: on boards, commissions, and tribunals. One, Mimi Fullerton, served on the Caplan-Sauvageau task force, then became director-general of TVOntario.[22] MacDonald appointed seven women to the CRTC,[23] more to the CBC, the National Arts Centre, the National Film Board, and Shirley Thomson to head up the National Gallery. The Canada Council now has equality in gender representation, and it was MacDonald who appointed the much-sought-after Joyce Zemans as its director.

Barbara McDougall

> If [Barbara McDougall] wants it, she could probably be the first woman prime minister.
>
> PAT CARNEY 1989[u]

Barbara McDougall has arrived in the right place at the right time in history and with the right credentials. A year earlier in Ottawa, the central Canadian politician with strong Western ties was about to address the convention on Women and Power. Minister of Employment and Immigration, and the Minister Responsible for the Status of Women, McDougall had flown in to the left-wing gathering with a right-wing mandate, one that included a record of disassembling banks in Alberta, privatizing twelve Crown corporations, and formulating a new immigration law to meet the global demands on Canada for the 1990s. The dark circles under her eyes testified to the endless hours of travel and jet lag, an occupational hazard of being an MP in this sprawling country.

McDougall was unpopular in that coalition of activists, many of whom were of NDP or Liberal persuasion as well as advocates of the NAC whose funding she would cut later that year. She would rather deal with failed banks or illegal aliens than the portfolio of status of women. Journalist Charlotte Gray wrote that McDougall had been ''appalled'' by that appointment.[v] Like any other politician aspiring to the major portfolios, she seems to fear that association with women's issues will trivialize her career. Even self-proclaimed feminist and former Liberal minister Monique Bégin once refused the portfolio, and Lloyd Axworthy will never forget the perils of that post. The self-help ideology of Conservatism is incompatible with the cry for more safety nets. McDougall operates as a politician, period. One can visualize her sigh of relief when Mulroney shifted the albatross from her neck to that of Mary Collins. But what she had to say at that conference was significant simply because she was perceived as the most powerful woman in the country. As a member of the eight-member Operations clique in the nineteen-member planning and priorities committee, McDougall had immediate access to the Prime Minister and his decisions. It is this tall, cool-headed yet friendly, tough-minded businessperson who has the personal potential and the public following to become Canada's first woman prime minister.

As the oldest of three children whose father died when she was eleven, McDougall became the surrogate parent while her mother went to work as a clerk in Queen's Park. Her mother's strength in dealing with the pain of bereavement while working to put all three daughters through university impressed upon McDougall an outlook that was both fatalistic and flexible. She learned that if the family could survive a crushing loss, no defeat could ever prevent her from carrying on, and she developed the rare skill of differentiating between political and personal attacks. That stood her well when she joined the world of finance on Hastings Street in Vancouver then Bay Street in Toronto,[24] and it made her an instant player in the inner sanctum of the West Block.

McDougall was the first woman to serve as a junior minister in the major portfolio of Finance, attending cabinet committee meetings and travelling on behalf of the Minister, Michael Wilson, her old business colleague from Bay Street. She had been through the mill with finance, in 1985 presiding with Alberta Minister of Consumer and Corporate Affairs Connie Osterman over the demise of two banks. When the Canadian Commercial and the Northland had first appealed to their colleagues for aid, McDougall had advised the government to let them sink or swim. Ignoring her advice, the government had joined with some of the big six banks in a bail out that ultimately failed. In 1985, the Department of Finance, fronted by Wilson's deputy, McDougall, closed them down.

As a loyal team member, McDougall took the heat, biting her tongue on "I told them so." Her impeccable deportment and resolute smile on national television won her widespread respect. The Deputy Minister conveyed silently that while she had to complete the unpalatable task, she clearly enjoyed playing hardball. The only irony lay in the charge from women's groups that she was being used as a scapegoat for Wilson and Mulroney. McDougall recoils from that kind of gender-driven protection.

Arguably more knowledgeable and influential in the fiscal business of Canada than any other woman politician, McDougall brings a private sector perspective in business to an understanding of the government's comprehensive agenda. She is, in the view of her former chief of staff Liz Roscoe, "always a key player at the table."[25] But by 1988, Carol Goar wrote that McDougall had brought some control to the portfolio, but privatization and regulatory reform were low priorities with the public. The Minister's image was waning,[w] and her status of women portfolio wasn't getting any easier. Compared to a career that had charged ahead full steam, McDougall must have felt as if she were standing still.

During the 1960s the Vancouver *Sun* had hired McDougall to compete with the *Province* business writer Pat Carney. McDougall had never been a journalist and couldn't type, but she was a success. As members of parliament, the two shared an apartment in Ottawa. They worked long hours on interrelated government disciplines and served together on the planning and priorities committee. For example, while Carney negotiated the energy policy, her bills went through Barbara McDougall as minister of state for finance.

When McDougall moved to Toronto she was welcomed socially by the business world and the Conservative Establishment, which included Jalynn Bennett, Hal Jackman, and lawyer Michael Meighen — against whom she nearly locked nomination squads in 1984. In the pre-nomination weeks Meighen, Jackman, and other prominent Conservatives held power lunches to decide who would run in St. Paul's. Vancouver lawyer Gowan Guest remembers telephoning his son Martin at the University of Toronto to ask if he would rally the students behind Meighen. A few days later Martin replied that Barbara McDougall had already *signed up* a thousand students. After running two campaigns for David Crombie, McDougall had spent a year quietly pounding the pavement, knocking on doors, and gathering support.

When the Prime Minister withheld endorsement of McDougall, hoping to announce the nomination to either his old friend Meighen, or Mike Wadsworth (a lawyer and former football player), McDougall supporters who had access to his office—Jalynn Bennett and Jane Pepino—assaulted him by telephone and telegram until he succumbed. Meighen and his Blue Team shelved their aspirations and gave McDougall one of the most prominent partisan groups in the country. She won with two-thirds of the vote.

During the actual campaign, choreographed by Julia Foster, supported in part by Jean Pigott's famous war chest, and bolstered by the fund-raising efforts of Bob McGavin and Jalynn Bennett, McDougall's own campaigning was bolstered by some eighty coffee parties held by women ranging through all socio-economic levels from her blue-collar neighbourhood to Rosedale's Kelly Meighen. With a team of 1,350 men and women whose enthusiasm grew to evangelist hype, she beat incumbent John Roberts by over 4,000 votes. During the 1988 campaign, her workers again attacked their jobs with the messianic fervour shown for a cult figure. McDougall clearly enjoyed the process of stomping her riding in the fresh air, one of the rare times politicians aren't jetting about the airways or meeting in offices.

Following Pat Carney's departure from Ottawa, Barbara McDougall was for a year the sole woman connected to the engine that runs Canada, yet by 1989, she had distanced herself from talk of power, snapped that she was sick of the subject, and refused to give an interview. The most powerful individuals recognize that tenure is reinforced by denial. So while McDougall joked her way through Pat Carney's Vancouver Roast, or drooped her eyelids and crooned at the John Crosbie Roast, "John. What can I say . . . about John. . . . What a body!", her reticence about her status had less to do with detaching herself from the women's movement than from an awareness of her altered state. Barbara McDougall had arrived as a force in the power systems of the land.

In the fall of 1990, McDougall was back in the headlines. The Minister of Employment and Immigration had won a major cabinet battle by convincing Michael Wilson that it made fiscal sense to raise the quota of immigrants to over one million during the coming five years. Stressing family unity, social support, and programs for integration and education for newcomers, McDougall's policy will have a significant effect on the future of the Canadian landscape. She has effected an overhaul of the Unemployment Insurance program by changing the methods for calculating UI benefits. Entry requirements are tougher, and she reallocated funds into job training and the upgrading of skills.

On April 22, 1991, McDougall was given the senior portfolio of minister for external affairs, a step closer to the seat of power. On a "Canada AM" interview, when asked what it felt like to be only the second woman in the position and one of the few women in the world to handle the post of External, she replied, "I always felt it was more uncomfortable for the men around me than for me. I have never felt like a second class citizen." Clearly she is pivotal to the basic systems that run this country, and when Mulroney decides to take his walk in a snowstorm—if the voters do not get him first—McDougall may well take a run at the PM's job.

CHAPTER 10 NOTES

1. In 1948 the newly married Maurice and Jeanne Sauvé travelled to London and then to Paris, where Jeanne worked for UNESCO's Youth Secretariat and earned the university degree she had coveted at the Sorbonne University at the age of thirty.
2. Sauvé was governor-general of Canada from 1984 to 1990.
3. Former NDP MLA British Columbia Rosemary Brown, who ran against Ed Broadbent for the federal leadership of the party, is featured in The Great Debate.
4. Rae's cabinet included the following: Ruth Grier, Evelyn Gigantes, Shelley Martel, Anne Swarbrick, Marion Boyd, Frances Lankin, Elaine Ziemba, Shelley Wark-Martyn, Zanana Akande, Shirley Coppen, and Jenny Carter. Judge Mary Hogan was appointed deputy attorney-general.
5. The NDP ruled in Manitoba from 1981 to 1988. When Premier Pawley nominated Myrna Phillips as speaker, the leader of the opposition, by tradition, seconds the nomination. But Gary Filmon refused, so Sharon Carstairs as the sole Liberal in the House, had to do it. Muriel Smith served as deputy premier from 1983-88, and minister of community services and corrections, as well as Minister of Economic Development. In the 1970s Smith had been a prominent activist for change in family law and established a large and successful family services agency in Winnipeg.
6. As vice-president of the International Confederation of Free Trade Unions, Carr claims to be connected to approximately one hundred million members of peripheral organizations from over one hundred countries. She also chairs the Commonwealth Trade Union Council, which comprises forty countries representing over thirty million workers.
7. The International Labour Organization is a United Nations agency that monitors labour standards in 150 member countries.
8. Experienced NDP women include western federal MPs Dawn Black and Margaret Mitchell, both of whom are well respected in their ridings by all parties. B.C. MLA Darlene Marzari will be a front runner for a cabinet posting if the government switches, and the former national president, Johanna den Hertog, may return as

a major player. Den Hertog narrowly lost to Kim Campbell in the 1988 federal campaign, then parachuted into the provincial riding of Point Grey to face further defeat.

9. McDougall and Carney have worked together on several issues including abortion, day-care, energy policy, and privatization.
10. The accords gave the provinces a bigger share of oil and gas revenues and moved toward the deregulation of prices. The Northern Accord is currently being negotiated.
11. Alberta Gas needed someone to guide it through the tangled system of territorial/federal government. Carney got her financing up front for Gemini and ran it debt free for ten years. She became fully conversant with American and Canadian energy companies, as well as government and Indian Affairs, for whom she did transportation and other studies. As the second largest shareholder of Denametrix, a company that priced natural gas, Carney dealt with Calgary oil executive Stella Thompson.
12. That line was really the brainchild of Ottawa *Citizen* columnist Marjorie Nichols.
13. The report showed that women account for 14 percent of senior management positions, and earn 70 cents for every dollar that men earn. It also showed that about 67 percent of women believe there is a glass ceiling; at the senior level that rises to 79 percent.
14. The Pat Carney Roast was a fund raiser for the Arthritis Society, B.C. and Yukon division, but Carney has long been supportive of the disabled. During the dinner, Rick Hansen appeared on video to note that in 1981, Carney had named him a young achiever and sent him to Ottawa to dine with the Queen. That sparked his momentum and Carney worked behind the scenes helping the Man in Motion tour get started. Upon Hansen's return from his global trip, Carney appointed him commissioner general to Expo 88 in Australia, sending a special message to the world about the potential of people with physical disabilities.
15. Senator Carney's directorships include the Asia Pacific Foundation (past), B.C. Sugar, Pacific Press, and Rogers Broadcasting. She was appointed to the Senate in 1990.
16. In 1987, Flora Macdonald, minister of communications (which now includes culture), would oversee the $50-

million cultural agreement with Ontario for the extension of the ROM, the AGO, and the restoration of the Elgin and Winter Garden, all masterminded by her old fund-raising friend, Eddie Goodman.

17. MacDonald's first experience in international negotiations occurred in the 1950s when Spain was a military dictatorship under Francisco Franco. She and another woman hitchhiker got a ride in an American limousine, which they discovered had been stolen from one of the embassies when they were arrested at the Spanish/French border. The border guards spoke only Spanish and threw them into jail.
18. One of MacDonald's plans for the free trade bill called for a strong Canadian licensing system for North American films. It elicited howls from Hollywood and its foremost supporter, then U.S. president Ronald Reagan.
19. MacDonald did win the copyright legislation for artists (opposed by distinguished artists such as Mary Pratt, who says it pits one artist against another), the $813,000 for authors in their Public Lending Rights program, $8 million extra for Canada Council performing arts, and a $380 million CBC broadcast centre in Toronto.
20. MacDonald's appointments to non-paying positions included—Canadian director of the Urban Institute in Washington and head of the Canadian delegation to the Quadrangular Forum (a meeting in Belgium of economic summit countries). The United Nations named her to an eleven-member panel in Geneva and Namibia to conduct hearings on multinational companies operating in South Africa. In the spring of 1990 she became visiting scholar to the University of Edinburgh.
21. Brown is executive director with MATCH International Centre, an organization supported by donations and by CIDA, linking Third World women with Canadians. Its aim is to combat poverty and violence among women. It works with child prostitutes in the Philippines and Thailand and concerns itself with such atrocities as the practices of bride burning in India and genital mutilation in Africa. Third World women design their own projects and come to MATCH. Said Brown, "We could be in many more places if I could raise the conzsciousness of Canadian women."

22. Also known as the Ontario Educational Communications Authority, TVOntario has as its chair and CEO Bernard Ostry, husband of Sylvia.
23. Women serving as full and part time commissioners on the CRTC, 1991, are Sally Warren, Gail Scott, Beverley Oda, and Adrienne Burn. Rosalie Gower and Monique Coupal retired in 1990.
24. McDougall worked first as a market research analyst for the Toronto *Star*, then as an investment analyst at Odlum Brown (1964-74), and from 1976 to 1981 as vice-president (the first woman) at A.E. Ames in Toronto (1976-81) before it merged with Dominion Securities (she lost her job in the merger).
25. Roscoe is now in the consulting business. McDougall's current chief of staff is former Tory organizer Ruth Archibald, a woman who is following the tried routes to power of such successes as Marjory LeBreton, Jocelyne Côté O'Hara, and Jodi White.

THE POWER OF THE LAW

CHAPTER ELEVEN

The Legacy of Irene Murdoch

> We learned . . . that the public demands no less respect from the law than it gives.
>
> ROSALIE ABELLA

In 1968, when Irene Murdoch's husband of twenty-five years broke her jaw in three places, she left their southern Alberta farm. No charges were laid against him and he was required only to make maintenance payments set by the court at $200 a month. Murdoch had never contributed money to the acquisition of real estate and assets, and therefore under Canadian matrimonial property law she had no legal right to a share of the lands that she had worked, either alongside him or alone for months at a time — driving trucks, tractors, teams, even dehorning cattle — to sustain the operation for a quarter-century.[1] Had the word "partner" been substituted for "wife," wrote *Chatelaine* editor Doris Anderson, "a man who had worked like Irene Murdoch would not only get half the property (valued at $240,000 with total assets at $312,000), but be recompensed for his injuries, and his assailant would go to jail."[a]

"Irene [Murdoch] was absolutely shattered, shafted by a legal decision," said Winnipeg homemaker/activist Berenice Sisler, recalling those events. They would lead to fundamental changes in the character of the law, which until then had decreed to an awed and uninformed public. But in a second battle in 1973, when the Supreme Court of Canada denied Murdoch reparation, the decision jangled a collective societal nerve and sparked a huge public outcry.[2] Irene Murdoch brought home to the general consciousness that women and children still had few legal rights. As former Judge Abella commented in her 1988 speech to the Canadian Club, "The family laws of property and support [had] created a systematic and generic dependency." As lawyer Anne Dubin put it, women were listed in the index of early legal textbooks with the incapacitated, the mental incompetents, and the chattels.

At the grassroots level, laypersons gathered, studied, and became an educated movement that made the Canadian Bar Association and the Law Reform Commission of Canada take notice, and recommend to the government the reform of matrimonial property law. The Berger Royal Commission on Family and Children's Law was influential in B.C., recomending that judges consider non-financial contributions of a spouse to the marriage. The Murdoch case, followed by the Canadian Charter of Rights and Freedoms, begins the era in which the law left the precincts of the ivory tower and became the property of the people.

In Manitoba, before the revised Marital Property Act could become law, Conservative Sterling Lyon—known as Canada's most aggressively chauvinist premier—won office and stopped the legislation. Alice Steinbart and Lindsay Taylor had formed the Coalition on Family Law Reform that had grown out of the Manitoba Action Committee on the Status of Women and comprised over twenty groups, including the Junior League and the YWCA. Two of the best informed activists were homemaker Berenice Sisler, and Muriel Smith, chair of the Manitoba Action Committee and future NDP cabinet minister. Sisler made presentations to the Manitoba Legislature, and she became known throughout the province and the country. A cool-headed, at times even humourous, presenter, Sisler was known to lose her temper with the intractable Lyon as her demands for family law reform were greeted with the same derision that the proposals of Thérèse Casgrain had faced in Quebec forty years earlier. Lyon continued having fun at Sisler's expense, unaware that public sympathy was shifting away from his style of iron-fisted power and towards the professional lobbying sphere of an informed public. On one occasion when accused of refusing to take family law reform seriously and of being anti-women, Premier Lyon grinned, "Conservatives like women. We're among the best breeders in the world."[3]

In response, Sisler, a Liberal supporter, crossed party lines to work with the NDP Opposition in her challenge to the recalcitrant Manitoba Conservatives. Former NDP premier Howard Pawley remembered that she came to know more than many lawyers about the nuances of family law. Then on election day in 1981, Lyon was out, Pawley and the NDP were in, and family law reform received top priority. With the co-operation of all parties, including the Tories who were inspired by Conservative MP Norma Price, the Manitoba Marital Property Act became law.

Suddenly homemakers across the country began examining their marital status and were shocked to learn that they possessed no more rights than Irene Murdoch. In Saskatchewan, Raynell Andreychuk, a lawyer,[4] had dozens of Irene Murdochs as clients, none of whom had any knowledge of their rights, and less than 3 percent of lawyers in the province were women who could advise them. In the 1960s, lawyer Nancy Morrison made it her practice to give her home telephone number to battered women so that they could call her when abused—usually around 3:00 a.m. She would then pick them up, awaken a justice of the peace, and assist the victims in laying charges. Morrison said that frequently, when women who were beaten by their drunken husbands called the authorities, "the police would come and just walk the guy around the block until he sobered up." One abused woman said that even after she was stitched and splinted, ambulance attendants would not help her press charges. Women felt like chattels, held hostage to an attitude fostered by the law and reinforced in society where, if they did not have full rights, they need not be afforded full respect.

Andreychuk remembered giving "hundreds of speeches on property rights in Saskatchewan to men and women. Women would rush up and say, 'My husband's left me. What are my rights?' I couldn't believe how they hadn't protected themselves." When she advised abused clients to leave their husbands, the victims would argue that they would lose their children, and they had no means of support.[5] Said Andreychuk, "There was an incredible, fearful dynamic in [just] not knowing."[6]

In all of Canada, except Nova Scotia where cruelty was a legal cause for divorce, committing adultery was virtually the only way an abused wife could get out of a marriage. Cooked-up adultery scenes were both degrading and fraudulent, leading to possible disbarment for the lawyer and public condemnation of the spouse. Should divorce proceedings follow, the wife would discover that family property and holdings—car, truck, home, farm, summer cottage, stocks, and bonds—were all registered in the husband's name. She was entitled to nothing, and jobs for untrained, middle-aged women, if found, were ill paying and demeaning. Women often chose to remain in tragic marriages because of the lack of economic alternatives. In examining Pettkus v. Becker, Janis Rose wrote of the reticence of Canadian courts to consider changes in societal attitudes towards marriage and cohabitation, "The court's treatment of economic realities of marriage and more informal relationships has been painfully slow."[b]

What gave Irene Murdoch's case such crucial importance was that it occurred when numerous activist streams were coalescing into a collective strength that was never again going to wither and fade away. The move to unite was manifested in the Royal Commission on the Status of Women and Laura Sabia's National Action Committee, followed by the Canadian Advisory Council on the Status of Women and boosted by the increasing number of women lawyers entering the profession.

In 1974 in the divorce case of Rathwell v. Rathwell, despite the fact that homemaker Helen Rathwell had financially contributed to the family business, Justice Donald Disbery of the Saskatchewan Court of Queen's Bench dismissed her claim for part of their property with, "Somebody has to defend the men from the present mode of the women's liberation movement."[c] The 1976 Court of Appeal decision to award one-half interest in the farm to Helen Rathwell recognized that marriage is an economic and social partnership of equals.[7] But fairness and justice did not always follow court decisions, particularly in family law when women depended more on good will than enforcement. If husbands left the province, there was no means of enforcing payment. As Abella observed, the attitudes and customs of centuries would not change without more legislation, and many women still choose the reliability of welfare over the uncertainty of receiving settlements.

In 1978, when Rosa Becker's nineteen-year common-law marriage to Lothar Pettkus ended, despite the fact that she had contributed financially to the union, the trial judge ruled that she was not entitled to an equitable share in the family farm and apiary business. Then the Ontario Court of Appeal reversed that decision, imposing a "constructive trust" of $185,000 on Pettkus. The Supreme Court of Canada unanimously dismissed Pettkus's appeal in 1980, but enforcement was almost impossible to execute. Pettkus never paid Becker a cent. Six years later, a poverty-stricken Rosa Becker sat down to write a letter about her futile attempts to collect maintenance, explaining that she felt impelled to make a public statement that might help other women. When she finished, Becker picked up a gun and shot herself in the head. Judges expressed anguish at their helplessness and press stories detailed the frustrations of enforcement. In March of 1988, the federal government made it possible for the courts to track down defaulters through their social insurance numbers and garnishee such incomes as wages, unemployment insurance, or income tax refunds to collect maintenance. But there is still no enforcement law. In February 1990, after a year of the British Columbia Family Maintenance Enforcement Program of collection, then British Columbia attorney general, Bud Smith, reported that whereas 85 percent of all former spouses in Canada had regularly defaulted on the payments, the $4 million collected by the new system in B.C. represented a still-dismal 46 percent payment rate. Nancy Morrison advised women, "You are on your own. Anything you get [out of divorce] is a bonus. You are capable. Get retrained. Become self-sufficient."

Enforcement problems aside, at no time in twentieth century history had there been such a dramatic overhaul of the legal system as in the 1980s, and in 1988 Morrison reflected that she never thought she would see it in her lifetime. Madame Justice Beverley McLachlin of the Supreme Court of Canada concurred: "It takes a while for social perceptions to find their way into legal principles, but it has certainly happened with rapidity when you look back on the usual speed of legal change." But reform has created enviable equality only for the wealthy. The 1991 reality of the new divorce laws can mean unmitigated suffering for the poor. A division of assets often means that lower income families must sell their only asset—their house—or continue to live in the same home in separate quarters by court orders. It can be, in Morrison's understatement, "a nightmare."

On the other hand, the wealthy divorcée has been launched on the path to unparallelled affluence of her own, thanks to the revisions wrought by the activists in family and property law. In a 1988 Ontario divorce case, Mariellen Black was awarded $6 million, a Toronto home worth $1.8 million, and monthly support payments of $6,500 from her former husband, Montegu Black, brother of Conrad and director of Argus and Hollinger corporations. Fairness meant providing Mariellen with the means to live in the manner to which she had become accustomed over their seventeen-year marriage. No longer will these divorcées live a diminished lifestyle in respectable anonymity. In one case, journalist Michael Salter noted in *Report on Business Magazine*[d] that a departing husband made his wife an out-of-court settlement of $15 million. The corollary of this ex-marital grand slam, of course, is that men can play the same game. Salter wrote of a wife who with two partners had established a clothing store chain worth $24 million, and was forced to take out a loan against the business in order to produce the $4-million cash, or 50 percent of her one-third share of the business, for her departing husband.

****

By April 17, 1985, when Section 15 of the Charter of Rights and Freedoms became law, many of the women who had lobbied for its inclusion had founded LEAF, the Legal Education and Action Fund. Part of its function is public education, but its primary focus is to undertake test litigation cases in the courts as interpreted through the Charter. As cases often reach the Supreme Court, LEAF is becoming a powerful vehicle for change in the country. Backed by a million-dollar gift from Nancy Jackman and her mother,[8] this non-profit organization epitomizes the thirty-year evolution from the volunteer grass-roots activists to the informed professionals functioning in the complex structures of the 1990s. LEAF lawyers Mary Eberts and UBC Dean of Law Lynn Smith represent the new-wave lawyers, conciliators who are calmly implacable in their pursuit of fairness, particularly in the fields of family and constitutional law.

Few institutions have been as affected as the law by the advent of women breaking into the ranks. Their increasing numbers, combined with the impetus of constitutional enshrinement of women's rights, are a catalyst that changes the way our society views itself. The concept of a gender power assaulting the customs integral to the judiciary may seem bizarre, but long before the grass-roots movement prodded the Canadian Bar to hasten legal reform, and decades before Alberta Judge Marjorie

Montgomery Bowker introduced the first Family Court Conciliation project, women were attempting to alter the climate of the courts and the quality of the law.

In a February 1990 address to Osgoode Hall, Madame Justice Bertha Wilson stunned the legal institution by calling for a more humane law to apply to both genders in society. She boldly stated that the law does not reflect the nature of 50 percent of the population. Systemic discrimination on the bench, or gender bias, as it is more commonly known, inspired her to challenge the quality of some judgements with: "Some aspects of the criminal law in particular cry out for change since they are based on pre-suppositions about the nature of women and women's sexuality that in this day and age are little short of ludicrous." Justice Wilson's words shocked the legal profession, partly because of their accusation, but particularly because they were made at all from a profession that has for centuries conducted its business in secrecy.

Then, one year later, Madame Justice Beverley McLachlin, also of the Supreme Court of Canada charged in a speech to the Elizabeth Fry Society in Calgary that some parts of criminal law are based on outdated sexual stereotypes that reflect unfairly on women. She cited prostitution and abortion laws, adding, "In the past, and to some extent the present, our criminal law has failed to accord equality to women."[e] Whether or not the judiciary condemns or condones these verbal fireworks, they happened, and the bench will never be viewed in the same way again. Simply by using the enormous power of their unassailable position, the justices have jolted the system and forced it towards more rigorous and public self-examination.

The universal reluctance of institutions to change is most often manifest in the law; its foundations build on perceived stability. If this recalcitrant profession had chosen to change its attitudes and self-disciplinary measures from within, the judiciary might have preserved its sanctity. At a 1986 "Socialization of Judges to Equality Issues" conference, Quebec Court of Appeal Justice Melvin Rothman and University of Calgary law professor Kathleen Mahoney called for re-education of judges, but not many bothered to attend, and nothing came of it.[f] Meanwhile, the public grew impatient over continuing examples of insensitivity towards victims of sexual assault and wife abuse, demonstrated by some judges socialized in an earlier era. In January 1987, only days before the story was to be told on the television show "Fifth Estate," the Nova Scotia judicial council finally recommended the removal of Judge Raymond Bartlett. Bartlett was known to quote from the Bible when advising battered women to return and be subservient to their husbands. Watchdog groups have became more outspoken about judgements made in cases of sexual assault, and the best known, METRAC,[9] is armed with facts and damning statistics on the lasting trauma of such assault. With the full support of the press, the cool-headed Pat Marshall, its executive director, is helping to break down the walls of judicial omnipotence as accounts of gender bias accumulate and burst into a public forum.

An increasing number of women lawyers and judges are demanding a new quality in court dynamics that, as Justice Wilson concluded in her Osgoode Hall speech, "will succeed in infusing the law with an understanding of what it means to be fully human." Quality has always been intrinsic to the judiciary, but if the flavour and interpretation of "the feminine perspective" is perceived to be lacking, the judgements can seem inequitable if not inhuman. Gender bias has been demonstrated from three viewpoints: that of the victims of sexual assault feeling dehumanized by judges citing mitigating circumstances for the guilty before handing down light sentences; that of women litigators who are treated differently from male counsel by some judges; and that of students still in law school.

On sexual assault sentencing, retired judge Marjorie Bowker defended the integrity of a legal system that must continue to evolve gradually as social conditions change. She considered the various changes in all aspects of women's lives to be relatively positive, but regarding what she called "the pathology of abuse," she observed that "there is a lack of understanding by judges of the essence of not only physical but sexual abuse and its lingering trauma." Then Bowker produced her burgeoning files on gender bias.

A sixteen-year-old James Frederick Deutsch raped a woman at gunpoint and was sentenced by Judge Stephen Borins to two and a half years in the penitentiary. The Appeal Court reduced his sentence to two years less a day in a reformatory and two years' probation because the assault was "not accompanied by many of the unpleasant features that often surround such an offence." In January 1988, Bruce Glassford was convicted of beating and attempting to rape a twenty-seven-year-old woman. Judge I. Anthony Vannini sentenced him to a ninety-day sentence served on weekends because he was "from a good family," and ruled that the woman had suffered no lasting emotional or psychological harm. An appeal raised his penalty to two years less a day.[10] In 1990, a judge gave a three-year suspended sentence to a man who had choked his "aggressive, vindictive" wife to death because she was considered to be mean-spirited: she had insulted his sexual prowess.

Lenient sentencing perpetuates the notion that women are still the property of their men, who in turn can be excused for crimes of passion.[11] In 1989, Quebec Court Judge Denys Dionne interrupted an argument about a point of law to remark, "Rules, like women, are made to be violated." As sentencing in cases of bank robbery and white-collar crime is more severe, it would appear that some male judges identify more easily with the wrench of losing their money than with the violence of physical sexual assault.

Like other institutional frameworks, the law itself evolved over centuries when women played no active part in the process. Justice Wilson argued in her 1990 Osgoode Hall address that the consummate power of jurisprudence, both punitive and inviolate, has developed from values that have systematically shut women out. She quoted from a 1989 paper by Rosalie Abella who wrote, "Every decision-maker who walks into a court room to hear a case is armed not only with the relevant legal text but with a set of values, experiences and assumptions that are thoroughly embedded."[h] Tevie Miller, the Associate Chief Justice of the Alberta Court of Queen's Bench, agreed, and in 1990, at the Canadian Judicial Council's[12] national seminars for judges, he included courses on elimination of gender bias similar to those the American Bar has been conducting in individual states for nearly a decade.

Justice Wilson accused the Canadian Bar of dragging its heels, but by that spring an international brotherhood of judges placed the issue of gender bias in the forefront of reform. That same summer, METRAC's Pat Marshall was invited to Edinburgh to speak on equality and judicial neutrality to the Society for the Reform of Criminal Law in Common Law Jurisdiction. The event was attended by judges from twenty-two countries.

Gender bias has tremendous consequences for women litigators arguing cases. Chief Justice Glube recalled appearing before some male judges more than a decade ago "who really didn't want to see a female lawyer in their courts," and the nearly 1,000 young Canadian women who have launched careers in the fractious field of criminal law are still feeling that hostility. Katherine Corrick, for one, noted that one judge greets all lawyers with "Good morning, gentlemen." Some presiding judges have been known to let two female counsel debate interminably as if mesmerized by the sight of women doing battle. Although Corrick enjoys the advantages of height and a well-modulated voice, several times when she has introduced herself in court to the presiding judge he has called her "young lady," and the male litigators "counsel." If the judge neither recognizes nor respects Corrick's professional position as equal to that of her male colleague, why should the jury?

The women members of the Criminal Lawyers Association met in January 1990, in Toronto to discuss forming a women's caucus to develop in a stronger voice. Their subsequent reluctance to do so reflected their wish not to polarize the judiciary. Women lawyers must survive like their corporate and political counterparts—by being tough, not complaining, and carrying on with their job. This is no field for wimps.

Today's law students are tomorrow's judges yet not all of them, including women, are sensitive to issues of gender bias. Despite high statistics of suicide attempts, not all are convinced of the lasting trauma inflicted on victims of sexual assault. John Hogarth, a law professor at UBC, has observed, "Sometimes the women [students] are far tougher on women —they have very little sympathy with the [battered,] self-effacing wife."

Reactions against gender biased courses still occur in law schools between students and teachers who seek progressive attitudinal change and the traditionalists such as Osgoode Hall law student Michael Reilly who in 1989, was so offended by the title of a course: "Radical Feminist Ideology: All Men Are Pigs In the Familial Relationship," that he complained in the student newspaper of its "unrelieved feminist content." It was taking time away from "substantive" studies on family law.[i] But equality, argued Kate Sutherland, 1988 University of Saskatchewan Law School Gold Medalist, is exactly what family law is all about. She recalled that when a course called "A Feminist Analysis of Law" was offered, even though it dealt with such subjects as the court's treatment of sexual assault and wife battery cases, men—and some women—argued that it was irrelevant. These provocative exchanges raise the question of whether the word "feminist" is counter-productive, repelling those people it seeks to reach. Once publicity was given to the content of the course, the class grew from twelve to twenty-five, 40 percent of whom were men. The surest route for women to permanently change established law is to work from inside the institution. The new trend to appoint female deans of law should mean a shift in focus from the traditional male-orientated emphasis to one which encompasses all of society.

CHAPTER 11 NOTES

1. In 1973, the Supreme Court of Canada upheld the 1971 Alberta ruling. In 1976, Irene filed a counterpetition and was awarded one quarter share in the property, worth $65,000.
2. The Canadian Advisory Council on the Status of Women endorsed a trust fund that was set up for Irene Murdoch by the Calgary Council of Women to help her repay legal debts.
3. Lyon and his legislature typified the outlook of the times. As recently as 1982, when NDP MP Margaret Mitchell rose in the House of Commons to table the Federal Task Force on Family Violence showing that one in ten wives were battered, federal Liberal and Conservative male MPs snickered, cracked jokes, and even jeered.
4. Andreychuk became a provincial court judge, Chancellor of the University of Regina from 1977-1983, was extensively involved in the YMCA at the international level, and then became high commissioner to Kenya. She is a permanent representative to Habitat in the United Nations and is presently the Canadian Ambassador to Portugal.
5. Although Andreychuk assured them that no court of law would take away their children, some years later MLA Colin Thatcher not only did that, but eventually had his abused ex-wife murdered. He was found guilty in 1984 and is serving a life sentence in prison with no eligibility for parole for twenty-five years. In 1991, abused mothers who cannot afford legal advice tell about husbands who file for custody of children first. As the courts are backlogged up to three years, those mothers do not have their children for that time.
6. Lawyers Claire L'Heureux Dubé and Lorraine Duguay (former journalist) in Quebec, Raynell Andreychuk in Saskatchewan, and Lynn Verge of Newfoundland, informed women that they had no rights. In Quebec, Monique Gagnon-Tremblay had trained as a secretary but, believing that women must become economically independent and responsible for creating change, she became a notary, then an MNA and the driving force behind revision of matrimonial property legislation. Quebec would be the last province to pass, in 1989, the 50-50 legislation that was devised by provinces throughout the 1980s.

7. In 1978 the Supreme Court of Canada upheld the decision.
8. Elizabeth Stikeman Rose (daughter of Heward Stikeman of Stikeman Elliott) and Judith Finlayson were the power behind the 1989 LEAF fund-raising roadshow that went across Canada. Marilou McPhedran and Marcia McClung chaired the huge Toronto effort. The Roadshow Advisory Committee included John Tory (junior),Carole Grafstein, Martha Cohen, Heward Stikeman, Tannis Richardson, Joan Sutton-Straus, Wendy Cecil-Cockwell, former lieutenant-governors Pauline McGibbon and Pearl McGonigal, and Reuben Cohen in New Brunswick, whose Central Guaranty Trustco was the national patron.
9. The Metro Action Committee on Violence Against Women and Children emerged from a Metro Toronto task force chaired by Jane Pepino.
10. Pat Marshall succeeded in registering a complaint with the Canadian Judicial Council because of Judge Vannini's "consistent misunderstanding of rape." He was not removed from the bench.
11. Journalist Judith Knelman wrote of the decree, "Are these qualities more acceptable in a man than in a woman?" She also wrote that in England, in 1846, the *Daily News* noted that juries considered wife-killing as "at the best, justifiable homicide; at the worst, manslaughter."
12. The Judicial Council is composed of Canada's federally appointed chief justices and is the most powerful governing body of the judiciary in the land.

CHAPTER TWELVE

The Judicial Hierarchy

> The Provincial court judges are the slave labour, the County Court judges are the harems, and the Supreme Court Judges are the sheiks. The Appeal Court is God.[1]
>
> ANONYMOUS JUDGE

The hierarchy and culture of the judicial system is a complex, sophisticated world designed to provide a fail-safe process for the public. At the base is the position of Justice of the Peace, epitomized by Lucy Jackson, a proud Dénê living in the isolated Northwest Territories community of Fort Good Hope. The mother of eleven children, Jackson displays a dignified bearing, pride in her people, and reverence for her office that make her an icon of the law in the North. She is famous for sentencing delinquent children to a few weeks out on her husband's trap line, a sort of northern Outward Bound from which they return healthy and with the first vestiges of self-esteem.

Up a step are the Provincial Court judges, the workhorses whose decisions may be overridden on appeal. Their courts are constitutionally separated from the province's Supreme and Appeal courts, the last recourse, before the Supreme Court of Canada. Some judges, such as Madame Justice Patricia Proudfoot of the B.C. Court of Appeal, begin at the bottom and work their way up to the top. Others, of whom Madame Justice Beverley McLachlin of the Supreme Court of Canada is one, enjoy instant elevation to a senior bench. Two chief justices serve in each province[2] for the Supreme and Appeal courts, and at the top is the Minister of Justice, Kim Campbell. The system of Federal Courts is separate, and includes Citizenship Judges whose appointments are not necessarily made from the legal profession and are famous for their patronage value.

****

In 1988, former Albertan and a professor of law at UBC Beverley Gietz McLachlin was appointed Chief Justice of the B.C. Supreme Court. As she was an outsider, street gossip was quick to pick up that she had helped former Alberta premier Peter Lougheed run his first campaign when no one had known who he was. "Patronage!" howled bereft colleagues, certain that the legendary Lougheed arm had reached over the mountains and touched the B.C. judiciary. The system functions with elaborate etiquette but, like any other hierarchy, lawyers and judges are known to manoeuvre for power and recognition. How could she understand their system and know the players? They soon had their answer. Members of the profession and judges conceded that she had impressed them with her extraordinary ability to sift through mountains of information, quickly emerging with a cogent analysis.

Madame Justice McLachlin, now of the Supreme Court of Canada, illustrates the theory that women now over forty rarely planned careers, but simply adapted to family situations as they arose. As a youngster she had enjoyed a carefree life that included wrangling cattle on her family's Pincher Creek ranch. Later, on a whim, she entered law school with the encouragement of University of Alberta Dean of Law, Wilbur Bowker (husband of Marjorie Montgomery Bowker). She was called to the bar, and joined Bull Housser and Tupper in Vancouver. Justice McLachlin seems to take on new assignments for the fun of the challenge. She "loved litigation," and in 1975 accepted the professorship at UBC because she "enjoyed the scholarship of law." She was first appointed a judge in 1981, and in 1988, shortly after being widowed with a young teenaged son, she accepted the position of Chief Justice "for the challenge," just six months later advancing to the country's highest court.

While serving as Chief Justice of the B.C. Supreme Court, McLachlin made a point of continuing to sit as well as executing her administrative duties, but her particular interest lay in the Justice Reform Committee's discussions on merging the court hierarchies. Judges do not have to be liked to be fair, but Justice McLachlin just happens to be one of the best-liked members of the bench in Canada, and some speculate that she could, become the first woman Chief Justice of the Supreme Court of Canada. Nancy Morrison considers Justice McLachlin to have been one of the best trial lawyers ever, remarking that "Everyone—counsels and litigants — emerge from her court feeling that they had got the best the system had to offer. She leaves you with a feeling of dignity.''

****

In 1982, Constance ''Connie'' Glube of Nova Scotia was appointed the first woman Chief Justice of a trial division of the Supreme Court. Considered tough minded but approachable, Justice Glube worked her way up from senior solicitor in the City of Halifax's legal department, becoming noted for her decisiveness and a no-nonsense court. On one occasion in the early 1980s, Justice Glube watched a divorcing couple with young children continually interrupt and harangue each other as their counsels quibbled over countless points of law. The bitter proceedings were going to take five days, and their custody demands promised future uncertainties for their children. Suddenly, the lawyers were shocked to see the exasperated Glube adjourn court, leave the bench, tell the couple she had seen better behaviour from two-year-old children, then send them home. The next morning they arrived in court to announce that they had worked out their differences.

Glube is on the road with the trial division nearly four months of the year, a nomad holding assizes in every one of Nova Scotia's eighteen counties. She lives in small town hotel rooms, preparing decisions or jury charges. As she told writer Ann Rhodes, ''You . . . stand on the edge and look in, and use all your mind and . . . feelings while you're dealing with it, then write a decision and put it away. If you relive the harrowing cases, you might lose your sanity.''[a] As in the lower courts, there is always the possibility that should the judgement be questioned, it can be appealed to the highest court in the land.

Life in The Provincial Court

> Kids have stopped me on the street and said, ''Remember me? I'm in university.'' Another said, ''Do you remember what you said to me in court? You changed my life.'' Then there are kids who didn't listen. They're in the penitentiary.
>
> RAYNELL ANDREYCHUK

Provincial Court judges may sit on the lowest bench in the hierarchy, but they deal with the majority of all criminal cases. These heroes and heroines of the court system hold vast powers to punish and to heal as they wrestle with the cauldron of court into which the fomenting brew of societal tragedy pours daily. There is family breakdown with all its ramifications — violence, incest, alcoholism. Then come B&Es, shoplifting, prostitution, and the lost teenaged souls who arrive drugged, drunk, assaulted, morose, defiant, dangerous, or, worst, with despair written across their every feature. Judge Andrée Ruffo's experience with the youth court in Quebec typified that of overburdened provincial court judges and social service ministries not only in this country, but in courts and bureaucracies around the world.

Dealing with persons charged under the criminal code gives provincial court judges authority to levy sentences in non-jury cases, and most of them deliver oral decisions as in frontier days. "You couldn't get through the day's work if you wrote," noted retired British Columbia judge Patricia Byrne, who often presided over the decaying Yale Street Family Court House. The diminutive Judge Byrne, clad in black robes and white wing collar, would sweep into a shabby room where defiant kids with big mouths and surly ways could peer down on her, yet with a few words establish authority in her court. Then, through the awesome responsibility of judgement, she was required to protect the public while patching up shattered lives through measures as varied as discipline, protection, punishment, and encouragement. Former Provincial Court judges Marjorie Bowker, Nancy Morrison, Patricia Byrne, and Raynell Andreychuk recalled that they could use their redoubtable power to reinforce an inner core of goodness that they perceived in the accused. Often the judge charged with repairing the damage is capable, through wise sentencing, of changing a life made wretched less by the child than by society itself. Rehabilitation is a major focus of the provincial court judges who keep seeing repeat offenders.

In Halifax, one young woman who had been through seventeen foster homes was charged with trafficking in marijuana. Judge Sandra Oxner noticed that there had been one period of eight months when the teenager had learned to type and even found a job. "You can just never give up on anybody," reflected Judge Oxner, "I have seen nobility in the strangest places." She concluded that, in this case, although a jail sentence was mandatory, her obligation to make her office socially useful was uppermost. With the agreement of the crown prosecutor to a program of education and total supervision, Judge Oxner telephoned church groups and her own prominent friends (among whom she counts the Oland brewing family) to enlist a volunteer group of thirty-two citizens to supervise, transport, and educate the young woman every minute of her life for the next year. After one minor backsliding, she was hired as a receptionist and is now married and a mother. Judge Oxner's plan illuminates the best use of community: institutional power combined with volunteer strength.

On the front line of crisis management, the Provincial Court judges are champions of seeking quality for society. In the 1960s, Alberta Family Court Judge Marjorie Montgomery Bowker, a member of the tiny band of Canadian women judges,[3] was the first to improve the protracted procedures in family breakdowns that required attendance in both the Provincial and Supreme courts. She could not change the law, but she saw a way to soften the hostile, painful impact by bringing divorcing couples to the negotiating table. In Ottawa, Bowker convinced the Ministry of Health and Welfare to fund a three-year project in the Family Court of Edmonton for court-centred marriage conciliation. Today it is known as the Family Mediation Service. She designed and initiated a system to function in concert with the existing law by housing mandatory professional counselling services within one courthouse complex. In 1975, after its three-year shakedown, the government of Alberta assumed responsibility for funding the services. ''Marjorie Bowker,'' noted Justice David McDonald of the Alberta Court of Queen's Bench, ''single-handedly forged the first mediation project in Canada.'' So superlative was the quality of her framework that it has been adopted in countries around the world.

Provincial Court judges can be surprisingly young. Ten years of law practice was customarily required, but affirmative action has sped up the process. In the spring of 1987, the police force and Nova Scotia justice system were under Royal Commission inquiry for the wrongful conviction for murder and eleven-year incarceration of Micmac Indian Donald Marshall. Halifax newspapers were carrying stories of racism and of a dictatorial justice reminiscent of the 1950s when blacks were excluded from ''white'' barbershops and private clubs except as servants.[b] In the midst of this and other problems, thirty-three-year-old Corrine Sparks, four generations away from slavery, was appointed Canada's first black female judge. A litigator who had worked her way through law school, established her own successful firm, and argued cases before a white male judiciary, Judge Sparks might well have been appointed to the bench anyway. But as a black, female lawyer in Nova Scotia, she was also there at the right time in history.

Fortunately for the citizens who appear in her family court, this bright young woman applies the wisdom born of childhood poverty in the black suburb of Cherrybrook, and of her slavery roots. Sparks has not forgotten that background. She is dedicated not only to her profession, but also to inspiring other young black women to fulfill their potential in the world beyond Cherrybrook. Encouraged by the then all-woman campus and individual tutors at Mount Saint Vincent University, Sparks graduated and then was accepted at Dalhousie Law School. Many of her classmates had come from privileged families with prestigious legal backgrounds; she brought her sense of history, parents who believed in her, the inspiration of longtime black activist and journalist Carrie Best, a strong Baptist faith, and the willingness to hold down two jobs to work her way through school. Judge Sparks is also marketable. An engaging woman whose softly styled chignon lends her a presence beyond her years, she has always shunned the aggressive approach in court, preferring as a litigator to fight with a relentless intellect, a gentle voice, and strong words. No one should underestimate her apparent softness. She is a Futurist to watch in the 1990s.

Why do lawyers accept the call to the bench? Certainly not for the money. Not for conviviality: most judges described their lives as lonely and isolated. Not for the workload. Michael Mandel of Osgoode Hall referred to "charter stress" to describe the increased pressure, even exhaustion, that have become side effects of the constitutional change that has swamped the judiciary.[c] In a 1989 address to the Canadian Bar Association in Ontario, lawyer Earl Levy noted, "With the greatest respect, I think that some provincial court judges are just losing it. . . . They are burning out."[d] Yet Judge Byrne's face lit up when she was asked why she had accepted. "Adults know the rules, but with children you're talking about protection, about the rest of that child's life. What you do may either save or destroy that child and it's a horrendous responsibility." What greater power can there be?

The Supreme Court

Ottawa, March 1988. Set far back from the Wellington Street slush, the concrete mass of the Supreme Court of Canada loomed out of the grey snow, a brooding, didactic temple of inviolate strength. Through the first two-thirds of this century, reverence for the law was reinforced by judges whose black robes and stern countenances personified that almighty power that next to God and Queen Victoria, ruled by absolutes. The concept of sin, intensified by corporal punishment, was so vast that children grew up regarding the legal system with awe and its disciplinary powers with fear. Subservience to that authority was intensified by the trappings of court: dark seats like pews in church, stone-faced policemen, black-robed judges meting out sentences in the sacred tones of a Gregorian chant. Everywhere in society the emphasis was on punishment more than reform, and few understood that much of it was the theatre that fortified institutional might. The purpose of a visit in 1988 to the Supreme Court was to meet with Madame Justice Claire L'Heureux-Dubé, only the second woman to be appointed to that bench in its then 113-year history. The first, Madame Justice Bertha Wilson, appointed in 1982, would not give an interview.

The traveller had first met Justice L'Heureux-Dubé a year earlier in Quebec City when she was a judge of the Quebec Court of Appeal. Instead of wearing robes, she had bounced into her office clad in old ski clothes. Her eyes gleamed behind substantial glasses as she laughed with the wicked delight of a student about to play hookey. A four-day blizzard had just ended and, gesturing at a cone-shaped mountain brilliantly etched against the cobalt sky, Justice L'Heureux-Dubé exclaimed, "Look at the snow on Mont Ste-Anne!" In six seconds this member of Quebec's high court had exploded the mystique of a forbidding judiciary and put a new, humane, face on the law.

Demands that would swamp an ordinary mortal have merely energized Justice L'Heureux Dubé. She has been a champion of family law reform as a litigator and a judge of three successive benches, sleeping only four hours a night before attacking the next day's problems with the same undiminished enthusiasm. Through some enviable inner drive, she is always up to date because, she explained, "Everything I have to do tomorrow, I do today. So, I am free!" The interview completed, Justice L'Heureux Dubé waved goodbye and headed for the hills.

On that grey day in Ottawa in 1988, negotiating security inside the Supreme Court meant removing outer clothing and surrendering purse and briefcase to undergo the scrutiny of X-ray machines and metal detectors. But then, with only cursory directions from the guards, the traveller took the elevator to the wrong floor and got lost. Footsteps echoed down dimly lit hallways of the perimeter circuit around a central core. Save for the spectral company of a century of chief justices presiding from oil paintings along the walls, this building seemed uninhabited, its doors without names or numbers, the silence oppressive — until an unseen mortal dropped some change, that reverberated like stones ricocheting down the walls of a well. Unlike the Provincial Court, which teemed with life, the Supreme Court was devoid of it: there were no shackled prisoners, police officers, hurrying counsel, witnesses, or even judges. With the honour of this highest appointment comes the cost of isolation. Justice L'Heureux-Dubé and her colleagues have been immured in a mausoleum and charged with ruling on society's fundamental values.

Since the advent in 1982 of the repatriation of the Constitution and the formation of the Charter of Rights and Freedoms, this court has had new powers to shape society. In a 1989 CBC "Morningside" conversation with host Peter Gzowski, Winnipeg lawyer Jack London said that the Canadian Charter of Rights and Freedoms has created a revolution, one that makes "appointed judges . . . partners in government." If society had not realized initially the extent of this monumental change, it became acutely aware of it on January 28, 1988, when the Supreme Court struck Section 251 — the abortion law — from the criminal code and left to a reluctant Parliament the politically explosive dilemma of either creating a new law or of leaving the country without one at all.[4]

Footsteps in the Supreme Court hallway could be heard drawing closer. A security officer appeared and, wielding a coded plastic card, escorted the traveller up an obscure staircase to the chambers of Justice L'Heureux-Dubé. The contrast to the hallways was startling. Here was all the warmth of a booklined, green-walled Victorian den. On the left, two overstuffed yellow chairs faced an immense stone fireplace. In the centre on the vast desk, applications for leave to appeal were piled beside thousand-page appeals themselves, and adjacent cupboards were filled with more reading to be done.

Justice L'Heureux-Dubé suddenly appeared from conference. Her "Welcome!" was sincere, but spontaneous laughter rarely punctuated the conversation of this judicial steward. Her convivial life had vanished. Participating in the 102 appeals that the Supreme Court heard in 1990, the 137 judgements that were handed down, and the hundreds of applications for leave to appeal that were read but refused, Justice L'Heureux Dubé writes all her deliberations by hand, declaring, "What I need to do is think. That's all. So I write longhand." Yet this court has reduced the waiting time for cases to be heard by up to three months, and in 1990 had eliminated more than a year's backlog. Reforms effected through the Canadian Bar Association in 1987 helped, but the progress resulted mostly from a full slate of workaholic judges who continued labouring into evenings and went home with briefcases on weekends. Peter Russell, a professor of political science at the University of Toronto, described the judges as "intellectually ambitious individuals, high-powered professionals . . . [who wish to confirm to the excellent counsel] who have appeared before [them] with buckets of . . . academic literature [that they are on top of it all.][11] Russell likened the added pressure of immediate public scrutiny from the electronic media to "writing perpetual final exams in public."

Justice L'Heureux-Dubé invited the traveller to lunch, then led the way down more gloomy hallways to two imposing doors, which she flung open to reveal a hospitable refectory and, deep in conversation at a mahogany dining room table, four judges of the Supreme Court of Canada. They turned and fell silent: Justices Jean Beetz of Quebec, William McIntyre of British Columbia, and Gerald Le Dain and Bertha Wilson of Ontario. Startled by this unexpected encounter with half the country's most powerful court, including the woman who wouldn't give an interview, the traveller braced for an inquisition. Instead, the judges rose graciously to welcome their visitor, and during the next hour in this quiet inner sanctum, over nouvelle cuisine served by uniformed waiters, the chimera of the old court gave way before a new dimension of humanity.

The talk was still on abortion law. Justice Bertha Wilson had applied abstract qualities of the human condition in her judgement, and it was her written decision in particular that continued to be applauded or damned across the land. A homey-looking woman with a soft Scottish accent, her shoulders slightly hunched from incessant hours at her desk, first in a private practice and then on the Court of Appeal of Ontario, she had become the most revolutionary member of the Supreme Court of Canada. In 1990, David Beatty, a professor of law at the University of Toronto, wrote in the *Globe and Mail* that "Of all of the people who have sat on the court, she was the staunchest defender of the Charter and the process of constitutional review . . . [hers] was, unquestionably, the court's most liberal and progressive theory of the Charter."[f] He went on to say that Justice Wilson held the government to account, requiring it to justify laws that might impinge on individual freedoms in its effort to meet its objectives.[5]

From a public perception, Justice Wilson emerged as a pre-eminent power with her 1988 Morgentaler decision. She had written of the "modern woman's struggle to assert *her* dignity and worth as a human being:" In the decision she wrote "The *Charter* and the right to individual liberty guaranteed under it are inextricably tied to the concept of human dignity . . . the right to make fundamental personal decisions without interference from the state." She concluded that, in making a woman's capacity to reproduce subject to the control of the state, "she is truly being treated as a means . . . to an end which she does not desire but over which she has no control. . . . Can there be anything that comports less with human dignity and self-respect?"

Employing the concept of dignity as well as fact is a mark of the breadth of constitutional reform and attitudinal change that has occurred in the judicial process over the past decade. It points to the infinite conundrums facing the judiciary about human rights, women, and the vast implications of modern day reproductive technology. Use or abuse of a woman's body, and the question of just who owns it and its foetus — herself or society — will continue to figure through the turn of this century among the most fundamental issues in civilized nations. They obtruded into the luncheon as the judges continued their impromptu debate. Justice Wilson's intention to seek the humane element had been revealed in 1982 when, after being appointed to the bench, she delivered a speech to the Ottawa Women's Canadian Club. As the wife of a small town Presbyterian clergyman, she had discovered how complicated people are, "how most of us are locked up tight inside ourselves most of the time, pretending to be something that we're not. . . . It is just as important to know about people as it is to know about the law."[g]

In a humorous aside, Justice Wilson described her visit with Justice Sandra Day O'Connor in the US Supreme Court where round-the-clock guards refused to leave her chambers, just in case, said the raconteuse, the Canadian Supreme Court Justice attacked the American Supreme Court Justice. Despite the threatening mail that still poured into Justice Wilson's chambers regarding the abortion decision, such overpowering security sounded laughable, metaphorically sketching a Canadian society whose quality of decency can be related to that of its judiciary.

The judges discussed their fatigue, the time spent away from their families, their monkish existence, and their work — a monumental and endless pilgrimage of papers, debate, and decisions. Yet as Justice L'Heureux-Dubé spoke, the old Gallic enthusiasm returned and the optimist who believes in the basic goodness of mankind laughed over Justice McIntyre's renditions of Mark Twain's anecdotes on the evil nature of man. Engrossed in the energy of their *inter pares* debates, the judges had become oblivious to the stranger sitting silently in their midst. Isolated as it is from the world, this judicial hybrid with nine fiercely independent minds has only itself for human interaction. It is a curious marriage of creativity and contention. Justice Wilson sprinkled the conversation with sage quotations and anecdotes, extracting them lightly from the air like a cellist plucking pizzicato strings in an impromptu symphony. The hour was filled with a spontaneous eloquence that might have been passé to the professionally sophisticated, but to a student of power it was riveting theatre. These guardians of the law were no longer practitioners of institutional inflexibility. Whether critics consider them right or wrong, brilliant or dull, few would disagree that the justices of the Supreme Court of Canada during the past decade have been anointed with even vaster powers and have introduced an era of compassionate jurisprudence to deal with a difficult, living law.

Justice Bertha Wilson's speech to Osgoode Hall Law School[h] created a predictable storm ranging from standing ovations to condemnations. Rosalie Abella called the speech "an extremely significant" benchmark, and Helena Orton, a LEAF litigation director, reported, "It was a very brave thing to do." On the other hand, lawyer Gwendolyn Landolt, a founding member of REAL Women, filed a formal complaint against Justice Wilson, arguing that regardless of constitutional change, public policy is not the authority and responsibility of the judiciary but of parliament. She charged that Justice Wilson's references were feminist in nature, and she took exception to Wilson's argument that men and women have fundamentally different values. Some women, she argued, thrive on confrontation just as some men are conciliators rather than fighters.

Debate aside, the hallmark of judges' power is their sacrosanct freedom to make judgements without fear of reprisal. *Globe and Mail* journalist Kirk Makin has charged that complaints about judges are examined in secrecy and usually disappear into a black hole. Allan Hutchinson, law professor at York University, told Makin that their power "is a classic case of self-regulation amounting to no regulation."[i] Judges' actions can be reviewed by the Canadian Judicial Council, but the removal procedure for a federally appointed judge goes beyond the justice minister to a joint address to the House of Commons and the Senate, all of which is so protracted that it creates a deterrent to initiating it. The point is, agree with her or not, Justice Bertha Wilson had the power to speak out, and she has probably forever altered the character of a judiciary that enjoys the greatest power in the land.

The traveller departed for the elevator, accompanied by a security escort and Justice L'Heureux-Dubé, who suddenly stepped into the elevator and rode down to the immense foyer, torn between duty and the gregariousness of a woman who once revelled in the vibrant society of Quebec. Turning to leave, she paused to share her own message: "We are seen as something beyond the people. We aren't. We are people too." Responsibility and sacrifice are the true, and inevitable, consequences of power.

CHAPTER 12 NOTES

1. An echelon above the Provincial Court, the British Columbia County Court, for one, was amalgamated in 1989 with the Supreme Court into one trial division.
2. Those women who have sat as chief justices in the provinces are Mary Batten, retired Chief Justice of the Court of Queen's Bench in Saskatchewan, Beverley McLachlin of British Columbia Supreme Court, and Constance Glube, Chief Justice, Trial Division, of the Supreme Court of Nova Scotia.
3. The talent pool for the less than one percent proportion of women judges was the barely 3 percent of women lawyers.
4. The only power that outweighs a Supreme Court decision is the Notwithstanding Clause in the constitution, used by Premier Robert Bourassa to reinstate Quebec's Bill 178 after the Supreme Court had decreed that French-only signs were unconstitutional.
5. According to Beatty, Madame Justice Wilson's thought has freed workers from sweeping restrictions on their right to strike, ensured refugees' guarantees of security, protected the legal rights of prostitutes as long as their activity does not offend the public, and given women unrestricted access to abortion during the first trimester of pregnancy.

CHAPTER THIRTEEN

The Portias

The only battle that women lawyers needed to win was won in 1897 when Clara Brett Martin won the right to become a lawyer.

MARGARET HYNDMAN[1]

We never mentioned affirmative action, or a women's movement. We just got on with it and practised law. . . . You can't sit around and whine about your life because you were born female. It's not a disability, for heaven's sake.

LAURA LEGGE

Laura Legge

When the entrepreneurial spirit functions from within the boundaries of institutions, it focusses on flexibility rather than wrestling with restrictions, and it fashions its own style to work to its advantage. It is generous, ignores intended insults, is usually accompanied by a sense of humour, and, while it embraces good luck, it applauds success based not on gender, but on excellence.

Laura Legge, founder in 1956 of her own law firm, epitomizes the women lawyers who "made it" before women were supposed to. She did not join her husband's law firm. He joined hers. With the candid perspective of one who fears neither institutions nor reprisals, Legge reflects from her comfortable but unadorned quarters at Yonge Street and St. Clair Avenue in Toronto, far from the glass and steel power symbols of her Queen Street colleagues. Law partner, past treasurer (president) of the Law Society of Upper Canada, a Life Bencher, former president of the Federation of Law Societies of Canada, Legge has done it all.

A secretary's toddler tumbled about, brought to work because a babysitter did not show. Legge has always made a place for working mothers in her office and has always watched out for the underdog. But never, ever label her a feminist. A nurse in her first career before she switched to law in 1948 and had her three children in the 1950s (while continuing to practise), Legge is less anti-feminist than she is pro-pragmatist, an empowered breed of women whose motto is "Just do it." Did Legge ever feel put down by her classmates at university in the 1940s? Certainly not. By her professors? Never. Has she ever had judges refer to her in court not as "counsel" but as "my dear"? Legge's nostrils flared at the insinuation, and the lawyer with the cameo hairdo and fragile wire glasses stated frostily, "They wouldn't dare."

Litigation has not been the centre of Legge's career, but she has commanded the respect of her peers, who broke with tradition and twice voted her treasurer of the Law Society of Upper Canada, one of the most prestigious law-related posts in the country. Former Supreme Court Justice Willard Estey said, "Laura Legge was clear, unemotional, as good as they come, maybe the best that we had." Like the politicians who have enjoyed success in the arena of debate, Legge has the gift of a voice that lends credibility and elicits a positive response. Judges and juries have been known to recoil from the shrill tones of a female litigator and miss the point because they had stopped listening.

Mid-year in 1988, Legge agreed to assume the position of treasurer of the Law Society. It was the year that the Economic Summit was being held in Canada and Legge understood that it had been agreed upon to invite Prime Minister Margaret Thatcher to be appointed an honorary bencher. When Legge sent the invitation and Thatcher accepted, howls of protest by some members of the Law Society exploded onto a bemused public. Lawyers Clayton Ruby, "our multi-millionaire socialist," Legge laughed—and Morris Manning, flew in a huff to the media. What should have been a private spat was broadcast by CBC Radio early one morning when Legge was phoned with Manning already on the air. Legge scoffingly blew him away, Thatcher arrived for the special convocation, remained to visit with everyone, and had a wonderful time. Subsequently, Legge received "vicious letters" from twelve women and two men who were, she announced, just "jealous of Thatcher because she's successful and militant feminists hate successful women."

Fed up with the cries for equal rights, affirmative action, and family law reform, Legge said, "It's rough out there for men too." She insists that the world is equally wide open for women, and she challenges them — with a cheerleader's conviction rather than critical diatribe — to stop whining, to get out, and prove themselves. "Whenever I have behaved like a lawyer I have been accepted as a lawyer. My sex is irrelevant. All that matters is my legal competence. Every woman who has practised law for as long as we [Margaret Hyndman and I] have will tell you the same thing." Of those who bemoan their ill-treatment or inability to break through the glass ceiling to partnerships she announced, "The profession doesn't need to prop up people who shouldn't be there, whether they're men or women, and as my husband jokingly says, affirmative action allows women to rise to the same level of incompetence to which men have been rising."

Legge's self-reliance was fostered in the Depression, as a daughter of self-educated Ontario farmers who were so determined their six children would be educated that they sent them all to high school seven miles away. She knows all about survival, achievement, and self-worth. When she began dating her future husband, Bruce Legge asked her what she was going to do when she graduated. "Practise law," she replied. Then he asked what she would do if she had children, and she reiterated, "Practise law." She smiled brightly in 1989 and said, "So we had no problem. I had three children and practised law." Then she mused, "I'm getting towards the end of my life, and I can tell you very candidly I have done exactly what I wanted to do. [Women] have as many rights as men today — we have had since I've been a lawyer." In 1973 her lawyer husband, Bruce, became a partner, and in the 1980s their son John joined them.

Legge's power is reminiscent of matriarchy *à la* Margaret Thatcher or Jean Pigott. Problems over which the rest of the country wrings its collective hands Legge dispenses as utter drivel. All this constitutional talk? She frowned, "What the devil they're talking about is beyond me, and the best thing that could have happened to us was that the Charter of Rights had never been brought in. Mr. Trudeau is a civil law lawyer. He didn't understand the English common law, which grows to meet all exigencies. The *Code Civile* does not."

Legge closed with Margaret Hyndman's favorite aphorism, "To define is to confine," before adding her final opinion: "[The charter] has been the most confining document. . . . We did not need it. [The Supreme Court is swamped.] Complete chaos. I told Pierre Genest, [one of] Trudeau's legal adviser[s], that he was out of his mind."

Anne Dubin

One who combined Establishment power with talent and a facility for practising in the male culture was Ann Dubin, whose mother wanted her to marry, stay home, and have children. Instead she enrolled in the University of Toronto law school with her business executive father's full support. Recalled Dubin of law school in the 1940s, when women were not only an anomaly but were often resented for taking up space, "I wasn't fighting any battle and I had a lot of fun." Dubin has never recognized discrimination against women in the profession. An insult cannot be an insult if you don't feel insulted. Her greatest strength, however, was practising from the beginning from within the core of institutional power. The year she graduated, she married Charles Dubin and joined his law firm as a partner. She recalled, "The work poured in." No one requested a male lawyer or even expressed dismay at having a young female lawyer do their corporate work. Respected for her professional talents as well as her community work, Dubin has enjoyed a long and prestigious practice from the centre of the legal universe.

Dubin does not agree with those who claim that the language of the court is male, and women have credibility problems. She stated, "Women in court today hold their own if they are able. A limited number of people can enjoy that ability. The same holds true with young men. Some of them are not great." Dubin was the first woman appointed to the Toronto Stock Exchange. She served eight years and made it "almost mandatory" thereafter that one of the two public governors be a woman. Economist Wendy Dobson succeeded her and was in turn replaced by Heather Reisman. Dubin is currently a partner at the prominent law firm Tory Tory Deslauriers & Binnington, is a director of Petro-Canada and Central Guaranty Trustco, serves as vice-chair of the Board of Governors at York University, and is a trustee at the Toronto General and Western Hospital Foundation. Her husband is Chief Justice of Ontario.

Jane Harvey

> The legal profession is almost pre-Industrial Revolution. It's been in the lawyers' interest to charge high fees, don't tell anybody what you're doing. The idea . . . frankly, protects the profession from competition. [Now] lawyers have priced themselves out of the market. Do you know how law firms are set up? From a business point of view, it's wacko.
>
> JANE HARVEY

In 1980, long before it was legal to advertise, lawyer Jane Harvey opened a storefront office on Bloor Street in the core of the Toronto uptown business district, then wrote to the Law Society of Upper Canada to ask if she could put a price list in her window. The answer was no. She wrote again and asked if she could put it in her reception area. When the society agreed, Harvey stood a man-sized cardboard sign in her reception area facing the street. Her listed services and accompanying fees could be read by the world as it passed by: MARRIAGE BREAKDOWN $150.00. DIVORCE-UNCONTESTED $299.00. BASIC WILL $75.00. BUSINESS INCORPORATION $299.00. CRIMINAL MATTERS: GUILTY PLEA $450.00 The sign met the Law Society's stated association rules yet shouted the underlying message. In retrospect, she muses of the risk she ran to her professional status: "It was stupid, but effective." And it was revolutionary.

Harvey's gambit might have bombed, but as a former lawyer for the Toronto *Star* she had media friends who were thrilled to give her challenge to the profession a boost. Positive publicity followed. Harvey the lawyer had become Harvey the merchant, selling legal advice with the enthusiasm of Fred Eaton let loose in his Seven Seas china shop during the Christmas rush. And from the start, the response from middle-to-upper-middle-class walk-in clients and medium-sized businesses was surprising. Each brought along a favourite horror story of previous legal expenses. Within three months the heavy workload impelled Harvey to hire another lawyer. The Law Society could do no more than send spot auditors and the Practice Adviser to examine Harvey's business. Both expressed polite concern that she couldn't know what she was doing, charging such low prices, and that the quality of service would suffer. "[My style]," she smiled, "was an unknown commodity." If not blatantly competing with senior members of her profession, she was certainly demonstrating what bare bones legal services could cost. By 1991 Harvey had one storefront office in the business centre of Adelaide, one on the Yuppie corner of Bay Street at Cumberland, and one each in the Yorkdale Mall, Fairview Mall, and the Scarborough Town Centre. Her future plans are to open in Western Canada.

Harvey has made the "informed client" her highest priority. She sees a discussion of all the options and consequences of the case as essential on the first visit, and structures her costs in stages. Then she sticks to them. The client can decide how far to go, and there are no surprises on the final bill. Clients can thank not only the tactics of the fat cat law firms for Harvey's attention to costs, but also an interior decorator she once hired who sent her an exorbitant bill for very little work. She sympathizes with clients who are quoted an hourly rate without knowing how many hours are involved. Her practice of pre-setting costs is the antithesis of some lawyers whose contentious dealings have been viewed as being designed to get clients into court.[a]

In 1974, after graduating from the University of Toronto law school in the first big class of women (22 percent), Harvey began articling with Smith Lyons Torrance Stevenson & Mayer, a Toronto law firm of over one hundred lawyers. From her vantage-point low in the hierarchy, she saw how unwieldy firms that followed traditional practices became. Worse, they lacked efficient management. The almost untenable overhead of mammoth law firms happened because partners, untrained in management, wasted time on decisions about personnel, salaries, equipment, and technology when they could be more effective working on legal matters. The unlucky partner elected manager for that year not only had to deal with his clients, but do the billing and run the firm. Mused Harvey, "It's amazing they've done as well as they have."

Years of success had made them believe their own myth. One night, Harvey found five of the six articling students in the library researching the same thing for different lawyers in the same firm. The next day she had the temerity to suggest to the head of the articling committee that he establish a central precedent file for greater efficiency. Harvey remembered, "He laughed and laughed. It was years before they put one in." Her decision to leave was precipitated by an incident in court when she was assisting a senior partner who not only refused to lunch with the client but stated in a voice chilled by arrogance, "Miss Harvey and I are going to the Barristers' dining lounge. We'll see you at 1:00." Harvey was appalled by the power games and politics.

Partners with awesome incomes still enjoy an ivory-tower lifestyle supported by what Harvey called "the cottage industry" below. But all those partners, junior or senior, have to be paid. Office space is lavish, business travel first class. All nonsense, said Harvey, as did Laura Legge, who pointed out that the clients are paying for those oak doors and interior staircases. Most major law firms have seen the light and are hiring business managers to streamline their systems before they price themselves out of the market. In May 1988, British Columbia Supreme Court Chief Justice Allan McEachern jarred the legal profession by publicly castigating lawyers for their cushy offices and exorbitant fees.

What particularly irritated Harvey was the rule outlawing advertising in the profession. The decree originally addressed the principle that ideals rather than money were what mattered to the practitioner. "Members of professions," recited Harvey, "neither discuss matters of money nor advertise. 'You must never look as if money counts' is a translation of, 'you must never diminish the dignity of your position by discussing it.' Yet [in the legal profession] they were charging higher and higher fees, [without fully informing the client]."

Envisioning a smaller firm, greater freedom for direct, individual control, and efficient cost-management, Harvey, by then twenty-eight, started her own firm and shaped it by pursuing a specific market. It had an excellent run until 1990 when the recession caused some contraction. She still has six lawyers, no articling students, and nine support staff. She trains each of her legal staff members in efficient business practices such as weekly, not monthly billing, which is also beneficial to her upscale clients. Over the years, Harvey has raised her prices only marginally, adhering to her formula of low prices and large volume. In firms of 200 lawyers, by the time a case reaches litigation, fees can run as high as $50,000. In a similar situation, Harvey's run at $5,000 and, she states, "the quality is the same." As for her staff, Harvey has introduced incentives by paying lawyers and staff as if they were self-employed. Her scale is based first on the business brought in and secondly on the work done. The salaries compare with those of larger firms with an entrepreneurial formula that includes bonuses for the secretaries as well as the professionals. There are no disagreements about what people are earning because salaries are common knowledge.

Rather than resenting Harvey, her professional peers applauded her for trend setting, particularly when law societies (and provincial legislation) prevented firms from expanding across the country and they were in potential danger of being overwhelmed by large American firms entering the Canadian market. In challenging the rules, she succeeded in shaking up the profession and opening its doors to better practices and greater freedom. The problems haven't ended. Harvey warned that unless lawyers improved their service to the public, clients will turn to paralegals, who have neither the training nor the supervision to offer reliable legal services. Mention "paralegal" to Laura Legge and she delivers an oratory of prime ministerial force on those pretenders to her profession. Would traditional law firms consider branch offices fashioned on Harvey's? "Why," laughed the legal retailer, "would they market Zellers products when they can sell Hermes scarves?" The traditionalists continue to ignore the signs posted by an increasing number of aggressive young men and women lawyers who are circumventing the bloated trappings of success. "They [big law firms] are still hoping," observed Harvey, "that nothing will change."

By 1989 Harvey was sitting as a bencher with Legge on the governing council of the Upper Canada Law Society. A decade ago she had begun an MBA course but found the evening hours impossible with two small children, so she took the accounting courses and still runs the business end of her five outlets. Her goal is to expand west after the recession, and she would not oppose the concept of franchising. She owns all her locations, enjoys summer holidays in France, and, of the challenge of being wife, mother and businessperson, sings the entrepreneurial anthem: "It's fun!"

Laura Legge, who considers Jane Harvey a businessperson rather than a lawyer, had the last word. She snorted, "My fees have always been lower than Jane's."

CHAPTER 13 NOTES

1. Called to the bar in 1926, Hyndman practised for sixty-four years, thirty of them while legally blind. Although an entrepreneurial-minded lawyer, some twenty years ago she had advised Laura Sabia in founding the National Action Committee, because of her concern for women who were locked in to poverty or someone else's economic control through marriage, had children to care for, and could not speak for themselves. She died in 1991.

MEDIA POWER

CHAPTER FOURTEEN

The Media

America is now wholly given over to a damned mob of scribbling women.

NATHANIEL HAWTHORNE 1855[a]

Marjorie Nichols . . . could eat this gang for breakfast and personally force this government into retreat on the American Express issue.

ALLAN FOTHERINGHAM[1b]

During Margaret Thatcher's 1983 visit to Canada, CBC-TV "Journal" host Barbara Frum conducted an interview with the British prime minister in which Thatcher seemed intent on diminishing Frum as decisively as she cheerfully demolished her opposition in the House of Commons. Patronizing, didactic, authoritative, Thatcher interrupted Frum's hard but valid queries to lecture her questioner with such missiles as: "I really *don't* quite *recognize* what you are saying. . . . The question you *should* be asking. . . . I *have* no rhetoric. . . . You still have to answer the question implicit in your question and to which you *will not address your mind*."

Weaker hearts might have suffered cardiac arrest, but a smiling, obdurate Frum would not succumb. When Thatcher interrupted, Frum interrupted her back to demand answers, which she then received. But Thatcher's dander was up, and when she appeared ready to walk out, Frum feigned contrition and asked, "Mrs. Thatcher, may I ask just two more questions?" The Prime Minister replied, "Quickies!" with the smile of a jaguar and the dangerous sweetness of the Queen thinking "Off with her head!"

Following Frum's experience, CTV host Pamela Wallin arrived at the British embassy to interview Thatcher live for "Canada AM." Having seen Frum's "Journal," the veteran reporter of the Falkland Islands War expected trouble. Wallin and her crew set up the room in the only way possible; then Thatcher arrived a half-hour early and ordered it all rearranged. "It was just such crap," snapped Wallin. "It was a power play. She was horrible." Eventually Thatcher expressed satisfaction and sat down. Said Wallin triumphantly, "She didn't realize that she had moved it all back. It was the same!" It was still ten long minutes to air time and Thatcher glared silently at Wallin who tried in vain to warm up the Prime Minister. It was going to be war. Two minutes before airing, Wallin looked meaningfully at the TV monitor in which the colour is always washed out and said to the make-up artist, "Mrs. Thatcher is looking a little pale. I think she needs a bit more blush."

Thatcher examined her image in the monitor and exclaimed, "Oh! You're quite right!" A powder puff was waved over Thatcher who was so grateful she gave Wallin the best interview of the host's life.

One of Adrienne Clarkson's more than 3,000 television interviews took place on the "Fifth Estate" with the Shah of Iran before his downfall. Clarkson stared coolly into the eyes of the potentate and with guts of steel asked, "Is there torture in Iran?"

The Shah: "Of course not, and I don't like the question."

Clarkson: "But I'm still asking it. Is there torture in Iran? We read about it in the papers like the [London] *Sunday Times*."

The Shah: "The *Times* is a rotten newspaper."

Clarkson: "Well, where I come from, the *Sunday Times* is not considered to be a rotten newspaper."

The Shah: "It is a rotten newspaper and don't ask me about torture! We don't have to torture people. Our methods are as sophisticated as yours are in the West."

****

Communication creates an intangible power, one unrestricted by bottom lines or social taboos. The writers, the television hosts, the media administrators, those who convey attitudes and present us with mirrors of ourselves or hype the next hero, have the single greatest connection to each individual in a society. Media personalities who survive this pressure-cooker enjoy international celebrity status and extraordinary influence. Barbara Frum talks with world authorities in the living rooms of the country. Should she care to utilize her potential power to influence the public, she has already won a trusting international constituency.

The media bring a dimension of discordant reality to public perceptions, reflecting social conditions and conscience, stripping façades away, raising questions about the past and future. Daily "the tribe" faces the task of interpreting a global humanity in astonishing flux, one whose fate is inseparably linked with our own. The media inform us. They may anger us with sensationalism, shallow analyses, or cynicism, but they can challenge us, shake us from complacency, and perhaps inspire attitudinal change. Some media personages claim, as did Frum in the spring of 1990, that the media are the power on this new world stage, a power enhanced by leaders who are playwrights rather than politicians or business executives. Rather than arbitrarily create political conditions of their own design, both Mikhail Gorbachev and F.W. de Klerk played to the pressure created by the international media's reflection of public opinion.

If the premise is true that global media influence world opinion, then television is the most powerful catalyst in civilized society. Magazines and newspapers demand the act of purchase, but the flick of a switch brings into our living rooms broadcasters who actually talk to us. In 1987, Environics Research found that people trust the TV news more than that found in papers or magazines.[2c] Long ago, fans of Dr. Kildare, television's first sitcom medic, wrote to their celluloid physician for professional advice, accepting their hero as an authentic doctor. Film, entertainment, and sports stars enjoy ready-made constituencies of millions that they can influence. Sting is out to save the Amazon. A former actor ruled in the White House. If Wayne Gretzky or Madonna backs your cause, it's a guaranteed success. The potential for power, or for producers, directors, and camera crews to access it, is immense. Of course, the power can work both ways, a fact well known by those who are skilled at seducing the media.

****

> They've lost sight of the issue. The pro-life movements have all these mini czarinas. . . . Prima donnas are holding onto power and they're getting away with it.
>
> BRENDA MONTGOMERY[3]

Tom Wolfe pointed it out in *The Bonfire of the Vanities:* all it takes to lure a camera operator is ten people simulating a crowd, leading more cynical viewers to wonder if the media reflect the news or create it. Time and again the media and radical groups play into each other's hands, and the Vancouver Right to Life Society president Elizabeth Green perfected the technique. A seasoned veteran of media exposure, Green has presided for eighteen years over the VRLS, which she co-founded with the Reverend Bernice Gerard, Vancouver's pentacostal televangelist, who has not only her own TV and radio programs but also a film production crew. Every time Green organized a rally, Gerard's film crew would roll in, cover the event, and then bill the VRLS.

But Green surpassed herself on December 15, 1988, when she launched the first Canadian Operation Rescue, a demonstration at the Everywoman's Health Clinic. While they were calling it "Big Betty's Event" around the clinic, Green was describing it as "something like a beach party." Her boast that she would be the first to be arrested came to pass when she led her group onto the street and demonstrators chained themselves by the neck with a Kryptonite bicycle lock to a concrete block in front of the clinic. The VRLS achieved national attention and played the media all the way to jail. Green's twenty-four-day sentence and a year's probation marked for her the success of her venture in a year of turbulent, even hostile demonstrations by pro-life factions across North America.

Access to media exposure is so vital to special interest groups and some individuals that people will fight for it even among themselves. At the April 1990 REAL Women's national conference in Vancouver, the brouhaha following their scandalous newsletter—its postage paid for by the provincial tourism department[4] — brought Gwendolyn Landolt, Ontario lawyer and co-founder of REAL Women, before the media to effect damage control. But she found herself pre-empted by VRLS president Betty Green, who was preening on prime-time news on behalf of REAL Women. Although a veteran of a hundred battles in the civility of the courtroom, Landolt lost her cool, shoved Green aside, and growled that the pro-life president was not the spokesperson for REAL Women. Veteran of a hundred street fights, Green shoved back and talked over Landolt to enraptured TV crews. The two demonstrated that, when it comes to prime-time national exposure, people cling to their territorial limelight with the tenacity of grizzlies protecting their lairs.

****

Breaking into the business of print, radio, and TV for women now forty-five and over provides trailblazing stories as varied as their adventures in these once male-dominated worlds. Today's senior media hosts are true entrepreneurs who ignored the rules of progression through the institutional hierarchies. None of them studied journalism, a discipline that was considered inappropriate for young ladies in the 1950s and 1960s. Most of them bluffed their way into their first jobs with pizazz and an indefatigable work ethic. Some, like *Saturday Night*, and *Chatelaine* journalist Charlotte Gray, were — and still are — homemakers. They began writing with their children racing around their knees, turning out, in Gray's case, well-informed articles on significant personalities in government and the national scene. Columnist Stevie Cameron considers Gray "one of the most perceptive political journalists in Canada." Gray's husband, like Cameron's, is a senior bureaucrat, which means she is privy to the various nuances of government issues. Cameron herself was a homemaker who commuted by bus from Ottawa to Toronto where she worked for the Toronto *Star* in an era when she was castigated for neglecting her family by everyone except her husband, mother, and mother-in-law.

Adrienne Clarkson started out reviewing books on the CBC's "Take 30," was its host within a year, and became an exacting TV interviewer when no one thought she could do it because she had studied liberal arts instead of journalism. Barbara Frum landed her first interview when she learned of a Torontonian who kept a town house full of pet snakes. Former CBC story editor Starr Solomon recalled that Frum nagged her for that job, but the show's producer grumbled that Frum was just the spoiled wife of a wealthy dentist out playing games. Solomon persuaded her boss to trust Frum, who interviewed the snakes' owner, impressed the crew, and launched her career.

A decade after the event, Pamela Wallin's eyes still glittered as she recalled the time when she was an unknown story producer for CBC radio's "As It Happens," and convinced a reporter in Delhi to give her the unlisted telephone number of Indira Gandhi. For three months Wallin kept telephoning the prime minister's house before she came to the phone and agreed to an interview with Barbara Frum. Wallin breathed, "You're this little pup journalist, just nobody, and you got Indira Gandhi on the phone. That's why [we] get bitten. This business is just so seductive."

Marjorie Nichols, parliamentary columnist for the Ottawa *Citizen* is the only anomaly in the bunch — she *knew* she wanted to be a political reporter in the 1960s, and after university and a job reporting on radio, she was hired by the Ottawa *Journal* on the night shift, police beat. She told author Susan Crean[d] that it was by hanging out on Parliament Hill that she met all the backbenchers, messengers, and secretaries, and she always got a story. Nichols spent a decade in Vancouver, and then returned to Ottawa. Mike Duffy, host of "Sunday Edition" for Baton Broadcasting, called the popular and courageous Nichols "a verbal cartoonist . . . [with] a Rodney Dangerfield delivery," adding that her "knowledge of the ins and outs of Canadian politics is encyclopedic."

Investigative Reporters

> . . . swarming, grunting, masses of jackals.
>
> CONRAD BLACK[e]

Stevie Cameron

The investigative reporters are the super sleuths of the media world, ferreting out information, sifting its relative value, and piecing together complex stories that otherwise might be missed. They hold vast powers over the lives of individuals simply by the way in which they and their producers research, structure, and focus their stories. The power of media exposure is rarely more evident than when it reveals the exploits or excesses of public figures, and imbedded in the hearts of investigative reporters is a cynicism that hones their natural curiosity to a fine art. Access to information is an essential requirement and few have better pipelines than Stevie Cameron. She knows half the secretaries on the Hill and has built up years of trust with her inside network: "It was my life as a housewife . . . as a volunteer at the Rockcliffe Park School book fair, and at Ottawa dinner parties. I had met all the players socially. Years of trust. People would tell me stuff and they would not see [their names] in the paper on Monday." Yet, when Cameron, as the then editor of Lifestyles for the Ottawa *Citizen*,[5] had asked to join the political team she was teased as the "editor of fluff."

Finally given a chance by her bosses — Nick Hills, Paddy Sherman, and Keith Spicer[6] — Cameron had her first success when she uncovered the avalanche of patronage posts that were Pierre Trudeau's retirement gifts in 1984. Her weekly source for the latest plums was a certain desk in the order-in-council office, and her scoops earned her both the envy of her Citizen colleagues, who had expected her to fall on her face, and respect as a first-rate sleuth in the ranks of Canadian journalism. Within the year she became part of the *Citizen's* special investigative reporting unit and a parliamentary columnist.

When the Conservatives took power, Cameron broke their patronage appointments as well. Then she stumbled onto a story about the redecoration of the official residences: 24 Sussex Drive, Stornoway, and the Speaker's house at Kingsmere. In 1984, interior decorator Giovanni Mowinckel received what would become the dubious honour of redecorating the prime ministerial homes. When Prime Minister Mulroney announced that he would spend only $97,000 on 24 Sussex and $25,000 on Harrington Lake from public funds, Cameron was impressed — until a senior Conservative insider told her, "That's bullshit. Don't you know about what they're doing over there? You're never going to get a press tour of that house, Stevie. The PC Canada fund is paying for a major part of it." As party war chests consist mostly of donations under $100, donors were entitled to pro-rated tax credits. If that were true, Cameron figured, then tax-credit money had been used for redecorating. By late autumn, 1986, racy stories began emerging about huge expenditures and their source, all of which Cameron documents in her book, *Ottawa Inside Out*. How she found the information is the stuff of cloak-and-dagger research.

In 1989, two years after a devastated Mowinckel fled Canada for Italy, Cameron had the sources—thanks to her friends-of-friends network who knew all the right unlisted telephone numbers for Mowinckel's friends, the Sussex Drive decorating teams, and the tradespeople who had built the famous dressing room with shelving space for eighty pairs of shoes. Cameron's supreme coup was winning power of attorney from Ken Cramer, Mowinckel's lawyer, to study the decorator's banked receivables. The bank manager, a Québécois who read only the French newspapers, had no idea that Cameron was a reporter. When he asked her if she worked for Ken Cramer, she replied, "No, but I'm a friend of Giovanni's. I'm helping prepare his defence," which was the truth if not the whole truth. When the manager told Cameron he would take her to the receivable files in a warehouse, she rented a portable photocopier and spent days pouring over the papers while he brought her coffee and studied for his CA exams. Long days in the vaults paid off. "My heart just stopped," Cameron recalled of her discoveries. "I found all the cancelled cheques from the PC Canada fund issued by its chair, David Angus, and cancelled cheques for [Giovanni's] donations to the PC Canada fund, the kick-backs that you have to pay." Occasionally the bank manager would look up from his reading and remark wonderingly to Cameron, "Do you know this stuff is leaking out to the press?"

The *Globe and Mail* ran Cameron's entire story, including the names of friends to whom Mila had given gifts. The full impact never struck, Cameron recalled, because "people were so overwhelmed by the image of Brian's closets full of Gucci loafers."[7] Cameron spent 1990 working as co-host of CBC-TV's renowned "Fifth Estate" with Victor Malarek, Linden McIntyre, and Hana Gartner, before returning to the *Globe and Mail* as a national affairs columnist.

Linda McQuaig

> We're using the ambiguity of the law. We as women are doing just what the guys do. . . . It's grey. We are as good as any group of guys.
>
> PATTI STARR[f]

In March 1987, B'nai Brith, a Jewish human rights organization, held a $200-dollar-a-plate dinner to honour Patti Starr, whose nets of influence were cast over the most prominent social, economic, and political seas of Ontario. The former president of the National Council of Jewish Women of Canada (Toronto section), she was still the head of its charitable foundation with sole signing power over a special capital fund within it; she was an insider Liberal fund raiser and close to Elvio DelZotto, a chief bagman for the Ontario Liberals and president of Tridel development. With his brother Angelo, Elvio also sat on the "brainstrust" committee of Ontario Place, chaired by Starr;[8g] and she had lobbied provincial politicians for subsidies for land development for such programs as the NCJW Prince Charles housing project, built by Tridel. The celebrity cast at Starr's dinner included Barbara McDougall, Lily Munro, then Ontario citizenship and culture minister, and former premier David Peterson. The words he spoke that evening must return to haunt him. He had risen, smiled at Starr, and gushed, "There isn't a person in this room she hasn't touched. . . . I can't tell you the number of times I've fallen victim to her enthusiasm."[h]

Patti Starr had it all—position, prominence, social access. Then in 1988 while *Globe and Mail* reporter Linda McQuaig was covering the federal Liberal nominations for the fall election, she started getting inside tips about Starr's riding association, and "weird" election donations linking the Jewish foundation charity to Queen's Park. The leaks may have been prompted by Starr's clash with John Sewell, chair of the Metro Toronto Housing Authority over the Tridel-built NCJW building. Sewell fought with Starr and the DelZottos over the Prince Charles Development (the contract terms of which violated the MTMA's business policy), and was subsequently fired by housing minister Chaviva Hosek, whose staunch supporters during her election campaign were the DelZottos and other developers.[9] The *Globe and Mail* gave Linda McQuaig time off to concentrate fully on the story, and she started digging.

Power can be as addictive as crack, and Starr's almost palpable desire for recognition became clear when McQuaig developed contacts inside the NCJW, where she discovered that Starr's influence was generated as much by intimidation as by enthusiasm.[i] McQuaig wrote about the almost endless supply of money available to Starr for whatever she needed in the spinning carousel of politicians, developers, fund raisers, entertaining, and donations. Starr smiled like a Cheshire cat and seemed almost boastful as she described her creative use of the gala, how she bought tickets to political fund raisers with money "earmarked for consulting services."[j] Once at the event, she would lobby politicians for her various needs. Each time McQuaig rephrased her queries about the use of NCJW funds for election purposes, Starr redirected the question towards the good works that were being done, all the while popping chocolates into her mouth, taking phone calls, sharing political gossip and revelling in her power as if she had no idea that she had crossed the line of legitimacy.[k]

An institutional caveat runs: beware of underlings, for they see all and have great power. Starr had come to believe her own myth. Betty Stone, former executive director and a twenty-six-year veteran of the NCJW, went to president Gloria Strom with the documents that showed political donations were being made from the charitable foundation. Strom confronted Starr, who assured the president that no such donations had been made. When Stone tried to investigate further, Starr fired her.[l]

McQuaig learned that Barbara McDougall had intervened on Starr's behalf to get charitable tax status for the NCJW foundation on the grounds that it was "providing housing exclusively for those in need of charity."[10m] This entitled them to a provincial sales tax rebate of $251,000 on the Prince Charles housing development, which was supposed to be used to improve the building or reduce the mortgage and rent. Instead, this money went into the charitable foundation's capital fund, which was the account controlled by Starr, and the money she drew upon to make political donations.[n]

When Linda McQuaig published her findings in the *Globe*, the fallout resembled Chernobyl. Five provincial ministers lost their cabinet posts, including the brilliant Chaviva Hosek[11] whose star had been rising ever since her impressive presidency of the National Action Committee and her year with Gordon Capital. Starr's government contact, Gordon Ashworth, who had received a refrigerator and a residential paint job arranged by Starr from a Tridel-related company controlled by the DelZottos, resigned;[12] the National Council of Jewish Women was devastated. When Peterson asked all members of the DelZotto family—including Elvio's wife, Marlene, who had nothing to do with any of it—to step down from their various public appointments during the subsequent inquiry, Conrad Black penned an impassioned article on the presumed innocence of his friends the DelZottos. In his same Toronto *Sun* column castigating investigative reporters as jackals, he called McQuaig a "weedy, and not very bright, leftist."[o] The *Financial Post* reprinted Black's column, as usual, but removed the epithets. Furious over the edits, Black resigned from his column in the *Post*, while new *Globe and Mail* editor-in-chief William Thorsell wrote a long letter to the Toronto *Sun* defending McQuaig and calling for Black to withdraw his comments about her.[p]

In a subsequent provincial government inquiry held as a direct result of McQuaig's reporting, Stone said that she knew of a NCJW six-figure bank account for which Starr was the sole signing officer. And it was Starr, said Stone, who was the "go-between" between Tridel and the NCJW, getting tax credits for the donations even though the developer had been repaid. Stone, reflecting on Starr's domination of the executive, said, "You had to either accept what Mrs. Starr said or you didn't function at all."[q] In November 1989, Starr and two other directors, Nita Goldband and Leslie Miller, were expelled for life from the NCJW. In March 1991, Starr faced seventeen counts of violating the Ontario Election Finances Act. Convicted on six counts, she was sentenced to jail for fraud and breach of trust. The scandal was thought by many to have been the catalyst that prompted the definitive defeat of the Ontario Liberals in 1990, and it inspired financial analyst Dian Cohen to tell a cautionary tale for new Premier Bob Rae on "Canada AM" the morning after the NDP sweep:

> Once upon a time when a new premier won an election, the outgoing premier left him three envelopes to open in time of need. The new premier put them at the back of his desk drawer. When his first economic crisis struck, the premier opened the first envelope. It said, "Blame me." It worked.

> When the second major economic crisis struck, the premier rushed to his desk drawer and opened the second envelope. It said, ''Blame Ottawa.'' It worked again.
>
> Then the scandals started within his own government, and on the eve of another election he opened the third envelope. It said, ''Prepare three envelopes.''

Linda McQuaig won a national newspaper award in 1990 for her investigation of Patti Starr. She is currently being sued by the DelZottos, and she has left the *Globe and Mail* to write a book on the Mulroney government.[13]

Diane Francis

The best known investigative reporter for years has been Diane Francis who writes financial columns for *Maclean's*, the Toronto *Sun*, and the *Financial Post*, where her column is called ''The Insiders.'' A regular commentator on CBC's ''Morningside'' and, in Toronto, on CFRB radio, Francis is not only articulate in explaining financial matters to the lay public but, when you read her books, *Controlling Interest: Who Owns Canada*, and *Contrepreneurs* (about stock market fraud), you know that there must be anonymous tips dropped on her doorstep in unmarked envelopes. Francis admits to loving gossip and she darts and hovers like a hummingbird, learning everything from how private companies are run to who attends influential and important private parties, such as the one on New Year's Eve held in 1983 by Paul and Jacquie Desmarais at their Palm Beach retreat.[14r] Born in Chicago, Francis operates with the fearlessness typical of American women. Her favourite sport is the journalistic equivalent of stripping the notorious Vancouver Stock Exchange to its boxer shorts, and then parading it about the country. A member of the advisory board of the Financial Post Company and a director of the Clarke Foundation, Francis has won business writing awards from the Royal Bank and the Canadian Petroleum Association, and *Toronto Life* recorded that, ''She has been named the most conspicuously well-connected financial journalist. . . . Or so she tells us.''[s] In the spring of 1991, Francis was appointed editor of the *Financial Post* and, complaining that we are overgoverned and overtaxed, she promised to challenge Canada's sacred cows.

The Television Hosts

Few men or women possess a gift for television interviewing, which Clarkson described as ''a cruel and mysterious process, not anything you can train for.'' Ask a certain question and you can lose your guest — or the surprise tactic may win you a revealing glimpse of the truth. Investigative broadcasters live under the constant fire of stopwatches and reticent guests. Most senior hosts today honed their skills with increasing electronic complexities that allow multiple, simultaneous interviews in order to bring all sides of a story into view. The interviewer may have a seasoned backup crew that has briefed them ahead of time and a producer guiding them through an ear phone but, as Roy Bonisteel said, ''There comes a time when you're on your own. This person has gone off from that and you can't bring them back, or he's said something more important than anything that's written down so you've got to follow that up.'' That is one of the great attractions for the viewer. The interview format provides a high-risk diversion that, like hang gliding or car racing, has a potential for disaster. The job is exhilarating and hazardous, giving the viewer a vicarious thrill watching Frum, Wallin, or Clarkson tackle Thatcher or the Shah.

Isabel Bassett

Central to the Canadian media and social universe, and the most powerful, best-connected media personage in the country, is Toronto journalist/author/CFTO writer/hostess Isabel Bassett.[15] The wife of CTV boss John Bassett,[16] the economic power (with the Eatons) behind Baton Broadcasting, Isabel Bassett is a pillar of the New Establishment. Her annual Grey Cup luncheon at the Park Plaza Hotel is attended by virtually everyone who plays the Toronto power game.

Bassett was a successful journalist before she married John, after which she wrote two books: *The Parlour Rebellion: Profiles in the Struggle for Women's Rights*, a tribute to turn-of-the-century women who coped with incredible restrictions; and then in 1985 *The Bassett Report: Career Success of Canadian Women*, a journalistic-statistical examination of women in the work force that demonstrated just how difficult it still was for them to advance. Currently she makes hard-hitting documentaries such as ''Children Take Care'' (a street-proofing show for kids), ''No Fixed Address'' (on the homeless in Canada), and ''Nightmare in the Neighbourhood'' (on crack, cocaine, and abuse in the neighbourhood).[17] Bassett's professional record is impeccable, but she also flies not quite under the wing of a man who embraces power with unabashed joy,[18] making her media power as secure as the seat of Madame Justice Beverley McLachlin on the Supreme Court of Canada. With her influence on programming in CFTO, her position on the inside track of the social elite of Canada, and her husband's staunch support, Isabel Bassett is one of the most influential and colourful forces in Canada for melding activist goals with Establishment power.

Pamela Wallin

> If you just act as if you have the right to do something, it's amazing how you can get things done.
>
> PAMELA WALLIN

In 1973, when a CBC producer asked Pamela Wallin, then a Prince Albert Penitentiary counsellor, to stand in for the sick host of a noon-hour open-line radio show, the young graduate quickly discovered that she had found her niche. As a psychology student and campus activist, she had become skilled at extemporaneous speech-making at the University of Regina. In the following decade, Wallin defined her life by marathon work schedules and sleep deprivation. She had come on the scene during women's early years in television media both as a broadcaster and researcher, which gave her control. So incensed did one male announcer become in those early days when Wallin teamed up with the first woman editor in Regina to run the morning show, that the men kept locking them out of the building. Women were not to be given keys. Wallin decided then that she would never demand equality because she was a woman; she would simply do her job ''so damned well that they could never complain.''

If media productions are a collaborative effort, as everyone in the business agrees, then the real power lies behind the screens. Somebody —or a team—has to put it all together. As a story producer and national editor of ''As It Happens''[19] in the early 1970s, Wallin recalled, ''I was one of the minions that made Barbara Frum look and sound great.'' Paying due respect to Frum's ability to speedily absorb large amounts of information, then reassemble it in a cohesive form, and present it without being intimidated by a Thatcher or a Kissinger, Wallin pointed out that no single person could handle twenty interviews pouring in from around the world every day: ''We had five minutes to do oral briefings and [wrote] out questions for Barbara as well.'' For the Indira Gandhi interview, Wallin had all her information prepared long before the event.

Wallin's association with politics through the program prompted her to ask Toronto *Star* national editor Lou Clancy for a job, and then admitted she knew nothing about writing for newspapers. She recalled, ''When Lou stopped laughing he agreed to have lunch with me.'' Convincing Clancy that she was smart and knew a lot about Canadian politics, she assured him that she could learn everything else on the job. An impressed Clancy catapulted her into the Ottawa bureau of the Toronto *Star*. Her immediate acceptance was due to the credibility she had won as a political reporter from ''As It Happens.''[20] When she moved to CTV, bureau chief Bruce Phillips used her on the panel show ''Question Period'' because she was one of the few women who could ad lib and hold her own. Wallin remains a formidable interviewer with the ability to sound extemporaneous while conveying a sense of friendly authority.

Wallin recalled that during Peter Lougheed's furious battles over the NEP and FIRA, the Premier had not spoken for six years with the *Star*—mainly because the paper was so focussed on Toronto. When she attended a press conference in Alberta and asked Lougheed a question, he retorted that, as an easterner, she could not possibly understand his answer. Everyone just stared when Wallin shot back that she resented the Premier's condescension, that she had been born and raised in western Canada, and understood the oil and gas issue. Repeating her question, she said she would appreciate his answering it. Lougheed not only answered the question, but he sent an aide over to invite Wallin to meet with him afterwards. She stayed on for four days of interviews and research, emerging with a major story that received top billing in the *Star* and prompted the paper to post a reporter in western Canada.

Eventually Wallin accepted the offer to co-host CTV's "Canada AM," but she also wanted to define the program, so she worked on it seventeen hours a day. "I never left that office before 8:30 at night and went to work at 3:30 a.m." After four years of this, she mused, "They should have committed me." One frightening night in the Falkland Islands while covering the 1982 war, Wallin and her crew were tear-gassed at a rally; Canadian flags were not something you wanted sewn on your knapsack after External had aligned Canada with British foreign policy. On the war's brighter side, she met camera operator Malcolm Fox, her future husband. In 1985 she became Bureau Chief of CTV News in Ottawa, as well as host of "Question Period," moved on to be CTV's national affairs correspondent, and is currently host of "Canada AM".

Barbara Frum

> I've always been spontaneous—I haven't plotted my life like Napoleon's campaigns. Anyway, look what happened to Napoleon.
>
> BARBARA FRUM[u]

Of all of Canada's undisputed celebrities, the most frequently watched is Barbara Frum, one of the few radio personalities to be chosen for television because of her journalistic ability rather than voluptuous looks.[21] The radio talk show "As It Happens" had allowed her great freedom, and her book, *As It Happened*,[v] provides often hilarious insights as much into the quick-thinking host herself as into the characters on the phone line. They ranged from the world famous, to a New York bank robber holding hostages while he talked, to a researcher studying urban stress on rodents by rattling their cages to the sound of subway noises. Frum still manages to circumvent the restrictive format of television by maintaining the fearless questioning and mental dexterity that enable her to discuss the nuances of Middle East peace talks, or to nail former premier Bill Vander Zalm to his chair when she tires of his smile.[22]

Pamela Wallin prefers the risks of live television, that like playing a spring salmon with a fly rod and ten-pound test line, gives the guest the same advantage as the host. On the other hand, "The Journal" goes for the more polished look of pre-taped shows. Any botched queries can be eliminated and new questions spliced in later, when the guests have no further comeback. The question of ethics, and of the potential power inherent in pre-taping is a subject of constant debate, but it is Frum who is perceived nightly to be the David Frost of Canada, the one who could get an immediate response from Mikhail Gorbachev, John Major, or George Bush. Bonisteel said of her tenacity, "[Barbara] is like a dog with a bone and she won't let up until she gets what she wants." One of the rare times Frum has faltered happened during a 1990 panel discussion of feminism with Margaret Atwood, Marilyn French, Anita Desai, and Betty Friedan. The playfully scheming Atwood startled Frum by asking, "Would you give up your job for a moment of swept-away passion, Barbara?"

Frum bumbled, "Not [for] one moment, but a lifetime of it," before gasping, "Why don't we take a break now that you're asking me questions so I can get the ball back." CBC flashed to a long commercial. When they returned, Atwood had been subdued and Frum continued the interview. Not many would so challenge Frum, whose tight-lipped expression has been known to chill with the sting of dry ice. Some have suffered from her abruptness off screen, and her peers believe that her tendency to keep people at a distance may date from her radio days. On the other hand, her warmth and generosity with friends is legendary. When Judy LaMarsh was dying and in debt, Frum organized friends to provide funds for her care, writing personally to each individual who became involved. When Ottawa columnist Marjorie Nichols was struck down with lung cancer, Frum called to check on her welfare with attention almost as frequent as that of Jack Webster who had flown to Nichols' side.

In terms of personal power, whether or not Frum single-handedly structures her own interviews matters little. It is the public's perception that counts. In her presumed access to world figures, the illusion is the power but, with Frum, her power is real. Allan Fotheringham described her as a "power broker [who] sifts and selects who is important. Ascendancy, and the opposite, on the popularity scale can be judged by who can be seen at the Frum dinner table."[v] And in an article he wrote of her, "[She] is . . . the den-mother, the traffic cop, among loving (and sometimes warring) personalities in broadcasting, journalism, the book industry and the arts world in general."[w] Early in 1989 when *Globe and Mail* editor Norman Webster and managing editor Geoffrey Stevens were fired in the upheaval at the paper, Frum moved quickly to honour the new *Globe* editor-in-chief William Thorsell. In his *Financial Post*[x] column, Fotheringham described the party she gave, which included Marcel Masse, then minister of communications, the Gotliebs just back from Washington, Conrad Black, Margaret Atwood, Robert Fulford, Anna

Porter, Sylvia and Bernard Ostry, Peter Mansbridge, and Robert Campeau (BB).[23]

Canada's most visible media mogul is also influential as the journalist[24] who, after receiving a BA degree in modern history from the University of Toronto, inspired women in the 1960s to enter politics and in the 1970s, as host on radio and television, paved the way for a legion of Futurists who are now after her job. It is unlikely they will get it in the near future. As Fotheringham concluded, "If you want to know where power is in Toronto, go to a Barbara Frum party."[y] If you can get an invitation. Failing that, others go to her beauty salon, where power Frum-style means she can take along her mammoth canine ball of black kinked curls. Those with allergies find other salons, but most customers are amused, a regular sneezer explaining in reverent tones, "That's Barbara Frum's dog, you know," her allergic attack a homage to superstardom.

Dian Cohen

CTV "Canada AM" business analyst Dian Cohen has always had a global vision and she calms viewers' financial confusion by putting complex monetary concepts or trends into comprehensible language. Cohen's cheerful presentation is fun to watch, and she inspires fan mail from business travellers who check out her early morning program from hotel rooms. Shift-workers and homemakers welcome the analyst over that first cup of coffee as she explains such mysteries as debt-to-equity ratio and interest rate arbitrage in conversational yet expert style. It is a comment on the power of being visible that, after twenty years of doing the same thing on CBC radio, Cohen said it was television that transformed her into a celebrity.

As a financial analyst speaking to the masses, Cohen has tremendous power potential. The inflexible structure of institutions, and particularly that of finance, was not designed for computerized selling and the danger of explosive change.[25] In the computer share sales of the last five years, chunks of cash as high as $15 trillion began darting around the world to take advantage of quick gains. In such volatile conditions, one irresponsible Orwellian comment could turn fear into panic, into a run on a stock, a bank, or the whole trading index. "You have to be accountable," Cohen said. Warning viewers at the beginning of the 1990/91 recession to cut up their credit cards and put their financial house in order was as far as she would go. Cohen detests the kind of reporting that fuels citizens' fears with needless doomsaying.

It is difficult to imagine Cohen as the blue-jeaned, gum-chewing, brat reporter that she was in the 1960s. She and Pat Carney used to hang out in the House of Commons budget lockup, and neither Turner nor Trudeau would give her interviews. At age fifteen she had fled school and a traditional home to work on a kibbutz at the beginning of Israel's independence. She returned to Canada intending to learn her father's grain brokerage business, but in the old double standard, he refused to let her. She said, "It was get an education and then be someone's wife." She did learn bookkeeping there, however, and she also hung around the office to learn about creative selling to the wheat board. Married at eighteen, Cohen took economic history at night school,[26] soon discovering that she had a natural talent for understanding issues and explaining them to the layperson. Now everyone she calls, from Lester Thurow to John Kenneth Galbraith, answers. Her goal is to inform her following, to provide guidelines so that individuals can see their options and take charge of their lives.

Cohen travels with a computer, turns out weekly editorials for newspaper and magazines, and speaks at conventions and symposiums for which her fee is approximately $5,000. The nomadic lifestyle suits this free spirit who raised three daughters and lives alone. She serves on the ECC and sits on several boards, including Canadian Pacific, Noranda Forest, and PanCanadian Petroleum, but to the day her father died, she said, "I don't think he ever believed that I could actually make a living."

Adrienne Clarkson

Adrienne's alarm clock doesn't ring, it applauds.

ALLAN FOTHERINGHAM

One night in 1942, a young Adrienne Poy Clarkson left Hong Kong with her parents and brother on a Japanese ship, which sailed to Mozambique and rendezvoused with another ship carrying American-based Japanese. Then they were traded one for one. From there the Poy family sailed for Ottawa via South America and New York. It was tough at first but, gradually, Clarkson's business executive father re-established himself in Canada. Had the Poys settled in Vancouver or Toronto, Clarkson might have been exposed to the worst of racism, but in Ottawa she was not even a member of an identifiable minority. There was only a handful of Chinese and virtually none in the public school system. The Poys started out in a multilingual city that melded race and culture, and respected intellectual curiosity. With the support of parents she regards as "heroic," Clarkson learned that she was capable not only of surviving but of accomplishing anything.

A leader in high school, she went on to be involved in campus politics and debating, while earning an Honours BA and an MA in English literature, then attending the Sorbonne to polish her French. In Paris she experienced what she called a "ruthlessly egalitarian meritocracy" in which women as well as men were expected to be adept at "tough intellectual play." It was a far cry from the British attitude toward women, which she described as retrograde and which has played such a major role in socializing Canadian women into subservience. During the 1970s she excelled at investigative reporting and at her host positions on "Take Thirty," "Adrienne at Large," and "Fifth Estate."

Integrating her French experience into her business style has not always won Clarkson support. In fact, the Canadian environment of consensus has never been conducive to developing the kind of tough-mindedness among women that caused former realtor Suzanne Lount to be called "the Barracuda" and Anna Porter the "Great White Shark." Clarkson said unapologetically, "Being tough-minded should not be confused with being inhumane." But when the presidency of the CBC and chair of the Canada Council were vacant in 1989 and Clarkson's name was suggested, one former cabinet minister shot down the idea with, "Adrienne Clarkson is out for Adrienne Clarkson." It is possibly her indomitable self-possession that causes confidence to be confused with arrogance.

Clarkson had made a host of friends at the Sorbonne who advanced to senior positions in the French civil service, and twenty years later, in the 1980s, she reconnected with them as agent general for Ontario in France. Using the civility of lunches, dinners, and various promotional events, she attracted high technology business, tourism, and culture while winning more credibility and press coverage for both Ontario and herself than any other Canadian ambassador. Although the number of joint ventures between French and Canadian firms increased dramatically during the recessive years, when Clarkson returned to Ontario many of the contacts began slipping away.

In 1987 when Clarkson accepted the position of publisher and COO at McClelland and Stewart, the publishing houses buzzed with speculation that she would fail. A year and a half later it was evident that her vision of taking Canadian publishing international, of making it more than just branch plants of American or British groups, was not going to materialize in her time frame. The purse strings of the company were controlled by business executive Avie Bennett, and bottom-line realities win all the time. Nevertheless, when Clarkson left the company in 1988, the media left her alone. She had struck a hard deal with Bennett, retaining her own imprint and, if street whispers are correct, some equity in the company.

In a crowded career spanning twenty-five years of high-pressure jobs, a personal commitment to dozens of speeches in 1988 to fight free trade, and trips in the name of PEN to observe elections in Chile, Clarkson acknowledged that she made sacrifices in her personal life. When her first marriage to Stephen Clarkson ended, so fervently did Clarkson believe in the empowering influence of fathers on daughters that she gave custody of their two girls to Stephen.

In 1988, Clarkson risked, if not relinquished her power base by taking the federal government to task for free trade policies and for cutbacks to the CBC by helping to mount "The Friends of Public Broadcasting." Her criticisms coincided with her departure from M&S, her search for a new job, and, just months later, the openings at the CBC and the Canada Council. Rather than promote herself for either job, however, she travelled the country, speaking to university students and anyone else who would listen on the importance of keeping the national network a strong and independent voice. In her attacks on free trade as a threat to Canadian sovereignty, her impassioned advocacy was hardly consistent with hungering after the government's plum chairships. Now only a change in government could put her back in the power game. For the time being, she is concentrating on "Adrienne Clarkson Presents," an arts and interview show that returns her to her first love, television. In her first two seasons she presented fabulous ballets, and interviewed such Canadian greats as John Polanyi, Morley Callaghan, Karen Kain, and the Peruvian novelist-would-be-politician Mario Vargas Llosa. Researching for Clarkson is her old friend Vivienne Moody, filmmaker, program developer, and bonne vivante who finds her boss's style of organization and leadership exhilarating. While the format of the show concentrates on entertainment through the performing arts, Clarkson's mandate is broad as she garners the crème de la crème of creative power.

Clarkson still works in the collaborative style in which she was trained by CBC veteran Dodi Robb and two producers, Donnalu Wigmore and Oscar-winner Cynthia Scott.[27] Once guidelines are established, Clarkson expects her talented staff to create their own routes to stated goals. As a child who watched her parents struggle through poverty, she said, "In a . . . country which is at a high level of development, [quality] should be not about how rich we can [be] but how well we can provide for, [and preserve] the dignity of, those who cannot make it [alone]. People cannot always help it. My family has been there. I do not believe that this is just a country of winners and losers [but one] of consensus. I want that to continue." Winner of four ACTRA awards for best TV documentary journalist and an Emmy, host of over 3,000 TV shows, author of three novels, defender of Canadian sovereignty, and crusader for PEN—those achievements and three honorary doctorates extrapolate into a kind of intangible power for the refugee child from Hong Kong.

The Managing Editors and the Administrators

> It is important that women not perpetuate the myths, the subjugation of women by themselves. [You must be able to say without apology], 'Why shouldn't I be associate editor of this newspaper? Why can't I think that one day maybe I'll be publisher. Why shouldn't I be powerful?'
>
> CATHERINE FORD

The number of women who have made it into executive or administrative positions of the media are practically as rare as women CEOs.[28] During the 1970s, the irrepressible Dodi Robb had struggled up the ladder to producer but never broke through the glass ceiling to the senior executive level. Phyllis Switzer was a founding partner of CITY-TV in Toronto.[29] When CTV won the post of Host Broadcaster for the Calgary Winter Olympics, it chose Switzer to set up and run the complex operation. Bill Pratt, the boorish president of the Olympiques Calgary Olympics, who was unhappy with the choice, pitched the insulting challenge at her: "With a name like Switzer, I expect you to bring it in on time and under budget." Stricken by cancer just as her term began, she underwent a mastectomy and within a week had signed herself out of the hospital to return to the pressure-cooker environment, explaining, "You have to hit the ground running, with a fabulous team, which I had." In a superhuman effort, the ailing Switzer brought the $88-million show in on budget, covered the Olympics superbly, and died a year later.

Lise Bissonette, a former journalist and newly named publisher of *Le Devoir,* intends to apply a hands-on style to save the historical, debt-ridden paper. It is a measure of the esteem in which she is held that she was the guest of honour at a fund-raising dinner in November 1990, at which some six hundred guests from the business, political, and cultural elite of Quebec showed up and paid $800 a plate to help reduce *Le Devoir's* $1.5-million debt. It took some power to bring together at a dinner political opposites Brian Mulroney, Jean Chretien, Jacques Parizeau, and cabinet ministers from the Bourassa government.[z] *Le Devoir* is struggling to survive, and Bissonnette has been ordained the one to save it.

In Alberta, Catherine Ford, Linda Hughes, and, until 1990,[30] Gillian Steward, have epitomized the joie de vivre of the wild west. Canada's only female managing editor at the time, Steward said that she "just fell into journalism." A graduate in political science, she was working in a University of Lethbridge research department that gave her material for a couple of articles in the local paper. When subsequently offered a job, she spent a frantic week learning how to write copy. Edmonton *Journal* editor-in-chief Linda Hughes graduated in arts from the University of Victoria, returned a piece of research borrowed from the Victoria *Times,* accepted a happenstance invitation to lunch with the editor, and was hired. She, too, scrambled to learn how the job was done. Catherine Ford, the feisty Calgary *Herald* associate editor, figures she got into newspaper work to defy her parents. Her traditionalist mother remains so uncomfortable with her daughter's position, that Ford suspects "she considers journalism only one step above prostitution."

At the Calgary *Herald,* Ford's ear-curling one-liners and bold editorial opinions melded well with Steward's quiet sense of humour, lyrical writing, and deadly pen. In Edmonton, Hughes is known to foster debate by taking unpopular stands such as advocating the right to name victims of sexual assault in court. Ford has described her position as associate editor at the *Herald* as running an ivory-tower thinktank and reflecting the opinion of the newspaper as a corporate citizen, even possibly the consensus of the city. It is her policy to not hire journalists with partisan interests, and she expects the same impartiality to govern their personal lives. It is a philosophy that creates isolation and drives those in the business closer together. As Steward noted, you can't be in the business for more than ten minutes without knowing your counterparts across the country. As managing editor, she oversaw the newsroom staff of two hundred—reporters, photographers, copy editors, librarians—and took responsibility for the editorial content of the paper.

Ford and Steward credited retired publisher Patrick O'Callaghan with opening the doors and creating an environment that encouraged the advancement of women. Those who have reached managing editor positions are extraordinary enough, but Ford is an anomaly of the restrictive 1950s. Raised in a traditionalist Southern Ontario home, in which the patriarchal structure included a grandfather judge and drop-in relatives who were lawyers and academics, she recalled the omnipresent ethic, "You had a responsibility to your God, your country, your church, your family. You were also your brother's keeper, you did what you had to do, and you didn't ask for anything if you could provide it for yourself. . . . Keep your head down and your mouth shut and get through it. Be the willow. Bend. No, no, I gotta be the goddamned oak. It was always a fight."

Shirley Sharzer was a newspaperwoman who aspired to reach the top at the *Globe and Mail*, but instead received the galling title of deputy managing editor. In the upheaval when William Thorsell assumed command, Sharzer was offered what Allan Fotheringham described as a "humiliating lateral arabesque."[aa] She left the paper to become training and development co-ordinator in the Southam Newspaper Group and prepared a report on the barriers to the advancement of women encountered in the Southam chain.[31] At a Vancouver conference in 1990 called Women, Words and Power, Sharzer said, "We found women were spinning their wheels, complaining about glass ceilings and being able to rise only so far."[bb] The number of women in administrative positions in the media world is diminutive and in 1990, CBC chief Patrick Watson admitted that corporation's record of advancing women was deplorable. Three who made it are Nada Harcourt, head of development of CBC television/dramatic series, and Joan Donaldson, chief of CBC's twenty-four-hour "Newsworld,"[32] both of whom report to Catherine "Trina" McQueen, CBC director of news and current affairs.[33] Charlotte Gray reported Barbara Frum as saying, "You've gotta hit [McQueen's] office if you want to get things done around here."[cc] These women are the programming engine behind the host/interviewers, and are most strategically positioned to influence policy such as how women are perceived on television. Having a voice at the administrative level holds a power quotient of enormous potential, but Charlotte Gray wrote[dd] that, as all of the glamour is on the screen, few women are attracted to the more anonymous offices where policy and budgets are decided. If and when they access sufficient power, and if enough of them take it and use it, the future of pornography and other forms of exploitation of women will become a whole new debate.[34] Ready to back such newsroom initiatives are women like Maude Barlow, a media outsider who founded the Canadian Coalition against Media Pornography, and formerly sat on the board of Media Watch Canada. These national women's organizations have been successful in getting the CRTC and the broadcasting industry to consider initiatives against the exploitation of women.

The Black Queen of King Street[ee]

> My dears, apart from Anatole France and Albert Schweitzer, there is no man interested in anything but sex.
>
> BARBARA AMIEL

> A witty woman is a treasure; a witty beauty is a power.
>
> GEORGE MEREDITH, 1885[ff]

Barbara Amiel's enemies are also her most impassioned fans. No media personality on two continents can enrage her wide readership so swiftly and completely as this renowned author, journalist, TV commentator and, since January 1991, first Canadian and first woman to be appointed lead political columnist of *The Sunday Times* of London. Her fearless dedication to classical liberalism in an age when society aspires to altruism makes her the devil's advocate to almost everything many women have fought for over the last century. The rage fostered by her contrarion writing and exacerbated by her extraordinary beauty is pure theatre. As the "black-haired vamp," as she has often been called, Amiel is the consummate power pundit, one who has not only learned how to play the game, but who manipulates her chessmen about the personal board of her own life with awesome skill. She has turned the tables on traditional male-female stereotypes by criticizing her own sex with such unmerciful lines as, "the feminists' 'superwoman' is "someone who holds down a job . . . and occasionally tucks the children into bed,"[gg] and turning the male species into sex objects when she commented to journalist Val Sears, "Men are . . . delicious. I wish they didn't have to talk."[hh] Barbara Amiel is the woman most women love to hate.

In November 1987, in Toronto, Amiel received the Colin M. Brown Freedom Medal and Award for her defence of basic political and economic freedoms at a fund-raising dinner for six hundred given by the ultra-right-wing National Citizens' Coalition (membership 36,000). Beside her at the head table sat her former second husband and mentor, George Jonas, who once told Rhoda Koenig of *Tatler*[ii] that when he had first met Amiel, he "found her very attractive and thoroughly unpleasant." Asked when he had changed his mind, Jonas replied, "Did I say that I changed my mind?" For the NCC event, Amiel's then husband, David Graham, sat far away at a guest table that he had purchased. By the end of her welcoming preamble, everyone in the room was leaning forward as intently as if Amiel were sharing an intimate secret with each of them. In a way she was, having spent the first ten minutes extolling the virtues of Jonas and his influence on her life, finishing with the definitive statement, "My life *is* George Jonas". Heads swivelled towards Graham. At the end of Amiel's address, during which she had attacked the "skeptical, antagonistic and sneering media" and "the idea of group parity that insists on the representation of different groups in all our institutions . . . according to their percentage in the population, be they women, Inuits, the handicapped, whatever group is in fashion . . . ," the audience leapt to its feet to give her a standing ovation.

Amiel is queen, the female warrior, battling against the espousal of social justice as manifested in affirmative action, legislation that she has equated with reverse discrimination and the Nuremberg laws.[jj] She provides a photographic dimension of stark opposites, crystallizing the edges of an ideology that condemns parity as heartily as it champions the honour inherent in self-reliance. This is the battle cry of a child who experienced family breakup first in England and then again in Canada, who lost faith in her mother as a protective force, and who left home at the age of fourteen and met her goal of finishing high school without succumbing to welfare by working in a factory. Intellectual journeys with Zweig and Schnitzler at the University of Toronto followed, as did codeine addiction, and an ideological turnaround that began with the Communist World Youth Festival in Helsinki, passed through jail in Mozambique, and emerged in classical liberalism.

Amiel looks mysterious but she is the most open book on two continents. No would-be detractor can drag some hidden horror from her past because she has already shared them all in her autobiography, *Confessions*. She has told us who, why, and what she is with an honesty as harsh as her history. Reading about her life leaves one numbed, as perhaps it has left Amiel herself. Asked by writer John MacKay in 1984, "Do you really like people enough to want good friends?" Amiel answered candidly, "No."[kk] Through tough-minded independence, education, and "bloody hard work," she advanced from *Maclean's*, an editorship at the Toronto *Sun*, and one year of column-writing for *The Times* to win, in 1987, a coveted British Press award. The British admire provocative thought, and appearances on a BBC TV commentary show followed.

Amiel gravitates to power the way oil spills flow into tidal estuaries. She enhances her territorial claim on it by writing in the first person, a practice frowned upon in schools of journalism. Even the irreverent Allan Fotheringham refers to himself as "your humble scribe," but Amiel wants you to know that she sits in the inner sanctum of power, and nowhere was this more evident than at London dinner tables during the

Thatcher reign. When her marriage to Graham fizzled out, she appeared at No. 10 Downing Street with Baron George Weidenfeld of Chelsea, an international publisher who, according to one observer, "oozes power." Anyone who has attended a dinner with Amiel is struck by her finesse in becoming the centre of attention. Rather than raise her voice with the rising decibel level of any convivial soirée she speaks in whispered modulation until, by some mysterious magnetic force, laughter and chatter diminish to pianissimo. By the champagne sorbet, cabinet ministers, moguls, and even prime ministers are listening to Barbara Amiel.

During her NCC speech, she let it slip that Margaret Thatcher once digressed at one of these dinners to discuss with Amiel where she buys her shoes. Amiel reveals her pipelines to the sweet wells of political dealing through such hilarious lines as "'If Gorbachev does want to withdraw meaningfully,' Henry Kissinger told me last week. . . . "[ll] Other journalists may have talked with the former US Secretary of State —by telephone through four secretaries and three security guards—but Amiel's quote evokes an image of candlelight and wine at Number 10 Downing, Kissinger whispering conspiratorially, leaning across the Beef Wellington towards Amiel's plunging neckline and welcoming smile, the better to hear her reply.

Amiel employs the art of seduction as freely as she does that of debate, and when *Confessions* was being launched, she confided to Val Sears, "If I'm attractive, I'll use that too."[mm] Sexual politics is, of course, the very selling factor from which a legion of women have been trying to disengage themselves. It's the kind of comment that inflames the women's movement, which Amiel calls "the Marxist Fog."[35nn] Sears correctly observed of Amiel, "There's no one—not a man, certainly not a woman —who doesn't glance at her covertly . . . and, for different reasons, just . . . burn." With her stinging delivery and décolletage, Amiel is the best form of entertainment on all fronts.

Few do-gooders escape her attention, and Amiel demolishes detractors not so much through her arguments — which attack the feminists (who "[may have] taken their private psychological problems and projected them on to the rest of us"[oo]), critics of the armed forces (in which "bullying . . . is a natural process of selection . . . "[pp]), and homosexuals ("[who] have the right to their freedom of choice in sexual predilection but not the right to my moral approval — or my tax money to promote it"[qq])—as by rendering her left-wing readers so apoplectic that they lose their capacity for intelligent rebuttal. By sending her critics into hyperventilating rage, Amiel scores repeatedly. In England, in reply to an article in which Amiel described the "misguided" philosophy of feminist Germaine Greer, Greer did not name her antagonist, but disguised her attacker so thinly that Amiel later said, "Oh my goodness, big feet, yes. That would be me." According to Greer, Amiel arrived for an interview four hours late, repeatedly interrupted Greer to ask for tea, bread, and other amenities, and then wrote a "vicious" article that had nothing to do with the interview. Greer rebutted by not only characterizing the "anorexic" Amiel as "a jerk" but describing her bosom as "break-front" and her feet as "gross."[rr]

Amiel once told journalist John MacKay[ss] that she has alienated everyone, which, if you are debating ideas, is lamentable. If you are attacking individuals, it is predictable. Mention her name at a party and women choke on their Perrier. Creating angst is her chilling game. No one plays it better, and like it or not, she has the power of the media to deliver her message. On the other hand, the media has also used Amiel. She sells newspapers, magazines, and advertising. No one compels people to read her column, but there is nothing like a good dose of healthy rage to get one through the week. Readers can reaffirm their own moral rectitude by observing, "What a terrible, narcissistic woman," before rushing out to read her next article.

That many Canadian readers are clinging earnestly to their colonial roots and the British syndrome of propriety is to Amiel the ultimate comedy. In a 1989 interview she told CBC radio host Vicki Gabereau that Canadians with a passionate allegiance to the throne are being duped by a mother country that "long ago left us swamped in polite and submissive colonialism. . . . English society is possibly the most malicious society I've ever been in. . . . [It's] a cutthroat, vicious, nasty piece of work."

Canadians also continue to take themselves too seriously. Amiel explained it all to Gabereau:

Amiel: The one thing that I prefer infinitely about England is that it has not lost its sense of humour. If there is anything that upsets me about Canada it is that it is so relentlessly earnest.

Gabereau: Oh. Wow. I'm stunned. You can't imagine. I thought we were a riot. . . .

Amiel: Unless there's someone like Professor — was it Professor Hummel? That marvellous professor at the University of Toronto who put on goggles and swam up and down the pool and was accused of sexual harassment?

Gabereau: You caused quite a scene about that one.

Amiel: This is the lunatic Alice in Wonderland side of Canada that you can rely on to give you material for columns ad infinitum. I tried to explain to English readers that in Canada they would actually prosecute a professor in goggles in the Hart House swimming pool for intense and prolonged staring. It's a hard one to sell. You can't quite get it across.

Gabereau: You got supreme hell for that one. People wrote letters up and down.

Amiel: on winning her newspaper award: You know it's funny. . . . All the time I was in Canada bashing away, I never once got even a nomination for column writing. . . . And I came to England and managed somehow or another after thirteen months of writing to get a British newspaper award. . . . I don't know how to account for it. . . .

Gabereau: It wasn't because you were whooping it up with Rupert Murdoch or anything.[tt]

CHAPTER 14 NOTES

1. "This gang," refers to Prime Minister Brian Mulroney, Joe Clark, former minister of external affairs, and Perrin Beatty, who had just switched from Minister of National Defense to Minister of National Health.
2. Despite twelve-second news clips, the poll found that Canadians go to TV for most of their news, believing the reporting is more accurate and the analyses more thorough than in newspapers, magazines, or radio.
3. Montgomery is a former vice-president of the Vancouver Right to Life Society.
4. The B.C. Ministry of Tourism had financed the mailing of what it had thought was a convention notice and only later learned that REAL Women's B.C. president, Peggy Steacy, had used the service to attack homosexuals and feminists.
5. Cameron had worked as food editor of the Toronto *Star*, then the Ottawa *Journal* before joining the Ottawa *Citizen*.
6. Nick Hills was head of Southam News Services; Paddy Sherman was publisher, and Keith Spicer, editor of the Ottawa *Citizen*.
7. In a September 1990 article in *City and Country Home* written by Nancy Southam about Hamilton Southam, chair of the Official Residences Council, Hamilton said Cameron's story was a "piece of fabricated fluff."
8. This was a position given either by Gordon Ashworth, former premier Peterson's executive director and close business liaison of Starr, or through Heather Peterson, the premier's bright and capable sister-in-law who, ewith Ashworth, was in charge of the 4,500 ABCs in Ontario. Columnist Michael Valpy suggested that it was Ashworth who was the main source of Starr's political clout.
9. Sewell's firing may have been co-incidental and unconnected to the Prince Charles Development project.
10. In fact, while they provided only 60 percent of apartments for charity, which did not meet Revenue Canada's requirements, they still got the charitable status. They did meet the Canada Mortgage and Housing Corp. requirement of a minimum 25 percent assisted housing. Consequently, it guaranteed the NCJW's $10-million loan and subsidized repayments.
11. Hosek has been applauded as the post-modern feminist, the new wave of negotiators who can bring

together the activist movement with the Establishment. She has been an associate professor of English, Canadian, and American literature at the University of Toronto, and held several administrative positions in the Faculty of English. She is an author and was also the first woman chair of the university's Academic Affairs committee of the Governing Council. She headed the National Action Committee in 1984 when she led the successful drive for the TV debate of the federal leaders on women's issues. In a rare move for a feminist, she left the world of university teaching and the National Action Committee to join the corporate world with Gordon Capital Corporation, and then won a seat in the Ontario Liberal government under David Peterson where she became Minister of Housing. Hosek lost her cabinet post in the Patti Starr scandal, lost her seat in the provincial election of 1990, and in 1991 was appointed Director of the Liberal Caucus Research Bureau, Ottawa.

12. Starr paid other perks such as $500 for a chauffeur-driven car of Monte Kwinter, Minister of Consumer and Commercial Relations as well as Minister of Financial Institutions. She was convicted of aiding and abetting the charity in paying this money, having moved over $90,000 of NCJW funds (Toronto section) to campaigns of at least twenty-five provincial and federal politicians. These donations are illegal under the federal Income Tax Act.
13. In 1987 McQuaig wrote, *Behind Closed Doors: How the Rich Won Control of Canada's Tax System . . . and Ended up Richer.*
14. The presence of Pierre Trudeau, Dinah Shore, Brian Mulroney, and Bill Davis proved that social and celebrity power supersedes political scraps any day.
15. Bassett is the former producer and co-host of "Hourlong," on CFTO.
16. John is the chair of the executive committee of Baton Broadcasting. CFTO is a CTV affiliate, with Baton being CTV's largest shareholder.
17. "Nightmare in the Neighbourhood" makes the point about the brutal underworld that the most vulnerable victims, single women and children, are left to fight the war on their own.
18. John Bassett once pre-empted regular programming on CTV to focus on a Wimbledon tennis match played by his unseeded teenaged granddaughter, Carling Bassett.

When a viewer called up to complain, the chair of Baton Broadcasting boomed cheerfully, "What's the point of having power if you never use it?"

19. Wallin credits "whiz kid" Mark Starowitz with popularizing first the famous radio program, then Barbara Frum, whom he recruited when he became executive producer at CBC's "The Journal," also his invention.
20. Wallin said that Toronto *Star*'s John Honderich (editor), Ian Urquhart (managing editor), Richard Gwyn (international affairs columnist), and Carol Goar (national affairs columnist), all helped her learn how to write for the press.
21. In the 1970s, Frum won four ACTRA awards, the National Press Club of Canada Award for outstanding contribution to Canadian journalism, and a Woman of the Year award from Canadian Press in literature, arts, and education category.
22. In January of 1990, Frum interviewed then premier Vander Zalm the evening following his famous address to the Canadian public in which he stated that well, yes, he had signed the Meech Lake agreement, but British Columbia might withdraw. Challenging Vander Zalm for reneging on a deal he had signed, Frum then sat blank faced as the Premier smiled from Toronto to the Rocky Mountains, said in patronizing tones, "Barbara, you've got it all wrong," and spun a phantasmagorical answer that contradicted his statements from the previous evening. When he finally paused for breath, Frum remained inscrutable, paused, then leaned toward her guest and asked in withering tones, "Excuse me, Mr. Premier, but isn't it a little late to be teasing?"
23. Before bankruptcy.
24. Frum wrote for *Maclean's, Chatelaine, Saturday Night*, and the *Globe and Mail*.
25. In October 1987, the world's computers locked into "sell" mode, contributing greatly to, if not causing, the disastrous plunge of the market.
26. Cohen eventually earned a BA from the University of Toronto in economic history and political science and an MA from McGill in economics.
27. Scott produced Clarkson's "Take 30" in the 1970s, and was formerly director in the famous Studio D of the National Film Board, which made the Oscar-winning nuclear warning *If You Love This Planet*. Now a director of Studio B, she won the Oscar for *Flamenco at 5:15*,

and her *The Company of Strangers*, which received a standing ovation at the 1990 Venice Film Festival, was shown in New York to rave reviews in the spring of 1991.

28. The most influential publishing figures among women in Canada today are: Martha Blackburn, who inherited the sprawling communication system in London, Ontario, including the *London Free Press*; Anna Porter, former chair of Doubleday Canada, president of McClelland-Bantam (Seal Books), and publisher/president/director of Key Porter Books; Nancy Colbert, publisher of HarperCollins Publishers. Colbert is also on the international editorial board of HarperCollins New York and HarperCollins UK; Dona Harvey has been editor of the Winnipeg *Tribune* and managing editor of the Vancouver *Province*; Barbara Amiel, former editor of the Toronto *Sun*, and Diane Francis, editor of the *Financial Post*.
29. Switzer also participated in launching First Choice TV, Canada's first national pay television station. She was senior vice-president of programming for both First Choice and CITY-TV.
30. Following an illness, Steward became a columnist for Southam News.
31. It was Joan Fraser, editor of the editorial page at the Montreal *Gazette*, who serves on a similar task force, who gave the idea to Sharzer. Sharzer's report, published in "Whither the Revolution," showed that although women make up approximately 50 percent of the enrolment in journalism schools and about 51 percent of newspaper readers, they represent only 22 percent of journalists at Southam, and only 5 percent (6 out of 126) of senior managers. The Canadian Daily Newspaper Publishers Association found that women make up 6 percent of publishers, 9 percent of editors-in-chief, and 6 percent of managing editors of daily newspapers.
32. In October 1990, Donaldson was struck down by a cyclist and in April 1991 was still in a coma.
33. McQueen graduated from journalism at Carleton University. She sits on the board of Visnews, and was formerly on the advisory boards of schools of journalism at the University of Regina and Ryerson Polytechnical College.
34. During her tenure as Minister of Communication, and even after she lost her seat, Flora MacDonald was the

invisible power promoting women into executive positions to affect broadcast programming. Mimi Fullerton of TVOntario, Trina McQueen, and Nancy Smith (vice-president of Global) all owe their jobs to her.

35. In 1984 Amiel attributed the term "Marxist Fog" to Tom Wolfe.

PART IV

INDIVIDUAL POWER

In battle or business, whatever the game
In law or in love, it is ever the same;
In the struggle for power, or the scramble for pelf,
Let this be your motto—
Rely on yourself!
For whether the prize be a ribbon or throne,
The victor is [she] who can go it alone!

JOHN GODFREY SAXE 1816–1887

THE GAME OF LIFE, ST. 7

CHAPTER FIFTEEN

The Entrepreneurs

To survive, you have to win.

You work your money, you take risks. Life is a gamble.
Rarely [do] I see anybody with such guts ending up a loser.
FETOUN YOSIF

During the 1970s, Torontonian Posy Chisholm was wintering away her usual six months in Cuernavaca, Mexico, with now deceased husband Robert Chisholm, then president of Dominion Stores. The energy-charged Posy Chisholm soon grew bored with sitting in the sun, went exploring, and wandered into one of the many poverty-stricken villages surrounding the city. She found women who were using bits of scrap cloth and their exceptional needle-working skills to create exquisite dolls. When they sold these and other handiwork in Cuernavaca, they were required to turn the money over to their husbands with no say in how it was spent. All too often, it wound up in the bars of Cuernavaca. Chisolm, seeing an entrepreneurial opportunity, formed a club for the women with a five-peso entry fee. She showed them how to pool their money, creating greater buying power for quality fabrics; then she designed models with muted European colours in contrast to the brilliant hues of Mexico. The women created a fabulous collection of dolls, embroidered tissue-box covers, hand towels, and tablecloths that Chisholm's friend Mary Carr-Harris took back to Toronto for a sellout Christmas bazaar.

Later, when Chisholm was distributing the profits in the village, she exercised the one rule of the club: the money had to be paid to the women who had earned it. Word spread fast. The next winter three more villages joined the club, then five, until communities of once-indigent families supported a thriving cottage industry. Chisholm and Carr-Harris linked up with Cuernavaca's only export distributor to deal with Neiman Marcus and with other prominent retailers across the United States.

The effect on the Mexican women was spectacular. They discovered that the power of money bestowed upon them the privilege of choice and a sense of personal empowerment. Centuries of subservience fell away. They stood taller, laughed openly, fed and dressed their children better. Then they went too far. When the women not only controlled their income but began to lay down ground rules for their husbands' lifestyles, the men grew surly and demanded that Chisholm give the money to them. She refused.

At the start of the sixth season, Chisholm arrived in Cuernavaca, hopped into a jeep, and headed for her villages. En route she found the road blocked by a phalanx of angry men who presented an ultimatum: turn the profits over to them or there would be no more industry. By demonstrating the route to independence through economic power and the dignity of self-sufficiency, Chisholm had also disrupted an entire culture. She was caught in a Catch-22 and sighed, "I did turn it over, for one more season. The men stopped working and were drunk all the time. We destroyed the community." Rather than finance the old system, Chisholm closed down the industry. She eventually learned through her chief liaison that it had taken five years for the villages "to return to normal" — that is, for the women to return to subservience as in the centuries before Chisholm.

****

Individual power brings, to those in control of the self, the ultimate freedom of action. In one decade Kaaydah Schatten, a West Coast native Indian, built a company from zero equity to an international franchise vendor worth over $20 million. She is committed to individualism and self-determination. Many such women reflect a right-wing perspective and profess to be apolitical. They view life as a game, disdaining programs such as affirmative action, and arguing that women can reach the top just as everyone in a democratic, capitalistic society is free to do.

Speak of the institutional beast to an entrepreneur and watch her face twist like a torn bun. Entrepreneurship is a state of mind in which men and women create situations rather than waiting for conditions to ripen for them. They function with the risk of a high-wire acrobat. They shun both titles and curriculum vitae, the leitmotif of corporate success in which each tiny line represents a painstakingly earned fingerprint of achievement won through years of conformity, training, patience, and cautious manoeuvring. When entrepreneurs list their deals, it matters little if they forget a few. Ask them how they made it and they not only tell all, but, like Kaaydah Schatten, they relate their mistakes as adventures rather than failures.

The entrepreneurial attitude can be found anywhere. Jetsetter Dale Mearns, Futurist Kaaydah Schatten, Mayor Elsie Wayne, and numerous women realtors[1] who in good times can make an annual income of $350,000-$1,000,000, do not subscribe to women's cry for equality. Rather, they champion the notion that democracy gives everyone the licence to strike it rich or go broke and be forgotten. Making concessions for those who haven't yet figured out the process simply diminishes, if not invalidates, the quality of individual potential and the dignity inherent in achievement.[2] Accepting any challenge and then improvising to meet it is the antithesis of the project-oriented committee meetings, carefully couched language, and hierarchal decision-making of corporations and government bureaucracies. Entrepreneurs wait for neither permission nor invitations, and, as they answer only to themselves, their ultimate power is being in control.

The greatest entrepreneurs often emerge during the worst economic times. They thrive on an insatiable curiosity about their own limits, repeatedly flirting with that ill-defined edge between success and failure. Dealing becomes a metaphor for life and death, each conquest melding them to the ecstasy of survival. It is their mainlining, the alchemy of moulding an idea to the engine of reality, and the close is an explosion that impels them on to the next deal.

Society tends to impute to entrepreneurs who cite the Donald Trump creed, "Deals are my art form," more odious motivations: greed, insecurity, revenge. Not so. The only difference between entrepreneurial impulsion and artistic creativity is that the latter is usually mired in respectable poverty. That entrepreneurs can grow wealthy makes their motives suspect, but some of Canada's greatest fortunes and major institutions were built by entrepreneurs who started with only a few dollars, and a dream that grew into the kind of mammoth corporate structures from which many of these rebels had fought to escape. H.R. MacMillan, the young tuberculosis patient from Ontario, headed west, founded in Vancouver what became the sprawling integrated forest products company MacMillan Bloedel, and lived into his nineties. He might have realized one of Canada's greatest fortunes if he hadn't given so many shares away to charity during his lifetime. For MacMillan, the fun of it was in the building.[3]

Sam Steinberg's mother started the $1.5-billion supermarket chain with a small Montreal grocery store, as did the widow Janet Cross in the Chateauguay, the 1828 inspirational precursor to the Montreal fortune of Alexander Cross and the Crosses of Alberta. Stephen Roman arrived in Canada as a penniless teenager and died leaving the $1.4-billion Roman Corporation; the Billes brothers founded the $3-billion Canadian

Tire with an $1,800 garage; and Sam Bronfman's entrepreneurial spirit is legendary. Thomas Bata created his global empire by salvaging funds from a shoe factory in a war-threatened Czechoslovakia. That he and his wife Sonja not only survived but also thrived in politically volatile countries such as Africa, underscores a major tenet of entrepreneurs: play by their rules but don't get involved in their politics.

The most brilliant female prospector-miner of the century was Viola MacMillan, who made millions of dollars staking over 2,000 claims. As president of the Prospectors and Developers Association of Canada from 1943 to 1965, and with legal secretary experience, she successfully pleaded cases for miners and built the association up from a handful to over four thousand. As well as doing, her own prospecting, she became privy to every strike and deal that was formulated in the mining world. She formed syndications, raising millions to drill, sink shafts, bring mines into production, and establish her equity. In her enthusiasm MacMillan also went to jail for stock manipulation,[4] but the only problem she ever had in a man's world was talking her way into her first cobalt mine before women were allowed underground (not because they were in danger, but because they were considered unlucky). Otherwise, the eighty-eight-year-old asserted, "I never had any opposition from men in my whole lifetime."

Most entrepreneurs thrive on surprise, some on terror, and all on amusement. The very best have a genius for putting together deals so that everyone benefits. *Saturday Night* writer Patricia Davies wrote about the "rush" of business, "When you are winning . . . juggling eight balls in the air and you keep them all up, when you are coming on confident to clients and bringing the big orders in, it is very, very exciting."[a] The bigger the risk, the bigger the score, the bigger the rush.

In putting together global deals, Edmontonian Audra Hollingshead has drunk gallons of tea with Charlie Chan, her Asian liaison, slogged through the jungles of Bolivia, and been mistakenly shot at in Japan by a gun-toting gang collecting a gambling debt. She has put an Edmonton drilling mud supplier in touch with a Bolivian merchant, linked a British company with the Beijing government to build turnkey hospitals, and confessed that the most terrifying experience of her life was moving in her teens from Morris, Saskatchewan, to the big city of Edmonton. About fifteen years later Hollingshead had turned $5,000 into two lodges, a motel, forty houses, properties in Mexico, Arizona, and Hawaii, and, just for fun, a string of thoroughbreds on the side. Her superior communications skills got her the job of chief of protocol for international sporting events ranging from the Commonwealth Games in Great Britain to the Calgary Olympics. Her most recent venture is an association with World Trade Compendium Partnership, strategic planners for business, import/export, and manufacturing, as well as political and diplomatic consulting.

As it seems unlikely that in the near future women will be running the large institutions, many of them are leaving to enter the entrepreneurial world where they can have freedom of action and, most important, the chance to build equity beyond a salary. Others never were inside. Kaaydah Schatten epitomizes those who come from the depths of poverty or minority disadvantage and have nothing to lose. These women in particular bear watching because they exemplify the spirit upon which Canada's early twentieth-century fortunes were made. And winning is not the only hallmark of their success. The greatest entrepreneurs do it with style.

The Dealers

> Waterfront property is not transportable. Bangkok is the place to be and gems are the new currency.
>
> DALE MEARNS

Vancouverite Dale Mearns was speaking from the riverside patio of the Oriental Hotel, Bangkok, in 1989. James Bond longboats roared past in random death charges, barely missing the match-box tugs towing up to eleven barges on the choppy Chao Phraya River. All along its myriad klongs, or canals, a teeming humanity hovered inches above the waterline, a symbol of impermanency. In Bangkok, everyone deals. The prize is life. This is the perfect city for Dale Mearns, age ''forty something,'' who is studying gemology and the Thai language. Daily she bargains for food, clothes, tuk tuk rides, and anything else that catches her fancy. She once spent ten minutes talking her way past the platoon of security men in the doorway of the Oriental Hotel. They were guarding Elizabeth Taylor, who was resting up after an AIDS benefit and strolling through the foyer wearing a diamond ring the size of a chandelier. Mearns was meeting guests in the Hotel and did not have to win their trust. She chose to. It was part of the fun.

Mearns first discovered far-eastern temptations in 1984 when she accompanied friend and guitarist Liona Boyd on a concert tour of China, Thailand, and Singapore. During a diplomatic bash in Beijing, Mearns overheard a conversation about exquisite sequined and beaded hangings called kalagas ''in a politically volatile country bordering Thailand.'' Only a handful of these had found their way to the United States since 1970, and Mearns sniffed an adventure. She left Liona to woo the Thais and, with friend Susan Thomson, secured a brief visitor's permit and headed off with virtually no contacts to search for the treasures.

Entrepreneurs have a spies-in-streetside-cafés look that makes them instantly recognizable to each other. Mearns quickly found a character who said he knew of ancient hangings among the hill tribes and off they went, slogging upwards through tropical forests in the rain and shin-deep muck. Murder never crossed her mind. Implicit in the risk-taking nature of deal makers is their capacity for trust. Eventually, in a diminutive village and through the veil of torrential rain, they saw an antique, blanket-sized kalaga tossed over a clothesline. Mearns bought it for a bottle of whiskey and a carton of cigarettes, promised to reimburse her guide sometime in the future, and then returned to the city. The export laws of this anonymous land remained hazy but soldiers wielding machine-guns inspired discretion. Within hours Mearns had found an official in a nameless embassy who agreed to send her kalaga out of the country if she would return with automobile parts and Speedo bathing suits.

In and out of the country in four days, she rejoined Boyd, finished the tour, and returned to Vancouver. Mearns knew she was onto a hot deal when the kalaga sold from a Canadian gallery for $3,000. Lugging two huge suitcases of bathing suits and auto parts back to Asia, she kept a rendezvous with the same guide, whom she paid generously. Then they returned to the mountains, where the villagers had somehow been forewarned. Kilos of kalagas awaited the Canadian. Mearns used all her cash to buy hangings, finally bartered away her camera equipment and everything else but her return airline ticket and her boots. Using donkeys to carry her treasures, she returned to the capital, where she delivered the suitcases of treasures to her delighted embassy contact. In turn he filled the empty bags with the kalagas, which were safely loaded onto a plane. Mearns returned to Vancouver where such art treasures can be imported duty free.

Selling the kalagas in North America was the other half of the fun. Mearns avoids telephones and does not believe in letters of introduction. The shock treatment of simply showing up underscores the element of surprise and hones the entrepreneur's skills. At Neimann-Marcus and Gump's, which specialize in Oriental Arts, Mearns just materialized, whipped out her treasures, and said, "Who do I show these to?" The kalagas sold for up to $25,000. One four-by-two-metre antique masterpiece hangs in a major national gallery. A year and a half later kalagas were being exported all over the world, but it was Mearns who had been on the leading edge of the business and had realized a small fortune. The mists of smuggling and forbidden lands swirl about this airy story, but once the open market was flooded by the hangings, the excitement was over, and Mearns moved on.

Mearns never has any idea what is going to happen next, which puts her on the cutting edge of opportunity. If nothing materializes, she makes it up as she goes along. Years ago, while covering the Philippine elections, she waved her old Inuvik *Drum* press pass and joined NBC, CBS, and ABC for what she called an intimate breakfast with Ferdinand Marcos. The next day it worked again and she breakfasted with Imelda. Dressing and acting as if she belonged were more important than the press pass;

they are elements of style employed by the most successful enterpreneurs. The right look gets you in almost anywhere.

Celebrity status provides an entrée around the world. When Mearns accompanied Liona Boyd to Cuba, she correctly anticipated meeting Fidel Castro and also arranged some business prospects beforehand. Acting on behalf of Keg Restaurants Ltd. and Canada Packers, Mearns offered to renegotiate with the Cuban export company that was giving them endless headaches on their purchase of Cuban lobster. ''You pull it off, name your price,'' they had said. At her first cocktail party in Cuba, she met Castro's minister of fisheries; the next day he went to work to solve the Keg's problem. Social access is power. Mearns stated frankly, ''Travel with a celebrity—you've got power.''

Only once did Mearns actually become entangled with a government bureaucracy, and neither has ever recovered. In 1978, when then Judge Lawrence Eckardt was appointed commissioner for the B.C. Royal Commission on Electoral Reform, he persuaded her to be his executive assistant,[5] Mearns intended to be operational within weeks. Instead, she was told by an executive bureaucrat that she would have to requisition everything from him, and setting up would take three months. She explained how ''Mr. Requisition'' operated: ''When these Royal Commissions are begun, the [bureaucrats] use you to buy all the best furniture that the government really wants for something else.'' Accustomed to the awesome power of his vouchers, Mr. Requisition responded to Mearns' expletives by swearing that she would not have telephones for three months. The game was on.

The game was on. Mearns went to the construction offices of the newly opened Vancouver Centre, bought their used desks with her own $200, found some cheap space that was finished but not leased, moved in her furniture, and got the telephones within three days by ordering them in the judge's name. When she found that paper supplies were far more expensive through the bureaucrat than from an independent printer, she bought from the latter. Her office was completely operative within days at minimal cost while Mr. Requisition fumed helplessly in the bureaucratic bowels of government. The royal commission was not only completed in record time, during which they rewrote the B.C. Elections Act, but, claimed Mearns, at a cost far less than that of other royal commissions. She sold her desks at a profit and swore never to work with government again.

In keeping with her promise to do something different every year, Mearns moved to Los Angeles, where she worked on Liona Boyd's career, and is considering an offer to build and manage a furniture factory in northern Thailand. Mearns travels through life with little baggage, no dependents, and no overhead. The only tools of her trade are fax machines in Vancouver, California, and the Orient. Through her various investments and entrepreneurial endeavours, she enjoys a six-figure income and the ultimate freedom of being completely in control of her life.

Eleni Skalbania

> There is a time in your life that you realize either you do it, or you go and work for somebody else. I knew I could do it. I knew it would work.
>
> ELENI SKALBANIA

Just across the street from Vancouver's Robson Square complex is the ninety-four-room Wedgewood Hotel, the miracle child of Eleni Skalbania. The elegant, European-style inn, which has run at over 90-percent occupancy ever since its second month, was once a decrepit apartment building that no developer would touch. Eleni accomplished the transformation during a tumultuous time in her life. It was a living Monopoly game filled with juggled hotels, foreign buyers, nervous partners, a $500,000 cheque, a $1.18-million payout to her husband's outstanding creditors, all complicated by seven years of disbelieving courts. She survived through sheer guts, an entrepreneurial alacrity for finding viable solutions to looming financial disasters, and a work schedule as frenetic as it was committed.

In 1979 Eleni Marinakis and her dealer friend Nelson Skalbania had just bought the $13.5-million Hotel Georgia, a prime if aging three-hundred-plus room edifice.[6] Two years later, with the country in a recession, the forty-odd-million-dollar financial empire of Nelson was disintegrating by the hour. He needed a buyer for his 50-percent share of the hotel, which was in fact registered under the name of the Wedgewood Village Estates of Eleni, who was by then his wife.

During the summer of 1981, while Eleni was in Greece visiting her father, Nelson made a long-distance deal with a Mrs. Chang Hsu Siu Pao in Hong Kong to sell his half-interest in the hotel for $15 million. As a down payment to the Wedgewood Village Estates, Pao wrote out a cheque for $500,000, and, despite the fact that it was Eleni's company in which she had sole signing authority, Nelson cashed it at the Royal Bank. The bank gave him the money on the basis that he was her husband. Humour can be defined as tragedy viewed over time. Eleni laughed softly as she retold the saga of racing home from Greece and reading the small print in Mrs. Pao's contract. The purchaser had placed a caveat on the hotel to secure her offer, but had made no assumption of the 50-percent mortgages for the next two years until the deal would close. This made the refinancing of the second mortgage, $5 million due in thirty days, totally impossible. The Royal Bank would only finance the $5-million mortgage payment provided ownership of the Hotel Georgia remained intact. "You cannot," explained Eleni, "mortgage half a hotel." When they tried to restructure the deal to meet the hotel's refinancing needs, Mrs. Pao became curiously unavailable, the crises exacerbated by delays in correspondence and claims of language difficulties between Vancouver and Hong Kong.

The mortgage date loomed. Eleni gestured with thumb and forefinger, "We were that close to foreclosure." Finally Mrs. Pao agreed to withdraw her caveat in return for the $500,000, and Nelson was back where he started. He now needed $20 million to survive. Eleni loved the Georgia and insisted she would never have sold it except to help her husband. The problem was, she did not want a fire sale, and news of Nelson's financial troubles had distanced friends. The Belzberg's First City Financial Corporation lent Eleni $6.5 million on condition that her Wedgewood Village Estates buy Nelson out and give her clear title to the hotel.

Instead of using the First City loan to meet the mortgage payments that were due in two months, Eleni bought Nelson's half to help him out, then scrambled to sell. In a frenetic period during which she ran the hotel on the strictest budget in concert with the Royal Bank and supervised essential renovations to avoid losing clientele, Eleni not only found a buyer, a Mr. Hii of Singapore, but she doubled their money to $30.5 million payable over two years. "To this day," Eleni noted, "if you ask Nelson which deal he made the most money on, it was the Hotel Georgia."

As soon as Nelson was paid, the trustee handling his crumbling empire slapped a lien on the Hotel Georgia, claiming that Wedgewood Village Estates had not paid fair market value for Nelson's half. It required WVE to put $3.5 million in escrow until the courts decided how much should go to the creditors. Eleni faced eight different legal actions over seven years, due in part to the bank cashing the $500,000 cheque because it did not recognize Eleni and her company as an entity separate from her husband. That reasoning was supported in court with the interpretation made by Justice Martin Taylor of Section 3 of the Bankruptcy Act, that husbands and wives by definition do not operate at arm's length.[7] Eleni gave determined testimony that she has always functioned in business as a separate entity but Justice Taylor ordered her to pay up an extra $2.35 million to Nelson's creditors. Trial followed trial all the way to the Supreme Court of Canada, after the B.C. Supreme Court ruling in 1988 that, while the Bankruptcy Act violated Eleni's right of contract and discriminated against married couples in presuming that, if married, you are not dealing with each other at arm's length, it nevertheless was the law. Justice Bruce MacDonald was bound by the Bankruptcy Act to order Eleni to pay her husband's creditors a reduced $1.18 million, the difference between the amount she had paid Nelson and what was deemed fair market value for the hotel. The court included Nelson's 50-percent share of the debt in the restructuring.

Eleni's lawyer Tom Berger then argued in his Leave to Appeal to the Supreme Court of Canada that "in British Columbia the last vestiges of spousal incapacity were repealed in 1985, when it was asserted by the Legislature that a married woman has a legal personality that is independent, separate and distinct from that of her husband.'' The Supreme Court refused to hear the appeal. The pain was taken out of the payment because the $3.5 million held in escrow pending the final decision had earned close to a million dollars in interest.

Dealing is in Eleni's blood. As a child in Greece, she watched her mother negotiate and buy apartments and stores in Athens, then act as her own contracter in remodelling. Eleni absorbed the process as well as her mother's fine hostess skills. Her family arranged her marriage at the age of seventeen, to lawyer Angelos Marinakis. The couple moved to Vancouver where Eleni studied commerce and accounting at UBC and then worked as a stockbroker, travel agent, and manager of her husband's law office and expanding properties. Such was her passion for business that she took only brief weeks off to give birth to her two daughters.

Eleni's hotel experiences began thirteen years ago with the Devonshire on Georgia Street. Her marriage had ended and, armed with funds from her divorce settlement, and with promoter Nelson Skalbania and realtors Robert Lee and Ronald Shon, she leased the Devonshire. At the time the hotel was losing money, due, Eleni surmised, to poor management. She spent three intensive months learning everything from the employees, then called the entire staff into the ballroom and, with their cheering support, fired the management team. Within the year she had turned a profit and knew she had found her creative niche.

During all the legal problems surrounding the Hotel Georgia, Eleni pushed forward. Quitting the hotel business never crossed her mind. She simply set her sights on a smaller, boutique hotel of her own. In the summer of 1983 she approached Vancouver financier Joe Segal with the offer of co-purchasing his dilapidated Mayfair Hotel. In order to finance it she had to be operative within six months, but Segal did not share her sense of urgency and structured a deal to sell to Eleni for $4.4 million. With Segal's support, the Royal Bank came on side, but she was so short of cash that she personally oversaw the contracting during which she tendered her own jobs, wrote detailed contracts, and waited at city hall until the staff responded with licences and permits. Eleni was hospitalized four times for exhaustion. Yet she did it, from gutting the building to installing the furniture just ten days before the arrival of her first guests. Exhilaration came over her as she remembered that time, telling how she then promoted herself in concert with the hotel because she did not have enough money to advertise. She stated, ''I had to establish the Wedgewood's name beyond that of the Mayfair.'' What has enabled the Wedgewood Hotel to capture the hearts of an international clientele is Skalbania herself. She will not even discuss selling it, but some realtors estimate its value to be $18 million, ''providing Eleni is there. She is the value.''

Comparing the Wedgewood with the Vancouver competition, Eleni said, "I don't compete. We're better. We've had the highest occupancy [in the city] for five years since I opened my doors." Frequently interrupted in her office when anyone from accountants to chambermaids slipped in to discuss a problem, Eleni is clearly the antithesis of New York hotelier horror Leona Helmsley. She is a perfectionist however, who synthesizes her deal-making talents and renovating skills with twenty-hour-a-day care and a fiercely loyal staff. All combine to make the Wedgewood a favourite oasis for high profile visitors seeking privacy.[8]

What drives her? Eleni pondered the question before answering with the fire of an entrepreneur: "I enjoy the business!" Her eyes shone as she described the first time she and her staff, standing across the street, watched the lights go on in her Wedgewood Hotel: "I thought, 'I created that. This is what it is all about.'" She is respected as a shrewd, sophisticated businessperson who is in for the long run. Quick witted, cool thinking, intuitive, and tenacious, Eleni also pays her debts. Running a hotel is the most difficult of businesses, and Eleni is as attuned to her creation as Liona Boyd is to her guitar. In the style of a true dealer, she harbours no bitterness over the long battle. She claims that she neither discusses finances nor competes with Nelson. In the perception of Vancouverites, she is a hotelier nonpareil. She is not only equal to her husband in business but, says business chat on the street, in quality deals, she has eclipsed him.

Sonja Bata

> In my own [working] life I forget that I'm a woman.
>
> SONJA BATA[b]

> There are two ways of [working] with her: Sonja's way and the wrong way, and sheer bloody-minded determination like that generally leaves casualties.
>
> ANONYMOUS[c]

To the Swiss manor born, the vibrant, black-haired Sonja Bata, who speaks five languages fluently, is the daughter of an internationally renowned idealist who set high standards for her. An architecture graduate, she married a family friend, Thomas Bata, in 1946. He was a Czechoslovakian shoe manufacturer who had left his country in 1939 one week before the Germans invaded to re-establish himself in Canada. Sonja joined her husband in what he refers to as an equal partnership. Whether or not she actually cut the deals, she has used her architectural skills to design stores and shoes, and to develop marketing strategies. Her avocation, developing a shoe museum, has turned into an accomplishment of extraordinary historical import.

Although she is criticized by the media for using cheap South African labour and for bowing to the whims of government decrees in the countries in which they operate, Bata's rebuttal reveals a ferocious protagonist for democratic rights. Everyone, she said, has the right to wear shoes regardless of politics, and everyone has the right to operate as an economic entity without partisan connections. Rather than make a statement about South African sanctions, they closed down. But, in Dhaka, Bangladesh, Muslim fundamentalists threw rocks at Bata shoe stores because the motif on a certain shoe resembled the Arabic characters for Allah. To restore peace, Thomas Bata issued a public apology but the couple adhere to their apolitical views while expanding their shoe manufacturing into a global empire of annual sales of 300-million pairs of shoes in over 6,000 retail outlets in ninety-three countries, with estimated sales of over $3 billion. As an unofficial ambassador, Sonja's connections to heads of state, potentates and mere bureaucracies are so vast that a telephone call from her can get you in to see almost anyone—or get you shut out of the country.

Asked what she cares about most, Bata turns evangelical about her work with the World Wildlife Fund before launching into her favourite challenge: inspiring children through Junior Achievement to learn creative self-reliance and self-determination. When chair of J.A., Bata was instrumental in getting the Bata Corporation to underwrite the cost of incorporating their program into the Ontario public school system at the Grade 5 level. With an almost fierce resolve she stated, "We must teach our children not to expect the government to provide jobs, but that they can create their own."

The directorships of this formidable woman fill pages. Known as a board member who can hold her own in any company, Bata is probably far less intimidated by men than they are by her, and she has little patience for women complaining about the glass ceiling. She believes that women may not be reaching the top because they do not really want the responsibility. Not only is she disdainful of legislation such as affirmative action for women, but, in true Thatcher style, Bata believes that rather than throwing out safety nets for women, you should provide a road map for others by making your own way to the top. She is the second woman in history to be inducted, in 1991, into the Canadian Business Hall of Fame. More than any other woman in Canada, Sonja Bata epitomizes the ultimate cliché of the most commanding CEO: "I don't get ulcers, I give ulcers."

The Impresarios

In a world of huge financial gambles in which the cost of one seat for a touring musical of the magnitude of *CATS* determines profit or loss, the moniker "impresario" evokes images of outdoor theatres plagued by July snow storms, of opening night at Stratford with the Stratford train broken down outside of New Hamburg, of Judith Forst, *Tosca,* and laryngitis. "The cost of touring is outrageous," noted seasoned impresario Marlene Smith. Impresarios rank among the biggest risk takers of the entrepreneurial world. Essential to their survival is toughness combined with the magic of Merlin in transmogrifying potential disaster into triumph.

Stars cost tens of thousands of dollars. In March 1989, just ten days before Maureen Forrester was to sing the world premiere of Margaret Atwood's poetry from *You Are Happy* in Vancouver's Orpheum Theatre, June Goldsmith, chair of the non-profit organization Music in the Morning, called the theatre to ask how many tickets had been sold. "Seven," was the answer. The veteran Goldsmith remained calm. The day before the show, the tickets sold out.

In preparation for Expo 86, Vancouverite Ann Farris Darling travelled the globe assembling the huge international arts program for the festival. She juggled and slotted and negotiated for two years, fending off such horrors as losing the theatre for La Scala by switching the performance to a hockey coliseum. During Expo, Farris Darling relied on her 500-member staff to help care for hundreds of artistic temperaments and technicians of varying disciplines, languages, and cultures. Just hours before his evening appearance, Placido Domingo called from Mexico City with the awful news that his father was ill and he could not make it. Darling convinced him to come, but at 6:00 p.m. he phoned to say his plane had just landed in Seattle. Farris Darling called Expo president Jim Pattison, who dispatched his jet to fetch the singer and fly him into Vancouver. There the limo service failed to meet him. Farris Darling scrambled again, and Domingo made the sold-out show just ten minutes late.

Being an impresario *is* theatre.

Bluma Appel said she would rather stage a play on Broadway, even if it folded in two weeks, than be given the Hope diamond. The camaraderie of the theatre world and the thrust toward opening night is heart-warming, gut-wrenching, fun, saddening, but always profoundly stimulating. For women who play the power game with blind trust, it can be utterly devastating:

****

[Marlene has] the gall of a canal horse.

TINA VANDERHEYDEN ABOUT MARLENE SMITH[d]

Contacts help when you need to raise a million or three, and Marlene Smith, veteran of at least forty-seven shows, is Canada's *grande dame* of theatre deal-makers. A member of the Old Toronto elite, she counts among her friends and investors Eaton's president Fredrik Eaton, Liz Tory, and Standard Broadcasting CEO Allan Slaight, with whom she sat on the Shaw Festival board. Smith has a smile that exudes the warmth of motherhood, and watching her knit by a fire on a Sunday afternoon makes it easy to imagine the parent of four children who won *Family Circle*'s Canadian Homemaker of the Year award. Switch to the office, however, and molten steel jets through her veins. She has survived as an impresario not only because she is good and has terrific financial contacts, but because, in the case of *CATS*, she bludgeoned her competition right out of T.S. Eliot's junkyard.

In April 1987, writer Jeremy Ferguson referred to *CATS* as "the remarkable triumph of Marlene Smith."[e] It was a remarkable show, perhaps the most successful, ambitious, and popular event ever to appear in Canadian theatre. The first musical to go on the road while the original was still playing on Broadway, *CATS* Canada grossed $42 million in its original run in Toronto and $75 million across Canada. But another, overlooked impresario, Tina VanderHeyden, a younger Dutch talent who had moved to Vancouver and worked under West Coast impresario David Y.H. Lui, and then went to the National Ballet in Toronto, claimed it was she who had been working since 1982 with the Shubert Organization in New York to secure the rights for *CATS* Canada. Smith disagreed, saying that around 1982, Gina Mallet, then entertainment writer for the Toronto *Star*, had said to her jokingly, "Why don't you do *CATS* at the Elgin?" That set Smith's wheels turning. Down the road, VanderHeyden believed she had *CATS* in the bag but no theatre, while Marlene Smith had a theatre but no show.

Smith and VanderHeyden agreed to collaborate and headed for New York to negotiate the rights with the Shubert Organization. It was then that VanderHeyden made her crucial mistake. At the signing of documents, she was prepared to list Smith's partner, Ernest Rubenstein, as a director and producer of *CATS* for Marlene Smith Enterprises, but for months she failed to realize that she had also cut him in for a third of the profits. Only after the signing did VanderHeyden learn that Smith did not actually have a theatre in hand. She was still juggling for the lease, but did get it.

Months later VanderHeyden, who was in charge of publicity, realized that she was being subtly cut out of things. Most people in the creative world can forgive a lot if they get fair recognition, but Rubenstein's profile was rising as producer, and Smith had somehow manoeuvred VanderHeyden into a perceived position of employee, gradually edging her out of meetings and daily operations in preparation of the show. In a *Toronto Life*[f] article, VanderHeyden told Rod McQueen that at the reception for the opening night of *CATS* she was placed at a table far away from the cast and investors, an organizer's decree that you're a nobody. When *CATS* made a quick profit and investors celebrated at the Hazelton Café, Smith almost excluded the younger impresario, who then realized that she was regarded not as an equal but as an assistant. Smith had gained control of information and built an increasingly higher profile for herself through her friends in the press. VanderHeyden became not only forgotten in magazine articles, but worse: in relation to the production, her absence made her appear inconsequential. In *Toronto Life's* ''Fifty Most Influential People for 1987,'' only Marlene Smith made the list for bringing *CATS* to Canada.[8]

VanderHeyden sued Smith for an equal share in Rubenstein's one-third cut, alleging that she had secured *CATS* for Canada, that Rubenstein had never been discussed as a partner, and that by virtue of Smith and Rubenstein's modus operandi, she had been rendered as anonymous as the *CATS* stars out of their costumes on the street. Each side produced sworn affidavits discrediting the other, and even though Bernard Jacobs, president of the Shubert Organization, agreed that his first contact and subsequent negotiations were with VanderHeyden, she had trusted Smith and signed the contract without reading the small print. She lost.

Marlene Smith had grown up with the entertainment business in her family. Her father, George Deller, was owner and operator of the Palais Royale Ballroom, and she became an active part in the theatre world while raising four children when John Bassett Jr. brought *Hair* to Toronto. Then came *Godspell* and Broadway producer Marvin Krauss. Smith the homemaker did the lowly jobs such as helping with ticket sales, but she was bitten, and the producers were so impressed with her organization that Krauss sent more work her way and became her mentor. Forty-seven shows later, up came *CATS*. Smith had combined business skills with her own social contacts to raise $2 million at just one cocktail party. She had accessed the monied crowd through Allan Slaight, and CATS was launched efficiently. Said Smith with equanimity, ''Raising money probably has to do with the fact that I'll always live in Rosedale.''

Slaight devised a limited partnership with a minimum investment of $25,000 to finance the company. Short months before opening, when Smith knew the costs were escalating, she called on the partners, who immediately threw in another million. They all got their money back sixteen weeks after opening, and from then on made money. Entrepreneur Liz Tory, one of the overjoyed investors, threw a party at the Rosedale Golf Club to celebrate and later cheerily gave tours through her renovated home announcing, ''This is our *CATS* bathroom, this is our *CATS* kitchen, our *CATS* sun room. . . . ''

The disintegration of a partnership, the acerbic court drama, and the terrible mental anguish suffered by VanderHeyden illustrate two tenets that otherwise competent women entering the business world must make part of their lives. The first is that to solidify your position means to build a public presence so that you are perceived by outsiders to be a force. Beyond ability, power is a perception, an image, being there. Secondly, women who believe in sisterhood are asking for disaster. Until women realize that a deal is a deal is a deal, they will be neither satisfied nor successful in a domain where only winners get standing ovations. VanderHeyden failed to understand that in business, kindness has no more weight than gender. Many men and women do business on a handshake but trust is not gender driven. In not reading the contract at least three times, she had made the most devastating mistake possible for women going into business with other women. Her gibe that Smith had the gall of a canal horse would delight the deal maker in Marlene Smith, who had hardly played by the Marquesse of Queensberry rules but had done nothing illegal. What counted was winning. Welcome to the real world.

VanderHeyden has come out a wiser woman with an MBA in street fighting, a degree that made her valuable to Gail Regan's battle with the maverick board of the Women's College Hospital. In the competitive world of theatre production, Smith and Rubenstein deposited a million dollars to the Ontario government's Heritage Foundation for a five-year licensing fee in the fabulously renovated Elgin & Winter Garden, with the stipulation that they produce works with 60 percent Canadian content. The two other main contenders for operation of the theatre, who lost, were Garth Drabinsky, formerly of Cineplex, and Tina VanderHeyden. But their coup was securing *The Phantom of the Opera* for the Pantages Theatre. VanderHeyden is co-producer and manager of that magnificent production. Down the street, so to speak, another famous impresario, David Mirvish, grabbed *Les Misérables*. Smith and Rubenstein promoted Kenneth Branagh's wild version of *A Midsummer Night's Dream*. And the game goes on.

The Fashion Entrepreneurs

> Think about the frame.
> The frame is carved, it is important,
>
> it exists, it does not reflect you,
> it does not recede and recede, it has
> limits . . .
>
> MARGARET ATWOOD[h]

> Beware of all enterprises that require new clothes.
>
> HENRY DAVID THOREAU[i]

"They'll never make a woman president of this company," scoffed Ted Leishman to Krystyne Romer Griffin in 1968. Leishman was manager of the fashion import section in Eaton's department store, flagship of one of Canada's greatest patriarchal dynasties. Romer worked on his staff.

"They will. This is what you do," commanded the columnar six-foot-plus Romer Griffin, who leaned toward Leishman with the sinister look of a Glenda Jackson plotting with Walter Matthau in a Frederick Forsythe thriller. Inheriting the wits and style of her Polish aristocrat parents, the youthful Romer was negotiating her entrée into Eaton's executive echelon, then a male enclave as unassailable as the financial institutions. She intended to shape Eaton's fashion empire into an image that would catapult it from 1950 blahs into 1960s rebellious chic. Glowering at Leishman, Romer commanded, "Go to your boss and advise him to open one European central buying office with me in charge. Instead of a crowd of buyers swarming all over the countryside and running up expense accounts, the European agents will bring their wares to me. In Paris. *I'll* run the operation and supervise the buying."

"He'll never go for that," balked Leishman, foreseeing the mutiny he'd face with his buying staff.

"He will. It's an excellent idea," persisted Romer. "Then he'll say, 'Who have you got in mind to run it?' and you say, 'Romer.' Nothing more. Say the idea is yours. You'll get the credit."

When Leishman nervously agreed to give it a try, Romer pushed harder, "Now. I must have the top job otherwise the Europeans will never go for a woman." Leishman blanched. Romer fixed him with a deadly eye and with tones rich in Polish inflection, hissed like Forsythe's archetypal antagonist, "I will know what happens. If this deal goes through and you do not use me, I will go to my friends in the media and give this story to the public."

So off Leishman went and presented the idea to his very senior executive as orchestrated. To his astonishment the executive replied, "I like it. Who have you got to run it?" Leishman gulped, "Romer — and the title of president is necessary to deal in the European community." Romer was on a plane heading for Europe before the Eatons realized that they had hired a thirty-one-year-old female president.

In Paris, Romer dismissed the old guard that had clung to the postwar code of mediocrity, and over the next ten years, under her aristocratic eye, Eaton's increased its women's clothing volume of imports and became known in the trade as Canada's Fashion Department Store. Its classiest shop in Montreal was referred to as Bloomingdale's North. Her rewards were a plush apartment, a style to which she had become accustomed during an earlier career with IBM International in Paris, and a chalet on the ski slopes of Val d'Isère. It was there that she fell in love with Scott Griffin, an adventurer from a FOOF who flies his own Cessna and lives on the wild side. They and their twelve-year-old daughter Chloe, live in Toronto.

Romer Griffin told the story of Chloe's birth (she was a breech birth, delivered by a veterinarian behind a Texaco station) in Fenton's, then Toronto's premiere power lunch restaurant. The traveller had arrived first, staving off the blustery chill of a November day by layering herself like a stylish renegade of the 1960s, topped off by the felt fedora of a spy. She was outdated for the late 1980s, but warm in the falling snow. Fortunately, none of the political and business cyclones who filled the restaurant had even noticed her arrival, and she preferred anonymity.

Then Romer Griffin appeared and paused at the entrance, all seven feet of her in six-inch stiletto heels. Conversations faded and forks froze in mid-air as men and women patrons caught sight of the apparition extending from floor to ceiling. She was authoritative rather than sultry, and no smile interfered with her up-tilted chin. The latest short, short pepper tweed Saint Laurent skirt barely wrapped her thighs. Snow still melted on her hip-length Saint Laurent jacket and her nearly naked legs filmed in sheer black Lycra. Weren't her knees cold? An eight-foot fur boa of charcoal grey with a touch of white fluff slunk from her right knee, up over her shoulder before tumbling down her back to her calf. Only when she had the attention of the entire restaurant did she move on, the boa flicking with every step she made towards the traveller, whose head had sunk beneath her shoulders.

Romer Griffin appeared to look nowhere while checking out everyone, and every eye in the restaurant tracked her like a heat-seeking missile. When she found the traveller at a table hidden behind a palm tree, she paused quizzically, unsure as to who, or what, was buried under the layers of clothing. Then she reached forward, tilted and peered under the fedora in silent reproach of arcane funk. The traveller was exposed. Only then did she descend to her chair. Fenton's patrons practically applauded before returning to their conversations, while the object of their delight announced in a voice heavy with the Polish accent and filled with satisfaction, "Fashion is entertainment. If not, it will fail."

Romer Griffin had established control of Fenton's and her interviewer without a single word. With that proclamation, she encompassed the philosophy of the multi-billion-dollar[9] women's fashion industry that costumes the theatre of life. Frozen knees are irrelevant. Designers and marketers tell it differently, but they lie. Throughout recorded history women have been defined by other people's opinions of how they look, and they still use fashion to present to the world their dramatic personas or their shady anonymity.

Romer Griffin is formidable and funny with a penchant for nudging the world off balance. She does not follow rules; she makes them. Her fashion maxim is those who take themselves too seriously should not play the game. Fashion is supposed to be fun. Henry VIII had a ball with it, as did Louis XIV and Madame de Pompadour. Another fashion maven, Holt Renfrew's vice-chair Hilary Weston, has been listed on the international best-dressed list—and its fashion hall of fame—despite the fact that she has committed such outrageous sacrileges as wearing her clothes backwards or, horrors, wearing three designers simultaneously. Joan Druxman, a Vancouver boutique owner who styles her jet-black hair as if struck by lightening, reasoned of style, "Well, why not look unique and terrific? You never go out and buy an ugly car or an ugly sofa!"

Every few years Romer Griffin moves on, either in search of new challenges, or because her institutional associates become exhausted by her entrepreneurial style. She is a risk-taker with other people's money, one who can win big if you can afford her. Functioning within the corporate milieu of department stores presents a paradox for Romer Griffin. Those who have the funds to afford the fashion world and its idiosyncrasies ultimately have the philosophical control, and in the eternal dilemma between art and finance, the bottom line eventually wins. That was why Romer Griffin's job as director of Holt Renfrew's Montreal and Toronto designer boutiques came to an end in 1989. Frustrated by the restrictions and choices placed on her by a department store faced with making that irritating thing called profit in a market as soft as silk, the fashion maven sniffed as she departed, "You do not put a $300 Calvin Klein next to a $6,000 Lacroix blouse." A pragmatist, as all entrepreneurs are, Romer Griffin believes in serving customers with what the market will bear, and in the spring of 1990 she made contacts in the Eastern European market to mass-market Mondi blouses out of Germany. She sits on the board of the Poland Canada Chamber of Commerce, and when the government changed in Poland she organized Lech Walesa's visit to Canada.

Romer Griffin's father was Polish aristocracy, and a civil engineer who moved his family to Quebec and became an international success. An urbane gentleman whom she idolized, he equated achievement with identity. Mr. Romer admonished his six children (Krystyne being the eldest), that "only when you give much and become outstanding, will you reflect your European aristocracy." Thus inspired, Romer Griffin set about to do both, using her talents to achieve the lifestyle of her family's entitlement. Raised to speak four languages, she finished school in Montreal, then headed for Paris and a secretarial job with IBM International. Before long she talked the multinational into a conference program headed by someone who knew instinctively how to hold a soup spoon, use a finger bowl, and take care of VIPs. She, of course, was their woman. Barely out of her teens, she laughed, "I lied about my age everywhere I went. . . . [IBM] had the money to do everything first-class—the hotels, the limos, the flowers, theatre." She had found her métier, providing first-class service for a financial power that in turn kept her in the manner to which she aspired.

In 1964 when Philippe de Gaspé Beaubien became the Director of Operations, Canadian Corp for the 1967 world exposition, he and a mutual friend—the Ambassador to France—recommended Romer Griffin run the VIP services at Expo. She was involved at the organizational stage, and for six months during Expo 67 she ran a staff of sixty-seven and threw 260 receptions. Responsible for all arrangements, she said of her expense account, "I had none. I just kept track of the bills. . . . I will deal only with people whose noses are long enough to know what is first class—people who like and expect the very best." Corporations or governments who wince at price tags need not apply.

Following her Eaton's career and a prominent Hazelton Lanes franchise with Saint Laurent, Romer Griffin was hired by Galen Weston to develop an image for his newly acquired Holt Renfrew's fashion boutiques. It was a natural acquisition for Galen, whose wife Hilary had begun her career in Ireland first as a fashion mannequin, then model, then buyer for Brown Thomas. If there is anything the Westons know well, it is the fashion world and those afficionados who can afford to enjoy its adventures and surprises. Hilary Weston was anxious to put her stamp on the HR boutiques, if not to join the management team. Meanwhile, she joined Romer Griffin on European buying trips, which, to the latter's delight, were first class all the way. They were the odd couple, the soft-spoken Weston with the hard-driving Romer Griffin, but the latter recalled that Weston took the mission so seriously she once cancelled her trip to China with Galen and the children. At the opening of the Fashion Boutiques in 1987, guests were served manhattans and given a kit containing an 8x10 photograph of Hilary Weston. The inference was that the Fashion Boutiques were hers, yet in his speech, Galen welcomed everyone on behalf of himself and his "spouse." Hilary remained a wise woman who understood the power of tradition, discretion, and timing. By 1989 Romer Griffin was gone, Hilary Weston was vice-chair, and the Fashion Boutiques reflected her buying influence — boosted by cameo appearances by her friend Paloma Picasso. By 1990 in the fashion world, Hilary was no longer "spouse": her name was synonymous with the Holt Renfrew Fashion Boutiques.

****

Krystyne Romer Griffin, Joan Druxman, and Fetoun Yousif — the voluptuous Lebanese Yorkville couturière of Fetoun — among other entrepreneurs in the fashion industry, are the gurus of human behaviour, the pop psychologists of cultural shifts or economic trends. Reflecting on the mystique of fashion and women's identity, Druxman observed that empowered women like media hosts Barbara Frum and Adrienne Clarkson use fashion as an art form to effect not an "in" look but an individual style in an industry that is fuelled by insecurity. Up to and through the late 1980s, fashion created a seasonal mania of women seeking individuality while clinging to the conformity of a singular look. The syndrome was supported by a multi-million-dollar sub-culture of fashion magazines that launched teenaged Monika Schnarre and other underfed youth into international stardom and six-figure incomes.

For many women, the most vivid manifestation of insecurity is wrapped up in their reaction to hapless journalists, political cartoonists, and authors who try to bring alive an individual for their readers when her appearance is off limits. Women spend billions of dollars annually on fashion foibles and face lifts, but describe a woman vice-president, politician, or litigator as blonde, beautiful, youthful, or stylish, and a stream of sexist accusations fall on the newspaper like the attack of a Stealth bomber. Try a humorous metaphor, such as Allan Fotheringham's description of publisher Doug Creighton's hair as looking as if it was combed by an eggbeater, or Peter Gzowski who looks like an unmade bed, or the time he took time out for a half-hour jog around Mike Duffy[j] —and howls about cheap meanness would bury the Letters editor. These men do not define themselves by their looks. They thought Foth was hilarious and got on with their business. Women who are so insecure about their professional image that they are loathe to be recognized, in part, by the myth of fashion, verify that it is fundamental to their identity. It may not be fair that they have been defined by other people's opinions for eons, but denying the reality increases its power. Nothing annoys businesswomen more than having their style of clothing described by the press when their financial, professional, and personal expertise should take the limelight. When world leaders debate at summits, Bush's ties are never a subject of discussion, while Barbara's dresses are. As long as women continue to use fashion to define themselves, they ask for it.

Whatever we think of it, fashion is elemental to our society. Even at the 1988 Economic Summit, which focussed in the Third World and its starving millions, Canada's showcase was not about agricultural technology or resources, but about its fashion industry, right there in prime time news along with survival. In one convention room world leaders struggled with the problem of starvation while elsewhere anorexic models pranced in a surrealistic parody of the Economic Summit.

Fashion victims are women who allow themselves to be defined by their wardrobes, with the result that no sooner are they clad in confidence than the designers change the game and render their clients' Scaasis and Roehms passé. The frenzy is easily perpetuated by lowering or raising hemlines, opening or closing heels, switching satin for silk, pouffe for slink, puce for aubergine, ecru for black, skirts for pants, wide leg for narrow. Slink, slank, slunk. Short, long, droop—switch the "in" whatever, and $86,000-quarterly wardrobes are abandoned in the stampede to be first to wear the newest look.[10] Plus ça change. . . .

Designers and salespeople are brilliant at the doubletalk inherent to the business. They will explain that they are in possession of the latest look sweeping Europe and New York, then put the clincher on the sale with the remark that their wildly expensive designs are, of course, not throw-aways. Joan Druxman described the paradox with, "It has to be chic and sophisticated but four years from now it's still going to be a classic."

Fashion can be women's most manipulative tool of power. Like the gala and the cause, using it to express one's personality fades in the face of the coercion, manipulation, and snippish cracks made by women consumed by envy, fear, or competitive mania. Druxman shakes her head in amazement at what "friends" say and do to control others. "I consider myself a reasonable authority on fashion. I know when somebody looks great [or terrible]. . . . The ones whose friends are getting married are green with envy and say such godawful things. I have also seen men who admire other glamorous women say terrible things to their wives in front of my staff. It's all about control—those men just didn't want them to look sensational.''

Many women are so uncertain of who they are that they cannot make decisions about what to wear. Even in the recessive 1990s, image consultants are making huge salaries advising mostly middle-aged women on their ''look.'' Sales clerks of lesser quality feel no compunction about convincing a five-foot three-inch woman that she will look terrific in the little number she has just seen on a six-foot, 112-pound model, but Druxman and Romer Griffin have been known to whip an unsightly outfit from their customers' backs because they refuse to jeopardize their own reputations just to make a sale.

The couturières noted that before women began earning their own money, very few would buy without first seeking permission from husbands who paid the bills and therefore had the right to judge. Some were prominent women, paradigms of competence and authority in their communities, yet they could not decide on how to dress themselves. When asked if women need their men to help them decide on an outfit, Toronto couturière Fetoun Yousif replied, ''Only if zey don't have zeroes from here to Zurich.''

Fashion is also used as a weapon for winning. When Torontonian Carole Grafstein slipped the word to *Globe and Mail* society columnist Rosemary Sexton that she was off to Paris to view the Chanel collection, in fashion parlance that was playing the power game in deadly earnest. It was Grafstein's clarion cry that she was there first. Marketers like Hilary Weston and Sharon Batten are expected to eye the merchandise. Shoppers like Grafstein are envied, resented, pitied, occasionally admired, and singled out as the one to beat. Women who take their fashion this seriously dress to win.

Then there is the Fashion Addiction syndrome. Romer Griffin related the story of one woman who arrived at the HR Fashion Boutique apologizing for her figure, which incorporated three sizes, and lamenting that she was neither as beautiful as Hilary Weston nor as strong as Romer Griffin. It never occurred to her that Romer Griffin is not as beautiful as Hilary Weston nor Weston as formidable as Romer Griffin nor as skinny as Monika Schnarre, and that these factors are irrelevant to fashion sense. The customer also noted that she could afford to spend only $5,000, which in 1991 would buy you one Ralph Lauren daytime outfit. ''She was afraid of me at first,'' remembered Romer Griffin who sent her off to get her hair cut and styled before shopping. Later, after four hours in the boutiques with lunch and champagne, the customer had fallen in love with everything she tried on. The image in the mirror was a transformed woman of fashion. Romer Griffin had seen it all before and warned, ''Your bill is currently running at $12,000. You are going to be furious with me.''

"I have to have it all," the elated customer insisted. Two weeks later, she made another appointment and spent another $12,000. Romer Griffin observed, "She was being seduced by clothes."

In the softer markets of 1991, some ateliers have hardly set aside a single needle because they cater to the carriage trade, that is above mere dips in the stock market. These entrepreneurs went for the big time by taking big risks, and Serge et Réal in Montreal, who designed creations for former governor-general Jeanne Sauvé, as well as Nancy Casselman, Zoe (Cokkinos) and Fetoun in Toronto, and Shenkofeh and Anna Marie Ochocki in Vancouver, simply continue to snip and stitch. Fetoun continues to fly to Mr. Chow's in New York for dinner and then return before her boutique opens the next morning.

Fetoun serves the vast ethnic societies that have moved into the haute couture world and every other haute world with greater wealth than the old guard ever dreamed. She uses her own name, her own designers, and makes a point of underselling the HR Fashion Boutiques. Of the soft market for women's fashions, she scoffed, "You cannot afford buying a Lacroix blouse for $1,000 and selling it for $4,000. Everything starts and ends by paying the bills." She also knows that spending is power, and once customers have the courage to enter a boutique, they will buy. Besides convenience and style, the boutiques provide a sense of privacy, the feeling of shopping in one's own home. The fashion psychologist added, "People love spending, whether it's shoes or groceries." In Vancouver, Catherine Guadagnuolo and Margaret Ross, owners of Boboli, the Italian fashion boutique, said in 1987 that some women would spend up to $50,000 in a morning. By 1991 that sum had slipped to a mere $25,000. In headier times, Boboli was known to sell out of entire shipments in days, then for weeks serve its faithful clientele cappuccino and cookies in the empty store until more merchandise arrived.

Joan Druxman is her own best advertisement. At fifty-two, she neither drinks nor smokes and looks smashing. In New York, where she keeps an apartment for her frequent visits to monitor the fashion trends, she has often been mistaken for Cher. In 1990 she moved from Winnipeg to Vancouver's chic South Granville — down the street from Boboli — to access the West Coast's continuing up-scale sales. Raised in Estevan, Saskatchewan, as Joan Zelcovich by Russian immigrant parents, Druxman took huge risks in opening her own business but said, "I have never, in all of my working life, had a door closed on me. [I am a gambler] . . . yet I have never been refused a request for a loan."

In 1975, Druxman left her husband and teenaged children and was disowned by her parents. "Nothing," she said quietly, "business failure, rejection, denial, whatever, could ever equal that wrench." Of the next month she said, "I went to a plastic surgeon, had my nose and boobs done. That September I borrowed $50,000 from the bank . . . bought an historic house at a tax sale . . . put in $200,000 of renovations . . . lived on $1,600, which was the refund on my pension, and opened up February

1977.'' She paid a seamstress by piecework, did all her own books and cleaned the shop on weekends. In six months she had paid back the $50,000 loan and that year grossed $285,000. So impassioned is Druxman with conveying her message of empowerment to other women that she volunteered her time when in Winnipeg at the Osborne House shelter for abused women. Criticized at first for looking like a *Vogue* cover shot, Druxman demonstrated that downcast women were inspired rather than intimidated by her appearance. She got their hair done, helped them put together a stylish outfit they could afford from second-hand stores, took them out to a terrific lunch, then sent them home feeling better about themselves.[11] The results proved astounding. Women who stand taller tend to command respect. She explained, ''Showing these women their own potential that not even their mothers told them they had, well, they start thinking, 'I'm somebody. I can take charge of my life.'''

Martha Sturdy and Zonda Nellis typify the West Coast entrepreneurial women who share a world view that has never restricted them to downtown Vancouver. From the start they joined the global village with such exuberance that, in turn, the world has welcomed them. Almost. Ontario-born Nellis, who weaves ''wearable art'' for customers in Japan (the first Canadian designer to show a collection in Tokyo in the fall of 1988), over forty U.S. department stores and boutiques, and the diplomatic women in Washington. Her clothes have been seen on The Cosby Show, Dynasty, and Hotel, but Nellis says she has never made it in Toronto. In 1985 when she was on her way to business appointments in New York, she stopped off at the Toronto Festival of Fashion only to be told, ''Oh, we're not interested in anything from B.C.''

Vancouver jewellery designer Martha Sturdy, struggling to put her life together following a broken marriage, created a collection at her kitchen table to pay the bills while completing her courses at the Emily Carr College of Art and Design. Then she, too, headed for New York. At the time she had never travelled without her husband, handled airline tickets, or even tipped a waiter, but her courage to go international paid off. Her annual sales exceed $2 million and her designs are sold through art galleries and some four hundred department stores across Canada, the United States, Saudi Arabia, Greece, and Japan. Her work has appeared in *Vogue, Flare, Harper's Bazaar,* and the Italian magazine *Donna*, and she was one of the few Canadians ever to be profiled in *Forbes*. Her jewellery is worn by top models, and she is sought out by Oscar de la Renta as well as Carolyne Roehm.[k]

****

Analysts attributed the dramatic slump at the end of the 80s in the fashion industry to amorphous seasonal designs, but they were ignoring the distinctive shift in women's feelings from subservience to empowerment. Rather than defining themselves by outside opinions, more women than ever before were players in the world outside their home and the fashion industry no longer had pre-eminent control of its customers. Women earning their own money are redefinining themselves, and whatever they choose, hemlines, colour schemes, shoe styles, and outrageous prices will no longer by dictated by the fashion industry.

This is not to say that women are no longer as concerned with their packaging, but they are looking for something more permanent in which to invest their dollar than fickle fashion. In the game of appearance, priorities have shifted from the cover-up to the body itself. Heal-thyself health spas and plastic surgeons are working overtime. Rather than pay $5,000 for a new outfit that becomes passé by the next season, women are opting for a week of working out, or having an eye tuck, liposuction, lip injections, or a face lift. Thus rejuvenated, they dust off clothes from four seasons ago and head out on the town. Said designer/entrepreneur Martha Sturdy to Barbara Sgroi of *Flare* magazine, "Fashion is so irrelevant in the big scheme of things."[1]

The Conduits to Power

> With our knowledge, we can facilitate and expedite [the process] by end-running a whole bureaucratic system.
>
> LIANE BENOÎT

The consultants are the seasoned intermediaries, the cross-pollinators between business, bureaucracy, and media. They are the new age lobbyists, presenting comprehensive propositions in a sophisticated yet entrepreneurial style that connects their clients to constructive action. However they come to the job, they come qualified, bringing a vast infrastructure of varied experience and a virtuoso talent for communicating with the inner sanctum of power. Traditional university degrees do not necessarily define their education, and each day, in a business that pays from $40,000 to $200,000 annually, they must justify, verify, and inspire organizations that they are of inestimable value.

In character the consultants are entrepreneurial yet they are skilled in institutional structure. Most cannot imagine working in corporate middle management. Many have had brutal experiences in backroom politics, others have reached the senior vice-presidency position in corporations, then have walked away. Like everyone else, consultants seek victory and, like the very best of entrepreneurs, they believe that everyone who comes to their table should benefit from what they have to offer. Jodi White, Liane Benoît, Jocelyne Côté-O'Hara, and Elizabeth Roscoe got their training in public policy while working on the Hill, assisting prime ministers Joe Clark (White, former chief of staff), and Brian Mulroney (O'Hara), Governor General Jeanne Sauvé (Benoît), cabinet ministers Barbara McDougall (Roscoe), and Michael Wilson. One of Heather Reisman's first major experiences was developing the organizational structure for the Abella Commission on Pay Equity. Jalynn Bennett and Susan Murray came from the corporate sector with strong political backroom experience, and Starr Solomon hails from the media, a former CTV producer, but each had become proficient in institutional systems before spinning out into their own freelance orbits.

****

Liane Benoît is typical in that her Delphi Group consists of seven men and herself, each of whom is politically connected, multidisciplinary, and has an influential international network. Each is concerned with altering the public perception of government as a coercive and negative force to one of a helpful partner in business. Their deals are socially progressive, environmentally sound, and financially lucrative. Benoît, a Futurist on the fast track, is pursuing the creation of an electronic education institute, an ''environmental network'' for a research base to link all education and related statistics across the country.[12]

Beyond her experience in business, she has powerful social connections to an international elite, developed while she served as aide to her governor general aunt, Jeanne Sauvé. Her company, Benoît and Associates does public affairs consulting and she is working with Indian Affairs regarding an alternate Indian act.

Susan Murray of S.A. Murray Consulting[13] started out with herself and a secretary, winning the $200-million equity guarantee from the Canadian and Ontario governments to restructure Massey-Ferguson. She happened to be cold-calling for business, and got chair Victor Rice facing foreclosure from the bank. In 1991, her offices in Toronto and Ottawa consist of eleven consultants, two researchers, and support staff, who focus on what she described as an intricate communication system between the private sector and key government operators.

One of the most powerful women in central Canada today is Montreal lawyer-entrepreneur-politico Manon Vennat, whose university buddies included Senator Michael Meighen, a university pal of Brian Mulroney. ''It all started at university,'' recalled Vennat, who says she is better known as a Liberal. Born and educated in Montreal, and active in the National Federation of Students, she was hired by the Liberal Secretary of State in 1969 to implement the recommendations of the Royal Commission on Bilingualism and Biculturalism. She was the first woman and the first francophone president, then chair, of the Montreal Board of Trade, at the time a lacklustre, anglophone-dominated board that she helped to revive by encouraging an alliance between anglophone and francophone business leaders. *Globe and Mail* writer Harvey Enchin called her ''the queen of Quebec capitalism.''[m]

Currently vice-president of Spencer Stuart and Associates, an executive-search firm, Vennat is best connected to power through her directorships.[14] Those who need her know she can play hardball —

Vennat claims a personal lobbying victory in winning the Canadair's CF-18 maintenance contract over a furious Manitoba. Winners must be indefatigable and always accessible. Richard Conrad wrote of Vennat in *Outlook '87*,[n] "Being with Manon is like being plugged directly into Hydro-Québec."

Rosemary McCarney, president of Cosult International, formerly Kanchar International,[15] is an international facilitator, lawyer, entrepreneur, educator; and she was also a policy-maker as former vice-president of the federal Liberal Party. She saw the potential for Kanchar in 1984-85 when she accompanied an armed convoy taking Canadian grain into Ethiopia through lands mined by Somalis who were after the provisions. McCarney is a global thinker and traveller, collaborating with CIDA in "Women in Development," which links the Business Co-operation Branch and the Canadian business community with women leaders in less developed countries. She teaches international business at the University of Toronto law school, her mind a vast repository of information and systems, many of which she has created herself and for which she has devised an interlocking network.

Jocelyne Côté-O'Hara, a social science graduate, worked in several public sector jobs, including Treasury Board, as a financial analyst, then was hired for the Mulroney PMO, first as policy adviser on women's issues and then as liaison between cabinet and the civil service. She subsequently moved into the private sector when B.C. Tel appointed her VP of government relations. Within the year Côté-O'Hara won for Microtel (a subsidiary of B.C. Tel) the biggest federal government communications contract ever awarded—a $268-million contract to build the communications portion of the North Warning radar network. For the western-based company, which had never before had a presence in Ottawa, it was a lesson in immediacy. "You have to work this town," Côté-O'Hara told Canadian Business .[16o]

Starr Solomon, formerly a CBC associate producer, CTV producer, and consultant with her own firm, has a particular talent for writing contracts and government policy in comprehensible language. She first polished it during her decade of living in Washington, D.C.[17] Through her own company, Waddell Solomon Associates, she did work for, among other companies, Petro-Canada, the Canadian Textile Institute, and the St. Lawrence National Bank in the United States. In 1989 she disbanded her company to work with Burson-Marsteller, the largest PR agency in the world.

Jalynn Bennett, of Jalynn Bennett and Associates, has connections extending into the financial, political, and social networks of Central Canada and sits on several boards and commissions.[18] Serving on ad hoc committees involving economic policy and government regulation, and committees in the Ontario Ministries of Finance and Education, Bennett had lines into the policy-making structures of the country. In Ontario, the NDP are now in power, but in 1988-89 Bennett sat on the Prime

Minister's advisory council to study Canada's free trade adjustment policies.

Paradigm Consulting's managing partner, Heather Reisman, is a dynamo with one of the widest networks in Canada and with a sophisticated awareness of how rigid institutional structures can shift their thinking to access the flexible, entrepreneurial spirit. She said she was inspired to get involved, to make a difference at the executive level in all her endeavours, by Senator Lorna Marsden. The fortyish Reisman has participated in policy development in the Liberal Party since the Trudeau era. Refreshingly frank and distinctly individualistic in her political views, Reisman remains a good friend of former Liberal leader John Turner in spite of being energetically opposed to his intransigent stand against free trade during the 1988 fall election campaign. Reisman speaks strongly in favour of a fiscal policy that would create a viable framework for entrepreneurship. She is a public governor of the Toronto Stock Exchange and a director of Canadian Pacific Hotels, a backroom politician with front-room aspirations, having served as vice-chair of the federal party's election platform committee and as a policy adviser to such politicians as Donald Johnston and David Peterson. Her husband, business executive Gerald "Gerry" Schwartz, promotes her, says Edward Greenspon, as an excellent candidate for Canada's first female prime minster."[p]

Reisman's company (formed after she had worked with Claude Frenette Intergroup and with Marc Gerstein, who has an MIT doctorate in organizational change) is designed to take the pain out of change, to strategize for the future, and to guide organizations through the ensuing evolution. She is typical of the women entering the institutional executive who place particular emphasis on employee needs. Her partners excel in technical, academic, and practical knowledge that capture opportunities for change within any company or situation. Her clients have included CTV Television Network (and its complex ownership structure), Spar Aerospace, Télémédia, and Domtar. In her volunteer sphere she did the strategic planning for the impressively successful LEAF, and she was a key strategist in developing the structure for the Abella Commission on Pay Equity.

Admirers worry that Reisman may be too thinly spread, but she is a highly organized Futurist who, with her husband's full support, can attack her briefcase in a chauffeur-driven limo while rushing between meetings. As a consultant, Reisman's futuristic visions are exciting because they bring together the best in institutional power with the flexible, up-beat thinking of the entrepreneur, and the compassionate overview of those who envision what was once considered a contradiction in terms: a society that is kinder, gentler, more entrepreneurial, and more competitive. Her strategizing could be extrapolated far beyond the corporate world and into the fields of education and the judiciary. The explosion in global awareness is not something to be feared, but to be enjoyed, and she wonders at the marvellous potential for growth: "It's like goldrush time. If you can see the world differently, you can . . . build your future forever.''

The Clash of the Titans

> What is power? I can walk in to see the Prime Minister when I want, but I can't get a cab in the rain.
>
> BLUMA APPEL

Entrepreneurship symbolizes individuality and freedom, and when its practitioners collide with the executive from the institutions, just who is running this country becomes arrestingly clear. It's the senior bureaucrats. Torontonian Bluma Appel is the apotheosis of the entrepreneur. Art patron, activist, back-room politician for the Liberals, creator and facilitator of ideas as magnificent as they can be bizarre, she is a nomad who touches down here and there, creating structures, legitimizing the disdained,[19] effecting change. Then, as her fledgling creations inevitably evolve into Establishment peer groups, she usually flees to do it all over again. Her buoyant personality is best reflected in her limited partnership of *Tamara* the New York play described in its brochure as ''A living movie. A walk-through soap opera, a voyeur's dream come true.'' The play takes place in a house and the audience is free to wander from room to room and ''choose the play they wish to see.''

A brilliant innovator, as long as she is able to operate in her own freewheeling style, Appel achieves seemingly impossible goals. Force her to work within someone else's organization, and everything flies apart. As a special project in the 1970s, Appel devised a way to expand the national museum's art inventory by inspiring Americans who had enjoyed the profits of Canadian business to express gratitude through art donations. Gifts, of course, would be encouraged through tax benefits. It was an audacious idea for the Canadian apologist mindset and its dedication to going by the book. In her enthusiasm to form an American Friends of Canada Committee, the entrepreneur never considered consulting Dr. Jean Sutherland Boggs,[20] a paladin of the institutional hierarchy and a pre-eminent force in the elite and powerful world of Canada's cultural icon, the National Gallery of Canada, which presumably was going to accept these fabulous gifts.

Boggs in fact operated in a style similar to Appel's, acting more like a CEO than a senior bureaucrat. After three years of repeated requests to the government to sanction a proper building for Canadian art, for example, she had bullied her bosses by resigning in a flood of publicity. The government responded not only by giving conditional approval for a new gallery but also by rehiring its tough executive as chair of the Canada Museums Construction Corporation. Michael Pantazzi, the National Gallery's associate curator of European and American Art, recalled that Boggs had the foundation dug and the walls up before the government knew what was happening. As chief of the construction board, Boggs had forged ahead in true entrepreneurial style aided by the divine right of institutional power.

Bluma Appel cheerily drew up an illustrious list of twenty-five founding members for her committee that included Henry Ford, David Rockefeller, and Armand Hammer. With the approval of Pierre Trudeau, future governor-general Jules Léger, then a senior bureaucrat, and diplomat, and her powerful pal Gérard Pelletier, she jaunted off to New York in 1972 to sell her idea. To reach all these renowned industrialists, Appel had only one contact, John Haverton, a New York PR executive for major corporations. Winning him over could open the door to such business luminaries as David Rockefeller of the Chase Manhattan Bank, who in turn could unlock other corporate doors. She won an interview with Haverton, to whom she outlined her plan to launch the committee at a special dinner with Prime Minister Trudeau at 24 Sussex Drive. Haverton was sceptical that Appel was legitimate until he proffered an idea and his visitor interjected, "I don't think Mr. Trudeau would go for that, but look, I'll phone him and find out." In America one does not just call the president about a dinner party, so Haverton quizzed, "Phone the Prime Minister from here?"

Appel responded, "Call 613-992-4211," which his secretary did, eyeing the Canadian suspiciously. When the call was answered with a cheerful, "Bureau du premier ministre," the secretary slammed down the telephone, exclaiming, "That was a prime minister's office!" With a parochialism that still makes Appel blush, she recalled saying, "Dial them collect. If he's not there, I don't want to waste your money." The Prime Minister's special assistant, Timothy Porteous, accepted the call. He knew of Appel's plan and began discussing the proposed event. On another telephone, Haverton dialed someone and whispered in an audible voice, "Make a hole in your diary, you must meet this woman." He was talking with Hoyt Ammidon, chair of U.S. Trust, who provided the entree to David Rockefeller. In two visits rather than the anticipated two years of diplomatic flip-flop and bureaucratic red tape, the American Friends of Canada Committee was conceived. Appel was quickly handed about the country to meet Rawleigh Warner, Jr., chair of Mobil Oil, Lynn Townsend, the CEO of Chrysler, James Roche, the CEO of General Motors, and Henry Ford. She recalled, "It went so fast it practically knocked me out, and without a structure, it practically knocked the whole thing out."

When Appel met Armand Hammer, the founder of Occidental Petroleum smiled and said, "Come on up—I'll give you this painting," and led her to a Goya. It was the entrepreneur's first coup. It was also a major mistake. Enter Boggs and the National Gallery, which has its own acquisitions committee. Faced with Appel's explosive success, Boggs, who had not been included in the process, was expected to welcome the Goya.

The museum chief was not about to have even the Mona Lisa foisted upon her and refused it. There is some suspicion that Hammer simply wanted to unload a lousy Goya. Boggs, of course, would have known that, but she did not inform Appel. Scowled the entrepreneur, "Armand Hammer took my idea and went off to Russia with his paintings. He gave [them] to Russia!"[21] Canadians, added Appel, just did not know how to operate in the sophisticated, international world of political gift-ing. It was the first of several power plays between Boggs and Appel that offended the Americans.

The American Friends of Canada Committee was launched as planned at 24 Sussex Drive. Canada would soon be the recipient of some marvellous gifts of art. David Rockefeller had already sent up a painting. Then Appel's face darkened as she described the historic clash between entrepreneur and institution, magnified by what the art patron identified regrettably as a battle between two powerful women, neither of whom would capitulate to the other. Having refused the Goya, Boggs returned David Rockefeller's painting as well. Then Alger Meadows offered to buy and donate a painting that was hanging at the Wildenstein Gallery in New York. Appel said it was the size of a wall and worth $250,000. Boggs saw it and decreed that it was too big. Not crummy art, just too big. When Appel expressed dismay over that rejection, another National Gallery executive quipped with the constipated thinking that has so characterized Canada, "Just tell them it's too big to fit in our elevator." No one seems to remember who the artist was but within a year it was sold to a museum in Los Angeles for $750,000. American-Canadian goodwill was running down the drain faster than melting snow. Trudeau knew that David Rockefeller was angry but not why. Appel recalled that the Prime Minister called her to ask if he could help. She might have played hardball and laid it all on the table, or she might have brought Boggs in as a full partner, just as the curator might have tried to inform Appel. Both women were into a power play and did neither. But Appel lacked the killer instinct to finish off the enemy. She did the historical old-boys' thing—refused to rat on Boggs, and took the fall herself.

Hoyt Ammidon called Appel and angrily demanded to know what was going on. She winced at the memory: "The whole thing came down on my head. At first I hadn't realized what [Boggs] was doing. Do you know, it was so gigantic that you cannot believe that this kind of thing can happen." The American Friends of Canada Committee faded away but was resurrected late in 1988 under the presidency of Gaetana Enders.[22] The committee was expanded to include, Shirley Thomson, the new director of the National Gallery, and among others, Sonja Bata, Liliane Stewart, Billie McCain, and former Glenbow Museum chair Jane Edwards, and, of course, Bluma Appel.

"It was a magnificent idea," mused Appel of her original Canadian Friends. Regarding her burgeoning files, which she is preparing for an autobiography, she acknowledged that it is also a cautionary tale on the danger of entrepreneurial drive clashing with institutional immobility. ''You know the saying, 'Oh, I don't compete with other women, I only help,' is nonsense. I think it was in her [Bogg's] nature that . . . she must be in control. Had I been a man, it might never have happened. Also, I went outside [the institution] to get this done because I never could have gotten it within—there is such a dust in the system.''[23]

Which is why entrepreneurs stay out of it.

CHAPTER 15 NOTES

1. Some of the most successful realtors are women who struck out into the world of real estate in the 1960s. Amongst those who first gained exponential success are Vancouver's Christine Dexter, the Regina mother-daughter team of Frances Olson and Denise Currie, Winnipeg's Suzanne Banfield Lount, Toronto's Sis Weld, and J.J. Jacobs of Montreal. More recently launched from the Futurist horizon, women are tapping the real estate explosion of Asian immigration: Vancouverites Patsy Hui and Andrea Eng and, in Toronto, Dee Dee Sung, whose specialty is dealing in golf courses.
2. In the North, where welfare and dependency is rampant, entrepreneurs are thriving. Some have come from the South—criminal lawyer Susan Green figured she made about $186,000 a year fresh out of university—before returning south. Two who stayed in Yellowknife are Ronne Hemming and Marion Lavigne, publishers whose annual revenues in Yellowknife Outcrop Ltd. are $2 million plus. Their assets include two magazines, economic consulting, advertising, public relations, a sixty-seven-foot Caribbean yacht, and shares in a Frobisher Bay Hotel.
3. H.R. MacMillan placed his family foundation under the umbrella of the Vancouver Foundation; during and after his lifetime his generous donations fell largely into the fields of education and science. His daughter, Jean Southam, has a particularly high profile in the dispersing of those funds.
4. Names indigenous to mining folklore of the country roll off MacMillan's tongue—the Hallnor gold mine which she sold to Noranda; Porcupine, Kirkland Lake, ViolaMac mine (lead, silver, and zinc) in BC, Lithium in Ontario, and the uranium mine at Lake Cinch that she sold to El Dorado. MacMillan and her husband George were convicted of fraud in connection with their April-August 1964 dealings in shares of what was then Windfall Oils & Mines. She served two months of a nine-month sentence. In 1989 she donated $1.25 million towards bringing the William Pinch mineral collection back to Canada and into the National Museum of Natural Sciences in Ottawa. In January 1991, she was the first woman to be inducted into the Canadian Mining Hall of Fame.

5. Judge Eckhardt wanted Mearns on side because she had written a critique of the Election Act after running the provincial campaign of Herb Capozzi.
6. Eleni had conceived the ambitious idea of buying the Hotel Georgia, then shortly thereafter she married Nelson and credited his ingenuity and connections for bringing them together with partners Bob Lee and Fred Wu for the Georgia deal. But two months later Lee and Wu pulled out, so Nelson and Eleni each bought half, and the saga began.
7. Not only were Eleni and Nelson operating at arm's length, but the story around town at the time was that, on the morning the deal was to be consummated, the couple arose, breakfasted, drove downtown together to the Georgia boardroom, greeted Mrs. Pao's agents, and called the meeting to order—then, to Nelson's amazement, Eleni refused to sell.
8. Tom Selleck, Sean Connery, Loni Anderson, and Burt Reynolds are all repeat visitors to the Wedgewood.
9. The sales for America designers, including Canadian sales, are awesome. In Nicholas Coleridge's *The Fashion Conspiracy,* the author wrote that Ralph Lauren's annual sales were more than $1.3 billion, with his personal fortune estimated at $350 million; Calvin Klein's sales were $1.1 billion, and Liz Claiborne's $1.8 billion.
10. Nicholas Coleridge claimed in *The Fashion Conspiracy* that in the United States the wealthy in-crowd divides the year into six party phases (p. 59), three or four houses, and about $347,000 worth of annual clothing purchases (p. 64).
11. Druxman also worked with a lawyer in helping the women press charges and file for protection, or for divorce, before helping them to find interim accommodation and get a job.
12. In the environmental field Benoît is also doing the environmental audit and strategic planning for the environmental initiatives of CP Hotels and Resorts, working with CIDA in environmental affairs. A self-acclaimed, "expedition junkie," she is managing an international polar expedition—four men doing an unsupported ski to the North Pole and back. There is no resupply and the trip must be completed in one hundred days, to prove the claims of Sir Robert Perry in 1909.

13. Murray has a background in business, government and politics. She studied political science at the University of Western Ontario and was a policy analyst in Government Members' Services at Queen's Park. She is a former vice-president of the Ontario PC party and has served as a strategy advisor in election campaigns and leadership battles.
14. Vennat's directorships include the C.D. Howe Institute, Bio-Mega, Canadian Chamber of Commerce, E-L Financial, Empire Life Insurance, Dominion of Canada General Insurance, Casualty Company of Canada, Canadian Indemnity, Canada Packers, McGraw-Hill Ryerson, and various educational institutions and cultural organizations.
15. McCarney's partners are an African, and Don Simpson, vice-president of the Banff School of Management.
16. Côté-O'Hara was one of the three women on Pat Carney's 1990 task force examining the barriers to women's advancement in the public service.
17. Solomon was the Washington adviser to a Canadian agency called International Development Research Centre. Then she monitored U.S. legislation on women's equality for the Status of Women Department and Treasury Board.
18. While a vice-president in corporate development at ManuLife, she was also co-chair of fund raising for Barbara McDougall's 1984 election campaign, and she serves as chair of the financial sector of SAGIT. She worked closely with then trade minister Pat Carney in the discussions leading up to the free trade agreement and SAGIT now deals with GATT. She also sits on ITAC, the International Trade Advisory Committee, is a commissioner on the Ontario Securities Commission, and is involved in an Asia Pacific study group with the Ontario government. She is a director of the Bank of Canada and of St. Mary's Cement.
19. Appel became a champion for AIDS victims before anyone else would even whisper the word. With the help of Cornelia Molson, she formed CanFar, the Canadian Foundation for AIDS Research, and criss-crossed the country dishing out both terrifying statistics and good sense, and winning media exposure in cities where no one had ever heard of her. By 1991 her CanFar fund raiser was an Establishment sellout, and Appel has successfully launched a CanFar Junior

Committee with such innovative an intriguing items as a $1 key-chain condom. CanFar's list of directors, advisers, and participants fills two pages with a constituency including Edward Bronfman, Sherrill Eaton, Maureen Forrester, David Peterson, Willard Estey, Mary Alice Stuart, and Geraldine A. Kenney-Wallace.

20. Among other accomplishments, the Peruvian-born Sutherland Boggs is a former head of the National Gallery, former chair and CEO of the controversial Canada Museums Construction Corporation, former professor at Harvard, former director of the Philadelphia Museum of Art, chair of the co-ordinating committee for the Paris/Ottawa/New York Dégas Exhibition, organizer of a Picasso Exhibition of similar significance, and former special adviser to the minister of communications of Canada.
21. Bill Jordan, the retired Texan curator for the Alger Meadows collection, reasoned that "Jean Boggs possibly turned down [the Goya] because she judged it of insufficient quality to hang in the gallery." In an article on Armand Hammer in *Vanity Fair*, March 1991, titled "Hammer Nailed," curator/author John Richardson described the Goya that was sent to Leningrad as a "dreary . . . third-rate Goya."
22. Wife of Tom Enders, former U.S. ambassador to Canada, Gaetana resurrected the committee with a dinner at the Citadel, Quebec, with then governor-general Jeanne Sauvé and the entire project is back on track. Described as "friendship through the arts," the American Friends of Canada have donated numerous objects of fine and decorative art to galleries and museums across the country and provided support for traveling exhibitions and performing artists, literary and cultural programs. However, none is of the magnitude of the gifts offered by Hammer, Meadows, and Rockefeller in 1972.
23. In 1975 Appel had moved on to new challenges. She convinced Marc Lalonde, then minister of state for the status of women, to hire her as a dollar-a-year woman —to perform a liaison between government and industry. For the next four years, Lalonde was delighted to have a hit-woman up front to implement some of the affirmative action recommendations in the report of the Royal Commission on the Status of Women. Bank CEOs were said to cower behind their

desks when they heard Bluma was in the building. She zoomed into executive offices like a one-woman SWAT team, hitting ''those dinosaurs'' Earle McLaughlin (Royal Bank), Frederick McNeil (Bank of Montreal), and Ian Sinclair (Canadian Pacific). No one could block her because, although she came sanctioned from the government, she was operating free of its hierarchy. Thanks to Appel's implacability, every bank put a woman on its board and began opening the doors to them for management training.

C H A P T E R   S I X T E E N

Inspirational Power

What is good, is given back.

LEWIS HYDE[a]

Societies are either redemptive or they are punishing and I would like to be part of a redemptive society. The best intellectual part of our society is the creative artist.

ADRIENNE CLARKSON

The power to nurture through inspiration is perhaps the most noble and treasured force of all. Traditionally, the triumph of faith over decree was the only power attainable by women, and many who are successful in all fields still want to identify with this positive force that eludes definition. Coercive power is immediate; inspirational power is incremental; based on trust, and evokes a mysticism so intangible that its revelation often comes only in hindsight. Its message is a masterpiece of subtlety, often slipping through implacable façades to capture the unsuspecting soul, before manifesting itself in ways as myriad as they are magnificent.

In his book *The Gift,* Lewis Hyde celebrates art as a gift rather than a commodity, one that provides a spiritual counterweight to our market-oriented society. In particular, the creative artists dedicate their lives to transporting us out of worldly concerns, enthralling us with the strength and magnificence of human creativity and, for a moment in time, transcending all human agony. In the presence of their gift, the beholder is drawn into a realm of detachment, and, ultimately, of self-revelation.

Evelyn Hart

Evelyn Hart, the ninety-five-pound principal dancer of the Royal Winnipeg Ballet and principal dancer for the Bayerisches Stattsballet of Germany, described herself as a stiff and "athletically clunky child," one who was "scared of life in general," a poor communicator. She realized at the age of ten that she had to be a dancer from the moment she saw Veronica Tennant performing Juliet on television. Recalling that moment she said, "It was so natural—all of a sudden what came out of me was an expression like the music speaking."

To achieve her power of the gift, Hart had first to cross the abyss separating desire from perfection. Each time a young dancer stands poised at the barre, or the recital pianist places hands over the keys, that artist must first conquer the spectre of failure. At times a paralyzing barrier prevents painters from slashing a cobalt arc across naked canvas, impels dancers to pitch pointe shoes out the window, or causes writers to stare wildly at the blank page and sweat blood. This fear drove a young Vladimir Horowitz to smash plates before a performance. It is a terror that has to do with conquering the Self, the only act that liberates the creative force, enabling artists to reach for excellence, to become the instrument through which they can share their creative power with the vicarious passions of others. This vanquishing and sharing is both the gift and the power, that unfathomable validation moulded in the crucible of denial, pain, failure, patience, discipline, hope, and often poverty. Incremental mastery follows each step, buoyed by the joy of expression until, at some subtle instant, the Self is consumed by the creation and emerges as a single power with illimitable parameters of expression.

When the youngster Hart first saw the fabulous Marcia Haydée, now artistic director of the Stuttgart Ballet, she recalled of the inspiration, "The sunlight came out of her and she wasn't there any more. Whatever it was, just touched me. . . . I felt like something within me went calm. It was . . . a spiritual experience." Then came the struggle to dance, not only to learn at the late age of eleven, but to convince her mother that the art was worthwhile. As the wife of a minister, Hart's mother agonized over what seemed the self-indulgence of dancing to pretty music glorified in chiffon and rhinestone costumes. What did that have to do with the starving millions? But Hart persevered, and as she grew in skill she met Yehudi Menuhin and compared the effect of his performance on her to that of Marcia Haydée. "He played for me and . . . there was the same quality in the eyes . . . in the spirit, and the soul. That is the thing that gives me the courage to go on; if I can share an ounce of what I have to give with others, then . . . I have this great commitment to . . . make a difference in anybody's life.'' Of the suffering and hunger in the world that haunted her mother Hart explained, ''I don't have medical talents. I've never been trained as a doctor. If I can in any way, by donating this experience, [give] someone . . . the courage to go on . . . [then I must dance].''

There would never have been an Evelyn Hart without Ludmilla Chiriaeff, Celia Franca, or Betty Oliphant — European dancers who arrived in post-war Canada with virtually nothing but their talents to share. All faced monumental privations, yet they found a way to create and to teach. In the 1950s in Montreal, Chiriaeff, a Latvian who had opened her first school in Geneva, was publicly condemned by the church in Quebec for showing her legs while dancing on television. Yet she founded Les Ballets Chiriaeff, a school where children blossomed along with the rising political consciousness of Quebeckers. It was a period when citizens were struggling for their independence from the repressive disciplines of church and state. In nurturing her students to discover the Self through dance, Chiriaeff inadvertently became a political force in the Quiet Revolution. Her school became a symbol of defiance and self-determination, and eventually was renamed Les Grands Ballets canadiens.

Sponsored in large part by the wealthy Establishment, Celia Franca and Betty Oliphant founded the National Ballet of Canada in Toronto. Betty Farrally and Gweneth Lloyd came to Canada in 1938 and eventually founded the Canadian School of Ballet in Winnipeg, which became the Royal Winnipeg Ballet. They then re-established the Canadian School of Ballet in Kelowna, British Columbia. From these schools emerged Evelyn Hart, Karen Kain, Veronica Tennant, Frank Augustyn, and a host of dancers who not only shared their artistry but also, in some cases, became teachers and used their gifts to open schools across the land.

One night in 1988, backstage at the O'Keefe Centre while a full house waited for the curtain to rise, Hart steeled herself against the pain of an infected big toe. A doctor injected a painkiller into her foot, she donned her pointes — torture boots, as they have been called — and floated on stage to dance a magnificent Giselle. The drug dosage was purposely insufficient to kill all sensation, but such was her obsession to connect with her audience that she conquered the pain. The performing artist knows that the only way to survive is to continue to share. Hart's frail form is little more than a flickering pilot light conveying its powerful message while daring the flame ever to be extinguished.

Maureen Forrester

The difficult situations in life are what make you grow.

MAUREEN FORRESTER[b]

It is a scene worthy of Fellini: in Toronto, during evening rush hour at the Bloor and Yonge intersection, neon lights flashing, street lamps reflecting off rain-slick streets, drivers anxious to get home, pedestrians dodging cars as they race across the streets. Amid the cacophony of gossiping crowds, blaring horns, screeching brakes, and roaring motors, a renowned contralto strolls peacefully down the street singing her latest aria—sotto voce. It is Maureen Forrester, testing her skill on a dissonant work demanding supreme concentration. Later she exulted, "If I can sing it in that noise, I know the orchestra can't put me off. I've got it!"

At the Orpheum Theatre in Vancouver, early in 1989, Forrester sang the world premiere of a collection of Margaret Atwood's poems from *You Are Happy*. The music had been commissioned by June Goldsmith of Music in the Morning, an organization that offers its audience education with performance. The Orpheum that held an audience included many who could not easily get out at night—the elderly, the disabled, and persons who lived long distances from downtown. In keeping with Music in the Morning's philosophy, Forrester explained the music for Atwood's poems in a way that evoked the friendly atmosphere of Goldsmith's den in which Music in the Morning was founded. Stephen Chatman, the composer, had touched the essence of Atwood's poetry with a finesse that allowed poet and singer to stand independent yet united, two disparate personalities and disciplines blended in an eerily beautiful reflection of their respective messages.

At the end, the diva who has helped so many other struggling artists said, "You know, one of the hardest things to do in this country is to get an original work performed, and if you do, it may never be heard again. We have time this morning, so I think I'll just sing it all over again." And, as an impromptu gift to poet, composer, and listeners, and in the style with which she has shared her fabulous gift for a lifetime, she did.

Forrester's spontaneous style grew in response to childhood poverty and the dual energies in Quebec of political repression and artistic expression. She is a fierce believer in helping yourself, "just getting on with it." Her awareness of gifts was nurtured as she developed the extraordinary potential of her voice and became the protégée of Montreal publisher/philanthropist J. W. McConnell. As her success grew with the size of her family (five children), nannies and a support system of friends made it possible for her to tour. Beyond singing, her way of giving back what was given to her has been to help fellow artists win rights, and to willingly relinquish over $500,000 in salary to fill the unpaid post as head of the Canada Council. She loves to inspire the wealthy into giving to the arts by starting her speeches with, "Ladies and gentlemen you have to face it—life is a terminal disease."

A passionate advocate for freedom in the arts, Forrester believes that excellence should be the only criterion of employment, and she abhors the principle of hiring artists just because they happen to be Canadian. She added that artists should not have to be accountable to political power, whether professional or governmental,[1] and she caused a brouhaha when she challenged ACTRA , the Alliance of Canadian Cinema, Television and Radio Artists, when it ordered the entire CBC cast of the Goldrush Follies to leave the stage. ACTRA's complaint was against American singer Joan Morris who had been denied a work permit. Forrester, who was playing Queenie Delarme, refused to walk, explaining of the incident, "Well sweetheart, nobody calls a fellow artist an 'unacceptable alien' to me. I go and sing Mahler in Vienna and they don't say 'Go home, we don't need Canadians to sing Mahler—he came from this part of the world.'" Never underestimate the power of a union. CBC had already spent $500,000 preparing the production but closed it down and never remounted it.

ACTRA suspended and fined Forrester and two others who had stood by her. Later at an unrelated union meeting concerning the hiring of American talent,[2] one young artist stood up to blame foreign artists because he had earned only $1,500 that past year. Forrester leaped to her feet and charged, "Young man, I want to tell you something and I want you to remember this for the rest of your life. You're lazy. Or maybe you're not good enough yet. Face facts. You're not good enough if you don't get hired. You don't go to enough auditions or you're not prepared. Does CBC owe you anything? You owe it to yourself to be better." The following year, Actor's Equity appointed Forrester to the board.

Even her attitude towards her voice contains an earthy exuberance bordering on the blasé. Warming up for a performance? She never does it, explaining that nervous divas have been known to wear out their voices behind stage. In her living room one afternoon, she leaned toward a tape recorder, boomed out a mellifluous note from the lowest register, before immediately striking High A, concluding with a sense of marvel, "My voice is an instrument. It is just there!" Then, for fun, she followed with a string of Russian, Italian, and German dialogue. Her zest for living brings constant hilarity on stage with such performers as Victor Borge, or in her private world, and once, when she locked herself naked out of a Dallas hotel room, Forrester embodied the credo that life is still only partly Wagnerian and mostly vaudevillian.

Diane Farris

In Vancouver, former dancer and homemaker Diane Farris claimed to know nothing about the world of art, but experienced the thunderbolt of inspiration when she saw the works of three young, unknown painters: Vicki Marshall, Angela Grossmann, and Attila Richard Lukacs. Although she had no financial resources, she wanted to share their paintings with the world. Inspired by nothing more than gut feeling, she opened a gallery and began to promote them in Vancouver. At the same time, by buying cheap seats on midnight flights, she travelled to New

York, Los Angeles, and Germany, and connected with the movers and shakers of the international art community. Contrary to a reputation for competitive snippiness, they welcomed and helped her. Nevertheless, two years later, she was teetering on the brink of bankruptcy.

Instead of quitting, Farris announced her tenuous position in the press, then moved from her Gastown studio up to South Granville, a tonier area and Vancouver's art gallery row. When friends learned that Farris was broke, one of them renovated warehouse space for her and created a soaring monument to space. Wholesalers supplied materials, artisans donated their skills, and bookkeepers their time to restructure the business to enable Farris to repay all her debts. At the same time, she won grants from the federal government to ship her pieces to the international shows. Response from international galleries, art magazines, and city periodicals such as *San Diego Magazine*[c] began pouring in. By 1990, all of Farris's young artists, and in particular Attila Richard Lukacs, had garnered an international following; and now when the cognoscenti arrive in Vancouver they head for Farris's gallery. Her Honda licence plate "BUY ART" reflects as much the mark of an entrepreneur as that of a former dancer with a new medium for sharing her creative gift.

****

Mary West Pratt is a New Brunswicker whose Harvard-educated father believed his daughters should all know how to play the piano, grow flowers, and paint. It was the last of these in which she excelled and wanted to pursue, but then she married Christopher Pratt, an exuberant Newfoundlander whose mother wanted him to be a doctor. Christopher, a talented artist, wasn't at all sure that was what he wanted to do. In the 1950s, women still subdued personal ambitions in deference to those of their husbands. Mary successfully encouraged her husband to paint, and when people said of an increasingly famous Christopher, "He has a huge ego. You keep his feet on the ground," Mary Pratt replied, "My job is not to keep Christopher's feet on the ground, but his head in the air."

A decade later Mary Pratt had discovered that she could be both homemaker and artist by painting the immediacy of her life: onions on a cutting board, lunch pails, baked apples, and, in time, her daughter's wedding in diaphanous brilliance. Mary's genius appears in her luminous revelations, less on the painted canvass than glowing from within, intricately blending her mixed media to create a three-dimensional illusion. Her first major exhibition in St. John's in 1967 was a sellout; her 1975 show at the National Gallery made her known across Canada; and in 1991, aficionados sign up for what can be a year-long wait at Elizabeth Nichol's Equinox Gallery, her Vancouver outlet, to purchase a Mary Pratt painting.

Fame has given Pratt a power beyond creativity, and she has used it to speak out for artists, to serve on the Canada Council Applebaum/Hébert Committee[3] investigating the relationship between government and the arts. But her greatest power is seeing with clarity the soul of Newfoundland, a land known better for its poverty than for its rugged beauty, where pastel-coloured homes that defy the fog are sprinkled like wildflowers around the craggy coastline. Mary Pratt gives dignity to the simple life with a realist perfection that is at once vital and pastoral. On the day when she visited with the traveller, she was wandering along the Salmonier River near Mt. Carmel. In her studio she had half completed the painting of a huge, glistening salmon tumbled over her wet steel sinks. Suddenly the sun broke through the clouds and bathed the rushing water, the wet stones, and the whiteness of her cottage in those shimmering colours that she shares with the world. "Look!" she cried, "the light!"

June Callwood

> She writes all morning and, at noon, she goes out and saves the world.
>
> TRENT FAYNE

She has aptly been called the Mother Teresa of Canada by Roy Bonisteel, and the conscience of Canadian law by lawyer Morris Manning. June Callwood's gifts create an awesome panorama of inspirational power that realizes concrete results. She has won the respect and love of Canadians in all levels of society. In celebration of Callwood's sixty-third birthday in 1987, Barbara Frum organized a celebration at the Inn on the Park in Don Mills. One thousand guests donated $120,000 for her Casey House, the first hospice for AIDS patients. Proudly opened by Callwood when the rest of the world was still shrinking from the disease with embarrassment and fear, she made the magnanimous gesture of naming it after Casey, her son, who at age twenty had been killed in a motorcycle accident. When asked if Casey was gay, she guffawed, "How he would have laughed at that!" Fund raising has always been a tough haul for Callwood because street kids and gay causes don't sell as well as ballet. At first, when she failed to win over corporate support for Casey House, she raised $30,000 with a drag-queen show. Then she lobbied all parties of the Ontario government to win a building grant, and gradually the corporate community came around.

Callwood's childhood, made lonely by an alcoholic father and a despairing mother, led to a teenage world in which she felt an outcast. It has made her a sensitive fighter for any injured soul in the land. Her desire for fairness began at the knee of an adoring grandfather judge who took her to his court. Her fierce certainty that she can succeed in her endeavours is intricately entwined with her childhood drive for survival and the intention to protect those who have also experienced the vicissitudes of a painful childhood. In 1967 she opened Yorkville Digger House for street kids. At the age of forty-four in 1968, she was charged with creating a disturbance when she interfered with a police officer hassling a youthful civil rights demonstrator at a rally. In 1974 she opened Nellie's, a refuge for battered women where she can still be found scrubbing the floors when she wants to think something through. Jessie's, for teenagers, was opened in 1982, and in 1987 it was the Casey House hospice. Then she travelled across the country for the *Globe and Mail*, writing a series about the homeless.

Throughout three decades, Callwood has authored and co-authored numerous books, magazine articles, and television and radio scripts, mostly about those who cannot speak for themselves. She has been involved with PEN Canada and Amnesty International; she is a lay bencher with the Law Society of Upper Canada; she has campaigned for such causes as pro-choice, abolition of the death penalty, breast-screening programs, justice for children, and the Canadian Organization for the Rights of Prostitutes. The list is endless. As Trent Fayne, her sportswriter husband, put it to Roy Bonisteel on ''Man Alive,'' the rest of us hope that someone will help the poor underdog and then we go about our business. Callwood goes down to the street and builds the structures that create change. She is not a do-gooder who applies Band-Aids to chronic wounds, but a facilitator who gets talented converts to co-operate in finding solutions. Each time she raises another million to build a Digger House, each time she establishes another educational program through which street kids or pregnant teenagers have a chance at a better life, she is demonstrating that process of empowerment. Any organization from which the upper crust has turned, Callwood has befriended, and in becoming a national icon for the dispossessed, she has validated them, won over the Establishment, and transformed herself into a Canadian institution.

Margaret Atwood

> This wonderful genius has made it. I know she's made it because a couple of times a month someone stops me and says, ''Excuse me, but aren't you Margaret Atwood? My wife just loves your books.''
>
> I'll know when I've made it when someone stops Margaret Atwood and says, ''Excuse me, but aren't you Rosie Abella? My wife just loves your decisions.''
>
> FORMER JUDGE ROSALIE ABELLA[d]

> Neurosurgeon to Atwood: When I retire, I'm going to write a book. Atwood to neurosurgeon: When I retire, I'm going to be a brain surgeon.

It was easy to take the wrong turning in the meandering streets of Yorkville looking for the home of the great novelist. The neighbourhood was characterized by old brick houses, whose sole uniqueness — downtown gardens — had a late-fall unkempt appearance. The windblown paper and plastic from the commercial zone tangled with ginger-coloured leaves in the mesh fences, and dried grass evoked a mood of mystery rather than mess. That was because *she* lived somewhere around there.

Atwood's home was different. It too was made of brick, but no paper tumbled about. A semi-circular driveway and large numbers discreetly placed beside the freshly painted black door gave to it a subtly cared-for look. This was not a home that advertised its presence or its owners. Like Atwood, it was presentable, even Establishment in character, but inscrutable. The traveller pressed the bell, remembering the warning of poet Susan Musgrave: "Margaret eats interviewers alive. And don't call her Peggy. She has publicly castigated a speaker who, uninvited, had the effrontery to introduce her as Peggy."

The kitchen, where Canada's most famous author was perched on a bar stool, was cluttered comfort. On the window ledge an aquarium bubbled oxygen desperately through green slime. The fish seemed content, but Atwood looked exhausted. She was sitting at the kitchen counter searching the morning *Globe* for her letter-to-the-editor with the intensity of a fledgling writer. She was also drinking *café au lait,* but neither offered coffee nor invited the traveller to sit. Musgrave had warned, "Boy, is she tough. A friend of mine interviewed Peggy and was so upset afterwards that she drove into a ditch." The traveller slid cautiously onto a bar stool ten feet away, like a game hunter approaching a wild beast poised for flight, fearful that the slightest misstep would cause Atwood to flee or attack.

"We walked in the country this morning . . . " Atwood suddenly intoned with that same hypnotic sound that mesmerizes audiences at the Harbourfront Reading Series. Atwood and Graeme Gibson had gone to the stables that morning with their daughter Jess, who rides rented horses — not because Atwood cannot afford a horse, but because, she explained, "rental horses have learned every trick in the book to outsmart and dominate their riders. They teach a young girl that she can have control over something — or someone — who is bigger and stronger than she is." The eyes were gleaming, the smile wicked. Atwood has a sense of theatre and loves to play with it.

"We'll walk to Avenue Road for brunch," Atwood suddenly said, looking dubiously at the traveller's black patent shoes. "Can you walk in those?" The traveller had just come from Isabel Bassett's power luncheon and looked like Valerie Rosedale. She wished she had stuffed running shoes into a briefcase and changed behind a tree. But adopting that façade would not have increased her understanding of *The Circle Game,* about which she knew little. Images. Atwood sees through them because she creates them:

you fit into me
like a hook into an eye

a fish hook
an open eye[e]

"[Atwood] is a literary creation," mused Sherrill Grace, "a metaphor which equates women and earth with the life-cycle process." A University of British Columbia English professor and author of the first book on Atwood's work, Grace noted that Canadians had been reluctant to acknowledge Atwood when American universities in the early 1980s were already including her in literature courses and reading Grace's *Violent Duality*. During the last twenty years Atwood endured, blossomed, and silenced those who would believe that she was a flash in the pan, realizing her international acclaim while Canadians continued to fear her or scorn her work.

Twenty-five years ago university students were told by professors of literature that "there are no Canadian authors worth reading," or Canadian heroes — or a Canadian identity they might have added. Twenty years ago Atwood described the victim/victor syndrome in her work *Survival*,[f] a seer describing the isolation and powerlessness of women with a clarity beyond her experience. Yet instead of seeking a clue to stumbling psyches through Canadian literature, budding scholars studied the British poets in a continuation of the colonial mindset. Atwood understood. Her ability to examine the minutiae of the Victorian jungle was absorbed from her entomologist father, who had taught her, on family trips to the backwoods, how to examine an insect subspecies or a mutant flower. A writer who evades being categorized, Atwood was raised to categorize. "It was never a red insect or a blue flower," she remembered. Her examination of a subject had to include those hierarchical kingdoms with their phyla, classes, tribes, subspecies, hybrids, all of which would be used in her merging of the animate with the inanimate, the organic with the human, joy with horror. Atwood sees human strengths and frailties with a chillingly detached eye. When she reads, her monotones give no hint to what is coming as she blends humour and beauty with the grotesque. She is an arch manipulator, lulling then shocking her audience into laughter or disgust.

yes at first you
go down smooth as
pills, all of me
breathes you in and then its

a kick in the head, orange
and brutal, sharp jewels
hit and my
hair splinters . . . [g]

It was her 1960s poetry and other writing that gave her the label of strident feminist. Critiques of her work during the 1970s and early 1980s are charged with an undercurrent of anger directed not toward the stories, but toward the author. When Urjo Kareda reviewed *Bodily Harm*, he wrote that ''zonked heroines'' like Rennie were passé, that Atwood had missed the boat, and that Rennie's opinion that men were creeps was probably Margaret Atwood's own opinion.[h] Did Atwood critics slam her because her content frightened them with her avalanche of seemingly disconnected imagery? And is she a strident feminist? ''Well, what is feminism? Let us begin,'' sighed Atwood. Time and again she disengages herself from any label that an admiring or vitriolic public foists upon her. She explained that she is for fairness, for educating women, for equal job opportunities, and equal pay for work of equal value. On the other hand, Atwood observed pragmatically, as women are the childbearers, and as a majority of them must also earn a living, ''If society wants them to continue having babies, it should make it possible for them to do so.'' In other words, provide quality day care. Feminism does not mean she has to support everything that other women do just because they are female. She protested, ''That means supporting Margaret Thatcher and Barbara Amiel. It's not asked of men that they should like and support any writing that's by men just because they're men.'' She aligns herself with the causes of PEN, Amnesty International, and the environmental crisis but takes pains to distance herself from any ''ism,'' a position that leaves her free from stereotype as women should be.

Atwood strode towards Avenue Road swathed in a spectrum of aubergine blended as subtly as the diverse images in her novels, all the while chatting in that detached monotone, a hovering spirit that seemed likely to disappear in a sudden gust of wind. She was preparing for a nine-month book tour across Canada, England, the States and Australia. Why? She admits the tours are fun, but if anyone thinks she does it to gain prominence, she dryly sums up her power by offering the chairship of the Writers' Union of Canada with: ''Obvious road to fame.'' Someone is conscripted into that unpaid job every two years. She took it on when authors did not even have guidelines for standard minimum contracts, before agents were well established in Canada, and when writers would have traded their first-born to get into print.[4] Performing artists have always embraced applause as part of the gift of sharing, of a dialogue of appreciation between these two participants that enriches the creative power. By tradition, writers were supposed to be anonymous recluses who remained locked in their attics, emerging only to visit their publisher with a completed manuscript.

Although Atwood denies currying public recognition, she has never hidden from her audience, never sought the writer's anonymity. Raised by parents who did not use guilt to control their children, she was not inhibited by Calvinist conventions from sharing her poetry with habitués of the coffee houses of the country. ''I began reading in the sixties,'' she shrugged matter-of-factly. "I was a poet. That's what poets did. I read in Toronto in the Bohemian Embassy, a coffee house painted black. We had sound effects. It had the first Espresso machine in Canada. It also had men and women's washrooms behind the stage. Just as I got to the most intense part of the poem, the Espresso machine would squelch or someone would flush the toilet and walk into the room." That element of unpredictability suits Atwood. It is the leitmotif of her work, keeping herself, as well as her audience, on edge. She is always current and relevant, and her ability to amuse can be as powerful as her propensity to terrify.

Atwood's greatest power emanates from the timelessness of her work. When *The Handmaid's Tale* was published in 1986, some found it a futuristic warning, some a medieval tale. For others, raised in the 1940s culture, it dredged up childhood nightmares. Then the horrifying policies of Nicolae and Elena Ceauşescu became an analogue for power gone mad. Atwood had known it all along. Her critical readers came to regard her novels less as man-hating diatribes than illuminations of the truth.

Late in the 1980s, in a discussion concerning overstressed budgets, Albertan MP Barbara "Bobbie" Sparrow, a former business executive, had said with sensible concern, "Look. We all know . . . when the budget's tight, music lessons are the first things which have to go." In the light of Atwood's *The Handmaid's Tale*, it seems that music lessons should be the last thing to go. Evelyn Hart observed that in Eastern bloc countries where materialism is non-existent, and truth and political freedom still remain distant visions, citizens' souls are nourished by the performing artists and authors. They are revered as North Americans worship their movie stars. In this country, support for the work of performers is possible only through the power of Establishment wealth. The gift circles. It works. Atwood understands the value of the gala fund-raising process, urging "We must protect it."

During the ten-minute walk, Atwood had led the traveller through a maze of streets like a guide who would lead you out of her woods but does not necessarily want you back. Suddenly she darted into the doorway of Arlequin, a café, where she leaned against a post to wait for a booth. People were discreet at first, stealing glances, then staring openly. She ignored them—not arrogantly but vacantly—her field of vision limited by her current thought. It is not Atwood's fame that unnerves everyone but her relentless brilliance, and few readers are able to separate the author cleanly from her literary images. She finds that tiresome, but must live with her occupational hazard.

Genius aside, it was media attention like the *New York Times* bestseller list and the rave reviews that helped promote Margaret Atwood to her status of world celebrity. It is media power that provides her with a vast forum for promoting her causes—defending freedom of speech, assisting persecuted authors in countries oppressed by dictatorships, or, in matters of the environment, saving the world: "We have [only] ten years," she warned. It seems that, rather than indulging in self-promotion, Atwood uses the media as a tool for her activist agenda. Artistic excellence combined with media power has made Atwood known in all circles and has won not only the respect, but also the adulation, of the Establishment. Its members admire her as "Atwood the luminary" rather than resenting her as Atwood the feminist, and while few would carry a banner for the rights of women or minorities, they will now join Atwood in her causes. Along with June Callwood and Isabel Bassett, Atwood ranks as one of the rare catalysts able to meld Activist persuasion with Establishment money.

Atwood described her real power, and that of all independent writers this way: "We don't have jobs. Nobody can fire us. We aren't bucking for political positions or speaking for formal political parties; we don't want to be senators; we're not running for office. We're self-supporting financially. We listen to what people have to say, to various sides of the story. So there's nothing anybody can do to us."

The traveller hailed a cab that got lost in Rosedale looking for the home of Maureen Forrester. When the traveller arrived Forrester confided, "I'm doing a world premiere in Vancouver next year singing poems by Margaret Atwood. They're called *You Are Happy*. They're weird."

Ann Petrie

> The true definition of heroism for me is, ordinary people who hear a call and answer in extraordinary ways. There is an essential goodness in us, and it is possible to manifest it. It is always miraculous, [never] planned, nothing sentimental. Once you get on that path, doors open, things happen that you could never imagine yourself —and not by manipulation or coercion.
>
> ANN PETRIE

In 1987, on a dark night just a few days before the fifteenth Moscow Film Festival was to begin, Red Square was adorned by the slick advertising posters of multi-million-dollar film companies. A Pravda reporter strolling through the square became curious when she saw Canadian filmmmaker Ann Petrie hanging up tacky little eight-by-ten flyers that had been photocopied in the Canadian Embassy. They were for her film, *Mother Teresa*, which, to her amazement, had been accepted for the Moscow Film Festival. Having made the film on her own resources, she was broke and making the best of it.

Petrie had felt so impelled to make this movie that she had quit her job as an ABC TV writer/producer of her own prime-time public affairs show in New York, to spend two years and her own money following the great humanitarian, just trying to get her permission to do the film. Eventually Mother Teresa had said, "First you must *do the work*"—help in her homes for the destitute and dying. Petrie did, and still does. Then one day on a train deep in the Indian mountains, Mother Teresa had suddenly announced that the time had come. Over a five-year period, Petrie roamed the world with her protagonist, shooting the film on a paltry production budget of $1.6 million, operating with her sister Jeanette as co-producer and co-director and a camera operator who was often conscripted by Mother Teresa to help in emergencies. Long before it was finished, the once hardboiled New York camera crew and a once cynical Ann Petrie would have followed Mother Teresa anywhere, even into the terrifying shelling of west Beirut.

That was in August 1982, when the troupe of five, including one Jewish camera operator, had arrived in Jôunié, then drove through the shelling and shooting as they approached the city. Petrie still cannot express her horror over the carnage. When they reached their hotel, it had just been bombed. Against the wishes of the terrified religious community, Mother Teresa intended to go into west Beirut and evacuate a hospital of children. She calmed her colleagues by saying that she would wait for a cease-fire, which she predicted would occur in five days. Suppressing smiles, they agreed with her to keep her from acting immediately. On the evening of the fourth day, she declared, "Tomorrow it will happen." That night missiles continued to zing over the city before plummeting to earth with devastating impact, but the next morning Beirut was bathed in silence.

Mother Teresa simply drove into west Beirut with the International Red Cross, but Petrie and her camera crew were not allowed to follow. A stringer for *Newsweek* took them through the Museum Crossing, filled with land mines and guarded by three checkpoints. No one knew the camera operator was Jewish. After they had stepped around land mines, strode past snipers and got through the Lebanese, Israeli, and Palestinian checkpoints, they were led by the guide to the Palestinian underground. They reached the shell-pocked hospital just as Mother Teresa began her evacuation, and the great woman handed babies to Petrie and the camera crew who helped as well as filmed. At the end of the day, when the crew was heading back through west Beirut towards safety, they were stopped at the final checkpoint. They had missed the curfew and would have to remain in west Beirut overnight. Petrie had the film in her purse, but worse, she had to get her Jewish crew member out. The *Newsweek* stringer looked the guard in the eye and said, "So shoot us," and continued walking.

Petrie said, "There was nothing to do but follow him. That was the longest walk I have ever taken in my life. We didn't looked back. We sweated bullets, but they didn't shoot."

So, five years later, there were the Petrie sisters in Red Square, tacking up their photocopied brochures, followed by a curious Soviet reporter and expecting a repeat of the Telluride Film Festival in Colorado when film critic Roger Ebert (of *Siskel and Ebert*) had to be dragged to it, whining,

"Who wants to see a movie about a nun?"[5] Thanks to the reporter, who wrote an expansive column in *Pravda*, and the global reputation of Mother Teresa herself, the theatre was filled to capacity on opening night. The Petries were petrified and sat at the back, steeling themselves for the worst. The clapping began after the first five minutes and continued in waves throughout the film. At the end, the Moscovites gave the film and its creators a standing ovation before turning on the house lights and bringing the Petries onto the stage. Then, in an extraordinary departure from the format of film festivals, the audience questioned them for over an hour. Extra showings of *Mother Teresa* were sold out, and at the end of the festival the Petries were awarded the Soviet Peace Committee Prize. Said Ann, "It was a miracle." And that was only the beginning.

In honour of its fortieth birthday in 1986, the United Nations had premiered *Mother Teresa* to a standing ovation. The movie went on to win fourteen international film awards. Months after the Moscow Film Festival, and after Mikhail Gorbachev had claimed there was no poverty in the Soviet Union, the General Secretary invited Mother Teresa and the Petries to return and open a shelter. "We were mobbed like celebrities," laughed Petrie. In December 1988, Mother Teresa established her care homes in Moscow, and later in the earthquake-stricken region of Armenia. When the film went to Rome during a synod of bishops and cardinals from all over the world, Petrie recalled, "We were told by Protocol that we would not be meeting the Pope, but *he* tracked us down. He was very warm, gracious, and for the first time ever he opened up a house for the dying at the Vatican. Then he went to Calcutta [to visit Mother Teresa]."[6]

Anna Richards French

In 1986 in Tianjin, China, a city with a secret military base, tens of thousands of Chinese thronged to see Rick Hansen, the Man in Motion.[7] Armed soldiers ran among the surging crowd, shouting at the accompanying cinematographers not to film the military planes screaming overhead. In the midst of the clamour and frenzy, a statuesque woman calmly followed her Vancouver camera crew. It was producer Anna French, whose blond hair, blue eyes, and chiselled features are more often seen on the screen than behind the lens. Thirty-year-old French moved with the aid of a black ebony cane and the halting grace of an amputee. During a seventeen-year battle with osteogenic carcinoma, she had established an enviable balance between accepting the inevitable and defying the ultimate consequence, as if each conquering of the insurmountable were a continuing validation of her life.

The monumental scope of her Man in Motion film typified French's glorying in challenges and her entrepreneurial style. She had never met Rick Hansen, had no funding, and undertook the project without contacting External Affairs. Ever since the death of Terry Fox from the same affliction as her own, French had intended to do a story on the capabilities of the disabled, and she was struck by the allegorical quality of Hansen's wheeling along the Great Wall in a country that hid its wheelchair-bound citizens. French didn't have time to wait for permission or to wade through the official channels of bureaucracy. Like Indiana Jones, she just made it up as she went along, and with her gentle humour and exuberant belief in whatever she did, she would repeatedly touch the chord of faith existing in the most confirmed cynic. She won over the Man in Motion office, the Asia Pacific Foundation, the complex bureaucracy of the Chinese consulate, corporate sponsors, creative artists, and eventually a reluctant Rick Hansen himself.

Cold-calling the office of B.C. Telephone vice-president of communications Jim MacInnes, French proposed that for the minuscule sum of $70,000 she would shoot a terrific film and be in and out of China in the impossible time of one week. At first MacInnes refused because the company was already considering making a $30,000 gift to the Man in Motion tour. French persuaded him to put that money behind her project with the prospect of earning much more for spinal research. Talented friends also rallied behind French. Top-salaried CBC camera operator Rob Douglas and Toronto cinematographer Derick Underschultz donated their services. Kodak drastically reduced the price of its film, and filmmaker Michael French, Anna's husband, volunteered his time as director. Still, the project almost collapsed.

Two days before they were to leave Vancouver, special permits from the Chinese government had not arrived, and what was then Canadian Pacific Airlines reneged on their free tickets. French was suddenly $12,000 short and without visas. Although her coterie of influential friends spans two continents, she did not call any of them. A Vancouver business friend who knew that the Asia Pacific Foundation of Canada was looking for a media production as a bridge to understanding between Asian and Canadian schools, called Foundation president Raymond Anderson, who in turn arranged an immediate meeting with Natalie Veiner Freeman, director of public affairs. Freeman had heard of neither French nor the project. She explained that the foundation could donate only for production, not flight expenses. French suggested that they trade off the allocation of funds with those of B.C. Telephone and went home, dubious. Indeed, her proposal to travel freely throughout China with cameras but without papers was almost fanciful.

Veiner Freeman's pipeline into high places is legendary. She instigated the calls that moved the Chinese consul-general to prepare papers instantly, and External to send an urgent message to the Canadian consul in Beijing to assist French's travel. Guy St. Jacques, then secretary to the consul-general in Beijing, recalled that camera crews without sponsors are rarely cleared. For French, it took less than twenty-four hours. The mission was expedited, he said, through the co-operative efforts of the

Asia Pacific Foundation, External, the Canadian embassy, the Chinese host organization for the Man in Motion tour, and good luck—all inspired by Rick Hansen and Anna French, who still had not met.

The next morning, and with mere hours to spare, Veiner Freeman called her to say, "Get your crew together, you're going." Later she mused, "You take risks in life; you take risks on people. I believed in Anna." The crew took off for Hong Kong without their permits, and with French unaware that a safety net had been cast around her trip. Forty-eight hours after her visit to Veiner Freeman, French and her crew were cleared by an immigration officer in Hong Kong who was amused to see a woman as "the boss." The required papers materialized from the consulate, and the troupe headed for China.

Once she caught up with the Man in Motion tour, already being filmed by CBC, French still had to persuade a sceptical and exhausted Rick Hansen to accept the interlopers. In the face of her quietly implacable pressure, he relented but would make no special concessions for her as they rolled through the teeming, astounded throngs in city after city. Always the eye of the hurricane, French symbolized an ethereal serenity as if she were merely hovering while everyone around her was dashing madly about. Yet her projects were always on time and consequential. By the end of a week with Hansen that culminated on the crest of the Great Wall, French had won his respect and friendship. But the challenge was far from over. Suspicious that French's sound equipment had picked up military frequencies, airport security guards demanded to X-ray the film. Agents of Cathay Pacific stepped in, convincing them to let the film through untouched, and French's crew left China.

Back in Vancouver, French inspired yet another round of volunteers to help complete the project. Rock star Bryan Adams wrote "Coming Home" while one of his merchandise managers, Craig McDowell, arranged the musical score. Gastown Productions and Shane Lunny Productions contributed $30,000 worth of editing, actor John Neville did the voice-over of French's script, and Baton Broadcasting's Doug Bassett bought the half-hour show called *Heart of a Dragon* for prime-time national television. The Asia Pacific Foundation had a French-language translation of the tape made and distributed to schools and libraries across Canada. Retail sales raised an estimated $150,000 for the Man in Motion Fund. An unconfirmed report has it that the film was also translated into Mandarin and sent to China. Beyond fund raising, and like most of French's other endeavours, the inspirational power of her film is unfathomable.

In the mid-1980s, following more films, and the birth of a daughter, Britt, French fought more medical battles with surgery and chemotherapy. The last occurred in 1988 while she was in England. French was the first Canadian to receive the Bish Medal for unusual achievements in the face of adversity. Back in Vancouver, she took scripts into hospital while undergoing treatment, and she again met a deadline. In July 1990, after winning the Canadian Programmer's Founders Award for her film

Canada's Choice about the national ski team, assuming a directorship with the Canadian-Soviet youth expedition Arctic Quest, and preparing to shoot a film in Australia, the thirty-four-year-old French was struck down for the fifth and final time, her life completed with the same quality of excellence she had applied to each of her endeavours.

French had understood that sense of immediacy that represents most acutely the precious gift of life. Although she claimed no obsession with mortality, she had proceeded with the calm and measured conviction of one who was living on borrowed time. She embodied the certainty that our society is driven not so much by marketing as by gifting, manifested in shared offerings neither traded nor returned in kind but flowing on, unimpeded, for millennia. The success of *Heart of a Dragon*, and of all creative gifts, derives from metaphysical qualities that bind a creative perseverance to the business of living and that render to the global community a power of immeasurable value and longevity.

CHAPTER 16 NOTES

1. Forrester lobbied against Bill C-24, designed to affect the distribution of funds to artists and arts organizations, and to make several Crown corporations including the CBC, Canada Council, and the National Arts Centre more accountable to the government. She and other artists feared that political pressures would affect the distribution of funds to artists and the arts.
2. At the time, ACTRA members had turned down a new collective agreement with CBC Television, complaining that the public broadcaster was hiring too many non-Canadian performers.
3. Its real name was the Federal Cultural Policy Review Committee. Its purpose was to study the state of culture in Canada and make policy recommendations.
4. In 1986, the Writer's Union won a Public Lending Right fee that pays money to writers whose works are used through libraries, and succeeded in getting the copyright law amended in 1988. It has lobbied the Department of Consumer and Corporate Affairs to plug an import loophole that allowed American-printed copies of Canadian books to be sold in Canada at prices undercutting the Canadian editions, creating a no-win situation for the Canadian publisher and writer.
5. By the end, Ebert was enthralled.
6. Petrie returned to Canada as co-producer of *Moonstruck* with Norman Jewison, spent a year at the Canadian Centre for Advanced Film Studies, and is completing a new screenplay, to be filmed in 1992, about a singer who loses her voice. In an unusual move, Maclean Hunter Broadcast Group, a private company, provided development funding for Petrie to do the film.
7. Rick Hansen, a paraplegic athlete from British Columbia, wheelchaired around the world during 1985-87 to foster an awareness of the disabled, and illustrate their ability to function as contributing members of society. His efforts raised over $20 million for spinal cord research, rehabilitation, and wheelchair sports.

PART V

THE POWER OF MERITOCRACY

I want to do it all.

JODY FREEMAN

CHAPTER SEVENTEEN

The Futurists

Let's Junk The Feminist Slogans: The War's Over.

DANIELLE CRITTENDEN[a]

Promote yourself, shout about your business, and if necessary, be brilliantly devious.

ANITA RODDICK[1b]

The Futurists, in their twenties or early thirties, arrive on the threshold of their professional lives with the social power of the Insider, the survival drive of the Outsider, and the passion of the Crusaders. Unfettered by a patriarchal childhood or by the inequities in the law that restricted their grandmothers, they have shed the diffidence of previous generations and they talk about their abilities, intentions, and mistakes with exuberance. Goal oriented, buoyed by academic credentials, they are the restless, confident devotees of a new order in which the right to self-fulfilment, success, and power has replaced the dual mantles of motherhood and stewardship.

Flexibility is their hallmark, self-reliance their anthem. Guilt does not exist in their vocabulary. Their lives are a continuum along which they range at will, from executive superstar to supermom to power volunteer, and "dropping out" means merely replacing the professions or big business for entrepreneurial enterprise.

Futurists are forthright rather than secretive, pragmatic rather than romantic. Seeking government support is abhorrent to them. They do things themselves. Competitive spirit is not an illusion that Futurists left on the playing fields of high school but a reality they carry proudly into their worlds of business, journalism, and the professions. Brassiness is not necessarily ingrained in their character, but neither is the trait "aggressive" considered negative. In 1987 at age sixty-five, Mary Batten, Chief Justice of the Saskatchewan Court of Queen's Bench, had said humbly of her extraordinary achievements, "I don't know how I got here; I didn't do anything." But thirty-one-year-old broker Heather Mackay and thirty-two-year-old business executive Kaaydah Schatten will tell you with a blend of self-assurance and charm that they are where they are because they're damn good at what they do, and they intend to go on to the top.

Rejecting the 1950s lesson of marriage and motherhood, they are preparing themselves for top spots in the marketplace and refuse to flinch from its hazards. The conundrum for the Futurist is not whom she is going to marry but which career she is going to choose. The most aggressive power seekers have honed their skills of winning to an art form, manifested in an avant garde look that implies they have already won. To this end, they are examining process, routes to achievement, and accomplishments to add to their CVs. Gentility and anonymous good deeds that characterized their parents' generation are no longer sufficient to sustain attention, let alone respect. Service must be seen and, like Guccis or Armanis, even causes are assessed as fashionable or passé. Looking over their shoulders to see if the competition is catching on, catching up, or surpassing can escalate the game to a frenzy until new goals seize their imagination and they are off again like a flock of sandpipers racing along the beach just one step from the crashing surf.

No Futurist will deny caring about the have-nots of this planet, even if she does subscribe to the theory that you get to the top only by making it happen for yourself. But some, the Crusaders, are especially conscious of also making a difference, of sharing their process of achievement. Whatever their characteristics, they are in pursuit of dazzling tomorrows.

These valiant young Futurists are a hybrid of the Ayn Rand "me" generation and the nineteenth-century male pioneers who raced to establish ranches or businesses before finding wives and producing children. Their drive to survive on their own terms runs in tandem with superlative achievement and a need for recognition. Men wishing to share their lives with Futurists must also be prepared to share them with their skyrocketing careers. In the 1988 rage film *Baby Boom,* Diane Keaton depicted a heroine more adept at juggling lovers and corporate negotiations than at Velcroing the baby into diapers. As one awed male litigator said of a female colleague, "No one runs into a Futurist—he just gets out of her way."

The Insiders
Linda Frum

Almost every time twenty-eight-year-old journalist Linda Frum picks up her pen she creates a national furor. Frum is a striking, younger version of the famous Barbara, her unruly copper hair electrified by the force field beneath. Frum is privileged, and knows it. In 1986 she denied in *Influence* magazine being a "stuffy, complacent, premature member of the Junior League."[c] She dismissed as unacceptable "young [women who are] ignorant of downtown Bay Street workings," and she has rejected her wealthy Establishment roots in favour of "associating with the intelligentsia class."[d] Her comments are hardly humble but neither are they frivolous. Frum was raised at a family dinner table that welcomed as guests the most provocative minds, the financially shrewd, and the back—and front—room media moguls. From childhood, Frum's parents encouraged their daughter to think independently, make her own choices, and participate in the heated discussions with writer friends June Callwood, Robert Fulford, and publisher Anna Porter. The ancient colonial precept of "Children should be seen and not heard" never existed in the Frum family. And Linda Frum knows that if anyone, besides the prime minister and the most prominent CEOs in the country, is plugged into the collective power source of Canada, it is her influential parents.

Two years after her *Influence* blast, Frum jetted across the country to research a book commissioned by friend and publisher Anna Porter: *Linda Frum's Guide to Canadian Universities*.[e] Following random interviews at forty-two universities and six colleges, she roasted these institutions with the gusto of a Viking spearing mounds of barbecued meat. Ignoring howls of fury during her cross-country tour, the recalcitrant Frum faced furious students, and then penned "Reach for the Mediocre" for *Saturday Night*, a scaled-down version of the opinions in her book. Saskatchewan, she opined, was too "small" and "impecunious" a province to handle two universities.[f] Regina University "should be closed and its 5,400 students moved to the U of S." Frum then carved up the universities of Manitoba, Toronto, and Windsor, and Laurentian University, all of which, she declared, are "glaring examples [of all that] helped drag Canadian higher education down to where it is today."[g] Subsequent letters to the editor[h] accused her of immaturity, "dubious research methods," poor preparation, and superficiality, which she shrugged off as whining. Frum's critique on quality was prescient. In the last three years the entire educational system in Canada has come under attack from a variety of sectors for sluggish administrations, outdated philosophy, and stagnant curricula.

Frum thrived on controversy even when she was a McGill University student. In 1983 she founded a right-wing campus newspaper to compete with the left-wing *McGill Daily*, which was financed by $80,000 from the students' annual fees. When Frum entitled her intended creation *The McGill University Magazine,* the board of governors threatened police intervention and lawsuits over what they deemed an illegal publication and unlawful use of the name "McGill." In reality, Frum's dastardly deed lay in challenging a tradition of an administration decreeing to its students. Some educational ivory towers, supposedly the repository of innovative ideas, staunchly resist the fresh air of independent thought. At first printing the paper by hand and using an underground distribution system, Frum then requested a meeting with McGill Principal David Johnston. He delayed for three weeks, perhaps hoping that Barbara's baby would go away. She would not; she published another issue, infuriating the McGill administration. The students were ecstatic. The Montreal *Gazette* ran front-page headlines. Thanks to this brouhaha, Frum's friend Peter Worthington published the cover story on her in *Influence* magazine titled, "What's a nice young lady like this doing to The Establishment?"[2] Linda Frum's career was launched.

Saskatchewan Report placed Frum's name first on a list of "People you would rather not have to dinner," and in its "Quote, Unquote" column, University of Regina President Lloyd Barber was quoted as saying, "Her problem is that she was born on third base and she thinks she just hit a triple."[i] In *Western Report* following Frum's *Saturday Night* article, a photo depicted Barber glaring past the rebellious Frum who was leaning elf-like on the gigantic letters of her book jacket. Barber grumbled, "Let's face it. If her name weren't Frum, that thing wouldn't have been published."[j]

Barber could be right. The insiders, well educated and empowered, start at the top. The "daughters of" are the leading edge of the New Establishment and hail from families with the power and prominence that usually comes from name and wealth. Linda Frum attacked the Establishment and the institutions of learning with the confidence of one who belongs. Her comments were less significant than the fact that, recognized as the offspring of famous and influential parents, she had a forum in which to make them.

Heather MacKay

Heather Mackay earns an ample six-figure commission in London as a vice-president selling Eurobonds for ScotiaMcLeod. She is the great-granddaughter of Senator and Mrs. John deBeque Farris, one of Vancouver's oldest and most venerable Establishment families. In her great-grandmother's era, the impropriety of it would have silenced women discussing money matters. But in 1988, Mackay breathed with the passion of a Jascha Heifetz upon receipt of his first Stradivarius violin, "One week after starting this job I knew I was meant to be here. I love money."

The glamorous, fast-talking Mackay can scrap with the best of traders, as she proved when applying for a job as a Eurobond salesperson. Armed with a BA in economics, she had arrived in London and spent three months living in a freezing flat while working as a receptionist in a sex-change clinic. Then she found a job in the finance department of a brewery and was promoted to inventory manager before approaching the brokerage house to apply for the job with what was then McLeod Young Weir. There the managing director asked her, "What do you know about Eurobonds?" Mackay replied brightly, "Nothing."

"Well, what the hell are you doing here then!" he snapped.

Mackay shot back, "You never said I had to know anything about bonds!" Startled, he hired her, wired her to a trader's phone for a week, then set her loose. At first European clients hung up the telephone, but Mackay always dialed right back with a cheerful, "We just got cut off." Within weeks they were referring her to their colleagues throughout Europe, and Mackay began working the Asian and then the American markets. She became so adept at juggling Deutsche mark, yen, and kroner in the fast-moving game of falling currencies and rising bonds that within the year she topped the sales force. By 1988 she had bought a house in London. Following a promotion in 1990, Mackay warned, "Don't tell my father what I'm making—it's more than he ever did."

Jennifer Taylor

In 1988, the sparkling twenty-seven-year-old Jennifer Sterling Taylor of Vancouver, a descendant of the prolific Wilson family of Victoria[3] and a fine arts major from Carleton University, headed for England to join the hot new sport of art sponsorship. The name Wilson meant nothing in London but one line in her brief CV noting that in 1987 she had topped corporate sales of art in Canada proved sufficient for her to beat out five hundred applicants for the head post of the new corporate membership plan of the Royal Academy of Arts. At the opening reception Taylor welcomed royalty, who "are really very nice," Prime Minister Margaret Thatcher, who said, "We must have tea," and Canadian Business and Arts impresario Belle Shenkman who smiled, "We must have lunch." Every one of her innumerable receptions drew the elite of Britain's social, business, and ambassadorial communities. Sterling Taylor's august position automatically placed her inside the system, not only socially but economically. Drawing on her automatic directorships in seven major corporate boards in the United Kingdom, she did the rounds and raised up to one million pounds a year.

After three years in the job, Taylor went off to pursue her painting career as well as taking on another fund-raising job with the Watford Palace Theatre, one of four Edwardian theatres in Great Britain. She is casting an eye about Europe for fresh sponsorships and expects, in her first year, to raise 150,000, pounds which should enable the popular Watford to retain its high standards of production while keeping ticket prices affordable.[k]

Lisa Woodward

Vancouverite Lisa Woodward, American-born daughter of Betsy and Austin Taylor,[4] masterminds Conservative strategy and campaigns. She is a thirty-five-year-old mother of four boys with deep American, Roman Catholic, Establishment roots and a politicized childhood in the Philippines where her father spent several years representing the Buckley business interests. It was the tangential relationship between democracy Filipino-style and her American heritage of freedom that have most affected her. The dreadful poverty beyond the presidential palace, the political murders, the armed guard around her school at election time, all impelled her father to impress upon his children the importance of protecting individual rights.

Woodward also learned about being on the outside. Instead of attending the exclusive American School in the inner compound, she was sent to the Roman Catholic school in the city, and as citizens of a nation that was hated in the Islands, she and another American child were repeatedly ganged up on by the wealthy Filipino students. Being on the inside, belonging, is not conducive to introspection, which is brought out when one is ostracized. Once that outside feeling is experienced, intransigent perspectives melt, enabling one to view the world from the refreshing perspective of an independent.

Woodward's vaguely upper-class mannerisms and New York accent contradict her fierce expression of democracy through Tories for Choice,[5] a nation-wide movement that endorses the pro-choice stance on abortion. The issue is thornier than any other in the Futurists' world, and her stand is a departure from former generations of Establishment propriety. Renewing her commitment to the Roman Catholic Church, Woodward nevertheless stated, "I'll be damned if anybody is going to legislate what I do."

****

Known as the third most important film festival in the world after Cannes and Berlin, Toronto's Festival of Festivals has spiralled to its lofty heights thanks to the style and talent of festival director Helga Stephenson, a niece of Signy Stephenson Eaton of Eaton's department stores. The irrepressible Stephenson trained for the job by managing a rock-'n-'roll band called Rosewood Daydream in the Far East, running a bar in Laos for off-duty Air America pilots during the Vietnam War, and working in public relations at the National Arts Centre. She then launched a successful career as a consultant.[1]

****

Many Futurists feel driven to super achievement because of their accomplished parents. Concerned that anyone might suspect her position with Télémédia was based on nepotism, the raven-haired Nanon Beaubien has armed herself with the same Harvard MBA as her two brothers before contemplating joining them in the family business. Nanon's sensational, accomplished parents, Nan-b and Philippe de Gaspé Beaubien, have always said, "Do what you want, but do it better than we did." With a challenge like that, the Beaubien children are committed to a lifetime expansion of the dynastic holdings, a metaphor for the pursuit of excellence. Most Insiders wouldn't want it any other way. Jennifer Tory Mingay, daughter of Elizabeth and John Tory, concurs. She is the manager of personal banking in the Royal Bank's Metro Toronto district, and enjoys privileges of the highest order such as accompanying her parents to the social events for the bank's annual board meeting. Providing her talent for business keeps pace with her social pipeline to power, she is a Futurist who may ultimately be seen in the executive offices of Canada's biggest bank.

Martha Tory, daughter of James and Marilyn and cousin to Jennifer, and Claire Sauder Wright in Vancouver,[6] are Insiders who subscribe to their family's tradition of low-profile public service outside the "in" charities. The former president of the Family Service Association of Toronto, Tory adheres to the traditional camouflage except in one regard: in Futuristic style, she uses her own high-profile name as a partner in the venerable chartered accountancy firm of Clarkson Gordon. Claire Wright also works with the Family Service Association in Vancouver and sits on the board of Family Service America. In the manner of June Callwood, Wright is a cheerful champion of the dispossessed. At a charity dinner in an elegant Vancouver home, Wright brought dignity to street kids by describing the Family Service programs with as much pride as if she were selling the National Ballet. With the awesome energy of the Futurists, she also parents six children and is working on her doctorate in English and French literature.

****

Other Futurists are enjoying stellar starts thanks to early installments on inheritances from parents who have bankrolled hefty ventures. Tina Koffler Boyman and Adam Koffler, along with their father Murray, formerly of Shoppers' Drug Mart, built and opened the King Ranch Health Spa and Fitness Resort in 1990, a $45-million, state-of-the-art health spa thirty-two kilometres north of Toronto. On the west coast, Mary Margaret

Young, a Finning Tractor heiress, backed her offspring in purchasing Whistler Mountain north of Vancouver. The relative price tags and headaches have proven equally monumental, but watchers are betting on the Koffler kids, rising cellulite being more dependable than falling snow.

****

Many Futurists are keeping their maiden names. A decade ago Maureen McTeer was condemned for refusing to be called Mrs. Joe Clark. Today, Barbara Pratt-Wangersky, award-winning artist-daughter of the famous Christopher and Mary, uses her name to market her talent. Pratt drew a prominent crowd and sold out in forty-five minutes at her debut in St. John's. "They came because of my name," acknowledged Barbara, "but they bought because they liked my work."

Some Futurists come from neither the inside nor the outside. They just arrive. Called "baby moguls" by *Globe and Mail* columnist Stevie Cameron[m] and referred to as "the new meritocracy of Canadian business" by James Fleming,[n] they come equipped with Harvard MBAs and CVs that would make older executives quiver with envy. Susan McArthur, a twenty-eight-year-old, sporty-looking blonde who comes from a professional family in Hudson, Quebec, is a whirling dirvish whose intellectual and physical firepower equals her penchant for switching jobs. As one who does not have a string of post-graduate degrees, McArthur spent her first few years using her jobs as courses in continuing education. She believes that women are more versatile in business than men, and she has an intuition for investment banking and a facility for getting the job done. She got her third job in as many months by accident. While she was walking up New York's Park Avenue one day, a limo roared by and splashed slush all over her. She jumped back, right against a lawyer from the Montreal law firm Stikeman Elliott, the same firm of former cabinet minister Marc Lalonde, McArthur's friend from her days as a page in the House of Commons. The lawyer and McArthur lunched and she left with the name of an executive with First Boston who subsequently hired her for the analyst program in corporate finance.

Futurists are highly adaptable and have no qualms about taking jobs lower than their sights until they get on track. McArthur had started out in backroom politics. After working as a legislative assistant for André Ouellet, then minister of labour, and volunteering for the 1984 Liberal campaign, she headed for New York with a pair of jeans and two business suits. She was hired as a sales clerk at Gucci's. While dining with a Montreal friend, she met "Mark," who worked at Morgan Stanley selling Hydro-Québec bonds. When McArthur expressed an interest in investment banking, Mark threw a dinner party for her at Raoul's in SoHo with some friends in the business. Soon afterwards, she left Gucci's to work in the world of finance. A few weeks later a Canadian friend invited

McArthur to a dinner for Prime Minister Brian Mulroney at the Economic Club, where she met more bankers. In 1987, after working for First Boston, she moved as an associate to Lazard Freres, the leading continental European investment bank. Working in mergers and acquisitions, she became involved in the Institut Mérieux acquisition of the Canadian company Connaught Biosciences. A year later, McArthur moved to the head office in Paris, met Lewis Reford of the old Quebec shipping family, and is getting married in 1991. McArthur had chosen New York and Paris over Toronto not only because of the work ethic, but because she views the Canadian world of finance and business as an elitist club. She warned that Canada's youth will flock to the United States until the country fosters an entrepreneurial spirit through greater opportunities. The fast-talking risk taker has a specific agenda: to establish herself before marriage, spend a decade raising a family and then enter politics. Becoming prime minister of Canada is to her neither joke nor fantasy. It's a potential goal.

****

The most distinctive feature of Futurists is pragmatism in viewing the economic realities of the 1990s. For couples, housing and general expenses demand two incomes, especially if there are children, and a generation raised in a material world in which former luxuries are now necessities is willing to work for the lifestyle. From childhood a vast information system exposed them to computer toys and skinny bodies in designer jeans and they are now on the leading edge of the consumer market. The syndrome is not the sole cachet of the Futurists: no one wants to start at the bottom anymore, but no generation has been better prepared academically and psychologically to reach the top faster. Business executive, former politician, and former bureaucrat Jean Pigott worried that young people were more concerned with fufilling their needs than with accountability or responsibility. "Women are obsessed," she frowned, "with the business of rights, perks, the right title, the right office, the big $200,000-a-year-salary." She wants to tell them, "My poor dear friend, you're going to be bypassed. That isn't what power is all about." Pigott believes Black Monday was a great day for young Canadians because it woke them up to reality. In the recession and social advocacy of the 1990s that seems to be contributing to a shift of focus towards the family, the Futurists are not only pursuing financial success, they are becoming more involved in changing the world around them. The pursuit of success through financial gain and executive power, combined with a crusading sense rising in the early 1990s, suggests that the Insiders are positioning themselves not just to belong to the New Establishment but to redefine it.

The Outsiders

What are you staring at, Chink?

BYPASSER AT YONGE AND BLOOR
TO SUSAN ENG, TORONTO 1986

Cultural exclusion is the single most punitive force in society, creating classes beyond those of wealth, and fostering in the dispossessed a continual pursuit of acceptance. The world will take notice of and respond to the Insiders first, but Futurists who come from the far corners of the universe face an eternal struggle that often fails to bring them peace of mind, although propelling them to exponential success. Old-guard Establishment values are of little more than arcane interest to the outsider. To Kaaydah Schatten, who worked her way from a Campbell River reserve to a multi-million-dollar business, power generated by name and nobility is insignificant compared to the leverage that emanates from wealth. Most Outsiders rely only on themselves and are ready to adapt quickly when change is profitable. In this extraordinary departure from the 1970s, when women clung to jobs like life preservers, just keeping track of a Futurist's fax number is a challenge. Changing jobs is a part of the survival strategy that accompanies entrepreneurial thinking. It keeps Futurists honed to a fine edge, and also makes many of them eminently successful.

Susan Eng

When Canadian-born Susan Eng expressed to her high school math teacher at Jarvis Collegiate Institute a desire to study law, he cautioned, ''I don't think you should, for two good reasons: first, you're a woman, second, you're Chinese.'' Her journey from Chinatown to the Premier's Council[7] is based on a multi-generational saga of privation and discrimination. Eng, a law partner with Blaney McMurtry, has a mind that is a vast repository of information and she can talk faster than a speeding subway train. This stylish Futurist is an outsider trying to get inside—not to the Old Establishment, but to a state of acceptance for both herself and others of Asian origin.[8]

Raised above her father's New Dainty Grill on the Yonge Street Strip, which served prostitutes, pimps, the terminally drunk, and the rough side of a gay community just coming out of the closet, she recalled of this valuable education, ''You learned the lay of the land, what to avoid, what was safe. You got a sense of the street and how to assess people.'' Eng speaks with wry affection about a heritage that includes a grandmother forced to work in the fields when her husband died and a father who arrived in Canada to discover that the Chinese were regarded as ''sub-human,'' laundrymen, gardeners, domestic help relegated to the basements of grand homes, and subject to Canada's Exclusion Act. That meant no wives or children.[9] In 1949 Eng's father, Tong Eng, finally returned to China, chose a wife — Chuey, Eng's mother — and brought her back to the Yonge Street café. Eng considers her family a microcosm of the Chinese experience in North America.

Aided by nothing more than hard work and a determination to leave the Strip she graduated from Osgoode Hall Law School. Now she contributes to her province economically, professionally, philanthropically, and politically. An international and domestic tax lawyer and Asia Pacific expert, Eng has access to institutional power through law, government, and business with Pacific Rim countries. On the Premier's Council her focus is encouraging business development, particularly among young people, and she has helped set up chairs of entrepreneurial studies at Ontario universities and colleges.

Eng's popularity, or lack of it, has run the gamut of public sentiment. In 1984, Eng was drafted to run as an Independent in a by-election for alderman of a Toronto ward. It turned out that she had cross-pollinated support so skilfully from both major parties that the electorate accused her of creating a Liberal-Conservative alliance and voted in the NDP. Her supporters had included federal Liberal power Jim Coutts and Conservative Larry Grossman, and at her first fund raiser even Premier Peterson came to present her with a personal cheque for her campaign.

If Eng has an identity crisis it is affected by the tug of her Asian roots, her wish to remain a free agent, and the need to belong. She admits to playing the game of haute couture and social conformity while abhorring its playing field, the cocktail ritual. As anyone will say, getting inside the system is a necessary evil; being there socially is the oldest way of opening doors and getting things done. While Eng claims to dislike labels such as president or chair, her denials are cavalier; few ABC positions could be more "inside" than the Premier's Council. An entrepreneur in spirit, she is exasperated by the sluggishness of institutional procedure. As a young lawyer fluent in Mandarin, Cantonese, and French, she was well equipped to capitalize on the economic explosion of the Pacific Rim, but she found Canadian companies reluctant to deal with Asians, still bound by the parochialism that had put the country on hold for so many decades.[o] They were even reluctant to hire translators. Journalist Judy Steed quoted Eng as saying that Canada was slow to "welcome Chinese-Canadians into the power structure," and was "dragging its heels" on trading with China.[p] Eng credits senior law partner Bill McMurtry for first recognizing the potential for Far East business.

Eng became an activist in 1979 when she began attacking stereotypes. It happened over a *W5* television program that depicted Asian students swarming into the universities and taking places away from Canadians. She felt impelled to pursue her goal of integration by publicly speaking out for the Asian people; as children, the Engs had let themselves be assimilated in order to be accepted, and the *W5* program had gone too far. An outraged Eng founded the Chinese Canadian National Council for Equality, which subsequently forced the president of CTV to apologize.[10] She went on to work for the protection of the rights of all minorities in Canada.[11]

When Eng formed the Chinese Canadian National Council for Equality, she approached Adrienne Clarkson to speak at the CCNCE inaugural dinner. To Eng's amazement, she was told that Clarkson's fee would be her usual $5,000. It was an obviously unaffordable sum for the fledgling council, so Eng chose someone else, but the incident said much about the two women's styles. As a distinguished member of the Canadian media, the Chinese-born Clarkson has earned her way inside and is recognized as a celebrity rather than an ethnic symbol. Although she has frequently discussed her roots in interviews, two survival techniques seemed to be afoot: Clarkson assimilates. Eng activates, and that may be the root of her problems.

In 1991, opposition to Eng's appointment as chair of the Metro Toronto Police Services Board, the force's governing civilian body, leaked to the press. Michael Valpy wrote of a "mean and vicious campaign . . . to block Eng's appointment."[q] In the past she had been known to criticize the police, she felt, with good cause, and after two years as a member of the board, Eng advocated that it serve the community more than the police. In spite of her innumerable acknowledged contributions, such as bringing Asian-speaking foot-patrol officers into Chinatown, Eng's style was too abrasive for some Torontonians.

The street-wise Eng is stubborn. She has learned how to benefit from the system yet refuses to succumb to its power. When she became a lawyer, she returned to Jarvis Collegiate for a class reunion, sought out the math teacher who had advised her against studying law, and politely told him that not only was she a practising lawyer but her salary exceeded his.

Kaaydah Schatten

> There are those who watch it happen, those who make it happen, and those who don't know what's happening. I intend to make it happen.
>
> KAAYDAH SCHATTEN

It took thirty-two-year-old Kaaydah Schatten less than ten years to parlay a $7,000 B.C. accident claim—awarded when she was eighteen—into her first $5 million. She lost it in 1981, headed for Toronto in 1983, and made it back in five years, including equity in real estate and an international franchise. Her estimated assets in 1990 were $20 million, and in the next ten years Schatten intends to make fifty million dollars. In 1989, with her Ceiling Doctor International franchised throughout Canada, the United States, and Europe, and a deal arranged with

Ohkawa Tekko Iron Works, one of the largest steel fabricators in the world, as well as upscale apartment holdings in Vancouver and Toronto, Schatten approached a major Canadian bank for a loan. As in the past, it refused. Turning to the United States, she secured $3 million from a Californian bank, a deal that included giving some equity, then she returned to Toronto and took her Canadian banker to lunch to tell him about it. He asked in amazement, "How did you do it!? Everything you did was against the rules." Schatten, who is famous for her soft-spoken, blunt repartees, replied sweetly, "You institutional thinkers have constipated colons in place of brains."

Since childhood, when she spoke only Kwakwala, Schatten has forged success out of historical neglect and cultural repression. Life on her reserve at Campbell River — where her name was anglicized to Crystal for the convenience of the Department of Indian Affairs — was a chaos of abandonment, alcoholism, and poverty. The steps she took while she was in Grade 1 are those by which she continues to build her assets, each new million widening the gap between childhood ghetto and adult success.

At the age of six when her Indian princess mother — Quoksistelia, anglicized to Quocksister — was sent to Vancouver for cancer surgery, and her father and the babysitter took off on a drunken binge, the grim-faced little girl quickly assessed her situation. She had four younger siblings who needed immediate care. She also knew even then that education was the only way out, and her mother had already moved the family to Lantzville so that Kaaydah could attend school off the reserve to learn to speak English. With this goal fixed in her mind, Schatten went to the local hotel and made her first deal: if owner Anne Caillet would care for the babies so that Schatten could attend school, the child would join the hotel cleaning staff. Caillet agreed, organizing the community women into shifts to care for the babies. Every Sunday for the next six years Schatten cleaned up the hotel bar, aware that, in place of giving handouts, Caillet had given her a sense of dignity, self-reliance, and a road map for success. From that beginning, Schatten studied as if her life depended upon it. She scrambled, made deals, and, at times when Quoksistelia feared there would be no food, found her mother jobs in the local cannery. Never on her trajectory to freedom would Kaaydah Schatten allow her family to experience the dishonour of welfare. At night, Schatten collected for the Bingo game and earned up to sixty dollars a week in tips, which she used for keeping the house, getting her mother's hair done, and buying her decent clothes. Schatten used whatever was left over to fix up her little room, to create harmony in a safe place. She still redecorates her real estate properties before renting or reselling, as if eliminating reminders of her sordid childhood.

Shatten quickly learned that survival meant learning the art of the possible or, as she described it, "If you never ask, you will never know whether it's a yes or a no, and if it's a no, it means not now.'' She became a child virtuoso in the art of the deal. She studied adult behaviour with the same intensity she devoted to arithmetic and reading. She was calculating about every person she met, every job she took, seeking out new angles to learn, and to win. When delivering eggs to homes of the wealthier set, she noticed that successful people put their money into land, and by her twelfth birthday she had found a job typing offers in a real estate office where she could ask about mortgages and study land values around Nanaimo. ''Was I tough? I am tough,'' said Schatten, her language veering from patient negotiator to tough-talking child-survivor.

When Schatten was fifteen, her father beat her mother and broke Schatten's arm. For the first time the teenager went to the police, and her father went to jail. The incident reinforced Schatten's opinion that marrying without monetary power meant subservience, and she became driven by a vision of freedom achieved through the wealth that she intended to generate and control. During her final year of high school she took a course entitled The Law and You, and with the help of Legal Aid got separation and protection papers drawn up for her mother. She sold the house and moved her family into an apartment for $150 a month. Then, with $90 in her pocket, she hitch-hiked to California. The trip confirmed for her that in a world of haves and have-nots, she would be a have.

Schatten stopped in San Francisco at a youth hostel located near Union Square, one of the classier plots of downtown land on the continent. After looking over the nearby residence on Nob Hill for women, she talked her way into a job as receptionist, demonstrated her enormous capacity for work, and so charmed the owners that they invited her to live with them in the posh suburb of Pacifica. Recognizing a young woman suffering from the effects of a dysfunctional childhood, they arranged counselling for her with Arthur Janov, author of *The Primal Scream*. She also met Shakti Gawain, who would go on to write *Creative Visualization*, a positive force for pursuing success. Schatten still considers them two of her most important mentors, along with Ayn Rand. Later, on a trip to Europe, Schatten would crash a tea party in Germany to meet Rand and then go to Spain to call on another hero, the surrealist painter Salvador Dali. Of those who have inspired her, Schatten observed, ''I am responsible for whom I meet and for what I learn.''

Schatten's career nearly ended when, during her second year at Malaspina College in Nanaimo, a car crash catapulted her through the windshield. She nearly lost a leg, but it was saved, she claimed, by a Shaman who, with the blessing of frustrated but sceptical doctors, performed a ritual healing in the hospital. Schatten evaluated her future and replaced chemistry studies, which she loved, with real estate development. She had already used the $7,000 accident insurance claim for a down payment on the Nanaimo fourplex in which her family lived. The former owner, who knew her, had let her make the deal with practically no cash and, of course, no bank loans. Laughed Schatten, "Banks loan money to a native teenager?"

During a year of recuperation, Schatten studied bookkeeping, worked for a logging company where she advanced into management, bought into a Nanaimo restaurant, and by the end of her nineteenth year had bought, traded or sold approximately ten properties. Just before her twentieth birthday she learned that developers from central Canada were searching for land for a shopping centre outside of Nanaimo. Visiting an old farmer friend on the outskirts of town who had repeatedly refused to sell to developers, Schatten convinced him that she was a nice native girl who wanted to farm. He sold his acreage to her for $50,000 with $10,000 down on a vendor-take-back mortgage. As soon as the deal was closed, Schatten telephoned a central-Canadian developer and two weeks later she flipped the land to the development company for $550,000. Shrugged the survivor, "We have to wear different masks for different things."

Seeking further knowledge of balance sheets and bottom lines, Schatten hired on as a junior account assistant at Tahsis, a B.C. lumber company. Within a year she became senior assistant responsible for $75 million in sub-contract work and log inventory systems. Schatten's windfall came when she invested $500 in the early days of Hemlo Mines and Corona Corp.[12] Bubbling with that innocent wonderment at which she is so adept, she explained, "I was a novice. I just followed the experts' tips. I made a ton of money."

Over the next seven years, Schatten continued to focus her energies on real estate development, investing with canny foresight in rundown Vancouver houses on the verge of becoming Yuppiedom's trendy Fairview Slopes. By her twenty-sixth birthday she had invested the bulk of her money in MURBs[13] and estimated her worth at $5 million. At the same time she fell in love with dentist Rob Forest, whom she rescued from protracted divorce proceedings by suggesting he sell his practice to his mother so that he had no assets. The price was a $10,000 gift and a Mercedes. Forest went to work for Schatten and is the father of her child. Had they married then, before Bill C31[14] was amended, their son would not have had native status.

To finance her Fairview Slopes project, Schatten had presold a MURB to thirteen partners in a sixteen-unit development for $50,000 cash each. A major Canadian bank had just expressed confidence in Schatten when the 1981 federal budget put an end to MURBs and double martinis were gulped down all over town. With that announcement, the bank pulled its financing and Schatten snapped that she was finished forever with "using Canadian banks who don't give a shit about Canadian investments." Instead of declaring bankruptcy and walking away from her friends, Schatten dialed the Hanil Bank of Canada (of Korea), which she says lent her $1.8 million. That, with a $1.5 million land loan, if she could get it, would enable her to complete the project. But she made a fatal mistake: she signed over the buildings as collateral. "That's where I learned about banking papers and what you sign," she remembered ruefully. "I gave them absolute control. They went in, quick claimed the property, and sold it out from underneath me." Her friends got their money back, but she lost everything, "Five million dollars of my own cash gone."

Rather than waste time in court, Schatten filed the information away, wiser for the experience. She drove to Mexico, lay on the beach, and dreamed of winning it all back. It may have been the clouds scudding overhead that shifted Schatten's thoughts to the thousands of dirty ceiling tiles she had replaced while renovating apartments. It's a messy, costly exercise and apartment managers automatically budget for tile replacement. If they could be cleaned, it would be big business. The chemist within Schatten surfaced, and with the help of a professional she invented both a formula, which remains secret, and jet spray equipment that she claims is superior to any other. Schatten was ready to move, but first she needed capital. In Canada, that meant going to Toronto.

In December of 1983, when the market had only just started to recover, Schatten and Forest headed for the big city with nothing but $10,000, the Mercedes, and a credit card. Driving into town, Schatten was amazed to see condominiums for sale at $30,000. She recalled, "They were giving them away—no money down and even paying for the legal fees." The cheapest accommodation they could find was in the poverty-stricken, crime-filled Jane-Finch corridor where the Mercedes stood out like Salvador Dali's cauliflower-filled Rolls-Royce. Using nothing but the credit card and the image of wealth the Mercedes implied, Schatten went shopping. From December through February 1984 she claims she bought fifty condominiums with no money down. Mortgages were then assumable without qualification. Then in a two-month frenzy she renovated every condo, juggling her funds and pending bills with the first and last months' rent to pay the mortgages and her costs.[15]

By March, Schatten had bought a customer list from a failed cleaning company and, with only herself and Rob to do the work, launched her ceiling business. How did she reach the big-time market with no advertising budget? Schatten claimed that she placed personal telephone calls to "the instant decision makers" — the CEOs or their counterparts in major businesses, banks, insurance companies, retail outlets, and the government. The thought of Brascan's Trevor Eyton or the Royal Bank of Canada's Allan Taylor seizing the telephone to talk with the Ceiling Doctor stretches credulity. How did she get through to them? Her wicked tones evoked images of the child-survivor: "It was easy. The secretary wouldn't dare not put me through. I'm not his wife . . . I'm, well . . . (snicker), I always got through," and before the power-that-be could hang up, the fast-talking Ceiling Doctor almost always closed the deal.

Schatten remembered that Trevor Eyton laughingly told her she had more balls than brains.

Schatten then registered Ceiling Doctor International and from 1986 to 1989 sold thirty-three North American franchises for $25,000 each. In 1988 she grossed $3 million in Canada alone with a minimum overhead and a skeletal staff. In August that same year she signed a $20-million franchise deal covering Southeast Asia and the Far East. She then sold out of the Japanese market for an undisclosed sum to concentrate on American and European expansion. She now has franchises in Ireland, Germany, and Hungary and is looking at South America and Eastern Europe. Moving her head office to Hamilton, opening an office in Texas, selling her Vancouver buildings, and winning refinancing for her Palace Pier apartments in May, 1991, she effectively dealt with her real estate problems, and believes she can ride out any economic storm. Claimed Schatten with that eternal optimism of the Futurists, ''We are recession proof.''

No longer limiting her goal to the pursuit of wealth, Schatten shifted into a new dimension, that of the gift society, the most honourable facet of her Indian culture. Although she was a main support of her family through the roughest of childhoods, Schatten has a theory that she lost her first five million through selfishness. ''I took. I never gave,'' she reasoned. ''Now I'm a capitalist with a social conscience.'' In 1987, she chose as her route to help others the Canadian Council for Native Business, which promotes entrepreneurship,[16] and she agreed to raise money for the Canadian Native Arts Foundation cross-country native ballet tour.[17] When the neophyte fund raiser walked into Northern Telecom and asked for $250,000, she got it. With that expression of wide-eyed innocence that makes her successes look like Lotto wins, she said, ''I just asked. And I got it. That's how you do it.''

Selling a native ballet performance to the cynical head of the National Arts Centre in Ottawa was tougher, and Schatten remains scornful of ''that pompous [ass] who runs it and didn't want the show. He got up at the University Women's Club in Ottawa and asked John Kim Bell [founder and president of the Canadian Native Arts Foundation] how many tickets had been sold. We hadn't even started marketing. He was totally out of line and I could have slugged him.'' Then Governor-General Jeanne Sauvé accepted an invitation to the opening event, entitled ''The Land of the Spirit.'' In 1988, at the sold-out opening night, the once abandoned child from the Campbell River reserve sat proudly beside the Queen's representative and noted with relish that ''the [man] whose name is forgettable was only too happy that night to come up and shake my hand.''

By 1989 Schatten's community profile had skyrocketed along with her trappings of success: a Maserati, a Jaguar, and the old Mercedes. Toronto applauds winners and respects the work ethic. Schatten explained unapologetically to Gordon Donaldson in *Canadian Business*, ''For every inch of fur on my coat, I've cleaned 100,000 square feet of ceiling. For every carat of diamond, I've cleaned a million square feet."[r] After reading Schatten's story in January 1989, Toronto investment dealer Mary Suzanne Lamont included the young entrepreneur in her power luncheons.

In her worst moments Schatten never doubted that she would make back her lost $5 million just as she is convinced she will increase it by a factor of at least ten. As she put it, "In Canada or the U.S., people are basically lazy. If you work to 80 percent of your maximum, it's easy to be successful." Placing the blame of the acceptance of mediocrity on the unions and government handouts, Schatten offers a simple solution: "The government should cut all the social security and unemployment insurance programs . . . until people become accountable. For those who are abusing the system, fuck them."

The Crusaders

Entrepreneurial confidence combined with humanitarianism is what drives the Crusaders. Buoyant, optimistic young women who would never consider themselves "victims" or, for that matter, "crusaders," some simply envision a better world. Leading the pack are the lawyers: Heather MacFadgen litigates for LEAF, Wendy Harvey is an advocate for screens to protect sexually assaulted children from facing the accused in court, University of Saskatchewan gold-medalist Kate Sutherland participates in the National Association of Women in the Law as does Harvard law student (master's) Jody Freeman,[18] who intends to specialize in constitutional law, litigation, and teaching. Alexandra Guest, a graduate of Queen's, Oxford, and University of Toronto law school, has been hired by the United Nations High Commissioner for Refugees. Her first posting was to Islamabad, where she is assisting refugees from Kashmir. A refugee from Uganda with British training, lawyer Mobina Jaffer tried in vain to get application forms from the Law Society of British Columbia in the mid-1970s. Finally she found a job working for former Supreme Court Justice Tom Dohm as a "girl Friday." When he learned of her problem, he got her the forms and advised her to tell the Law Society she was working for him. Ten days later her credentials were accepted. She received her Canadian citizenship, became a law partner with Dohm, and founded the group called Immigrant and Visible Minority Women of B.C.

Vancouverite and Queen's University graduate Catherine Mulholland is a technical officer for the director general of the World Health Organization and is posted in Geneva. She is involved in five projects, one of which, in the slums of Cairo, has the support of Madame Mubarak, wife of the Egyptian president. Twenty-eight-year-old Karen Ridd, a member of the Peace Brigade International, boldly refused to leave a Salvadoran jail when released by her captors until the police also released her Colombian cell-mate and friend.[19] Twenty-three-year-old Judi Tyabji of Kelowna campaigned, carrying her small child, on a Liberal ticket in a provincial by-election to protest the government's cutback in welfare and the former premier Bill Vander Zalm's "pray to Jesus" solution for single mothers.

In 1980, environmentalist Margot Franssen joined with her sister Betty-Ann, then nineteen, to start the Canadian franchise of the United Kingdom-based Body Shop. Using only environmentally friendly substances and a minimum of recycled packaging, they grossed $195,000 in their first year and by 1990 posted retail sales of $60 million.[20] "We're going to try to shame our industry," Franssen told the Toronto *Star*.[s] And she told Michael Valpy of the *Globe and Mail*, "The end-goal with Body Shop is not to make money but to be able to sleep at night with a clear conscience and have fun at what you're doing." Valpy concluded, "She gives capitalism a good name. She sets a pace for corporate responsibility."[t]

****

Other Crusaders have experienced the pain of defeat, the rejection of society, or the tenuity of life. In their darkest moments, they have healed themselves from some profound internal wellspring and then, through subtle metaphor, they have shared their process with the world.

Diane Dupuy

On the eve of the Calgary Winter Olympics, January 1988, Jeanne Lougheed, wife of the former premier Peter Lougheed, and the inspiration behind many of the extraordinary health services and resources for the performing arts in Alberta,[21] reflected upon the fund-raising galas and various causes to which she often lends her name. The prairie sun was glimmering off bobsled runs and ski jumps, soon to be challenged by the most able young athletes in the world, but Lougheed's thoughts were on the disabled. She had just toured ARBI, the Association for the Rehabilitation of the Brain Injured, and had seen a young woman curled up in a corner, isolated from, and perhaps barely aware of, the world. Lougheed recalled sadly, "I felt I should be visiting this woman regularly, getting down on my knees with her, and maybe some day we could communicate . . . but I don't have that time. So I go to a charity ball, have fun, see my friends, and hope the money I give will enable someone else to get down on their knees and try to reach that young woman." Lougheed's candid observations reflected the sense of guilt and even helplessness experienced by most of us who rationalize that our visits and concern might not do any good anyway, so we give money and we don't go.

Torontonian Diane Dupuy did go. She not only got down on her knees but caught up young mentally handicapped people and in a whirl of creativity spun them to unimagined heights. Through equal measures of patience, encouragement, and bullying, Dupuy created a skilled professional troupe known as the Famous People Players (FPP).[23] In its nearly two decades of existence, it has toured Canada, China and the United States, and in 1986 achieved the impossible dream — playing to critical acclaim on Broadway. Its medium, the magic of black-light puppetry once suggested to her by Bill Cosby, came in fact from Dupuy's own terrified childhood.

A dyslexic child who was herself called "retard" by classmates, Dupuy suffered under her father's discipline at home. He punished her by banishing her to a darkened basement, and she struggled through childhood as an angry, frightened outcast. That heavy baggage fostered in Dupuy a defiant will to survive and to heal others. When she was a twenty-year-old skilled puppeteer giving shows at the CNE, a woman named Audrey Watson asked her to perform for some mentally disabled children at Surrey Place Centre in Toronto. During the program the children calmly aided a victim of an epileptic attack, then returned to watching the puppets. Dupuy was amazed by their concern and captivated by their warmth. She thought of the classmates who had ridiculed her and an epileptic girl in her class in Grade 8, and wondered just who were the retards. Inspired to discover their potential, Dupuy collected a group of mentally disabled youth and trained them to handle the life-sized puppets for her black-light show.

Initially, one disaster followed another. Dupuy could have sought professionals for her innovative show, but her alter ego was going along with her or she would not go at all. She took her troupe home when they needed a place to stay, taught them personal hygiene, and rode the subway with one young man considered so grotesque that his mother rarely let him out of the house. With Dupuy's help he gained the confidence to travel everywhere with pride and became one of the most valuable members of the troupe.

That Dupuy succeeded at all is a tribute to her determination in an atmosphere of professional disbelief. For years even the medical profession shied away from her. Hers is a purity of power to which almost all men and women aspire. An Outsider, she could not benefit from boardroom manipulations, or win through style. She simply coupled her own wounded spirit with the desire of the disabled to become contributing members of society. Over the years, Dupuy and the FPPs meshed in a symbiosis of healing. The black basement of punishment became the magic of black-light, and the childhood fantasies through which she escaped that horror became the scenarios for the brilliantly coloured puppets swooping and dancing to "The Sorcerer's Apprentice," "The Carnival of the Animals," and "Scheherazade."

Gambling that a lifesize puppet of Liberace playing his candelabra-laden piano would be a smashing success, Dupuy determined to meet the entertainer one evening following his performance at the Toronto O'Keefe Centre. Gate-crashing a reception being held in his honour by the city's fund-raising elite, Dupuy cut in on the pianist who was dancing with the wife of the O'Keefe Centre general manager. Using her big smile and hooded eyes, Dupuy talked faster than Liberace could sweep her around the floor, telling him all about her show and her envisioned puppet. He responded by having his manager, Seymour Heller, give her his card. It was a token gesture, but Dupuy now had the great man's telephone number, or almost, and she began building a major sequence around Liberace. In the summer of 1974, less than a year later, when FPP was hired to do a CNE puppet show during August,[23] Dupuy called Seymour Heller to see if Liberace would attend. Heller neither returned her calls nor answered her letters. Still determined, in February 1975 Dupuy suggested to the fund raisers for the Ontario Association for the Mentally Retarded that they invite the Famous People Players to be their entertainment for their annual event. The association hesitated, but Dupuy promised that Liberace would attend their planned luncheon. The OAMR capitulated, not realizing that Liberace knew nothing about it.

Dupuy probably missed a career as an impersonator. Over a two-week period, she kept calling Heller, claiming first that she was a Mrs. Bradshaw of Prime Minister Trudeau's office trying to track down the Liberace puppet to perform at 24 Sussex Drive, then calling back as a society maven from Forest Hill who wanted to hire the puppet for a country OAMR luncheon, and finally as an organizer of the OAMR who wanted Liberace to appear as a surprise for the prime minister. For weeks Dupuy juggled characters like kited cheques, tantalizing Heller until he finally called to say that Liberace would attend the luncheon.

Dupuy's inspiration was prophetic. Not only did the Toronto glitterati finally awake to this remarkable troupe, but Liberace was so delighted by the fantasy and so impressed when he met the troupe members that he hired FPP for his Las Vegas show. For the next ten years FPP travelled to Las Vegas, expanded their repertoire to include complicated symphonic accompaniments, and enthralled audiences and orchestras throughout North America. Corporations, politicians, and celebrities flocked to help fund the troupe and volunteer their time.[24] Funds soared, and when the Broadway show became a possibility, citizens dropped in at Swiss Chalet restaurants across Toronto to buy FPP T-shirts. Canadians contributed $25,000 and then made $15,000 selling FPP buttons from street corners and gas stations across the country. Truck drivers, elderly women, and children stopped to buy one button and left with an entire bagful. Eventually, the troupe made it to Broadway and earned $350,000 from the gala benefit on October 23, 1986.

Dupuy is uncompromising in demanding excellence and has been known to roar and bellow at her sponsors as well as at the slightest hint of self-pity in her troupe. Despite her bullying tactics, the elite of fund raisers were drawn to her dream. Like the busy Jeanne Lougheed, supporters saw in her a vicarious opportunity to share in something they could not do themselves. Frequently asked to speak to women's groups Dupuy roundly scolds the "Wives Of" for spending their lives pursuing fancy causes and fashionable clothes out of fear and insecurity. "You," she blasts them, "are afraid to stand up for something, to get out and take a chance." And then she fires that unsettling reproach: "*You* are the disabled!" Requests for speaking engagements continue to roll in. Asked how she feels about blind men selling pencils on the street, Dupuy snapped, "I'd snatch those pencils out of their hands, throw them in the gutter, and tell them to stop. Why should the affliction be the sell?"

Because affliction does sell. As Dupuy tells it, one morning in 1976 when FPP was due on stage in Las Vegas that evening, the U.S. immigration officer at the Toronto airport refused to let them board the plane because their work permits were not in order. Forty-five minutes before the last plane was to leave for Vegas, Dupuy called the White House and asked to speak to the President. She got through to two secretaries, each presumably closer to the Oval Office, explained the problem, and shamelessly used the future jeopardy of the mental retardation cause to enhance her argument. Within minutes a special assistant to the President called back to say that the Famous People Players would be cleared through his office. They made the flight and their show.[u]

Dupuy is on the defensive if anyone refers to her players as disabled, yet it is precisely their achievement in the face of that adversity that skyrocketed the players to fame and realized Dupuy's objective of fostering respect for the disabled. Her dream that her players would become famous as professionals and not as mentally disabled was a paradox, for how could she expect the world to alter entrenched opinions if they were unaware of the special nature of whom they were watching? Dupuy uses her troupe in part as inspiration and in part as weapon, and therein lies a whole sector of clout that few dare to either criticize or ignore. Her own response is a contradiction. When the traveller referred to the "mentally retarded," because Dupuy had used the phrase, the tightly coiled Futurist boomed, "You are the retard!" The traveller then referred to the "professional troupe" and was corrected with, "'Handicapped.' Call it like it is!" When, in a final effort to get it right, the traveller tried "the learning delayed," Dupuy shot her down with, "Don't use cute terms!"

"Everywhere she goes, she builds a barrier around herself—and everywhere she goes, she only bumps into herself,"[v] wrote Dupuy, depicting herself with a quote from the movie *Breakfast at Tiffany's*. Should she exhaust the goodwill of her gala committees, Dupuy may attain her most fervent desire, which is to go it all alone.

Jody Freeman

A twenty-seven-year-old Vancouver scholar who studied human biology and international relations at Stanford University, Jody Freeman backpacked around Asia, won the Dean's Key from the University of Toronto for her academic and extracurricular campus activities while earning her law degree, and in 1990 was awarded several fellowships with full funding to attend Harvard University for her master's in law.[25] Freeman is a popular, empowered Futurist who holds within her world view the concerns of a Judge Abella, a Judge Ruffo, a Doris Anderson, a Mary Eberts. The daughter of Natalie Veiner Freeman, Jody is among the handful of her generation's crusaders for social justice, whether the Futurists see the need for it or not.

''You could say I have made it,'' observed Freeman in a self-assured voice whose mellow timbre is destined to capture the respect of judges and juries. ''I'm privileged and I'm educated. [What I have been able to do] does not mean that the changes within institutions are deep and profound.'' Of the restrictions put upon her mother's and grandmother's generations, Freeman believes that while the cosmetics have changed, ''systemic discrimination continues in subtler, more insidious ways.'' Said Freeman, ''In the courts, for example, it is one thing to alter the terminology from rape to sexual assault but quite another to change the way rape victims are treated in the courtroom and by the public. Fundamentally, the world has not changed.''

Freeman agreed that this may be the time to soften feminist language, but she said, ''It is a question of strategy. We need to evaluate what works and what doesn't work with a given audience and a given set of goals. I don't believe that to be effective we must always be non-threatening.'' Although Freeman sees the value in compromise and moderated language, she also thinks that disagreement and conflict are essential to progress for women. ''Radicalism extends the outer limits of the philosophical spectrum and makes room for a variety of voices. It pushes people to think through their position.'' Subscribing to a broad feminist view, Freeman acknowledges the personal challenge to choose a strategy that neither allows the issues to degenerate in a syrup of subtleties nor compromises her integrity or her style.

****

The Futurists are poised to inherit an earth burdened with the moral conundrums of overpopulation, genetic manipulation, surrogate motherhood, ecological disaster, AIDS, the economic monstrosity posed by unyielding national debts, educational systems that have failed to prepare many of them for competition in the global market place, and inadequate, non-existent or mammoth health care services that may prove the most oppressive power of all.

The freedoms enjoyed by Futurists are also unprecedented. They can no longer be made into brides at age twelve; they can legally enter into and practise the profession of their choice; their salaries are becoming equal to those of men of similar titles; and in the executive suites, they will find that hierarchical power is flattening into shared decision making. Should they marry, which many do not intend to do, they may keep their maiden names without recrimination; should they become pregnant, human rights laws decree that they can take maternity leave without losing their jobs, or if they do, LEAF will intercede for them, if necessary, all the way to the Supreme Court of Canada. Should they divorce, they will receive 50 percent of the family assets accrued during marriage. It may take another thirty years or it may happen in the next decade, but Futurists who are financially focussed are firmly launched on a trajectory that could give them the equity and fortunes that for centuries have been the basis of power for men.

The Futurists readily confess to only one fear. Liane Benoît is single, successful, and head of her own Benoît and Associates consulting group. Her dilemma, like that of other Futurists, is how to juggle stellar success with her biological clock. Futurists in their mid-thirties who are enjoying success in the marketplace are not only facing the deadline for having children but also have to choose whether or not to walk away from a career in order to raise a family, whether to have children and continue to compete for the top job, whether to marry solely for the purpose of having a child, or whether to bear a child out of wedlock either with a friend's assistance or through artificial insemination. Romance, let alone love and marriage, is no longer an essential criterion, any more than the family is still considered the sole, impregnable nucleus of a civilized society.

This freedom of choice is the Futurists' Wall. Never in their grandmothers' wildest nightmares could they have imagined such scenarios for motherhood. The defeat in the Senate on January 31, 1991, of the abortion bill was a milestone in women's freedom, but a Royal Commission on New Reproductive Technologies portends new laws, and the Futurists' fundamental right as individuals to control their own bodies may once again be relinquished to the state. Individual provinces are already claiming the right to take funding of abortions into their own hands. That could be the Waterloo for those Futurists who currently see no further need for the women's movement.

CHAPTER 17 NOTES

1. Anita and Gordon Roddick founded The Body Shop in the United Kingdom in 1976. It is an environmentally conscious cosmetic franchise headed in Canada by Margot Franssen.
2. In 1990, Linda Frum published *The Newsmakers: Behind the Camera with Canada's Top TV Journalists*, a compilation of excerpts from interviews with some forty-nine TV journalists. All royalties go to CBC camera man Jean-Guy Nault, who broke his neck while on the job in 1985.
3. ''Wilson's'' is the Victoria Establishment store in which even royalty might stop to shop for the finest in British woollens and tweeds. The Wilsons have also been landowners, and municipal politicians, including mayors, and the family tree is as high quality as the cashmeres sold in their store.
4. Austin Taylor is old, old Vancouver. His mother, Kathleen Taylor, presided over the block-square Georgian estate of Shannon and was a volunteer power in the city. Taylor is chair and CEO of ScotiaMcLeod, brother of Pat Buckley, New York's most famous society maven, and, therefore, brother-in-law of William F. Buckley.
5. The organization was founded in 1988 by a group of Vancouver Conservative friends, including Woodward, Sally Warren, Virginia Richards, Diana Lam, Brenda Kinsella, LEAF lawyer Heather MacFadgen, and Pat Carney aide Donna Mackey. It expanded when they received media exposure in Toronto.
6. Interfor, her family's forest products company, is a successful international conglomerate run from the West Coast and notable for its intense privacy.
7. The Premier's Council is a select Ontario group whose mandate is to spend $100 million a year for ten years to design an economic strategy for Ontario and to attract global business to the province. The council consists of twenty-eight members who have included Roberta Bondar, astronaut; Donald Webster, chair of Helix Investment; Moses Znaimer, president and CEO of CITYTV; George Peapples, president of General Motors of Canada; Geraldine Kenney-Wallace, president of McMaster University; and Dr. Fraser Mustard, president of the Canadian Institute for Advanced Research.

8. Her sister Rose is a geneticist with an MBA who worked in management for a bio-technical firm before moving to the Federal Business Development Bank as a project manager in the venture capital division. Her brother Hubert studied at the University of Toronto School of Music before earning an MBA, and brother Henry is a doctor.
9. The Acts were designed, Eng assumed, to prevent reproduction by the resident Chinese. It allowed only a handful of Chinese—men only—to enter the country in a twenty-four-year period, and was not changed until after the Second World War in 1947.
10. The CCNCE now has twenty-nine chapters across Canada, and is attempting to emphasize the truer image of Chinese as professionals and international entrepreneurs.
11. Eng has been connected with the Urban Alliance on Race Relations, a member of an Ad Hoc Committee on Media and Race Relations, and a contributor to the Special Parliamentary Committee on Participation of Visible Minorities in Canadian Society.
12. Nell Dragovan, who had founded Corona Resources, brought Murray Pezim, wizard of the Vancouver Stock Exchange, into the fledgling Hemlo Gold Mines deal on the north shore of Lake Superior. Dragovan was pivotal to securing the land leases; the cost of taking the mine to production was $80 million. An ownership battle with LAC Minerals followed, which Corona won in 1989. The collective gold deposits are said to be one of the largest in Canadian history, and Nell Dragovan's big stake makes her one of the all-time great women entrepreneurs.
13. "Multiple Unit Residential Buildings" were a means of sheltering money from taxation, sanctioned by the federal government. The sudden cancellation of the program in the 1981 budget destroyed the assets of many who had used it.
14. Thanks to efforts by numerous native women such as Mary Two-Axe Earley, Blanche Macdonald, the late fashion school founder, and Schatten herself, the law was amended in 1985. Only after the change did Schatten and Forrest marry. In 1991, LEAF is fighting the Indian Act based on the Charter. It is challenging the second-generation cut-off that discriminates against women in Bill C31. To date, children of people whose mothers lost their status because they married a non-

status Indian will not get Indian status. Children who have Indian lineage through the paternal line have status.

15. As each of Schatten's fifty condos realized about $500 per month, she could pay out $450 on the mortgages including interest, principal, and taxes, which left her with a positive cash flow of above $3,000 per month for living and renovating expenses.
16. Its board includes as directors Murray Koffler, Barbara McDougall, Edward Bronfman, Maureen McTeer, Monique Bégin, and Judy Erola.
17. The purpose of the foundation is to promote the arts for native youth by providing scholarship and bursaries.
18. Jody is the daughter of Natalie Veiner Freeman.
19. Ridd was acting as a witness for the Peace Brigades International, an organization that believes a passive witness can hamper or even stop violent disputes.
20. Body Shop Canada stores have devoted their display windows to the charitable donations group, Imagine. They have raised funds for the World Wildlife Federation and for Friends of the Earth.
21. When premier, Peter Lougheed gave Jeanne credit for directing his attention towards health and the arts. ARBI (Association for the Rehabilitation of the Brain Injured), the Head Injured Relearning Centre, and the William Watson Lodge for recreation for the disabled in Canmore have pioneered special services for re-education and recreation for the brain injured.
22. Guided by puppeteers made invisible through the use of black cloaks and ultraviolet light, phosphorescent puppets create an illusion of a choreographed, floating fantasia. Dupuy's mother, Mary Thornton, designs and makes the costumes, props, and puppets.
23. The CNE thought it was doing her a favour and in return, Dupuy agreed to do sixteen puppet shows a day, apart from the FPP show, for the month.
24. Supporters included former lieutenant-governor Pauline McGibbon, ballet great Celia Franca, actor Lorne Green, Anne Murray, and Maureen McTeer, who organized an Ottawa fundraiser for the future Broadway show. Outside Canada, Jack Lemmon and Paul Newman offered support. Newman donated $10,000 for an FPP show, dropped in beforehand as a courtesy, and was so entranced by the sight of the

Liberace puppet floating toward the piano that he remained for the entire show.

25. As a law student Freeman was active in mooting, worked in a legal clinic for those who could not afford a lawyer, acted as an associate editor of the *Law Review,* and published one paper in the University of Toronto *Faculty of Law Review* and another in the Berkeley *Women's Law Journal* on radical feminists and Liberal feminists concerning prostitution reform.

CHAPTER EIGHTEEN

TUUM EST: It's Up To You.

Women do not want pity. They want process. [Believe you're] a winner and people will treat you like one.

JOAN DRUXMAN

The political analyses of women in power proves that women have failed. . . . We are here [in Ottawa], so close to Parliament Hill, but so far from parity. Women are still standing outside, watching, because they have failed to effectively infiltrate the institutions which run this country.

YOLANDE COHEN

In March 1988, women from across the country slogged through the Ottawa slush to register for a symposium entitled "Women and Power." The event was one of several being sponsored by the Canadian Advisory Council on the Status of Women. Like the nationally successful "Winning Women" organization founded by Senator Mira Spivak that holds symposiums across Canada on how to get into politics, it featured panel discussions and was sold out. A convivial atmosphere prevailed in the converted railway station as women central to the feminist movement over the past twenty years milled about greeting the converted. Many women there were the so-called militants who had struggled to win the 1967 Royal Commission on the Status of Women, changes in family law, human rights commissions, and the enshrinement of women's rights in the Constitution. Just seeing these congenial veterans of a hundred battles demystified the myth of stridency that has surrounded them. These were professional women, their collective expertise ranging through the fields of education, publishing, law, medicine, and government.

From Quebec there was then Liberal MP Lucie Pépin, who co-founded Quebec's first (then illegal) vasectomy clinic, and who, in 1984, stepped into the traditionally Liberal federal riding of Outremont with the blessing of the departing Marc Lalonde. She would lose her seat in the fall of 1988 because of the free trade issue. There was Parti Québécois member Pauline Marois, a woman whose significance in the 1990s could increase in direct proportion to the popularity of Quebec sovereignty.[1] There were two university professors who are prolific authors on the subject of power: Yolande Cohen, from l'Université du Québec à Montréal, and Jill Vickers, director of the Institute of Canadian Studies at Carlton University. Monique Bégin was there; while minister of health and welfare, she had introduced a new law to strengthen medicare, and in 1991 is joint chair of Women's Studies at the University of Ottawa and Carleton University. Judith Ramirez from Toronto, who championed the coalition of domestic workers into a group called Intercede, was accompanied by a Portuguese woman who wept with anger and gratitude as she spoke of former abuse in Canada and new-found rights. Prior to the late 1980s, who would have imagined non-English-speaking immigrant cleaning ladies, as they were called, having rights? Intercede embodies the feminist victories of the century.

Every one of these women had helped create change and, in some distinctive way, penetrated institutional structures to set in place certain inviolable systems of protection for society. One such organization is the Canadian Advisory Council on the Status of Women, and its then president, Sylvia Gold, opened the conference with a story about activist Emma Goldman, who was jailed at the turn of the century for being an anarchist, and for warning that legislation alone would not change the nature of institutions. Doris Anderson, the den mother to modern activists, spoke. She has remained a presence in the women's movement since her resignation as president of CACSW in 1981, writing her newspaper columns on the realities of life for women and minorities.

But does a society that reveres competition know much about the campaign to win the rights contained in Sections 15 and 28 of the Charter of Rights and Freedoms? If so, does it care? A year earlier, during a similar panel discussion on women and power, when Senator Lorna Marsden had referred to the "events of 1981," a young *Globe and Mail* reporter had asked, "What happened in 1981?" Six years earlier as a teenaged high school student, she had been unaware of feminist fights. At the time, guaranteeing women's rights had been for many the most consequential milestone of the century, a victory that lay less in the result than in the brilliant lobby that finally caused politicians to view women as both a formidable power and a political asset. Yet, if they even know, the reaction from the Futurists often is, "Who cares?"

The question illuminates the ephemeral nature of the women's movement. Each new generation is born into greater freedom, and women who have never felt subjugated are impatient with those who continue to flog the concept of gender equality. In 1988, *enfant terrible* Linda Frum condensed her own view of a century of equality struggles into one paragraph for *Chatelaine*:

> Men have always acceded to any demand for "female advancement," sensible or silly. When we asked them to help with the dishes and diapers, we got it. When we asked them to stop excluding women from important government, corporate and judicial positions, we got that. When we announced our plan to replace market wages with a whimsical "pay equity" scheme, we got—good God!—that too.[a]

Fearless Frum outraged a legion of older women with her glib criticism, but they should have known that she represents a recurring force of history. Ninety-five-year-old Albertan Irene Stainton recalled in 1990 that when she was nineteen, she had watched her mother campaign with Nellie McClung for the right to vote and had considered it all to be just nonsensical fun. Stainton did not appreciate the significance of her mother's efforts until she married, bore three children, and experienced the restrictions of society on women for herself. While Frum intends never to fall into the victim category, her attitude shows why seasoned activists portend a reversal in women's fortune. Believing that complacency could jeopardize the rights women have already won, many ardent feminists see their influence being eroded. Their power base has shifted from the amateur, though skilful, community lobbyists of Irene Murdoch's day to the professionals like Mary Eberts, who can interpret legal technicalities such as how the 1990 Meech Lake accord could have negated women's constitutional rights. Women who lament this change reflect the poignancy of feminists who loved doing battle, and regret what many view as the end of the war.

That the battles of the 1990s will be fought in the courts, or simply on an individual basis in the offices of the nation, rather than with demonstrations on the streets has defeminized the issues, reduced their pejorative aura, and led to what Barbara McDougall, then minister responsible for the status of women, described at the 1988 conference as the "Third Stage of Power."[b] She replaced the complaint of "Look at what we still cannot do," with her upbeat message of "Look what we can do now." Those who contemplate political careers are learning the secrets from mentors who have already made it and are willing to share their knowledge. In three levels of government throughout the country there have been, as of the spring of 1991, hundreds of women mayors and councillors, over one hundred female MLAs, forty women MPs (at one time), four deputy premiers[2], and one premier. The example set by NDP Premier Bob Rae of appointing eleven women to the Ontario provincial cabinet could forever change the composition of Canadian political parties. McDougall's declaration that "men are interested in the game and women in the issues" might sound derogatory, but she identified those differences as a synergy through which "the political arena will be strengthened." She also challenged women not only to respond to current legislation but to initiate it: "We need to lead through the front [door]," to win at least an equal say in the decision-making processes of this country.[c]

The gap between the feminists and the status quo has narrowed not only because women are becoming empowered, but also because women freed from the old patriarchal bonds are using their voice. Largely through feminist-generated initiatives, society has legitimized the concept of human rights, changed family law, brought sexual abuse into the open, set the framework for equality in employment, and made choices available to the Futurists. Natalie Veiner Freeman noted that feminism defined a crucial segment of history from 1960 to 1988, but suggested that it has yet to come to grips with the new-found confidence of the 1990s. In fact, the feminist movement has become an institution in its own right but, ironically, like those it strove to change, is reluctant to alter even its language. The great reformer Thérèse Casgrain always referred to herself as a "humanist" rather than a feminist. In reality, most feminists are not strident agitators at all, but the abrasive image lingers, and unless they redefine themselves and modernize their rhetoric, they could find themselves anachronistic to today's society.

In recent years, corporate attitudes have been shifting towards more open, non-confrontational dialogue. In labour-management arbitration, for example, the language of negotiation has changed from combative demands to courteous mediation. Individuals in law, business, religion, health care, and government are complying with alternatives in their everyday speech. Non-sexist language can lead to tongue-tanglers such as "waiterperson," and "alderperson" which evolved into "councillor." Almost everyone is trying, although Jean Pigott remains intransigent. She declared, "There's no such word as chairwoman in the English language. I'm a chairman."

As for style, Julie Davis, who is second-in-command at the Ontario Federation of Labour, noted, "If you want someone to listen to you, don't shout — lower your voice." She must know, having successfully negotiated a $1.5-million annual grant from the Ontario government to launch the largest workplace literacy program in North America. Experienced negotiators Judi Korbin, Louise Roy, and Helen Sinclair epitomize the new style of mediator, and Shirley Carr, president of the Canadian Labour Congress and trailblazer in the caustic world of labour negotiations, has responded affirmatively to warnings from other, formerly volatile union leaders to soften her attacks.

Three years have passed since Rosalie Abella in her Canadian Club speech defined the 1980s thus: "The lines in this decade seem clearly drawn, as equality and fundamentalism assert competitive claims to superior ideologies. Both sides have abandoned their timidity and donned the confident gloves of legitimacy."[d] Yet by the spring of 1991, the two major organizations speaking for women — NAC for equality, REAL Women for fundamentalism[3]—had lost their media power to journalists like Danielle Crittenden and her sister-in-law Linda Frum. Both young women consider NAC's continued cries for equality as little more than whining. Theirs are the voices of neo-Conservatism, and may not be any more representative of society than are NAC or REAL, but by winning the attention of the media during the late 1980s, Crittenden, Frum, and other journalists of like mind are the opinion makers who will be heard. Prominent Quebec journalist Lise Payette, a former MNA , described a growing mood across the country when she said "People need to be won, inspired, not forced." As the catalyst for one of the largest demonstrations by women in Quebec history,[4] she warned that radical feminism destroys consensus. Today Futurists seeking activist power are more likely to use party politics than women's special interest groups. Demonstrators who shroud themselves in black and lie down in the Toronto traffic to protest "capitalism's exploitation and enslavement of women"[e] may find that no one even bothers to notice them.

The irony is that although NAC and REAL differ on the key issue of abortion, they share some goals. REAL's belief that every woman should be treated with respect regardless of the lifestyle she chooses for herself, echoes the NAC manifesto once advocated by founder Laura Sabia. On the other hand, what could be more provocative than the term "REAL," which implies that non-members are imposters. To many women who have never identified with either group, their battles sound like schoolyard scraps devised by Margaret Atwood's Cordelia.[f] Marjorie LeBreton, Deputy Chief of Staff to the Prime Minister, worried that shrill public statements by any special interest group that claims to speak for women, do a disservice to all women because they reinforce the mistaken notion that women are unable to deal rationally with issues. If she reacted emotionally every time a crisis arose, LeBreton said, "I wouldn't survive one week in this job. The difference is, I don't think of myself as a victim." Even Laura Sabia called for NAC's dissolution and argued that as most of the Royal Commission's recommendations had been implemented, women should now be able to make it on their own. In a Toronto *Sun* article Sabia went further: "Women no longer need child-like protection. . . . Instead of standing . . . tall and doing for ourselves, we're wallowing in self-pity and demanding that the state coddle us."[g] In the urgent need to save our damaged planet from ecological disaster, there seems to be more to guard against together than to fight about in isolation, and the REAL and NAC conflicts reflect the outlook of the 1990s: if you cannot offer a solution, you are part of the problem.

This is the age of Meritocracy, a time in which an increasing number of women thrive on competition, believe they have power, and regard gender issues and safety nets as both confining and detrimental to their goals. They are more interested in examining the national debt than in worrying about something called women's issues, and they recoil from slotting subjects into gender categories. It is particularly offensive to many senior women executives who have adapted successfully to a predominantly male environment to be accused of language or mannerisms that define them as "men in skirts." Feminists who use this weapon are guilty of reverse discrimination, reintroducing the daunting stereotypes of the 1950s and 1960s. More and more women in all sectors of society spurn anyone who claims to speak on their behalf or who imposes constraints or expectations on a gender that has spent so much energy struggling for an independent identity. Many women at the executive level are operating in a professional world beyond gender.

The no-help-needed view is nevertheless anathema to the woman whose history ranges from the Holocaust to the federal Pay Equity Act. For Rosalie Abella, equality must be safely framed in law, and she stated to the Vancouver Canadian Clubs, as if reading a judgement from the bench: "Laws reflect commitment. They entrench objectives. [They] represent a minimum standard below which conduct will not be tolerated. . . . The matter of equality is thus not left to the vagaries of human nature or individual tolerance, but rather is promulgated through law as a social requirement and entitlement."

Doris Anderson maintains her vigilance, writing of the wave of refugees—four out of five of whom are women and children—that is already breaking up into cultural ghettoes across the country.[h] Isolated from integrated Canadian communities, many new mothers remain subject to the cultural shackles of societies criticized by Amnesty International for their mistreatment of women. Outside immigrant cultures, abuse of women in established Canadian communities remains endemic. Journalist Stephen Hume reported that in 1990, two-thirds of the women killed in Canada died in the so-called safety of their homes, and although the massacre at l'École Polytechnique de Montréal was front-page news, only six months later the tragedy of nine Montreal wives and children who were murdered "in one bloody month by vengeful husbands and jealous lovers . . . sank beneath our apathy."[i]

In closing her 1988 speech, Abella emphasized that a support system is vital to the concept of fairness: "Declaring that women have an equal right to work without providing accessible child care makes the right a shibboleth. [We must] end the insidious double standard that acts as a form of psychological contraceptive blackmail for women contemplating combining families with jobs." And that, she asserted, means making accommodation for "the historical and biological differences of women, the child bearers, the economic shock absorbers of society."

Today the reality is that women are entering the workforce in record numbers either because they enjoy the challenge, want to be responsible for their lives, or need the money to survive. Whatever the reason, working women are here to stay, and consultant Heather Reisman is concerned that if we stop the effort to change corporations that remain even subtly hostile to the notion of working mothers, "we are giving up on children. We are forfeiting our grandchildren." Women who aspire to become executives are simply going to stop having children because many are coming to believe that they cannot do it all.

Statistics are always open to interpretation,[5j] but until industry alters its policies to accommodate women employees who have children, many cannot take advantage of the improved climate for advancement. For them, protection by law seems to remain a necessary evil. The statistics make a bleak background for what is being called "the feminization of poverty" or, as Yolande Cohen put it, "the welfare state which is mainly for women." Negative conclusions about women's advancement in institutions can always be made by the statistically armed,[6k] however Futurists interpret the bad news not as discrimination, but as part of paying their dues. Their irrepressible belief is that women *can* make it to the top, and if they do not, they may be sabotaging themselves.

Those who are enjoying the power game dismiss the Abella creed. As Montreal litigator Lorraine Duguay said, "We've made it. Men accept us as colleagues. We are not having problems, we're having fun." With so many women graduating from the professional faculties and gaining proficiency in their respective disciplines, the success of a clear-thinking, assertive meritocracy is overshadowing the 1960s principle of advancement through seniority and the 1980s use of affirmative action. Expertise is superseding notions of age or gender. Women have become so comfortable with their positions that they are tossing out the gorilla-shouldered power suits, painting their law and publishing offices dusty-rose, and then doing battle in the marketplace with the zeal of their male colleagues. As Natalie Veiner Freeman put it, "It's tough out there for men, too. It always has been. The Futurists have no illusions about who their enemies are. They are just a different kind of troop heading into the field." In 1982, Peter C. Newman said of corporate power, "They [men] are warring over the exponential growth of their power. . . . These guys spend their energy trying to kill each other off. That is the meaning of free enterprise. It's a Darwinian jungle."[l] There are women who enjoy playing that game, too, just as there are men who pursue excellence through consensus.

Competition, strategy, and winning are all human characteristics, and in a utopia ruled by women, power plays would still abound. In 1984, Brascan chief Trevor Eyton told author Patricia Best, "I'm not sure I've met very many women who would look me in the eye and say: 'I want to be the chief executive officer of this company.'"[m] Mary Suzanne Lamont phoned him with a challenge: if she could find some women who wanted his job, would he entertain them? Eyton cheerfully agreed. It cost him lunch for seventy women at the Toronto Four Seasons Hotel.

Futurists like Crittenden or Frum who denounce the feminist movement do not seem to realize that they personify it. The tenets that call for fair play and respect are integral to their psyches. Today, a woman executive who discovers her salary is less than her male counterpart marches to the boss's office and thrashes it out with demands for retroactive pay. She knows that human rights tribunals protect her from being fired for her temerity. Hiring practices have improved immeasurably since the years when Bruna Giacomazzi was told that women were not eligible for management positions, or when a Manitoba separate school board would not employ Sharon Carstairs because she was married and might become pregnant. And while Rosann Cashin fought a seven-year "conflict of interest" dismissal from the CBC just because her then husband, Richard Cashin, president of NFFAWU the fisheries union, was also on the board of Petro-Canada,[7] CBC bureau chief Terry Hargreaves kept his job even though his wife, Jodi White, was serving as Chief of Staff in the office of Cabinet Minister Joe Clark, before becoming the executive director of the Conservative Party of Canada.

No one relinquishes power willingly. "Don't look to men (or anyone) to give up power; you've got to fight for it,"[n] Jean Pigott has said. But the corporate climate of hierarchical control is changing. The chasms between executive dictatorships and secretarial pools, unions and management, feminists and fundamentalists are shrinking. The increasing presence of women at the executive level in business has led to a corporate vernacular that includes "team participation" and "co-operative decision making." Those who still complain about systemic discrimination in the institutions are having difficulties being heard. No one wants to write about them any more, particularly in the light of the sweeping decisions announced by former trade-union lawyer Beth Symes as chair of the Ontario pay-equity hearings tribunal.[8o]

Although the Carney task force on barriers to women's advancing in the public service concluded that opportunities for promotion remain limited, and that the corporate culture is still hostile, an unquenchable optimism can be felt among women executives who believe they are sufficiently equipped to get on with it. As journalist Brenda Dalglish said,[p] "If being a woman is the problem, there is no solution."

Just how to use power is a conundrum with which many women are still struggling. The number of role models is increasing, but women are still learning not to apologize for power and to own it with grace. Calgary *Herald* associate editor Catherine Ford warned, "Nobody can give you power. They can give you a powerful job [but not] the power that goes with it. You have to have that internal sense of leadership."

Heather Reisman, whose specialty is organizational change, encourages women to acknowledge their power, to stop feeling guilty about how it was acquired. She said, "Canadians in general are intimidated by the notion of power. It doesn't matter *how* you are central to it — whether you have married it, or have accessed it politically, business-wise, socially, or how high you are in the official hierarchy. It just matters that you are close to the nerve centre of what is going on in your organization.'' A conviction of their individual and unlimited potential is becoming a source of increasing strength to many women.

Ultimately, the greatest power is internal, an inner sanctum of strength that has less to do with world views, feminist associations, or legislated protection than it does with self-esteem. Women who view themselves as victims will continue to be treated as victims. None of the winners in *Invisible Power* succeeded because they demanded equality or were protected by pay equity. They made it because they recognized no interior barriers; they *knew* they could do it. Neither practising subservience nor depending on government safety nets, they rose to the top using their own resources of confidence, perseverance, and discipline, while pursuing the concept of excellence. Many benefitted from extensive university educations, but only a handful had the doors opened for them by wealth and name. That some of them like Rosalie Abella devote their lives to the pursuit of fairness, has little to do with the fact that they succeeded by themselves. Like Abella, many acknowledge phenomenal luck as well as caring mentors, but neither can sustain success without that internal empowerment.

Perhaps the Kaaydah Schattens were really the privileged children. They started with less than nothing, but they possessed an unshakeable self-reliance peculiar to the dispossessed. Independent thinkers rejected by society, they refused to succumb to a siege mentality, and were thus unhampered by society's cultural restrictions. Society would have understood if Kaaydah Schatten's tragic childhood had left her a welfare dependent. But on the day the six-year-old made a deal to work in exchange for her siblings' care, she discovered the powerful alchemy of harsh reality bound to faith in oneself. A grateful Schatten said of the woman who hired her, ''I learned that I could control my life. After that, anything was possible.''

The cycle that fosters the notion of perpetual victim must be stopped somewhere. If empowerment rather than safety-nets is the answer, then the first step must be for society to stop accepting atrocities such as battered women. As that is not going to happen immediately, women must influence change by helping themselves. Children of both sexes need to develop self-esteem and mutual respect, together with a sense of responsibilty for the quality of their lives. Girls need to learn how to avoid getting into abusive relationships, let alone bearing children into them. Psychologist Lynda Bentall would add an Outward Bound course to the education of every twelve-year-old girl to let her discover that she can conquer fear, and succeed, through her own potential and the positive power of teamwork.

Rosalie Abella and Barbara Amiel illustrate the extremes of a societal seesaw balanced on the fulcrum of democracy. The former judge seeks a kinder, fairer society through legislation, while the controversial commentator warns that lurking within state paternalism are humiliation, degradation, and inertia for those citizens who have never known how to help themselves. Barbara Amiel's credo that everyone has the right to leave home at fourteen and thrash her way to the top is severe but significant. Universal care is the bond from which many women are struggling to be liberated. In the superlative democratic society there would be no need for affirmative action programs. In casting social safety nets across this land, Canadians must guard against becoming a society that will never know what constitutes initiative and the power of creativity.

Maureen Sabia, current chair of the Economic Development Council, daughter of NAC founder Laura Sabia, and pal of Barbara Amiel, is a vociferous antagonist of safety nets for women. In the late 1960s, after successfully articling with the all-male law firm McCarthy and McCarthy, she was told that she could not continue on there because clients would think they were getting second best from a woman. Sabia went on to disprove this on her own, and argues that women who demand legislated intervention for fairness are simply replacing parents or spouses with government control and are no freer than before.

The key to infinite empowerment is education, yet it remains the last of the institutions to respond to changes in society. In 1989, Carol Goar, national affairs columnist with the Toronto *Star*, emphasized the need for a national system of public education based on a federal philosophy backed by funds and a vehicle for implementation.[9] Goar warned that the provinces' insular perspective and constant bickering with Ottawa will leave education in a morass of confusion, ill prepared to help anyone with the future.[q] That future begins now, and the educational system does have an opportunity for substantial change by the end of this decade when large numbers of tenured academic and administrative staff will retire.

Sylvia Ostry charged in a 1991 speech to the Vancouver Board of Trade[r] that the Canadian economic system lacks innovation, and the solution must be sought through extensive public education changes, as well as increased research and development programs beyond the post secondary level. But few institutions hate change more than the universities,[10s] particularly as new structures could shatter the educational Richter scale. Educators with fresh, flexible ideas must become a part of the new executive structure and this must include women. A decade ago, the progressive views of Margaret Fulton, then president of Mount Saint Vincent University, caused some colleagues to describe her as a "lethal opponent." Yet Fulton was held in such high esteem elsewhere that in 1987 Prime Minister Gro Harlem Brundtland invited her to come to Norway to devise the administration and curricula for a new university. Attitudes towards women university administrators have changed in the last few years, and Patricia Marchak, the first woman Dean of Arts in the seventy-five-year history of the University of British Columbia[11] is optimistic that as well as being welcomed as productive research scholars, qualified women in far greater numbers will become integral components of the executive and policy-making structure.[12] [13]

The 1991 appointment of economist and former Shell Canada executive Elizabeth Parr-Johnston as president of Mount Saint Vincent emphasizes that innovative business management is of genuine interest to a campus population that is 85 percent female. Retiring president Naomi Hersom had already expressed the need to prepare students for an economically tougher and more competitive decade. The appointment of scientist Geraldine Kenney-Wallace, former chair of the Science Council of Canada, as president of McMaster University[14] makes a significant statement in an era when many girls are still advised that math and science are not important to their careers. Global warming, dying rain forests, and explosive reproductive technology underscore that it is the scientists[15] who not only affect the quality of our lives but hold in their collective hands the physical, and to some extent the moral, fate of our universe.

Native activist Yvonne Lavallee has observed, "Education, not government assistance, is the critical tool [for women]. [It] is the key to open the doors to manage our lives, our resources, our future." Everyone is a potential educator: everyone has the power to inspire positive change. It can be as basic as fashion maven Joan Druxman's showing a battered woman how to get legal protection, how to find a job, how to become self-sufficient. Canada's great humanist June Callwood encourages the young guests at her Toronto homes to change their lives through re-education programs. Helping children to discover their abilities through the performing arts is an innovation of Vancouver dancer/sculptor Carol Henriquez, creator of Arts Umbrella. It began with forty-five children in a church basement and currently, through its school outreach program, affects 20,000 children annually.[16] In the summer of 1991, Lynda and Robert Bentall designed, financed, and launched their own "Ailanthus,"[17] a sophisticated creative arts program co-ordinated with the Vancouver Public School Board and focused specifically on underprivileged inner-city kids. Henriquez and the Bentalls believe children who discover an internal creative force fire the spark of self-esteem, personal commitment, and desire for excellence.

Education can flow from structured organizations such as Junior Achievement, which, under former chair Sonja Bata, introduced entrepreneurial classes into the Ontario elementary schools. The YMCA's Youth Enterprise Centres, where the advisory board is chaired by Dian Cohen, provides warehouse space and guidance for young entrepreneurs. One project completed by the Canadian Foundation for Economic Education is a video series, "Entrepreneurship for Canadians," distributed to high schools, colleges, and universities.[18] The Calmeadow Foundation, created by Martin Connell and Linda Haynes, encourages micro-enterprises and economic self-reliance among the disadvantaged.[19] Deanna Rosenswig, a senior vice-president at the Bank of Montreal, is the vice-chair of Connell's board and also a member of the Finance Committee of Women's World Banking, a non-profit organization dedicated to guaranteeing small loans to women who lack access to credit. In her own league is Claudette MacKay-Lassonde, former president of the Association of Professional Engineers of Ontario and a graduate of l'École Polytechnique de Montréal. Chair of the Canadian Engineering Manpower Board, the forty-three-year-old MacKay-Lassonde is perceived to be one of the most powerful role models for women in the professional fields.

****

Empowerment and self-sufficiency are bringing winners the thrill of participating in the various systems that run this country, and the numbers are growing. Caldwell Partners International, the executive search firm, said that in 2,000 searches since 1985, 28 percent of the jobs have gone to women. The reason, said chair Douglas Caldwell, is not affirmative action but a growing expertise among women.[20t] The number of senior women managers has more than doubled over the last five years and the next generation of women executives could sweep past the trailblazers who coined the phrase "the glass ceiling." Valerie Casselton, Vancouver *Sun* labour columnist, dared women to stop cataloguing past injustices in favour of making the most of the power they have now and claiming jobs and salaries within their reach.[u] In the past ten years when governments were hastily meeting demands for equality by appointing women to the ABCs, hundreds ignored accusations of accepting token appointments or patronage to seize this opportunity first to learn and then to assume positions of leadership. All across Canada women continue to seek responsibility by participating in the game as it exists, and then, if they wish, instilling into it a subtle feminine ambience.

Those women who cannot break through invisible barriers or who tire of the corporate game simply become entrepreneurs. A 1988 CACSW study, "Women Entrepreneurs: Building a Strong Canadian Economy," predicted that by 1990 women would start 65 percent of the new small businesses and their failure rate would be half that of men. The study was correct. This aptitude for flexibility indicates that women can create their own corporate institutions. Breaking through to the top may ultimately be less significant than the success of those who left the corporations to start their own companies.

****

Will the advent of more women at policy-making levels humanize institutions? Professor Jill Vickers remains unconvinced that some magic number of women will transform everything. She advised women to "develop a conscious strategy for change."[v] NDP Leader Audrey McLaughlin observed in 1990 that bringing more women into politics or other institutions is not necessarily going to advance women's interests. Citing the records of Conservative women members of parliament as examples, she said that she would rather see the needs of women represented by male social democrats than by women who expect other women to tough it out independently.[w] Her remark emphasizes the point that we'll have achieved civilized society when women *and* men can take any place on the human spectrum rather than be limited to the confines of paleolithic stereotypes.

Still, there is some proof that women are changing attitudes in the corporate institutions. Journalist Jane Allan discovered that a new breed of executives "are team builders motivated by a vision for the company instead of personal power. . . . And they're often women."[x] In the closing arguments of her debate with Barbara Amiel, Rosemary Brown claimed the increase in prosecutions for child abuse in British Columbia was directly related to the larger number of women lawyers in the prosecutor's office. Only 9 percent of federally appointed judges are women, but the appearance of women on the Supreme Court of Canada—beginning with Bertha Wilson in 1982—has changed the character of that body. For example, the "battered wife syndrome" was recognized and accepted as a defence by the Supreme Court, and women such as Judge Andrée Ruffo presiding on the provincial benches are making a difference.

Justice Carol Huddart of the B.C. Supreme Court jailed a father of two for contempt of court after he had defied orders to pay child maintenance for five years, even though his annual income exceeded $200,000. That judgement sent shock waves across the country, warning the thousands of parents delinquent in support payments that their neglect will no longer be tolerated.

The University of Victoria's Maureen Maloney is typical of the women deans in four law faculties across the country[21] in placing a greater emphasis on the feminine perspective in the evolving curriculum. The University of British Columbia dean of law, Lynn Smith, and assistant professor Isabel Grant were commissioned by Rosalie Abella and the Ontario Law Reform Commission to study "Gender Representation in the Canadian Judiciary."[y] The professors studied the method, philosophy, and politics involved in appointing judges, and the results, published widely in 1991, called for more stringent and equitable guidelines in the appointment of judges. Their findings were underscored by forty-two-year-old Mary Hogan who said, when appointed Ontario's deputy attorney-general in 1991, that she aims to expand legal clinics for the public, come to grips with the cost of litigation, and take aim at "the [judicial] system's white male dominance."[z]

The organizations LEAF and NAWL are intervening powers that ensure the protection of minorities in the courts, and the native law program at universities has enabled native lawyers to argue on their own behalf for land claims. Justice Minister Kim Campbell held a symposium in June 1991 called Women, Law, and the Administration of Justice.[22] Also in 1991, the Canadian Bar Association appointed Bertha Wilson, now retired from the Supreme Court of Canada, to head a task force for a two-year study of women and the legal profession that will include gender equality in the courts and "gender sensitization" of judges. By May 1991, Wilson was already garnering a lot of media print on her speeches about family violence and in a speech to B'nai Brith, she made a plea to police, the courts, and society to end "Band-Aid remedies" for the crimes of wife assault and incest.[aa]

Women in positions of power are affecting the traditional outlook of the judiciary, if not by statute, then by convincing the legal profession to impose programs for re-education upon itself. Just how much the judiciary has changed in one year became evident in May 1991 when Gwendolyn Landoldt, representing REAL Women, placed an official complaint against Justice Beverley McLachlin for her "partisan" views in charging that some criminal laws lead to unfair and unequal treatment of women.[bb] The Canadian Judicial Council not only dismissed the complaint, but praised Justice McLachlin for making the comments.[cc]

While she was Police Commissioner of Metro Toronto, Jane Pepino influenced employment equity, child-care services for officers and staff, and equitable promotions in the police force. She supports the argument that the increased numbers of women at executive levels and on boards of institutions have had an impact on the amelioration of society, or at least on the laws and attitudes that more accurately reflect a sense of fairness in attempting to accommodate the needs of all people.

These are times when the awareness of gender equality, human need, and social justice could find a balance with the entrepreneurial drive of the Futurists. The next ten years should see a monumental increase of young women in leadership positions. It still may be another decade before the current Futurists show a preference for the CEO's chair over starting their own businesses, but Beverley McLachlin could become the first female Chief Justice of the Supreme Court of Canada. In July 1991 we saw Rita Johnston wrest the premiership of British Columbia away from Grace McCarthy by sixty votes. We could see Kim Campbell and Barbara McDougall competing for the leadership of the federal Conservative party, or, with Audrey McLaughlin heading a revitalized NDP party, possibly the first woman prime minister of Canada.

Of all the forces of power, it is the economic that reigns supreme. As June Callwood put it, "Those who value the human spirit might deplore the idea but in modern society, money is mobility, money is dignity, and money is protection. A woman who can earn as much as a man . . . has her future in her own hands. . . . Few people attack their equals.''[23dd] When the Martha Blackburns and Jeannine Guillevin-Woods are dealing in hundreds of millions of dollars, the issue is not gender. It is power. Barbara Amiel touched on women's need for women to learn the basics of money management when she said to Vicki Gabereau, ''If I could start all over again . . . I would train women not about their rights but . . . about the wonders of compound interest. . . . If we had financial freedom, we wouldn't need any of the other stuff.''[ee]

Generations of Establishment homemakers/socialites had the key—money power—behind them. Throughout this century they have exhibited a canny resourcefulness in outmanoeuvring many restrictions of their culture to become an amalgam of ambassador and power player. Today's Establishment woman remains a shrewd operator, still camouflaging her routes to that power with secrecy and grace, but through boards, tribunals, order-in-council positions, and the proverbial dinner table she is also emerging as a not-so-subtle activist. The once compliant Establishment ladies have evolved into the Lisa Woodwards and Heather Mackays—an elitist, Futurist scrum who will not be pushed around. CFTO documentary producer Isabel Bassett hits hard with her films on the deterioration of neighbourhoods plagued by drugs, the victims of which are frequently single-parent mothers and children. And Gail Regan, backed by her mother, Helen Phelan, commandeered the Women's College Hospital board from her own peers, fighting for a principle in a public way once forbidden by her culture. That the Establishment is speaking out reflects the opinion of Gillian Steward who said, ''All of us are born with a different spirit, a different personality [that some have subjugated for too long]. At some point it is going to come out no matter what happens.''

Wealthy Establishment Women like Elizabeth Tory, Ruth Goldbloom, Countess Dobrzensky, Brenda Norris, Hilary Weston, Mary Alice Stuart, Tannis Richardson, Isabel Diamond, Ruth Grant, Jenny Belzberg, Eve MacDougall, and Sandra Kolber know that subscribing to the principles of a liberal democracy means volunteering the energy and expertise to make the country work. Government simply cannot handle all the demands for social and cultural assistance, and these are the players who can both give it and get it for those who cannot. Charities and non-profit organizations are far and away the winners, but these savvy strategists are also enjoying either the participation in choosing the projects of family foundations or the entrepreneurial flavour of deal making—of juggling the risks and complexities inherent in every fund-raising undertaking. Intimately connected to corporate power—after all, they sleep with it—and familiar with its complexities and processes, they welcome the influence generated by vast wealth. If feminists want to share in that power for their causes, they must win the Establishment's trust.[24] The most successful organization to be accepted by the New Establishment is LEAF, which has replaced what was feared as strident activism with the legitimacy of the courts. With the aid of broad-based funding from the general public and increasingly from the Establishment, litigators are providing the essential professionalism and diplomacy to fight the new-age war.

On Vancouver Island in the spring of 1991, another symposium was held. Many of the sixty women attending Women Toward the Millennium can be found in the pages of *Invisible Power,* and the composition was markedly different from that of the 1988 Ottawa conference. Present were not only the professional theorists such as Rosalie Abella, who spoke about the long-term "cost benefits" of equality in employment,[ff] but also the women vice-presidents of banks and businesses ranging from forestry products and airlines to multinationals, all of which face the bottom-line challenge of implementing pay equity while they are trying to survive in a global marketplace. Speaking of the pay equity hikes being made to women across the country, Helen Sinclair welcomed the principle but warned of dangers in consuming wealth without regenerating it. There is an urgent need for a viable strategy to create wealth, she said, warning that "you cannot build rights on the backs of future generations."[gg]

Present at the millennium conference were some proud to call themselves feminist and others who wouldn't be caught dead with the label. There were at least three raised in Establishment wealth, a Liberal senator, the Conservative justice minister, several members of the NDP, labour negotiators, deans of law and other educators. In an atmosphere charged with intellectual energy and good will, women debated from their disparate ideological views, seeking practical solutions to the hard-core issues facing society. The event moved toward meeting the challenge made by Jill Vickers in her closing remarks at the 1988 Ottawa symposium. Vickers had called upon women to create new institutions, to join traditional economic power with professionally presented activist goals marketed in non-inflammatory ways. The result, she predicted, would be a shared power in which women could not only determine their own destiny, but could change the world.

CHAPTER 18 NOTES

1. Marois served as minister of various portfolios before being defeated in the 1985 election when the PQ lost power. She also ran unsuccessfully for the leadership of the party but was its vice-president, and is president of the Commission on Social affairs for the PQ. She was re-elected in the general election of 1989 in the Taillon riding.
2. Deputy premiers in British Columbia were Grace McCarthy and Rita Johnston, who became premier. Althea Landry serves in New Brunswick, and Lise Bacon in Quebec.
3. NAC's umbrella has covered as many as four million women while REAL claims a national membership of around 50,000. Nevertheless, the smaller organization is significant in terms of power because it has won a voice through the media.
4. Payette, who was a minister in the PQ government, is remembered for her comment during the 1980 sovereignty referendum debate that the late Madeleine Ryan, wife of then Liberal leader Claude Ryan, was an "Yvette," the housewife character in Quebec elementary school textbooks. Many Quebeckers believe Payette was responsible for disrupting the momentum of the pro-sovereignty "oui" side. Furious women turned out in record numbers to vote against the proposition.
5. Statistics Canada and the National Council of Welfare report that 59 percent of the poor are women, usually single mothers whose child-care problems make it difficult to work or upgrade their skills; that women still earn 64 cents for every dollar earned by men, and that men with high school diplomas can earn the same amount as women with a university degree; that in divorce cases before recent enforcement programs were put in place, 85 percent of husbands defaulted on child-support payments, and that percentage since enforcement has dropped by 42 percent; that following divorce, living standards for many women and children drop by 73 percent while men's rise by 42 percent.
6. In 1988, the *Globe and Mail* reported that of 211 directors on boards of Canada's major banks, only 5.7 percent were women. Statistics from the Canadian Bankers' Association in 1990 put the number of women

at the vice-president level and higher at 60 out of 1,019, or 6 percent. Of 4,538 managers in the public service, 481 were women. ''Beneath the Veneer,'' the 1990 report on barriers to women in the public service, found that women make up almost half the federal public service but account for 14 percent of its senior management positions. In a 1988 paper, ''Women in Power: The Real Threat to Corporate Culture,'' CACSW president Gladys Symons reported that since 1979, ten of fifty senate appointments have gone to women. Since the Conservative government took power in 1984, it has appointed women to 31 percent of order-in-council positions, increased women deputy ministers from seven to twenty-three, and appointed thirteen women to diplomatic missions abroad. In 1990, 14 percent of the Members of Parliament were women, but they constituted 21 percent of the membership on female-oriented, ''soft issues'' committees such as health, social service, tourism, and culture, and only 7 percent on ''hard issues'' committees.

7. In Newfoundland in September 1981, when Rosann Cashin, resources broadcaster for CBC radio, was fired, she sued for wrongful dismissal. Following seven years of expensive battles, she was reinstated with lost wages, $2,500 for hurt feelings and loss of self-respect, and her request to work in Ottawa granted. She is currently writing and broadcasting for CBC radio's ''Open House'' in Ottawa, and still fighting to get her legal fees paid by the Canadian Human Rights Commission, which had ruled initially that she did not have a case.
8. Rosalie Abella's 1986 observation that the impact of her pay-equity commission could be monumental was referring to its impact on social justice, but the up-front financial impact is equally enormous. The Manitoba board of commissioners estimated a $16-million cost over four years to realize pay equity just for the city of Winnipeg's 10,000 employees. In 1991, Ontario's new NDP government extended what the *Economist* described as ''the world's toughest pay-equity law'' to include all of the private sector firms and government agencies in the province that employ more than ten workers. In Ontario, these amendments to the pay-equity law affect a total of 1.7 million women workers. In 1990, the extra cost to Ontario public hospitals to make necessary wage hikes was $50 million. Employers

are required to set aside at least 1 percent of their total payroll annually to achieve pay-equity.

9. While it was hardly the national philosophy of which Goar wrote, Barbara McDougall when Minister of Employment and Immigration re-allocated almost $1.3 billion of unemployment insurance funds into job-training and upgrading skills.
10. In his 1987 book about doctoral programs in North American universities, *The PhD Trap*, Wilfred Cude wrote that PhD programs were ''inflexible, cumbersome, restrictive and deplorably wasteful.''
11. At the University of Toronto, Ann Saddlemyer is Master of Massey College; Marcia Chandler was appointed dean of the faculty of Arts and Science, and was short-listed in 1989 for the presidency of the prestigious Radcliffe College in Cambridge, Massachusetts.
12. Dean Marchak was a key member of a 1960s group that pushed for Canadian Studies programs and Canadian texts during a time when Canadian economic studies were presented by American theorists employing American research material.
13. Professor of Architecture Blanche van Ginkel was not only a trailblazer for women in design, but in 1980 she became the first woman dean of architecture in Canada and the second in North America when she assumed the position at the University of Toronto from 1980 to 1982. In 1986 she became president of the Association of Collegiate Schools of Architecture, a North American, internationally connected body.
14. Other women who are currently presidents of Canadian universities are Eva Kushner of Victoria University in the University of Toronto, who promotes appointment of qualified women into the faculty, Marsha Hanen, University of Winnipeg, who advocates incorporating women's studies into the mainstream studies of history and law, and Marion Fry, King's College, associated with Dalhousie University, who places emphasis on creative thinking.
15. Among Canada's most influential scientists are UBC professor Edith McGeer, microbiology; Science Council of Canada chair Janet Halliwell; Julia Levy of Quadralogic, cancer research; Ursula Franklin, professor of metallurgy and material science, University of Toronto, who also focusses on furthering peace and fostering international understanding; Sylvia Fedoruk, currently lieutenant-governor of Saskatchewan, who studied

with physicist Dr. Harold Johns, the inventor of radioactive cobalt treatment of cancer; geneticist Penelope Allerdice at Memorial University of Newfoundland, who identified the Allerdice Syndrome; geneticist Patricia Baird of UBC, chair of the Royal Commission on New Reproductive Technologies; and ethicist Margaret Somerville, director of the McGill University Centre for Medicine, Ethics and Law. Roberta Bondar, Canada's only woman astronaut, is an MD and has a doctorate in neurobiology. She is currently working with NASA.

16. Named by Trudi Pekarsky, Arts Umbrella is supported by government for only 5 percent of its budget and raises funds at an annual art auction supported by prominent artists and by corporations such as Alcan. Its two vans, "Van Go" and "Stage Coach," visit schools in the East End and inner city.
17. The Ailanthus is a tree in China that is impervious to the grimiest, most dismal conditions. The worse its surroundings are, the more it blooms. This program will target 200 high risk children annually in thirteen schools where gang recruitment begins at the Grade 5 level—75 percent of these children belong to single parents and homes where violence, drugs, alcohol, and teenage pregnancy are common. Ailanthus aims to break this despairing cycle.
18. This foundation is backed by business and all the provincial governments to inspire youth to respond creatively to change. The video series committee was co-chaired by Jalynn Bennett and Timothy Casgrain of Hees International Bancorp, with David Culver and Senator Trevor Eyton as honorary co-chairs, and included businesspeople who succeeded, such as Jim Pattison, and those such as Nelson Skalbania who failed but returned to try again.
19. The Calmeadow Foundation provides through its First People's Fund small loans of $50 to $1,200 to home enterprises for persons locked out of the traditional credit sources. Four Indian reserves in particular are using the program with impressive results: Kettle and Stoney Point, Sachigo Lake, Wikwemikong, and Whitefish River First Nation Reserve, all in Ontario.
20. In 1990 at the University of Toronto, women made up 36 percent of all MBA students, 41 percent of law students, and 17 percent of engineering students. Figures show a 38 percent increase from 1984 to 1989 of

women into middle management compared to 12 percent for men. The senior management level remains low at 12 percent.

21. The University of Calgary appointed Margaret Hughes in 1984, followed in 1989 by Constance Hunt; Hélène Dumont is the Dean of Law at l'Université de Montréal; Maureen Maloney and Lynn Smith are Deans of Law at the University of Victoria and the University of British Columbia respectively.
22. The symposium addressed three wide-ranging issues that include all facets of justice from law school to the bench: the substantive law as it relates to women, women and the administration of justice, and women and the legal profession.
23. No one would agree more than battered women who are still losing custody of their children because of insufficient funds to access lawyers fast enough to claim custody before their abusive husbands do.
24. Post-Establishment Nancy Jackman created the Canadian Women's Foundation to encourage women to donate to causes not usually supported by men. Jackman said that less than one percent of foundation money goes to women's causes such as battered women's or street kids' shelters, or girls' schools.

ENDNOTES

INTRODUCTION: THE ILLUSION OF POWER/1

a. Barbara Sgroi, ''Beauty Queens,'' *Flare*, September 1989.
b. Douglas O'Neill, ''Money, Power, Influence: The Top 50,'' *Toronto Life*, May 1990.

CHAPTER 1, THE CEOs OF SOCIAL POWER/9

a. Margaret Atwood, ''Weight,'' *Vogue*, August 1990.
b. Nicholas Coleridge, *The Fashion Conspiracy*, London: Heinemann-Mandarin (Octopus Publishing Group), 1988, p. 56.
c. Alyse Frampton, ''Sold! To the woman in the black dress,'' *Saturday Night*, March 1989.
d. Jack Todd, ''The Very Rich do 'the right thing' for $300 a plate,'' Montreal *Gazette*, 23 Sept. 1989.
e. Diane Dupuy (with Liane Heller), *Dare to Dream*, Toronto: Key Porter Books, 1988, pp. 226-30.
f. Ibid., p. 229.

CHAPTER 2, THE NEW ESTABLISHMENT/35

a. Yvonne Cox, ''When push came to shove at Women's College Hospital,'' *Chatelaine*, September 1990.
b. Ibid.
c. Doris French, *Ishbel and the Empire: A Biography of Lady Aberdeen*, Toronto and Oxford: Dunern Press, 1988.
d. Penney Kome, *Women of Influence*, Toronto: Doubleday Canada, 1985, p. 23.
e. Nelson W. Aldrich Jr., *Old Money*, New York: Alfred A. Knopf, 1988, p. 41.
f. Julie Connelly, ''The CEO's second wife,'' *Fortune*, 28 Aug. 1989.
g. Peter C. Newman, ''Adventures in the Rich Art Trade,'' *Maclean's*, 22 May 1989.

h. Peter C. Newman, *The Acquisitors: The Canadian Establishment*, Volume 2, Toronto: McClelland and Stewart, 1981, p. 24.
i. Tina Brown, ''Gayfryd Takes Over,'' Vanity Fair, November 1986.

PART II, ACTIVIST POWER/59

a. Natalie Veiner Freeman, ''Student of Power,'' *City Woman*, Fall 1982.

CHAPTER 3, THE GRASSROOTS MOVEMENT/61

a. Stevie Cameron, ''People always feel better after they talk to Rosalie Abella,'' *Globe and Mail*, 20 Nov. 1986.
b. Rosalie Abella, ''The Impact of Equality,'' speech to the Vancouver Canadian Clubs, 5 Feb. 1988.
c. Thérèse F. Casgrain, *A Woman in a Man's World*, Toronto: McClelland and Stewart, 1972, p. 72.
d. Ibid, p. 113.
e. Ibid, p. 138.

CHAPTER 4, THE TURBULENT DECADES/73

a. Rosalie Abella, speech to the Vancouver Canadian Clubs, 5 Feb. 1988.
b. Barry Craig, ''Women's march may back call for rights probe,'' *Globe and Mail*, 5 Jan. 1967.
c. Mary Lile Benham, ''Headline History Interpreted for Youthful Listeners,'' *Saturday Night*, 3 March 1945.
d. Florence, Bird *Anne Francis: An Autobiography*, Toronto and Vancouver: Clarke, Irwin & Company, 1974.
e. Craig McKie, ''The Law: A Changing Profession,'' *Canadian Social Trends—Statistics Canada*, Summer 1986.
f. Penney Kome, *Women of Influence*, Toronto: Doubleday Canada, 1985.
g. Penney Kome, *The Taking of Twenty-Eight*, Toronto: The Women's Press, 1983.
h. Reference by Kome, *Women of Influence*, p. 134.
i. Ibid, pp. 135-36.
j. Penney Kome, *The Taking of Twenty-Eight*, Toronto: The Women's Press, 1983, p. 108.

k. Ibid, p. 104.
l. M.P. Connelly, "Women in the Labour Force," *Canadian Encyclopedia*, 2nd edition, Edmonton: Hurtig Publishers, 1988, p. 2326.

CHAPTER 5, WINNERS IN THE POWER GAME/101

a. Vladimir Il'ich Lenin, *The Three Sources and Three Component Parts of Marxism*, translated by Max Eastman, United States: republished by Imported Publications, 1976.
b. Angela Miles, "Integrative Feminism," *Fireweed: A Feminist Quarterly*, Summer/Fall 1984.
c. Kelly McParland, "Hongkong Bank will shift assets overseas," *Financial Post*, 18 Dec. 1990.
d. Anne Collins, "Why We're not Number One," *Canadian Business*, November 1988.
e. Greg Weston, "Blais-Grenier quits cabinet over oil refinery closure," *Ottawa Citizen*, 2 Jan. 1986.
f. Carol Goar, "McDougall: A victim of circumstance," Toronto *Star*, 24 March 1988.
g. Bertha Wilson, "Will Women Judges Really Make a Difference?" speech presented at Osgoode Hall Law School, 8 Feb. 1990.
h. Robert Matas, "Change attitudes not laws, feminists told," *Globe and Mail*, 5 Nov. 1990.
i. Maureen Forrester with Marci McDonald, *Out of Character*, Toronto: McClelland and Stewart, 1986, p. 208.
j. Jane Allan, "When Women Set The Rules," *Canadian Business*, April 1991.
k. Robert Mason Lee, "Nobody's Baby," *Saturday Night*, November 1985.
l. Leslie Scrivener, "Coping With Copps," Toronto *Star*, 6 March 1988.
m. Hugo Young, *One of Us*, London: Macmillan, 1989, p. 312.
n. Anne Collins, "Why We're Not Number One," *Canadian Business*, Nov. 1988, Pelchat's words are, "The importance of the issue of your sex diminishes directly in proportion to the rise in your personal power."
o. Ibid.
p. Linda Crompton, Letter to the Editor, *Globe and Mail Report on Business Magazine*, December 1990.

q. Canadian Press, ''Conduct charges hit youth judge,'' Vancouver *Province,* 23 Oct. 1990.
r. Benoit Aubin, ''Residents protest route for huge hydro power line,'' Montreal *Gazette,* 17 July 1986.

CHAPTER 6, THE SENIOR EXECUTIVES/133

a. Claudia Glenn Dowling, ''The Testing of Dory Yochum,'' *Life,* August 1990, p. 55.
b. Brenda Dalglish, ''Having It All,'' *Maclean's,* 3 Sept. 1990.
c. Jonathan Ferguson, ''Canadian Bankers' Association presents more than a new face,'' Toronto *Star,* 30 Oct. 1989.
d. Bob Power, ''Let's Make A Deal,'' *B.C. Business,* October 1989.
e. Peter Black, ''The Bus Stops Here,'' Montreal *Magazine,* March 1986.
f. ''Women At The Top, A Progress Report,'' *Globe and Mail Report on Business Magazine,* October 1990, cover photo of Stella Thompson, article p. 56.

CHAPTER 7, THE INHERITORS/153

a. Charles Lamb, *Last Essays of Elia,* 1832.
b. Mark Evans, ''Newly bold Cara is on the lookout for a $100M acquisition,'' *Financial Post,* 23 Jan. 1990.
c. Alexander Ross and Natalie Veiner Freeman, ''The Richest Refugees,'' *Canadian Business,* May 1987.
d. James Fleming, ''Glory Days,'' *Globe and Mail Report on Business Magazine,* July 1988.
e. Diane Francis, ''Ballard,'' *Financial Post,* 31 Jan. 1991.
f. Alan Gray, ''Suit over Steinberg trust lays bare a family feud,'' *Financial Times of Canada,* 18 Jan. 1988.
g. Ian Brown, *Freewheeling,* Toronto: HarperCollins, 1989, p. 223.
h. Ibid, p. 6.
i. Catherine Dunphy, ''Rebels with a Cause,'' Toronto *Star,* 13 Feb. 1988.
j. Phyllis Lambert's address at the opening ceremonies of the CCA, reported by Pamela Young in ''A capital of design,'' *Maclean's,* 22 May 1989.
k. Fred Bernstein, ''Joan of Architecture,'' *Metropolitan Home,* November 1989.

l. Paul Goldberger, ''A Tresurehouse for Architecture,'' New York *Times*, 7 May, 1989.
m. Nelson Aldrich Jr., *Old Money*, New York: Alfred Knopf, 1988, p. 114.
n. Patricia Poirier, ''Bronfman heiress supports sovereignty for Quebec,'' *Globe and Mail*, 22 Nov. 1990.
o. Alexander Bruce, ''Buy, Buy, Blackburn,'' *Financial Times of Canada*, 30 Jan. 1989.
p. Jennifer Wells, ''The Roman Empress,'' *Financial Times of Canada*, 29 Aug. 1988.
q. Alexander Bruce, ''Buy, Buy, Blackburn,'' *Financial Times of Canada*, 30 Jan. 1989.
r. Michael Nolan, *Walter J. Blackburn, A Man For All Media*, Toronto: Macmillan of Canada, 1989.
s. Rod McQueen, ''A Media Empire in Transition,'' *London Magazine*, November 1987.
t. Alexander Bruce, ''Buy, Buy, Blackburn,'' *Financial Times of Canada*, 30 Jan. 1989.

CHAPTER 8, THE POLITICAL PYRAMID/193

a. Charlotte Gray, ''Capital Gains,'' *Saturday Night*, December 1988.
b. Susan Riley, ''The Power of Positive Networking,'' *Chatelaine*, September 1985.
c. Charlotte Gray, ''Capital Gains,'' *Saturday Night*, December 1988.
d. Michael Bociurkiw, ''King of the hill,'' *Globe and Mail*, 14 Nov. 1987.
e. Mary Ann Smythe, ''Keeper of the Green,'' Ottawa *Magazine*, June 1985.
f. Harvey Enchin, ''Judge who killed deal on Texaco cuts wide swath'', *Globe and Mail*, 21 Nov. 1989.
g. Montreal *Standard*, 27 Sept. 1941.
h. Carol Goar, ''Some bad news for the lady in the bath,'' Vancouver *Sun*, 23 June 1988.

CHAPTER 9 THE MAYORS/215

a. Lewis Harris, ''Westmount mayor faces feisty challenger in Monday vote,'' Montreal *Gazette*, 31 Oct. 1987.
b. Ibid.

c. Ibid.
d. Matthew Fraser, ''May Cutler is one for the book,'' *Globe and Mail,* 14 Jan. 1988.

CHAPTER 10 THE PARTIES/223

a. Mary Ann Smythe, ''Keeper of the Green,'' Ottawa *Magazine,* June 1985.
b. Jeanne Sauvé, ''A controversial farewell,'' Toronto *Star,* 30 Dec. 1990.
c. Gary Mason, ''Manitoba Liberals revived,'' Vancouver *Sun,* 22 April 1988.
d. Miro Cernetig, ''Carstairs accuses opponents of sexist stance on hustings,'' *Globe and Mail,* 10 Sept. 1990; Miro Cernetig, ''Carstairs support takes a beating,'' *Globe and Mail,* 12 Sept. 1990.
e. Leslie Scrivener, ''Coping with Copps,'' Toronto *Star,* 6 March 1988.
f. Gord McIntosh, ''NDP chose an 'also-ran,' Liberal Copps says,'' The Whitehorse *Star,* 5 Dec. 1989.
g. Susan Delacourt, ''Choice of McLaughlin blazes trail. . . . '' *Globe and Mail,* 5 Dec. 1989.
h. Vicki Gabereau, CBC Radio, 29 Nov. 1989.
i. Jack Munro and Jane O'Hara, *Union Jack,* Vancouver and Toronto: Douglas & McIntyre, 1988. p. 168.
j. Charlotte Gray, ''Can Shirley Carr Give the CLC More Clout?'' *Chatelaine,* August 1987.
k. Doris Andersen, *To Change the World: A Biography of Pauline Jewett,* Richmond Hill, Ontario: Irwin Publishing, 1987, pp. 55-56.
l. Doug Ward, ''Leadership bid a matter of moxie,'' Vancouver *Sun,* 1 Sept. 1989.
m. Chris Wood, ''A Race Without Stars,'' *Maclean's,* 5 June 1989.
n. Charles Lynch, ''NDP bound to fail with McLaughlin,'' Vancouver *Sun,* 8 Sept. 1989.
o. Tim Harper, ''It's been a very good year for McLaughlin,'' Toronto *Star,* 1 Dec. 1990.
p. Juliet O'Neil, ''Battle-axe image unfair . . . '' Montreal *Gazette,* 16 Jan. 1988.
q. Stevie Cameron, *Ottawa Inside Out,* Toronto: Key Porter Books, 1989, p. 221.
r. Heather Robertson, ''A Woman for our Time,'' *Canadian Magazine,* 3 May 1975.

s. Hugh Winsor, ''Fuss over CBC's news service masks a more important issue,'' *Globe and Mail,* 1 Feb. 1988.
t. Rick Groen, ''Flora,'' *Globe and Mail,* 11 April 1987.
u. Jill Vardy, ''Rising Stars,'' *Financial Post,* 1 Jan. 1990.
v. Charlotte Gray, ''A Woman's Place,'' *Saturday Night,* May 1987.
w. Carol Goar, ''McDougall: A victim of circumstances,'' Toronto *Star,* 24 March 1988.

CHAPTER 11, THE LEGACY OF IRENE MURDOCH/257

a. Doris Anderson, ''Two Cases where Women Lost Heavily,'' *Chatelaine,* Winter 1974.
b. Janis Rose, ''Pettkus v. Becker,'' *Canadian Community Law Journal,* C#KN 180 C353, Vol. 5-6, 1981-83.
c. Eleanor Wachtel, ''The Ten Lousiest Legal Judgments of the Seventies,'' *Chatelaine,* March 1978.
d. Michael Salter, ''The High Cost of Leaving,'' *Report On Business,* October 1988.
e. Stephen Bindman, ''System unfair to women, judge says,'' Vancouver *Sun,* 19 April 1990.
f. Suzanne Zwarun, ''Why are Judges so lenient in Sexual Assault cases?'' *Chatelaine,* September 1988.
g. Judith Knelman, ''Courtroom tradition: taking it easy on wife killers,'' *Globe and Mail,* 12 Dec. 1990.
h. S. Martin and K. Mahoney (eds.), *Equality and Judicial Neutrality* (1987), Carswell, pp. 3-9 and pp. 8-9. From the speech of Madam Justice Bertha Wilson, ''Will Women Judges Really Make a Difference?'' Osgoode Hall Law School, 8 Feb. 1990.
i. Kirk Makin, ''Feminist content in courses stirs debate at law schools,'' *Globe and Mail,* 26 Dec. 1989.

CHAPTER 12, THE JUDICIAL HIERARCHY/269

a. Ann Rhodes, ''Women Judges: A New Breed,'' *Chatelaine,* June 1985.
b. Howard Palmer, ''Prejudice and Discrimination,'' *Canadian Encyclopedia,* 2nd edition, Edmonton: Hurtig Publishers, 1988.
c. Editorial, ''Two for the court,'' *Globe and Mail,* 25 Jan. 1989.

d. Kirk Makin, ''Burnout in judges linked to poor pay, heavy workloads,'' *Globe and Mail,* 6 March 1989.
e. Peter Gzowski, CBC *Morningside,* 24 April 1989.
f. David Beatty, ''A matter of finding the right justice.'' *Globe and Mail,* 26 Nov. 1990.
g. Ann Rhodes, ''Women Judges: A New Breed,'' *Chatelaine,* June 1985.
h. Bertha Wilson, ''Will Women Judges Really Make a Difference?'' Osgoode Hall Law School, Feb. 1990.
i. Kirk Makin, ''Conduct of Judges rarely censured by peers, observers say.'' *Globe and Mail,* 4 March 1989.

CHAPTER 13, THE PORTIAS/281

a. Canadian Press, ''Lawyers could improve service and reputation by talking to their clients, report advises.'' (*Globe and Mail,* 21 Feb. 1990).

CHAPTER 14, MEDIA POWER/291

a. Caroline Ticknor, *Hawthorne And His Publisher,* Port Washington: Kennikat Press, 1913, p. 141.
b. Allan Fotheringham. ''Cromwell Rules in the Nation's Capital,'' *Maclean's,* 3 April 1989.
c. Duncan McMonagle, ''TV favored as source of news, survey finds,'' *Globe and Mail,* 27 Jan. 1988.
d. Susan Crean, *Newsworthy: The Lives of Media Women,* Halifax: Goodread Biographies, 1985, p. 54
e. Conrad Black, ''What happened to presumed innocence?'' Toronto *Sun,* 29 June 1989.
f. Linda McQuaig, ''Video showing Starr as leading lady has familiar faces in supporting cast,'' *Globe and Mail,* 10 July 1989.
g. Michael Valpy, ''Starr's rise improbable without guardian angel,'' *Globe and Mail,* 21 June 1989.
h. Linda McQuaig, ''Video showing Starr as leading lady has familiar faces in supporting cast,'' *Globe and Mail,* 10 July 1989.
i. Ibid.
j. Thomas Walkom, ''Starr's slush fund for politicians: where the money came from,'' Toronto *Star,* 17 June 1989.

k. Linda McQuaig, ''Video showing Starr as leading lady has familiar faces in supporting cast,'' *Globe and Mail*, 10 July 1989.
l. Gene Allen, ''Starr misled group about political gifts, charity's head says,'' *Globe and Mail*, 21, Sept. 1989.
m. Linda McQuaig, ''Minister linked to federal approval of charitable status for Starr's fund,'' *Globe and Mail*, 21 June 1989.
n. Michael Valpy, ''Just who was needy in the Starr building?'' *Globe and Mail*, 22 June 1989.
o. Conrad Black, ''What happened to presumed innocence?'' Toronto *Sun*, 29 June, 1989.
p. William Thorsell, Editorial, Toronto *Sun*, 5 July 1989.
q. Gene Allen, ''Starr group fired executive staffer after political donations queried.'' *Globe and Mail* 4 Oct. 1989.
r. Diane Francis, *Controlling Interest: Who Owns Canada?* Toronto, Macmillan of Canada, 1986, pp. 48-49.
s. Doug O'Neill, ''The Top 50,'' *Toronto Life*, May 1990.
t. Mark Abley, ''Person behind the voice,'' Vancouver *Sun*, 16 April 1988.
u. Barbara Frum, *As It Happened*, Toronto: McClelland and Stewart, 1976.
v. Allan Fotheringham, *Birds of a Feather: The Press and the Politicians*, Toronto: Key Porter Books, 1989, p. 147.
w. Allan Fotheringham, ''Hostess with mostest of powerful friends,'' *Financial Post*, 14 Feb. 1989.
x. Ibid.
y. Ibid.
z. Patricia Poirier, ''Foes bury hatchet at *Le Devoir* gala,'' *Globe and Mail*, 17 Nov. 1990.
aa. Allan Fotheringham, ''Drama escalating in the Globe soap opera, *Financial Post*, 12 April 1990.
bb. Shirley Sharzer, requoted by Mia Stainsby, ''Media tough on women, forum hears,'' Vancouver *Sun*, 1 Oct. 1990.
cc. Charlotte Gray, ''Women in TV: A Status Report,'' *Chatelaine*, April 1990.
dd. Ibid.
ee. Judi McLeod, ''Hail the Black Queen of King St.'' Toronto *Sun*, 14 Nov. 1987. McLeod attributes the sobriquet, ''The Black Queen,'' to the Toronto press.
ff. George Meredith, *Diana of the Crossways*, Chapter I (1885).

gg. Barbara Amiel, ''Narcissus, thy name is woman,'' *Maclean's*, 13 Feb. 1989.
hh. Val Sears, ''Barbara's not entirely conservative,'' Toronto *Star*, 4 May 1980.
ii. Rhoda Koenig, ''Make Amiel of it,'' *Tatler*, August 1988.
jj. Barbara Amiel, Canadian Bar Association Debate, 27 Aug. 1984.
kk. John MacKay, ''Barbara Amiel Explains It All For You,'' *Toronto Life Fashion*, Summer, 1984.
ll. Barbara Amiel, ''What makes news at the CBC,'' *Maclean's*, 8 Feb. 1988.
mm. Val Sears, ''Barbara's not entirely conservative,'' Toronto *Star*, 4 May 1980.
nn. Barbara Amiel, ''How the feminists hurt women,'' *Maclean's*, 1 Oct. 1984.
oo. Rhoda Koenig, ''Make Amiel of it,'' *The Times*, reprinted in *Tatler*, August 1988.
pp. Ibid.
qq. Ibid.
rr. Germaine Greer, ''Germaine Greer on the Celebrity Journalist,'' *The Independent Magazine*, 6 Oct. 1990.
ss. John MacKay, ''Barbara Amiel Explains it all for you,'' *Toronto Life Fashion*, Summer 1984.
tt. Vicki Gabereau with Barbara Amiel, ''The Vicki Gabereau Show,'' CBC Radio, 6 Oct. 1989.

CHAPTER 15, THE ENTREPRENEURS/323

a. Patricia Davies, *Globe and Mail Report on Business Magazine*, September 1989.
b. Ibid.
c. Wendy Dennis, ''The Power and Influence of Sonja Bata,'' *Toronto Life*, August 1983.
d. Rod McQueen, ''Cats Fight,'' *Toronto Life*, November 1987.
e. Jeremy Ferguson, ''Summoning the Angels,'' *Empress Magazine*, April 1987.
f. Rod McQueen, ''Cats Fight,'' *Toronto Life*, November 1987.
g. Harriet Eisenkraft, ''The Top 50,'' *Toronto Life*, May 1987.
h. Margaret Atwood, ''Tricks With Mirrors,'' *You Are Happy*, Toronto: Oxford University Press, 1974, pp. 24-27.

i. Henry David Thoreau, ed., Owen Thomas, *Walden and Civil Disobedience*, New York and London: W.W. Norton, 1966. p. 15.
j. Allan Fotheringham, ''Gentility with tennis and gin,'' *Maclean's*, 3 Aug. 1987.
k. Don Mitchell, ''My Way,'' *The Province*, 24 Jan. 1982.
l. Barbara Sgroi, ''Lifestyle,'' *Flare*, March 1989.
m. Harvey Enchin, ''Quebec's Queen Bee of capitalism,'' *Globe and Mail*, 24 Sept. 1986.
n. Richard Conrad, ''Lady Capitalist,'' *Outlook '87*, Montreal *Gazette*, 27 Jan. 1987.
o. Ian Allaby, ''The Successors,'' *Canadian Business*, August 1988.
p. Edward Greenspon, ''The Acquisitor,'' *Globe and Mail Report on Business Magazine*, October 1987.

CHAPTER 16, INSPIRATIONAL POWER/361

a. Lewis Hyde, *The Gift: Imagination and the Erotic Life of Property*, New York: Vintage, 1979, dedication page.
b. Maureen Forrester with Marci McDonald, *Out Of Character*, Toronto: McClelland and Stewart, 1986, p. 237.
c. Mark-Elliott Lugo, ''Art Fix in L.A.,'' *San Diego Magazine*, March 1990.
d. Rosalie Abella, ''A Celebration of Person's Day,'' speech at the LEAF Person's Day Breakfast, 18 Oct. 1988.
e. Margaret Atwood, *Power Politics*, Toronto: House of Anansi Press, 1972, p. 1.
f. Atwood, *Survival: A Thematic Guide to Canadian Literature*, Toronto: House of Anansi Press, 1972.
g. Atwood, *Power Politics*, p. 22.
h. Urjo Kareda, ''Atwood on Automatic,'' *Saturday Night*, November 1981.
i. Margaret Atwood, *The Handmaid's Tale*, Toronto: McClelland and Stewart, 1985.

CHAPTER 17, THE FUTURISTS/383

a. Danielle Crittenden, ''Let's Junk The Feminist Slogans: The War's Over,'' *Chatelaine*, August 1990.
b. Deborah Cowley, ''The Woman From The Body Shop,'' *Reader's Digest*, September 1989.

c. Linda Frum, ''Rocking The Establishment,'' *Influence*, October 1986.
d. Debra Black, ''Growing Up Rich,'' *Toronto Life*, September 1986.
e. Linda Frum, *Linda Frum's Guide to Canadian Universities*, Toronto: Key Porter, 1987.
f. Linda Frum, ''*Reach for the Mediocre*,'' *Saturday Night*, September 1988.
g. Ibid.
h. *Saturday Night*, December 1988.
i. Lloyd Barber, Saskatchewan *Report*, September 1988.
j. Virginia Byfield with Patrick McManus and Rene Mauthe, ''Bitten by Barbara's baby,'' *Western Report*, 12 Sept. 1988
k. Grelle White, ''Jenny stars as Miss Money-maker,'' Watsford *Observer*, 26 Oct. 1990.
l. Mildred Istona, Editorial, *Chatelaine*, January 1991.
m. Stevie Cameron, ''The Canadian contingent at Harvard,'' *Globe and Mail*, 23 March 1987.
n. James Fleming, ''The Top 25,'' *Globe and Mail Report on Business Magazine*, December 1988.
o. Judy Steed, ''Getting out of the ghetto,'' *Globe and Mail*, 31 May 1986.
p. Ibid.
q. Michael Valpy, ''Smear campaign debases Toronto,'' *Globe and Mail*, 27 March 1991.
r. Gordon Donaldson, ''Vaulting Ambition,'' *Canadian Business*, January 1989.
s. Allan Swift, ''Chain of boutiques sells cosmetics for the environmentally concerned,'' Toronto *Star*, 9 March 1988.
t. Michael Valpy, ''A clear conscience can also make money,'' *Globe and Mail*, 25 Aug. 1989.
u. Diane Dupuy with Liane Heller, *Dare To Dream*, Toronto: Key Porter Books, 1988, pp. 118-119.
v. Ibid, p. 24.

CHAPTER 18, TUUM EST/411

a. Linda Frum, ''Do men still hold women back?'' *Chatelaine*, October 1988.
b. Barbara McDougall, ''Power: The Third Stage,'' Women and Power Conference, Canadian Advisory Council on the Status of Women, Ottawa, 13-15 March 1988.

c. Ibid.
d. Rosalie Abella, speech, "A Celebration of Person's Day," 18 Oct. 1988.
e. Danielle Crittenden, "Let's Junk the Feminist Slogans: The War's Over," *Chatelaine*, August 1990.
f. Margaret Atwood, Cordelia is a character in *Cat's Eye*, Toronto: McClelland and Stewart, 1988.
g. Laura Sabia, Toronto *Sun*, 10 June 1987.
h. Doris Anderson, "New bill leaves refugee women living in limbo," Toronto *Star*, 9 July 1988.
i. Stephen Hume, "No ceasefires in the war on women," Vancouver *Sun*, 4 January 1991.
j. *Divorce and Family Mediation: Research Study in Three Canadian Cities*, Ottawa: Department of Justice, 1988. *Women in Canada*, Stats Canada. Catalogue # 89-503. E. Lenore Weitzman, *Divorce Revolution: The Unexpected Social and Economic Consequences for Women and Children in America*, 1981. *The B.C. Family Maintenance Enforcement Program*, Victoria: Ministry of the Attorney General, January 1990.
k. Lisa Young, The Royal Commission on Electoral Reform, Ottawa, 1991.
l. Natalie Veiner Freeman, "Student of power," *City Woman*, Fall 1982.
m. Patricia Best, "Man talk: What do men of power say about women in the work world? Or have they even noticed?" *City Woman*, Fall 1984.
n. Susan Riley, "Jean Pigott and the power of positive networking," *Chatelaine*, September 1985.
o. "Papering over the sex gap," *Economist*, 12 Jan. 1991.
p. Brenda Dalglish, "Having it all," *Maclean's*, 3 Sept. 1990.
q. Carol Goar, "National education system badly in need of leadership," reprinted in the Vancouver *Sun*, 7 Feb. 1989.
r. Sylvia Ostry, "Canada and Competitiveness in the International Economy," Canadian Institute of International Affairs/Vancouver Board of Trade, 1 May, 1991.
s. Wilfred Cude, *The Ph.D. Trap*, West Bay, Nova Scotia: Medicine Label Press, 1987.
t. University of Toronto Office of Academic Statistics and Records; Brenda Dalglish, "Having it All," *Maclean's*, 3 Sept. 1990.
u. Valerie Casselton, "Women at work: power and profits," Vancouver *Sun*, 16 Oct. 1990.

v. Jill Vickers, "Four Questions in Search of a Theory," Women and Power Conference, Ottawa, 13-15 March 1988.
w. Canadian Press, "McLaughlin takes swing at Tories' three top women," Vancouver *Sun*, 16 Nov. 1990.
x. Jane Allan, "When women set the rules," *Canadian Business*, April 1991.
y. Lynn Smith, Isabel Grant, "Gender Representation in the Canadian Judiciary," a report commissioned by the Ontario Law Reform Commission, 1991.
z. Michael Valpy, "Ex-Judge ideal choice for daunting challenge," *Globe and Mail*, 30 Jan. 1991.
aa. Bertha Wilson, speech to B'nai Brith Women of Canada, Toronto, 26 May 1991.
bb. Beverley McLachlin, "Crime and Women—Feminine Equalty and the Criminal Law." Address to the Elizabeth Fry Society, Calgary, 17 April 1991.
cc. Stephen Bindman, "Female judge 1; REAL Women 0," Vancouver *Sun*, 24 May 1991.
dd. June Callwood, "Male rage," *Homemaker's Magazine*, March 1990.
ee. "The Vicki Gabereau Show," CBC, 6 Oct. 1989.
ff. Rosalie Abella, "Women Towards the Millennium," a speech, Parksville, British Columbia, 5 May 1991.
gg. Helen Sinclair, Closing Address, "Women Towards the Millennium," Parksville, British Columbia, 5 May 1991.

Index

An "n" beside the page number indicates a reference in the chapter notes.